Assessments in Forensic Pra

Assessments in Forensic Practice: A Handbook

Edited by

**Kevin D. Browne, Anthony R. Beech,
Leam A. Craig, and Shihning Chou**

WILEY Blackwell

This edition first published 2017
© 2017 John Wiley & Sons Ltd

Registered Office
John Wiley & Sons Ltd, The Atrium, Southern Gate, Chichester, West Sussex, PO19 8SQ, UK

Editorial Offices
350 Main Street, Malden, MA 02148-5020, USA
9600 Garsington Road, Oxford, OX4 2DQ, UK
The Atrium, Southern Gate, Chichester, West Sussex, PO19 8SQ, UK

For details of our global editorial offices, for customer services, and for information about
how to apply for permission to reuse the copyright material in this book please see our website at
www.wiley.com/wiley-blackwell.

The right of Kevin D. Browne, Anthony R. Beech, Leam A. Craig, and Shihning Chou to be identified
as the authors of the editorial material in this work has been asserted in accordance with the UK
Copyright, Designs and Patents Act 1988.

Library of Congress Cataloging-in-Publication Data

Names: Browne, Kevin D., editor. | Beech, Anthony R., editor. | Craig, Leam A., editor. |
    Chou, Shihning, editor.
Title: Assessments in forensic practice : a handbook / edited by Kevin D. Browne,
    Anthony R. Beech, Leam A. Craig and Shihning Chou.
Description: Chichester, West Sussex ; Malden, MA : John Wiley & Sons Inc., 2017. |
    Includes bibliographical references and index.
Identifiers: LCCN 2016046916| ISBN 9780470019016 (cloth) | ISBN 9780470019023 (pbk.) |
    ISBN 9780470515853 (pdf) | ISBN 9781118314555 (ePUB)
Subjects: LCSH: Forensic psychiatry–Handbooks, manuals, etc.
Classification: LCC RA1151 .A84 2017 | DDC 614/.15–dc23
LC record available at https://lccn.loc.gov/2016046916

A catalogue record for this book is available from the British Library.

Cover image: (Hands) © Image Source/Gettyimages; (Texture) © da-kuk/Gettyimages
Cover design: Wiley

Set in 10.5/13pt Times by SPi Global, Pondicherry, India
Printed and bound in Malaysia by Vivar Printing Sdn Bhd

10 9 8 7 6 5 4 3 2 1

Contents

About the Editors

Kevin D. Browne, PhD, CPsychol (Foren), FSB, EuroPsy is Director of the Centre for Forensic and Family Psychology and Director of Forensic Psychology Programmes in the Division of Psychiatry and Applied Psychology, School of Medicine, University of Nottingham, UK. As a Registered and Chartered Forensic Psychology Practitioner, he has written books and articles extensively in the areas of family violence, child maltreatment, institutional care, and deinstitutionalization of children and has been working as a consultant to UNICEF and WHO. In the past, he was Head of the World Health Organization Collaborating Centre on Child Care and Protection (2006 to 2009) and the Chief Executive of the High Level Group for Children in Romania (2003 to 2006). He acts as an expert witness to civil and criminal courts in the assessment of parenting, child maltreatment, sexual and violent offenses in the home, and matters concerning child rights, care, and protection.

Anthony R. Beech, DPhil, FBPsS is the Head of the Centre for Forensic and Criminological Psychology at the University of Birmingham, UK. He has authored over 180 peer-reviewed articles, over 50 book chapters, and six books in the area of forensic science/criminal justice. His particular areas of research interests are risk assessment; the neurobiological bases of offending; reducing online exploitation of children; and increasing psychotherapeutic effectiveness of the treatment given to offenders. In 2009 he received the Significant Achievement Award from the Association for the Treatment of Sexual Abusers in Dallas, Texas, and the Senior Award from the Division of Forensic Psychology, British Psychological Society, for recognition of his work in this area.

Leam A. Craig, BA (Hons), MSc, PhD, MAE, CSci, CPsychol, FBPsS, FAcSS, EuroPsy is a consultant forensic and clinical psychologist and partner at Forensic Psychology Practice Ltd. He is Professor (Hon) of Forensic Psychology, the Centre for Forensic and Criminological Psychology, University of Birmingham, and Visiting Professor of Forensic Clinical Psychology, School of Social Sciences, Birmingham City University, UK. He is a Chartered and Registered (Forensic and Clinical) Psychologist, a Chartered Scientist, and holder of the European Certificate in Psychology. He is a Full Member of The Academy of Experts. He is a Fellow of the British Psychological Society, Fellow of the Academy of Social Sciences and recipient of the Senior Academic Award from the Division of Forensic Psychology for distinguished contributions to academic knowledge in forensic psychology. He has previously worked in forensic psychiatric secure services, learning disability hospitals, and consultancy to prison and probation services throughout England, Wales, and Northern Ireland, specializing in high-risk complex cases. He is currently a Consultant to the National Probation Service on working with offenders with personality disorders. He has previously been instructed by the Catholic and Church of England Dioceses, South African Police Service, and the United States Air Force as an expert witness. He acts as an expert witness to civil and criminal courts in the assessment of sexual and violent offenders and in matters of child protection. In 2015 he co-authored a Ministry of Justice research report into the use of expert witnesses in family law. He sits on the editorial boards of several international journals. He has published over 80 articles and chapters in a range of research and professional journals. He has authored and edited 10 books focusing on the assessment and treatment of sexual and violent offenders, offenders with intellectual disabilities, and what works in offender rehabilitation. He is a series editor for the What Works in Offender Rehabilitation book series published by Wiley-Blackwell. His research interests include sexual and violent offenders, personality disorder and forensic risk assessment, and the use of expert witnesses in civil and criminal courts.

Shihning Chou, PhD is an assistant professor and forensic psychologist. She is the Deputy Director of the Centre for Forensic and Family Psychology, Division of Psychiatry and Applied Psychology, School of Medicine, University of Nottingham and has carried out research on international adoption, deinstitutionalization of children, and parenting interventions. Her practice focuses on psychological and risk assessment in parenting, childcare and protection, and family violence. Her current research interests lie in the development of offending/harmful behavior and psychological vulnerability, childhood victimization, child-to-parent violence, psychological sequelae, and recovery and family well-being after political violence. She is also interested in forensic occupational and health issues such as the impact of staff and situational variables on patients/residents.

Contributors

Karen Bailey, CPsychol is a principal forensic psychologist in Birmingham and Solihull Mental Health Foundation Trust and trained to facilitate Safeguarding Children training within the trust. Her practice focuses on psychological and risk assessment in parenting, childcare and protection, family violence, child abuse, and neglect. Her experience also includes risk assessments of sexual and violent offenders via the Prison and Probation Services and preparation of expert witness reports of mandatory and discretionary life-sentenced and indeterminate sentenced prisoners. She has experience of providing oral evidence at lifer Parole Board reviews as well as in Family Courts and has presented research at conferences on child abuse and neglect and the role of criminality in poor parenting.

Taljinder Basra, DClinPsy is a HCPC registered clinical and forensic psychologist employed at Birmingham and Solihull Mental Health Foundation Trust, working in the Severe and Complex Care Directorate. He has several years' experience in assessing risk in parents suspected of neglect and/or abuse, and offenders in a mental health hospital and in the community. He has also been involved in training and teaching risk-related topics to mental health professionals and university graduates in both the UK and India. His research has included investigating the demographic, personality styles, coping strategies, anger, and parental stress differences between abusive and neglectful parents. He is currently interested in exploring the role and prevalence of self-conscious emotions, such as shame in inpatient adult mental health service users who are in forensic settings.

Anthony R. Beech, DPhil, FBPsS is the Head of the Centre for Forensic and Criminological Psychology at the University of Birmingham, UK. He has authored over 180 peer-reviewed articles, over 50 book chapters, and six books, all in the area of forensic science/criminal justice. His particular areas of research interests are risk assessment; the neurobiological bases of offending; reducing online exploitation of children; and increasing psychotherapeutic effectiveness of the treatment given to offenders. In 2009 he received the Significant Achievement Award from the Association for the Treatment of Sexual Abusers in Dallas, Texas, and the Senior Award from the Division of Forensic Psychology, British Psychological Society, for recognition of his work in this area.

Louise Bowers, ForenPsyD is a chartered and registered forensic psychologist and a director of the Forensic Psychologist Service Ltd. Louise splits her time between giving expert evidence (Crown Court and Parole Board), providing therapy, delivering training, university lecturing, and working for the Health and Care Professions Council (HCPC). She was the first psychologist appointed to the Parole Board (2003–2010), where she was instrumental in developing the role of forensic psychology on the board. Louise's doctorate research was an investigation of offense supportive cognition in young adult sexual offenders. Previous roles have included senior positions within the HM Prison Service, the NHS, and with a range of private providers of forensic services.

Kevin D. Browne, PhD, CPsychol FIBiol is the Head of the Centre for Forensic and Family Psychology at the University of Nottingham, UK. He has written extensively in the areas of family violence, institutional care, and deinstitutionalization of children, and has been working as a consultant to UNICEF. In the past, he has also been a temporary advisor to the World Health Organization on child health and the Chief Executive of the High Level Group for the Children in Romania. He was the Head of the World Health Organization Collaborating Centre for Child Care and Protection from 2006 to its closure in 2009.

Shihning Chou, PhD is an assistant professor and forensic psychologist. She is the Deputy Director of the Centre for Forensic and Family Psychology, Division of Psychiatry and Applied Psychology, School of Medicine, University of Nottingham and has carried out research on international adoption, deinstitutionalization of children, and parenting interventions. Her practice focuses on psychological and risk assessment in parenting, childcare and protection, and family violence. Her current research interests lie in the development of offending/harmful behavior and psychological vulnerability, childhood victimization, child-to-parent violence, psychological sequelae, and recovery and family well-being after political violence. She is also interested in forensic occupational and health issues such as the impact of staff and situational variables on patients/residents.

Franca Cortoni, PhD, CPsych is a clinical and forensic psychologist. She is an associate professor at the School of Criminology of the Université de Montréal and a research fellow at the International Centre for Comparative Criminology. Since 1989, she has worked with and conducted research on male and female sexual offenders. Dr Cortoni has published extensively and made numerous presentations at national and international conferences on sexual offender issues. Among others, she has co-edited a book on female sexual offenders and a book on criminal violence (published in French). She is also a member of the editorial board of *Sexual Abuse: A Journal of Research and Treatment* and of the *Journal of Sexual Aggression.*

Leam A. Craig, PhD, CPsychol FBPsS, FAcSS is a consultant forensic and clinical psychologist and partner at Forensic Psychology Practice Ltd. He is Professor (Hon) of Forensic Psychology at the Centre for Forensic and Criminological Psychology, University of Birmingham, and Visiting Professor of Forensic Clinical Psychology at the School of Social Sciences, Birmingham City University, UK. He is a Fellow of the British Psychological Society, Fellow of the Academy of Social Sciences and recipient of the Senior Academic Award from the Division of Forensic Psychology for distinguished contributions to academic knowledge in forensic psychology. He is a chartered and registered (forensic and clinical) psychologist, a chartered scientist, holder of the European Certificate in Psychology and a Full Member of the Academy of Experts. He is currently a Consultant to the National Probation Service on working with offenders with personality disorders. He has previously been instructed by the Catholic and Church of England Dioceses, the South African Police Service, and the United States Air Force as an expert witness. He has published over 80 research articles in a range of research and professional journals along with 10 books. He is a series editor for the What Works in Offender Rehabilitation book series published by Wiley-Blackwell. His research interests include sexual and violent offenders, personality disorder and forensic risk assessment, and the use of expert witnesses in civil and criminal courts. He sits on the editorial boards of several international journals.

Louise Dixon, PhD is a forensic psychologist who has specialized in the prevention of and intervention in violent behavior for over a decade, with a particular focus on the family, children, and young people. She is currently a reader at Victoria University at Wellington. She specializes in the prevention of interpersonal aggression and violence. Primarily, her research has centered on the study of intimate partner violence and abuse, and the overlap with child maltreatment in the family. Louise has received funding from prestigious UK research councils such as the Economic and Social Research Council, Higher Education Funding Council for England, and the Police Knowledge fund. She is a series editor for the What Works in Offender Rehabilitation book series published by Wiley-Blackwell.

Simon Duff, PhD is a chartered and registered forensic psychologist working academically at the Centre for Forensic and Family Psychology, Division of Psychiatry and Applied Psychology, School of Medicine, University of Nottingham and clinically at the Mersey Forensic Psychology Service in Liverpool. He has carried out research concerned with aspects of stalking, sexual offending, working memory, and hypnosis. His practice focuses on working with individuals who have sexually abused children, and individuals with sexual fetishes that have led to prosecution. His current research interests lie in stalking, sexual offending, fetishes, non-offending partners of men who have offended against children, and aspects of denial.

Caroline Friendship, PhD is a chartered and registered forensic psychologist who is a psychologist member of the Parole Board and also works in private practice. Her current roles involve the risk assessment of prisoners and the provision of research consultancy services to criminal justice organizations. Previous posts include Principal Psychologist with Her Majesty's Prison Service and Principal Research Officer for the Home Office (now Ministry of Justice). She has written over 20 peer-reviewed publications relating to the use of reconviction as an outcome measure and evaluating offending behavior programs.

Eleanor M. Gittens, PhD is a recognized teacher in Forensic and Investigative Psychology. She has carried out research on the spatial behavior of offenders, criminal careers, violence, and violent offenders. Her current research interests lie in the development of criminal behavior and the progression of the criminal career; offender and geographical profiling; investigative interviewing; and intelligence-led policing.

Lynsey F. Gozna, PhD is a Chartered Psychologist and Scientist, Associate Fellow of the British Psychological Society and a member of the National Arson Prevention Forum in the UK. She is a Teaching Fellow in Forensic Psychology at the University of Leicester and an Honorary Visiting Fellow at the University of Lincoln, UK. Her research interests relate to interviewing in forensic settings to enhance the effectiveness of practitioners making high stake judgements of risk incorporating consideration of personality, motive, and mind set across a range of offence types. Recently she has been investigating the concept of revenge including how this applies to offending behaviour and accompanying decision-making in the context of forensic mental health. She additionally works in a multi-agency child sexual exploitation team where she has been developing the CAPTIVE psychological formulation model to enhance the intervention, investigation and management of cases.

Ruth M. Hatcher, PhD is a lecturer in Forensic Psychology at the University of Leicester, a chartered forensic psychologist (British Psychological Society), and a registered psychologist (Health and Care Professions Council). She has 15 years' experience conducting forensic psychological research and has managed a number of research projects including evaluations of offending behavior programs (for the Ministry of Justice and the Northern Ireland Office). In addition, she has been involved in evaluations for bodies such as the Home Office, Ministry of Justice, Leicestershire Probation Area, and the Department for Education and Skills in Ireland. She has published numerous peer-reviewed publications, book chapters, and books.

Clive R. Hollin, PhD is Emeritus Professor at the University of Leicester, UK. He wrote the best-selling textbook *Psychology and Crime: An Introduction to Criminological Psychology* (2nd ed., 2013, Routledge); and also *The Psychology of Interpersonal Violence* (2016, Wiley-Blackwell). In all, he has published 21 books alongside over 300 other academic publications; he was for 20 years lead editor of *Psychology, Crime, & Law*. Alongside various university appointments, he has worked as a psychologist in prisons, the Youth Treatment Service, special hospitals, and regional secure units. In 1998 he received the Senior Award for Distinguished Contribution to the Field of Legal, Criminological, and Forensic Psychology from the British Psychological Society.

Kevin Howells, PhD is Emeritus Professor at the University of Nottingham and a clinical psychologist who has worked both as a practitioner and an academic in the forensic field. He has worked in forensic and mental health services in the United Kingdom, Australia, and the United States. He has been a professor at the Universities of Birmingham, South Australia, and Nottingham and was Head of the Peaks Academic and Research Unit at Rampton Hospital. He has published extensively in the fields of anger and aggression, violent and sexual offending, and mental disorder in relation to offending behavior. He is a Fellow of the British Psychological Society and a chartered clinical and forensic psychologist.

Roger B. Hutchinson, MSc, CPsychol is a consultant psychologist, and a director of Forensic Psychology Practice Ltd. He initially trained as a botanist and worked as a research technician before qualifying as a clinical psychologist in 1981. He has worked within the NHS primarily in developmental pediatrics, neuropsychology, learning disability, and forensic services, becoming the clinical director of a large learning disability service which won national awards for "best patient environment," "best mental health team," and "risk management team of the year." He has an NHS management qualification and also trained as a Master NLP Practitioner. His has specialist interests in profound disability and complex needs, lecturing throughout the world in the area of Snoezelen and multisensory activity. Through his work as an expert witness he continues to try to ensure that people with a disability are afforded equality of choice and opportunity.

Carol A. Ireland, PhD is a chartered psychologist, forensic psychologist, and chartered scientist. She acts as an advisor in crisis/conflict situations and is lead trainer and developer of training for a high-secure psychiatric hospital. Carol currently acts as a consultant for the police as a national advisor for critical incidents. She also works at the University of Central Lancashire, where she is the Director of Studies for the MSc in Forensic Psychology. She is one of the lead trainers for the International Organisation of Forensic Practitioners. She has written over 50 publications, including journal articles, book chapters, and books, mainly on offending, consultancy, and crisis (hostage) negotiation.

Vicki Jackson-Hollis, PhD is an evaluation officer at the National Society for the Prevention of Cruelty to Children (NSPCC). In this role she designs and conducts qualitative and quantitative evaluations exploring the delivery and outcomes of intervention programs to prevent child maltreatment. She has carried out a body of research into the victimization of children and young people in the school and community environments (extrafamilial victimization), exploring its characteristics, impact, and the risk factors for victimization. She is particularly interested in the role of victimization in the development and continuation of offending behavior in young people. While completing a PhD in Applied Forensic Psychology at the University of Nottingham, she was also involved in an EU Daphne funded study of child abandonment involving nine European countries.

Lawrence Jones, CPsychol is the Head of Psychology at Rampton Hospital, Nottinghamshire Health Care Trust and an honorary associate professor at the University of Nottingham. He has worked in community prison and health settings with offenders and is qualified as a clinical and a forensic psychologist. He has published on a range of subjects including therapeutic communities, offense paralleling behavior, case formulation, and working with people with personality disorder diagnoses who have sexually offended, and teaches on the Leicester and Sheffield clinical psychology doctorates and the Nottingham forensic psychology course.

William R. Lindsay, PhD, FBPS, FIASSID, FAcSS is Consultant Clinical and Forensic Psychologist and Clinical Director in Scotland for Danshell Healthcare. He is Professor of Learning Disabilities at the University of Abertay, Dundee and Honorary Professor at Deakin University, Melbourne. He has published over 300 research articles and book chapters, published five books, held around 2 million pounds in research grants, and given many presentations and workshops on cognitive therapy and the assessment and treatment of offenders with intellectual disability. His current research and clinical interests are in dynamic risk assessment, sex offenders, personality disorder, alcohol-related violence, and CBT, all in relation to intellectual disability.

James McGuire, PhD is Professor of Forensic Clinical Psychology at the University of Liverpool, where he was also Director of the Doctorate in Clinical Psychology program 1995–2013. Prior to that he worked in a high-security hospital and has carried out psycho-legal work involving the assessment of individuals for criminal courts for hearings of the Mental Health Review Tribunal and the Parole Board. He has conducted research in prisons, probation services, juvenile justice, and other settings on aspects of psychosocial rehabilitation with offenders, and has published widely on this and related issues. He has acted as a consultant to criminal justice agencies in a number of countries.

Eugene Ostapiuk, MSc, CPsychol is a consultant forensic clinical psychologist (retired) and Honorary Professor at the University of Birmingham School of Psychology and Centre for Forensic and Criminological Psychology. He has worked in the public sector and in private practice, specializing in working with families in crisis, psychological assessment of risk, and evaluation of parenting skills in family proceedings. He has been associated with postgraduate teaching in social learning theory, behavioral interventions with offenders, consultancy, and with professional training courses in forensic and clinical psychology at the Universities of Leicester and Birmingham, and has published in these areas.

Kerry Sheldon, PhD, DClinPsy is a HCPC Registered Principal Clinical Psychologist in an Older People's NHS Integrated Mental Health Service. Her practice currently focuses on older people with organic and/or functional disorders within community and inpatient settings. Her career includes working for the probation service, managing a NHS research department, teaching undergraduate and postgraduate psychology, criminology and forensic psychology as well as consultancy work for Pearson's Education Limited. Dr Sheldon has carried out research on men who download child abuse images from the Internet, personality disorders, the effects of pornography, as well as a number of service evaluations. She has a number of publications including Sheldon, K. (2012). Internet Sex Offences, In B. Winder & P. Banyard (Eds.) In A Psychologist's Casebook of Crime: From Arson to Voyeurism. Palgrave Macmillan; Sheldon, K. Davies, J., Howells, K (Eds.) (2011). Research Methods for Forensic Practitioners, Willan Publishing; Sheldon, K and Howitt, D. (2007). Child Pornography and the Internet. John Wiley & Sons.

Ian Stringer, MSc, CPsychol is a consultant psychologist, and a director of Forensic Psychology Practice Ltd. He is an honorary research fellow in the Centre for Forensic and Criminological Psychology, University of Birmingham. He graduated in Clinical Psychology in 1985. His career has included work in a specialist residential unit for children (up to ten years of age) with severe behavioral problems; a long-stay adult mental health hospital for adults with chronic mental illness; special hospitals; regional secure units, and youth treatment services. His work has included children with extreme emotional and behavioral problems; adolescent offenders and adolescents with behavioral problems; sex offenders (including risk assessments for clergy of various denominations, screening both while in training and after subsequent offending), and violent and aggressive people across a wide age range (childhood to old age). He is currently a consultant to both the Youth Offender Service and the National Probation Service in the development of a transition framework, and the development of a framework for the assessment of personality disordered offenders, and management programs and treatment frameworks. He has published in the areas of assessing risk in sexual offenders and treating sexual offenders with intellectual disabilities.

Peter Sturmey, PhD is Professor of Psychology at the Graduate Center and Queens College, City University of New York. He has published over 200 journal articles, 50 book chapters, and nearly 20 books mostly related to behavior analysis, staff and parent training, developmental disabilities, case formulation, and severe challenging behavior.

James Vess, PhD has over 30 years of clinical and research experience with offender populations in the United States, New Zealand, and Australia. He served in a variety of clinical, supervision, and program evaluation roles at Atascadero State Hospital, a high-security forensic treatment facility in California, and has held academic positions at Victoria University of Wellington, New Zealand and Deakin University in Australia. His research has focused on assessment, risk management, and public policy relating to violent and sexual offenders. He is currently a senior psychologist specialist with the California Department of Corrections and Rehabilitation.

Tony Ward, **PhD**, **DipClinPsyc** is Professor of Clinical Psychology at Victoria University of Wellington. He was director of the Kia Marama treatment center for sex in Christchurch, New Zealand and has taught clinical and forensic psychology at the Universities of Canterbury, Victoria, Melbourne, and Deakin. Professor Ward's current research interests include offender rehabilitation and desistance, restorative justice and ethical issues in forensic psychology, and theoretical psychopathology and cognition in offenders. He is the creator of the Good Lives Model of offender rehabilitation and gives numerous workshops, keynote addresses, and consultations around the world on this model. He has published over 350 academic articles and is an adjunct professor at the Universities of Birmingham and Kent.

Kate Whitfield, PhD is a senior lecturer in Forensic Psychology at Sheffield Hallam University. She has carried out research on critical and major incident management, crisis negotiation, and child abandonment in Europe. Her current research interests relate to online offending and victimization, organizational concerns in forensic settings, preventing violence against children, and leadership during critical incidents.

Phil Willmot, PhD is a consultant forensic and clinical psychologist with the Men's Personality Disorder Service and Mental Health Service, Rampton Hospital and a Senior Fellow of the Institute of Mental Health, University of Nottingham. He has previously worked in a number of public sector prisons where he specialized in the assessment, treatment, and management of high-risk offenders, particularly sexual offenders. His research interests include the mechanisms of change in the treatment of personality disorder, and developing treatment programs for offenders who have committed a combination of sexual, violent, and firesetting offenses.

Pamela M. Yates, PhD has worked as a clinician and researcher in various capacities since 1987. She has worked with adults and youths, including sexual offenders, violent offenders, individuals with substance abuse problems, and victims of violence, and has developed accredited offender treatment programs. Her research and publications include offender rehabilitation, assessment and treatment of sexual offenders, program evaluation, risk assessment, treatment effectiveness, psychopathy, and sexual sadism. She has written extensively on the Self-Regulation and Good Lives Models of sexual offender intervention.

1

Introduction

KEVIN D. BROWNE, ANTHONY R. BEECH, LEAM A. CRAIG AND SHIHNING CHOU

Research and practice in forensic psychology involves a wide range of activities within secure and community settings. Secure settings include Her Majesty's Prison Service, private prisons, Local Authority homes for young people and secure units for adult and young offenders with mental health issues and/or personality disorders run by the National Health Service (NHS) or private organizations. Furthermore, there are similar secure services offered to adults or young people with intellectual disabilities who are also deemed to be a danger to themselves or others. Community settings involve psychologists working with the police, social services, youth offending services, and community health services, especially in the areas of violence in the community, domestic violence, child abandonment, abuse, and neglect.

The aim of psychological interventions in forensic settings is to reduce the possibility of harmful behavior directed toward self or others or that threatens the rights and safety of adults and children. This involves the prevention of violent and antisocial behavior and helps with the detection and identification of those perpetrators who have already committed a violent or antisocial offense. These activities are usually carried out in community settings.

Forensic psychologists working in secure settings are usually working with people who have already committed an act of violence and/or antisocial behavior. The aim of their work is to assess the factors that led to their index offense and ameliorate or reduce the chances of the same behavior being repeated within the secure setting or after release. Risk factors associated with violent and antisocial

Assessments in Forensic Practice: A Handbook, First Edition. Edited by Kevin D. Browne, Anthony R. Beech, Leam A. Craig, and Shihning Chou.
© 2017 John Wiley & Sons Ltd. Published 2017 by John Wiley & Sons Ltd.

acts include mental health problems, addiction and substance misuse, intellectual disabilities, personality disorders, and adverse experiences in childhood.

Hence, one of the most frequent activities of a forensic psychologist, in both community and secure settings, is to carry out "psychological assessments" in relation to the risk of violent and antisocial behavior (including acquisitive crime) and the formulation of criminogenic needs that direct interventions in terms of treatment and rehabilitation. The formulation balances the assessment of dynamic risk and background static risk factors, with protective factors that may help prevent people in conflict with the law from reoffending.

Furthermore, forensic psychologists advise law enforcement agencies and the criminal justice system on behavioral assessment in the investigation of offenders, eyewitness testimony, psychological influences on jury decision-making, and the preparation of vulnerable children and adults in court.

Similar to clinical psychologists, forensic psychologists must be proficient and competent in skills such as clinical/forensic assessment, interviewing and observation, written and verbal communication, and psychological report writing. Often, they are invited as expert witnesses into court and/or to make case presentations informing courts about an offender's ability to stand trial, about Parole Board hearings, and about the multidisciplinary teams who are making decisions about the future placement of offenders.

With respect to victims of crime, forensic psychologists are involved in the assessment of re-victimization and victim support, child custody evaluations, parenting assessments, counseling services to victims, and the assessment of post-traumatic stress disorder and its relation to the victim to offender concept.

The criminal justice system and the professionals, policymakers, politicians, and the general public often see offenders and victims as a strict dichotomy, that is a person is either a victim or an offender. However, in reality, the distinction is blurred if current and life histories are taken into account. In fact, the majority of offenders have been previously victimized and a significant proportion of victims later develop behavior harmful to themselves or to others. This can be within their family environment only or it can be within the family and the community.

STRUCTURE OF THE BOOK

This book contains four sections, covering the assessment of various client groups in different legal and professional contexts.

Part One covers psychological and risk assessment in investigations and in the criminal justice system:
   Risk assessment and formulation
   Violent offenders and murderers

Sexual offenders
Firesetters
Parole assessments
Behavioral assessment in investigative psychology.

Part Two focuses on the assessment of clients in mental health and specialist health
services:
Assessing risk of violence in mentally disordered offenders
Assessing mental capacity in offenders with intellectual and developmental
disabilities
Offenders with personality disorders
Offenders and substance abuse.

Part Three covers the assessment of violence in the family and the community and
its relevance to prevention:
Community approaches to the assessment and prevention of intimate partner
violence and child maltreatment
Parental assessments in childcare proceedings
Perpetrators of domestic violence.

Part Four engages readers in discussions on policies and practice issues in forensic
assessment:
Assessment of hostage situations and their perpetrators
Assessing the sexually abused child as a witness
Working with young offenders
Ethics of risk assessment.

PART ONE

Criminal Justice Assessments

2

Case Formulation and Risk Assessment

PETER STURMEY AND WILLIAM R. LINDSAY

INTRODUCTION

Effective and appropriate assessment is the cornerstone of offender management and treatment. Thus, mental health professionals often assess risk of recidivism and conduct case formulations to identify the most effective intervention for a specific offender. Risk assessment and case formulation are interdependent clinical activities. Case formulations may result in interventions which produce both beneficial changes in offender behavior and may also subsequently impact risk assessment. For example, teaching an offender generalized problem solving and vocational and alcohol management skills that are based on the formulation of their case may well reduce the offender's risk and may result in an increased likelihood of less restrictive placement. Alternatively, an inappropriate, ineffective, or iatrogenic treatment plan may result in increased offender risk and result in an increased likelihood of restrictive placement and continued costs of incarceration and of treatment. For example, an inappropriate cognitive treatment plan might inadvertently teach an offender to minimize his or her problems by teaching that person to describe his or her private verbal behavior in a manner consonant with treatment progress, even though his or her private verbal behavior has not truly changed. Thus, risk assessment and formulation for treatment planning are two central aspects of the assessment of offenders.

This chapter will provide an overview of risk assessment and case formulation within the context of offender services. The first section will describe risk assessment and illustrate the application of the risk assessment of offenders. The second section will describe case formulation generally and its application to offenders, and will specifically illustrate its application to persons with personality disorders. The final section will summarize outstanding issues in risk assessment and case formulation when working with offenders.

RISK ASSESSMENT

Risk assessment refers to the evaluation of a risk and the likely cost of such risk. Diverse fields such as economics and public health, and ensuring the safety of food, use risk analysis. Thus, in forensic psychology risk analysis involves the estimation of the costs of reoffending and violence to others, and the costs of such risks to individuals and society. Traditionally, forensic risk assessment involves assessment of static/historical risks and dynamic risks. Static/historical risk assessment contains unchangeable factors in the person's history and, since one cannot change one's history, the value of a static risk assessment for a particular individual will never reduce but will increase if they commit another offense. Dynamic risk assessment refers to the assessment of variables that are more open to change through clinical intervention and other variables.

Static/Historical Risk Assessment

Throughout the 1970s and 1980s, it became clearer that clinical judgment was extremely poor in predicting who would and would not reoffend in cases where there was a judicial or mental health review (Quinsey, Harris, Rice, & Cormier, 1998; Steadman, Fabisiak, Dvoskin, & Holohean, 1987). There were many reports in the literature concerning the poor predictive validity of clinical judgment when clinical judgment is unsupported by any actuarial prediction (Elbogen, 2002; Litwack, 2001; Quinsey et al., 1998). Throughout the 1970s and 1980s, research appeared using statistical prediction instruments applied to forensic issues. In relation to general criminal recidivism, predictive accuracy, based on actuarial prediction, rose to around 60–80% (Andrews & Bonata, 2010). Research on the prediction of violent and sexual recidivism also produced a range of promising variables (Harris, Rice, & Quinsey, 1993; Monahan, 1981). Harris et al. (1993) studied 695 men submitted to a maximum security psychiatric institution for varying lengths of time. These authors followed up all but a few of the participants and compared recidivists ($N=191$) with non-recidivists ($N=427$) on a range of variables which might predict future violence. These variables subsequently formed the basis of several of the risk assessment instruments used at present. For example, work on the *Historical/Clinical/Risk Management* (HCR-20) (Webster, Eaves, Douglas, & Wintrup, 1995), cites Harris et al. (1993) as evidence for eight of the ten historical actuarial variables in the HCR-20.

In Harris et al. (1993), several childhood variables emerged as showing highly statistically significant differences between recidivists and non-recidivists, such as childhood aggression and maladjustment in early schooling, being expelled or suspended from school, and being arrested before the age of 16 years. All of these variables can be considered to be indications of violence and disruption in childhood, and this cluster of predictive variables has continued to feature in all subsequent historically based risk assessments. Another childhood predictor was whether or not the individual had been separated from their parents prior to the age of 16 years. All these predictors may perhaps be assessed reliably and accurately, at least under some circumstances; however, these variables may be thought of as proxies for learning experiences. For example, although separation from parents prior to the age of 16 years is a fairly easy item to assess, it probably points to a range of developmental and attachment difficulties which the individual may have experienced associated with parental separation, the subsequent effects of that separation, and pathways to offending.

In relation to adult variables, Harris et al. (1993) found that employment history, previous violence, absconding from institutions, failure of prior conditional release, and whether or not the individual had previously been in a relationship all distinguished recidivists from non-recidivists. Again, these variables were incorporated into subsequent assessments.

In relation to the index offense, perpetrator age distinguished the groups and this variable was retained in subsequent assessments. The Psychopathy Checklist – Revised score (Hare, 1991) was higher and a diagnosis of personality disorder was more common in the recidivist group.

While considering the Harris et al. (1993) study, it is worth noting the somewhat counterintuitive predictors which had not been included in some later risk assessments. For example, victim injury was significantly lower in the recidivist group. The percentages of offenses against women and in which the perpetrator knew the victim were also lower in the recidivist group. In other words, more violent offenses, offenses against strangers, and offenses against women were more frequent in those who did not reoffend. Interestingly, a diagnosis of schizophrenia occurred more than twice as often in the non-recidivist than the recidivist group. Harris et al. (1993) also included two proximal or dynamic variables including pro-criminal values and attitudes unfavorable to convention, which were both more common in the recidivist group.

These authors then combined these variables into a successful predictive instrument that included the following variables: separation from parents when under 16 years, whether or not the person had been married, elementary school maladjustment, failure in prior conditional release, age at index offense, diagnosis of personality disorder, alcohol abuse history, victim injury in the index offense, diagnosis of schizophrenia, whether or not there had been a female victim, and offense history. The *Psychopathy Checklist – Revised* was also included in the item list. This risk assessment was called the *Violence Risk Appraisal Guide* (VRAG) (Quinsey et al., 1998). Because of its extensive empirical derivation, the VRAG and its accompanying assessment for sexual offenses, the *Sex Offender Risk Appraisal Guide* (SORAG), have become standard instruments against which other risk assessments have been compared for predictive accuracy. Both the VRAG and SORAG have been cross-validated on a variety of forensic psychiatric populations and prisoner samples (Harris, Rice, Quinsey, & Cormier, 2015). These authors found that the VRAG predicted those who would and those who would not perpetrate a future violent offense with significant accuracy and a medium to large effect size, and produced significantly more accurate predictions than unstructured clinical judgment.

Around the same time, *Structured Clinical Judgment* was developed by Webster et al. (1995) in the form of the Historical/Clinical/Risk Management – 20 Items (HCR-20) Assessment. This is the most widely used *Structured Clinical Judgment* and is organized into three sections: historical (ten items), clinical (five items), and risk (five items). The clinician rates each item on a three-point scale: 0, no evidence of the variable; 1, some evidence of the variable; 2, clear evidence of the variable. The total score is the sum of the items. The authors do not generally recommend making decisions on the basis of the total score; rather, they recommended that the items are structured in order to help the consideration of a comprehensive range of variables with a view to arriving at a final judgment. In this way, actuarial, historical variables are combined with an assessment of current clinical status and consideration of future risk variables.

The HCR-20 has been revised more recently to accommodate changes in clinical practice. The HCR-20 V3 (Douglas, Hart, Webster, & Belfrage, 2013) is a much expanded manual that accommodates shifts that have occurred in clinical and forensic practice, and principally incorporates greater attention to formulation and risk management plans. The HCR-20 V3 describes a seven-step process of gathering case information, evaluating the presence of the 20 risk factors, evaluating the relevance of risk factors, developing a risk formulation, developing future scenarios relevant to the person being assessed, considering risk management strategies, and concluding on the seriousness and imminence of the risk. The 20 items have also changed significantly since first published according to clinical experience and new research over the years.

Several groups of researchers have compared the predictive accuracy of both the VRAG and the HCR-20 (original versions) on a range of databases. Generally, studies have used Receiver Operator Characteristics (ROC) to evaluate the significance of risk prevention. A ROC curve is a two-dimensional plot of the true positives on the *y*-axis and false positive on the *x*-axis. Researchers use the Area Under the Curve (AUC) to measure the accuracy of a prediction. An AUC of .7 indicates a significant prediction with a medium effect. For example, Kroner and Mills (2001) followed up 79 male offenders who had been convicted of various violent offenses, excluding sexual offenses. In their comparison of predictive accuracy, they found that the

VRAG achieved an AUC value of .75 and the HCR-20 had an AUC value of .72. Both of these are significantly better than chance with a medium to large effect size, and there was no meaningful difference between the AUCs for each measure. Barbaree, Seto, Langton, and Peacock (2001) compared the predictive accuracy of the VRAG, SORAG, and Static-99 (Hanson & Thornton, 1999). The Static-99 is an actuarial assessment for future sexual offending. These authors employed a Canadian database of 215 sex offenders who had been released from prison for an average of 4.5 years. They found that the VRAG, SORAG, and Static-99 successfully predicted general recidivism and sexual recidivism.

As has been indicated, the HCR-20 has a highly respectable scientific background in common with other risk assessments. *Structured Clinical Judgment*, in the form of the HCR-20, is the most frequently used form of risk assessment. It has now been subject to a considerable quantity of research work in a range of settings for offenders in both correctional and mental health facilities. Since it has a range of clinical scales, it is unsurprising that much of the research has been carried out in forensic psychiatric settings or with mentally disordered offenders. For example, Grann, Belfrage, and Tengstrom (2000) conducted a two-year follow-up of 404 forensic patients who had committed violent offenses. They found that the HCR-20 H scale (historical section) predicted violence significantly for both offenders with a diagnosis of schizophrenia (AUC=.71) and offenders with personality disorder (AUC=.71). In a two-year follow-up of 70 psychiatric patients who had committed violent acts, Dolan and Khawaja (2004) reported that the HCR-20 total score significantly predicted self or collateral reports of violence (AUC=.76) and documented incidents of reoffending (AUC=.71).

Work on the HCR-20 has begun to investigate a range of other variables with mentally disordered offenders. Douglas and Ogloff (2003) investigated the relationship between rater confidence and accuracy of the prediction of risk. They followed up 100 forensic psychiatric patients, 79% of whom had a violent index offense. In addition to completing HCR-20 judgments, raters were asked to indicate their confidence in the judgment on a 10-point scale. They found that the AUC value for the high confidence group was much greater than for the low confidence group for predicting any violence.

The HCR-20 has also been employed with female participants. In a comparison of male and female forensic patients, Strand and Belfrage (2001) found no difference in scale or total scores between the two groups. The only significant gender differences were on individual items: males scored higher on previous violence, violence at a young age, substance use, and negative attitudes, with females scoring higher on personality disorder, impulsivity, and stress. On the other hand, de Vogel and de Ruiter (2005) compared 42 women and 42 men in a forensic psychiatric service and found that the HCR-20 was a better violence predictor for men (AUCs for total scaled score ranged between .75 and .88) than for women (AUCs ranged from .52 to .63). Grevatt, Thomas-Peter, and Hughes (2004) investigated the extent to which the HCR-20 predicted short-term violence within six months of admission to a forensic unit. Although the H scale and total score were poor predictors of short-term violence, the clinical (C) scale significantly predicted any incidents (AUC = .72) and verbal abuse (AUC = .81). They also found that the C and risk (R) scales reduced significantly in response to treatment in hospital.

In a follow-up to Barbaree et al. (2001), Langton, Barbaree, Seto, Peacock, Harkins, and Hanson (2007) extended the original database to include 468 sexual offenders followed up for an average of 5.9 years. Langton and colleagues found that the VRAG was a significant predictor of serious violent incidents (AUC = .73), while the Static-99 significantly predicted future sexual incidents (AUC = .75). They found that all instruments had predictive validity for the types of incidents for which they were designed. Harris et al. (2015) made a further evaluation of the VRAG and SORAG, predicting serious violent and sexual recidivism in a sample of 396 sexual offenders. For serious violent recidivism, both the VRAG and the SORAG were found to have AUC values of .73, and for sexual recidivism corresponding AUC values were .65 and .66, respectively. Therefore, the various studies are consistent, showing the VRAG and HCR-20 to have predictive values that are significant with a medium to large effect size.

Risk assessment instruments have been found to predict with significant accuracy a range of types of violent incident in different populations, including offenders with Intellectual Disability (ID). For example, Quinsey, Book, and Skilling (2004) investigated the predictive validity of the VRAG in men with ID. Their study employed 58 men with serious histories of antisocial and aggressive behavior, who were followed up for an average of 16 months. Eighty percent of participants had at least one additional diagnosis: 56% had a diagnosis of some type of personality disorder; 36% had been diagnosed with some type of paraphilia; 11% had a diagnosis of psychosis; and 9% were diagnosed with affective disorder. Thirty-nine had at least one incident of antisocial or aggressive behavior over the follow-up period. Quinsey et al. (2004) found that the VRAG showed significant predictive value with a medium effect size (AUC = .69), and that monthly staff ratings of client behavior were significantly related to antisocial incidents.

Two subsequent studies compared the relevant predictive accuracy of a number of risk assessments, including the VRAG. Gray, Fitzgerald, Taylor, MacCulloch, and Snowden (2007) compared the VRAG, PCL-Screening version (Hart, Cox, & Hare, 1995), and the HCR-20 in a group of 145 offenders with ID and 996 offenders without ID, all discharged from four independent sector hospitals and followed up for a minimum of two years. All instruments showed significant predictive validity for all groups and, for the ID group, all the assessments predicted future incidents with a medium to large effect size for both violent and general recidivism. Indeed, all the risk predictors showed greater accuracy with the ID group than with the mainstream non-ID offenders. Lindsay et al. (2008) completed a further evaluation of a number of risk assessments on a sample of 212 offenders with ID from a range of community and secure settings. They followed participants up for a period of one year and compared the VRAG, HCR-20, Static-99 (Hanson & Thornton, 1999), and Risk Matrix (RM) 2000 (Thornton, Mann, Webster, Blud, Travers, Friendship, & Erikson, 2003), and used two measures of proximal risk assessment (see below). The VRAG and HCR-20 both showed significant predictive accuracy (AUC = .71 and .72, respectively). The RM 2000 had poorer predictive accuracy with a small AUC, but the authors noted that the assessment was promising since the scoring criteria were relatively straightforward. Thus, the results from these various studies suggest that the predictive validity of actuarial risk assessment with offenders with ID was at least as good as other offender groups. These studies attest to the value of actuarial risk assessment and *Structured Clinical Judgment* in the assessment of risk for offenders across cultures and settings.

The more recent iterations of the HCR-20 and the VRAG have also been evaluated. The VRAG-R was evaluated by Rice, Harris, and Lang (2013) with 1,261 sexual and violent offenders released from maximum security establishments. It was found to have very good predictive accuracy with large effect sizes up to 49 years after discharge. The HCR-20 V3 was evaluated in a special issue of the *International Journal of Forensic Mental Health* and studies reported good inter-rater reliability (Douglas & Belfrage, 2014), validity for different aspects of the assessment (Strub, Douglas, & Nicholls, 2014), and violence prediction (Doyle, Archer Power, Coid, Kallis, Ullrich, & Shaw, 2014).

Dynamic/Proximal Risk Assessment

As mentioned earlier, Harris et al. (1993) found that two dynamic variables – attitudes unfavorable to convention and pro-criminal values – showed highly significant differences between recidivists and non-recidivists. Thornton (2002) also incorporated antisocial attitudes into his framework for assessing dynamic risk in sex offenders, and demonstrated the difference between sex offenders and non-sex offenders on attitudes supportive of sexual offending.

Hanson and colleagues (Hanson & Harris 2000; Hanson & Morton-Bourgon, 2004) developed an important approach to the understanding and assessment of dynamic risk. They separated such factors into "stable" and "acute" factors. Stable dynamic factors include dispositions, such as a propensity to anger, and states that may have been learned through a person's life, such as alcohol dependence. These stable dynamics are amenable to treatment. In this way the risk can be reduced through learning a range of personal skills or controlled through environmental manipulation. Acute dynamic factors are events that are closest in time to the behavior to be predicted; for example, a person may be drunk and/or provoked to anger when a family member insults them, both acute factors sharply increasing the dynamic risk. (Note that acute dynamic factors overlap with the controlling variables, such as establishing operations, discriminative stimuli, and current contingencies used in applied behavior analysis.)

An example of this approach comes from Hanson and Harris (2000) who studied a sample of offenders in probation settings. They found that dynamic factors were indeed predictive of supervision breakdown caused by the person reoffending. Both Hanson and Harris (2000) and Hanson and Morton-Bourgon (2004) have reported that dynamic factors had additional predictive value over static risk assessment in relation to both violent and sexual incidents. It is with these factors that clinicians would start when considering appropriate intervention. Thus, acute dynamic risk assessment informs forensic case formulation by identifying significant target behaviors that pose risk, and also by identifying manipulable variables that may be part of the case formulation and be the basis of the treatment plan. Note, however, that the relationships between acute dynamic risk factors observed in group studies may have little or no relevance to the case formulation of individual cases. For example, a group study might find a correlation of .3 between an acute dynamic predictor such as drunkenness with a group of participants. For one offender there may be a very strong positive correlation between drunkenness and offending; for a second person there may be a weak relationship that is only strongly predictive of violence when other variables, such as insults from family members, are present; and, finally, for a third person being drunk may have a large negative correlation with offending, for example, when someone drinks to reduce arousal and arousal is related to offending. Thus, clinicians should consider the relationship between group studies of acute dynamic risk factors cautiously when formulating individual cases.

Monahan (1981), while acknowledging the crucial value of static risk factors, also stressed the importance of understanding contextual dynamic factors as antecedents to crime or indeed as protective factors preventing individuals from committing crime. If a person has a long-standing love of the Rolling Stones, has all their albums, and has a ticket for their concert tonight, it is reasonable to predict that this person will go to a Rolling Stones concert tonight; however, if that person breaks their leg seriously on the morning of the concert, this will significantly alter the event prediction. In this way, it is clear that even with the strongest predictive factors, proximal variables can intervene to make significant changes. (In this case, proximal variables increased the likelihood of competing responses negatively reinforced by pain reduction and increased the response cost of engaging in activities reinforced by the Rolling Stones.) Short-term fluctuations in mood, substance abuse, or victim access can sharply change the risk of onset of offending. Controlling these factors through self-regulation or environmental manipulation can be correspondingly protective against the onset of antisocial behavior or criminal acts.

Lindsay et al. (2004) and Steptoe, Lindsay, Murphy, and Young (2008) have demonstrated the importance of dynamic risk factors in two separate reports on offenders with intellectual disabilities in maximum security hospitals. They developed the *Dynamic Risk Assessment and Management System* (DRAMS), which employed variables from previous studies, including mood, antisocial behavior, abhorrent thoughts, psychotic symptoms, self-regulation, therapeutic alliance, substance abuse, compliance, emotional relationships, and victim access. Since their participants were drawn from a high-security setting, there were no opportunities for substance abuse or victim access. By gathering daily ratings of participant behavior, they related them into independently collected incident data. They found that for individual participants, ratings taken on the day before an incident were significantly higher than ratings taken at least seven days distant from any incident. The significant predictors were mood, antisocial behavior, abhorrent thoughts, and total score. In a subsequent larger-scale study, Steptoe et al. (2008) found that sections of the DRAMS on mood, antisocial behavior, and intolerance/agreeableness had significant predictive values with future incidents (AUC > .70). There were also highly significant differences with large effect sizes between assessments taken one or two days prior to an incident and the control assessments conducted at least seven days distant from an incident. This study confirms the importance of dynamic variables and in particular dynamic antisociality in relation to future incidents for offenders with ID.

Conclusions

There have been significant developments in the evaluation of risk assessments for sex offenders and violent offenders. The available evidence suggests that risk assessments based on actuarial variables predict significantly better than chance and significantly better than unstructured clinical judgment. Dynamic variables are also important considerations and, as Hanson and Harris (2000) have shown, provide additional predictive value over static risk assessment. Consideration of these proximal factors is likely to be the point at which clinical intervention will begin. This now leads us to consideration of that very task.

CASE FORMULATION

General Features of Case Formulation

Eells (2007a) offered a generic definition of case formulation as "a hypothesis about the causes, precipitants, and maintaining influences of a person's psychological, interpersonal, and behavioral problems … A case formulation also serves as a blueprint guiding treatment and as a marker for change. It should help the therapist experience greater empathy for the patent and anticipate possible ruptures in the therapy alliance …" (p. 4). For example, psychodynamic approaches may place substantial emphasis on uncovering the alleged developmental roots of a problem, since within this theoretical framework uncovering these apparent causes is not merely a part of the formulation, but also part of the treatment. Cognitive behavioral approaches vary in the weight they place on history. Some Cognitive Behavior

Therapy (CBT) approaches de-emphasize history, as it may add little of substance to the formulation and the subsequent development of a treatment plan (Kuyken, Padesky, & Dudley, 2009), whereas other CBT approaches place some weight on understanding where a client's schema might have come from and developed. Various behavioral approaches to case formulation also differ on the emphasis given to history. For example, some transcripts of Wolpe interviewing clients show him searching for a conditioning event that a client has not yet identified. Other approaches, such as the Functional Analytic Clinical Case Model, only place emphasis on the current controlling variables that have a large causal impact on target behaviors and that the client and therapist can readily manipulate to produce the largest, most meaningful benefits to clients (Haynes & O'Brien, 2000; Lapaalainen, Timonen, & Haynes, 2009). Thus, there is general agreement that case formulations should be brief, should abstract out key features of the case, should integrate diverse aspects of the case, perhaps including history, and should guide idiographic treatment.

Despite this agreement on these general features of case formulation, there is significant disagreement on key questions (Sturmey, 2009b). For example, approaches to case formulation differ on the nature of the target behaviors that formulations should address, the status of cognitions and emotions as causes of behavior or behavior to be changed, and the reality of inferred constructs, such as alleged cognitive structures, and the desirability of mono-theoretical versus integrated case formulations, and so on.

There is general agreement that the main function of case formulation is to predict the most effective treatment beyond treatment implied by diagnosis and treatment as usual. Case formulation may unify diverse information, such as different target behaviors that serve the same function, repeated patterns of interactions, social relationships, and reactions to different stressors or events. Case formulation can be a tool to use with the clients. For example, clients may participate in varying degrees in developing and using the formulation. In so doing, it is possible that case formulation may be more respectful of client autonomy and dignity. Involving a client in developing their own formulation may also begin the process of behavior change by gradually teaching the client discriminations about their own behavior and its relationship to the environment. This may subtly begin the process of behavior change before initiating a formal treatment plan and thereby make client behavior change more likely (Skinner, 1953). It may assist the client in understanding their problems and the rationale for their treatment better than if the formulation is delivered cold without client participation. Finally, a formulation may enhance the therapeutic alliance and help the therapist understand and repair disruptions to the therapeutic alliance (Eells, 2007a).

There are many approaches to case formulation. Approaches differ both in terms of theoretical orientation and in terms of the specific technology used to make a formulation. Thus, formulations may be made from cognitive behavioral, behavior analytic, psychodynamic, eclectic, and other approaches (Eells, 2007b; Sturmey, 2009b). Case formulation may use interviews, questionnaires, observations, and specific guidelines on how to conduct an assessment to make a formulation, and may use written summaries, letters to clients (Dunn, 2009), or diagrams to summarize the current variables related to current problems, and may or may not also diagram the development of the presenting problems (Lapaalainen et al., 2009). Different approaches to case formulation also vary in the extent and manner in which clients participate in making the formulation.

Despite the current popularity of client participation in developing formulations, there is very little evidence to support the ideologically seductive views of client participation. There are two related problems. First, no studies to date have operationally defined client participation. Thus, it is difficult to know exactly what participants do when they participate in formulation and whether different studies and advocates of case formulation are referring to different things. Second, the only study to date that has reported data on client reaction to formulations produced mixed results. Chadwick, Williams, and MacKenzie (2003) found that although some clients with psychosis reacted positively to their formulations, others viewed their formulations negatively, perhaps because their formulations traced their current problems back to early in their history and thus appeared to present their problems as fixed in their history and overwhelming. This latter point may be particularly relevant to formulation with offenders, many of whom have long forensic histories and extensive histories of abuse and deprivation. Due to the limited quantity of data on this point no firm generalization can be made on the role of client participation in case formulation, but it is clearly an area that is ripe for empirical investigation.

Forensic Case Formulation

Forensic Case Formulation (FCF) is but one form of case formulation, so it shares many features with other forms of formulation, but also faces additional special challenges. Offenders often present with many of the same problems as general clinical populations, such as anxiety, depression, and social skills deficits and excesses, and also present with higher rates of other problems, such as personality disorders, substance abuse, and violence than clinicians encounter in other contexts. Thus, clinicians working in forensic settings must have generic case formulation skills, as well as specialist skills in formulating problems more commonly encountered in forensic settings.

FCF also presents at least three specific challenges to clinicians: offenders often have extensive histories, may live in settings that are very different from the place where clinically significant problems occurred, and their clinical problems are intricately bound up with the justice system. Offenders often have forensic histories that date back to childhood and adolescence; some have histories of abuse, deprivation, and unusual experiences dating back even earlier. In addition, many offenders – especially those who are incarcerated – have extensive histories with the justice system. Thus, clinicians attempting to formulate forensic cases have to digest, analyze, and synthesize an unusually large quantity of client history. Further, clinicians have to evaluate histories that may be incomplete and presented with many forms of biases from the offender, family members and significant others, other clinicians, and members of the justice system.

A second challenge for FCF is that index offenses and other forensically and clinically relevant behavior often cannot occur in restricted forensic settings. For example, if an offender is incarcerated they may have no access to alcohol, illicit substances, or minors. Thus, if substance use is a key element in an FCF it may be difficult or there may be no opportunity to observe the clinically relevant behavior and in the context in which it occurred prior to incarceration. One potential solution to this problem comes from the recent development of the notion of offense paralleling behavior (OPB), which refers to the possibility that behavior observed in a restrictive forensic setting may be functionally similar to offending behavior even if it is topographically different from the offending behavior. For example, an offender with a history of violent, acquisitive offenses might show a pattern of coercive or threatening behavior in order to obtain items that are valuable to him or her. Likewise, an offender who retreats into violent fantasy when alone prior to an offense might also engage in this behavior in a forensic setting. If these behaviors do indeed parallel the functions of index offenses they may afford the clinician the opportunity to formulate a case and, indeed, to implement a treatment plan based on a formulation (Daffern et al., 2007).

Finally, clinicians in forensic services have to interact with the justice system, which significantly impacts treatment delivery and disposal of the offender. For example, a clinicians' evaluation of risk and treatment progress might lead them to recommend discharge. In contrast, a facility board, sensitive to the politics and community reaction to discharging violent sexual offenders, may be reluctant to concur with clinicians' judgments. Similarly, the behavior of staff in a residential setting might maintain or exacerbate clinically relevant behavior. For example, Shepherd and Lavender (1999) reported that aggressive episodes in a juvenile setting were more often directed toward non-professional staff than to professional staff. This observation suggests that some aspect of non-professional staff behavior might precipitate or reinforce offender aggression and that some form of staff training might be appropriate, especially for non-professional staff.

Understanding the Development of Offending Behavior

Many authors have proposed that a case formulation should both account for the development of the presenting problem and integrate the development with the presenting problem, and that this should be one of the criteria for a good formulation and should be part of professional training in case formulation (Eells, 2007a).

For example, many forensic case formulations note the absence of appropriate social behavior and compensatory inappropriate social behavior in offenders; often forensic case formulations attempt to describe how appropriate social behavior was not learned and how socially inappropriate behavior came to take its place and serve the same purpose as the absent appropriate social behavior (Gresswell & Hollin, 1994). Many FCF also note the unusual family histories of many offenders. These histories might include the absence of models for appropriate behavior, the presence of models for socially inappropriate behavior, punishment for appropriate behavior, and reinforcement of behavior that subsequently develops into offending behavior. Thus, an offender's history might reveal that as a child his or her family members routinely engaged in violence, presented few models and opportunities to learn problem solving, and punished delaying of gratification. If as an adolescent, the future offender subsequently becomes part of a subculture that punishes typical social behavior and reinforces deviant behavior socially and through the material benefits of offendings, such as through acquisitive offenses, then the clinician might link this history to the current presenting problems of violence, acquisitive offenses, lack of problem-solving skills, and intolerance for delay of gratification. Of course, an offender may present with the same main problems, but through a different learning history. These differences in learning histories might make a significant difference in treatment, for example, if a second person presented with the same problems – aggression and acquisitive offenses – but learned these behaviors with a history of anxiety, avoidance of criticism.

A second potential benefit of FCF is that it may make sense of apparently senseless behavior, such as offending behavior that is harmful to the person or that, at least at first blush, appears to be a random and bizarre act of violence that occurred out of the blue. A good example of how a history-based FCF can account for a seemingly meaningless highly violent offense and guide a treatment plan comes from Gresswell and Hollin (1994), who reported a case formulation of the development of offending behavior in a murderer.

Understanding the development of offending behavior and how this relates to the current problems and their maintaining factors may also be helpful to the clinician in developing an integrated FCF and a better treatment plan. For example, if a history consistently identifies deficits in certain social or problem-solving skills that are repeatedly related to offending or clinically important behavior, then this aspect of the history may point the clinician toward an appropriate and powerful intervention strategy that addresses many of the offender's significant problems. The potential benefit of incorporating history into a case formulation when it relates to current important variables comes from Wolpe's annotated case formulations (Wolpe & Turkat, 1985). These reveal Wolpe conducting detailed clinical interviews to search for potential conditioning events that can be important for some clinical problems. Wolpe then uses the results of these history-based interviews to identify variables in the *present* environment that can be manipulated to conduct treatment. For example, Wolpe and Turkat (1985, pp. 13–22) reported a case study of a woman with a fear of passing out. Only after extensive interviewing did Wolpe find a possible conditioning event that might have accounted for the onset of the problem. She finally revealed that when she was five years old she was taken to hospital without her parents and told that she would have an unannounced eye operation which she experienced as "total terror" (p. 16). Thus, Wolpe could now formulate the case as a fear of passing out and losing control based on this early conditioning event. This formulation also accounted for other specific fears, such as a fear of begin in deep water where she also feared passing out. Kuyken et al. (2009, pp. 225–228) used a similar process when they linked a client's core beliefs of being "a waste of space" and "useless" to specific historical traumatic events. Again, though, they use history to inform an understanding of current behavior and its relationship to the environment to develop a treatment plan based on current variables that can be changed. In the end we are not Time Lords: history is not a variable that we can manipulate; current environmental variables and behavior can be changed and sometimes client history helps us to identify what those current environmental variables might be.

Case Formulation of Current Problems: Personality Disorders

Offenders present with a very wide range of current problems which often include more severe mental health issues, including personality disorders, psychoses, aggressive behavior, concurrent substance abuse problems, and sexual disorders. Additionally, they may present with skill deficits, such as unassertiveness and lack of sexual knowledge and behavior, and excessive behaviors, such as bullying and lying. These current problems are often the focus of clinical interest, including case formulation. These problems are too diverse for this chapter to review comprehensively, and the reader is referred to generic volumes on case formulation (Eells, 2007a; Hersen & Rosqvist, 2009; Sturmey, 2007, 2008, 2009a). This section will illustrate the applications of case formulation to two common forensic problems: personality disorders and aggression.

Personality disorders seem an unlikely candidate for case formulation; many people see them as ingrained structural characteristics of a person reflecting the person's underlying, unchanging, and perhaps unchangeable biology. Yet the classic psychology literature on personality is replete with the well-established finding that personality and environment interact with one another, resulting in considerable variability in behavior within and across people. Sometimes environment swamps personality and all people behave in the same manner; sometimes extraverts behave in a timid fashion and very anxious people are sometimes brave in the face of extreme threats. Thus, whatever the status of the construct of personality, one must allow for environmental variables to influence behavior.

Diagnostic labels such as personality disorders serve a number of useful purposes, such as shorthand ways of communicating something about clients, service planning, and legal functions; however, the use of constructs such as personality disorders as explanations of observed behavior is illogical, since behavior is used to infer the presence of the alleged construct and then the alleged, unobserved construct is used to explain the observed behavior used to infer the construct itself. Skinner (1953: 284) writes that: "The personality, like the self, is said to be responsible for features of behavior. For example, delinquent behavior is sometimes attributed to a psychopathic personality … We may quarrel with any analysis which appeals to a self or personality as an inner determiner of action, but the facts which have been represented with such devices cannot be ignored." Skinner went on to discuss which observations of behavior lead to the inference of personality. He noted that responses can be organized by environmental variables such as reinforcer deprivation. For example, a person who is hungry adjourns a meeting and eats, but a sated person no longer speaks or behaves as the hungry person he formally was. The timid person made angry shows all the characteristic behavior of a person whose behavior is reinforced by observing other people suffer: they watch aggressive movies, yell at others, and see the other people cower. Skinner went on to suggest that a single personality is not a useful construct, but rather that the environmental variables related to reinforcement organize our responses. Thus, the pious personality of a Sunday Christian religious congregation is replaced by the angry and aggressive business person on Monday morning at work. These two so-called personalities perhaps inhabit the same skin, but they come and go with available contingencies.

There have been several interesting applications of case formulation to personality disorder. For example, Turkat's (1985) important volume on behavioral case formulation includes case descriptions of antisocial (Sutker & King, 1985), paranoid (Turkat, 1985), and histrionic personality disorders (Bantley & Callon, 1985). All three of these functional assessments of personality disorders share several things in common. They operationalize the patterns of behavior denoted by the shorthand of "personality disorder," and identify the reinforcers that hold those patterns of behavior together. Intervention, where possible, involves addressing each cluster of behavior and its associated reinforcer by teaching new ways of obtaining these reinforcers or devaluing them. The most pertinent example for this chapter is the example of antisocial personality disorder (ASPD), and this chapter will discuss this example in some detail.

Sutker and King (1985) offered a behavioral case formulation of Mr V, a 28-year-old man who met DSM-III criteria for ASPD. Mr V's primary physician referred him for assessment after he had a car accident. He subsequently reported lower back pain without any known organic origin and requested medication for his lower back pain. The authors conducted a behavioral assessment using a clinical interview, a review of medication charts, interviews with significant others in Mr V's life, including his wife, and an extensive psychometric assessment.

During the initial interview Mr V was cooperative, verbally facile, emotionally responsive, and uninhibited. He was unclear about the direction of his life and concerned about his marriage and some apparently minor legal problems. Although he admitted a history of legal problems and drug abuse in the past, he asserted that he had grown out of these problems. Based on this and two weeks of self-monitoring, Sutker and King developed four main domains of problems, including back pain, depression, marital discord, and legal difficulties and their associated situational factors. For example, legal difficulties included driving while drunk, speeding tickets, and the injury litigation. These problems were influenced by situations such as alcohol and drug use, and increased idle time.

Subsequent assessment with his wife and reviews of his medical records revealed an extensive history of legal and illegal drug and alcohol abuse, marital problems related to repeated flagrant sexual infidelity, and changing jobs without warning with subsequent financial problems. The psychometric assessment and a further interview with Mr V revealed yet further problems throughout his development. Intelligence tests results were scattered and suggested someone who was able, but was easily distracted and had failed to maximize his intellectual abilities. Other assessment information revealed that his family home had lacked supervision and his parents frequently fought in relation to his father's drinking and staying out late at night. His parents divorced when he was 11 years old. During adolescence he engaged in extraverted, sensation seeking behaviors, including drug use, sexual behavior, and criminal behavior. He avoided the academic aspects of school and his home because his mother was too critical for him. After marrying a young woman because she was pregnant by him he obtained employment. He led a relatively settled life for two years, but became bored of his wife and this lifestyle and returned to his former habits. After joining the marines for two years this pattern continued and he had further easy access to illegal drugs. He enjoyed being in the marines because of the physical aspects of the job, a culture condoning sexual promiscuity, and its camaraderie. After his recent drunk driving offense his wife, who had threatened divorce previously on many occasions, then filed for divorce for the first time. This precipitated his most depressed episode and he reflected that his drug use caused more problems that it solved.

Sutker and King's case formulation noted that this man had several significant strengths, including intelligence, responsiveness to structured environments, such as the marines, and some motivation to escape the negative emotions he experienced. During the development of his problems he experienced few negative consequences for deviant behavior. His drug abuse was initially effective in reducing negative emotions, but eventually was ineffective in achieving happiness and a personally satisfying life.

The formulation of his current problem identified four problem areas. These included (i) antisocial psychopathology, such as alcohol and substance abuse, and impulsive reckless behavior, such as promiscuity and drunk driving; (ii) depression, such as complaints of boredom, reduced activity, and exaggeration of pain; (iii) cognitive and behavioral dyscontrol, such as little impulse control and poor self-discipline in many areas of his life; and (iv) social immaturity and dependence, such as being both demanding of significant others and simultaneously not investing in personal relationships. This case formulation suggested several treatment goals, such as maintaining an alcohol and drug-abuse-free life, finding exciting alternatives to drug-abuse and promiscuity, learning skills to manage his negative emotions, acquiring some self-discipline in his life, and improving relationships with his wife or divorcing and gaining clear goals for work and education. Based on this formulation, Sutker and King derived several elements of a possible treatment plan. These included (i) forming a good therapeutic relationship that avoided any appearance of superficiality or manipulation to which Mr V might be especially sensitive; (ii) reduction of alcohol and substance abuse, and subsequent possible relapses, perhaps through in-patient treatment; (iii) use of positive reinforcement, rather than punishment during the therapeutic relationship; (iv) maximizing personal strengths, such as social facility and physical prowess; and (v) removal of antecedent stimuli associated with drug abuse and antisocial behavior. As mentioned earlier, behavioral case formulation and assessment of acute dynamic risk factors overlap, and this case illustrates this. For example, a risk assessment might identify alcohol and substance abuse antecedent stimuli related to drug use and antisocial behavior as acute, dynamic risk factors that are modifiable and that could be the basis for a treatment plan, such as Sutker and King suggested.

This approach to formulation of ASPD emphasizes breaking down the global construct of "personality" into a matrix of response classes and their controlling environmental variables, such as situations that influence each response class. The problem of distortion and lying from clients who may have a lifetime of deceit and minimization of personal problems is addressed by using multiple informants and sources of information. Treatment is potentially difficult because the construct of "personality" in part denotes that the problems to be addressed are pervasive throughout many of the person's life domains and hence treatment may include many independent and/or interdependent problems to be addressed. For example, in Sutker and King's treatment plan they gave preeminence to treatment of drug and alcohol abuse as an essential area for change which, if not addressed, was likely to undermine treatment of other domains. Nevertheless, effective treatment of this problem domain may have some benefit to other domains, but would be unlikely to change all four problem domains, which would probably require other interventions.

Outstanding Issues in Case Formulation

There is now an extensive literature – if not, indeed, book industry – on case formulation, which provides many models for clinicians to use in case formulation, including FCF (Sturmey & McMurran, 2011). Yet, despite the surfeit of case formulation books, the research literature is meager. There are many issues relating to case formulation that remain troubling, leading some to refer to case formulation as "the Emperor's clothes" and to call for some modest covering of this naked emperor (Kuyken, 2006).

CONCLUSIONS

Forensic mental health professionals conduct risk assessments and cases formulations to reduce the public's exposure to risk and to provide case formulations as the basis for idiographic treatments. There is now an extensive battery of risk assessment instruments and there is a substantial research literature on their use with offenders, including offenders with ID. Case formulation is a core clinical function for many mental health professionals which can be applied to FCF, but it faces special challenges. Although there are models for clinicians to use when conducting forensic case formulation, there is relatively little research available so far. Future research should focus on developing a more extensive research base, which should address the generic kinds of issues in case formulation, such as reliability, validity, how to use formulations with clients, and professional training, as applied to forensic services.

REFERENCES

Andrews, D.A., & Bonta, J. (2010). *The psychology of criminal conduct* (5th ed.). New Providence, NJ: LexisNexis.

Bantley, P.J., & Callon, E.B. (1985). The case of Ms. H. In I.D. Turkat (Ed.), *Behavioral case formulation* (pp. 199–252). New York: Plenum.

Barbaree, H.E., Seto, M.C., Langton, C.M., & Peacock, E.J. (2001). Evaluating the predictive accuracy of six risk assessment instruments for adult sex offenders. *Criminal Justice and Behavior, 28*, 490–521.

Chadwick, P., Williams, C., & Mackenzie, J. (2003). Impact of case formulation in cognitive behaviour therapy for psychosis. *Behaviour Research and Therapy, 41*, 671–680.

Daffern, M., Jones, L., Howells, K., Shine, J., Mikton, C., & Tunbridge, V. (2007). Refining the definition of offence paralleling behaviour. *Criminal Behaviour and Mental Health, 17*, 265–273

de Vogel, V., & de Ruiter, C. (2005). The HCR-20 in personal disordered female offenders: A comparison with a matched sample of males. *Clinical Psychology and Psychotherapy, 21*, 226–240.

Dolan, M., & Khawaja, A. (2004). The HCR-20 and post discharge outcome in male patients discharged from medium security in the UK. *Aggressive Behavior, 30*, 469–483.

Douglas, K.S., & Belfrage, H. (2014). Interrater reliability and concurrent validity of the HCR-20 Version 3. *International Journal of Forensic Mental Health, 13*, 130–139.

Douglas, K.S., Hart, S., Webster, C., & Belfrage, H. (2013). *HCR-20 V3: Assessing risk for violence, user guide*. Burnaby, BC: Mental Health, Law and Policy Institute, Simon Fraser University.

Douglas, K.S., & Ogloff, J.R. (2003). The impact of confidence on the accuracy of structured professional and actuarial violence risk judgements in a sample of forensic psychiatric patients. *Law and Human Behaviour, 27*, 573–587.

Doyle, M., Archer Power, L., Coid, J., Kallis, C., Ullrich, S., & Shaw, J. (2014). Predicting post-discharge community violence in England and Wales using the HCR-20 V3. *International Journal of Forensic Mental Health, 13*, 140–147.

Dunn, M. (2009). A cognitive analytic formulation. In P. Sturmey (Ed.), *Clinical case formulation: Varieties of approaches* (pp. 199–213). Chichester, UK: John Wiley & Sons, Ltd.

Eells, T.D. (Ed.) (2007a). *Handbook of psychotherapy case formulation*. New York: Guilford Press.

Eells, T.D. (2007b). Psychotherapy case formulation: History and current status. In T.D. Eells (Ed.), *Handbook of psychotherapy case formulation* (pp. 1–25). New York: Guilford Press.

Elbogen, E.B. (2002). The process of violence risk assessment: A review of descriptive research. *Aggression and Violent Behaviour, 7*, 591–604.

Grann, M., Belfrage, H., & Tengstrom, A. (2000). Actuarial assessment of risk for violence: Predictive validity of the VRAG and the historical part of the HCR-20. *Criminal Justice and Behavior, 27*, 97–114.

Gray, N.S., Fitzgerald, S., Taylor, J., MacCulloch, M., & Snowden, R. (2007). Predicting future reconviction in offenders with intellectual disabilities: The predictive efficacy of the VRAG, PCL-SV and the HCR-20. *Psychological Assessment, 19*, 474–479.

Gresswell, D.M., & Hollin, C.R. (1994). Multiple murder: A review. *British Journal of Criminology, 34*, 1–14.

Grevatt, M., Thomas-Peter, B., & Hughes, G. (2004). Violence, mental disorder and risk assessment: Can structured clinical assessments predict the short-term risk of inpatient violence? *Journal of Forensic Psychiatry and Psychology, 15*, 278–292.

Hanson, R.K., & Harris, A.J.R. (2000). Where should we intervene? Dynamic predictors of sexual offence recidivism. *Criminal Justice and Behavior, 27*, 6–35.

Hanson, R.K., & Morton-Bourgon, K. (2004). *Predictors of sexual recidivism: An updated meta-analysis* (Corrections Research User Report No. 2004-02). Ottawa: Public Safety Canada.

Hanson, R.K., & Thornton, D. (1999). *Static-99: Improving actuarial risk assessments for sex offenders* (User Report 1999-02). Ottawa: Department of the Solicitor General of Canada.

Hare, R.D. (1991). *The Hare Psychopathy Checklist: Revised*. Toronto: Multi-Health Systems.

Harris, G.T., Rice, M.E., & Quinsey, V.L. (1993). Violent recidivism of mentally disordered offenders: The development of a statistical prediction instrument. *Criminal Justice and Behavior, 20*, 315–335.

Harris, G., Rice M., Quinsey V., & Cormier C. (2015). *Violent offenders: Appraising and managing risk* (3rd ed.). Washington, DC: American Psychological Association.

Hart, S.D., Cox, D.N., & Hare, R.D. (1995). *The Hare PCL: SV*. Toronto: Multi-Health Systems.

Haynes, S.N., & O'Brien, W.H. (2000). *Principles and practice of behavioral assessment.* New York: Springer.

Hersen, M., & Rosqvist, J. (2009). *Handbook of psychological assessment, case conceptualization, and treatment. Volume 1: Adults.* Chichester, UK: John Wiley & Sons, Ltd.

Kroner, D.G., & Mills, J.F. (2001). The accuracy of five risk appraisal instruments in predicting institutional misconduct and in new convictions. *Criminal Justice and Behavior*, *28*, 471–489.

Kuyken, W. (2006). Evidence-based case formulation: Is the emperor clothed? In N. Tarrier (Ed.), *Case formulation in cognitive behaviour therapy: The treatment of challenging and complex clinical cases* (pp. 12–35). London,: Brunner-Routledge.

Kuyken, W., Padesky, C.A., & Dudley, R. (2009). *Collaborative case conceptualization: Working effectively with clients in cognitive-behavioral therapy.* New York: Guilford Press.

Langton, C.M., Barbaree, H.E., Seto, M.C., Peacock, E.J., Harkins, L., & Hanson, K.T. (2007). Actuarial assessment of risk for re-offence amongst adult sex offenders: Evaluating the predictive accuracy of the Static-2002 and five other instruments. *Criminal Justice and Behavior*, *24*, 37–59.

Lapaalainen, R., Timonen, T., & Haynes, S.N. (2009). Theoretical orientation and rationale. In P. Sturmey (Ed.), *Clinical case formulation: Varieties of approaches* (pp. 157–178). Chichester, UK: John Wiley & Sons, Ltd.

Lindsay, W.R., Hogue, T., Taylor, J.L., Steptoe, L., Mooney, P., Johnston, S., O'Brien, G., & Smith, A.H.W. (2008). Risk assessment in offenders with intellectual disabilities: A comparison across three levels of security. *International Journal of Offender Therapy and Comparative Criminology*, *52*, 90–111.

Lindsay, W.R., Murphy, L., Smith, G., Murphy, D., Edwards, Z., Grieve, A., Chettock, C., & Young, S.J. (2004). The dynamic risk assessment and management system: An assessment of immediate risk of violence for individuals with intellectual disabilities, and offending and challenging behaviour. *Journal of Applied Research in Intellectual Disabilities*, *17*, 267–274.

Litwack, T.R. (2001). Actuarial versus clinical assessments of dangerousness. *Psychology, Public Policy, and Law*, *7*, 409–443.

Monahan, J. (1981). *The clinical prediction of violent behavior.* Washington, DC: US Government Printing Office.

Quinsey, V.L., Book, A., & Skilling, T.A. (2004). A follow-up of deinstitutionalised men with intellectual disabilities and histories of antisocial behaviour. *Journal of Applied Research in Intellectual Disabilities*, *17*, 243–254.

Quinsey, V.L., Harris, G.T., Rice, M.E., & Cormier, C.A. (1998). *Violent offenders: Appraising and managing risk.* Washington, DC: American Psychological Association.

Rice, M., Harris, G., & Lang, C. (2013). Validation of and revision to the VRAG and SORAG: The Violence Risk Appraisal Guide – Revised (VRAG-R). *Psychological Assessment*, *25*, 951–965.

Shepherd, M., & Lavender, T. (1999). Putting aggression into context: An investigation into contextual factors influencing the rate of aggressive incidents in a psychiatric hospital. *Journal of Mental Health*, *8*, 159–170.

Skinner, B.F. (1953). *Science and human behavior.* New York: Simon & Schuster.

Steadman, H., Fabisiak, S., Dvoskin, J., & Holohean, E. (1987). A survey of mental disability among state prison inmates. *Hospital and Community Psychiatry*, *38*, 1086–1090.

Steptoe, L., Lindsay, W.R., Murphy, L., & Young, S.J. (2008). Construct validity, reliability and predictive validity of the Dynamic Risk Assessment and Management System (DRAMS) in offenders with intellectual disability. *Legal and Criminological Psychology*, *13*, 309–321.

Strand, S., & Belfrage, H. (2001). Comparison of HCR-20 scores in violent mentally disordered men and women: Gender differences and similarities. *Psychology, Crime & Law*, *7*, 71–79.

Strub, D.S., Douglas, K., & Nicholls, T.L. (2014). The validity of version 3 of the HCR-20 violence risk assessment scheme amongst offenders and civil psychiatric patients. *International Journal of Forensic Mental Health*, *13*, 148–159.

Sturmey, P. (Ed.) (2007). *Functional analysis in clinical treatment*. New York: Academic Press.

Sturmey, P. (2008). *Behavioral case formulation and intervention: A functional analytic approach*. Chichester, UK: John Wiley & Sons, Ltd.

Sturmey, P. (Ed.) (2009a). *Varieties of case formulation*. Chichester, UK: John Wiley & Sons, Ltd.

Sturmey, P. (2009b). Case formulation: A review and overview of this volume. In P. Sturmey (Ed.), *Varieties of case formulation* (pp. 3–30). Chichester, UK: John Wiley & Sons, Ltd.

Sturmey, P., & McMurran, M. (Eds.) (2011). *Forensic case formulation*. Chichester, UK: John Wiley & Sons, Ltd.

Sutker, P.B., & King, A.R. (1985). Antisocial personality disorder. In I.D. Turkey (Ed.), *Behavioral case formulation* (pp. 115–153). New York: Springer.

Thornton, D. (2002). Constructing and testing a framework for dynamic risk assessment. *Sexual Abuse: A Journal of Research and Treatment*, *14*, 139–153.

Thornton, D., Mann, R., Webster, S., Blud, L., Travers, R., Friendship, C., & Erikson, M. (2003). Distinguishing and combining risks for sexual and violent recidivism. *Annals of the New York Academy of Sciences*, *989*, 225–235.

Turkat, I.D. (Ed.) (1985). *Behavioral case formulation*. New York: Springer.

Webster, C.D., Eaves, D., Douglas, K.S., & Wintrup, A. (1995). *The HCR-20: The assessment of dangerousness and risk*. Vancouver, BC: Simon Fraser University and British Colombia Forensic Psychiatric Services Commission.

Wolpe, J., & Turkat, I.D. (1985). Behavioral formulation of clinical cases. In I.D. Turkat (Ed.), *Behavioral case formulation* (pp. 5–36). New York: Springer.

3

Assessment of Violence and Homicide

KERRY SHELDON AND KEVIN HOWELLS

Practitioners working with perpetrators of violence typically have a number of important assessment tasks. Although these tasks may appear at first to be relatively discrete, closer examination reveals that they are strongly interrelated and that they all depend, ultimately, on two conditions (themselves interrelated): (i) the availability of an adequate theory of violence and its causation; and (ii) an empirical research base. Some practitioners and theorists focus on one particular facet of violence assessment, for example the prediction of future violence (risk assessment) or conducting assessments for treatment, while others are required to span a broad range of assessment tasks. For the purposes of this chapter, we identify the following types of assessment task: (i) assessment for prediction, (ii) assessment for understanding and formulation of the individual case, and (iii) assessment relating to treatment. Finally, we consider assessment in relation to a specific form of violence-homicide. First, however, violence needs to be defined.

VIOLENCE: DEFINITIONS AND CONCEPTIONS

There are many variations in the definition of violence. Anderson and Bushman (2002), for example, define violence as aggression that has extreme harm as its goal. Webster, Douglas, Eaves, and Hart (1997a) define violence as actual, attempted, or threatened harm to a person or persons that is deliberate and non-consenting.

Assessments in Forensic Practice: A Handbook, First Edition. Edited by Kevin D. Browne, Anthony R. Beech, Leam A. Craig, and Shihning Chou.
© 2017 John Wiley & Sons Ltd. Published 2017 by John Wiley & Sons Ltd.

This would include behavior that is fear-inducing, for example stalking. The World Health Organization (WHO) defines violence as the "intentional use of physical force or power, threatened or actual, against oneself, another person, or against a group or community, that either results in or has a high likelihood of resulting in injury, death, psychological harm, maldevelopment or deprivation" (Krug, Dahlberg, Mercy, Zwi, & Lozano, 2002, p. 5). This definition covers a broad range of outcomes – including psychological harm, deprivation, and maldevelopment. The WHO argues that this reflects a growing recognition among researchers and practitioners of the need to include violence that does not necessarily result in physical injury or death, but that nonetheless imposes a substantial burden on individuals, families, communities, and health-care systems. More commonly, however, the label of violence is restricted to behavior where physical harm is inflicted. It would also seem that the "intent" of the perpetrator is an important aspect when defining whether an act is violent, thereby requiring knowledge of the internal processes of the individual committing the behavior.

Violent offending forms a subcategory of violence, referring to acts of violence that contravene the legal code. However, defining an individual as a violent offender on the basis of whether they have committed a particular violent offense is highly problematic (Kenny & Press, 2006). The latter authors point out that considerable differences in behavior exist between acts that meet a legal definition for violence, such as assault, and have called for a reliable coding system for classifying violent acts and offenses. There are also many ways of distinguishing *within* the violent offender group. Serin (2004) suggests that imminence, severity, its nature, victim affiliation, and weapon use/preference are important aspects and that violent offenders can be defined in terms of their motivations (affective versus instrumental), victim choice (spouse versus not), and type of offense. The issue of the demonstrated *heterogeneity* of violent acts and violent actors is an important one for practitioners to consider (Howells, 2010; McGuire, 2008).

The uncertainty and complexity of the definition of violence has important implications for everything that clinical and forensic practitioners do. How violent behavior is defined and classified has a major impact when assessing violence, when attempting to predict it, and for defining the level of treatment needed in a specific population. For instance, a restricted definition will create a smaller group of individuals requiring treatment than will an inclusive one. In addition, drawing comparisons between studies is difficult where there are wide variations in clinical and research practice, with violent offender status sometimes ascribed on the basis of their index offense alone, at other times on the basis of their whole criminal history, and for others on the basis of the most frequent offense (Howells, Daffern, & Day, 2008). Furthermore, definitional problems can also affect the frequency of violence and the pattern of its relationship with other variables (Kenny & Press, 2006).

Assessment for Risk Prediction

Risk, in this context, typically refers to the probability of an individual reoffending after release from prison, or at some other stage in the future. The concept dates back to the early twentieth century when researchers used official files that held information about the demographic and criminal history of the offender (Howitt, 2006). Conceptually, there is a distinction between the likelihood that an individual will commit a further crime in the future (risk) and the level of danger or adverse consequences to the victim from a crime (dangerousness). Therefore, a person might be judged at a high risk of reoffending, but the predicted act may be no more than shoplifting. On the other hand, a person may have a low risk of reoffending but, if they do, very serious consequences are expected for the victim (Clark, 1999).

Making judgments of risk is an inexact and even speculative exercise, so practitioners need a clear rationale and structure underpinning their approach to risk assessment. A good risk assessment estimates the risk and danger to the public a person may pose, and thus may enhance public safety via prevention and risk management plans. Although not always perceived as such by the person being assessed, a good quality risk assessment may also be in the long-term best interests of the individual being assessed, as well as society more widely. A good risk assessment maximizes professional accountability, improving the transparency and consistency of decisions.

The assessment of risk of violence is best considered within two frameworks: first, that provided by the aggression theory (Howells et al., 2008) and, second, that provided within the "What Works" framework or "Risk-Needs-Responsivity (RNR)" model (Andrews & Bonta, 2006). The RNR approach highlights three important assessment tasks in relation to violent offenders, following on from the accepted rehabilitation principles of risk, criminogenic needs, and responsivity. First, the *risk* principle suggests that high-risk offenders should receive the most intensive treatment whereas those of low risk require less intensive intervention. Second, the *need* principle recognizes that the factors causally linked to violent offending need to be the focus of intervention and, by implication, of assessment. These "criminogenic needs" relate to an offender's lifestyle, cognitions, and behavior. Third, the *responsivity* principle posits that treatments should be tailored to the characteristics, abilities, and learning styles of the offender. Adherence to the risk-need-responsivity principles has provided meaningful guideposts from which to construct valid instruments for the purposes of violence risk assessment.

Turning first to the implications of the *risk* principle for assessment purposes, it is notable that the principle justification for the existence of specialized forensic services is to conduct violence risk assessment and management (Doyle & Dolan, 2008). The development of risk assessment has become a major activity in forensic and clinical practice and being a high-risk-status offender is central to admission to some forensic services. For instance, to be admitted to one of the Dangerous and Severe Personality Disordered services in England, the offender must be shown to pose a high risk, in combination with meeting other criteria (Sheldon & Krishnan, 2009). Violent offenders clearly need to be assessed to determine whether their level of risk is such that intensive treatment and rehabilitation are required.

Generations of Risk Assessment

It is now widely acknowledged in the literature that there are three "generations" of risk assessment: *clinical judgment*, the *actuarial approach*, and *structured professional judgment*. Historically, first-generation risk instruments were based on unstructured, non-systematic subjective clinical judgments. The approach had the advantage of being flexible, allowing clinicians to focus on idiosyncratic influences and violence prevention (Hart, 1998). There is, however, a general consensus that clinical inference is not a powerful tool for assessing the level of risk a person may pose because of a number of limitations, including inadequate interrater reliability across assessors, and a failure to specify the decision-making process (Hart, 1998; Monahan, 1981). In his classic review of the field in 1981, Monahan criticized the accuracy of this approach and later concluded that only one in three positive predictions of violence made by mental health professionals was accurate (Monahan, 1984). Further limitations associated with this approach include a lack of specificity in defining either violent behavior or dangerousness leading to personal biases affecting prediction (Monahan, 1981); a reliance on illusory correlations in which we assume that there is a correlation between two behaviors if they appear to coexist (Chapman & Chapman, 1969); a lack of corrective feedback concerning the results of clinician's predictions (Loza, 2003); discounting the influence of situational or environmental factors on behavior (Bandura, 1971); and ignoring the low base rate for violent recidivism which increases the chance of making false predictions (Webster & Menzies, 1988).

In light of these limitations, the second-generation risk prediction methods were purely statistical driven, that is, actuarial (Bonta, 2002). In other words, only items that were maximally predictive of recidivism were included (e.g., having a previous violent offense), regardless of their theoretical or rehabilitative value. Grove and Meehl (1996) advocated for the actuarial approach to risk assessment over clinical judgment primarily on the basis of superior accuracy, demonstrating that actuarial measures were statistically better at predictive accuracy than unaided clinical judgment. But there are other identified advantages of actuarial measures, beyond that of accuracy for instance: their underlying logic and methodology are more transparent to, and understandable by, those involved in predicting violence (Baird, 1985; Gottfredson, 1987; Mossman, 2000).

VRAG as an Example of Actuarial Assessment

Efforts to produce actuarial assessments which combine risk factors that predict future violent behavior have been met with some success. For instance, the most widely used scale is the Violence Risk Appraisal Guide (VRAG; Webster, Harris, Rice, Cormier, & Quinsey, 1994) used to predict violent recidivism within a psychiatric sample, upon release to the community. This is a 12-item scale developed using data from the files of 618 male criminal offenders and forensic patients who were either being evaluated for criminal responsibility or fitness to stand trial, or were being treated in a forensic facility, and who were then followed up archivally for seven years (Harris, Rice, & Quinsey, 1993). It was recalibrated on an extended sample of more than 800 such patients followed for 10 years (Quinsey, Harris, Rice, & Cormier, 1998). The 12 items, or risk factors, selected were those that produced significant independent relationships with violence in multivariate analyses (multiple regression) using violence (yes/no) as the criterion. Three items (separation from parents before age 16, elementary school adjustment, and scores on the Psychopathy Checklist – Revised (PCL-R; Hare, 1991, 2003)) refer to development issues; four items are based on the index offense (age at index offense, victim injury, alcohol abuse, gender of victim); and the other items are diagnosis of personality disorder, diagnosis of schizophrenia, marital status, failure on prior conditional release, and non violent offense score. Due to the reliance on previous convictions to rate three of the items, it is better suited to prison and forensic populations (Doyle & Dolan, 2008). As well as producing a total score, the VRAG is used to allocate an individual to one of nine categories; each category is associated with an estimated probability of violent recidivism. Participants in category 1 have the lowest score and are considered as having a very low risk of violent recidivism and those in category 9 are considered as having a very high risk of recidivism. For example, 33% of the individuals who were in VRAG category 5 recidivated violently within seven years, whereas 100% of those in VRAG category 9 recidivated violently within seven years (Cooke, 2000).

The accuracy of the VRAG in predicting violence in the original sample, as represented by area under the curve (AUC), was .76 (Webster et al., 1994). AUC is a statistic of receiver operating characteristic (ROC) analysis, and it represents the likelihood that a randomly chosen recidivist would have a higher score than a randomly chosen non-recidivist. Therefore, an AUC of .76 means that a randomly chosen recidivist would have a higher score than a non-recidivist 76% of the time. AUCs greater than .70 are considered large effect sizes. In subsequent studies the VRAG has been shown to predict violent recidivism moderately well (Rice, 1997; Rice & Harris, 1995; Rice & Harris, 1997). For example, Rice and Harris (1995) reported ROCs with an AUC statistic of .75 for violence at follow-up periods of 3.5 years in 799 men. In a cross-validation study of Swedish mentally disordered offenders (schizophrenia cohort and personality disordered cohort), Grann, Belfrage, and Tengstrom (2000) found that the VRAG predicted violent reconviction within two years of release/discharge, with a ROC of .68 in both cohorts taken together. The VRAG fared better with the group of personality disordered offenders.

The VRAG has also been shown to predict non-violent (AUC = .68; Kroner & Mills, 2001) and violent convictions (AUC = .67; Mills, Kroner, & Hemmati, 2007) as well as revocations (AUC = .75; Kroner & Mills, 2001) in non-mentally disordered incarcerated males. Despite the fact that the scale was designed to predict violent recidivism over periods of up to 10 years after release, it can moderately predict short-term inpatient violence although not as successfully as the HCR-20 or the PCL:SV (Doyle, Dolan, & McGovern, 2002). The VRAG scale relies heavily on the psychopathy item for successful prediction and this individual item tends to outperform the VRAG total score in terms of prediction accuracy (Doyle, Dolan, & McGovern, 2002; Grann, Belfrage, & Tengstrom, 2000).

Despite the fact that the VRAG and other risk instruments demonstrate fairly good predictive validity, commentators have noted shortcomings associated with these strict models of prediction. Such limitations include a lack of potential generalizability beyond the samples of development; ignoring individual variations in risk; a tendency of actuarial models to exclude factors which, although not empirically associated with violent recidivism, may be logically associated, for example homicidal ideation and threats; and a failure to identify the nature, severity, frequency, or imminence of future violence (Cooke, 2000; Hart, 1998); and minimizing the role of professional judgment (Douglas & Skeem, 2005). It is also argued that the function of actuarial measures is only that of prediction (Doyle & Dolan, 2008). Historically, risk instruments would have been developed to make one-time predictions of violence associated with civil commitment, release decisions, or long-term institutionalization (Douglas & Skeem, 2005). However risk assessment in mental health services, for instance, have broader functions beyond prediction, such as the prevention and management of violent risk (Heilbrun, 2002). Critics of actuarial instruments argue that the true goal of risk assessment should be to inform risk reduction, rather than solely to predict risk (Wong & Gordon, 2006). The clinical reality is that risk does not remain at one point indefinitely, rather practitioners will focus on risk factors that can be changed, such as through treatment (Douglas & Skeem, 2005; Heilbrun, 2002; Webster, Douglas, Belfrage, & Link, 2000).

Assessment of Dynamic Factors

The limitations above not withstanding, the main criticism of actuarial assessments is that they are predominately composed of static factors (Andrews & Bonta, 2006). Static factors are historical, and/or are unchanging (e.g., gender, age at first offense). Although some causal factors for violence are stable and enduring (Hodgins, 2008), the need for measures that include dynamic risk factors has been well described and analyzed by Douglas and Skeem (2005). Douglas and Kropp (2002) similarly argue that static risk can give direction as to the intensity of the treatment required to lessen future violence, but it does little to assist a clinician in (i) deciding how to manage that patient's risk or (ii) identifying treatment targets that might reduce risk levels. In contrast, dynamic risk factors are concerned with understanding change in a person's risk *over time*. Variation can occur as a result of changes in the internal affective or cognitive states of an individual (e.g., he is prone to violence only when under stress, after being disinhibited by alcohol, and when "humiliated" by a woman), or variation may occur according to the situation in which an individual finds himself in (e.g., he is violent only in group settings). Neglect of dynamic risk factors diminishes the formulation of an individual case and the implementation of effective risk-reduction strategies (Howells et al., 2008). As will be apparent from a later section in this chapter, the focus on dynamic risk is congruent with the functional analytical approach to violence risk assessment.

As clinicians are concerned with the clinical task of managing and preventing rather than violence prediction per se, a third generation of risk assessment, known as the *structured professional judgment* (SPJ), developed. This is a composite of the actuarial and clinical approaches (Doyle & Dolan, 2008). The emphasis of the SPJ model is on developing guidelines that structure the exercise of professional discretion. These frameworks are evidence based and promote systemization and consistency but are flexible enough for practitioners to take into account individual specific details of the case and the contexts in which assessments are conducted (Doyle & Dolan, 2008). Consequently, the SPJ approach adheres to the *Needs* principle – where the focus moves from risk judgments to the characteristics which are amenable to intervention and that when changed are associated with a reduced likelihood of reoffending (Andrews & Bonta, 2006; Wong & Gordon, 2006). Although static and dynamic risk factors have both been shown to be useful in predicting risk (Wong & Gordon, 2006), current theorists would argue that dynamic risk factors are more relevant where the focus is on risk reduction (Douglas & Skeem, 2005; Heilbrun, 1997). In practice, it is the ongoing and repeated administration of dynamic risk factors that can tell a practitioner what case-specific intervention strategies to use with an offender and to what extent treatment has been effective – which can, in itself, aid in the decision-making process (Daffern, 2007; Heilbrun, 1997). Langton (2007) argues that this is of considerable importance in settings such as secure services where the principle focus of violence risk assessment is the more immediate timeframe rather than years after transfer/release and where the aim is to identify targets that might be amenable to intervention in order to lower the risk of violence.

Webster, Douglas, Eaves, & Hart (1997b), who are the leading proponents of the SPJ model, argue that clinical violence risk prediction can be improved significantly if:

1. assessments are conducted using well-defined published schema;
2. agreement between assessors is good, through training, knowledge, and expertise;
3. prediction is for a defined type of violent behavior over a set period;

4. violent acts are detectable and recorded;
5. all relevant information is available and substantiated; and
6. actuarial estimates are adjusted only if there is sufficient justification.

SPJ has been implemented on a large scale in some secure forensic mental health services (e.g., at Rampton Hospital in the United Kingdom), with all patients being subjected to comprehensive SPJ assessments. Typically, these include the use of multiple assessment methods and information sources including extensive use of historical and current case information, (e.g., substance misuse); formal consideration of the presence and relevance of risk factors associated with increased risk; identifying the presence and relevance of risk factors which decrease risk (historical, current, and contextual); producing a comprehensive formulation of the person's risk (e.g., the nature, severity, imminence, likelihood, risk-reducing/enhancing factors for violence); and identifying management interventions (e.g., treatment, supervision, monitoring, victim safety planning) which can be developed into a risk management plan (Doyle & Dolan, 2008).

HCR-20 as an Example of a Structured Professional Judgment

Several promising sets of assessment tools have been developed under the SPJ model and would reflect the RNR approach, including the Historical/Clinical/Risk Management-20 (HCR-20; Webster et al., 1997a). The HCR-20 (Webster et al., 1997a) was developed with applicability to a wide variety of settings. It contains 20 items of which 10 relate to *historical*, largely static risk factors (e.g., previous violence and prior supervision failure) included in earlier actuarial tools; five relate to dynamic *clinical* risk factors (e.g., unresponsiveness to treatment and symptoms of major mental illness); and five relate to future situational risk factors which focus on the *management* of the individual (e.g., plans lack feasibility, lack of personal support, and contextual factors such as stress). The items are scored as *not present*, *possible present*, and *definitely present*. The HCR-20 does not provide numerical cut-offs that mandate categorization of individuals into risk levels. Rather, based on the assessment of risk factors, their perceived importance for the individual, the degree of intervention the case will require, and the likelihood that they will be managed effectively, clinicians are encouraged to arrive at a structured final risk judgment of low, moderate, or high.

The usefulness of the HCR-20 as a predictor of post-discharge violence has been explored in a number of studies. For research purposes, it is possible to treat the HCR-20 as an actuarial scale and simply sum the items to produce four-dimensional scores, including a total, which ranges from 0 to 40. Douglas, Ogloff, and Hart (2003) evaluated the predictive ability of the HCR-20 more generally, and the SPJ specifically, in a sample of 100 forensic psychiatric patients who had been found not guilty by reason of a mental disorder and were subsequently released to the community. Violence in the community was established from multiple file based sources. The clinical scale scores, total scores, and structured professional judgments predicted post-release community physical violence and non-physical violence with moderate to large statistical effects (AUC ranged from .67 to .74). In addition multivariate analyses showed that the HCR-20 structured final risk judgments were most strongly related to violence over and above the actuarial scores. A review by Dolan and Doyle (2000) explored the predictive validity of the HCR-20 in small samples of North American non-forensic and civil psychiatric patients. Its ability to predict violent outcomes once individuals were released into the community (as measured by AUC) was moderate to good (.63 to .80). In the United Kingdom, the HCR-20 has been found to significantly predict community violence post-discharge with the dynamic clinical and risk management items adding incremental validity to the historical static factors (Doyle & Dolan, 2006). It has also been shown to have superior predictive ability over Hare's screening version of the psychopathy checklist (Doyle & Dolan, 2006; Douglas, Ogloff, Nicholls, & Grant, 1999).

Research has also focused on the HCR-20's ability to predict short-term inpatient violence (Belfrage, Fransson, & Strand, 2000; Gray et al., 2003; Grevatt, Thomas-Peter, & Hughes, 2004). Daffern (2007) argues that the results of such studies demonstrate the need to be mindful of sample characteristics where there is limited variance in the scores as the scale will show reduced capacity to discriminate between violent and non-violent individuals.

Violence Rating Scale

A more recent fourth generation of risk instrument has been specifically designed to be integrated into (i) the process of risk management; (ii) the selection of intervention methods and treatment targets; and (iii) the assessment of treatment progress (Andrews, Bonta, & Wormith, 2006). These instruments can be administered repeatedly and can document changes in specific criminogenic needs and in the overall risk potential of an individual. Instruments such as this are not very common at present (Bonta, 2002), but one such example is the Violence Rating Scale 2 (VRS; Wong & Gordon, 2000, 2006).

The VRS assesses the risk of violent recidivism in forensic patients. It contains items that are either empirically or theoretically linked to violent recidivism. There are six static or historical items (e.g., age at first violent conviction, number of young offender convictions) and 20 dynamic factors (e.g., mental disorder, weapon use, impulsivity). Each item is rated between 0 (not present/not applicable) and 3 (definitely present/applicable) using descriptive criteria. Published research on the tool is limited (Doyle & Dolan, 2008) but the authors (Wong & Gordon, 2000) report that it has been used to assess the effect of treatment on risk in a violence reduction program in Canada and results indicate that the measure is predictive of violent recidivism at a two-year follow-up (AUC=0.81). In addition, the static factors on this scale have some moderate predictive validity for isolated incidents of inpatient physical assault (AUC = .63) whereas the clinical factors seem most predictive of repetitive inpatient violence (AUC = .60), although the HCR-20 has shown superior accuracy in this regard (Grevatt et al., 2004).

Most of the measures explored in this chapter are general violence risk instruments (e.g., VRAG, HCR-20; VRS). In a few cases instruments have been designed to predict a specific form of violence, such as sexual recidivism (Sexual Violence Risk-20 – SVR-20; Boer, Hart, Kropp, & Webster, 1997). Hence professionals have a choice of assessment tools for the production of general violence, as well as certain types of violent behavior. Although not developed as a risk measure, psychopathic personality traits as assessed by the Psychopathy Checklist – Revised (PCL-R; Hare, 1991, 2003) and more recently the Psychopathy Checklist: Screening Version (PCL:SV) (Hart, Cox, & Hare, 1995) have also been shown to be useful in the prediction of future violence (Gendreau, Goggin, & Smith, 2002; Hare, Clark, Grann, & Thornton, 2000; Hart, Hare, & Forth, 1994; Hemphill, Hare, & Wong, 1998; Monahan, 1996; Salekin, Roger, & Sewell, 1996). In addition, general recidivism risk measures such as the Level of Supervision Inventory – Revised (LSI-R) (Andrews & Bonta, 1995) have been shown to predict future violence with some moderate success (Gendreau et al., 2002; Harris et al., 1993). The utility of more general recidivism measures for predicting violence may in part be due to the overlap in risk factors or violent and general recidivism (Bonta, 2002). Thus, in addition to violence-specific instruments, measures designed for other purposes may also assist in the prediction of violence.

The Functional Approach to Assessment

The range of variables functionally (causally) related to violence has been demonstrated to be large. For an overall review see Howells et al. (2008) and Figure 3.1.

It follows that all such factors need to be addressed in a comprehensive assessment of the individual.

As previously noted, it is increasingly acknowledged that risk assessment for violence needs to include dynamic measures as well as static measures. Consideration of state and situational factors and their effects on disturbed behavior have been bread-and-butter tasks in clinical assessments in general mental health for many years, a product, perhaps, of the emphasis on comprehensive formulation in clinical psychology (Sturmey, 2008), but has been curiously neglected, until recently, in violent offender assessment. The state and situational emphasis is congruent with the functional analytic approach to violence assessment described below. Douglas and Skeem (2005) have described methodologies for assessing dynamic factors influencing violence. Ogloff and Daffern (2002; 2006; 2007) have devised a method for 24-hour prediction of violence (the dynamic appraisal of situational aggression (DASA)), based on daily ratings of behavior by staff, which is based on the variation in violence propensity from day to day.

- Social learning

- Triggering external events and situational factors

- Cognitive appraisals, beliefs, and information-processing styles

- Empathy and perspective-taking deficits

- Negative affective states

- Anger

- Inhibitory and self-regulatory deficits

- Personality traits conducive to aggression

- Personality disorders, including psychopathy

- Substance misuse

- Mental disorder

- Victimization in childhood

Figure 3.1   Factors identified as linked to violence in the literature. (Summarized from Howells et al., 2008.)

Theoretical and empirically derived knowledge about important causal influences for aggression and violence is of critical importance in devising treatment approaches for violent offenders. First, however, the violent behavior of offenders needs to be formulated. Such a formulation may be either idiographic (that is, at the individual level) or nomothetic (at the population level). A nomothetic needs analysis might suggest, for example, that alcohol misuse and emotional dysregulation are known antecedents of aggression in the offender population being addressed and that, therefore, treatment programs to address these problems are required. An idiographic analysis of an individual (rather than the group) might suggest, on the other hand, that a particular person's aggression is influenced by, for example, very particular factors such as exposure to humiliating provocations and subsequent paranoid ideation. Population analyses are essential in service planning while individual analysis is required to plan treatment for the individual offender. Idiographic assessment of causal influences allows for the likelihood that some influences will be idiosyncratic and specific to the individual under consideration. Such analysis is likely to be particularly important in complex populations such as those with Dangerous and Severe Personality Disorders (DSPD) (Howells, Krishnan, & Daffern, 2007).

Functional analytic assessments (Daffern & Howells, 2002, 2009; Daffern, Howells, & Ogloff, 2007; Sturmey, 1996, 2008) seek to clarify the factors responsible for the development, expression, and maintenance of problem behaviors. Such methods may be of assistance in understanding the factors contributing to the development, expression, and maintenance of violence. Functional analytic assessments are typically achieved through assessment of the behavior of interest, assessment of the individual's predisposing characteristics, and consideration of the antecedent events, which are important for the initiation of the behavior, and the consequences of the behavior, that maintain and direct its developmental course (Haynes, 1998; Haynes, Yoshioka, Kloezeman, & Bello 2009).

Assessment and Classification of Function (ACF)

An assessment framework for analyzing the functions of aggressive actions (assessed through review of proximal antecedents and consequences within the context of the individual's predisposing personal attributes and limitations) has been proposed by Daffern and colleagues (Daffern et al., 2007; Daffern & Howells, 2002, 2009). This classification system, the 'Assessment and Classification of Function' (ACF; Daffern et al., 2007), acknowledges that multiple functions may be present for any particular act and that perpetrators may have different goals for different acts. These functions are *Demand avoidance, To force compliance, To express anger, To reduce tension (catharsis), To obtain tangibles, Social distance reduction (attention-seeking), To enhance status or social approval, Compliance with instruction,* and *To observe suffering.* For the ACF, each function is recognized through its characteristic antecedents and consequences and scored as present or absent for a particular aggressive behavior. The ACF acknowledges that violence may have multiple functions and goals for the individual as well as for the group. Indeed any one violent act may have multiple functions, suggesting it is unhelpful to think of functions as necessarily characteristic of the individual offender. Thus methods such as the ACF classify acts rather than actors.

So far the major applications of the ACF have been to mentally disordered violent offenders (Daffern et al., 2007) and to personality disordered offenders (Daffern & Howells, 2009). In a study of 502 aggressive incidents in a high-security forensic psychiatric hospital in Victoria, Australia, Daffern et al. (2007) found that anger expression was the most frequent function of aggression but that functions differed for aggressive behaviors toward staff and those toward fellow patients. Demand avoidance was a common function for aggression toward staff but rare for aggression to patients. To obtain tangibles (an instrumental function) was rare for all incidents. Daffern and Howells (2009) have recently extended this work to high-risk offenders with personality disorders in Rampton Hospital in the United Kingdom and added two further categories of function to the original nine functions, namely "sensation-seeking" and "sexual gratification," to capture apparent sexual/sadistic functions occurring in this very high-risk and complex population. In the latter study the function of the violent offenses leading to admission (index offenses) proved to differ substantially from the functions of violent behaviors within the institution.

The ACF seems to hold promise as a method for assessing violent offenders in the criminal justice system. Howells, McMurran, Howard, and Jinks (2009), for example, have reported using the ACF to analyze the functions of violence in violent juvenile offenders whose violent acts occurred in the context of alcohol use.

Assessing Responsivity in the Violence Perpetrator

As has already been discussed, the assessment of violence may have many purposes: to identify causal or explanatory variables for the violent behavior, to identify consequent treatment targets, and to estimate the probability of future recurrence of violent behavior (risk assessment). The assessment of the violent individual for treatment, however, needs to go beyond the assessment of causal factors and identification of targets, to investigate factors likely to affect response to treatment. The responsivity principle within the RNR model (Andrews & Bonta, 2006) is concerned with exactly this and with the need to ensure that the style and content of interventions is matched to the characteristics of those being treated. The responsivity principle has been neglected relative to the efforts directed to the assessment of risk and need (Ogloff & Davis, 2004).

In recent years interest has developed in the notion that treatment readiness constitutes a vital responsivity factor for violent and other offenders (Howells & Day, 2003; Ward, Day, Howells, & Birgden, 2004; Serin, Donna, Mailloux, & Kennedy, 2007). The high drop-out rates frequently observed in offender programs (Dowden & Serin, 2002; McMurran, 2004; McMurran & Theodosi, 2007) are likely to be attributable in part to low readiness and motivation for the treatment on offer. In relation to the present chapter, the issue arises as to how readiness and motivation can be measured. A prerequisite for a useful readiness assessment is that it be multifactorial, reflecting the many domains within which low readiness may be manifested, including intrapersonal cognitive (Chambers, Eccleston, Day, Ward, & Howells, 2008), affective, behavioral, volitional (goals), and identity factors as well as a range of situational and organizational variables (Ward et al., 2004). There have been attempts to construct readiness measures in some studies of the treatment of violent offenders (Howells et al., 2005; Williamson, Day, Howells, Bubner, & Jauncey, 2003), though these have been often based on "stages of change" theoretical models which have been subject to recent critiques (Casey, Day, & Howells, 2005).

The Violence Treatment Readiness Questionnaire (VTRQ) and the Multifactorial Offender Readiness Model (MORM)

Casey et al. (2007) and Day et al. (2009) have described a brief measure of readiness – the Violence Treatment Readiness Questionnaire (VTRQ) – developed originally from the Multifactorial Offender Readiness Model (MORM) outlined by Ward et al. (2004). Interview-based assessments of similar readiness variables have also been devised by Serin et al. (2007). In the Day et al. (2009) study the VTRQ scale was shown to predict subsequent engagement in a violence treatment program, though this finding needs to be replicated with larger numbers and in relation to different types of violence interventions. The VTRQ scale (Day et al., 2009) is brief (20 items) and proved to be a better predictor of engagement than a longer semi-structured interview assessing the same readiness variables.

The MORM model includes external, situational factors as potential determinants of engagement. Thus there is a need for the practitioner to consider the assessment of these factors. The therapeutic climate of the setting or service within which treatment is delivered is an obvious target for assessment. The EssenCES climate measure, designed and developed by Schalast in Germany (Schalast, Redies, Collins, Stacey, & Howells, 2007), is a promising tool for this task.

Assessment of Homicide

Homicide is not one form of crime or one type of violent behavior but is perpetrated under very different circumstances and for very different reasons. Killing of an intimate partner because of sexual jealousy, killing a biological child due to temporary psychosis, homicide in the course of another crime, racially motivated homicide, and the more unusual cases of serial murder, mass homicide, terrorism, and homicide among children are likely to be very different.

Risk factors for homicide and violent behavior are usually evaluated at the social/community level and at the individual level. At the social/community level, social disorganization has been identified as a risk factor. This includes a lack of social control, high population density, a high percentage of young people, a tolerance for violence, income and racial inequality, poverty, low levels of education, and high unemployment. However, the relative strength of these variables in predicting homicide rates has varied widely in different studies.

At an individual level, there are risk factors associated with specific manifestations of homicide. A risk factor associated with homicide (and indeed violence generally), especially between unrelated males, is alcohol consumption: the offender, victim, or both commonly consume alcohol, usually to excess (Boles & Miotto, 2003; Haggard-Grann, Hallqvist, Langstrom, & Moller, 2006). Offenses often occur in or around the victim's home, in licensed premises, or on the streets, and are often not planned or involve the intention to kill (Brookman, 2005). This suggests that alcohol-related homicides present, for the most part, an extreme version of a common type of violent crime rather than a distinct form of behavior. In contrast, the risk factors associated with infant homicide include mental disturbance of the mother, social deprivation, single parenthood, and violent relationships (Brookman, 2005). While these risk factors may help narrow down the population at highest risk of abuse, it still remains difficult to translate this knowledge into practical and effective ways of identifying particular parents who may need to be the target of prevention strategies for serious abuse – let alone homicide.

Domestic or partner homicide also makes up approximately 40% of homicides in the United Kingdom (Aldridge & Browne, 2003). For instance, of all women murdered between 1995 and 2000, 57% were killed by their current or former partner (husband, boyfriend, or lover), yet less than 7% were killed by a stranger (Brookman, 2005). The indicators seen as most appropriate to assessing the risk of domestic homicide are mainly derived from studies within North America. Some factors are probably more applicable to the United States than the United Kingdom, such as access to guns. But there is a range of factors that may be equally important in both contexts:

- serious injury in a prior abuse incident;
- drug/alcohol abuse;
- access to a weapon/weapons in the household;
- previous threats with a weapon;
- threats to kill;
- threats of suicide should the partner leave;
- forced sex of female partner (Campbell et al., 2003); and
- extensive jealousy (Mullen, 2008).

However, even if these are salient risk factors, some of them, such as threats to kill, do not lead to homicide in a great majority of cases (Aldridge & Browne, 2003)

A significant proportion of intimate partner homicides are preceded by domestic violence by the male before the homicide and frequently occur in the aftermath of a separation, or the woman leaving for another partner (Arbuckle et al., 1996; Brookman, 2005; Campbell, 1992; Campbell et al., 2003; Ellis & DeKeseredy, 1997). Therefore, one of the major ways to decrease intimate partner homicide is to identify those battered women at risk and those perpetrators who are at most at risk of perpetrating domestic violence.

Recently, formal risk assessments for domestic violence and homicide have appeared in the psychological literature. One early attempt is the "Danger Assessment" (DA) instrument (Campbell, 1986) – a 15-item yes/no instrument compiled from a review of research on risk factors for homicide or serious injury in wife-battering relationships. It includes such items as the presence of psychological abuse, escalation of violence, generality of violence, and the perpetrator's misuse of substances, and was originally developed to assess risk of homicide among batterers. It elicits information solely from the victim where she uses a calendar to record incidents and answers the questions herself. (See Campbell, 1995 for a discussion of psychologically based risk assessments for lethality within domestic violence settings.)

In preliminary research with a sample of African American women whose partners had been arrested for domestic violence, scores on the DA were found to be predictive of re-victimization (defined as threatened or actual violence) in the three months after contact (Goodman, Dutton, & Bennett, 2000). Although these data are promising, several limitations to the study make it somewhat difficult to generalize the results to the question of identifying individuals at risk. In particular, it used samples drawn from the legal system, and therefore it is unclear whether the findings may be applied to domestic violence cases in which the courts have not been involved. Furthermore, the outcome of re-abuse was also only measured with one question that did not differentiate between threats and actual assault and therefore did not capture the potential escalation of domestic violence. Importantly, a recent study found that a subset of the DA items were not particularly effective at identifying future risk for severe victimization (including threats of killing the victim) over a four-month period (Weisz, Tolman, & Saunders, 2000). The contradictory results in these two studies may be attributable to methodological differences between the studies (e.g., demographic characteristics of the samples, scoring procedures for the DA, definition/assessment of re-victimization). As such it is difficult to determine how useful this instrument is for the prediction of risk and it may be best seen as a tool for increasing victim awareness regarding risk of homicide and the risk factors that apply in his/her situation (Campbell, 1995).

The Spousal Assault Risk Assessment (SARA)

The Spousal Assault Risk Assessment (SARA; Kropp, Hart, Webster, & Eaves, 1998) is a 20-item instrument for the SPJ of risk for partner violence. The 20 items are divided into two equal sections. Part one comprises factors that are statistically associated with risk of future violence in general – substance misuse, employment problems, mental illness and personality disorder, and items that reflect domestic conflict including exposure to family violence, violation of conditional release, and past assault of family members. Part two includes risk factors that are thought specifically related to partner violence such as recent escalation, sexual jealousy, past use of weapons and/or credible death threats, and attitudes that support spousal assault. The manual instructs raters to use the items, especially the critical items, to form a clinical judgment of low, moderate, or high risk. However, interrater reliability was poor for both the critical items and the clinical risk ratings (Hilton et al., 2004). The limited research available would suggest that it is the risk rating and scores on part two of the SARA that are higher among recidivists than non-recidivists (Grann & Wedin, 2002; Kropp & Hart, 2000). Similarly, that only some of the SARA items are useful predictors of recidivism, such as past violation of a conditional release, personality disorder (including psychopathy), and minimization or denial of spousal assault history (Grann & Wedin, 2002). However, both the DA and SARA are of little value for the police and others who must make quick decisions about the detention of a perpetrator, risk to the victim, and victim assistance (Hilton et al., 2004). But the police are in a unique position to assess risk factors and can interview the victim concerning her fears. Research suggests, for example, that women's ratings of the likelihood that their partners would be aggressive again in the future are more effective at predicting severe violence over short periods than risk factors drawn from the literature (Weisz et al., 2000). It should be noted, however, that the research by Weiss et al. examined only the risk of serious violence; it did not test the woman's assessment of mortal risk (Brookman, 2005).

However, the fact remains that intimate homicides are very difficult to predict because domestic violence is much more widespread than domestic homicide thereby making it difficult to identify who, from the large numbers of women abused, are at mortal risk. Moreover, the majority of even the most serious and repetitive acts of domestic violence do not end in murder. Equally a fair proportion of domestic homicides have no reported history of domestic abuse (Brookman, 2005; Sherman, 1993; Walker & Meloy, 1998).

CONCLUSIONS

In essence, the assessment of homicide requires the same general approach as that advocated above for violent offenders. Individuals who have committed homicide are likely to be over-represented in populations defined as high risk, by virtue of the dangerousness or severity of the act itself, though not necessarily by virtue of the probability of reoffending per se. The presence of "over-control" of angry and aggressive impulses has been suggested as being present in some homicidal offenders (Blackburn, 1971; Davey, Day, & Howells, 2005), though this is not a well-researched area. Where the over-control pattern is present, particular attention would need to be paid to the assessment and potential breakdown of self-regulatory processes. In general, however, mapping the antecedents and functions of a homicidal act requires the same methods as for serious non-homicidal acts, though the high social salience and impact of homicide may warrant a more intensive psychological investigation.

In summary, the practitioner involved in assessing violence has available to them a significant and growing body of empirical research, theoretical ideas, and clinical methods. The role of assessment extends far beyond the determination of risk and is vital in the future development of treatment interventions aimed at the reduction of violence. It is also possible to discern a growing appreciation of the need to understand the individual person who has acted violently – the idiographic approach. Such an approach may enrich knowledge derived from the nomothetic tradition.

REFERENCES

Aldridge, M.L., & Browne, K.D. (2003). Perpetrators of spousal homicide: A review. *Trauma, Violence, & Abuse, 4* (3), 265–276. doi:10.1177/1524838003004003005

Anderson, C.A., & Bushman, B.J. (2002). Human aggression. *Annual Review of Psychology, 53*, 27–51.

Andrews, D., & Bonta, J. (1995). *Level of Service Inventory – Revised.* Toronto, ON: Multi-Health Systems.

Andrews, D., & Bonta, J. (2006). *The psychology of criminal conduct* (3rd ed.). Cincinnati, OH: Anderson.

Andrews, D., Bonta, J., & Wormith, J.S. (2006). The recent past and near future of risk and/or need assessment. *Crime & Delinquency, 52,* 7–22.

Arbuckle, J., Olson, L., Howard, M., Brillman, J., Anctil, C., & Sklar, D. (1996). Safe at home: Domestic violence and other homicides among women in New Mexico. *Annals of Emergency Medicine, 27,* 210–215.

Baird, C. (1985). Classifying juveniles: Making the most out of an important management tool. *Corrections Today, 47,* 32–38.

Bandura, A. (1971). Social learning theory of aggression. In J.F. Knutson (Ed.), *The control of aggression: Implications from basic research.* Chicago, IL: Aldine.

Belfrage, H., Fransson, G., & Strand, S. (2000). Prediction of violence using the HCR-20: A prospective study in two maximum-security correctional institutions. *Journal of Forensic Psychiatry, 11* (1), 167–175.

Blackburn, R. (1971). Personality types among abnormal homicides. *British Journal of Criminology, 11* (1), 14–31.

Boer, D.P., Hart, S.D., Knopp, P.R., & Webster, S. (1997). *Manual for the Sexual Violence Risk-20: Professional guidelines for assessing risk of sexual violence.* Vancouver: British Columbia Institute Against Family Violence.

Boles, S.M., & Miotto, K. (2003). Substance abuse and violence: A review of the literature. *Aggression and Violent Behaviour, 8,* 155–174.

Bonta, K. (2002). Offender risk assessment: Guidelines for selection and use. *Criminal Justice and Behaviour, 29,* 355–379.

Brookman, F. (2005). *Understanding homicide.* London: Sage.

Campbell, J.C. (1986). Nursing assessment for risk of homicide with battered women. *Advances in Nursing Science, 8,* 36–51.

Campbell, J.C. (1992). "If I can't have you, no one can": Power and control in homicide of female partners. In J. Radford & D.E.H. Russel (Eds.), *Femicide: The politics of woman killing* (pp. 99–113). New York: Twayne.

Campbell, J.C. (1995). Prediction of homicide of and by battered women. In J.C. Campbell (Ed.), *Assessing dangerousness: Violence by sexual offenders, batterers and child abusers* (pp. 96–113). Thousand Oaks, CA: Sage.

Campbell, J.C., Webster, D., Koziol-Mclain, J., Block, C., Campbell, D., Curry, M.A., … & Laughton, K. (2003). Risk factors for femicide in abuse relationships: Results from a multisite case control study. *American Journal of Public Health, 93* (7), 1089–1097.

Casey, S., Day, A., & Howells, K. (2005). The application of the trans-theoretical model to offender populations: Some critical issues. *Legal and Criminological Psychology, 10,* 1–15.

Casey, S., Day, A., Howells, K., & Ward, T. (2007). Assessing suitability for offender rehabilitation. *Criminal Justice and Behavior, 34,* 1427–1440.

Chambers, K.C., Eccleston, L., Day, A., Ward, T., & Howells, K. (2008). Treatment readiness in violent offenders: The influence of cognitive factors on engagement in violence programs. *Aggression and Violent Behavior, 13,* 276–284.

Chapman, L., & Chapman, J. (1969). Illusory correlations as an obstacle to the use of valid psychodiagnostic signs. *Journal of Abnormal Psychology*, *74*, 271–280.

Clark, D. (1999). Risk assessment in prisons and probation. *Forensic Update*, *1*, 15–18.

Cooke, D.L. (2000). *Current risk assessment instruments*, *Report of the Committee on Serious Violent and Sexual Offenders (The MacLean Committee)*, Edinburgh: The Scottish Executive. Available from: www.gov.scot/Resource/Doc/158910/0043170.pdf (last retrieved July 10, 2016).

Daffern, M. (2007). The predictive validity and practical utility of structured schemes used to assess risk for aggression in psychiatric inpatient settings. *Aggression and Violent Behaviour*, *12*, 116–130.

Daffern, M., & Howells, K. (2002). Psychiatric inpatient aggression: A review of structural and functional assessment approaches. *Aggression and Violent Behaviour*, *3*, 1–21.

Daffern, M., & Howells, K. (2009). The function of aggression in personality disordered patients. *Journal of Interpersonal Violence*, *24* (4), 586–600.

Daffern, M., Howells, K., & Ogloff, J.R.P. (2007). What's the point? Towards a methodology for assessing the function of psychiatric inpatient aggression. *Behaviour Research and Therapy*, *45*, 101–111.

Davey, L., Day, A., & Howells, K. (2005). Anger, over-control and serious violent offending. *Aggression and Violent Behavior*, *10*, 624–635.

Day, A., Howells, K., Casey, S., Ward, T., Chambers, J.C., & Birgden A. (2009). Assessing treatment readiness in violent offenders. *Journal of Interpersonal Violence*, *24* (4), 618–635.

Dolan, M., & Doyle, M. (2000). Violence risk prediction. *British Journal of Psychiatry*, *177*, 303–311.

Douglas, K.S., & Kropp, P.R. (2002). A prevention-based paradigm for violence risk assessment: Clinical and research applications. *Criminal Justice and Behaviour*, *29*, 617–658.

Doyle, M., & Dolan, M. (2006). Predicting community violence from patients discharged from mental health services. *British Journal of Psychiatry*, *189*, 520–526.

Doyle, M., & Dolan, M. (2008). Understanding and managing risk. In M. Soothill, P. Rogers, & M. Dolan (Eds.), *Handbook of forensic mental health*. Cullompton, UK: Willan.

Doyle, M., Dolan, M., & McGovern, J. (2002). The validity of North American risk assessment tools in predicting in-patient violent behaviour in England. *Legal and Criminological Psychology*, *7*, 141–154.

Douglas, K.S., Ogloff, J.R.P., & Hart, S.D. (2003). Evaluation of a model of violence risk assessment among forensic psychiatric patients. *Psychiatric Services*, *54* (10), 1372–1379.

Douglas, K.S., Ogloff, J.R.P., Nicholls, T.L., & Grant, I. (1999). Assessing risk for violence among psychiatric patients: The HCR-20 violence risk assessment scheme and the Psychopathy Checklist: Screening Version. *Journal of Consulting and Clinical Psychology*, *67*, 917–930.

Douglas, K.S., & Skeem, J.L. (2005). Violence risk assessment: Getting specific about being dynamic. *Psychology, Public Policy and Law*, *11* (3), 347–383.

Dowden, C., & Serin, R. (2002). *Anger management programming for federal male inmates: The impact of dropouts and other program performance variables on recidivism*. Research Branch, Correctional Service Canada. Available from: www.csc-scc.gc.ca/research/092/r82_e.pdf (last retrieved July 10, 2016).

Ellis, D., & DeKeseredy, W.S. (1997). Rethinking estrangement, interventions, and intimate femicide. *Violence Against Women*, *3*, 590–609.

Gendreau, P., Goggin, C., & Smith, P. (2002). Is the PCL-R really the "unparalleled" measure of offender risk? A lesson in knowledge cumulation. *Criminal Justice and Behaviour*, *29*, 397–426.

Goodman, L.A., Dutton, M.A., & Bennett, L. (2000). Predicting repeat abuse among arrested batterers: Use of the Danger Assessment Scale in the criminal justice system. *Journal of Interpersonal Violence*, *15* (1), 63–74.

Gottfredson, D. (1987). Statistical and actuarial considerations. In F. Dutile & C. Foust (Eds.), *The prediction of violence* (pp. 71–81). Springfield, IL: Charles C. Thomas.

Grann, M., Belfrage, H., & Tengstrom, A. (2000). Actuarial assessment of risk for violence: Predictive validity of the VRAG and the historical part of the HCR-20. *Criminal Justice and Behavior*, *27*, 97–114.

Grann, M., & Wedin, I. (2002). Risk factors for recidivism among spousal assault and spousal homicide offenders. *Psychology, Crime & Law*, *8*, 5–23.

Gray, N.S., McGleish, A., MacCulloch, M.J., Hill, C., Timmons, D., & Snowden, R.J. (2003). Prediction of violence and self-harm in mentally disordered offenders: A prospective study of the efficacy of HCR-20, PCL-R and psychiatric symptomatology. *Journal of Consulting and Clinical Psychology*, *71* (3), 443–445.

Grevatt, M., Thomas-Peter, B., & Hughes, G. (2004). Violence, mental disorder and risk assessment: Can structured clinical assessments predict the short-term risk of inpatient violence? *Journal of Forensic Psychiatry and Psychology*, *15* (2), 278–292.

Grove, W.M., & Meehl, P.E. (1996). Comparative efficiency of informal (subjective, impressionistic) and formal (mechanical, algorithmic) prediction procedures: The clinical–statistical controversy. *Psychology, Public Policy, and Law*, *2*, 293–323.

Haggard-Grann, U., Hallqvist, J., Langstrom, N., & Moller, J. (2006). The role of alcohol and drugs in triggering criminal violence: A case-crossover study. *Addiction*, *101*, 100–108.

Hare, R.D. (1991). *Manual for the Hare Psychopathy Checklist – Revised*. Toronto, ON: Multi-Health Systems.

Hare, R.D. (2003). *Manual for the Hare Psychopathy Checklist – Revised* (2nd ed.). Toronto, ON: Multi-Health Systems.

Hare, R.D., Clark, D., Grann, M., & Thornton, D. (2000). Psychopathy and the prediction validity of the PCL-R: An international perspective. *Behavioural Sciences & the Law*, *18*, 623–645.

Harris, G.T., Rice, M.E., & Quinsey, V.L. (1993). Violent recidivism of mentally disordered offenders: The development of a statistical prediction instrument. *Criminal Justice and Behaviour*, *20*, 315–335.

Hart, S.D. (1998). The role of psychopathy in assessing risk for violence: Conceptual and methodological issues. *Legal and Criminological Psychology*, *3*, 121–137.

Hart, S., Cox, D., & Hare, R. (1995). *The Hare PCL:SV Psychopathy Checklist: Screening Version*. New York: Multi-Health Systems.

Hart, S.D., Hare, R.D., & Forth, A.E. (Eds.) (1994). Psychopathy as a risk marker for violence: Development and validation of a screening version. In *Violence and mental disorder: Developments on risk assessment* (pp. 81–97). Chicago, IL: University of Chicago Press.

Haynes, S. (1998). The changing nature of behavioural assessment. In A. Bellack & M. Hersen (Eds.), *Behavioral assessment: A practical handbook* (pp. 1–21). Boston, MA: Allyn and Bacon.

Haynes, S.N., Yoshioka, D.T., Kloezeman, K., & Bello, I. (2009). Clinical applications of behavioural assessment: Identifying and explaining behaviour problems in clinical assessment. In J. Butcher (Ed.), *Oxford handbook of clinical assessment*. New York: Oxford University Press.

Heilbrun, K. (1997). Prediction versus management models of relevant risk assessment: The importance of legal decision making context. *Law and Human Behaviour*, *21*, 347–359.

Heilbrun, K. (2002). Violence risk: From prediction to risk management. In D. Carson & R. Bull (Eds.), *Handbook of psychology in legal contexts* (2nd ed., pp. 127–143). Chichester, UK: John Wiley & Sons, Ltd.

Hemphill, J.F., Hare, R.D., & Wong, S. (1998). Psychopathy and recidivism: A review. *Legal and Criminological Psychology*, *3*, 139–170.

Hilton, N.Z., Harris, G.T., Rice, M.E., Lang, C., Cormier, C.A., & Lines, K.J. (2004). A brief actuarial assessment for the prediction of wife assault recidivism: The Ontario domestic assault risk assessment. *Psychological Assessment*, *16* (3), 267–275.

Hodgins, S. (2008). Criminality among persons with severe mental illness. In M. Soothill, P. Rogers, & M. Dolan (Eds.), *Handbook of forensic mental health* (pp. 400–423). Cullompton, UK: Willan.

Howells, K. (2010). Distinctions within distinctions: The challenges of heterogeneity and causality in the formulation and treatment of violence. In M. Daffern, L. Jones, & J. Shine, (Eds.), *Offence paralleling behaviour* (pp. 53–71). Oxford: Wiley-Blackwell.

Howells, K., Daffern, M., & Day, A. (2008). Aggression and violence. In M. Soothill, P. Rogers, & M. Dolan (Eds.), *Handbook of forensic mental health* (pp. 351–374). Cullompton, UK: Willan.

Howells, K., & Day, A. (2003). Readiness for anger management: Clinical and theoretical issues. *Clinical Psychology Review*, *23*, 319–337.

Howells, K., Day, A., Williamson, P., Bubner, S., Jauncey, S., Parker, A., & Heseltine, K. (2005). Brief anger management programs with offenders: Outcomes and predictors of change. *Journal of Forensic Psychiatry and Psychology*, *16*, 296–311.

Howells, K., Krishnan, G., & Daffern, M. (2007). Challenges in the treatment of dangerous and severe personality disorder. *Advances in Psychiatric Treatment*, *13*, 325–332.

Howells, K., McMurran, M., Howard, R., & Jinks, M. (2009). *The functions of violence in juvenile offenders using alcohol*. Conference of the International Association for Forensic Mental Health Services, Edinburgh (June).

Howitt, D. (2006). *Introduction to Forensic and Criminal Psychology* (2nd ed.). Harlow, UK: Pearson Prentice Hall.

Kenny, D.T., & Press, A.L. (2006). Violence classifications and their impact on observed relationships with key factors in young offenders. *Psychology, Public Policy and the Law*, *12*, 86–105.

Kroner, D.G., & Mills, J.F. (2001). The accuracy of five risk appraisal instruments in predicting institutional misconduct and new convictions. *Criminal Justice and Behavior*, *28*, 471–489.

Kropp, P.R., & Hart, S.D. (2000). The Spousal Assault Risk Assessment (SARA). Guide: Reliability and validity in adult male offenders. *Law and Human Behaviour*, *24* (1), 101–118.

Kropp, P.R., Hart, S.D., Webster, C., & Eaves, D. (1998). *Spousal Assault Risk Assessment: User's guide*. Toronto, ON: Multi-Health Systems.

Krug, E.G., Dahlberg, L.L., Mercy, J.A., Zwi, A.B., & Lozano, R. (Eds.). (2002). *World report on violence and health*. Geneva: World Health Organization.

Langton, C.M. (2007). Assessment implications of "What Works" research for Dangerous and Severe Personality Disorder (DSPD) service evaluation. *Psychology, Crime & Law, 13*, 97–111.

Loza, W. (2003). Predicting violent and non-violent recidivism of incarcerated male offenders. *Aggression and Violent Behaviour, 8*, 175–203.

McGuire, J. (2008). A review of effective interventions for reducing aggression and violence. *Philosophical Transactions of the Royal Society of London Series B, Biological Sciences, 12*, 1–21.

McMurran, M. (Ed.) (2004). *Motivating offenders to change*. Chichester, UK: John Wiley & Sons, Ltd.

McMurran, M., & Theodosi, R. (2007). Is treatment non-completion associated with increased risk of reconviction over no treatment? *Psychology, Crime & Law, 13* (4), 333–343.

Mills, J.F., Kroner, D.G., and Hemmati, T. (2007). The validity of violence risk estimates: An issue of item performance. *Psychological Services, 4* (1), 1–12.

Monahan, J. (1981). *Predicting violent behaviour*. Beverley Hills, CA: Sage Library of Social Research.

Monahan, J. (1984). The prediction of violent behavior: Toward a second generation of theory and policy. *American Journal of Psychiatry, 141*, 10–15.

Monahan, J. (1996). Violence prediction: The last 20 and the next 20 years. *Criminal Justice and Behaviour, 23*, 107–120.

Mossman, D. (2000). Commentary: Assessing the risk of violence – Are accurate predictions useful? *Journal of the American Academy of Psychiatry and the Law, 28*, 272–281.

Mullen, P. (2008). The crimes and pathologies of passion: Love, jealousy and the pursuit of justice. In M. Soothill, P. Rogers, & M. Dolan (Eds.), *Handbook of forensic mental health* (pp. 555–588). Cullompton, UK: Willan.

Ogloff, J., & Daffern, M. (2002). *Dynamic Appraisal of Situational Aggression: Inpatient Version*. Melbourne, Victoria, Australia: Monash University and Forensicare.

Ogloff, J.R.P., & Daffern, M. (2006). The Dynamic Appraisal of Situational Aggression: An instrument to assess risk for imminent aggression in psychiatric inpatients. *Behavioral Sciences and the Law, 24*, 799–813.

Ogloff, J.R.P., & Daffern, M. (2007). The assessment of risk for inpatient aggression in psychiatric inpatients: Introducing the Dynamic Appraisal of Situational Aggression: Inpatient Version.

Ogloff, J., & Davis, M. (2004). Advances in offender assessment and rehabilitation. *Psychology, Crime & Law, 10*, 229–242.

Quinsey, V.L., Harris, G.T, Rice, M.E., & Cormier, C.A. (1998). *Violent offenders: Appraising and managing risk*. Washington, DC: American Psychological Association.

Rice, M. (1997). Violent offender research and implications for the criminal justice system. *American Psychologist, 52*, 414–423.

Rice, M., & Harris, G.T. (1995). Violent recidivism: Assessing predictive validity. *Journal of Consulting and Clinical Psychology, 63*, 737–748.

Rice, M., & Harris, G.T. (1997). Cross validation and extension of the Violence Risk Appraisal Guide for child molesters and rapists. *Law and Human Behaviour*, *21*, 231–241.

Salekin, R.T., Roger, R., & Sewell, K.W. (1996). A review and meta-analysis of the Psychopathy Checklist – Revised: Prediction validity of dangerousness. *Clinical Psychology: Science and Practice*, *3*, 203–215.

Schalast, N., Redies, M., Collins, M., Stacey, J., & Howells, K. (2007). EssenCES: A short questionnaire for assessing the social climate of forensic psychiatric wards. *Criminal Behaviour and Mental Health*, *18*, 49–58.

Serin, R.C. (2004). Understanding violent offenders. In D.H. Fishbein (Ed.), *The science, treatment and prevention of antisocial behaviours. Volume 2: Evidence-based practice* (pp. 12–13). Kingston, NJ: Civic Research Institute.

Serin, R.C., Donna L., Mailloux, D.L., & Kennedy, S.M. (2007). Development of a clinical rating scale for offender readiness: Implications for assessment and offender change. *Issues in Forensic Psychology*, *7*, 70–80.

Sheldon, K., & Krishnan, G. (2009, September). The clinical and risk characteristics of patients admitted to a secure hospital based "Dangerous and Severe Personality Disorder" unit. *British Journal of Forensic Practice*, *11* (3), 19–27.

Sherman, L.W. (1993). Preventing homicide through trial and error. In H. Strang & S.A. Gerull (Eds.), *Homicide: Patterns, prevention and control*. Canberra: Australian Institute of Criminology Conference Proceedings, ALC.

Sturmey, P. (1996). *Functional analysis in clinical psychology*. Chichester, UK: John Wiley & Sons, Ltd.

Sturmey, P. (2008). *Behavioral case formulation and intervention: A functional analytic approach*. Chichester, UK: John Wiley & Sons, Ltd.

Walker, L.E., & Meloy, J.R. (1998). Stalking and domestic violence. In J.R. Meloy (Ed.), *The psychology of stalking: Clinical and forensic perspectives* (pp. 139–161). San Diego, CA: Academic Press.

Ward, T., Day, A., Howells, K., & Birgden, A. (2004). The multifactor offender readiness model. *Aggression and Violent Behavior*, *9*, 645–673.

Webster, C.D., Douglas, K.S., Belfrage, H., & Link, B. (2000). Capturing change: An approach to managing violence and improving mental health. In S. Hodgins & R. Muller-Isberner (Eds.), *Violence among the mentally ill* (pp. 119–144). Dordrecht, Netherlands: Kluwer Academic.

Webster, C.D., Douglas, K., Eaves, D., & Hart, S. (1997a). *HCR-20: Assessing Risk for Violence – Version 2*. Vancouver, BC: Simon Fraser University.

Webster, C.D., Douglas, K.S., Eaves, D., & Hart, S. (1997b). Assessing risk of violence to others. In C.D. Webster & M.A. Jackson (Eds.), *Impulsivity: Theory, assessment and treatment*. New York: Guilford Press.

Webster, C.D., Harris, G., Rice, M., Cormier, C., & Quinsey, V. (1994). *The Violence Prediction Scheme: Assessing dangerousness in high risk men*. Toronto, ON: University of Toronto, Centre for Criminology.

Webster, C.D., & Menzies, R.J. (1988). The clinical prediction of dangerousness. In D.N. Weisstub (Ed.), *Law and mental health: International perspectives, Vol. 3* (pp. 158–208). New York: Pergamon Press.

Weisz, A.N., Tolman, R.M., & Saunders, D.G. (2000). Assessing the risk of severe domestic violence: The importance of survivors' predictions. *Journal of Interpersonal Violence*, *15* (1), 75–90.

Williamson, P., Day, A., Howells, K., Bubner, S., & Jauncey, S. (2003). Assessing offender motivation to address problems with anger. *Psychology, Crime and Law*, *9*, 295–307.

Wong, S., & Gordon, A. (2000). *The Violence Risk Scale, Version 2*. Unpublished. Distributed from Research Unit, Regional Psychiatric Centre, Saskatoon, Canada.

Wong, S., & Gordon, A. (2006). The validity and reliability of the Violence Risk Scale: A treatment friendly violence risk assessment tool. *Psychology, Public Policy and Law*, *12* (3), 279–309.

4

Sexual Offenders

FRANCA CORTONI, ANTHONY R. BEECH AND LEAM A. CRAIG

INTRODUCTION

During the past 20 years, there have been great advances in what we know about sexual offenders and how to assess their risk of recidivism and treatment needs (Beech, Craig, & Browne, 2009; Craig, Browne, & Beech, 2008). This chapter considers a number of approaches to assessing risk in sexual offenders and measures used to assess levels of deviancy in sexual offenders and how this relates to treatment. In addition, it discusses assessment considerations for Internet, juvenile, and female sexual offenders, and sexual offenders with intellectual disabilities, special subgroups that are increasingly coming to the attention of the criminal justice system.

ASSESSING RISK OF RECIDIVISM AND TREATMENT NEEDS

The assessment of sexual offenders is predominantly driven by the need to establish the likelihood of future occurrences of sexual offending behavior (Hanson & Morton-Bourgon, 2005; Hart, Laws, & Kropp, 2003; Quinsey, Harris, Rice, & Cormier, 2006). The risk assessment considers the individual characteristics of the offender that increase or decrease the probability of recidivism. These characteristics, referred to as *risk factors*, can be subsumed under two main dimensions – an

Assessments in Forensic Practice: A Handbook, First Edition. Edited by Kevin D. Browne, Anthony R. Beech, Leam A. Craig, and Shihning Chou.
© 2017 John Wiley & Sons Ltd. Published 2017 by John Wiley & Sons Ltd.

antisocial orientation and sexual deviance (Hanson & Morton-Bourgon, 2004, 2005; Quinsey et al. 2006; Roberts, Doren, & Thornton, 2002) – each consisting of static and dynamic factors.

Static factors are unchangeable aspects in the offender's history that are related to recidivism. Among sexual offenders, and indeed all offenders, static risk factors for general and violent (non-sexual) recidivism include being at a younger age, being single, and having a history of lifestyle instability, rule violations, and criminal activity (Andrews & Bonta, 2010; Hanson & Morton-Bourgon, 2005). Static factors specifically related to sexual recidivism include prior sexual offenses, and having male, stranger, and/or unrelated victims (Hanson & Thornton, 2000). Risk assessments based strictly on static risk factors, however, do not provide information on areas related to sexual recidivism that may predict the onset of the further offending behavior. Similarly, they do not provide information on the areas that would benefit from intervention. Given that risk of reoffending is not a static state, dynamic factors add an important dimension to the evaluation of risk: they improve the accuracy of risk prediction and provide focused avenues for the treatment and management of sexual offenders (Beech, Erikson, Friendship, & Hanson, 2002; Hanson, 2006; Quinsey et al., 2006; Thornton, 2002).

Dynamic factors are those aspects of the offender that are amenable to change, and may identify when an offender is most at risk (Hanson, 2006). Within dynamic risk factors, *stable* factors are relatively enduring characteristics that are related to the potential for recidivism, while *acute* factors can be viewed as short-term states that create conditions for sexual offending. Three converging bodies of research have demonstrated that dynamic risk factors predict sexual reoffending independently from static factors, providing evidence of the importance of not only assessing these factors, but also addressing them in treatment (Beech, Fisher, & Thornton, 2003; Craig, Thornton, Beech, & Browne, 2007; Hanson & Harris, 2001; Hanson & Morton-Bourgon, 2005; Thornton, 2002, 2005). While there are some slight variations among the three lines of research, there is a general agreement that the main changeable characteristics associated with sexual offending are deviant sexual interests, distorted cognitions supportive of sexual offending, problematic socio-affective functioning, and poor self-regulation.

Dynamic Risk Factors

A sexual interest and arousal to children or violence has long been established as a powerful predictor of sexual recidivism, particularly when combined with high levels of psychopathy (Hanson & Morton-Bourgon, 2005; Quinsey et al., 2006). Typically, a physiological assessment, such as penile plethysmography, is the best method to establish sexual deviance, although such tests are not without their limitations (Laws, 2003). Many offenders fail to demonstrate arousal under assessment conditions and this lack of arousal does not mean that an individual is automatically at lower risk of offending. Many factors influence whether sexual deviancy can be detected during a physiological assessment, including the ability by the offender to suppress his arousal (see Laws, 2003 for a review). When a physiological assessment of arousal is not possible, sexual deviance can be inferred from an examination of the history of sexual offending, or through the use of various psychometric instruments (Beech et al., 2003; Craig & Beech, 2009; Craig et al., 2007; Seto, Harris, Rice, & Barbaree, 2004).

The extent to which an offender is generally preoccupied with sex is also related to sexual reoffending (Craig, Browne, Beech, & Stringer, 2006; Hanson & Bussière, 1998; Hanson, Harris, Scott, & Helmus, 2007; Hanson & Morton-Bourgon, 2005). Sexual offenders tend to give sex an exaggerated importance in their lives, and tend to believe they have stronger sexual urges and needs than most people (Hanson & Harris, 1998). Further, sexual offenders utilize both consenting and deviant sex to cope with life's difficulties and manage negative emotional states (Cortoni & Marshall, 2001; Looman, 1995; McKibben, Proulx, & Lusignan, 1994; Proulx, McKibben, & Lusignan, 1996) and this particular tendency is strongly related to sexual recidivism (Hanson et al., 2007). The determination of the sexual self-regulation patterns of sexual offenders are therefore an important component of their assessment. Indicators of sexual preoccupation include the frequency in which offenders engage in any type of sexual activity such as masturbation, and the use of pornography or other similar sex-related activities such as attending strip bars or prostitutes. The presence of paraphilias such as fetishism, particularly if they are related to the offending behavior, provides another indication of sexual preoccupation (Thornton, 2005).

Cognitions supportive of sexual offending refers to a general cognitive disposition that facilitates sexual offending behavior (Bumby, 1996; Hudson, Wales, Bakker, & Ward, 2002; Thornton, 2002). Sexual aggressors typically adhere to stereotypical, hostile, or distorted views of women, children, and sex (Hanson & Harris, 2001; Mann & Beech, 2003). They also have core beliefs about themselves and the world that predispose them to interpret ambiguous or threatening information in a hostile fashion. This predisposing, in turn, interacts with other factors such as deviant arousal or impulsivity to lead to sexual offending (Beech, Fisher, & Ward, 2005; Beech, Ward, & Fisher, 2006; Mann & Beech, 2003; Ward & Keenan, 1999). A number of psychometric instruments were developed for the assessment of pro-offending attitudes and cognitive distortions (e.g., Abel, Becker, & Cunningham-Rathner, 1984; Bumby, 1996; Check, 1984), and higher scores on these scales tend to be related to persistence in sexual offending (Hudson et al., 2002). Hanson and Harris (2001) have also demonstrated that these problematic cognitions are easily evaluated during an interview. The areas of importance to assess include attitudes that excuse, permit, or condone sexual offending, attitudes that indicate a sense of entitlement to sex, and maladaptive beliefs about relationships, gender roles, and children (Thornton, 2002).

Socio-affective difficulties typically include interpersonal difficulties and emotional identification with children. Inherent in the interpersonal difficulties exhibited by sexual offenders is a lack of intimacy in relationships. Both a lack of intimate partners and the presence of conflicts within an existing intimate relationship are predictive of sexual reoffending (Hanson & Bussière, 1998; Hanson & Morton-Bourgon, 2005). For rapists, difficulties in intimate relationships may be related to their experiences of adversarial or impersonal relationships with family and peers, thereby leading to a general lack of concerns for others (Hanson, 2006). For child molesters, a presence of emotional identification with children may interfere with their ability to establish healthy adult relationships (Wilson, 1999). The presence of emotional identification with children is a powerful predictor of sexual recidivism among child molesters (Hanson et al., 2007; Hanson & Morton-Bourgon, 2005). The interview will typically reveal the extent to which sexual offenders engage in adversarial intimate relationships or report feeling emotionally closer to children than to adults.

Poor self-regulation, also known as poor self-management abilities, is marked by a poor ability to self-monitor and to inhibit impulsive, irresponsible, and rule-breaking decisions (Thornton, 2002). Among sexual offenders, evidence of lifestyle instability and low levels of self-control are indicative of difficulties in anticipating the consequences of one's actions, and establishing and working toward long-term goals. Within the context of supervision, poor self-regulation is evidenced by a tendency to break conditions of community supervision and failure to meet other commitments such as work or treatment demands (Hanson et al., 2007; Thornton, 2002). Offenders with poor self-regulation also typically minimize their risk, and fail to engage in identified strategies to prevent a return to offending behavior, including dropping out of treatment (Hanson & Morton-Bourgon, 2005).

Treatment Needs

As discussed above, dynamic risk factors are changeable characteristics of the offender that have a demonstrated empirical relationship with sexual offending behavior and that, when reduced, lead to reductions in recidivism (Hanson, 2006). Consequently, they constitute the elements that need to be addressed in treatment. Unfortunately, there is some disconnect between established dynamic risk factors of sexual offenders and the issues that are typically addressed in contemporary treatment for sexual offenders. As evidenced in the research of risk prediction (e.g., Hanson & Morton-Bourgon, 2005; Quinsey et al., 2006), there are clear indications that antisociality is related to sexual offending patterns. Interestingly, though, assessments for treatment typically focus on the factors unique to sexual offenders such as deviant sexual interests and intimacy deficits (Ward & Marshall, 2004), and have mostly neglected to consider the antisocial characteristics of these offenders (Cortoni, 2005; Lalumière, Harris, Quinsey, & Rice, 2005). As Hanson and Morton-Bourgon (2005) point out, "The prototypical sexual recidivist is not upset or lonely; instead he leads an unstable, antisocial lifestyle and ruminates on sexually deviant themes" (p. 1158). The assessment for the treatment of sexual offenders therefore needs to examine the more general antisocial characteristics exhibited by the offender as well as sexual deviancy issues.

The method of treatment used in North America and the United Kingdom is best described as cognitive behavioral therapy (CBT). This approach has developed through the combination of both cognitive and behavioral approaches to therapy. For an overview of the CBT approach see Marshall, Anderson, and Fernandez (1999). To give a brief synopsis, the behavioral component addresses the overt and covert behavior of an individual and the principles of learning theory. Originally this was confined to the use of procedures to alter behavior, that is, rewarding desired behaviors and punishing unwanted behaviors, but has since broadened out to include modeling (demonstrating a desired behavior) and skills training (teaching specific skills through behavioral rehearsal). The cognitive component of the CBT approach addresses the thoughts or cognitions that individuals experience, which are known to affect mood state and hence have an influence upon subsequent behavior. Cognitive therapy therefore aims to encourage an individual to think differently about events, thus giving rise to different affect and behavior. The use of self-instruction and self-monitoring, and the development of an awareness of how one thinks affects how one feels and behaves, are vital components in cognitive therapy. By combining these two approaches, CBT provides a comprehensive approach to treating sexual offenders that now has research evidence to support its efficacy (e.g., Friendship, Mann & Beech, 2003; Hanson et al., 2002; Lösel & Schmucker, 2005). CBT has been shown in the "What Works" literature (Andrews & Bonta, 2010) to be the most effective method of treating offenders.

Group, rather than individual work, is the usual method of delivery of CBT. The group work approach is seen as being suitable for all types of sexual offender. Beech and Fordham (1997) outlined the benefits of being in a group and group work as the following: groups provide an environment that can offer both support and challenge to the individual; group work provides the opportunity for discussion with peers, and provides opportunities for increasing self-esteem and empathic responding; groups also offer a forum for support and sharing of problems which may be a completely new experience for many child sex abusers who are generally isolated individuals, often with interpersonal deficits and feelings of inadequacy. Having the experience of being valued, being able to help others, practicing social skills, and getting to know others in detail can greatly improve an individual's self-esteem and interpersonal functioning. Given that feelings of inadequacy and lack of appropriate relationships may be an important vulnerability factor for many sexual offenders, improvement in these areas is an important element in reducing reoffending.

Risk Assessment Strategies

There are three main assessment strategies broadly used in the assessment of risk and treatment need in sexual offenders (Craig & Beech, 2010). The first strategy is the *functional analysis*, a clinical tool used to investigate the antecedents, behaviors, and consequences of the offense (Ireland & Craig, 2011). This type of analysis is an important first step to ascertain the type of goals and strategies a sexual offender has toward offending (Craig, Browne, & Beech, 2008). The second strategy is the *actuarial risk* assessment. This assessment consists of the completion of an empirically established scale that codifies the presence or absence of static risk factors. Actuarial scales provide estimates or probabilities of risk based on the total score obtained on the scale. Finally, dynamic risk assessment is where research meets clinical perceptions. Within this strategy, the *stable and acute dynamic risk factors* are assessed.

Several actuarial scales have been developed to specifically assess the risk of sexual recidivism: the STATIC-99 (Hanson & Thornton, 2000; see Helmus, Thornton, Hanson, & Babchishin, 2012 for STATIC-99R), a 10-item scale, and the Sex Offender Risk Appraisal Guide (SORAG; Quinsey et al., 2006) and STATIC-2002 (Hanson & Thornton, 2003; see Helmus et al., 2012 for STATIC-2002R), both of which have 14 items, and are examples of static risk assessment tools that take into account the antisocial and sexual deviance domains to predict both violent and sexual recidivism. These scales provide superior predictive utility than unstructured clinical judgment based on traditional models of psychopathology or clinical experience (Hanson & Bussière, 1998; Hanson & Morton-Bourgon, 2009; Quinsey et al., 2006).

The most commonly used actuarial risk assessment in the United Kingdom is the Risk-Matrix 2000 (RM2000; Thornton et al., 2003). RM2000 has two scales, one for measuring risk of sexual recidivism and one for measuring risk of non-sexual violent recidivism in sexual offenders. The sexual recidivism scale, RM2000/S, uses a two-step system to risk assessment. Step 1 contains three risk items (number of previous sexual appearances, number of criminal appearances, and age) the sum of which is translated into a risk category (Low, Medium, High, Very High). Step 2 considers four aggravating risk factors: any conviction for sexual offense against a male; any conviction for a sexual offense against a stranger; any conviction for a non-contact sex offense; and single – never been married. The presence of two or four aggravating factors raises the risk category by one or two levels respectively. These actuarial scales have been shown to demonstrate good predictive accuracy in assessing sexual recidivism risk in sexual offenders.

The following tools are currently available to assess stable dynamic risk factors: (i) the Structured Assessment of Risk and Need (SARN, Thornton, 2002; Webster et al., 2006); and (ii) the STABLE-2007 and the ACUTE-2007 (Hanson et al., 2007). SARN uses clinical ratings assessing 16 dynamic risk factors, categorized into each of Thornton's dynamic risk domains (sexual interests, offense supportive attitudes, relationships, and self-management). The STABLE-2007 contains 13 items that assess various aspects of the following dimensions: significant social influences, intimacy deficits, attitudes supportive of sexual assault, cooperation with supervision, sexual self-regulation, and general self-regulation. The ACUTE-2007 (Hanson et al., 2007) assesses the following acute risk factors: victim access; emotional collapse (i.e., evidence of severe emotional disturbance/emotional crisis), collapse of social supports; hostility; substance abuse; sexual preoccupations; and rejection of supervision. The items assessing victim access, sexual preoccupations, hostility, and rejection of supervision, taken together, are particularly predictive of new sexual or violent offenses (Hanson et al., 2007). An understanding of the literature on risk assessment and risk factors (e.g., see Craig, Browne, & Beech, 2008) and training in the scoring methods of these risk assessment tools are recommended prior to their utilization.

SPECIAL POPULATIONS

While most is known about the assessment of adult male sexual offenders who have committed contact offenses, Internet, juvenile, women, and offenders with intellectual disabilities who sexually offend are increasingly coming to the attention of the criminal justice system. Efforts have been devoted in recent years to better understand the dynamics of the offending behavior of these subtypes of sexual offenders, but as will be seen, much remains to be known. The assessment of these types of offenders is typically guided by clinically derived risk assessment tools and what little empirical evidence exists on the factors linked to the offending patterns of these offenders.

Internet Sexual Offenders

Internet sexual offenders are those who have been charged or convicted of downloading illegal sexual material (usually child pornography) from the Internet (Beech, Elliott, Findlater, & Birgen, 2008). Internet offenders can be broadly categorized into four categories (Krone, 2004; Wortley & Smallbone, 2006): (1) individuals who access abusive images sporadically, impulsively, and/or out of curiosity; (2) individuals who access/trade abusive images to fuel their sexual interest in children; (3) individuals who use the Internet as part of a pattern of offline contact offending, including (3a) those who use the Internet as a tool for locating and/or grooming contact victims and (3b) those who use the Internet to disseminate images that they have produced; and (4) individuals who access abusive images for seemingly non-sexual reasons (e.g., for financial profit).

Research has yet to establish empirically validated tools for the assessment of risk of sexual offending among Internet offenders. In a study examining patterns of Internet offending and subsequent contact sexual offenses, Seto and Eke (2005) found no evidence that the use of standard assessment tools can predict future sexual offending among those child pornography offenders who have no history of attempted or completed contact sexual offenses. They did find that, just like with contact offenders, greater sexual arousal to children appears to be related to a greater risk of committing a contact offense. In addition, they found that the absence of prior criminal history lowers the risk of new offenses of any type in those non-contact Internet offenders.

In a meta-analytical review of the recidivism rates of 2,630 Internet offenders, Seto, Hanson, and Babchishin (2011) found a sexual recidivism rate of 4.6% and a violent recidivism rate of 4.2%. They noted that 2% of the sexual recidivists had committed a new sexual offense of some kind while 3.4% committed a new child pornography offense. The follow-up times ranged from 1.5 to 6 years. In an extended follow-up of 541 Internet offenders, with an average follow-up period of 4.1 years, Eke and Seto (Eke & Seto, 2008; Seto & Eke, 2008) found a 4% recidivism rate for new contact sexual offenses, a 6.6% rate for violent (including sexual) recidivism, and a 7% recidivism rate for new child pornography offenses. It is noted that 30% of the sample had prior or concurrent sexual offenses. Seto and Eke (2008) found that offenders with no prior criminal history have lower recidivism rates of any types and that past criminal history variables are predictive of new recidivism. Specifically, predictors of sexual and child pornography recidivism included prior failures while under supervision for the current or past offenses, a younger age at first charge, and a juvenile criminal history. In addition, the presence of a hebephilic (roughly corresponds to ages 11 to 14 years) interest was specifically predictive of new child pornography offenses.

Based on these findings, the presence of prior criminal history and other sexual offenses should be examined. For those Internet offenders with prior or concurrent contact sexual offenses, standard risk assessment tools should be utilized. For those with no contact sexual offenses and a lack of other criminal history, it is unclear whether risk assessment tools are applicable. In fact, the STATIC-99 is specifically *not* to be used for these offenders (Harris, Phoenix, Hanson, & Thornton, 2003). Overall, risk of future contact offenses appears to be low for Internet offenders with no other criminal history. In those cases, the assessment should focus on the functional analysis of the offending behavior to determine what elements played a part in the Internet behavior.

Juvenile Sexual Offenders

Although juvenile sexual offenders used to be considered "miniature adults," it is now recognized that they in fact constitute a population distinct from adult offenders (Worling & Långström, 2006). Juvenile offenders appear to be responsible for approximately 20% of all rapes and 30 to 50% of all child molestation (Barbaree & Marshall, 2006), but their rates of sexual recidivism, while widely variable, appear to be low although their rates of general recidivism are much higher. In their review of 22 studies of recidivism rates in juvenile sexual offenders, Worling and Långström (2006) found that sexual recidivism rates varied from 0 to 40% across studies. Overall, across studies, these authors found an average sexual recidivism rate of 14%, and an overall recidivism rate of 42%. These rates included subsequent recidivism as an adult. As is commonly found in recidivism studies with adult offenders, a linear relationship between elapsed time and rates of recidivism is also found for juvenile offenders.

Juvenile sexual offenders are not heterogeneous. Their victims vary from children to peers and adults. They have diverse developmental experiences; they vary in their levels of emotional and behavioral control; they demonstrate different sexual interests; and they present with varying levels of antisocial characteristics (Hunter, 2006; Worling & Långström, 2006). Preliminary work by Hunter (2006) indicates the presence of three broad categories of juvenile sexual offenders. The first category, *Life Style Persistent*, consists of youth with a history of conduct disorder since childhood. Compared to the offenders in the other categories, these youth engage in all types of criminal behavior, including sexual offending, and their victims are typically peers or adults (Hunter, 2006). It is hypothesized that this group will persist in their generalized criminal activities in adulthood. This group is most consistent with the early-onset, life-course persistent offenders proposed by Moffitt (1993). These offenders are typically characterized by early neuropsychological deficits and negative environments. Those neuropsychological deficits manifest themselves through a series of difficulties (e.g., hyperactivity, impulsivity, difficult temper) leading to negative reactions from the environment (i.e., coercion, rejection, etc.) thus limiting the opportunities for the child to learn prosocial attitudes and behaviors. The successive negative interactions will lead to an early onset, persistence, diversification, and aggravation of antisocial manifestations over the life course (Moffitt, 1993).

The second category, *Adolescent Onset – Non Paraphilic*, is comprised essentially of youth whose sexual offending is transient and typically directed toward young girls. The offending behavior appears related to deficits in social competence and self-confidence or to adolescent experimentation. These offenders may turn to young girls because they are unable or too afraid to establish sexual relationships with appropriately aged peers. These offenders tend to demonstrate high levels of psychosocial deficits, but very little criminal or sexual deviancy characteristics (Hunter, 2006). This category of offenders appears more closely related to the adolescence-limited type of juvenile offender outlined by Moffitt (1993). For these offenders, the offending behavior appears to be primarily attributable to more contextual/situational explanatory factors. In other words, the offending behavior is viewed as the results of a gap between biological maturity and social maturity in adolescence. As the deviance of those youth would not be a manifestation of an underlying propensity for sexual deviance, desistance is the norm as they reach adulthood (Moffitt, 1993). Hunter (2006) hypothesized that these youths would likely have the best long-term outcomes, provided they do not start associating with antisocial peers or become involved in substance abuse.

The final category, *Early Adolescent Onset – Paraphilic*, appears to predominantly reflect an underlying dimension of developing sexually deviant interests. Offenders in this group demonstrate deviant sexual interests, particularly toward children, and are likely to have victims of both genders. These youths are predicted to have the poorer outcomes in terms of sexual recidivism and long-term psycho-social adjustments (Hunter, 2006). In their preliminary research, Hunter (2006) found that youths in this group demonstrated high sexual interests in children and the highest index of sexual offending against boys. A validation of this typology, including long-term follow-up of the 330 male juvenile sexual offenders in the study, is currently under way (Hunter, 2006).

To our knowledge, there has not yet been a statistical meta-analytical review of the risk factors related to sexual and other recidivism among juvenile sexual offenders. In narrative reviews of risk factors for juvenile sexual offenders, Gerhold, Browne, and Beckett (2007) and Worling and Långström (2006) noted a number of risk factors that had received empirical validation among youths. Specifically, deviant sexual interests, prior convictions for sexual offenses, more than one victim, stranger victims, social isolation, and failure to attend specialized treatment have all received empirical support. Problematic parent–adolescent relationships and attitudes supportive of sexual offending were also found to be promising risk factors, although their empirical support is much more limited. Finally, although research is still lacking, a high-stress family environment, impulsivity, an antisocial orientation and antisocial peers, the presence of pronounced sexual preoccupation, and offending against children, particularly males, are viewed as promising risk factors among youth who sexually offend (Worling and Långström, 2006). It is noted that there is no evidence that the established risk factors for male juveniles apply to female juvenile sexual offenders. Hence, extreme caution must be exercised when conducting an assessment for risk of sexual recidivism among female juvenile offenders (Frey, 2010).

A number of risk tools have been developed specifically to assess risk of sexual recidivism among male juvenile sexual offenders. These include the Juvenile Sexual Offense Recidivism Risk Assessment Tool-II (J-SORRAT-II; Epperson, Ralston, Fowers, DeWitt, & Gore, 2006), the Juvenile Sex Offender Assessment Protocol-II (J-SOAP-II; Prentky & Righthand, 2003), and the Estimate of Risk of Adolescent Sexual Offense Recidivism (ERASOR; Worling & Curwen, 2001). The JSORRAT-II is an actuarial scale that consists of 12 historical items covering areas such as prior offenses, victim variables, and disciplinary concerns. While developed on a large sample of youths (N=636), the instrument has never been cross-validated. The J-SOAP and the ERASOR both provide empirically guided clinical judgment of risk and identifies areas for interventions. The J-SOAP assesses four factors: sexual drive and preoccupation; impulsivity and antisocial behavior; intervention; and level of community stability. The ERASOR includes both static and dynamic factors, but the total score of the scale may not be the primary consideration. Rather, the presence of some risk factors, on their own, may warrant a finding of high risk as they may indicate the presence of particularly problematic pathways to offending such as antisociality or sexual deviance (Worling & Curwen, 2001).

These assessment tools were specifically designed for male juvenile sexual offenders between the ages of 12 and 18. All three scales require that evaluators have an understanding of the literature on the risk factors related to juvenile sexual offending; an understanding of the difficulties inherent in assessing risk among youths (e.g., see Prescott, 2007); and a thorough understanding of the scoring methods of each tool.

Another instrument potentially useful in the assessment of juvenile sexual offenders is the Structured Assessment of Violence Risk in Youth (SAVRY; Borum, Bartel, & Forth, 2003). This scale was designed to assess risk of violence in general as opposed to only risk of sexual recidivism. The scale, however, may provide additional information regarding general risk for violence not contained in the other tools. This scale contains historical and contextual items as well as individual and protective factors.

Research is still required to validate risk assessment tools for male juvenile sexual offenders. Much of the research on these tools was conducted on the developmental samples and cross-validation studies are sparse. Viljoen et al. (2008) examined the predictive utility of the J-SOAP-II, the J-SORRAT-II, and the SAVRY in an independent sample of juvenile sexual offenders. Their study included 169 youths with an average follow-up time of 6.5 years. Their results showed that total scores on the SAVRY and J-SOAP-II predicted non-sexual violent recidivism with some degree of accuracy. Scores on the J-SOAP-II and the J-SORRAT-II, however, did not significantly predict new sexual offenses in their sample. Further, they found significantly higher false positive rates (false positive occurs when someone is inaccurately judged to be a high risk of reoffending) for juveniles aged 12 to 15, indicating that the predictive utility of the instruments became unstable for this younger group. These authors suggested this problem may be due to developmental differences between younger and older adolescents. Rajlick and Gretton (2010) examined the predictive utility of the J-SOAP-II and the ERASOR among 128 juveniles with only sexual offenses and 140 juveniles with sexual and non-sexual offenses. Recidivism was defined as a new charge or conviction. The mean follow-up time was 6.6 years. The sexual recidivism rate was 9.4% and the non-sexual recidivism rate was 34%. The analyses showed that there was an interaction between offender type and predictive validity of both the J-SOAP-II and the ERASOR. While both measures had strong predictive utility for the sexual-only juvenile offenders, neither measures predicted sexual recidivism among the juvenile offenders with sexual and non-sexual offenses. The findings from these studies demonstrate the difficulties inherent in assessing juvenile sexual offenders (Prescott, 2007): professionals tasked with assessing juvenile sexual offenders, particularly those under age 16, are faced with a complex task that requires an understanding of developmental as well as risk assessment issues for this unique population.

Adult Female Sexual Offenders

It is estimated that adult female sexual offenders constitute approximately 12% of all sexual offenders (Cortoni, Babchishin, & Rat, 2016). In contrast to male offenders, female sexual offenders have much lower recidivism rates. In their meta-analytical review of recidivism among 2,490 women who had been convicted of sexual offenses, Cortoni, Hanson, and Coache (2010) found, in a follow-up period of approximately six years, a 1.5% sexual recidivism rate, a 6% violent recidivism rate, and an overall rate of any type of recidivism of 20%. In comparison, male sexual offenders, for a five-year follow-up period, have respectively 13%, 25%, and 36% recidivism rates (Hanson & Morton-Bourgon, 2004).

These lower recidivism rates, combined with the much smaller prevalence of female sexual offenders, have to date precluded the development of risk assessment tools for this type of offender. Because tools for male sexual offenders have not been validated for women, using these tools to assess female sexual offenders would be inappropriate as they would grossly overestimate the risk of recidivism in women on the basis of factors that have no demonstrated empirical relationship with sexual recidivism among women. In addition, simply extrapolating from the male sexual offender literature to assess risk in female sexual offenders is likely to lead to invalid risk appraisal and unintended consequences. For example, in the United States, female sexual offenders have been civilly committed as sexually violent predators despite the lack of evidence regarding the risk of recidivism posed by these women (Vess, 2011).

Until sufficient empirical knowledge has accumulated to establish validated risk tools, the assessment of the risk of sexual recidivism among female sexual offenders should be based on factors that have been linked to recidivism among these women (see Cortoni, 2010 for a review). Research has shown that female offenders do share some of the same static factors as males. Specifically, in her study of 471 female sexual offenders, Vandiver (2007) found that the prior number of any offenses predicted re-arrest for new general and violent offenses but that no factor predicted new sexual offenses. In their examination of 1,466 female sexual offenders registered in the State of New York, Sandler and Freeman (2009) found that prior misdemeanors, prior drug offenses, and prior violent offenses were related to non-sexual recidivism. The only factor related to new sexual offenses was the presence of prior child (non-sexual) abuse offenses.

As dynamic risk factors for female sexual offenders have yet to be empirically identified, the assessment of risk of women who sexually offend should be based on the elements that appear linked to their offending behavior. Research suggests that attitudes and cognitions that support the offending behavior, relationship problems, the use of sex to regulate emotional states, and emotional dysregulation problems are common among female sexual offenders (Eldridge & Saradjian, 2000; Grayston & De Luca, 1999; Nathan & Ward, 2002). Sexual gratification, a desire for intimacy (with either a victim or a co-defendant), or instrumental goals such as revenge or humiliation are also associated with female sexual offending (Gannon, Rose, & Ward, 2008). Finally, as female sexual offenders, just like their male counterparts, also engage in other criminal behavior, factors such as the presence and extent of antisocial attitudes, antisocial associates, and substance abuse as a precursor to the offending behavior should also be assessed (Cortoni, 2010).

Problematic relationships appear particularly relevant for female sexual offenders. Between a third and two-thirds of female sexual offenders are estimated to offend in the company of an accomplice (Vandiver, 2006). This co-offender is typically male although female co-offending does occur. Within co-offending situations, the woman may be coerced into the offending via force or fear, or she may co-offend willingly or initiate the sexual offending behavior (Gannon et al., 2008). Interestingly, Williams and Nicholaichuk (2001) found that only those women who had engaged in solo offending committed new sexual offenses. In their review of 61 Canadian women convicted of sexual offenses, with an average follow-up time of seven years, no woman with a co-offender in the index sexual offense was subsequently re-arrested for a new sexual offense. It is important to note that as the recidivism rate was very low (N=2), further research is needed before the impact of a co-offender on recidivism rates can be fully examined. Gannon et al. (2008) provide further evidence that problematic relationships are inherent among female sexual offenders. In their examination of the offense pathways of female sexual offenders, these authors found that practical and emotional support from family and friends were lacking in all cases, and that they were frequent victims of domestic violence. Similarly, in their study of 139 female sexual offenders, Wijkman and Bijleveld (2008) found that those women with more than one documented sexual offense were particularly vulnerable, socially abused women. The accumulation of research findings of female sexual offenders indicate that not only are the presence and dynamics of the relationship with the co-offender important components of the evaluation of female sexual offenders, but also the general quality of their social and familial support.

Sexual Offenders with Intellectual Disabilities

Unlike their mainstream counterparts, it is only relatively recently that researchers and clinicians have begun to assess sexual offenders with intellectual and developmental disabilities (IDD). With the advent of community care policies throughout the Western world, there has been a decrease in the provisions of custodial care for people with IDD (Lindsay et al., 2002) which has led to an increase in the number of sex offenders with IDD under community supervision (Craig, 2010).

Accurate estimations concerning the prevalence of sex offenders with IDD are notoriously difficult to establish since sexually abusive behavior by men with IDD often goes unreported (Murphy, 2007). Indeed, a significant increase in research of sexual offenders with IDD has led to an awareness that sexual offenses by men with special needs may be more prevalent than previously acknowledged (Dolan, Holloway, Bailey, & Kroll, 1996). Some studies have highlighted IDD as more prevalent among those who offend and those who offend sexually (Gross, 1985; Lund, 1990). Walker and McCabe (1973) reviewed 331 men with IDD who had committed offenses and had been detained under hospital orders in secure provision in England and Wales. They found high rates of fire raising (15%) and sexual offenses (28%) when compared with other groups in the secure hospital sample. McBrien, Hodgetts, and Gregory (2003) found that 41% of a sample of adults with IDD referred to a local authority engaged in challenging behaviors defined as "sex related," of which 17% had police contact and 4% were convicted of sexual offenses. However, as Lindsay, Hastings, Griffiths, and Hayes (2007) have pointed out, studies conducted in different settings have produced different prevalences of offenders and types of offending. The methodological difficulties between studies make it extremely difficult to make sound estimates of offenders with IDD in a range of criminal populations.

While there is some evidence that prevalence rates are higher for sexual offenders with IDD, it is important to note that the higher prevalence rate may be, to some extent, an artifact of several sources. It has to be remembered that people with IDD are generally under greater scrutiny from relatives and carers than those in the general population. Lindsay (2002) argues that although some studies have suggested an increase in incidents of sexual offenses among offenders with IDD, there is no compelling evidence for the over- or under-representation of people with IDD among sex offenders. For a detailed discussion on prevalence and theories of sexual offending in people with IDD see Craig and Lindsay (2010).

Turning to reconviction rates for this client group, Klimecki, Jenkinson, and Wilson (1994) reported an overall reoffending rate of 41.3% in previous prison inmates with IDD at a two-year follow-up, and 34% recidivism rate for sexual offenders. Day (1993, 1994) found that reoffending was more likely to occur in the first year following discharge and Klimecki et al. (1994) reported that 84% of overall reoffending occurred within the first 12 months. However, Klimecki et al. noted that several individuals who had received prison sentences for sex offenses were still incarcerated and were, therefore, unable to reoffend. More recently, in a review of treatment services for sexual offenders with IDD (N=62), Lindsay et al. (2002) found that 4% of IDD sex offenders reoffended within the first year and 21% reoffended after four years. However, direct comparisons between the studies by Lindsay et al. and Klimecki et al. should be made with caution. Lindsay et al. and Klimecki et al. used different definitions as indications of offending (i.e., "reoffending" and "reoffense" respectively) which may limit the extent to which the rates of recidivism of the two studies can be compared. A review of UK mainstream (non-IDD) sex offender follow-up studies reported the mean sexual reconviction rate was 5% at two years and 6% at four years (Craig, Browne, Stringer, & Hogue, 2008). Using Klimecki et al.'s (1994) reoffense rates of 34% at two years and Lindsay et al.'s (2002) reoffense rate of 21% at four years, Craig and Hutchinson (2005) calculated that the re-conviction rate for sex offenders with IDD is 6.8 times and 3.5 times that of sex offenders without IDD at two years and four years follow up respectively. However, it is not clear whether this reflects a greater rate of reoffending of this client group or is merely a reflection of detection rates in a group of people who often receive increased community supervision.

Few studies have investigated the relationship between static risk factors and sexual offense recidivism in sexual offenders with IDD. Lindsay, Elliot, and Astell (2004) conducted a study to review the predictive potential of a range of previously identified variables and to assess their relationship with recidivism. They followed 52 male sex offenders who had an average IQ of 64.3. At least one year had elapsed since conviction for the index offense; the mean period of discharge was 3.3 years. They examined 15 static/historical variables and 35 proximal/dynamic variables, all of which had either been identified in previous research or were added on the basis of clinical experience. From the combined (static and dynamic) 50 risk items they found that antisocial attitude, poor maternal relationship, low self-esteem, lack of assertiveness, poor response to treatment, offences involving physical violence, staff complacency, an attitude tolerant of sexual crimes, low treatment motivation, erratic attendance and unexplained breaks from routine, deterioration of family attitudes, unplanned discharge, and poor response to treatment were significantly related to recidivism. This is consistent with MacMillan, Hastings, and Coldwell (2004) who followed up 124 individuals with IDD and found that an individual's history of violence predicted future violence. While employment history, criminal lifestyle, criminal companions (antisocial influences), diverse sexual crimes, and victim choice have been associated with recidivism in studies on non-IDD sex offenders, these factors did not emerge from Lindsay et al.'s (2004) study. However, as Lindsay and Taylor (2009) argue, these results are perhaps not surprising as very few individuals with IDD have an employment history but often have alternative regimes of special educational placements and occupational placements which serve to make up the weekly routine. Indeed, Boer, Frize, Pappas, Morrissey and Lindsay (2010) offers guidance on adaptations of using structured clinical judgment risk assessment scales such as the Sexual Violence Risk-20 (SVR-20: Boer, Hart, Kropp, & Webster, 1997) with sexual offenders with IDD as the definitions of many items such as employment and relationship problems, psychopathy, past supervision failures, and attitudes toward treatment will not reflect the needs of this client group. Lindsay et al. (2004) did find "non-compliance" to be a significant factor which suggests that the levels of compliance in individuals with IDD should be judged in relation to their peers rather than to non-IDD clients.

The application of actuarial risk scales in sexual offenders with IDD has also been investigated. The majority of actuarial instruments are developed using multivariate statistical techniques of which the cohort samples have often been mainstream non-IDD sex offenders. The actuarial method compares similarities of an individual's profile to the aggregated knowledge of past events. This can have the effect of reducing the predictive accuracy of the scale when applied to an individual with characteristics that differ from the data cohort. Most actuarial risk measures include factors such as number of previous criminal convictions, prior sexual convictions, and prior non-sexual violence. However, as Green, Gray, and Willner (2002) found, sexual offenders with IDD were more likely to be convicted of a sexual offense if they had targeted children and males as victims. Those with differing victim characteristics were less likely to have been convicted and thus were less likely to have a history of prior convictions. In these circumstances, actuarial measures may under- or over estimate the risk of those offenders diverted from the criminal justice system to mental health services. Indeed, in a cross-validation study using the STATIC-99 with a sample of sex offenders with IDD, Tough (2001) found that STATIC-99 may overestimate the risk.

Although Harris and Tough (2004) note that nobody has developed a reliable static actuarial measure specifically for the population of sex offenders with IDD, they argue there is no scientific reason to believe that static and stable factors that reliably predict risk for a normal offender will not reliably predict risk in offenders with IDD. Harris and Tough have successfully applied the Rapid Risk Assessment of Sexual Offense Recidivism (RRASOR: Hanson, 1997) to a sample of sex offenders with IDD in an attempt to best direct services consistent with the risk principle (i.e., the most effective treatment resources target truly high-risk offenders). Although they did not present any data to support the predictive accuracy of the RRASOR with sex offenders with IDD, they used the scale in order to allocate services to 81 sex offenders with IDD based on the level of risk. They found that the distribution of the level of risk in this sample was consistent with that of the original scale development study. While research into this area is ongoing, others have successfully applied a number of actuarial scales to IDD sex offenders using the Violence Risk Appraisal Guide (Lindsay et al., 2008; Quinsey et al., 2006), RRASOR (Craig, Stringer, & Sanders, 2012; Lindsay et al., 2008), STATIC-99 (Lindsay et al., 2008), and RM2000 (Lindsay et al., 2008; Quinsey, Book, and Skilling, 2004).

Based on a sample of 56 sexual offenders with IDD, Embregts et al. (2010) developed a risk scale based on dynamic and environmental risk factors identified from the literature as being relevant to sexual offenders with IDD – the Risk Inventarization Scale on Sexually Offensive Behavior of Clients with Intellectual Disabilities (RISC-V). The RISC-V assesses client and environmental factors using 50 questionnaire items: 15 items address static client factors and 35 items address dynamic client or environmental factors. Dynamic client factors are measured in terms of two subscales: (i) offending behavior (11 items); and (ii) emotional and social stability (11 items). Dynamic environmental factors are measured in terms of a single subscale: quality of supervision (13 items). The RISC-V is not designed to predict future risk of reoffending, due to the absence of validity studies, but utilizes client and environmental factors as risk factors for sex offending behavior in this client group. A component analysis of the dynamic client and environmental variables revealed three different subscales, namely quality of supervision, offending behavior, and emotional and social stability.

In a follow-up validation study, van den Bogaard, Embregts, Hendriks, and Heestermans (2013) compared the RISC-V dynamic and environmental factors in a sample of 30 sexual offenders with IDD with 39 non-sexual offenders with IDD. They found some significant differences between the groups on dynamic client factors with the non-sexual offenders group displaying more rule-breaking behavior and using more alcohol and drugs than the sex offender group. However, there were no significant differences in offending behavior and social emotional stability.

While sexual offenders with IDD share a great many characteristics with their mainstream counterparts, there is a suggestion that the range of relevant factors to be considered regarding the IDD sexual offender may be wider than for the non-IDD sexual offender.

CONCLUSIONS

The accurate assessment of treatment need and recidivism risk in sexual offenders is the cornerstone of effective practice in treating and managing sexual offenders in the community. In this chapter, we have summarized the current literature on assessing treatment need in sexual offenders and risk factors associated with sexual recidivism. Throughout the literature, the dynamic factors often identified as being associated with sexual offending are deviant sexual interests, distorted cognitions supportive of sexual offending, intimacy deficits and problems with socio-affective functioning, and poor self-regulation and self-management. It is often these factors that form the basis of effective treatment and management initiatives. While actuarial static risk instruments are effective in providing long-term estimations of sexual recidivism risk, attention should also be paid to both stable and acute dynamic risk factors that are likely to provide information on where and when.

Aside from "mainstream" adult male perpetrators of sexual abuse, there is a developing interest in special populations of sexual offenders such as Internet offenders, juveniles, adult female offenders, and sexual offenders with IDD. While assessment of these subgroups of sexual offenders is typically guided by structured clinical judgment, there is a growing body of research examining theories, treatment approaches, and risk assessment and management strategies within these groups.

REFERENCES

Abel, G.G., Becker, J.V, & Cunningham-Rathner (1984). Complications, consent and cognitions in sex between children and adults. *International Journal of Law and Psychiatry*, 7, 89–103.
Andrews, D.A., & Bonta, J. (2010). *The psychology of criminal conduct* (5th ed.). Cincinnati, OH: Anderson.

Barbaree, H.E., & Marshall, W.L. (2006). An introduction to the juvenile sex offender: Terms, concepts, and definitions. In H.E. Barbaree & W.L. Marshall (Eds.), *The juvenile sexual offender* (pp. 1–18). New York: Guilford Press.

Beech, A.R., Craig, L.A., & Browne, K.D. (2009). *Assessment and treatment of sex offenders: A handbook*. Oxford: Wiley-Blackwell.

Beech, A.R, Elliott, I.A., Findlater, D., & Birgen, A. (2008). The Internet and child sexual offending: A criminological review. *Aggression and Violent Behavior*, *13*, 216–228.

Beech, A.R., Erikson, M, Friendship, C., & Hanson, R.K. (2002). Static and dynamic predictors of reconviction. *Sexual Abuse: A Journal of Research and Treatment*, *14*, 153–165.

Beech, A.R., Fisher, D.D., & Thornton, D. (2003). Risk assessment of sex offenders. *Professional Psychology: Research and Practice*, *34*, 339–352.

Beech, A., Fisher, D., & Ward, T. (2005). Sexual murderers' implicit theories. *Journal of Interpersonal Violence*, *20*, 1366–1389.

Beech, A.R., & Fordham, A.S. (1997). Therapeutic climate of sex offender treatment programmes. *Sexual Abuse: A Journal of Research and Treatment*, *9*, 219–237.

Beech, A.R., Ward, T., & Fisher, D. (2006). The identification of sexual and violent motivations in men who assault women: Implication for treatment. *Journal of Interpersonal Violence*, *21*, 1635–1653.

Boer, D.P., Frize, M., Pappas, R., Morrissey, C., & Lindsay, W.R. (2010). Suggested adaptations to the SVR-20 for offenders with intellectual disabilities. In, L.A. Craig, W.R. Lindsay and K.D. Browne (Eds.), *Assessment and treatment of sexual offenders with intellectual disabilities* (pp. 193–209). Chichester, Wiley-Blackwell.

Boer, D.P., Hart, S.D., Kropp, P.R., & Webster, C.D. (1997). *Manual for the Sexual Violence Risk—20 professional guidelines for assessing risk of sexual violence*. Vancouver, BC: Mental Health, Law, and Policy Institute, Simon Frazer University.

Borum, R., Bartel, P., & Forth, A. (2003). *Manual for the structured assessment of violence risk in youth*. Tampa, FL: University of South Florida. Available from: www.fmhi.usf.edu.

Bumby, K.M. (1996). Assessing the cognitive distortions of child molesters and rapists: Development and validation of the MOLEST and RAPE scales. *Sexual Abuse: A Journal of Research and Treatment*, *8*, 37–54.

Check, J.V.P. (1984). The hostility towards women scale. Unpublished doctoral dissertation. University of Manitoba, Canada.

Cortoni, F. (2005, November). *Criminal career pathways of sexual offenders: Clinical implications*. Paper presented at the 24th Annual Research and Treatment Conference of the Association for the Treatment of Sexual Abusers, New Orleans, Louisiana, USA.

Cortoni, F. (2010). The assessment of female sexual offenders. In T.A. Gannon & F. Cortoni (Eds.), *Female sexual offenders: Theory, assessment and treatment* (pp. 87–100). Oxford: Wiley-Blackwell.

Cortoni, F., Babchishin, K.M., & Rat, C. (2016). The proportion of sexual offenders who are female is higher than thought: A meta-analysis. *Criminal Justice and Behavior*. OnlineFirst: DOI:10.1177/0093854816658923.

Cortoni, F., Hanson, R.K., & Coache, M.E. (2010). The recidivism rates of female sexual offenders are low: A meta-analysis. *Sexual Abuse: A Journal of Research and Treatment*, *22*, 387–401.

Cortoni, F.A., & Marshall, W.L. (2001). Sex as a coping strategy and its relationship to juvenile sexual history and intimacy in sexual offenders. *Sexual Abuse: A Journal of Research and Treatment, 13*, 27–43.

Craig, L.A. (2010). Controversies in assessing risk and deviancy in sex offenders with intellectual disabilities. *Psychology, Crime & Law, 16* (1), 75–101.

Craig, L.A., & Beech, A.R. (2009). Psychometric assessment of sexual deviance. In A.R. Beech, L.A. Craig, & K.D. Browne (Eds.), *Assessment and treatment of sexual offenders: A handbook* (pp. 89–107). Oxford: Wiley-Blackwell.

Craig, L.A., & Beech, A.R. (2010). Towards a best practice in conducting actuarial risk assessments with adult sexual offenders. *Aggression and Violet Behavior, 15*, 278–293.

Craig, L.A., Browne, K.D., & Beech, A.R. (2008). *Assessing risk in sex offenders: A practitioner's guide*. Chichester, UK: John Wiley & Sons, Ltd.

Craig, L.A., Browne, K.D., Beech, A., & Stringer, I. (2006). Psychosexual characteristics of sexual offenders and the relationship to reconviction. *Psychology, Crime & Law, 12* (3), 231–244.

Craig, L.A., Browne, K.D., Stringer, I., & Hogue, T.E. (2008). Sexual reconviction rates in the United Kingdom and actuarial estimates. *Child Abuse & Neglect, 32*, 121–138.

Craig, L.A., & Hutchinson, R. (2005). Sexual offenders with learning disabilities: Risk recidivism and treatment. *Journal of Sexual Aggression, 11* (3), 289–304.

Craig, L.A., & Lindsay, W.R. (2010). Sexual offenders with intellectual disabilities: Characteristics and prevalence. In L.A. Craig, W.R. Lindsay, & K.D. Browne (Eds.), *Assessment and treatment of sexual offenders with intellectual disabilities: A handbook* (pp. 13–35). Oxford: Wiley-Blackwell.

Craig, L.A., Stringer, I., & Sanders, C.E. (2012). Treating sexual offenders with intellectual limitations in the community. *British Journal of Forensic Practice, 14* (1), 5020.

Craig, L.A., Thornton, D., Beech, A.R., & Browne, K.D. (2007). The relationship of statistical and psychological risk markers to sexual reconviction in child molesters. *Criminal Justice and Behavior, 34*, 314–329.

Day, K. (1993). Crime and mental retardation: A review. In K. Howells & C.R. Hollin (Eds.), *Clinical approaches to the mentally disordered offender*. Chichester, UK: John Wiley & Sons, Ltd.

Day, K. (1994). Male mentally handicapped sex offenders. *British Journal of Psychiatry, 165*, 630–639.

Dolan, M., Holloway, J., Bailey, S., & Kroll, L. (1996). The psychosocial characteristics of juvenile sexual offenders referred to an adolescent forensic service in the UK. *Medicine, Science and the Law, 4*, 343–352.

Eke, A.W., & Seto, M.C. (2008, October). *Examining the criminal history and recidivism of registered child pornography offenders*. Paper presented at the 27th Annual Research and Treatment Conference of the Association for the Treatment of Sexual Abusers, Atlanta, GA, USA.

Eldridge, H., & Saradjian, J. (2000). Replacing the function of abusive behaviors for the offender: Remaking relapse prevention in working with women who sexually abuse children. In D.R. Laws, S.M. Hudson, & T. Ward (Eds.), *Remaking relapse prevention with sex offenders: A sourcebook* (pp. 402–426). Thousand Oaks, CA: Sage.

Embregts, P., van den Bogaard, K., Hendriks, L., Heestermans, M., Schuitemaker, M., & van Wouwee, H. (2010). Sexual risk assessment for people with intellectual disabilities. *Research in Developmental Disabilities, 31*, 760–767.

Epperson, D.L., Ralston, C.A., Fowers, D., DeWitt, J., & Gore, K.S. (2006). Actuarial risk assessment with juveniles who sexually offend: Development of the Juvenile Sexual Offence Recidivism Assessment Tool-II (JSORRAT-II). In D.L. Prescott (Ed.), *Risk assessment of youth who have sexually abused: Theory, controversy, and emerging strategies* (pp. 118–169). Oklahoma City: Wood 'N' Barnes.

Frey, L.L. (2010). The juvenile female sexual offender: Characteristics, treatment and research. In T.A. Gannon & F. Cortoni (Eds.), *Female sexual offenders: Theory, assessment and treatment* (pp. 53–71). Oxford: Wiley-Blackwell.

Friendship, C., Mann R., & Beech, A.R. (2003). Evaluation of a national prison-based treatment program for sexual offenders in England and Wales. *Journal of Interpersonal Violence, 18*, 744–759.

Gannon, T.A., Rose, M., & Ward, T. (2008). A descriptive model of the offense process for female sexual offenders. *Sexual Abuse: A Journal of Research and Treatment, 20*, 352–374.

Gerhold, C.K., Browne, K.D., & Beckett, R. (2007). Predicting recidivism in adolescent sexual offenders. *Aggression and Violent Behavior, 12*, 427–438.

Grayston, A.D., & De Luca, R.V. (1999). Female perpetrators of child sexual abuse: A review of the clinical and empirical literature. *Aggression and Violent Behavior, 4*, 93–106.

Green, G., Gray, N.S., & Willner, P. (2002). Factors associated with criminal convictions for sexually inappropriate behaviour in men with ID. *Journal of Forensic Psychiatry, 13*, 578–607.

Gross, C. (1985). Activities of a development disabilities adult offender project. Olympia, WA: Washington State Developmental Disabilities Planning Council.

Hanson, R.K. (1997). *The development of a brief actuarial risk scale for sexual offence recidivism.* (User Report No. 1997-04). Ottawa: Corrections Research, Public Safety Canada.

Hanson, R.K. (2006). Stability and changes: Dynamic risk factors for sexual offenders. In W.L. Marshall, Y.M. Fernandez, L.E. Marshall, & G.A. Serran (Eds.), *Sexual offender treatment: Controversial issues* (pp. 17–31). Chichester, UK: John Wiley & Sons, Ltd.

Hanson, R.K., & Bussière, M.T. (1998). Predicting relapse: A meta-analysis of sexual offender recidivism studies. *Journal of Consulting and Clinical Psychology, 66*, 348–362.

Hanson, R.K., Gordon, A., Harris, A.J.R., Marques, J.K., Murphy, W., Quinsey, V.L., & Seto, M.C. (2002). First report of the collaborative outcome data project on the effectiveness of psychological treatment for sex offenders. *Sexual Abuse: A Journal of Research and Treatment, 14*, 169–194.

Hanson, R.K., & Harris, A. (1998). *Dynamic predictors of sexual recidivism.* (User Report No. 98-01). Ottawa: Corrections Research, Public Safety Canada.

Hanson, R.K. & Harris, J.R. (2001). A structured approach to evaluating change among sexual offenders. *Sexual Abuse: A Journal of Research and Treatment, 13*, 105–122.

Hanson, R.K., Harris, A.J.R., Scott, T.L., & Helmus, T. (2007). *Assessing the risk of sexual offenders on community supervision: The Dynamic Supervision Project.* (User Report

No. 2007-05). Ottawa: Corrections Research, Public Safety Canada. Available from: http://www.publicsafety.gc.ca/cnt/rsrcs/pblctns/ssssng-rsk-sxl-ffndrs/index-en.aspx (last retrieved July 11, 2016).

Hanson, R.K., & Morton-Bourgon, K.E. (2004). *Predictors of sexual recidivism: An updated meta-analysis. User Report No. 2004-02*. Available online from: http://www.publicsafety. gc.ca/cnt/rsrcs/pblctns/2004-02-prdctrs-sxl-rcdvsm-pdtd/index-en.aspx (last retrieved July 20, 2016).

Hanson, R.K., & Morton-Bourgon, K.E. (2005). The characteristics of persistent sexual offenders: A meta-analysis of recidivism studies. *Journal of Consulting and Clinical Psychology, 73,* 1154–1163.

Hanson, R.K., & Morton-Bourgon, K.E. (2009). The accuracy of recidivism risk assessments for sexual offenders: A meta-analysis. *Psychological Assessment, 21,* 1–21.

Hanson, R.K., & Thornton, D. (2000). Improving risk assessments for sex offenders: A comparison of three actuarial scales. *Law and Human Behavior, 24,* 119–136.

Hanson, R.K., & Thornton, D. (2003). *Notes on the development of a Static-2002*. Available online from: http://www.publicsafety.gc.ca/cnt/rsrcs/pblctns/nts-dvlpmnt-sttc/index-en.aspx (last retrieved July 11, 2016).

Harris, A.J.R., Phoenix, A., Hanson, R.K., & Thornton, D. (2003). STATIC-99 coding rules: Revised-2003. (User Report No. 2003-03). Ottawa: Corrections Research, Public Safety Canada. Available from: www.static99.org.

Harris, A.J., & Tough, S. (2004). Should actuarial risk assessments be used with sex offenders who are intellectually disabled? *Journal of Applied Research in Intellectual Disabilities, 17,* 235–241.

Hart, S., Laws, D.R., & Kropp, P.R. (2003). The promise and the peril of sex offender risk assessment. In T. Ward, D.R. Laws, & S.M. Hudson (Eds.), *Sexual deviance: Issues and controversies* (pp. 207–243). Thousand Oaks, CA: Sage.

Helmus, L., Thornton, D., Hanson, R.K., & Babchishin, K.M. (2012). Improving the predictive accuracy of Static-99 and Static-2002 with older sex offenders: Revised age weights. *Sexual Abuse: A Journal of Research and Treatment, 24* (1), 64–101.

Hudson, S.M, Wales, D.S., Bakker, L., & Ward, T. (2002). Dynamic risk factors: The Kia Marama evaluation. *Sexual Abuse: A Journal of Research and Treatment, 14,* 101–117.

Hunter, J. (2006). Understanding diversity in juvenile sexual offenders: Implications for assessment, treatment, and legal management. In R.E. Longo & D.S. Prescott (Eds.), *Current perspectives: Working with sexually aggressive youth and youth with sexual behavior problems* (pp. 63–78). Holyoke, MA: NEARI Press.

Ireland, C., & Craig. L.A. (2011). Adult sex offender assessment. In D.P. Boer, R. Eher, L.A. Craig, M.H. Miner, & F. Pfafflin, (Eds.), *International perspectives on the assessment and treatment of sexual offenders: Theory, practice and research.* (pp. 13–33). Oxford: Wiley-Blackwell.

Klimecki, M., Jenkinson, J., & Wilson, L. (1994). A study of recidivism amongst offenders with an ID. *Australian and New Zealand Journal of Developmental Disabilities, 19,* 209–219.

Krone, T. (2004). A typology of online child pornography offending. *Trends and Issues in Crime and Criminal Justice, 279,* 1–6.

Lalumière, M.L., Harris, G.T., Quinsey, V.L., & Rice, M.E. (2005). *The causes of rape*. Washington, DC: American Psychological Association.

Laws, D.R. (2003). Behavioral economic approaches to the assessment and treatment of sexual deviation. In T. Ward, D.R. Laws, & S.M. Hudson (Eds.), *Sexual deviance: Issues and controversies* (pp. 65–81). Thousand Oaks, CA: Sage.

Lindsay, W.R. (2002). Research and literature on sex offenders with intellectual and developmental disabilities. *Journal of Intellectual Disability Research, 46* (1), 74–85.

Lindsay, W.R., Elliot, S.F., & Astell, A. (2004). Predictors of sexual offence recidivism in offenders with intellectual disabilities. *Journal of Applied Research in Intellectual Disabilities, 17,* 299–305.

Lindsay, W.R., Hastings, R.P., Griffiths, D.M., & Hayes, S.C. (2007). Trends and challenges in forensic research on offenders with intellectual disability. *Journal of Intellectual and Developmental Disabilities, 32,* 55–61.

Lindsay, W.R., Hogue, T.E., Taylor, J.L., Steptoe, L., Mooney, P., O'Brien, G., Johnston, S., & Smith, A.H.W. (2008). Risk assessment in offenders with intellectual disability: A comparison across three levels of security. *International Journal of Offender Therapy and Comparative Criminology, 52* (1), 90–111.

Lindsay, W.R., Smith, A.H.W., Law, J., Quinn, L., Anderson, A., Smith, A., Overend, T., & Allan, R. (2002). A treatment service for sex offenders and abusers with ID: Characteristics of referral and evaluation. *Journal of Applied Research in Intellectual Disabilities, 15,* 166–174.

Lindsay, W.R., & Taylor, J.L. (2009). The assessment of treatment related issues and risk in sexual offenders and abusers with ID. In A.R. Beech, L.A. Craig & K.D. Browne (Eds.), *Assessment and treatment of sexual offenders: A handbook* (pp. 217–236). Oxford: Wiley-Blackwell.

Looman, J. (1995). Sexual fantasies of child molesters. *Canadian Journal of Behavioral Science, 27,* 321–332.

Lösel, F., & Schmucker, M. (2005). The effectiveness of treatment for sexual offenders: A comprehensive meta-analysis. *Journal of Experimental Criminology, 1,* 117–146.

Lund, J. (1990). Mentally retarded criminal offenders in Denmark. *British Journal of Psychiatry, 156,* 726–731.

MacMillan, D., Hastings, R., & Coldwell, J. (2004). Clinical and actuarial prediction of physical violence in a forensic intellectual disability hospital: A longitudinal study. *Journal of Applied Research in Intellectual Disabilities, 17,* 255–266.

Mann, R., & Beech, A.R. (2003). Cognitive distortions, schemas and implicit theories. In T. Ward, D.R. Laws, & S.M. Hudson (Eds.) *Theoretical issues and controversies in sexual deviance* (pp. 135–153). London: Sage.

Marshall, W.L., Anderson, D., & Fernandez, Y. (1999). *Cognitive behavioural treatment of sexual offenders.* Chichester, UK: John Wiley & Sons, Ltd.

McBrien, J., Hodgetts, A., & Gregory, J. (2003). Offending behaviour in services for people with learning disabilities in one local authority. *Journal of Forensic Psychiatry & Psychology, 14* (2), 280–297.

McKibben, A., Proulx, J., & Lusignan, R. (1994). Relationships between conflict, affect and deviant sexual behaviors in rapists and pedophiles. *Behaviour Research and Therapy, 13,* 571–575.

Moffitt, T. (1993). Adolescence-limited and life-course-persistent antisocial behavior: A developmental taxonomy. *Psychological Review, 100,* 674–701.

Murphy, G.H. (2007). Intellectual disabilities, sexual abuse and sexual offending. In A. Carr, J. McEvoy, P. Noonan-Walsh., & G. O'Rielly (Eds.), *Handbook of intellectual disability and clinical psychology practice* (pp. 831–866). London: Routledge.

Nathan, P., & Ward, T. (2002). Female sex offenders: Clinical and demographic features. *Journal of Sexual Aggression*, *8*, 5–21.

Prentky, R., & Righthand, S. (2003). Juvenile Sex Offender Assessment Protocol-II (JSOAP-II). Available online from the Center for Sex Offender Management at www.csom.org.

Prescott, D.S. (2007). *Assessing youth who have sexually abused: A primer*. Holyoke, MA: NEARI Press.

Proulx, J., McKibben, A., & Lusignan, R. (1996). Relationships between affective components and sexual behaviours in sexual aggressors. *Sexual Abuse: A Journal of Research and Treatment*, *8*, 279–289.

Quinsey, V.L., Book, A., & Skilling, T.A. (2004). A follow-up of deinstitutionalised men with intellectual disabilities and histories of antisocial behaviour. *Journal of Applied Research in Intellectual Disabilities*, *17*, 243–254.

Quinsey, V.L., Harris, G.T., Rice, M.E., & Cormier, C.L. (2006). *Violent offenders: Appraising and managing risk* (2nd ed.). Washington, DC: American Psychological Association.

Rajlick, G., & Gretton, H.M. (2010). An examination of two sexual recidivism risk measures in adolescent offenders: The moderating effect of offender type. *Criminal Justice and Behavior*, *37*, 1066–1085.

Roberts, C.F., Doren, D.M., & Thornton, D. (2002). Dimensions associated with assessments of sex offender recidivism risk. *Criminal Justice and Behavior*, *29*, 569–589.

Sandler, J.C., & Freeman, N.J. (2009). Female sex offender recidivism: A large-scale empirical analysis. *Sexual Abuse: A Journal of Research and Treatment*, *21*, 455–473.

Seto, M.C., & Eke, A.W. (2005). The criminal histories and later offending of child pornography offenders. *Sexual Abuse: A Journal of Research and Treatment*, *17*, 201–210.

Seto, M.C., & Eke, A.W. (2008, October). *Predicting new offences by child pornography offenders*. Paper presented at the 27th Annual Research and Treatment Conference of the Association for the Treatment of Sexual Abusers, Atlanta, GA, USA.

Seto, M.C., Hanson, R.K., & Babchishin, K.M. (2011). Contact sexual offending by men with online sexual offenses. *Sexual Abuse: A Journal of Research and Treatment*, *23*, 124–145.

Seto, M.C., Harris, G.T., Rice, M.E., & Barbaree, H.E. (2004). The Screening Scale for Pedophilic Interests and recidivism among adult sex offenders with child victims. *Archives of Sexual Behavior*, *33*, 455–466.

Thornton, D. (2002). Constructing and testing a framework for dynamic risk assessment. *Sexual Abuse: A Journal of Research and Treatment*, *14*, 137–151.

Thornton, D. (2005, November). *Evaluating risk factor domain and clusters*. Paper presented at the 24th Research and Treatment Conference of the Association for the Treatment of Sexual Abusers, Salt Lake City, UT, USA.

Thornton, D., Mann, R., Webster, S., Blud, L., Travers, R, Friendship, C., & Erikson, M. (2003). Distinguishing and combining risks for sexual and violent recidivism. In R. Prentky, E. Janus, M. Seto, & A.W. Burgess (Eds.), *Understanding and managing sexually coercive behavior. Annals of the New York Academy of Sciences*, *989*, 225–235.

Tough S. (2001). Validation of two standard assessments (RRASOR, 1997; STATIC-99, 1999) on a sample of adult males who are intellectually disabled with significant cognitive deficits. Master's thesis. University of Toronto, ON, Canada.

van den Bogaard, K.J.H.M., Embregts, P.J.C.M., Hendriks, A.H.C., & Heestermans, M. (2013). Comparison of intellectually disabled offenders with a combined history of sexual offenses and other offenses versus intellectually disabled offenders without a history of sexual offenses on dynamic client and environmental factors. *Research in Developmental Disabilities, 34*, 3226–3234.

Vandiver, D.M. (2006). Female sex offenders: A comparison of solo offenders and co-offenders. *Violence and Victims, 21*, 339–354.

Vandiver, D.M. (2007, November). *An examination of re-arrest rates of 942 male and 471 female registered sex offenders*. Paper presented at the Annual American Society of Criminology Conference, Atlanta, GA, USA.

Vess, J. (2011). Risk assessment with female sex offenders: Can women meet the criteria of community protection laws? *Journal of Sexual Aggression, 17*, 77–91.

Viljoen, J.L., Scalora, M., Cuadra, L., Bader, S., Chávez, V., Ullman, D., & Lawrence, L. (2008). Assessing risk for violence in adolescents who have sexually offended: A Comparison of the J-SOAP-II, J-SORRAT-II, and SAVRY. *Criminal Justice and Behavior, 35*, 5–23.

Walker, N., & McCabe, S. (1973). *Crime and insanity in England*. Edinburgh: Edinburgh University Press.

Ward, T., & Keenan, T. (1999). Child molesters' implicit theories. *Journal of Interpersonal Violence, 14*, 821–838.

Ward, T., & Marshall, W.L. (2004). Good lives, aetiology, and the rehabilitation of sex offenders: A bridging theory. *Journal of Sexual Aggression, 10*, 153–169.

Webster, S.D., Mann, R.E., Carter, A.J., Long, J., Milner, R.J., O'Brien, M.D., Wakeling, H.C., & Ray, N.L. (2006). Inter-rater reliability of dynamic risk assessment with sexual offenders. *Psychology, Crime & Law, 12*, 439–452.

Wijkman, M., & Bijleveld, C. (2008, September). *Female sex offenders: Recidivism and criminal careers*. Paper presented at the 8th Annual Conference of the European Society of Criminology, Edinburgh, Scotland.

Williams, S.M., & Nicholaichuk, T. (2001, November). *Assessing static risk factors in adult female sex offenders under federal jurisdiction*. Paper presented at the 20th Research and Treatment Conference, Association for the Treatment of Sexual Abusers, San Antonio, TX, USA.

Wilson, R.J. (1999). Emotional congruence in sexual offenders against children. *Sexual Abuse: A Journal of Research and Treatment, 11*, 33–47.

Worling, J.R., & Curwen, R. (2001). Estimate of Risk of Adolescent Sexual Recidivism (ERASOR: Version 2). In M.C. Calder (Ed.), *Juveniles and children who sexually abuse: Frameworks for assessment* (pp. 372–397). Lyme Regis, UK: Russell House.

Worling, J.R., & Långström, N. (2006). Risk of sexual recidivism in adolescents who offend sexually. In H.E. Barbaree & W.L. Marshall (Eds.), *The juvenile sexual offender* (pp. 219–247). New York: Guilford Press.

Wortley, R., & Smallbone, S. (2006). *Child pornography on the Internet*. Washington, DC: Office of Community Orientated Policing Services, US Department of Justice.

5

The Assessment of Firesetters

LYNSEY F. GOZNA

The fire you kindle for your enemy often burns
yourself more than them.
                                        Chinese proverb

INTRODUCTION

Arson or deliberate firesetting[1] behavior can be difficult to comprehend owing to the
highly destructive nature of such actions, and it is unsurprising therefore that this
offense can result in a tariff of life imprisonment. In law, arson is considered
"criminal damage" and is dealt with under the Criminal Damage Act 1971. It is
perhaps the minimization of the offense – destruction of property through fire – that
has made this offense less attractive to researchers and practitioners, some highlighting that firesetting is just another weapon of choice instead of a gun or a knife.
However, the complexities of personality and behavior of those who engage
in firesetting can be challenging for practitioners to interpret and assess and the
range of motivations relevant to this offense reveal the idiosyncratic nature of cases.
This in turn increases the need for tailored methods to be utilized when assessing
individuals and undertaking focused treatment interventions.

The ethos of this chapter is to provide a discussion of the current understanding
of deliberate firesetting and firesetters and to present a framework within which to
assess individuals. Illustrations of these will be furnished with relevant case examples

Assessments in Forensic Practice: A Handbook, First Edition. Edited by Kevin D. Browne,
Anthony R. Beech, Leam A. Craig, and Shihning Chou.
© 2017 John Wiley & Sons Ltd. Published 2017 by John Wiley & Sons Ltd.

that articulate different motivational themes. In addition – with the objective of helping those charged with the task of arson assessment – the practicalities of undertaking such assessments are discussed.

UNDERSTANDING THE BEHAVIOR

The offense of arson is multifaceted and while many researchers have attempted to gain an understanding to assist police and fire investigation and practitioners conducting assessments in post-conviction settings, little overall consensus about the behavior has emerged, nor is there much crossover of knowledge between pre- and post-conviction settings. While there are apparent themes in the backgrounds and behaviors of samples of arsonists (Doley & Fritzon, 2008), ultimately it is necessary to acknowledge the idiosyncrasies and incorporate these into the overall comprehension of arson offending. Indeed, this broadens the consideration of fire-setting beyond the development of the MacDonald Triad (MacDonald, 1963, 1977; Slavkin, 2001), which comprised the three elements of firesetting, enuresis, and animal cruelty.

Assessing individuals convicted of arson requires an awareness of the relation-ship with fire and any relevant associated behavior. This requires a broader under-standing than purely gaining information about the severity of an offense (e.g., victim's injuries or death) and the accompanying conviction (e.g., arson with intent to endanger life) (Section 1 (2) Criminal Damage Act 1971). The crucial require-ment for practitioners is to identify and explore the motivation and intent of the arsonist in order to identify the psychological needs that are being realized through firesetting.

The relevance of fire in the overall context of wider offending is crucial to under-stand. It is likely that the true extent of firesetting will not be reflected in the previ-ous convictions of an individual, partly due to the low rates of detection or because fires have not come to the attention of the authorities. Therefore disclosure by individuals of wider interests and activities relevant to firesetting might occur but not have been formally recorded. Often what appears to be insignificant can be overlooked and hence the assessment of a firesetter is not always fully developed through discussion.

ARSON

Knowledge of the legal decision-making in relation to convictions of arson is, as mentioned earlier, based upon the appropriate sections under the Criminal Damage Act 1971. This allows for an awareness of sentencing decisions and the severity of the offense committed. The two key factors at play for assessment purposes are: (i) Arson – *reckless as to whether life endangered*, and (ii) Arson – *with intent to endanger life*. Both of these offenses are indictable only and there are aggravating and mitigating factors that influence sentence tariffs.

The case examples presented in this chapter illustrate some of the difficulties in assessing motivation, intent, and severity of such offenses, particularly because of the unpredictable nature of fire. Intent and motivation are considerations for legal decision-making and can also be pursued in post-conviction settings to gain a thorough insight into offender motivation and accompanying offense decision-making and behavior. A number of factors assist legal interpretation of the severity of the offense:

1. offenses with evidence of intent or recklessness;
2. motivation;
3. planning;
4. use of accelerants;
5. injuries sustained by third parties;
6. extent of the damage caused;
7. risk of fire spreading;
8. dwelling attacked; and
9. location being public building or school.
   (Criminal Damage Act 1971)

An assessment of firesetting should take account of these factors and whether the perception at the time of the offense by the police or fire service was accurately reflected. Police and fire investigations where the burden of proof rests with the Crown are more challenging when there is an absence of interview evidence, that is, a suspect gives a "no comment" interview or denies any involvement in the offense. This can result in the collection of evidence for the prosecution illustrating a different chain of events than actually occurred or would be disclosed by an offender post-conviction. The motive and intent of firesetting will not always be reflected in the commission of the offense and from evidence gathered at the crime scene, sometimes resulting in inaccurate interpretations of offender actions. Although during the investigation it will not always be possible to identify the motivation or intent of an individual, this can be relevant when considering the offense for the purpose of an assessment, particularly in relation to risk.

OFFENDER MOTIVATION

Assessing motive and intent can assist in the development of a tailored understanding of offense behaviors. Understanding the reasoning behind the offense and how this influenced the decision-making of the individual before, during, and after informs judgments made in relation to likely recidivism.

A number of practitioners (e.g., Fritzon, Canter, & Wilton, 2001; Inciardi, 1970; Prins, 1994; Stadolnik, 2000; Williams, 2005) have attempted to develop and define a typology approach to understand arsonists by concentrating on the motive. Typologies, while not without limitation in terms of mutual exclusivity, can assist with the investigation of arson and enable offenses to be distinguished in terms of motivation (Gozna, 2010). Distinguishing individuals through their motive for the offense has the potential to aid an initial assessment and the tailoring of interventions post-conviction. Although the samples (e.g., females, young persons, mentally ill, prison populations) used to develop typologies are diverse, there are sufficient parallels to enable distinctions to be drawn (for a detailed review, see Dickens, Sugarman, & Gannon, 2012; Gannon & Pina, 2010; Willis, 2004).

Edmunds (1978), in describing types of aggressive behavior, focused on separating the motivation for such acts as (i) Acquisitive – targeting individual or property for gain; (ii) Vindictive – actions aims at hurting a perceived aggressor (e.g., revenge, jealousy); (iii) Instrumental – actions designed to achieve an end in response to some environmental stimulus (e.g., criminal, cry for help, self-destruction, children, "hero" type); and (iv) Cathartic – an expression of emotion, whether anger, tension, or despair, but toward a random target (e.g., sexual pleasure, pleasure or excitement, vandalism, boredom, or relief of tension) (in Barker, 1994, p. 71).

Ravataheino (1989) identified seven categories that form descriptions of the offense itself, the motivation, or the individual committing the offense. Specifically these categories comprise (i) insurance fraud; (ii) revenge, jealousy, hatred, envy, grudge; (iii) sensation-seeking; (iv) alcoholic/mental patients and the temporarily disturbed; (v) vandalism; (vi) pyromaniacs; and (vii) children under 15 years. Distinctions drawn between these categories enables some indication of the underlying motivations to be identified. Additional development by Prins (1994) resulted in a detailed typology of firesetting which considers a range of motivations and comprises (i) *financial* reward; (ii) covering up a collateral offense; (iii) *political* purposes; (iv) *self-immolation* as a political gesture; (v) *mixed motivations* (including reactive minor depression, cry for help, alcohol intoxication); (vi) *attention-seeking*; (vii) presence of an actual *psychiatric* or associated disorder, including severe affective disorder, schizophrenia, "organic" disorders (e.g., brain tumor or injury, temporal lobe epilepsy, dementing process, or disturbed metabolic processes), mental subnormality (retardation, learning disability), mental impairment; and (viii) *revenge* (against individuals, society, generally).

Similarly to the work of Inciardi (1970), the outcome of the work conducted at the National Center for the Analysis of Violent Crime (NCAVC) by Douglas, Burgess, Burgess, and Ressler (1992, 2006) focused on motive, modus operandi, and consequences of arson. This resulted in the development of six "types" of arson and can assist not only the investigation of such offenses but the assessment of the offender prior to or post-conviction: (i) vandalism; (ii) excitement; (iii) revenge; (iv) crime concealment; (v) profit-motivated; and (vi) extremist (pp. 59–60).

The basis for the Douglas et al. (1992, 2006) research was the analysis of real-life arson offense cases to provide a differentiation of motive, choice of target/victim, and post-offense behavior. However, the additional utility of understanding in detail these "types" is to gain wider understanding of the offenders' perspective and hence likelihood of recidivism. This is particularly beneficial because it allows for knowledge developed mainly for investigative purposes to be utilized in clinical settings and for the divide between the two to be bridged (see Boon, 1998; Gozna & Prendergast, 2008). Before the six motivations are considered in relation to implications for assessment, it is necessary to incorporate an additional aspect of firesetting: that of pathological firesetting (pyromania), which is considered within F63 Habit and Impulse Disorders of the ICD-10 (World Health Organization, 2010, p. 166) but was removed from the recent revision of the Diagnostic and Statistical Manual of Mental Disorders (DSM-V; APA, 2013). Further, the motivation of "emotional displacement," which although not fully explored by the Douglas et al. (1992, 2006) typology, is relevant to the police investigation of deliberate firesetting/arson, and to treatment and assessment in forensic settings.

Pyromania

From the perspective of clinical diagnoses, firesetting takes the form of pyromania (F63.1 – ICD-10; World Health Organization, 2010), an impulse disorder "which is characterized by acts of, or attempts at setting fire to property or other objects, without apparent motive, and by a persistent preoccupation with subjects related to fire and burning. There may also be an abnormal interest in fire engines and other firefighting equipment, in other associations of fires, and in calling out the fire service" (p. 166). Therefore the essential features are (i) repeated firesetting without any obvious motive such as monetary gain, revenge, or political extremism; (ii) an intense interest in watching fires burn; and (iii) reported feelings of increasing tensions before the act, and intense excitement immediately after it has been carried out (p. 166). The differential diagnosis for pathological firesetting enables distinctions to be made across a range of broader disorders contained within the ICD-10 and where firesetting occurs within the context of (i) observation for suspected mental disorder (Z03.2); (ii) conduct disorder (F91.1); (iii) sociopathic personality disorder (F60.2); (iv) schizophrenia (F20.-); and (v) organic psychiatric disorders (F00-F09). It is also beneficial to acknowledge the occurrence of inadvertent firesetting in relation to dementia, acute drunkenness, chronic alcoholism, and other drug intoxication. However, within the context of forensic settings, the interpretation of motive for firesetting could become blurred when drug or alcohol intoxication is an aspect of a broader set of circumstances (e.g., Harris & Rice, 1984, 1996).

The pathological component of firesetting (pyromania) is considered relatively low in terms of diagnosis in forensic/clinical settings, particularly because the differential diagnosis oftentimes will result in negation of the pathological aspect

(Davis & Lauber, 1999; Geller, Erlen, & Pinkus, 1986; Kelly, Goodwill, Keene, & Thrift, 1999). Despite this seemingly low prevalence, the impulsivity more broadly, and feelings of excitement and tension release, remain a relevant consideration for practitioners conducting assessments.

Emotional Displacement

The acknowledgment of a displacement of emotional reactions to situations is relevant to the undertaking of assessment for arson. The "Displaced Aggression Hypothesis" (McKerracher & Dacre, 1966) states that that the sole motivating force for firesetting is a misplaced, internally driven anger which is "directed at an organism or object that is not responsible for the factors that initially stimulated the behaviour" (Reber, 1995, p. 17). Although this ultimately suggests that the anger has been displaced away from the person to an external target (e.g., a property), there is potential for harm to occur regardless of intent.

Prins (1994) incorporated this into a "mixed motives" category that considers individuals suffering a mild form of reactive depression, those acting out a cry for help, or individuals who are intoxicated with alcohol and/or drugs. Lewis and Yarnell (1951) recorded a subset of their arson case analysis as being "at the height of jealous resentment in injured vanity when the women of their choice seemed to be directing their affections towards others" (p. 32).

There is evidence to show that in a situation where an individual feels rejected or disempowered, the response could be sheer anger and frustration; however, the act of firesetting is related to confirming or reassuring oneself of power and this can be in the form of sexual potency. The case of "Mr L" highlights how this can manifest in offending behavior.

Case Example

Mr L

Index offense: Mr L was walking back from a nightclub alone. He had arranged to meet a girl for a date, but on arriving observed her speaking with other men. On walking back to his flat Mr L set fire to a wheelie bin in the garden of a house. The fire in the wheelie bin spread to a nearby shed causing extensive damage. A second bin was vandalized in an identical manner further down the same road although the damage was limited to the immediate area. In interview, Mr L admits his offenses and outlines that he felt frustrated and just needed to let off steam but did not feel able to confront his situation. His presentation is one that lacks self-confidence and self-esteem.

Relevant history: Mr L is 25 years old and has no previous convictions. He has a successful job as a computer programmer. Mr L lives with his father and stepmother. He has had no long-term relationships and little overall involvement with women.

Vandalism

Vandalism has been purported by Douglas et al. (1992, 2006) as encompassing malicious and mischievous motivation that results in destruction or damage. This can be separated into experimentation with fire or explosives, reporting or causing false alarms, and hoax devices. This also considers the potential for peer group pressure with multiple offenders setting fires with likely targets including school premises, residential areas, and areas of general vegetation such as fields, grassland, and forest. Therefore such firesetting is generally committed by younger individuals either independently or within a group scenario. In addition to the firesetting behavior is the potential within this motive for attacks toward fire crews attending a scene, an area of concern that is growing with the intent of the firesetting to lure the fire service to the location where they are vulnerable to planned attacks (Foley, 2008). This can be considered as part of a wider presentation of antisocial behavior or something malign in intent. Douglas et al. (1992, 2006) identify two responses following the commission of the offense: to leave the scene or to watch from a safe distance. This assists practitioners assessing the offense to establish whether a wider need is being met in the manner in which individuals/groups react or behave following an offense. The observation of the fire once it has been set could have a number of interpretations for an assessment – issues of gaining power, establishing it, or projecting it.

Case Example

Mr C

Index offense: Mr C was walking home through his local town when he saw his old school playing fields being set up for a public firework and bonfire night display. The poster on the school gate highlighted that the display would be held the following weekend on the Saturday night. Mr C returned to the school later in the week with three of his friends and set light to the bonfire. The fire service responded to calls from local residents although the boys ran off but watched the scene from a nearby location.

Relevant history: Mr C is 15 years old and was expelled from his school at the age of 14 years and following this received education from an independent organization. He has a prior conviction for arson where he attempted to set fire to the roof of the children's home he lived in from 10 to 13 years following a succession of failed foster care placements. He is suspected of setting fire to the playground climbing area in his local town. His friends are involved in general antisocial behavior and more generalized criminal damage.

The relevance of remaining at or fleeing the scene can assist in determining the personal benefit that an individual gains from firesetting. In terms of mischief making, watching the events unfold when the fire service responds and deals with a blaze can continue the "buzz" and enhance feelings of power. In the case of Mr C above, the fire enabled feelings of power and anger to be expressed as he made his mark on the local community through negative spoiling behavior. Remaining at the scene allowed an increase in the perception of his handiwork through watching the response of the fire personnel to the scene.

In cases where the offender/s leave/s the scene, this provides an alternative take on the interpretation. The target of the fire will help to establish whether it is the act of setting the fire or the subsequent events that are relevant. Both of these offender responses have the potential to identify likely personality and criminogenic need (that which is being met through the commission of the offense). The case of Mr X illustrates the use of firesetting to vandalize and meet a need to react negatively to those in authority.

Case Example

Mr X

Index offense: Mr X was in the vicinity when the police attended a house call following a report being made about young people behaving in an antisocial manner spraying graffiti on a nearby wall. The police attended and the officers entered the property of the complainant. Mr X used lighter fluid as an accelerant to set fire to the police car. The car set alight easily and was engulfed in flames requiring the fire service to respond to the scene. Once the fire service personnel arrived the group of young people, largely goaded by Mr X, began throwing missiles at the crew. Mr X was arrested and brought into custody.

   Relevant history: Mr X is 15 years old and has a history of vandalism, antisocial behavior, and public order offenses. He has been excluded from school and is currently on an Intensive Supervision and Surveillance Programme (ISSP) with the local Youth Offending Team. His attitude to authority has been and continues to be a considerable challenge to professionals working with him.

Excitement

This form of firesetting emphasizes the need for the arsonist to achieve a level of excitement and emotional or sexual arousal through the commission of the act and subsequent events. This motivation is more commonly focused on meeting an internal need and therefore the intent to harm others in this respect is reduced. Douglas et al. (1992, 2006) further distinguish this type of offense as a result of the focus of the crime for the offender into four motives: (i) thrill-seeking; (ii) attention-seeking; (iii) recognition (to achieve hero status); and (iv) sexual perversion.

The distinctions between the four subsets of excitement-motivated firesetting are important to understand because they have direct impact on the assessment of risk and for evaluating the utility of treatment. Thrill-seeking can be one of the most prevalent forms of excitement-motivated firesetting because setting fires results in feelings of excitement, power, and thrills. This means that the entire experience of firesetting is relevant, from lighting the fire through to the response by the fire crews attending the scene, hence individuals remain at the scene. This motive is perhaps the most challenging to eradicate because the individual gains so much positive emotional reinforcement from their actions. The case of Miss B aptly illustrates the challenges faced.

Case Example

Miss B

Index offense: Miss B set fire to a field at night while under surveillance by the police for a spate of arsons in the county. She remained at the scene to watch the fire but was arrested driving away. She claimed that she was returning home from a night out with friends and no firesetting paraphernalia was found. Miss B had been recorded on video committing the offense although when shown this evidence in police interview claimed that "it could have been anyone."

Relevant history: Miss B is 19 years old and her parents report that she had a fascination with fire from an early age, and that it appeared to begin following a major incident on a farm near where the family lived where a barn and haystacks burnt down. Miss B has been arrested and interviewed on seven previous occasions and charged with arson offenses on two occasions. In the five other instances no further action has been taken due to a lack of evidence and denial. Miss B is suspected by police as responsible for a further 96 offenses although has not been charged due to lack of evidence.

Attention-seeking and recognition (hero status) motives are similar in that they both involve gaining some form of attention, whether covert or overt. The individual seeking attention through their firesetting will light small fires in open locations in order to gain the kind of attention that results in an unknown individual engaging in such activity. In this case, there is no intent to harm others and the attention is achieved by the focus on the fires and associated media or community coverage. Recognition, however, tends to be gained through a greater degree of involvement in firesetting, making the call to the emergency services, assisting the fire service, and remaining on hand at the scene. This can variously involve individuals who are retained or part-time firefighters and only paid per fire they respond to; individuals wanting to make a family or parent proud through the act of rescuing others; or individuals with wannabe firefighter mentality who wants to be immersed in the entire experience.

Finally, the sexual perversion motive (Douglas et al., 1992) is most closely linked to the paraphilia (DSM-IV-TR) of "pyrophilia" where individuals experience sexual arousal associated with fires, recurring intense sexual fantasies, and sexual urges involving fires, sexual interest in fire, and sexual arousal from fire. Although early explanations focused on the link between sexual gratification and firesetting (Freud, 1932), and this has been supported by cases of convicted arsonists (e.g., Rice & Harris, 1991), ultimately there is little evidence leading to substantial links between the two (Lewis & Yarnell, 1951; Prins, Tennent, & Trick, 1985; Rice & Harris, 1991). Concluding anything meaningful with regard to sexual interest in firesetting is challenging – fires tend to be small, private, and focus on the internal gratification of the individual, perhaps decreasing the likelihood of arrest. There is evidence that ejaculate, faecal deposits, and pornography can all be left at the scene of such fires (Douglas et al., 1992). It is also important to consider the content of computers used by the arsonist. Hence this is a hypothesis that should not be disregarded due to a lack of compelling evidence in the field.

Revenge

A motivation underpinning many interpersonal offenses is revenge (Douglas et al., 1992), and this is especially dangerous and destructive when fire is utilized as a weapon. The setting of the fire where revenge is the motive is in response to or retaliation for a perceived injustice that has occurred – be it real or imagined (Douglas et al., 1992). This therefore increases the potential for heightened emotional arousal and the need for the offender to exact revenge via various means. Within this it is crucial to consider the use of fire to commit murder. For example, cause of death by burning can be strongly associated, or reflective of, an underlying motive of anger, suggesting that a large proportion of offenders are known to the victims in some way (Canter & Fritzon, 1998). The violence demonstrated in these deaths was extreme, with injuries far beyond that which was necessary to kill. Further evidence of this is illustrated by injuries to buttocks and genitalia that are inflicted on the victim. The second function is crime concealment (see the section below).

The danger or risk posed by an offender in this instance will occur on a vast continuum and be influenced by many different factors. Accordingly, understanding revenge as a relevant factor in an offender's motivation has to be an initial consideration with in-depth follow-up of information to identify the range and depth of feeling. Douglas et al. (1992) distinguish this by the identification of the victimization that can occur on a personal, societal, or institutional level. In addition, the form of the firesetting could be as group retaliation (e.g., against a particular religious group) or for the purpose of intimidation. There is therefore a requirement to understand the way in which the feelings and need for revenge manifest, and timescales where offenses could occur.

Case Example

Mr G

Index offense: Mr G threw a firebomb at the door of a house occupied by a witness who had given evidence against him and his co-defendants in a case of an armed robbery of a petrol station. Mr G had previously sent threatening letters to the witness that included threats to kill. The firebomb caused serious damage to the front of the property and removed the front door. The witness and their family had to move home as a result of the offense due to fear of further reprisals. In police custody, Mr G refused to discuss the offense and gave a "no comment" interview. He initially pleaded "Not Guilty" at court, later changing this to "Guilty," which was considered by police to be a result of the overwhelming evidence against him but also in order to reduce the sentence he served. An informant testified that Mr G intended to kill the witness and their family although this had not been successful. Mr G has previously set fires to intimidate witnesses.

Offending history: Mr G is 37 years old and has previous convictions for violent and drug offenses, and is a member of a "criminal family" and a traveler community. His first conviction was at 12 years when he stole a stereo from an electrical shop. Since then, he has been arrested 68 times and convicted in 43 of these. Mr G has spent a total of 19 years in prison or secure forensic settings as a result of his offending.

The case of Mr G illustrates how pervasive vengeful thoughts can be and that in some instances fire will be used as the most convenient or effective weapon against a specified target.

Crime Concealment

This motivational orientation is perhaps less key to a psychological understanding of firesetting activity because the act of setting fire is a secondary response to a primary need. The objective is to cover up another offense, be it murder, car crime, fraud, or burglary, in order to avoid arrest and prosecution. As such, crime concealment can occur to destroy evidence and is distinct from that which is profit motivated, in that financial gain is not the key consideration.

Cases can range in sophistication depending on the relative familiarity an offender has with firesetting methods. In one case of the murder of two men in a flat, the individuals were tortured for their credit card details and then stabbed extensively. One of the two offenders panicked following the death of the victims and torched the flat to reduce the physical evidence left at the scene. However, he received significant burns to his face and arms in the process.

The significance of firesetting in crime concealment cases is as a means to an end; hence assessments are likely to concentrate on the primary offending behavior rather than fire. Such individuals are more likely to be assessed in the context of violence or property offending, with fire as a secondary consideration.

Profit

The purpose of firesetting here is the monetary benefit that is gained as a result of the commission of the offense. In such instances, the fire is set to result in financial gain. Individuals who engage in firesetting tend to be focused, planned, and can be employed as a "hired torch" (Douglas et al., 1992), and as such is similar to contract killing. The motive is business oriented, therefore the likely targets are those where assets are held either by the offender themselves or by third parties (e.g., claiming on insurance following a car being stolen and burnt out), or for wider financial gain through business (e.g., a nightclub fire). It is therefore possible that the fire would conceal not only bad business practice or potential bankruptcy, but also the accompanying profit as a result of the offense.

Extremist Motivated

The motivation of arson which is related to extremist belief is to further a range of causes (social, political, or religious). It is perhaps less relevant here to consider arson in terms of a traditional assessment due to the nature of the offense. Hence, here the use of fire is a direct result of wider criminal activity such as pursuing a "cause" through terrorism, discrimination, or rioting within a civil disturbance. These are all separate offenses within a wider set of crimes, although the target of the arson is a representation of the antithesis of the offender's belief (Douglas et al., 1992). The chosen targets of such offenses are varied and range from directed

---

Case Example

Mr K

Index offense: Mr K was struggling to respond to debt collectors and other financiers from his lap dancing club and was aware that the extent of the debts was beyond the profits of the business. The creditors were becoming impatient and making threats to Mr K that they were going to recuperate their finances by taking his personal assets. Mr K had previously been visited at his home by a business associate who had threatened him and his family. The interest being collected on the loans was taking up all the profit from the business and therefore Mr K arranged to burn down the club by staging the incident as an accidental fire. Following an investigation into the fire at the nightclub, evidence of accelerants was identified by fire investigation dogs and Mr K was arrested. During interview in police custody, Mr K denied the offense and refused to discuss anything with the officers.

Relevant history: Mr K has a history of suspected involvement in organized criminal networks including a charge of conspiracy to murder, which was not proven, and handling stolen goods.

---

attacks on individuals to groups, scientific research laboratories, slaughter houses, religious institutions, and "right to life" groups. The importance and intent of such targeting and bombings and the association of fire within such offenses is more global in scale. This can concern the management of perceptions through the killing of targeted individuals, which may or may not include collateral damage (i.e., those who are not the intended target). Death and carnage associated with such offenses impacts on two main levels: (i) the physical injury/death of victims and the proliferation of images of the offense through the viral nature of the Internet; and (ii) related communication mediums.

CONSIDERATION OF INTENT

As noted above – the level of intent of an offender could be at variance with the actual events as they occurred. In terms of the law, there is the obvious distinction between accident – which may include recklessness – and intentional arson. The purposeful behavior of a firesetter can be identified from that which is more impulsive and spontaneous. If an individual is instrumental and goal directed, then it is still possible that what they had initially planned changed somewhat when they came to commit the offense. If there is a relationship between the firesetter and those who are the victims of the offense, then this can evidence particular targeting.

However, while someone can intend to do something specific to an individual or group, the logistics of completing the offense can lead to a change of events. The mental state of the offender at the time of the arson can provide more insight into the likely intention. For example, the act of checking whether people and animals were safe prior to setting a fire can show a reduction in the severity of the offense, which might be more focused on damage to property rather than risk to others. If the arson is used as a method of committing murder, then the intent would be established more from the perspective of that offense and the relevance of fire could be seen as a weapon of death, much like a knife or firearm. The offender might have intended the firesetting to result in injury or intimidation to others or to lead to self-injury (e.g., suicidal intent). It is possible that there was damage limitation following the firesetting by informing those at risk or the fire service. While firesetting can be unpredictable in outcome, and this may increase the attraction to fire for some, there is an initial expectation by firesetters of the extent of the fire they will create and the level of destruction it will cause. However identifying knowledge of fire spread and damage can assist in determining their likely intent.

ASSESSMENT LOGISTICS

Across the firesetting literature, there are a number of attempts to develop a comprehensive approach to the assessment of arson in order to develop a complete understanding of an offender/patient (e.g., Fineman, 1995; Jackson, 1994; Jackson, Glass, & Hope, 1987; Gannon & Pina, 2010; Ó Ciardha & Gannon, 2012). The focus of this section of the chapter is to develop the firesetting assessment incorporating the various elements from recommendations in the literature and to incorporate a consideration of the legal, investigative (e.g., Brunt, 2009), and behavioral elements of the offense(s).

Interview Preparation

Practitioners are often under pressure to respond to the challenges presented by prisoners/patients within forensic settings. Gozna and Boon (2007, 2010) emphasize the importance of a tailored approach to assessment and in particular in interviewing. The Chameleon Interview Approach provides a framework for understanding the multitude of factors requiring consideration when preparing to interview, including personality (including disorder and psychopathy), client and offense history and behavior, and the mindset, motive, and modus operandi. The focus of assessment in the context of firesetting should be on gaining an understanding of the offense itself, wider offenses (proven and suspected), and the formulation of a holistic view of the internal and/or external needs that are being met.

Knowledge

The offense of arson rarely occurs in isolation of other offenses or indeed a wider interest in fire and so it is important to establish where firesetting sits within a wider set of relevant factors. Therefore, in order to prepare for interviewing an individual awaiting trial, sentencing, or following conviction, the index offense should be focused upon in addition to a broader set of factors that may or may not be peripheral to the decision-making of risk. Moreover, it is important to establish whether the individual has undergone previous historical assessments or treatment interventions relating to arson offenses, and to establish their prior thinking about arson offenses and also the views of other practitioners who have engaged in work with them. It is possible that if an individual has already addressed prior firesetting behavior, that they will have increased insight into current incident/s. It is important to consider that such insights can be presented as "treatment speak"[2] or jargon, to emphasize or de-emphasize information to professionals to create a particular impression – whether in regard of faking good/faking bad and implications of risk.

To avoid being caught on the back foot, practitioners require a broad and deep understanding of the offense of arson, legally, investigatively, and behaviorally. An effective approach to underpin the assessment of firesetting is through the use of Functional Analysis (see Jackson, 1994; Jackson, Glass, & Hope, 1987), which is a process that assists in determining the psychological function of the fire for the individual concerned. In addition, a process that enables a number of features to be assessed, the BAREPCS (Perkins, 1991: Behaviors, Attitudes, Relationships, Emotions, Physical conditions, Cognitions, and Sexual interests), enables the practitioner to take a focused approach to the understanding of the offense and incorporates a focused interview strategy to identify pertinent factors. Most recently, work in this area has considered the psychopathology of arson within the context of treatment (Gannon & Pina, 2010) and has developed a theoretical model to account for the various trajectories of firesetters and argue that distinct psychological vulnerabilities predominate for different individuals (Gannon, Ó Ciardha, Doley, & Alleyne, 2012; Ó Ciardha & Gannon, 2012). The Multi-Trajectory Theory of Adult Firesetting (M-TAFF) conceptualizes individuals into "one of five prototypical trajectories leading to firesetting: antisocial cognition; grievance; fire interest; emotionally expressive/need for recognition; and multi-faceted" (Ó Ciardha & Gannon, 2012, p. 123). The theory has much to give toward understanding adult firesetting and can be usefull employed in the consideration of case formulation and assessment.

In addition to the collateral information[3] available, an assessment interview enables the perspective of the individual to be obtained. However, it is beneficial for practitioners to consider peripheral elements which further aid decision-making about risk. An overall picture of the offense(s) will have been gained in the preparation for interview; however an additional focus is required on the manner in which the information is disclosed to the practitioner in terms of credibility and consistency. It is beneficial to consider the following thoughts before, during, and after an individual is interviewed to allow for reflection on what has been presented:

- What information or events are they choosing to disclose or avoid in an interview?
- Are they comfortable discussing their firesetting behavior?
- Are they overemphasizing or de-emphasizing particular factors in the detail of the offense? Why is this likely to be?
- Who do they feel is ultimately to blame for the offense?
- Do they feel that the official version of events is a true reflection of what happened?
- In what way does the official version alter from their perception of the offense? Which version do you believe?
- How do you feel when the individual is describing their offending? Does it make sense to you in terms of likely credibility and the logistics of the firesetting (if in doubt, speak to a fire investigation officer)?

During and following any assessment of firesetting, consideration should be given to imminent risk regardless of whether the interview occurs in a secure setting or in the community. When assessing prolific firesetters, it is unlikely that discussion of every fire will be possible, some even being forgotten by the individual, although the themes or motivations behind the offending should be ascertained from salient offenses identified in the collateral information for more in-depth discussion. Therefore it is necessary to identify Antecedents, Behaviors, and Consequences (ABC, see Lee-Evans, 1994) of those offenses that are officially recorded and those that have been disclosed post-conviction. Once the discussion is underway, it is likely that individuals will disclose wider offenses or interests in fire as relevant to them. However, such discussions require trust to be developed and time and reflection on the part of the practitioner.

Historical Firesetting

The historical involvement with fire – both functional and dysfunctional – can assist in the understanding of the offense(s). The emphasis here is the historical signifi-cance of fire during childhood: whether this was a healthy curiosity or interest in playing with matches and watching controlled fires, or tended toward a more patho-logical involvement or exposure to firesetting constituting concern from others. If an individual has been in a variety of institutions for 20 years and not set any fires, then their history of firesetting needs to account for the factors that were relevant at the time of the offense and whether such problems would lead to further offenses. It is therefore the appropriate and inappropriate nature of the firesetting or the poten-tially dangerous implications that need to be recorded and considered in the overall assessment of an individual.

Questioning childhood involvement in fire is necessary to locate when the interest commenced and can be taken as an opportunity to identify the level of insight the individual has; the focus should be on their prior behavior and whether they are willing/able to identify any particular link to their current offending behavior. In some instances the early witnessing of fires will become especially important to the child owing to their broader circumstances and could become a pertinent memory for them. For example, observing a large fire could be the first exposure a child has to a feeling of power whether through prosocial or antisocial ways. Hence this could result in a child aspiring to become a firefighter or commence an interest in firesetting. This has the potential to be of relevance as an influence for their later interest and in any use of fire in an offending capacity.

ABC ANALYSIS

Establishing the Antecedents, Behaviors, and Consequences of the offense(s) can assist in gaining a holistic view and allow for more focused discussion on particularly pertinent points (Perkins, 1991). The following section presents some questions and factors that assist in an assessment of firesetting, although these are not all-encompassing. It is relevant to consider some of the pertinent and peripheral issues, a few of which will result in direct questions for practitioners to pose, and others, it is suggested, are for the practitioner to reflect upon during the assessment process. However, the result of covering these relevant topics will enable a focused visualization of the individual and will be informative regarding the potential risk implications.

The Role of Parents – Dysfunction in Relationship

The nature of the "parental" relationships to the individual can reveal issues of parental deprivation or abuse. Where relevant this may assist in the formulation of the understanding of offense motivation and the related concerns of reoffending. Example questions include: What is the relationship with parents like (if relevant)? How often does the individual see close family or communicate with them? What influence do siblings have on the wider relationship with parental figures? Is the individual themselves a parent – how has their experience influenced their views?

Employment Problems and Links to Firesetting

This concerns any potential link between arson in the workplace and problems in employment. It is possible that problems at work will be a factor in triggering the need to set fires. Arson attacks in the workplace can be difficult to identify and there may be a number of parallel hypotheses relating to the motivation of the offense. Example questions include: Have you ever set fires as a reaction to something that has happened to you at work? Have you ever set a fire as a response to losing your job? Have you ever wanted to get back at colleagues or the organization where you have worked?

Previous Dysfunction in Relationships Including Sexual Problems

The presence of problems in relationships can be a factor in understanding the need that is being met through firesetting behavior. However, it is possible this is unrelated and a parallel problem. Therefore, it is important to understand the nature of domestic or sexual conflicts in order to develop an awareness of a link with arson or a wider problem. This can incorporate consideration of:

• Domestic violence – victimized as a child or adult, perpetrated as an adult.
• Sexual abuse – victimization or perpetration of sexual offenses.
• Short-term or brief sexual relationships.
• Any link between sexual activity and firesetting behavior.

Dependence on Alcohol or Drugs

It is common to encounter a level of substance misuse among the offending population, but whether the consumption of alcohol or drugs is relevant to firesetting has to be ascertained (Gozna, 2010). That is to say, is it a disinhibitor that will increase the likelihood of an offense being committed or increase its severity? Reports from previously undertaken interventions relating to drugs or alcohol will assist in this assessment. Example questions include: How does your use of alcohol impact on your reactions to others and your accompanying behavior? What is your pattern of alcohol use or drug use? Does the use of alcohol or drugs impact on your mood? How do you behave when you have been drinking? In what way does it affect you? Do certain types of alcohol or drugs influence your reactions or moods?

Deliberate Self-Harm

The relevance of self-harm and suicidal ideology when assessing arson is critical, particularly in prisons and forensic mental health settings. From clinical and prison observations it is apparent that it is necessary to identify how this manifests and whether fire has ever been employed as a method with which to harm, for example setting fire to a person's own clothing or body parts. This can occur in situations where a person deliberately sets fire to their property and remains inside in an attempt to commit suicide, or sets fire to their clothing in order to sustain considerable injuries. However, self-harm can also be parallel to firesetting acts and therefore needs to be understood in the appropriate context. Relevant example questions here include: Have you ever used fire as a method of self-harm? Is your self-harm related to your firesetting? How do you feel about using fire to harm yourself? Have you ever set a fire as a method of suicide? What happened and what did you intend to happen?

Feelings at the Time of the Offense – Psychological State

This has the potential to unveil the motivation behind the offending behavior and what the likely triggers were that led up to the chain of events. It is possible that the initial views developed by practitioners about the likely motive could alter once a discussion is held with an offender about the offense. It is also interesting at this point to identify the level of insight and reflection an individual has about their firesetting behaviors. However it is worth bearing in mind that any motivations might not be willingly identifiable for reasons such as denial of involvement, lack of insight, self-deception, or genuine lack of understanding.

The apparent spontaneity or planning of an offense can highlight whether the firesetting is an immediate reaction to an event, or whether there is a slow build up to the event in the mind of the offender over a period of time. Example questions to consider posing include: How were you feeling on the day of the offense? Did you think about setting the fire in advance? Were you aware of your emotions when you set the fire? How did you plan the fire? What was the outcome of the fire in terms of your resulting mood?

Was There a Particular Event or Experience that Led to the Firesetting?

This relates to the circumstance that preceded the event of setting the fire and therefore particular triggers. It is important to consider wider fire-related behavior such as hoax calling or malicious attacks on fire service personnel. This can also focus on a positive interest in fire moving into a more pathological interest. Example questions include: Why did you set the fire? What happened for you to make that decision? Was the fire planned or a spontaneous decision? Did you feel justified reacting like that when you think about what was happening at the time?

Reason for the Particular Fire and Its Significance

The target of the arson could be significant to the offender although this might not initially be apparent to the practitioner. It is important to focus on the links that the individual has with particular places. The significance of the site will be related to a historical location where the person frequented (e.g., school), or a site which has emotional significance attached to another individual (e.g., property), or a symbolic representation of heightened emotional relevance (e.g., a particular church, a place of worship associated with a particular faith). This further assists in the assessment of risk for future fires and which locations or individuals would be considered as high risk. Example questions include: What was the significance to you of the location or area where you set the fire? What made you feel like this about the location? What was your intent when you set the fire? Did it go according to plan?

Prior Supervision/Treatment Interventions

Depending on the historical/collateral information gained about firesetting behavior, it is possible that individuals will have engaged in prior supervision or taken part in offending behavior programs. It is important to identify the success or otherwise of such programs and whether there were any challenges in regard to levels of cooperation or engagement by the offender and any accompanying interpretation for this. Example questions include: Did the individual respond well to supervision? How have they behaved in treatment interventions? Were they disruptive and how was this exhibited? Are they displaying/did they display passive aggression in sessions? Are/were they "complying" superficially rather than legitimately? In what way are/were they able to illustrate reflection and insight into their past offending as a result of prior interventions? Have you ever taken part in any awareness groups for firesetting or specific-offense-related work? What do you remember from your prior experiences of doing these treatment programs? How did you feel it helped you to understand your own firesetting actions?

Self-Awareness and Insight into Behavior

The level of awareness and insight displayed can provide a wealth of information for the practitioner. There are a number of important factors that need to be taken into account. To what extent does the individual understand the needs that are being met through their firesetting behavior? Do they think that such incidents are likely to occur in the future? In what way do they recall their actions – with regret, distress, pride, and so on?

Offense Supportive Beliefs

Similar to wider offense supportive beliefs, it is necessary to gain information about the beliefs and attitudes that the individual holds. How do they feel about their offense(s) and to what extent do they accept responsibility for their actions? Do they believe the offense was justified and they were responding normally to a situation? Are there distortions in the manner in which they discuss their offense and have responded subsequently? How do their views impact on the likelihood of future offending?

Emotional Impact of Firesetting

How does the individual cope with general situations and how has this impacted on their firesetting behavior? Is it serial in nature or have they committed a one-off offense? Do they sit comfortably with their actions or feel compelled to continue to offend? What are the emotions that are displayed before, during, and after the offense? Do they report a release of tension or other emotions during and following firesetting? What impact will this have on future offending?

Recent Firesetting Activity or Offenses

The seriousness and frequency of firesetting behavior needs to be established, in particular the nature and extent of any escalation. It is possible that the official record of convictions will not truly match the actual behavior that has occurred or the extent of offenses committed. Therefore it is important to establish the full picture of the behavior, which includes convicted and committed offenses and non-problematic firesetting. Example questions include: How many offenses of fire-related acts have you been arrested/convicted for? Have you ever set any fires and not been caught? Is there a difference between the offenses you were arrested for and those where you were not identified?

Progression of Firesetting Behavior

This refers to the progression in the skills, methods, or actions of firesetting over the course of time. In what way has an individual developed their firesetting actions over time? If they have set a significant number of fires historically, how have the fires been set? Is there consistency in the offending or evidence of increased sophistication and improvements made?

This will also be influenced by whether offenses were planned (in fantasy or reality) or spontaneous. A greater expertise and awareness of firesetting can be established through the use of accelerants, timing devices, or learning how to increase the spread of fire by setting multiple seats. Any progression could be indicative of recidivism and therefore the picture of the growth in experience and skill in firesetting should be noted. Example questions include: What have you learned about fire and firesetting since you started committing offenses? Are you more considered or better organized when you set fires now than you were in the past? How do you think your knowledge of fire has improved? Are you also more aware of the dangers of fire? Have you ever been injured (inadvertently) as a result of setting a fire?

Independent Firesetting Activity

The interpretation of the firesetting behavior can be hugely influenced by the presence or involvement of other individuals. It is possible that individuals who set fires with peers or collaborators will do this for wholly different reasons than when they are acting alone. Is the firesetting occurring with the intent of involving others as victims or is the response from third parties confined to the fire service and possible bystanders? In what way does the personality of the individual provide the impetus for them to set fire? Example questions include: Have you ever shared you interest in fire with other people? Have you always set fires when you were alone? Why do you think you act alone when engaging in firesetting acts? Is firesetting an intensely personal experience for you?

Group Firesetting

In some circumstances, firesetting occurs as an action with other individuals, possibly a collaborator or wider group, including peers.

It is likely therefore that the offense will be differentiated from independent acts through, for example, intent, offense actions, and post-offense behavior. Hence the occurrence of firesetting within a group requires the identification of instigators and followers and the ability of the practitioner to ascertain the needs that are being met through this group dynamic. Example questions include: Has your firesetting ever involved offending with other people? What role did they play in the firesetting? Did you feel you were more or less successful in the act as a result of being with others? What was your involvement in the offense?

Internal Influences

One trigger that can be influential in firesetting actions is the experience of emotion and the way in which an individual copes with this. The displacement of emotion or aggression can occur as a result of an internal state that has become unbearable for the individual. This can inevitably increase the need to act upon these emotions and can influence the likelihood of firesetting. In addition, other factors to consider include the influence of hormones, Axis I and II disorders (DSM-IV-TR, APA, 1994), and wider considerations. These should be identified to ensure that their relevance is considered in the wider assessment. Example questions include: How do you manage your emotions when you are experiencing problems? What do you do to respond to stress? Have you ever been diagnosed with a psychiatric disorder? Do you think this has had an influence on your interest or use of fire in offending?

External Influences

In addition to internal influences, there are wider factors that have the potential to impact on the offense(s). These can be wide-ranging and will be linked to the motivation for the firesetting. It is also relevant to incorporate knowledge of which situations or people influence the individual's decision-making process or will cause them to emotionally/psychologically destabilize and trigger an offense (firesetting or other). If the fire is in response to external triggers then the identification of these allows for a focused understanding of the risk posed. Example questions include: Have external influences or situations ever impacted on your firesetting? Have you ever set a fire in response to something someone has done to you?

The Perception of Fire

This factor emphasizes the importance of identifying the perception held of fire and its accompanying dangers. This is particularly in relation to the fires that are set by the individual and the destructive nature. Depending on the severity of firesetting, it is crucial to highlight what could happen in a worst-case scenario if this were to occur. Example questions include: If you think of the worst-case scenario for your firesetting, what would be the situation and who would be the target of the fire? What are the likely injuries? Do you think you are in control of the fires that you set? Has anything ever gone wrong or not gone to plan when you have set a fire? Have you ever imagined or fantasized about setting fires?

Fascination with/Attraction to Fire

The emphasis is to establish the way in which the individual is attracted to fire and whether fire is perceived in a positive manner. Does fire hold a particular fascination for the individual being assessed? What is the situational context for this? What is the nature of the fascination and how does this potentially put others at risk? Is the fascination confined to less severe fires which, while resulting in monetary loss, have no impact on life?

Benefits of Firesetting

The benefit of firesetting can result in a cathartic experience for an offender. For example, firesetters will sometimes report that they experience a release (of emotional pressure or stress) as a result of setting a fire, which has been described as paralleling self-harm acts. The resulting feeling from firesetting can additionally result in a hugely empowering experience, which is accompanied by a surge of energy. It is therefore helpful to identify the nature of the emotional response (if any) that is experienced and the underpinning meaning. In this case, gratification is based on the motivation for the fire and this includes emotional release, power, pleasure, sense of justice or revenge, relief of boredom, and control. It is the perception of the individual rather than the inference from the practitioner that is important here to establish the needs that are being met. Example questions that practitioners may want to consider asking include: What benefit do you gain from firesetting? Do you get a buzz when you think about your past firesetting? What, if any, positive emotions do you experience when you set fires?

Planning and Spontaneity

It is beneficial to differentiate between expressive and instrumental acts within firesetting, which are caused by the behavioral underpinnings of the offense. Fesbach (1964) introduced the hostile (expressive) and instrumental dichotomy as a method of understanding the function of aggression. An understanding of violent behavior cannot be disregarded when considering firesetting and should be investigated depending on the relevance for the individual being assessed. Expressive aggression is in response to the need to change what can be an intolerable emotional state. Instrumentally aggressive acts tend to be goal-oriented in their focus and are intended to change something in individuals or the wider environment. Therefore in this situation, fire is used as a means to an end.

Firesetting as Self-Protection

If an individual feels they are on the receiving end of a threat (real or perceived), then there is the potential to respond with fire as a method of protection. The threat could include perceived status of the individual, self-esteem, and physical safety. The medium of fire highlights that the individual does not hold the capacity to respond to such threats through typical acceptable methods but instead uses fire to react. This has implications for coping strategies when threats to self are perceived as high. Such maladaptive coping can impact on recidivism and the focus on triggers that cause an individual to react to threats in dysfunctional ways. Example questions include: Was your firesetting in response to something or someone who threatened you? What was the reason you felt threatened?

Impact of Violence

Violent offending can occur in parallel to firesetting or fire can be the method employed as a response to a situation. This includes offenses against the person and offenses more akin to criminal damage. Therefore the emphasis here is to identify whether violent offenses are relevant to the assessment of firesetting, or exclusive. The understanding of violence here will establish whether fire is a method of indirectly reacting in an aggressive manner to a situation, or if it is directly used to cause harm in addition to other physical violence, the use of weapons, and focused aggression.

CONCLUSIONS

The assessment of firesetting is challenging and requires practitioners to be aware of many of the issues prior to embarking on a face-to-face discussion with an offender. This chapter has attempted to discuss the main factors that enable the preparation of a bespoke method of individual assessment and the importance of establishing motive, intent, and offender decision-making. The cases presented throughout the chapter illustrate the variety of offenses that can be considered under the remit of deliberate firesetting, regardless of whether they are legally defined as such. The desired outcome of understanding a firesetter's motives from collateral file information and an assessment interview is that it will be possible for the practitioner and individual to develop a visualization of the antecedents, offense behaviors, and the consequences, with a view to identifying areas of treatment need and interventions.

ACKNOWLEDGMENTS

Thanks to Julian Boon for his comments on an earlier version of this chapter.

NOTES

1 The terms "arson" and deliberate "firesetting" will be used interchangeably throughout this chapter. However it is the deliberate nature of firesetting that meets the criteria for consideration under the Criminal Damage Act 1971 in England and Wales.
2 "Treatment speak'" is a concept whereby offenders/patients employ in their vocabulary certain words or phrases they have been exposed to during therapy, treatment programs, or from other offenders. The use of such "speak" within discussions of offending behavior is entirely for instrumental gain and giving a false impression of progress or risk. This does though need to be distinguished from individuals who are legitimate.
3 Although there is often little communication of information from pre- to post-conviction settings, in arson offenses there is a requirement to understand the reality of the offense and associated damage because this will assist in establishing ground truth prior to assessment.

REFERENCES

American Psychiatric Association (2013). *Diagnostic and Statistical Manual of Mental Disorders (4th ed.) – DSM IV-TR*. Washington, DC: APA.
Barker, A.F. (1994). *Arson: A review of the psychiatric literature*. Oxford: Oxford University Press.
Boon, J.C.W. (1998). Science, psychology and psychological profiling: An epistemological perspective. In M. Baurmann & H. Dern (Eds.), *Methods of case analysis: An international symposium* (pp. 143–155). Wiesbaden, Germany: Bundeskriminalamt.
Brunt, D. (2009). *How to investigate arson: A guide to investigators*. Guildford: Mi Print.
Canter, D., & Fritzon, K. (1998). Differentiating arsonists: A model of firesetting actions and characteristics. *Legal and Criminological Psychology, 3*, 73–96.

Davis, J.A., & Lauber, K.M. (1999). Criminal behavioural assessment of arsonists, pyromaniacs and multiple firesetters: The burning question. *Journal of Contemporary Criminal Justice, 15* (3), 273–290.

Dickens, G.L., Sugarman, P.A., & Gannon, T.A. (Eds.) (2012). *Firesetting and mental health.* London: RCPsych Publications.

Doley, R., & Fritzon, K. (2008). Assessment and treatment of fire-setters. In K. Fritzon & P. Wilson (Eds.), *Forensic psychology and criminology* (pp. 101–109). Sydney: McGraw-Hill.

Douglas, J., Burgess, A.W., Burgess, A.G., & Ressler, R. (1992). *Crime classification manual.* Lexington, MA: Lexington.

Douglas, J., Burgess, A.W., Burgess, A.G., & Ressler, R. (2006). *Crime classification manual* (2nd ed.). San Francisco, CA: Jossey-Bass.

Edmunds, G. (1978). Judgements on different types of aggressive behaviour. *British Journal of Social and Clinical Psychology, 17,* 121–125.

Fesbach, S. (1964). The function of aggression on the regulation of aggressive drive. *Psychological Review, 71,* 257–272.

Fineman, K.R. (1995). A model for the qualitative analysis of child and adult fire deviant behavior. *American Journal of Forensic Psychology, 13,* 31–60.

Foley, M. (2008). *Attacks on fire-fighters: The nature of the problem.* Unpublished MSc thesis. University of Surrey, UK.

Freud, S. (1932). The acquisition of fire. *Psychoanalytic Quarterly, 1,* 210–215.

Fritzon, K., Canter, D., & Wilton, Z. (2001). The application of an action system model to destructive behaviour: The examples of arson and terrorism. *Behavioral Sciences and the Law, 19* (5–6), 657–690.

Gannon, T., Ó Ciardha, C., Doley, R. & Alleyne, E. (2012). The Multi-Trajectory Theory of Adult Firesetting (M-TAFF). *Aggression and Violent Behavior, 17* (2), 107–121.

Gannon, T.A., & Pina, A. (2010). Firesetting: Psychopathology, theory and treatment. *Aggression and Violent Behavior, 15,* 224–238.

Geller, J.L., Erlen, J., & Pinkus, R.L. (1986). A historical appraisal of America's experience with "pyromania": A diagnosis in search of a disorder. *International Journal of law and Psychiatry, 9,* 201–229.

Gozna, L.F. (2010). *Fascination with fire: The psychology of arson.* Invited talk given to Cleveland Fire Service Bonfire Campaign Conference, Wynyard Rooms, Cleveland, October 22.

Gozna, L.F., & Boon, J.C.W. (2007). *The chameleon offender: The synergising of psychology and psychiatry to meet the challenge.* Paper presented at the Conference of Research in Forensic Psychiatry, Regensburg, Germany, May 29–31.

Gozna, L.F., & Boon, J.C.W. (2010). Interpersonal deception detection. In J. Brown & E. Campbell (Eds.), *The Cambridge handbook of forensic psychology* (pp. 484–491). Cambridge: Cambridge University Press.

Gozna, L.F., & Prendergast, J. (2008). Increasing innovation in applied research: Bridging the investigative-clinical divide. In L. Rayment & L. Falshaw (Eds.), *Issues in Forensic Psychology (8)* (pp. 12–22). Leicester: The British Psychological Society.

Harris, G.T., & Rice, M.E. (1984). Mentally disordered firesetters: Psychodynamic versus empirical approaches. *International Journal of Law and Psychiatry, 9,* 267–285.

Harris, G.T., & Rice, M.E. (1996). A typology of mentally disordered firesetters. *Journal of Interpersonal Violence, 11* (3), 351–363.

Inciardi, J.A. (1970). The adult firesetter: A typology. *Criminology, 8*, 145–155.

Jackson, H.F. (1994). Assessment of firesetters. In M. McMurran & J. Hodge (Eds.), *The assessment of criminal behaviours of clients in secure settings* (pp. 94–126). London: Jessica Kingsley Publishers.

Jackson, H.F., Glass, C.A., & Hope, S. (1987). A functional analysis of recidivist arson. *British Journal of Clinical Psychology, 26*, 175–185.

Kelly, J., Goodwill, A., Keene, N., & Thrift, S. (1999). A retrospective study of historical risk factors for pathological arson in adults with mild learning disabilities. *British Journal of Forensic Practice, 11* (2), 17–23.

Lee-Evans, J.M. (1994). Background to behaviour analysis. In M. McMurran & J. Hodge (Eds.), *The assessment of criminal behaviours of clients in secure settings* (pp. 6–34). London: Jessica Kingsley Publishers.

Lewis, N.D.C., & Yarnell, H. (1951). Pathological firesetting (pyromania). *Nervous and Mental Disease Monographs, No. 82*. New York: Coolidge Foundation.

MacDonald, J.M. (1963). The threat to kill. *American Journal of Psychiatry, 120* (2), 125–130.

MacDonald, J.M. (1977). *Bombers and firesetters*. Springfield, IL: Charles C. Thomas.

McKerracher, D.W., & Dacre, J.I. (1966). A study of arsonists in a special security hospital. *British Journal of Psychiatry, 112*, 1151–1154.

Ó Ciardha, C., & Gannon, T. (2012). The implicit theories of firesetters: A preliminary conceptualization. *Aggression and Violent Behavior, 17*, 122–128.

Perkins, D.E. (1991). A psychological treatment programme for sexual offenders. In B. McGurk, D. Thornton, & M. Williams (Eds.), *Applying psychology to imprisonment* (pp. 191–218). London: HMSO.

Prins, H. (1994). *Fire raising: Its motivation and management*. London: Routledge.

Prins, H., Tennent, G., & Trick, K. (1985). Motives for arson (fire raising). *Medicine, Science and the Law, 25*, 275–278.

Ravateheino, J. (1989). Finnish study of 180 arsonists arrested in Helsinki. *Fire Prevention, 223*, 30–34.

Reber, A. (1995). *Penguin dictionary of psychology*. London: Penguin.

Rice, M.E., & Harris, G.T. (1991). Firesetters admitted to a maximum security psychiatric institution. *Journal of Interpersonal Violence, 6*, 461–475.

Slavkin, M.L. (2001). Enuresis, firesetting, and cruelty to animals: Does the ego triad show predictive validity? *Adolescence, 36*, 461–466.

Stadolnik, R.F. (2000). *Drawn to the flame: Assessment and treatment of juvenile firesetting behavior*. Sarasota, FL: Professional Resource Press.

Williams, D.L. (2005). *Understanding the arsonist: From assessment to confession*. Tucson, AZ: Lawyers & Judges Publishing Company, Inc.

Willis, M. (2004). Bushfire arson: A review of the literature. *Research in Public Policy Series (No. 61)*. Canberra: Australian Institute of Criminology.

World Health Organization (2010). *The ICD-10 classification of mental and behavioural disorders: Clinical descriptions and diagnostic guidelines*. Geneva: World Health Organization.

6

Forensic Psychological Risk Assessment for the Parole Board

LOUISE BOWERS AND CAROLINE FRIENDSHIP

INTRODUCTION

The Parole Board of England and Wales is "an independent body that works with its criminal justice partners to protect the public by risk assessing prisoners to determine whether they can safely be released into the community" (Parole Board, 2013). Parole Board decisions are based on evidence mainly provided by prison and probation service staff regarding the prisoner. One of the sources of evidence comes from psychologists who predominately, but not exclusively, specialize in forensic psychology. Some are employed directly by the prison and probation services, others are instructed on behalf of the prisoner to provide a view that is independent of these organizations.

Parole Boards in Canada, the United States, and Europe have increasingly relied on the opinion of forensic psychologists who act as expert witnesses assessing the risk of serious harm a prisoner poses to the public at the point of potential release (Craig & Beech, 2010). Forensic psychologists use their theoretical knowledge of risk among criminal groups to make evidence-based predictions about future offending behavior for an individual in order to make a recommendation to the Parole Board about progression. A decision whether or not to release a prisoner into the community has a profound effect on the prisoner, the victim(s) of the offense, the victim's family, and the general public. Prisoners do not forfeit their human rights just because they have caused harm to others (Coyle, 2008) and balancing the rights of the prisoner against a duty to protect the public is a key Parole Board consideration.

Assessments in Forensic Practice: A Handbook, First Edition. Edited by Kevin D. Browne, Anthony R. Beech, Leam A. Craig, and Shihning Chou.
© 2017 John Wiley & Sons Ltd. Published 2017 by John Wiley & Sons Ltd.

Underestimating the risk a prisoner presents can be catastrophic as in the case of Anthony Rice (HM Inspectorate of Probation, 2006). Equally, overestimating the risk can lead to prolonged and unnecessary incarceration. Given what is at stake, psychologists need to ensure they are professionally competent to undertake risk assessments.

This chapter is intended to assist psychologists in providing relevant, useful, and defensible risk assessment reports for the Parole Board. It outlines the historical context and powers of the Parole Board, details what should be included in a psychological report, and concludes with some ethical and practical considerations.

THE HISTORICAL CONTEXT OF THE PAROLE BOARD

The Parole Board for England and Wales was established in 1968 under the Criminal Justice Act 1967. It became an independent executive non-departmental public body (ENDPB) on July 1, 1996 under the Criminal Justice and Public Order Act 1994. The Board was initially sponsored by the Prison Service, then by the Home Office, and from May 2007, by the Ministry of Justice. Its stated role is to assess the level of risk presented by prisoners and to decide if they can safely be released into the community (Parole Board, 2013). The overarching aim of the Parole Board is to work with others to protect the public and to contribute to the rehabilitation of prisoners.

Initially the Parole Board was an executive body with limited powers. Its primary function was to advise and make recommendations to the Home Secretary regarding the continued detention or release of prisoners. Panels considered written reports in the absence of the prisoner or their representative. When asked to contribute, psychologists would typically submit a report to the Board with no further input. In the early 1990s, a series of key rulings led to the Parole Board changing from an executive body into a court-like body, with significant implications for the provision of psychological evidence. *Thynne* (and others)[1] in the European Court of Human Rights confirmed that discretionary life-sentenced prisoners should have the decision to release them made by a court-like body with the possibility of an oral hearing, and so, in 1992, the Parole Board was granted the power to preside over such a court and direct the release of such prisoners. In 1997, the Board's authority to direct release was extended to Her Majesty's Prison detainees (those convicted of murder when under 18 years of age at the time of the offense) and to those serving automatic life sentence and, in 2002, following the case of *Stafford*,[2] to mandatory lifers.

In 2007, in the case of *Brooke*,[3] the Parole Board was deemed not to demonstrate the level of objective independence from the Ministry of Justice or the Secretary of State for Justice that is required of a court. As a result, further administrative and procedural changes have been made to increase the objectivity of the Parole Board and its independence from the Secretary of State. The Parole Board has therefore become a court-like body where decisions about the most dangerous offenders are more often than not made at oral hearings with the prisoner and their representative present. The implications for psychologists is that when asked to produce a risk assessment report for the Parole Board they will frequently be directed to attend an oral hearing as a witness and their evidence will be subject to cross-examination by members of the Board and by the prisoner's representative.

The most recent ruling to influence Parole Board practice is a Supreme Court Judgment in the case of *Osborn, Booth, and Reilly*,[4] handed down in October 2013, which widens the range of circumstances in which the Parole Board is required to hold an oral hearing. Many more prisoners will now receive an oral hearing but it is not yet clear how the Parole Board will deal with this increased demand on its resources and how it will impact the provision of psychological assessments.

PAROLE BOARD REVIEWS

When eligible, a prisoner is entitled to a Parole Board review. There are two methods of review: a paper panel or an oral hearing. Traditionally, determinate sentence prisoners had their case considered at a paper panel and indeterminate sentence prisoners at an oral hearing, but this has changed over time. Following the Osborn judgment, more cases are entitled to an oral hearing, and as psychological risk assessments are mainly provided for oral hearings, the latter will be the focus of this section.

Oral hearings usually take place in the prison where the prisoner is located, providing the Parole Board panel with face to face contact with the prisoner and also the witnesses directed to attend the hearing. In recent years, the Board has been piloting the use of video link technology, which allows the panel to be located at a central point while the prisoner and other witnesses are at a prison and/or probation offices.

Oral hearings are typically heard by three-member panels with the exception of some recall hearings, which are heard by a single member. The Parole Board is currently reviewing their practice in order to accommodate the expected increase in the number of oral hearings following the Osborn judgment; the number of panel members required for an oral hearing may vary in the future with possibly only two-member panels required.

Panels are chaired by either a judge or a specially trained member of the Parole Board. The other two panel members may be an independent member (who may not have worked in criminal justice) or a probation member. Where the case warrants, a specialist member, either a psychiatrist or psychologist, is allocated to a panel. The prisoner is often represented, in most cases by a legally qualified representative, although recent changes to Legal Aid entitlements may mean that more prisoners will be representing themselves in future. Witnesses usually include the Offender Manager, the Offender Supervisor, and anyone else who can add something to the risk assessment decision. Typically, witnesses have prepared a written report prior to attending the hearing. Other attendees at an oral hearing may include the Secretary of State's representative or an observer. Observers tend to be professionals working in criminal justice but may include members of the prisoner's family. In addition, a victim liaison officer and/or the victim of the offense (or a family member of the victim) may attend the beginning of the hearing to read out a victim personal statement.

Arnott and Creighton (2014) noted that the style of oral hearings should be as informal as possible with the panel having an inquisitorial role. The panel is free to conduct the hearing in the manner it feels most appropriate to the matters to be decided. In reality hearings tend to be conducted in the preferred style of the panel chair, which may be inquisitorial but can be adversarial. Although hearings are a court-like process, the standard of proof is, as in civil matters, the balance of probabilities.

Psychologist members of the Parole Board contribute to the quality assurance of psychological risk assessments provided at oral hearings. Their role is to advise a panel on the qualifications and experience of the expert, on any specific psychological issues relevant to the case, on the quality of the risk assessment, and to help make sense of differing psychological opinions. The first psychologist members were appointed to the Board in 2003 and there are currently about 20 psychologist members. All are chartered psychologists (British Psychological Society) and registered forensic psychologists (Health and Care Professions Council); some are also registered clinical psychologists.

WHO DOES THE PAROLE BOARD ASSESS?

The Parole Board currently has a responsibility to consider the risk posed by *all* indeterminate (except for a handful of life-sentence prisoners given whole-life terms) and *some* determinate sentenced prisoners, in order to make a decision about the suitability of release. The Parole Board has different powers depending on the type of prisoner and the stage of sentence.

Determinate Sentenced Prisoners

All offenders sentenced under the provisions of either the Criminal Justice Act 2003 or the Criminal Justice and Immigration Act 2008 are automatically released at the half-way point of their sentence without referral to the Parole Board. Other determinate sentence prisoners are subject to discretionary conditional release (DCR) by the Parole Board if serving four or more years for an offense committed before April 4, 2005, or if given extended sentences for public protection (EPP) for offenses committed on or after April 4, 2005. From December 3, 2012, a new sentence called an extended determinate sentence (EDS) replaced the EPP. The Parole Board considers whether these prisoners are safe to release into the community once they have completed the minimum time they must spend in prison. All determinate sentences have had the same statutory test for release since the Legal Aid, Sentencing and Punishment of Offenders Act 2012 came into place: "the Parole Board must not give a direction [for release] … unless the Board is satisfied that it is no longer necessary for the protection of the public that a person should be confined." The Board also considers any determinate sentence prisoner referred by the Secretary of State following recall to prison for a breach of their parole license conditions. In terms of numbers there are fewer Parole Board reviews of determinate sentenced prisoners than indeterminate sentence prisoners.

Indeterminate Sentenced Prisoners

The Parole Board considers whether indeterminate sentence prisoners, including those recalled to prison for breaching their license conditions, are safe to be released into the community once they have completed their tariff (the minimum time they must spend in prison). There are six different types of indeterminate sentence:

Mandatory life for those convicted of murder.

Detention at Her Majesty's Pleasure (HMP detainee) for those convicted of murder when under 18 years of age at the time of the offense.[5]

Discretionary life for those convicted of other very serious offenses where life is the maximum sentence (e.g., manslaughter, rape, arson with intent to endanger life, armed robbery).

Automatic life for those convicted for a second time of a variety of serious specified offenses, such as armed robbery or rape from October 1, 1997. This sentence ceased to be available to the sentencing courts after April 3, 2005. The sentence was based on the presumption that anyone who was found guilty of a second serious offense must be "dangerous." The sentence of life was automatically imposed in these circumstances unless the offender could prove that there were "exceptional circumstances" and that they did not pose a continuing danger to the public.

Indeterminate sentence for public protection (IPP) replaced the Automatic Life sentence on April 4, 2005. Under the provisions of the Criminal Justice Act 2003, this sentence was mandatory when an offender was convicted of any of the 96 "serious specified" sexual or violent offenses listed in Schedule 15 of that Act and the court subsequently made the assessment that the offender was "dangerous."[6] These provisions were subsequently revised in the Criminal Justice and Immigration Act 2008 where an IPP could now only be passed when the corresponding determinate sentence would have been at least four years. Judges were also given back discretion in passing IPP sentences in all other circumstances.

This sentence can also be imposed on young people under the age of 18 at the time the offense was committed but in these circumstances it is referred to as Detention for Public Protection (DPP). On December 3, 2012 this sentence ceased to be available; however, it is estimated that 5,500 IPP/DPP prisoners currently remain in custody (Arnott & Creighton, 2014).

New automatic life sentence was introduced for offenders who are convicted and sentenced for a second "serious specified" sexual or violent offense (as outlined in the IPP sentence above) where a sentence of 10 or more years' imprisonment was imposed for the first offense, and the second offense merits a sentence of 10 or more years' imprisonment (taking account of any guilty plea). This was outlined in the Legal Aid, Sentencing and Punishment of Offenders Act 2012 and came into place after December 3, 2012.

While the Parole Board treats all types of indeterminate prisoners administratively in the same way, Arnott and Creighton (2014) highlight that the reason for imposing a life sentence can have relevance when assessing risk issues for the purposes of parole and it would be wrong for psychologists not to take this into consideration when making their risk assessment.

PAROLE BOARD POWERS IN RELATION TO INDETERMINATE SENTENCED PRISONERS

Under the Crime (Sentences) Act 1997 and the Criminal Justice Act 2003, once an indeterminate prisoner has completed his tariff or minimum term[7] the Parole Board has the authority to *direct* immediate release. If the Parole Board makes a direction to release a prisoner on life license, written reasons are prepared which outline the decision and the conditions of the license. The Parole Board, therefore, sets the license conditions. The life license remains in force until death although the supervision element of the license can be cancelled. If risk is seen to be escalating, further offenses are committed on license, or probation supervision breaks down, an indeterminate sentenced prisoner can be recalled to prison at any time. For IPP prisoners, the situation is slightly different in that after 10 years of being supervised in the community they can apply to the Parole Board to have the license imposed at release terminated. The life license may contain standard conditions and additional conditions tailored to manage the prisoner's specific circumstances. Conditions may relate to where the prisoner must live, any areas of exclusion, no contact conditions, a curfew, prohibited activity requirements, and any type of offending behavior work to be undertaken on license (reviewed in Arnott & Creighton, 2014). All of the conditions must be both necessary and proportionate to protect the public and/or existing victims. License conditions are an important part of the Parole Board's role and irrespective of whether or not a psychologist is recommending release, an opinion should be given to the Parole Board about relevant license conditions that would help the Probation Service manage the prisoner's risk in the community.

If a released indeterminate sentenced prisoner breaches the conditions of their life license, the license can be revoked by the Secretary of State, resulting in a recall to custody. The Parole Board then has the authority to decide whether it is safe for the prisoner to be re-released or progress to open conditions. Sometimes a prisoner is returned to closed conditions following a failure in open conditions and in these cases the Board is asked to advise the Secretary of State on a return to open conditions. It is common for psychologists to be called upon to provide a risk assessment for indeterminate sentenced prisoners in any of these situations.

The Test for Release for Indeterminate Prisoners

Section 28 of the Crime (Sentences) Act 1997 states that the Parole Board can release an indeterminate sentenced prisoner only if it "is satisfied that it is no longer necessary for the protection of the public that the prisoner should be confined." The Parole Board considers "whether the lifer's level of risk to the life and limb of others is considered to be more than minimal," referred to as the "life and limb test." The relevance for psychologists is that when assessing an indeterminate sentenced prisoner for possible release, it is not "any risk" that should be assessed but only risks that mean the prisoner could cause serious harm to another, which includes physical and psychological harm. The importance of understanding this test cannot be underestimated, and when providing evidence to the Parole Board a clear statement of exactly what the risk is and how serious harm might manifest should be given. Assessments should cover the risk of both imminent and longer-term serious harm.

The test for transfer to open conditions in the case of indeterminate sentenced prisoners is slightly different. When considering release the Parole Board considers only the likely risk of serious harm. In a transfer to open conditions, the Parole Board is also directed to take account of the likely benefits for the prisoner of a progress to lower-security conditions. The directions state that the Parole Board "should balance the risks against the benefits to be gained from such a move." A move to open conditions needs to consider the progress the prisoner has made in reducing his risk and whether the prisoner is likely to cause serious harm. The risk of absconding and likely adherence to license conditions when undertaking any resettlement leave into the community also need to be considered.

Considering a Transfer to Open Conditions and Release

When a prisoner is at tariff or beyond their tariff date, they are entitled to apply to the Parole Board for release regardless of the conditions of security under which they are detained. If a prisoner reaches the tariff date and is still in closed conditions, the panel will consider both release and a move to open conditions. The Parole Board's policy on the transfer of indeterminate sentenced prisoners to open conditions states that it would be unusual for an indeterminate prisoner to be released directly from closed conditions without a period of testing in open conditions, and that there need to be exceptional circumstances. If direct release from closed conditions is recommended, clear evidence must be given to assure the Parole Board that there is no more than minimal risk to life and limb without the need for testing and monitoring in open conditions and what circumstances merit such a move.

Some cases have a pre-tariff review hearing held about three years before the expiry of the tariff and so prior to any consideration for release. Here the Parole Board is asked to advise the Secretary of State as to whether sufficient progress has been made for the risk to be low enough for the prisoner to be transferred to open conditions. The Secretary of State has more recently exercised his own power in making such decisions and tends now only to seek advice from the Parole Board on finely balanced cases.

It must be noted that if the Parole Board does not direct release or recommend a move to open conditions, it has no powers over a prisoner's security classification. For example, the Board cannot recommend a progression from a category B to a category C prison. It also cannot recommend what programs a prisoner must do in order to reduce their risk. These operational matters are the responsibility of Prison Service management.

When an Indeterminate Prisoner Has Been Recalled to Prison

When an indeterminate sentenced prisoner has been recalled it is usually because he has demonstrated risk-related behavior, been charged or convicted of a further offense(s), or the supervision arrangements with the Probation Service have broken down. Once recalled, the prisoner has the right to have the lawfulness of his continued detention reviewed by the Parole Board at an oral hearing. The Parole Board must assess the risk currently posed by the prisoner and decide whether it is safe to re-release. It is unlikely that a psychologist would be asked to give an opinion on whether the recall was justified, but they are often asked to make an assessment of the risk the prisoner poses if re-released; the circumstances of recall or behavior displayed while on license may well be relevant to this assessment. The test for re-release is the same as for initial release, that is, a no more than minimal risk to life and limb.

Directions Issued by the Secretary of State to the Parole Board

For many years the Secretary of State issued directions to the Parole Board instructing them what factors they must take into account when assessing prisoners for release, transfer to open conditions, or a re-release following recall. Recently, the courts in

England and Wales ruled that it is unlawful for him to issue binding directions to the Parole Board when it is sitting as a court, but at the same hearing it was decided that it was quite right for the Parole Board to take into account the matters contained in the directions as a matter of common sense. In July 2013 it was announced that the Secretary of State was withdrawing the directions issued to the Parole Board in relation to its decisions on early release. The Parole Board issued its own guidance to panels, which reflected the previous directions. The Secretary of State directions still remain binding on the Board when considering open conditions. It is important that psychologists are familiar with these factors and that the evidence for each of them is outlined in risk assessment reports. The factors are listed in the Appendix to this chapter.

RISK ASSESSMENT REPORTS

The Civil Procedure Rules, Part 35 Practice Direction provides information about how expert reports should be presented. The format is prescribed for civil courts rather than criminal courts, but many practitioners follow it closely for criminal cases. As more psychologists use the format in other areas of their work it is likely that it will be increasingly used for Parole Board reports, but it is ultimately for individual psychologists to decide on the content and presentation of their reports based on their own experience and perception of best practice. See: http://www. justice.gov.uk/courts/procedure-rules/civil/rules/part35/pd_part35.

There are several key texts that describe the process and best practice for risk assessment (Craig & Beech, 2010; Ireland, Ireland, & Birch, 2009; Logan & Johnstone, 2013). The key stages in this process are:

- Collect and record information from different sources for a comprehensive picture.
- Use different methods of assessment, for instance interview (offender and staff), risk assessment tools, and psychometric measures.
- Critically analyze, interpret, and integrate information gathered.
- Make evidence-based and defensible decisions regarding risk.
- Communicate and share information with others.
- Engage in ongoing monitoring and review to ensure the assessment is up to date.

Best practice in risk assessment has evolved from relying entirely on clinical judgment to supplementing with other approaches such as actuarial risk assessment. The more recent SPJ approach combines the best elements of clinical judgment and actuarial assessment (Helibrun, Douglas, & Yasuhara, 2009). There has been an explosion in the development, validation, and use of SPJ tools (Fazel, Singh, Doll, & Grann, 2012), and when preparing risk assessments for the Parole Board there is an expectation that, where available, a SPJ tool will be used. This is a rapidly developing area and it is incumbent on professionals to keep abreast of research developments and best practice.

Developments in risk assessment have led to the recognition of the importance of protective factors, which are defined as "those factors that can compensate for a person's risk factors and thus play an important part in the overall risk judgement" (De Vries Robbé & De Vogel, 2013, p. 293). Some SPJ tools specifically identify protective factors (e.g., Structured Assessment of Violence Risk in Youth, SAVRY; Borum, Bartel, & Forth, 2006), and there are also stand-alone protective factor assessments (e.g., Guidelines for the Assessment of Protective Factors for Violence Risk, SAPROF; De Vogel, De Ruiter, Bouman, & De Vries Robbé, 2009). There is now an expectation that to provide a comprehensive risk assessment, protective factors should also be considered.

What to Include in a Risk Assessment Report

Psychological assessment reports should cover the following as a minimum:

- A clear statement of exactly what type of risk is being assessed.
- A clear statement setting out the scope and purpose of the report and specifying exactly what risks are being assessed.
- All psychologists need to bear in mind that the Parole Board is mainly concerned with risk of serious harm, which by default usually means the risk of violent or sexual reoffending. In some cases other clinical assessments are relevant, for instance mental health, learning difficulty, or personality assessment.

HOW THE RISK WILL BE ASSESSED

Having decided what risk is going to be assessed it is important that the psychologist explains the methods that will be used to assess this risk. This should usually include a review of file information and interviews with the offender and other professionals involved in the case. An SPJ tool should be used if available and it is the psychologist's responsibility to ensure they are using a tool that is reliable and valid. Psychometric measures may be appropriate to assess a particular risk factor or clinical feature but need to be supported by a clear explanation of the purpose of the assessment. Psychometric assessments should be tailored to a prisoner's needs – it is unhelpful for psychologists to use a standard battery of measures for all their reports. Psychometric measures (unlike some risk assessment tools which are in essence professional guidelines) are subject to their own code of good practice when used in court (British Psychological Society, 2005, and see www.psychtesting.org.uk).

A summary and interpretation of the results of risk assessment tools or psychometric tests should be in the main body of the report; details of the full results may be given in an appendix. It is unhelpful to structure a psychological report around a single SPJ tool, as the findings need to be integrated with the information collected from other methods. Psychologists need to ensure they have received appropriate training for the risk assessment or psychometric measures they use and be prepared to answer questions about this.

BACKGROUND AND CRIMINAL HISTORY

A comprehensive life history needs to be reported in order to identify experiences, attitudes, and patterns of behavior that have influenced offending. This includes a critical analysis of any offending behavior and criminal convictions. This should not just be a list: consideration should be given to circumstances and patterns of offending and this may include frequency, severity, and escalation of offending. Convictions that relate to non-compliance, escape from custody, and/or other risk factors such as drug or alcohol misuse are also useful. Analysis of offense-free periods can give important information about protective factors. Techniques to explore specific offenses can be useful in order to understand how risk may manifest, for instance functional analysis methods (see Daffern, 2011). A common failing of risk assessments is focusing on the index offense or one type of offending and not exploring other relevant previous offenses.

For some offenders, there may be information available about offenses they are alleged to have committed. Alleged offenses may occur at any stage of life history, for example prior to an index offense or as a reason for recall to custody. There is no single way to deal with alleged offenses but a psychologist needs to clearly explain how the alleged offenses have contributed to their risk assessment. It can be helpful to consider the impact on the risk assessment if it is assumed that the offending occurred and also if it did not.

CLINICAL RISK FORMULATION

There are many different definitions of and theoretical approaches to case formulation, but they are all underpinned by a set of common features (see Ireland & Craig, 2011; Sturmey & McMurran, 2011). In essence, a case formulation for forensic psychology is a theoretically driven procedure for organizing, integrating, and summarizing risk assessment information in such a way that the factors that contributed to and maintained the offending can be understood. Case formulation can also assist with the identification of risk factors, their interrelationship, treatment needs, and the core elements of risk management plans. It is unhelpful for the Parole Board to receive a list of risk factors such as "criminal lifestyle and peers" or "offense related sexual interests." A good case formulation should explain the origins and nature of the individual risk factors, how they manifest, and their relevance for that individual (see Douglas & Reeves, 2010).

When a prisoner denies all or aspects of his offending, it can make risk formulation of offending more difficult. It is possible, however, to analyze the prisoner's life history and the circumstances of the offenses to arrive at potential risk factors and offer a theoretically driven hypothesis about how the offending came about. It must be remembered that denial is not a categorical concept; it is multifaceted and dynamic and can include minimization, partial denial, claimed memory loss, or categorical denial (Jung & Daniels, 2012). There are many reasons why a prisoner may deny or minimize their offending that a psychologist should consider (Maruna & Mann, 2006). In any case, a psychologist should make clear how they have treated any form of prisoner denial in their assessment.

PROGRESS IN TREATMENT AND CUSTODIAL BEHAVIOR

When considering progress made on treatment programs it is often assumed that this means completion of accredited offending behavior programs. A report should consider a broader range of activities such as educational or vocational qualifications, which are also important (e.g., Harper & Chitty, 2004). The starting point for assessing progress is to review the risk factors that have been established as playing a role in the offending and assessing how far the interventions that have taken place mitigate these risks. If accredited offending behavior programs have been undertaken it is worth bearing in mind that no one program is likely to cover all of an individual's risk factors and a prisoner may well have other treatment needs. For some types of offenses, for example arson and acts of terrorism, there are limited or no programs available, and more creative solutions to assisting prisoners to change have to be considered. Some offenders are ineligible for the standard programs available due to issues such as literacy levels, cognitive ability, high levels of psychopathic traits, and mental health issues.

A report needs to give clear evidence of how an intervention has assisted the prisoner to make positive change and thereby reduce risk. It is useful for a report to give examples of behavioral and attitudinal changes. This may come from changes observed while the intervention was being undertaken (e.g., post-program review or report) or how new skills are being implemented in the wider environment. Some prisoners complete a wide range of relevant offending behavior programs without achieving the desired attitudinal or behavioral change. It is helpful if the reason for this can be established, which may require further assessment. It could be that the prisoner is not motivated to change, may not have understood the program content, may not have retained program information, or may be unable to put the skills learned into practice.

Assessing the progress made by prisoners who remain in partial or total denial of their offending can pose some difficulties, because these prisoners often refuse or are ineligible to undertake offense-focused work. As stated above, however, all prisoners can demonstrate a reduced risk of reoffending in many other ways apart from attending accredited offending behavior programs. Depending on what the individual risk factors are, it is possible that a prisoner could maintain their innocence and still show evidence of reduced risk or increased levels of protection by, for example, abstaining from taking drugs, severing links with criminal peers, or learning to read and write. The Court of Appeal has deemed it unlawful for the Parole Board to deny a recommendation for parole *solely on the grounds* that the prisoner continues to deny his or her guilt (Arnott & Creighton, 2014). It is important, therefore, that psychologists providing evidence to the Parole Board in these circumstances describe the full range of ways in which the prisoner has or *could* have demonstrated a reduced risk of reoffending, while respecting his or her right to maintain his innocence.

A review of custodial behavior provides evidence of change, in particular as to whether offending behavior programmes have had an impact. Negative custodial behavior should be analyzed, including gaining an understanding from the offender about the thoughts, attitudes, and emotions that underpinned the behavior. The concept of offense paralleling behavior is often used in forensic risk assessment, defined by Jones (2004) as "any form of offense related behavioral (or fantasized behavior) pattern that emerges at any point before or after an offense. It does not have to result in an offense; it simply needs to resemble, in some significant respect, the sequence of behaviors leading up to the offense" (p. 38). It is important to emphasize that the behavior of concern does not have to be identical to the original offending behavior but it needs to serve the same purpose and function (for further reading see Daffern, Jones, & Shine, 2010).

COMMUNICATING THE RISK ASSESSMENT

A risk assessment report should make some clear and firm conclusions about risk. This should include an opinion about the level of risk (e.g., low, moderate, or high), which may differ according to setting (e.g., closed prison, open establishment, or community). The type of harm a prisoner is likely to commit if reoffending occurs is also important as well as the imminence of that harm. It is useful to identify potential victims (e.g., female partners, male members of the public not known to the offender, related female children). It should be clear by the evidence reported from the risk assessment how these risk conclusions were reached. A report should make a clear statement regarding any outstanding risk factors and treatment needs. For some offenders, no further intervention will be recommended, but if required a recommendation for future assessment or intervention(s) should be made. A report should also cover the circumstances in which risk can be lowered or raised.

When preparing a risk assessment for the Parole Board, it is important to remember that the risk a prisoner poses will be contextual or a function of the circumstances in which they find themselves. Borum et al. (2006) describe how there has been a welcome shift away from a prediction model of risk, where a person was either assessed as dangerous or not, to a more contemporary conceptualization of risk as contextual, dynamic, and subject to change. They summarize the task for the contemporary risk assessor as being "to determine the nature and degree of risk a given individual may pose for certain kinds of behaviours in light of anticipated conditions and contexts." If the processes outlined above have been conducted effectively it should be relatively easy to provide evidence to the Parole Board regarding the circumstances and contexts in which the risk of reoffending a prisoner poses may be raised or reduced. A review of the release and risk management plan may establish if the circumstances of release are likely to expose the prisoner to situations that may destabilize them or alternatively offer a degree of protection. It is important for a psychologist to read and comment on the proposed risk management plan as their assessment feeds directly into this.

HAS THE TEST FOR RELEASE OR TRANSFER TO OPEN CONDITIONS BEEN MET?

There are statutory tests that must be applied before an indeterminate sentenced prisoner can be recommended for a transfer to open conditions or a direction for release can be made by the Parole Board. Psychologists providing risk assessments to the Parole Board should familiarize themselves with the various tests that apply, and in each individual case, based on everything that they know about the prisoner, reach a conclusion about whether the test has been met or not. A psychological assessment report should make a clear recommendation to the Board. A conclusion ideally is made not solely on opinion or clinical judgment but on a balance of evidence taking risk and protective factors and the prisoner's progress into account.

ETHICAL AND PRACTICAL CONSIDERATIONS

Professional Practice

When any professional is writing a report for or giving evidence to the Parole Board they should ensure that they comply with the Code of Conduct and standards set by their regulatory body. For psychologists, this is the Health and Care Professions Council (HCPC). A psychologist needs to recognize the limits of their knowledge, skill, training, education, and experience when conducting a risk assessment.

Human Rights

Ward (2008) provides an overview of human rights legislation and its relevance to forensic psychology. This is important because the prisoners that appear before the Parole Board have committed the most serious offenses and in doing so they have often violated the human rights of others. These sorts of offenses often create feelings of revulsion and disgust, but Coyle (2008) argues that although these prisoners have their human rights curtailed, they have not forfeited their human rights but they should be treated with dignity and respect and be involved in decisions about their treatment. Vess (2008) argues that in order to avoid human rights abuses, it is vital that (professionals) providing any form of risk assessment make the accuracy and limitations of their assessment explicit in terms that the recipients can understand. He also raises concerns about the inadequate protection provided to offenders when professionals with "less than adequate expertise" produce poor quality reports in circumstances that could "substantially influence judicial outcomes." He suggests that, overall, prisoners have limited avenues open to them to challenge the opinions of risk assessors employed by the state who they may perceive as wishing to keep them in custody.

Making Defensible Decisions

It is perhaps worth remembering that no risk assessment procedure will ever be 100% accurate and all risk assessors have to live with the uncertainty that this brings. The Parole Board work very much in the public eye and the decisions they make and the evidence that they rely on is subject to public scrutiny. It is essential, therefore, that professionals reach defensible and reasoned conclusions. Carson (1996) defines a defensible decision as one where "a responsible body of co-professionals would have made the same decision" and Kemshall (2009) sets out the standards for *defensible* rather then *defensive* decision-making. This includes ensuring that the assessor has an appropriate level of knowledge, skill, and experience, reliable assessment methods are used, risk assessments are evidenced based, information is evaluated to avoid bias, communication with others has taken place, and that decisions are fully recorded.

Differing Psychological Opinions

Arnott and Creighton (2014) suggest that a psychology report provided by a psychologist external to the prison and probation services is most likely to be requested when the prisoner disagrees with a prison risk assessment. This is more commonly referred to as an independent psychology report. If the prisoner is unhappy with the "independent" view there is no requirement for this report to be disclosed to the Parole Board or for it to be included in the prisoner's dossier.

In some cases an independent practitioner may have reached a different conclusion to that reported by the psychologist employed by HM Prison Service and in these cases both professionals are often directed to attend the hearing to give their evidence. There are many reasons for differences in psychological opinion. It could be that different amounts and types of information have been used to form an opinion, or different assessment tools have been used, or the same tools have been used but interpreted differently. Diverse views of a prisoner can also be formed due to differences in the quality of the relationships with the prisoner. Following the Anthony Rice further serious offense case review (HM Inspectorate of Probation, 2006) it was recommend that treatment providers should not be involved in writing risk assessment reports in order to maintain objectivity.

Giving Oral Evidence at Parole Board Hearings

Psychologist expert witnesses attending a Parole Board hearing should ensure that they come prepared. They should bring a copy of their report to the oral hearing having carefully reread it together with a copy of anything they may want to rely on such as case notes and assessment materials: the Parole Board may ask about something which is not covered in the report but is covered in other material. Often the report will have been made at some point in the past and it is good practice to be aware of any prisoner developments in the period between writing the report and the date of the hearing. A written addendum will be required only if directed by the Parole Board, but the witness should be in a position to give the panel an oral update on anything which may impact the risk assessment and recommendation. It may be necessary to have contact with the relevant prison or to have read the latest reports provided for the hearing. A second psychologist may attend the hearing. This could be another psychologist employed by HM Prison or Probation Services or a psychologist from an external organization that is independent of prison and probation. It is important for psychologists to check the hearing timetable to see who else is attending and to have read any other psychological reports. It is good practice to consider points of agreement and points of disagreement between the two assessment reports and, in some cases, the Parole Board may direct that psychological witnesses with differences of opinion meet and prepare a written statement of these points. The British Psychological Society's expert witness guidance group provides useful advice to psychologists on providing expert witness testimony (see British Psychological Society, 2010; Crighton, 2013).

CONCLUSIONS

The Parole Board essentially makes two types of decisions: whether to release a prisoner or make a recommendation for the prisoner to transfer to open conditions. The amount of information required to make these decisions is wide-ranging.

Psychologists are increasingly being asked to assist the Parole Board in providing risk assessment reports and giving evidence in person at oral hearings. Before taking on this role, psychologists must satisfy themselves that they have the skills and competencies to complete the task effectively and also that they have sufficient knowledge about Parole Board practice to enable them to provide the type of information required. It is vital that psychologist professionals ensure that they are practicing ethically and that in the pursuit of protecting the public they do not compromise the rights of the prisoner.

APPENDIX

Parole Board guidance to its own members to take the place of the Secretary of State's directions. In most cases a panel will consider the following, where appropriate and available, in reaching its decision:

1. the nature and circumstances of the index offense and any previous offenses;
2. any information relating to the offender's personal circumstances and background;
3. any reports prepared for the trial and the sentencing remarks and any judgment of the Court of Appeal, House of Lords, or Supreme Court in the case;
4. the prisoner's attitude and behavior toward, and relationships with, others, including authority figures;
5. assessments resulting from programs, courses of treatment, or other activities designed either directly or indirectly to address his offending behavior;
6. any medical, psychiatric, or psychological considerations where relevant to the assessment of risk;
7. actuarial assessments of risk;
8. the prisoner's behavior during outside activities throughout the sentence and any such periods in the past, including periods spent on license or bail;
9. in the case of an indeterminate sentenced prisoner, the time spent in custody since expiry of the tariff;
10. representations from a victim;
11. the prisoner's attitude to, and the likelihood of compliance with, conditions of release on license;
12. plans for supervision on release and the suitability of the release address;
13. written or verbal representations made by the prisoner and his representative;
14. any other material, information, or fact deemed by the panel to be relevant to the assessment of risk.

Each case will be treated on its merits and without discrimination on any grounds.

NOTES

1 *Thynne, Wilson, and Gunnell v UK (1991) 13 EHRR 666.*
2 *Stafford v UK (2002) 35 EHRR 32.*
3 *R (on the application of Brooke) v Parole Board (2007) EWHC (Admin) 2036.*
4 *Osborn and others v Parole Board* [2013] *UKSC 61.*
5 *Powers of the Criminal Courts (Sentencing) Act 2000.*
6 Dangerousness is defined as "there is a significant risk to members of the public of serious harm, occasioned by the commission of him of further such offenses."
7 The time that the trial Judge states the prisoner must spend in prison for the purposes of punishment.

REFERENCES

Arnott, H., & Creighton, S. (2014). *Parole Board hearings: Law and practice* (3rd ed.). London: Legal Action Group.

Borum, R., Bartel, P., & Forth, A. (2006). *SAVRY: Structured Assessment of Violence Risk in Youth. Professional Manual.* Lutz, FL: Psychological Assessment Resources, Inc.

British Psychological Society (2005). *Code of good practice for psychological testing.* Leicester, UK: BPS.

British Psychological Society (2010). *Psychologists as expert witnesses: Guidelines and procedure for England and Wales* (3rd ed.). Report commissioned by the Professional Practice Board (PPB) and Research Board (RB) of the British Psychological Society. British Psychological Society Expert Witness Advisory Group. Leicester, UK: BPS.

Carson, D. (1996). Risking legal repercussions. In H. Kemshall & J. Pritchard (Eds.), *Good practice in risk assessment and risk management* (pp. 3–12). London: Jessica Kingsley Publishers.

Coyle, A. (2008). The treatment of prisoners: International standards and case law. *Legal and Criminological Psychology, 13*, 219–230.

Craig, L.A., & Beech, A.R. (2010). Towards a best practice in conducting actuarial risk assessments with adult sexual offenders. *Aggression and Violent Behavior, 15*, 278–293.

Crighton, D. (2013). Expert witness work – time to step up to the plate. *The Psychologist, 26*, Part 7, July 2013, 486–487.

Daffern, M. (2011). Functional analysis. In K. Sheldon, J. Davies, & K. Howells (Eds.), *Research and practice in forensic psychology* (pp. 216–230). Abingdon, UK: Routledge.

Daffern, M., Jones, L., & Shine, J. (Eds.) (2010). *Offence paralleling behaviour: A case formulation approach to offender assessment and intervention.* Chichester, UK: John Wiley & Sons, Ltd.

De Vogel, V., De Ruiter, C., Bouman, Y., & De Vries Robbé, M. (2009). *SAPROF Guidelines for the assessment of protective factors for violence risk.* Utrecht: Forum Educatief.

De Vries Robbé, M., & De Vogel, V. (2013). Protective factors for violence risk: Bringing balance to risk assessment and management. In C. Logan & L. Johnstone (Eds.), *Managing clinical risk: A guide to effective practice* (pp. 291–310). London: Routledge.

Douglas, K.S., & Reeves, K. (2010). The HCR-20 violence risk assessment scheme: Overview and review of the research. In R.K. Otto & K.S. Douglas (Eds.), *Handbook of violence risk assessment* (pp. 147–185). New York: Routledge.

Fazel, S., Singh, J.P., Doll, H., & Grann, M. (2012). Use of risk assessment instruments to predict violence and antisocial behaviour in 73 samples involving 24 827 people: Systematic review and meta-analysis. *British Medical Journal*, *345* (24:2), 4692–4692. doi:10.1136/bmj.e4692

Harper, G., & Chitty, C. (Eds.) (2004). The impact of corrections on re-offending: A review of "What Works". *Home Office, Research, Development and Statistics, Research Study No. 291*. London: Home Office.

Helibrun, K., Douglas, K.S., & Yasuhara, K. (2009). Violence risk assessment: Core controversies. In J.L. Skeem, K.S. Douglas, & O. Lilienfield (Eds.), *Psychological science in the courtroom: Consensus and controversy* (pp. 333–357). New York: Guilford Press.

HM Inspectorate of Probation (2006). *An independent review of a further serious offence case: Anthony Rice*. London: HMIP.

Ireland, C.A., & Craig. L.A. (2011). Adult sex offender assessment. In D.P. Boer, R. Eher, L.A. Craig, M.H. Miner, & F. Pfafflin (Eds.), *International perspectives on the assessment and treatment of sexual offenders: Theory, practice and research* (pp. 13–34). Chichester, UK: John Wiley & Sons, Ltd.

Ireland, J.L., Ireland, C.A., & Birch, P. (2009). *Violent and sexual offenders: Assessment, treatment and management*. Portland, OR: Willan.

Jones, L. (2004). Offence Paralleling Behaviour (OBP) as a framework for assessment and interventions with offenders. In A. Needs & G. Towl (Eds.), *Applying psychology to forensic practice* (pp. 34–63). London: British Psychological Society; and Oxford: Blackwell.

Jung, S., & Daniels, M. (2012). Conceptualizing sex offender denial from a multifaceted framework: Investigating the psychometric qualities of a new instrument. *Journal of Addictions & Offender Counseling*, *33* (1), 2–17.

Kemshall, H. (2009). Working with sex offenders in a climate of public blame and anxiety: How to make defensible decisions for risk. *Journal of Sexual Aggression*, *15* (3), 331–343.

Logan, C., & Johnstone, L. (Eds.). (2013). *Managing clinical risk: A guide to effective practice*. London: Routledge.

Maruna, S., & Mann, R.E. (2006). A fundamental attribution error? Rethinking cognitive distortions. *Legal and Criminological Psychology*, *11* (2), 155–177.

Parole Board (2013). *Parole Board for England and Wales: Annual report and accounts 2012/2013*. London: The Stationery Office.

Sturmey, P., & McMurran, M. (Eds.) (2011). *Forensic Case Formulation*. Chichester, UK: John Wiley & Sons, Ltd.

Vess, J. (2008). Sex offender risk assessment: Consideration of human rights in community protection legislation. *Legal and Criminological Psychology*, *13*, 245–256.

Ward, T. (2008). Human rights and forensic psychology. *Legal and Criminological Psychology*, *13*, 209–218.

7

Behavioral Assessment in Investigative Psychology

ELEANOR M. GITTENS AND KATE WHITFIELD

Behavioral assessment in investigative psychology (popularly known as offender profiling) increasingly features in fictional works, such as films, television series, and books. There is widespread fascination with how the hero or heroine is able to determine the villain's personality, location, and future actions by analyzing what is known about his or her behavior. The assessment of these offenders is largely based on the work of the Federal Bureau of Investigation's (FBI) Behavioral Science Unit (BSU). Despite their pioneering efforts in assessing the behavior of offenders (see Ressler, Burgess, Douglas, Hartman, & D'Agostino, 1986; Ressler & Shachtman, 1992), very few of their bold statements are based on empirical research (Canter, Alison, Alison, & Wentink, 2004). Canter and Youngs (2003) refer to this phenomenon of accepting theories that have no empirical foundation, simply because of their continued appearance in films and television series, as the "Hollywood Effect."

In an effort to build a more scientific discipline and move away from the under-researched theories of the FBI, the field of investigative psychology was born (Canter, 1994). Investigative psychology grounds its brand of profiling in established psychological theories and promotes a more scientific assessment of criminal behavior. However, investigative psychology is more than just the practice of developing offender profiles. It is an area of applied psychology that encompasses police investigations, different aspects of criminality, and issues that are not conventionally managed by the police, but rather by their partner agencies (Canter, 1994, 2004; Canter & Youngs, 2003). This chapter will focus on the origins of offender profiling,

Assessments in Forensic Practice: A Handbook, First Edition. Edited by Kevin D. Browne, Anthony R. Beech, Leam A. Craig, and Shihning Chou.
© 2017 John Wiley & Sons Ltd. Published 2017 by John Wiley & Sons Ltd.

the emergence of investigative psychology, behavioral assessment in investigative psychology, and offender profiling in the United Kingdom today.

THE ORIGINS OF OFFENDER PROFILING

In 1887, Sir Arthur Conan Doyle created a fictional detective named Sherlock Holmes, who is famous for his assessment of human behavior and astute observations. In the stories, Holmes makes inferences about crimes only after careful reflection and consideration of the data. According to Canter and Youngs (2009), "Holmes' process of reasoning lays the foundation for scientific approaches to the investigation of crime" (p. 52). He uses inductive reasoning to arrive at his conclusions, drawing on fine details to develop general principles. Inductive reasoning differs from deductive reasoning in that deductive reasoning is based on a premise. Thus, if the premise is incorrect so too will be the reasoning (Canter & Youngs, 2009).

In order to understand how behavioral assessment was established in investigative psychology, it is important to examine the history and development of offender profiling. Over the years, numerous synonyms have been used to describe offender profiling, such as criminal profiling, psychological profiling, crime scene analysis, and behavioral profiling (Ainsworth, 2001). However, over the last decade, in the United Kingdom, a broader term for offender profiling has emerged, namely "behavioral investigative advice." This advice is firmly grounded in behavioral science and is considered in the context of investigating serious crime (Rainbow & Gregory, 2009). It has taken a long time to arrive at the notion of behavioral investigative advice, with many academic debates occurring in the interim (see Alison, Bennell, Mokros, & Ormerod, 2002; Alison, Smith, & Morgan, 2003; Alison, West, & Goodwill, 2004; Canter et al., 2004; Snook, Cullen, Bennell, Taylor, & Gendreau, 2008; Mokros & Alison, 2010).

It is common that many offender profiling practices today draw on classification systems that relate to criminal behavior, crime scenes, and offender characteristics (Snook et al., 2008). The most well-known classification system is the FBI's organized/disorganized dichotomy (Ressler et al., 1986), made famous in the film *The Silence of the Lambs*. However, long before the fictional characters of Hannibal Lecter and Clarice Starling, there was an Italian criminologist by the name of Cesare Lombroso, whose work is said to have influenced a number of the early profilers, such as James Brussel and Robert Ressler (Canter & Youngs, 2009). Lombroso developed a theory of anthropological criminology, which proposed that criminality is inherited and that there is a distinct part of the population who are "born criminals." Further, these individuals can be identified by physical features, such as a strong jawline, high cheekbones, large eye sockets, unusually sized ears, and tattoos. They are also characterized by laziness, insensitivity toward pain, vanity, impulsiveness, and cruelty (Lombroso, 1911). Despite research proving that physical characteristics cannot predict criminality (Goring, 1913), Lombroso's ideas continue to have some influence today (Canter, 1994).

It is worth noting that a number of individuals have created behavioral assessments that later became known as profiles. For example, in 1942, at the request of the United States Office of Strategic Services, Walter Langer wrote a report on Adolf Hitler which suggested that Hitler would commit suicide if the war turned against him (Langer, 1972). This report is now popularly referred to as a "profile of Adolf Hitler" (Canter & Youngs, 2009). Another person who created what would later become known as a profile is Dr Thomas Bond, who described the features of the person who was responsible for the murder and mutilation of five women in Whitechapel, London. The account he provided to the police of Jack the Ripper was based on crime scene information, previous reports, and an autopsy he performed on one of the victims. By deriving the possible physical and psychological attributes of the offender from this information, Bond is likely to be responsible for the first recorded profile (Canter, 2004).

Examples of similar occurrences, where experts offer advice to the police, are present throughout history. One of the more renowned advisors is American psychiatrist Dr James Brussel, who provided the police with advice in relation to the "Mad Bomber" of New York. Between 1940 and 1956, homemade bombs had been left at different locations in and around New York. The bomber had also sent threatening letters to the newspapers and police. As a result of the bomber's focus on the Consolidated Edison Company, throughout the investigation it was thought that he or she was a former employee holding a grudge. In order to create a profile, Brussel analyzed the threatening letters and crime scene information. Upon completion of the profile, Brussel persuaded the police to publicize it. This resulted in a clerk at the company, Alice Kelly, singling out George Metesky from worker's compensation files. Metesky was arrested and several of his characteristics were found to fit the profile provided by Brussel (Canter, 1994; Canter & Youngs, 2009).

Brussel's profile of the "Mad Bomber" highlighted the usefulness of profiling, logic, and reasoning to law enforcement agencies. In particular, it came to the attention of Howard Teton who, in collaboration with Patrick Mullaney, introduced offender profiling to the FBI (Theoharis, Poveda, Rosenfeld, & Powers, 1999). The BSU's first case occurred in 1973 at a Rocky Mountain's campsite, where a seven-year-old girl, Susan Jaeger, was kidnapped from her tent. Teton, Mullaney, and Robert Ressler developed a profile of a young, white, male offender, who was likely to be a loner with above average intelligence. An informant contacted the FBI and suggested that David Meirhofer may be a suspect; however, there was no evidence to support this. Then, in 1974, Meirhofer became a suspect in a murder investigation. He volunteered to take a lie detector test and be injected with "truth serum" so as to prove that he was not the offender. He passed both tests so well that many thought he was innocent. However, the team at the BSU knew that some offenders will purposefully look for ways to get in contact with the investigating team or people connected to the investigation. They suggested that Susan Jaeger's parents keep a tape-recorder by their telephone and, one year later, Meirhofer called them. During the conversation he had with Susan's mother, Meirhofer broke down in tears. Unfortunately, the tape was not enough to prove his guilt. Mullaney suggested that more information might be gained if the Jaegers met with Meirhofer in person. This was arranged, but proved uneventful. However, soon after the meeting, the Jaegers received another call from Meirhofer. This time, as a result of the telephone call, the FBI were able to obtain a search warrant and, while searching Meirhofer's home, found body parts from both victims. Meirhofer thus became the first serial killer to be caught with the aid of the BSU's profiling technique (Wilson & Seaman, 1990).

THE EMERGENCE OF INVESTIGATIVE PSYCHOLOGY

By 1986, the FBI's offender profilers were reportedly being requested to provide advice in 600 investigations a year (Douglas & Burgess, 1986). Their efforts were described as being a combination of "brainstorming, intuition, and educated guesswork" (Douglas, Ressler, Burgess, & Hartman, 1986, p. 405), but nevertheless marked the point where it was realized that in order to effectively contribute to an investigation, research needed to be conducted in relation to the offenders and their offenses (Canter & Youngs, 2009). The team at the FBI's BSU set about developing classification systems – the most widely cited being the organized/disorganized dichotomy (Ressler et al., 1986). Based on case file information and interviews with 36 offenders, this classification system suggests that offenders and their offenses can be categorized as organized or disorganized. Organized offenders are likely to be intelligent, socially competent, have a neat appearance, and carefully plan all their activities (including their offense). In terms of their offense, they are likely to plan who their victim will be, the weapon they will use, how they will remove evidence, and their escape route. On the other hand, disorganized offenders are likely to be of average intelligence, lack social skills, have an untidy appearance, and be impulsive in their actions. They tend to leave a crime scene that is chaotic in nature, reflecting that very little of their actions are planned (Ressler et al., 1986). The organized/disorganized dichotomy, and the BSU's approach to offender profiling, has received much criticism over the years. This is primarily due to a number of methodological weaknesses, such as lacking a representative sample and conducting interviews that lacked reliability and validity (see Canter et al., 2004 for a full overview). Indeed, Canter et al. (2004) note that the developers of the organized/disorganized dichotomy "never set out to test the discriminatory power of their dichotomy on a sample that was not specifically drawn up to illustrate this dichotomy" (p. 296). Despite these deficiencies, the work of the BSU was very important to the emergence of investigative psychology.

Around the same time that the BSU were developing their organized/disorganized dichotomy, Professor David Canter was approached by the UK police for advice regarding an investigation into a series of rapes and murders that had occurred in London. The police had already linked the crimes to a common offender, based on blood typing and the surviving victims' reports. However, they wanted further advice in terms of the behavior of the offender. Canter was a social psychologist and had not conducted any previous research regarding criminals and their behavior. As such, he had to resort to the basic tenets of psychology to assist him with his analysis (Canter, 1994; Canter & Youngs, 2009).

Canter began by listing all the actions that had occurred in every crime and then compared the crimes with each other. This effort showed that some offenses were very similar in terms of the offender's actions. Indeed, it was believed that sometimes the offender worked alone, while at other times he may have had an accomplice. Consistencies were also identified in terms of how the offender approached his victims, how he bound his victims, and the typical discussion he would have with them. Canter and his colleagues then mapped the offenses, in order of occurrence, on a map of London. As a result of this exercise, they were able to estimate where the offender was likely to live, as well as how his behavior was changing over time. The preliminary "profile" that Canter provided the police was surprisingly accurate, and helped the police to narrow down their list of 2,000 possible suspects. John Duffy was 1,505th on the list, but closely matched the "profile" Canter had produced. He was also the only suspect to live in the area that Canter had predicted. The police launched a large-scale surveillance operation to monitor Duffy's activities. Soon after this, Duffy was arrested (Canter, 1994, 2003; Canter & Youngs, 2009).

WHAT IS INVESTIGATIVE PSYCHOLOGY?

The success achieved in the Duffy case paved the way for Canter's continued contribution to a number of police investigations. However, he also saw the need to ground offender profiling in scientific research. By contributing to further investigations, Canter built links with the police that enabled him to gain access to data on offenders and their offenses. He envisaged a wide range of research activities, using these data, on which a scientific discipline could be built. This discipline was to become known as investigative psychology (Canter & Youngs, 2009).

There are three processes in an investigation that can be viewed as giving rise to investigative psychology. These are investigative information, police decision-making, and inferences from offenders' actions. Investigative psychology is the scientific study of these three processes, such that investigations and the legal process can be improved (Canter & Youngs, 2003). The first process, investigative information, includes how information is collected, analyzed, and used. Information can range from crime scene evaluations to interview transcripts, through to crime reports and the geographic locations of criminal offenses. However, as this information is collected for the purpose of investigating crime, and not conducting scientific research, it may present challenges for the researcher. Investigative psychology considers how evidence can be transformed into data, such that it may be used in empirically grounded studies that may assist the police in their investigations (Alison, Snook, & Stein, 2001; Canter & Alison, 2003).

The second process, police decision-making, refers to how decisions can be enhanced and supported (Canter & Youngs, 2003). An approach that has been recognized by several researchers (e.g., Alison & Crego, 2008; Crichton & Flin, 2002) as assisting with understanding decision-making during critical incidents and police investigations is the Naturalistic Decision-Making (NDM) approach (Zsambok & Klein, 1997). This approach developed as a result of growing recognition that people are required to make decisions in stressful and uncertain situations, and indeed do so effectively, yet little is known regarding *how* they actually do it (Klein, 1997). NDM is defined as "the way people use their experience to make decisions in field settings" (Zsambok & Klein, 1997, p. 4). Indeed, it has been suggested that key to this definition is the term "experience," as police leaders can use heuristics gained through experience to make decisions and develop a plan of action (Klein, 1997). There are a wide range of heuristics that individuals can use; however, they are commonly perceived as contributing to biased judgments and less than adequate performance, as when individuals use them they are not considering alternative courses of action (Tversky & Kahneman, 1974). Traditional decision-making research advocates that effective decision-makers must evaluate several courses of action before selecting the most appropriate; however, NDM research suggests that this is unrealistic given the time-pressured nature of real-world settings (Kahneman & Klein, 2009). Investigative psychology considers the heuristics and biases used in police decision-making (see Almond, Alison, Eyre, Crego, & Goodwill, 2008), as well as training programs that can be used to enhance and support police decision-making during stressful situations (see Eyre, Crego, & Alison, 2008).

The third process, making inferences from offenders' actions, includes how offending behavior develops, differentiates, and can be predicted. In order to make inferences, models regarding offenders' actions are required. These models should be the outcome of empirical studies and robust hypothesis testing (Canter & Youngs, 2003). Canter (1995) describes such studies as attempting to find the link between the offender's actions and his or her personal characteristics. Often referred to as the A–C equation, where A equals Actions and C equals Characteristics, this concept of linking actions to personal characteristics is concerned with the *structure* of offending (i.e., in terms of common themes that are present) and what this says about the offender (Canter & Youngs, 2003).

One way of determining the underlying themes of offending behavior is to employ non-metric multidimensional scaling procedures (Canter, 2000). Possibly the most well-known of these procedures, used widely by Canter's students and colleagues (see Alison & Stein, 2001; Canter, Bennell, Alison, & Reddy, 2003; Canter & Fritzon, 1998; Canter & Heritage, 1990; Salfati, 2000; Santtila, Häkkänen, Alison, & Whyte, 2003), is Smallest Space Analysis (SSA). SSA, also referred to as Similarity Structure Analysis (Borg & Shye, 1995), was developed in 1954 (Guttman, 1954). It transforms a correlation matrix into a visual representation of points in a geometric space. Each point represents a variable, and the rank order of the distance between each point inversely represents the ranks of the correlations between variables. This means a Monotone Mapping Condition exists, whereby the higher the correlation between two variables, the smaller the distance between them in the related space (Shye, Elizur, & Hoffman, 1994).

The space occupied by the content universe (or domain) of the investigated concept is continuous. This means that there is also continuity of meaning; thus variables are not considered significant on their own, but rather always in relation to the other observed variables in the content universe. Additionally, any variables studied in the content universe are only a sample of that content universe. This is because each variable is just a point in the concept's space and does not represent the whole concept. Indeed, according to the Continuity Principle, there are an infinite number of points between any two variables. Therefore, the investigated concept should be viewed as a continuum of points, rather than a collection of scattered points (Shye et al., 1994).

SSA provides a spatial representation of the variables in a form that makes it easy to interpret and to examine emergent patterns in the data. By means of regional contiguity, variables that have a common facet element are located in the same region of space. Unlike cluster analysis, variables may be close together but part of different regions. This is as a result of the Continuity Principle. Regional contiguity patterns and their assistance in building hypotheses and constructing theory are a major strength of SSA, and provide a different way of examining the structure of the data which is not possible in cluster or factor analysis. Indeed, unlike these other data-analytic procedures, SSA not only shows how the variables are grouped, but also how these groups relate to each other, and which variables are on the cusp of a specific region (Shye et al., 1994).

SSA is flexible by allowing a certain amount of freedom regarding where a point is mapped in the geometric space. The Smallest Space Principle assists in selecting where the point should be mapped by opting for the space with the lowest dimensionality. The smallest space mappings are chosen because they have the most concise, compact representation of the variables and their correlations (Shye et al., 1994). According to Canter (2000), SSA has proven to be useful in determining behavioral salience, models of offender differentiation, and themes in offending behavior. By using SSA to determine the relationships between co-occurring criminal actions, one can not only uncover common themes, but also how offenders differ. Thus, Canter (1994) suggests that studying offenders' actions at the scene of their crimes is important in terms of revealing further information about the individual offenders. This approach rests on the assumption that the way in which a crime is carried out is in some way a reflection of the everyday life of the offender.

AREAS OF RESEARCH IN INVESTIGATIVE PSYCHOLOGY

The central premise of investigative psychology is that aspects of criminal and civil investigations can be made more effective and efficient by drawing on the behavioral science of psychology. The lack of scientific rigor evident in past profiling procedures has driven researchers to map a scientific discipline that can underpin and systematize contributions to police investigations. This academically grounded approach has opened up potential applications way beyond the initial "profiling" (Canter, 2004). Studies in investigative psychology have covered crimes such as burglary (Bennell & Canter, 2002), arson (Canter & Fritzon, 1998), stalking (Canter & Ioannou, 2004), robbery (Porter & Alison, 2006), and domestic violence (Riggs, Caulfield, & Street, 2000). Research has also been conducted in relation to investigative issues, for example, investigative interviewing (Milne & Bull, 1999), critical incident management (Alison & Crego, 2008), detecting deception (Vrij, 2008), confessions (Gudjonsson, 1992), eyewitness testimony (Wells & Olson, 2003), hostage negotiation (Almond & Budden, 2012), and counterterrorism (Mullins, 2009).

One area of research that has attracted much interest is that of geographical profiling. This is defined as using offense locations to understand the offender's characteristics and predict his or her place of residence (Canter, 2003). Geographical profiling has the potential to assist police investigations by prioritizing suspects based on where they live (Rossmo, 2000). Indeed, it has been found that the majority of offenders who are identified commit offenses in their home vicinity, or at least in places that are familiar to them (Canter, 1994). Routine activity theory (Cohen & Felson, 1979) suggests that this is due to offenders "discovering" opportunities to commit offenses as they go about their everyday lives.

Several geographic profiling systems have been developed (e.g., see Canter, Coffey, Huntley, & Missen, 2000) that are based on research relating to the spatial behavior of offenders (e.g., Brantingham & Brantingham, 1981). These systems use specific algorithms to determine where an offender is likely to live. The algorithms, or distance decay functions as they are also known, assume that the number of crimes committed decrease as the distance from home increases. However, included in the distance between an offender's home and the location of his or her crime is a "buffer zone," where the offender is less likely to commit any offenses. This is possibly due to the associated risk (Turner, 1969). Geographic profiling systems are increasing in popularity, as they claim to narrow down the area where an offender lives by approximately 90% (Canter et al., 2000; Rossmo, 2000). However, emerging research suggests that expensive computerized systems may not be necessary, as appropriately trained police officers could make equally accurate predictions regarding the home base of an offender (Bennell, Snook, Taylor, Corey, & Keyton, 2007; Snook, Taylor, & Bennell, 2004).

OFFENDER PROFILING IN THE UNITED KINGDOM TODAY

In the United Kingdom, it has become increasingly recognized that the term "offender profiling" is narrow in definition, frequently misunderstood, and governed by myths in popular fiction. As such, in 2001, the Association of Chief Police Officers (ACPO) replaced the term "offender profiler" with "behavioral investigative advisor." Behavioral investigative advice involves more than making inferences about an offender's characteristics. It is a discipline that offers an additional perspective and assists with making informed decisions at different stages of an investigation (Rainbow & Gregory, 2009). Indeed, Rainbow and Gregory (2009) argue that the value of behavioral investigative advice lies in this additional perspective, which is different from that which is usually employed when conducting an investigation. Behavioral investigative advisors offer support in terms of crime scene assessment, hypothesis generation, linking crimes, offender background assessment, suspect generation, suspect prioritization, interviewing advice, and risk assessment (Rainbow & Gregory, 2009).

There are three factors that are fundamental in terms of achieving high-quality behavioral investigative advice. First, all behavioral investigative advisors are required to agree to specific working conditions. These dictate the responsibilities of behavioral investigative advisors, including report writing (as well as the type of information that should be reported), administrative procedures, and a willingness to have work audited on an annual basis. The second factor relates to quality assurance, or more specifically, the annual audit. Every 12 months an independent panel reviews the work of all behavioral investigative advisors, and determines whether or not an individual will remain an "ACPO approved" behavioral investigative advisor. The third factor refers to ensuring the strategic development and resilience of behavioral investigative advice. This includes a clear process that individuals need to go through in order to become an ACPO approved behavioral investigative advisor. Indeed, as a *minimum* requirement, a civilian would need (i) a psychology or criminology degree, (ii) a professional qualification, (iii) membership of a professional body, (iv) experience of working with offenders and/or victims, and (v) chartership (Rainbow, 2011).

Most behavioral investigative advisors that are consulted by the police are permanently employed by the National Policing Improvement Agency (NPIA). However, on certain occasions, advice may be required that is beyond the expertise of the team at the NPIA. In such instances, an ACPO approved behavioral investigative advisor outside of the NPIA may be called in to provide specific advice in relation to the investigation (Rainbow, 2011). There are no regulations that state that the police must seek behavioral investigative advice during an investigation (although it is suggested in guidance manuals). As such, it is an investigative decision on the part of the senior investigating officer (SIO) to request advice (Rainbow & Gregory, 2011).

Once this request has been made, the behavioral investigative advisor and SIO meet to establish clear terms of reference with regards to what is expected of both sides. This is finalized in writing before the behavioral investigative advisor receives any of the material relating to the investigation. Such material could include briefings, statements, crime reports, pathology reports, photographs, crime scene visits, and access to the investigating team. Once the behavioral investigative advisor has all the information he or she needs, preparing the report can begin. It is worth noting that behavioral investigative advisors seldom work in the same room, or even on the same premises, as the investigating team. This enables a certain amount of objectivity and easier access to resources, such as libraries and statistical programs (Rainbow & Gregory, 2011).

Once the data have been analyzed, a report is sent to the SIO. In a recent study of 47 reports produced by the NPIA (see Almond, Alison, & Porter, 2011), there were on average 17 (SD = 7.58) claims made per report. Of these claims, 38% were about the offender's characteristics, 35% were about the offender's behavior, and 13% were about the offender's geographic location in relation to the crime scene. In 98% of the reports, there were valid grounds for making the claims, and in two-thirds of the reports a clear rationale was provided that linked the grounds for making the claims to specific details of the case. Additionally, on average, five (SD = 3.9) recommendations were made per report. These related primarily to new lines of inquiry (15.7%) and prioritization of suspects (11.8%). A small percentage of the recommendations were related to forensic analysis (1.5%) and the risk of future offending (0.7%).

The report produced by the behavioral investigative advisor is not a final document, but rather a work in progress that helps facilitate dialogue between the behavioral investigative advisor and SIO. Discussion is essential in order to ensure accurate understanding of the recommendations being made, and to re-evaluate advice based on any new information that may emerge. The SIO should always be critical of any recommendations proposed and not blindly accept advice without careful reflection. It is only by challenging the advice that its validity can be established, and it is used in the way that the behavioral investigative advisor intended. For instance, the advice cannot be considered as absolute certainty (Rainbow & Gregory, 2011).

Based on the above, it should be clear that today "profiling" in the United Kindom does not mean making decisions for the investigating team. It does not mean single-handedly implementing a strategy that will outfox the killer. It does not mean that a maverick hero or heroine is required to sweep in, find the offender, and to only do so based on their wits and a "special kind of intuition." Instead, it is about providing *advice*, with each recommendation having a sound rationale behind it. It is an audited process that ensures quality and transparency. It is certainly not shrouded in the myth and mystery as depicted on the silver screen.

REFERENCES

Ainsworth, P.B. (2001). *Offender profiling and crime analysis.* Cullompton, UK: Willan.

Alison, L.J., Bennell, C., Mokros, A., & Ormerod, D. (2002). The personality paradox in offender profiling: A theoretical review of the processes involved in deriving background characteristics from crime scene actions. *Psychology, Public Policy and Law, 8,* 115–135.

Alison, L.J., & Crego, J. (2008). *Policing critical incidents: Leadership and critical incident management.* Cullompton, UK: Willan.

Alison, L.J., Smith, M.D., & Morgan, K. (2003). Interpreting the accuracy of offender profiles. *Psychology, Crime & Law, 9,* 185–195.

Alison, L.J., Snook, B., & Stein, K.L. (2001). Unobtrusive measurement: Using police information for forensic research. *Qualitative Research, 1,* 241–254.

Alison, L.J., & Stein, K.L. (2001). Vicious circles: Accounts of stranger sexual assault reflect abusive variants of conventional interactions. *Journal of Forensic Psychiatry and Psychology, 12,* 515–538.

Alison, L.J., West, A., & Goodwill, A. (2004). The academic and the practitioner: Pragmatists' views of offender profiling. *Psychology, Public Policy and Law, 10,* 71–101.

Almond, L., Alison, L.J., Eyre, M., Crego, J., & Goodwill, A. (2008). Heuristics and biases in decision-making. In L.J. Alison & J. Crego (Eds.), *Policing critical incidents: Leadership and critical incident management* (pp. 151–180). Cullompton, UK: Willan.

Almond, L., Alison, L.J., & Porter, L.E. (2011). An evaluation and comparison of claims made in behavioural investigative advice reports compiled by the National Policing Improvement Agency in the United Kingdom. In L.J. Alison & L. Rainbow (Eds.), *Professionalizing offender profiling: Forensic and investigative psychology in practice* (pp. 250–263). New York: Routledge.

Almond, L., & Budden, M. (2012). The use of text messages within a crisis negotiation: Help or hindrance? *Journal of Police Crisis Negotiations, 12,* 1–27.

Bennell, C., & Canter, D.V. (2002). Linking commercial burglaries by modus operandi: Tests using regression and ROC analysis. *Science and Justice, 42,* 153–164.

Bennell, C., Snook, B., Taylor, P.J., Corey, S., & Keyton, J. (2007). It's no riddle, choose the middle: The effect of number of crimes and topographical detail on police officer predictions of serial burglars' home locations. *Criminal Justice and Behavior, 34,* 119–132.

Borg, I., & Shye, S. (1995). *Facet theory: Form and content.* London: Sage.

Brantingham, P.J., & Brantingham, P.L. (1981). *Environmental criminology.* Prospect Heights, NY: Waveland Press.

Canter, D.V. (1994). *Criminal shadows: Inside the mind of the serial killer.* London: HarperCollins.

Canter, D.V. (1995). The psychology of offender profiling. In R. Bull & D. Carson (Eds.), *Handbook of psychology in legal contexts* (pp. 343–355). Chichester, UK: John Wiley & Sons, Ltd.

Canter, D.V. (2000). Offender profiling and criminal differentiation. *Legal and Criminological Psychology*, *5*, 23–46.

Canter, D.V. (2003). *Mapping murder: The secrets of geographical profiling*. London: Virgin Books.

Canter, D.V. (2004). Offender profiling and investigative psychology. *Journal of Investigative Psychology and Offender Profiling*, *1*, 1–15.

Canter, D.V., & Alison, L.J. (2003). Converting evidence into data: The use of law enforcement archives as unobtrusive measurement. *The Qualitative Report*, *8*, 151–176.

Canter, D.V., Alison, L.J., Alison, E., & Wentink, N. (2004). The organized/disorganized typology of serial murder: Myth or model? *Psychology, Public Policy and Law*, *10*, 293–320.

Canter, D.V., Bennell, C., Alison, L.J., & Reddy, S. (2003). Differentiating sex offences: A behaviorally based thematic classification of stranger rapes. *Behavioral Sciences and the Law*, *21*, 157–174.

Canter, D.V., Coffey, T., Huntley, M., & Missen, C. (2000). Predicting serial killers' home base using a decision support system. *Journal of Quantitative Criminology*, *16*, 457–478.

Canter, D.V., & Fritzon, K. (1998). Differentiating arsonists: A model of firesetting actions and characteristics. *Legal and Criminological Psychology*, *3*, 73–96.

Canter, D.V., & Heritage, R. (1990). A multivariate model of sexual offence behaviour: Developments in "offender profiling." *Journal of Forensic Psychiatry*, *1*, 185–212.

Canter, D.V., & Ioannou, M. (2004). A multivariate model of stalking behaviours. *Behaviormetrika*, *31*, 113–130.

Canter, D.V., & Youngs, D. (2003). Beyond "offender profiling": The need for an investigative psychology. In D. Carson & R. Bull (Eds.), *Handbook of psychology in legal contexts* (pp. 171–205). Chichester, UK: John Wiley & Sons, Ltd.

Canter, D.V., & Youngs, D. (2009). *Investigative psychology: Offender profiling and the analysis of criminal action*. Chichester, UK: John Wiley & Sons, Ltd.

Cohen, L.E., & Felson, M. (1979). Social change and crime rate trends: A routine activity approach. *American Sociological Review*, *44*, 588–608.

Crichton, M., & Flin, R. (2002). Command decision making. In R. Flin & K. Arbuthnot (Eds.), *Incident command: Tales from the hot seat* (pp. 201–238). Aldershot, UK: Ashgate.

Douglas, J.E., & Burgess, A.E. (1986). Criminal profiling: A viable investigative tool against violent crime. *FBI Law Enforcement Bulletin*, *55*, 9–13.

Douglas, J.E., Ressler, R.K., Burgess, A.W., & Hartman, C.R. (1986). Criminal profiling from crime scene analysis. *Behavioral Sciences and the Law*, *4*, 401–421.

Eyre, M., Crego, J., & Alison, L.J. (2008). Electronic debriefs and simulations as descriptive methods for defining the critical incident landscape. In L.J. Alison & J. Crego (Eds.), *Policing critical incidents: Leadership and critical incident management* (pp. 24–53). Cullompton, UK: Willan.

Goring, C.B. (1913). *The English convict: A statistical study*. London: Darling and Son.

Gudjonsson, G. (1992). *The psychology of interrogations, confessions and testimony*. Chichester, UK: John Wiley & Sons, Ltd.

Guttman, L. (1954). A new approach to factor analysis: The radex. In P.F. Lazarsfeld (Ed.), *Mathematical thinking in the social sciences* (pp. 258–348). Glencoe, IL: Free Press.

Kahneman, D., & Klein, G.A. (2009). Conditions for intuitive expertise: A failure to disagree. *American Psychologist*, *64*, 515–526.

Klein, G.A. (1997). The current status of the naturalistic decision-making framework. In R. Flin, E. Salas, M. Strub, & L. Martin (Eds.), *Decision making under stress: Emerging themes and applications* (pp. 11–28). Aldershot, UK: Ashgate.

Langer, W.C. (1972). *The mind of Adolf Hitler: The secret wartime report*. New York: Basic Books.

Lombroso, C. (1911). Introduction. In G. Lombroso-Ferrero (Ed.), *Criminal man: According to the classification of Cesare Lombroso* (pp. xi–xx). New York: Knickerbocker Press.

Milne, R., & Bull, R. (1999). *Investigative interviewing: Psychology and practice*. Chichester, UK: John Wiley & Sons, Ltd.

Mokros, A., & Alison, L.J. (2010). Is offender profiling possible? Testing the predicted homology of crime scene actions and background characteristics in a sample of rapists. *Legal and Criminological Psychology*, *7*, 25–43.

Mullins, S. (2009). Terrorist networks and small group psychology. In D. Canter (Ed.), *The faces of terrorism: Multi-disciplinary perspectives* (pp. 137–150). Chichester, UK: John Wiley & Sons, Ltd.

Porter, L.E., & Alison, L.J. (2006). Leadership and hierarchies in criminal groups: Scaling degrees of leader behaviour in group robbery. *Legal and Criminological Psychology*, *11*, 245–265.

Rainbow, L. (2011). Taming the beast: The UK approach to the management of behavioral investigative advice. In L.J. Alison & L. Rainbow (Eds.), *Professionalizing offender profiling: Forensic and investigative psychology in practice* (pp. 5–17). New York: Routledge.

Rainbow, L., & Gregory, A. (2009). Behavioural investigative advice: A contemporary view. *Journal of Homicide and Major Incident Investigation*, *5*, 71–82.

Rainbow, L., & Gregory, A. (2011). What behavioral investigative advisors actually do. In L.J. Alison & L. Rainbow (Eds.), *Professionalizing offender profiling: Forensic and investigative psychology in practice* (pp. 18–34). New York: Routledge.

Ressler, R.K., Burgess, A.W., Douglas, J.E., Hartman, C.R., & D'Agostino, R.B. (1986). Sexual killers and their victims: Identifying patterns through crime scene analysis. *Journal of Interpersonal Violence*, *1*, 288–308.

Ressler, R.K., & Shachtman, T. (1992). *Whoever fights monsters*. New York: St. Martin's Press.

Riggs, D.S., Caulfield, M.B., & Street, A.E. (2000). Risk for domestic violence: Factors associated with perpetration and victimization. *Journal of Clinical Psychology*, *56*, 1289–1316.

Rossmo, D.K. (2000). *Geographic profiling*. Boca Raton, FL: CRC Press.

Salfati, C.G. (2000). The nature of expressiveness and instrumentality in homicide: Implications for offender profiling. *Homicide Studies*, *4*, 265–293.

Santtila, P., Häkkänen, H., Alison, L.J., & Whyte, C. (2003). Juvenile firesetters: Crime scene actions and offender characteristics. *Legal and Criminological Psychology*, *8*, 1–20.

Shye, S., Elizur, D., & Hoffman, M. (1994). *Introduction to facet theory: Content design and intrinsic data analysis in behavioral research*. London: Sage.

Snook, B., Cullen, R.M., Bennell, C., Taylor, P.J., & Gendreau, P. (2008). The criminal profiling illusion: What's behind the smoke and mirrors? *Criminal Justice and Behavior*, *35*, 1257–1276.

Snook, B., Taylor, P.J., & Bennell, C. (2004). Geographic profiling: The fast, frugal, and accurate way. *Applied Cognitive Psychology*, *18*, 105–121.

Theoharis, A.G., Poveda, T.G., Rosenfeld, S., & Powers, R.G. (1999). *The FBI: A comprehensive reference guide*. Phoenix, AZ: Oryx Press.

Turner, S. (1969). Delinquency and distance. In J.T. Sellin & M.E. Wolfgang (Eds.), *Delinquency: Selected studies* (pp. 11–26). Chichester, UK: John Wiley & Sons, Ltd.

Tversky, A., & Kahneman, D. (1974). Judgement under uncertainty: Heuristics and biases. *Science, 185*, 1124–1131.

Vrij, A. (2008). *Detecting lies and deceit: Pitfalls and opportunities*. Chichester, UK: John Wiley & Sons, Ltd.

Wells, G.L., & Olson, E.A. (2003). Eyewitness testimony. *Annual Review of Psychology, 54*, 277–295.

Wilson, C., & Seaman, D. (1990). *The serial killers: A study in the psychology of violence*. London: Virgin Books.

Zsambok, C.E., & Klein, G. (1997). *Naturalistic decision-making*. Mahwah, NJ: Lawrence Erlbaum.

PART TWO

Offenders with Mental Disorders

8

Assessing Risk of Violence in Offenders with Mental Disorders

JAMES McGUIRE

Several decades following the advent of the deinstitutionalization movement, stigmatization of mental ill-health appears to remain a perturbing problem in many societies. Surveys by both the World Health Organization (2001) and the World Psychiatric Association have produced disturbing evidence to that effect. The latter considered social stigma to be "the main obstacle to better mental health care and better quality of life of people who have the illness, of their families, of their communities and of health service staff" (Sartorius & Schulze, 2005, p. xiii). Mehta, Kassam, Leese, Butler, and Thornicroft (2009) summarized a succession of surveys in England and Scotland using representative community samples interviewed at several points in the period 1994–2003. Disturbingly, the researchers found a "significant deterioration" (p. 281) in public attitudes over the study period on most of the survey items.

STIGMA, SOCIAL DISTANCE, AND RISK PERCEPTION

What are the reasons for the perseveration of these unreceptive attitudes? One element that may play an influential part is a long-standing assumption that people with some types of mental health problems are inherently dangerous. The resultant fear appears not just to have persisted; it may even have increased. Phelan, Link, Stueve, and Pescosolido (2000; Link, Phelan, Bresnahan, Stueve, & Pescosolido, 1999) were able to compare perceptions of mental illness in the United States

Assessments in Forensic Practice: A Handbook, First Edition. Edited by Kevin D. Browne, Anthony R. Beech, Leam A. Craig, and Shihning Chou.
© 2017 John Wiley & Sons Ltd. Published 2017 by John Wiley & Sons Ltd.

between 1950 and 1996. They found that the American public's concept of mental disorder had broadened during that period, such that many mental health problems were perceived as "less alien and less extreme" (p. 200); essentially as something that could happen to anyone. Over the same timescale, however, the expectation that people who suffered from psychosis were potentially dangerous had multiplied by a factor of 2.5. In a study conducted in Germany, reporting of violent incidents that involved persons with schizophrenia increased the "social distance" between them and others, and reinforced existing negative stereotypes. The intensity of this varied as a function of news stories (Angermeyer & Matschinger, 1996).

Public attitudes and anxieties often have a fairly tangential relationship to the objective risk of harm, in the sense of the number of relevant adverse events that actually occur. During the period 2000–2005 there were on average over 900 homicides per annum in England and Wales; people diagnosed with severe mental disorders were responsible on average for 52 per year (Appleby et al., 2006). Despite evidence of a later rise in the frequency of homicide due to mental disorder (National Confidential Inquiry, 2009), after increasing between 1950 and 1980, it has been generally declining since then (Large, Smith, Swinson, Shaw, & Nielssen, 2009). Moreover the pattern of homicides committed by people with major mental disorders is essentially similar to that for people without such disorders, in that most victims are relatives or acquaintances. In a leading survey to be discussed below, "perpetrators of stranger homicide were less likely to have a lifetime history of mental disorder" (Appleby et al., 2006, p. 101). In the already very unlikely event that we are to be the target of a homicidal assault by someone unknown to us, that person is more likely *not* to suffer from a major mental disorder than to do so, by a factor of roughly 20:1 (*Medical News Today*, 2009).

RISK ASSESSMENT AND VIOLENCE PREVENTION

These contradictions notwithstanding, if an adverse event can be predicted and thereby averted, it appears natural that people will search for ways to accomplish this. The *National Confidential Inquiry into Suicide and Homicide by People with Mental Illness* (Appleby et al., 2006) considered that 18% of the suicides and 14% of the homicides examined were preventable. Maden (2007) analyzed aspects of a series of 25 homicides committed by people with severe mental disorders and concluded that several could have been prevented through use of a structured risk assessment procedure (the HCR-20, described below). The development of risk assessment research should be placed in this context. How far is it possible to predict a violent event such as a homicide or assault, and to take action that will reduce the likelihood of its occurring? This question and others are the focus of this chapter, with reference to individuals convicted of crimes, and who are also diagnosed with mental disorders.

Integrating several sets of findings, the case for violence risk assessment is fairly solidly supported. First, it has been recognized for some time that it is possible to predict general criminal recidivism, and that information gathered for that purpose can also be used to design and deliver interventions to reduce it (Andrews, 1989; Andrews & Bonta, 2010a; Andrews, Bonta, & Wormith, 2006). This discovery led to the formulation of the "risk principle": that the amount and intensity of intervention should be tailored to an individual's risk of reoffending. Two large-scale reviews have shown that approaches guided by that principle have yielded higher success rates in this respect than those not so guided (Andrews & Dowden, 2006; Lowenkamp, Latessa, & Holsinger, 2006). Second, from a different area of research, there is also sound evidence that aggressiveness is relatively stable over periods of several years. This has been found in two meta-analyses of longitudinal studies (Olweus, 1988; Zumkley, 1994). Third, a substantial amount of evidence indicates that aggression and violent offending can be reduced (McGuire, 2008, 2013). Accomplishing this, of course, depends on successful assessment of risk-need factors and allocation to the most appropriate services, treatment programs, and strategies for risk management (Hollin, 2002). Arguably, use of the best validated methods can potentially "optimise the balance between public safety and offenders' civil liberties" (Harris, Rice, & Quinsey, 2008, p. 154). Currently, violence risk assessment has become virtually "standard practice" in forensic mental health and in some jurisdictions plays a pivotal role in the application of mental health law.

Before proceeding, we should note that a large proportion of the discussion in this area is couched in psychiatric terminology. The diagnostic manuals, the DSM-5 (American Psychiatric Association, 2013) and ICD-10 (World Health Organization, 1992) – the latter at the time of writing, under revision – set the scene for virtually all research in this field. By providing definitional criteria, they have a dominant influence on how persons who experience acute mental distress are classified, and which combinations of problems are thought to form distinct "syndromes." This approach is not without its critics, and in the most serious accusations, it has been shown to be scientifically weak, and its empirical basis questionable (Clark, Watson, & Reynolds, 1995). Space does not permit addressing this debate in the present chapter. The net effect, however, is that it is extremely difficult to review any facet of this topic without employing the language of psychiatric classification.

MENTAL DISORDER AND VIOLENCE RISK

A first question in this area is whether the presence of a major mental health problem increases the likelihood of violent behavior. Disentangling the possible contribution of mental disorder to an elevated risk of criminal offending, and especially violence, has proved to be a formidable task. Part of the reason for this resides in the elusiveness of some of the variables that need to be defined and measured to make any firm conclusions possible. Certainly, epidemiological studies of the mental health of prisoners yield strong evidence that levels of disorder are significantly higher than in the outside community (Fazel & Seewald, 2012; Sirdifield, Gojkovic, Brooker, & Ferriter, 2009; Steadman, Osher, Robbins, Case, & Samuels, 2009). However, this discovery does not in itself signify the presence of a cause–effect relationship. Another difficulty arises from the recurrent finding that many factors associated with serious offending are also correlated with each other. Thus economic hardship, neighborhood disorganization, family dysfunction, parental neglect, childhood victimization, low educational attainment, erratic lifestyle, and a history of substance abuse, have all been associated with *both* of the target variables of interest here (crime and mental disorder respectively).

Reviewing the voluminous research literature pertaining to this issue is beyond the scope of the present chapter, and there is currently no consensus position regarding it. However there appears to be a majority of opinion permitting some broad-spectrum, if tentative conclusions.

First, there is very little evidence that mental health problems in general are associated with a heightened risk of committing crimes of violence. What is very clear is that people suffering from severe and enduring mental health problems are much more likely to harm themselves than others. Second, however, recent large-scale reviews suggest that some diagnosed mental disorders, notably schizophrenia and other psychoses, are associated with an increased risk of violence. Fazel, Gulati, Linsell, Geddes, and Grann (2009) reviewed 20 studies with an aggregate sample of 18,423 individuals and after discounting the influence of concurrent substance abuse, found an odds ratio of 2:1 for the relationship between schizophrenia and violence. Douglas, Guy, and Hart (2009) reviewed a total of 204 studies, subsuming 166 independent samples, and concluded that "psychosis was reliably and significantly associated with an approximately 49% to 68% increase in the odds of violence relative to the odds of violence in the absence of psychosis" (p. 687). If this sounds large, note also that "the average effect size for psychosis … is comparable to numerous individual risk factors" found in other research (p. 693). Furthermore there was considerable heterogeneity in the findings surveyed, with one quarter of the effect sizes obtained being below zero (with a mean odds ratio of 0.73), while another quarter were large (above an odds ratio of 3.30). (An odds ratio of 1 indicates that violence is equally likely whether or not psychosis is present. Below 1, an association with violence is less likely; above 1, it is more likely). Third, the strength of the association between psychosis and violence varies considerably as a function of the number of moderator variables, and these often operate in combination. For example, high rates of mental disorder, abuse of alcohol or other substances, and violence may be a function of neighborhood factors such as deprivation and disorganization (Elbogen & Johnson, 2009; Fazel, Långström, Hjern, Grann, & Lichtenstein, 2009; Silver, Mulvey, & Monahan, 1999; Steadman et al., 1998). Thus it is possible that even if people with psychoses commit acts of violence, that may not be a result of any predisposition intrinsic to their mental states per se, but a function of events in their lives, such as family conflict or victimization by others (Silver, 2006).

Some of these findings appear to contradict suggestions made at the opening of this chapter. Could it be that public fears of those with serious mental disorders, given their increased community presence following dehospitalization, are entirely warranted? Some authors have repeatedly cautioned against the underestimation of violence risk associated with schizophrenia (Hodgins, 2009). However, the only research available in which crime trends have been analyzed across the period when deinstitutionalization occurred found no evidence that it was associated with an increase in crime attributable to people with mental disorders (Wallace, Mullen, & Burgess, 2004); although we should note that this was in a location (Victoria, Australia) where community care was fiscally well supported. Note too that where homicide rates by people with mental disorders have increased, they have done so at a rate commensurate with that in the rest of the population (Large, Smith, & Nielssen, 2009).

On various other points, research findings are inconsistent. For example, earlier indications that violence might be likely to occur as a result of *threat/control-override delusions* (Link & Stueve, 1994) or *command hallucinations* (McNiel, 1994), were not corroborated by the MacArthur study on risk assessment, the largest of its kind conducted to date, in which a cohort of 1,136 patients was followed up at 10-week intervals for a period of one year after discharge from hospital (Appelbaum, Robbins, & Monahan, 2000).

Whether these findings translate into designating psychosis as a *predictor* in violence risk assessment also remains unclear. Bonta, Law, and Hanson (1998) reported a meta-analysis of predictor–outcome relationships, extracting data from 68 independent studies, with a cumulative sample size of 15,245. Risk factors were classified into four broad sets: *demographic*; *criminal history*; *deviant lifestyle*; and *clinical*. The most accurate were demographic and criminal history variables: indeed the overall pattern obtained was a close parallel to that typically found with offender populations in the penal system. The weakest predictors of recidivism were clinical variables. Although a diagnosis of Antisocial Personality Disorder was associated with a greater risk of future criminality, no other diagnostic category emerged as significant. Psychosis was negatively correlated with future general and violent recidivism. Other studies since then have obtained analogous findings (e.g., Gray et al., 2004; Phillips et al., 2005).

DEVELOPMENT OF RISK ASSESSMENT

Both the usage and the study of risk assessment in mental health care are often described as having passed through several "generations" of activity, each characterized by a particular approach to the appraisal and prediction of violent behavior (Andrade, O'Neill, & Diener, 2009; Bonta & Wormith, 2008). Initially, research followed practice, evaluating outcomes of decisions made by clinical judgment. Later, research guided practice making it gradually more "evidence based," with the development first of an *actuarial* approach to risk assessment and later of structured professional judgment (SPJ) to help make clinical decisions and manage risk. This is a loose and broad-brush conceptual framework, however. The boundaries between the successive phases are by no means firm or clear-cut.

First Generation. The earliest research in this field comprised what have been called naturalistic studies in which, for example, patients who had been released from secure hospitals were retrospectively followed up in the community and their rates of reconviction or of return to institutions were recorded. Melton, Petrila, Poythress, and Slobogin (2007) portray this phase as approximately occupying the period from 1960 to 1980. Most assessments undertaken during this phase (and probably for several decades beforehand) were based primarily on the exercise by experienced practitioners of "unaided" professional *clinical judgment*. This was grounded for the most part on their intuitions, probably based on their accumulated recollections of individual casework, and its end product was typically a statement of opinion. Without any specially provided training or formalized assessment protocols, this approach is nowadays considered inadvisable. When it was subjected to more rigorous evaluation, its low reliability (agreement between different clinicians judging the same case) and validity (predictive power in relation to the outcome) became readily apparent. One recurrent finding was that rates of predicted "dangerousness" were often far higher than later findings confirmed (Monahan, 1984).

In an attempt to systematize the task of assessing risk, researchers were therefore urged to move toward an approach centered on the measurement of variables for which there was an empirically demonstrable association with a violent outcome (Monahan, 1981). In terms of research, the discovery that a methodology of this kind was superior to individual judgment had been shown as long ago as the mid-1950s when Meehl (1954) published his groundbreaking study comparing the relative accuracy of the two approaches. Although this was not focused on violence as such, the implications for all efforts at prediction were far-reaching. This led to the emergence of the "actuarial" approach, entailing "… use of formulas that are experimentally derived" (Melton et al., 2007, p. 308), often contrasted with the "clinical" approach that preceded it. The apparent divide between these two approaches is by no means a neat one: what is called clinical judgment can take a variety of forms, with different methods placed on a continuum (Conroy and Murrie, 2007). On the failings of unstructured judgment, however, ensuing studies and reviews in successive decades have solidified support for the conclusions originally drawn by Meehl (e.g., Sawyer, 1966; Grove & Meehl, 1996). This has been further amplified using meta-analysis, replicating and extending those conclusions (Ægisdóttir et al., 2006; Grove, Zald, Lebow, Snitz, & Nelson, 2000).

Second Generation. In actuarially based risk assessment, specified variables that have been found to be correlated with the occurrence of adverse events (in this case violent offenses) are measured, and predictions then made, based empirically on discerning the combination of them with the greatest prognostic accuracy. Because this approach has typically relied on complex statistical analysis, it has often been mistakenly called the "statistical" approach, and contrasted with the earlier predominantly "clinical" one. That is, however, something of a misnomer, as in principle aspects of clinical judgment could be quantified and statistically analyzed. The key difference between the two approaches lies in whether or not the basis for making the judgments is rooted in systematic observation of relationships, or demonstrated in research findings, rather than drawing on the judgments of individual clinicians working independently.

This approach is also believed to make the reasons for risk decisions more transparent. Many clinicians might find it difficult to articulate how or why they arrived at their conclusions regarding someone's level of risk. It also results in an impressive increase in predictive accuracy: it has been estimated that it led to an improvement in predicting general recidivism from 60% to 80%, and violent recidivism from 40% to 53% (Loza, 2003). Examples of second-generation actuarial predictors include the *Offender Group Reconviction Scale* (OGRS; Copas & Marshall, 1998; Howard, Francis, Soothill, & Humphreys, 2009), and the *Violence Risk Appraisal Guide* (VRAG; Quinsey, Harris, Rice, & Cormier, 2005). Hollin (2002) has provided a survey and critique of several other prediction tools used in mainstream penal services (prisons, probation, youth justice). Collectively, as a type of method, these measures have come to be called *Actuarial Risk Assessment Instruments* (ARAIs). Their distinguishing feature is the use of explicit rules for combining items into a global risk assessment, usually in the form of a score (Bonta, 1996).

Third Generation. But the tendency of second generation risk assessments to focus almost exclusively on "static" factors has in turn proved to have its limitations. Such factors are insensitive to change over time and to the fluctuations in variables that have clear potency as influences on risk. The resultant picture is inevitably incomplete as many aspects of individual functioning are excluded from the process. Could accuracy be increased by reintroducing them? In a third generation of assessments, therefore, "dynamic" factors were incorporated into risk assessment. This also allowed the reintroduction of some elements of clinical judgment, as there are recurrent situations on which little nomothetic data can be brought to bear. In forensic and clinical work, it is probably not an exaggeration (though it might be an oxymoron) to say that novel and unprecedented scenarios appear with surprising regularity. However, in third-generation assessments, clinical judgment is structured according to reproducible criteria, and is "anchored" in statements or observations that can be made explicit, so facilitating calibration between assessors. Thus, these risk assessments combine actuarial and clinical methods of prediction, though usually in highly systematized ways. Collectively they have come to be grouped together under the heading of "structured professional judgment" (SPJ). Some approaches represent "dynamic risk factors" using alternative terminology, that of "criminogenic need," and therefore call this model "risk-needs assessment" (Andrews, Bonta, & Wormith, 2006; Wong, Gordon, & Gu, 2007). The *History-Clinical-Risk Management* framework (HCR-20) is an example of an assessment of this type (Webster & Hucker, 2007). To use the majority of these methods, training is usually required, designed and sometimes provided by a scale's authors. Recently Guy, Packer, and Warnken (2012) identified a total of 19 extant SPJ tools.

Fourth Generation. The emergent, fourth wave of risk assessment is even less easy to define than the preceding three. It builds on all the findings of previous approaches, but adds a further element, that of *risk management* (Heilbrun, 2003). Information on broad risk categories may be used for allocating individuals to levels of service, or to varying types and intensities of treatment and support. Information on dynamic risk factors is then added, focusing on those variables associated with relapse, and attempting to reduce their potential impact, monitoring progress over time, and adjusting interventions as necessary. Thus a "feedback loop" is built into risk assessment procedures. The *Level of Service/Case Management Inventory* is an illustration of this generation of methods (Andrews, Bonta, & Wormith, 2004).

It is not necessarily the case that each successive generation of tools represents an unequivocal improvement on the one before. The choice of method should be guided by the assessor's objective. For example, Campbell, French, and Gendreau (2009) found that second-generation static instruments were best for predicting institutional violence, whereas third-generation methods were superior predictors of long-term post-release outcome.

What is still almost invariably neglected in risk assessment is the environment: the circumstances in which an individual finds him- or herself. In the earlier generations of research, when the language of dangerousness was more commonly used, most risk assessments were almost entirely *dispositional* in their orientation; that is, they located the likely causes of potential future violence within individuals (Otto, 2000). Although behavioral, social learning and interactionist approaches to personality place emphasis on environmental factors at a theoretical level, proposals and methods for recording information about it and incorporating them in risk assessments have remained relatively undeveloped. Unfortunately much risk assessment retains its internal, intrapersonal emphasis.

METHODOLOGY OF RISK ASSESSMENT RESEARCH

Risk assessment requires a sound empirical basis if it is to maximize its likelihood of being effective. Evidence is crucial to underwriting both its clinical usefulness – or lack of it, if that is how things turn out – and its credibility in the legal process. To evaluate risk assessment instruments themselves, several indicators are used, and before employing any single method it is advisable to check on how well supported it is in this respect. In this section, we briefly overview some of the indices used for this before embarking on a short survey of some of the instruments in current use.

The following are some of the statistics that are commonly cited as evidence that any given assessment is worth using. There are three pairs of definitions and an additional, more elaborate concept combining one of the pairs in a single measure (Blackburn, 2000).

- *Positive* and *negative predictive value*: these terms refer respectively to the proportion of a study sample predicted to be violent or not to be violent who are correctly predicted.
- *False positive* and *false negative rate*: the former is the proportion of the actually non-violent who are incorrectly predicted (i.e., who were predicted to be violent), while the latter is the proportion of the actually violent who were incorrectly predicted (i.e., were predicted to be non-violent).
- *Sensitivity* is the proportion of those who are actually violent who were correctly predicted to be, whereas *specificity* is the proportion of those who are actually not violent who were correctly predicted to be.

The last two measures can be combined in a statistic developed from a "signal detection" model of appraising accuracy. This involves the use of *Receiver Operating Characteristics* (ROC) curves, where the relative accuracy of prediction is computed across the range of possible scores on an assessment. As a risk prediction score increases (on whatever scale we are testing), the proportion of those who are actually violent should increase while the proportion of those not violent should fall. A perfect predictor would (by definition) get this right every time. The extent to which an actual predictor falls below this ceiling can be plotted graphically, and the resultant statistic is therefore known as the *area under the curve* (AUC) (Mossman, 1994).

Other indices have also been devised but are less commonly quoted. They include, for example, the *Diagnostic Odds Ratio* (DOR) that entails a procedure similar to that utilized in medical diagnosis where there is a dichotomous outcome (thus violence yes/no is equivalent to disease present/absent). However, attempts to anticipate the likelihood of a violent or sexual assault are of limited usefulness in binary form, and prognostic estimates will only be of practical use in this field if they generate a continuous variable (risk level) or one with several categories.

Using data of these kinds from risk assessment research, the accuracy of different methods can be compared with each other. The AUC offers particular advantages in providing a common metric developed from the relative balance of an instrument's sensitivity and specificity, and is independent of sample size. This provides an indicator of the comparative success of each measure, that is, its accuracy as a means of predicting a violent event. For approximately the last 20 years or so, the AUC has been widely used as the key indicator of the predictive validity of most risk assessment scales. However, this is not a universally supported recommendation. Several recent reviews have questioned some aspects of it (Mossman, 2013; Singh, 2013). One important suggestion is that it is not advisable to use the AUC on its own, and other indicators (such as positive and negative predictive value) should also be included in research and evaluation reports. Another is that published manuals of risk assessment instruments should include calibration tables and other material as essential reference points for interpreting risk scores.

Reviews of Risk Assessment Instruments

There have been several recent major reviews of this field, although it is crucial to note that each of them integrates data from studies of offenders with and without mental disorders. Most had the objective of drawing together findings of predictive/outcome studies within a given area, but others have addressed methodological questions. All have sounded notes of caution regarding the predictive validity of assessment measures.

Farrington, Jolliffe, and Johnstone (2008) succeeded in comparing a number of risk assessment methods for criminal recidivism in terms of the average AUC each of them generated across a number of prediction–outcome studies. A selection of their findings is shown in Table 8.1. Campbell et al. (2009) undertook a similar task but confined their main analysis to those measures on which data were available from 10 or more effect-size calculations, focusing therefore on just five instruments (HCR-20, LSI-R, PCL:R, SIR, and VRAG). Yang, Wong, and Coid (2010) ranged more broadly and analyzed data on nine separate tools. These authors concluded that "there is no appreciable or clinically significant difference in the violence-predictive efficacies

Table 8.1 Predicting violence: Comparison of areas under the curve for the most widely researched risk assessments (Farrington, Jolliffe, & Johnstone 2008).

Device	Number of comparisons (k)	AUC	Lower CI	Upper CI
GSIR: General Statistical Information on Recidivism	4	0.73	0.68	0.79
OGRS: Offender Group Reconviction Scale	4	0.71	0.66	0.75
Historical-Clinical-Risk Management (HCR-20)	13	0.70	0.66	0.74
Psychopathy Check List (Revised) (PCL:R)	18	0.69	0.66	0.73
Violence Risk Appraisal Guide (VRAG)	18	0.69	0.67	0.72
Level of Service Inventory (Revised) (LSI-R)	7	0.64	0.63	0.66

of the nine tools … if prediction of violence is the only criterion for the selection of a risk assessment tool, then the tools included in the present study are essentially interchangeable" (p. 759). That conclusion is perhaps not surprising given the findings of a factor-analytic study by Kroner, Mills, and Reddon (2005). These authors separated out the items from four established scales and then recombined them in a series of random selections. The resultant incarnations yielded predictions of post-release recidivism or revocation of parole as accurately as their formal counterparts, suggesting that all assessments tap into essentially the same pool of predictor variables.

Singh and Fazel (2010) reported a "meta-review," a sweeping survey of previous efforts at evaluation of the field of violence risk assessment. They identified 40 reviews (9 systematic reviews and 31 meta-analyses) of this area, encompassing 2,232 primary studies and no fewer than 126 separate risk assessment instruments. No single measure emerged as consistently superior to any of the others in terms of its predictive validity. In many other respects, there was sizeable inconsistency among the findings, and of particular note for present purposes, there was "no clear evidence of risk assessments' validity in psychiatric samples" (p. 982). There were "significant methodological weaknesses" in many reviews; among them the problem that moderator effects were rarely analyzed, such as the differential impact of settings on results (e.g., differences between prison, secure hospital, and community samples).

Singh, Grann, and Fazel (2011) and Fazel, Singh, Doll, and Grann (2012) reported two related systematic reviews also comparing nine risk assessment tools (but a different selection from Yang et al.). The former integrated a set of 68 studies, involving 88 independent samples with a cumulative total of 25,980 participants; the latter a set of 73 samples with an aggregate of 24,827 participants. These authors found wide variation in the predictive accuracy of the selected measures. They concluded, somewhat gloomily, that "even after 30 years of development, the view that violence, sexual, or criminal risk can be predicted in most cases is not evidence based" (Fazel et al., 2012, p. 5). They recommended that risk assessments be combined with other information, and should be used only to "roughly classify" individuals in different risk categories.

Whittington et al. (2013) reviewed studies of violence risk assessments published in the period 2002–2008 used in either mental health or criminal justice settings. Integrating data from 65 studies where AUCs were reported, these authors too found a wide range of predictive values. The mean AUC across all studies was 0.69 with a range from 0.44 to 0.88. However, the upper reaches of this range (above 0.75) were populated by only five studies derived from four different assessments, with the two highest figures obtained from a far shorter follow-up interval (84 days) than for the other instruments (which varied from 350 to 4,143 days).

Rossegger et al. (2013) conducted a review of studies on the three ARAIs reported to be the most widely used in clinical practice: the VRAG (described below); a related measure, the *Sex Offender Risk Appraisal Guide* (SORAG); and another sexual reoffense predictor, the *Static-99*. These authors located 84 replication studies based on 108 separate samples. They discovered that there was a sizeable gap between the reporting of an evaluation study by an instrument's developers, and evaluations conducted by other researchers. To the extent that some studies were designed as replication tests to check the validity of the selected tools, the "matching" between how measures were implemented in original (developer-led) and later (replication) studies was often poor. It would appear that without independent evaluations of measures – that is, ones conducted by researchers other than their developers – the validity of those instruments remains in doubt. Singh, Desmarais, and Van Dorn (2013) reported a "second order" systematic review of 47 predictive validity studies published in the period 1990–2011, dealing with 25 risk assessment instruments. This included both actuarially based methods and others using structured clinical judgment. The standards of reporting in risk assessment research were found to be very variable across studies; AUC values were interpreted in only one-third (34%) of the studies, and possible limitations discussed in fewer than one in five (19%). The authors identified a need for more standardized approaches to analysis and reporting across the field of risk assessment research.

While less directly relevant to the field of risk and mental disorder, there have been recent systematic reviews of risk assessment in other areas of offending behavior. This includes the work of Nicholls, Pritchard, Reeves, and Hilterman (2013) who conducted a review of risk assessment approaches in the area of intimate partner violence (IPV). Nicholls et al. located a set of 39 studies published in the period 1990–2011, encompassing 19 different risk assessment measures. Some of them showed that most professionals working with IPV "continued to rely on their intuition and subjective judgment despite the limitations" of that approach (p. 87). Results showed there was a wide variability in the quality and rigor of the studies that were found, although assessments with a specific IPV focus performed slightly better than those with a general violence focus. Overall, the authors characterized the usage of risk assessment methods in IPV as being in need of considerable development and refinement. Tully, Chou, and Browne (2013) reported a systematic review of risk assessment tools used in the area of sexual offending. These authors integrated data from 43 studies, with a cumulative sample size of 31,426, and after applying extensive quality-control procedures, data were collated on nine measures. In both this and the Nicholls et al. (2013) review, predictive validity was found to be in the moderate range. Some measures doing better than this in the study by Tully et al. (2013) were unfortunately based on only two outcomes in each case. As in the Rossegger et al. (2013) review, there was evidence of better outcomes from studies reported by developers of measures than were found in independent studies.

Classification and Decision Trees

In technical terms, all the methods subsumed in the above reviews are derived from a *linear model*. That is, they involve numerical analysis of continuous variables meeting certain statistical assumptions. However, risk assessment can also be undertaken via a quite different route, entailing the use of what is called a *classification-based* approach. Here, cases are assigned to risk levels, using specified features, and classed as high or low in violence propensity in a succession of dichotomous (yes/no) decisions (Gardner, Lidz, Mulvey, & Shaw, 1996). A sequence of such binary comparisons ("recursive partitioning") thereby generates a tree-like structure. The more features an individual possesses that are associated with violence, the likelier it is he or she will emerge in the higher-risk branches of the tree. This type of procedure was employed to analyze data from the first 20 weeks of the MacArthur Risk Assessment study (Monahan et al., 2001). Where some research participants were not neatly classified at the first attempt, the procedure was repeated until all had been allocated to a risk-level group. This is known as an *iterative classification tree* (ICT). Using a total of 106 potential risk factors, individuals were ultimately allocated to one of five groups. As risk levels increased, the size of the group declined. Figure 8.1 shows the risk of violence in each of the resultant groups.

Banks et al. (2004) have described a still more elaborate analysis in which the MacArthur sample was successively classified using as many as five different risk assessment models (where a "model" means a selected combination of risk factors).

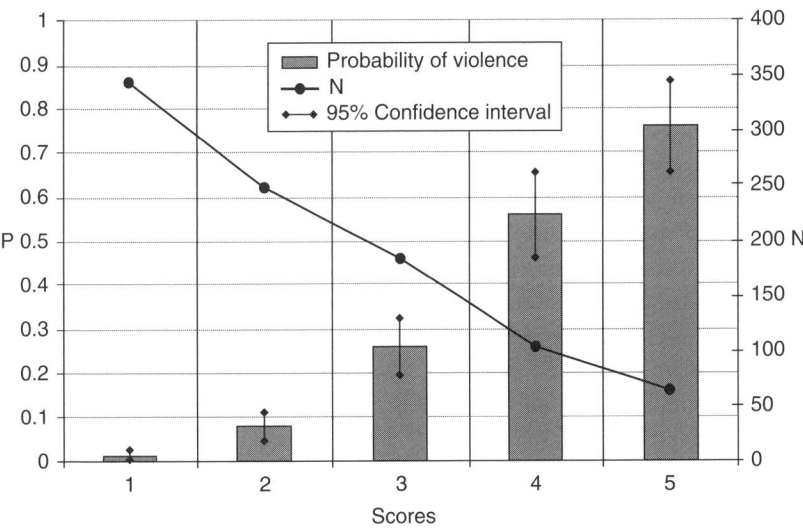

Figure 8.1 Number of cases and percentage violent in each risk class. Reproduced with permission of SAGE publications.

The authors argued that rather than trying to identify a single "best" model, a preferable approach might be to combine prediction models, employing different sets of variables each time. Such analyses have been conducted converging data from up to ten distinct models.

SPECIFIC ASSESSMENTS

There is now, if perhaps not a plethora, certainly an abundance of discrete instruments designed for assessing risk of future violence among people with severe mental health problems. A survey of 29 medium secure forensic units by Khiroya, Weaver, and Maden (2009) showed they were being extensively used in those settings. The following is a selection of the more commonly employed scales and allied methods. They are presented in an order that approximately reflects a movement from exclusive reliance on static factors to one that includes a gradually increasing proportion of dynamic factors.

Offender Group Reconviction Scale (OGRS). Most available outcome data on the OGRS pertain to its second version (OGRS-2; Copas & Marshall, 1998). However, this has now been supplanted by an updated version (OGRS-3) that has been validated on a sample of 76,000 offenders and offers an additional advantage in requiring only six pieces of information (as opposed to nine), and in yielding one-year as well as two-year prediction scores. Howard et al. (2009) describe details of the background research and state that the AUC is improved to 80% and for prisoners only it is 84%. The OGRS appears to be only infrequently used in forensic mental health services, despite quite strong evidence that as a predictor it outperforms the other instruments currently available (Gray et al., 2004). However, being a static/actuarial method it does not incorporate the assessment of dynamic factors providing indications of what areas might be useful to address for risk management purposes.

Violence Risk Appraisal Guide (VRAG). The development of the VRAG arose from long-term follow-up research with men discharged from the secure mental health center at Penetanguishene, Ontario (Quinsey et al., 2005) and has been described as the "most researched" actuarial tool (Fogel, 2009, p. 57). There are 12 constituent items, covering areas such as early school adjustment, history of alcohol problems, marital status, and victim injury, in addition to the standard criminal history and clinical diagnostic indicators. Outcome studies generally support the validity of the VRAG, with an AUC as high as 0.80 in a study by Harris, Rice, and Cormier (2002); though a lower figure of 0.70 was found in a later replication in Germany (Kröner, Stadtland, Eidt, & Nedopil, 2007).

Psychopathy Check List. This instrument exists in several forms: the full adult version, the *Psychopathy Check List: Revised* (PCL:R; Hare, 1999, 2003); a short, screening version (PCL:SV); and a youth version (PCL:YV). The first comprises 20 items designed to take account of criminal history and lifestyle variables, alongside aspects of interpersonal and emotional functioning. Although the information required for completing the check list can be extracted from case files, it is recommended that this be accompanied by a specially designed interview (for which training is required). While the scoring of some items is determined almost algorithmically, others require the exercise of judgment on the part of the assessor. There are ongoing, and as yet unresolved, disputes concerning the core factor structure of the PCL:R with two, three, and four factor solutions obtained in different studies, and there is disagreement over interpretation of these results (Blackburn, 2007; Cooke, Michie, Hart, & Clark, 2004; Hare & Neumann, 2008). Although the PCL:R is reputed to be among the best currently available predictors of serious violence, some researchers have expressed reservations about it (Gendreau, Goggin, & Smith, 2002; Leistico, Salekin, DeCoster, & Rogers, 2008). A meta-analysis of 95 studies by the latter group showed significant heterogeneity in effect sizes. In the review by Yang et al. (2010), "Factor 1 of the PCL:R, which assesses the core psychopathic personality features, demonstrated practically no predictive efficacy" (p. 757). Such accuracy as it has derives from Factor 2 (criminal history and lifestyle variables). Note that PCL:R or PCL:SV scores are entered as an item in both the VRAG and the HCR-20.

History-Clinical-Risk Management-20. The *HCR-20* (Webster, Douglas, Eaves, & Hart, 1997) is so called because it requires the combination of information under 20 separate headings: 10 are *Historical*, 5 are *Clinical*, and 5 denote *Risk Management* issues. The potential added value of methods such as the *HCR-20* resides in their usefulness for specifying intervention targets with individuals, which may help to reduce the chances that antisocial behavior will recur. As seen earlier in Table 8.1, the HCR-20 emerged from the review by Farrington et al. (2008) as having the highest average AUC (0.74) of the combined actuarial-clinical or SPJ measures. However the difference was only marginal and no such advantage was found by Yang et al. (2010). The mean AUC among 16 studies found in the review by Whittington et al. (2013) was 0.68, not an especially impressive figure for such a widely used instrument that had emerged from the survey by Khiroya et al. (2009) as by far the most frequently employed risk assessment in mental health services. Given the need to keep pace with research findings, a revised version of the instrument has been developed (HCR: Version 3: Douglas, Hart, Webster, & Belfrage, 2013). Douglas (2014) discusses the adaptations made to the HCR-20 of particular relevance in assessment and management of conditional release from secure forensic services. A special issue of the *International Journal of Forensic Mental Health* (April 2014) reported initial studies of the HCR-20-V3. Subsequently Hogan and Olver (2016) found that the HCR-20-V3 clinical scale emerged well in comparison with other assessments in prediction of inpatient aggression.

Level of Service/Case Management Inventory (LS/CMI). The LS/CMI is probably more frequently utilized in criminal justice than mental health settings, but is potentially applicable in both (Andrews et al., 2004). Designed both as a risk assessment and a management and monitoring tool, the LS/CMI is classed as a fourth-generation instrument. Comparative outcomes to date, however, draw mainly on research with its predecessor, the *Level of Supervision Inventory* (LSI). This emerged very favorably from a comparative review by Campbell et al. (2009); however, Farrington et al. (2008) found lower average predictive accuracy, with a significant difference between its mean AUC and that of the best-performing static predictors. For the LS/CMI itself there are as yet only a few outcome studies reported.

Violence Risk Scale (VRS). The VRS is grounded in the *psychology of criminal conduct* (PCC) model developed by Andrews and Bonta (2010b), and is also designed for evaluation of variations in risk factors. The latter aspect applies the *stages of change* model, transposed from the field of addictions research (Prochaska, DiClemente, & Norcross, 1992). For these reasons it too can be considered a fourth-generation measure. The scale contains proportionally more items focused on dynamic risk factors than any of the preceding measures: it comprises 6 items focused on static and 20 items focused on dynamic risk variables (Wong, Olver, & Stockdale, 2009). In a 4.4-year follow-up of 918 male prisoners, the VRS yielded AUCs between 0.71 and 0.75 (Wong & Gordon, 2006). In contrast to many previous findings, predictive validity (dividing VRS scores into five-point intervals) was particularly high for the relationship between dynamic risk variables and violent recidivism, a very promising result.

Classification of Violence Risk (COVR). As described earlier the classification-based approach applies a different logic from that used in correlation and regression-based risk research. Some researchers consider that this leaves scope for great flexibility in that, potentially, many more variables can be encompassed. The *multiple models* procedure tested by Banks et al. (2004) produced an AUC of 0.88, one of the highest reported in the literature. Although the methodology does not readily lend itself to everyday use in its initial form, it has since been supported by more accessible computer software (Monahan et al., 2005, 2006). These findings are among the strongest evidence to date for the possibility of using risk assessments to predict future likelihood of violence among persons with severe mental disorders.

Actual Outcomes

Just how "risky" are those who commit serious violence; that is, what is their likelihood of reoffending following discharge from custody? Broadly speaking, the more serious the crime, the less likely it is to be repeated. Clearly, those who commit mass, serial, or spree murders (adopting a widely used typology of homicide) are customarily detained for life (or in some instances, in some locations, executed), hence there are no follow-up studies of their progress following release. The fact that these and other individuals assessed as posing the highest risk are rarely if ever released, while self-evidently desirable from a public safety perspective, has been described as a fundamental impediment for risk assessment research (Litwack, 1993).

The overwhelming majority of homicides involves a single victim only, and studies indicate that the likelihood of repeating such an act is very low. In Finland, Eronen, Hakola, and Tiihonen (1996) found a rate for homicide recidivism over 13 years of 2.2%; factors most strongly associated with its recurrence were alcohol problems and a diagnosis of personality disorder. Bjørkly and Waage (2005) reviewed the available literature on *recidivistic single-victim homicide*, finding only 11 relevant studies and only three that examined the phenomenon specifically. Prevalence rates were typically in the range 1–3.5%. Subsequently Roberts, Zgoba, and Shahidullah (2007) reported post-release data on a random sample of 336 homicide perpetrators in New Jersey; none had committed another murder, though the follow-up period was only five years. Hill, Habermann, Klusmann, Berner, & Briken (2008) have reported a 20-year follow-up of 166 sexual homicide perpetrators in Germany. During that quite lengthy period only three of this sample committed a further homicide; 23.1% committed a further sexual offense and 18.3% a non-sexual violent offense.

With respect to those who commit serious violent crimes, including homicide, and who suffer from mental disorders, there is a modest amount of research showing outcomes in the years after discharge from institutions. Buchanan (1998) described a 10.5-year community follow-up of 425 patients discharged from high-security hospitals in England. Over that period, 14% were convicted of a serious offense, 14% of a violent offense, and 7% of a sexual offense. Jamieson and Taylor (2004) analyzed outcomes for a cohort of 197 patients over a total period of 12 years. Of this group, 38% were reconvicted of at least one offense; 26% were reconvicted of a serious offense. The median time to a first serious reoffense was 2.2 years (mean = 3.2 years). In most respects, broadly consistent patterns of results have emerged from these studies. Factors associated with greater likelihood of reconviction included being younger, male, unmarried, and having a legal classification of psychopathic disorder (as defined by the Mental Health Act 1983). Where analyzed, the strongest single predictor was number of previous convictions.

The rate of violent reoffending and of reconviction of those discharged from high-security hospitals is on average lower than for those released from prison, and for discharges from medium security it is lower still. For example, Maden, Scott, Burnett, Lewis, and Skapinakis (2004) followed up 959 patients discharged from medium secure units in England and Wales between April 1997 and March 1998. Within two years the general reconviction rate was 15% and the violence reconviction rate only 6%. Again the "strongest association with offending was previous offending" (p. 1534). Davies, Clarke, Hollin, and Duggan (2007) followed up 550 first admissions to a single medium secure unit over a 20-year period. A sizeable proportion was reported to have been involved in some form of violent behavior (28% after two years, 42% after five years), and a large proportion were re-admitted to secure units at some later stage. However the number convicted of grave offenses (murder, attempted murder, robbery, rape, and arson) at two and five years respectively were: for those classified as suffering from mental illness, 5.6% and 10.5%; and for those classed as suffering from personality disorder, 9% and 13.8%. Coid et al. (2007) examined reconviction histories of 1,344 patients discharged from medium secure units over an average follow-up period of 6.2 years. The mean conviction rate across all offenses was 34.3% for men and 15.3% for women; corresponding figures for violent offenses were 18.1% and 5.1% respectively; and for grave offenses 12.2% and 6.2%. In Scotland, Ho, Thomson, and Darjee (2009) carried out a two-year follow-up of 96 patients discharged from the country's first medium secure unit (opened in 2001). Of this group only 4.2% were subsequently involved in violent incidents, with 2.1% being convicted of serious and 8.3% of minor violent offenses.

These findings could be interpreted as showing that the secure hospital system is reasonably effective; although without relevant comparative outcome data such a conclusion is somewhat speculative, and recall again that discharge is less likely the higher the assessed risk. One worrying inference is that risk levels may be consistently overestimated and that in all likelihood there are many more false positives than false negatives, that is, more people who probably do not need to be detained who are, than there are people discharged who should not be.

RISK ASSESSMENT IN PRACTICE

Advances in risk assessment methodology raise another fundamental challenge: that of transferring findings obtained from aggregate estimates and applying them to individual cases. As in all measurement, there is a problem of standard error and the use of confidence intervals. This has been a focus of some disagreement in risk assessment research. Hart, Michie, and Cooke (2007) called the entire enterprise into question in arguing that the scope for error when scores are considered at the individual level is unacceptably wide. Their arguments constitute virtually a wholesale rejection of the possibility of evidence-based prediction on a case-by-case basis. Other researchers have responded that in arriving at these conclusions Hart et al. misapplied statistical techniques: for example, the notion of confidence intervals around the score for a single individual was described as meaningless (Gendreau & Cullen, 2008; Harris et al., 2008; Mossman & Selke, 2007). However, Hart and Cooke (2013) have responded vigorously to these and other criticisms, sustaining their argument with an empirical study of 90 convicted male sexual offenders followed up over a 3.5–5.0-year period. On the basis of their analyses they concluded that "it was virtually impossible to make meaningful distinctions among subjects based on individual risk estimates made using ARAI scores" (2013, p. 93).

Nevertheless it is unquestionably vital that practitioners should exercise substantial caution when conducting risk assessments and basing conclusions or recommendations on them. In an effort to resolve the problems of translation from large-scale to individual levels of risk assessment, Conroy and Murrie (2007) have proposed a scheme comprising six elements or steps. As this framework is very broad-ranging, designed to cover diverse risk assessment contexts, the following represents an adapted version of their proposals applied to assessment of offenders with mental disorders.

- As Conroy and Murrie (2007) point out, all risk is domain specific. Therefore a first step in any assessment should be to clarify the referral question and the intended objective. Put another way, it is essential to specify what is the nature of risk to be assessed, in terms of the type of offense or harm, over what timescale, and under what conditions (e.g., transfers between different levels of security or supervision). It is important to avoid simply providing a score that implies "dangerousness" is an inherent feature of individuals; though regrettably, that is often what is done. Also, sometimes risk cannot be adequately estimated: for an individual who has been under detention for over 20 years, there is no firm evidential basis that can inform forecasts of his or her likely future behavior.
- A second step is to locate the assessment in the context of what is generally known about the problem in question (the knowledge base). That is, assessors should draw upon whatever relevant actuarial or normative data are available, as close to the defined risk area as we can obtain, and examine base rates of the target behavior for the appropriate comparison population. This might include scrutiny of official criminal statistics or other relevant data sources.
- The third step is to consider the "nomothetic" evidence concerning the target behavior. This includes identifying the general and specific risk and protective factors associated with its occurrence, then evaluating the extent to which they apply to the individual being assessed. Practitioners often regard this as the core risk assessment activity, but in Conroy and Murrie's (2007) approach it forms only part of the overall process.
- Attention next turns to the use of "idiographic" assessment information: details of the case history, and of unique factors that may influence an individual's future actions. This is a disputed point as some experts explicitly prohibit the introduction of this kind of material, on the grounds that it will reduce predictive accuracy. Others, however, regard it as fundamental, because the individual being assessed will almost certainly differ in some respects from the population on whom normative or nomothetic data are available; or because there are unusual issues applying to the case. Ideally this stage would be guided by a clinical case formulation or explanatory account of the individual's problem behavior and functioning. It should also incorporate "anamnestic" information, which refers to the study of the circumstances in which an individual's previous violence occurred and the risk factors that were operative within them.
- The purpose of risk assessment is of course to facilitate legal or clinical decision-making. Thus for its output to be used it has to be conveyed effectively to those empowered to make that decision. Research has shown that the format of

communication of risk assessments results has an influence on how information is perceived and employed. (This issue will be considered below.)

• Finally, risk assessment is nowadays conjoined to risk management, which requires identifying what services, intensity of supervision, staff qualifications and training, are needed to ensure risk factors are monitored and kept to a minimum. This should focus on both individual factors and contextual variables, entailing compilation of an inventory of the environment and the situations the person is likely to encounter, and factors operating within each of them.

Proposals for embedding risk assessment within a carefully articulated sequence of decisions have been endorsed by other clinical researchers. Monahan and his colleagues (2001) have urged that all risk assessment be carried out within an explicit, structured framework. This should be informed by the use of well-attested actuarial instruments, and Monahan et al. advocate that when this is done it should be repeated using a different approach each time (as in the multiple-models perspective). Only when there is sufficient agreement between assessments carried out in different ways can practitioners place confidence in the predictions made (Monahan et al., 2001). Bonta (2002) similarly espouses the use of multiple predictors and provides other guidelines for undertaking sound risk assessment. Farrington et al. (2008) emphasize the importance of training in use of risk assessments, and the integration of other information such as case formulations into assessment decisions. Hanson (2009) echoes such points, provides a list of features to which competent risk assessors should aspire, and summarizes examples of the sometimes striking differences in predictive accuracy when risk assessments are used by trained versus untrained, or by "conscientious" versus "non-conscientious," operators respectively.

COMMUNICATING RISK INFORMATION

As numerous authors working in this area have noted, in the typical case, risk information has to be relayed from an assessor (usually a clinical or forensic practitioner) to a legal decision-making forum (e.g., a jury, parole hearing, or mental health review tribunal). As succinctly summarized by Heilbrun, Dvoskin, Hart, and McNiel (1999, p. 94), "risk communication is the link between risk assessment and decision-making about risk." Heilbrun and his colleagues forwarded a rationale for the study of risk communication and have devoted considerable thought to dissecting the parameters of the process.

For example, it has been shown that the format used to present risk information has an impact on perceptions of risk. Predictions can be represented in terms of categories (low, medium, high), as percentages ("a 60% risk of reoffending"), or frequencies ("six out of every ten"), and these have differential effects with frequency estimates resulting in perceptions of higher risk (Slovic, Monahan, & MacGregor,

2000). In addition to the choice of metric or mode of expression of risk information, it is often considered better practice to, rather than provide summary risk-level scores, offer conditional statements regarding what would be likely to alter (increase or reduce) levels of risk under different circumstances. This can be phrased perhaps as a sequence of "if … then …" statements, for example, "the risk of assault would be higher if …; it would be lower if …," itemizing the various contingencies applying to that event involving that individual. This seems preferable on both scientific and ethical grounds to the issuing of simple prediction scores, which also transmit an impression of being immutable over time, when voluminous evidence shows that this is not the case (Heilbrun, Douglas, & Yasuhara, 2009). Securing change through effective risk management is the goal most services are seeking to pursue.

Heilbrun, O'Neill, Strohman, Bowman, and Philipson (2000) found that respondents to a specially conducted survey using hypothetical case vignettes showed a preference for receiving risk information that consisted of a list of identified risk factors coupled with strategies for the management of each one – focusing, in other words, on risk management. The least favored option was the use of percentage likelihood scores as simple predictions. In a later and larger-scale survey, Heilbrun et al. (2004) found more complex interactions between risk level, mode of presentation, and focus (prediction versus management). Conroy and Murrie (2007) summarize this literature and other studies in the area, offering valuable guidelines on the entire process of how to convey risk assessment reports.

Ethically sound risk evaluation, according to Tolman and Rotzien (2007), is not centered on the production of prediction scores with the sole or primary preoccupation being their degree of accuracy. Rather, the objective is to "provide information on risk factors, describe whether or not those factors apply in the current context, describe and elaborate the person's history of previous violent behaviors and relate those previous contexts to the person's current and reasonably estimated future situations, and suggest strategies to reduce risk" (2007, p. 76).

ETHICAL ISSUES IN RISK ASSESSMENT

As Melton et al. (2007, p. 299) have observed, "clinicians' involvement in violence prediction is extremely controversial. With years of confinement or possibly the offender's life hanging in the balance, there is no other area of the law in which expert testimony may exert so significant an impact." The advent and steadily expanding use of risk assessment raises some fundamental ethical issues and moral dilemmas for practitioners and for the agencies within which they work (McGuire, 2004).

One issue, noted earlier, that has persisted throughout the history of risk assessment research is "error through overprediction" (Pfohl, 1979, p. 57). The findings of follow-up studies, briefly reviewed above, raise a general question concerning the impact of risk assessment. It is probably the case that a large proportion of those who continue to be detained would be "false positives" if discharged. Has the net effect of disseminating risk assessment been the unnecessary restriction of liberty for a sizeable number of patients?

There are, of course, several factors to be considered when making detention and discharge decisions, risk being only one of them. But as Conroy and Murrie (2007) have commented, clinicians all too often pay insufficient attention to base rates when conducting risk assessments and making decisions. This has been ascribed to a common cognitive fallacy called *base rate neglect*, which arises in many decision-making tasks. That in turn raises human rights issues regarding the fate of persons with mental disorders who may be unnecessarily detained. In the present author's experience it remains too often true that "the team uses the materials in the past record to make theoretical inferences about the patient in the present. The appearance of the patient (through second hand reports inscribed in the record) are taken as documents of an invariant underlying pattern" (Pfohl, 1979, p. 63).

The most worrying potential outcome of erroneous predictions on the basis of risk assessment is its use in capital cases. Undoubtedly, predictions made by juries presiding in such cases have been shown to be "alarmingly poor" (Cunningham, Sorensen, & Reidy, 2009, p. 240). However whether formal procedures result in an adequate improvement is also open to question. In the state of Texas, "by far the most active death-penalty state" (Sorensen, Wrinkle, Brewer, & Marquart, 1999, p. 483), this has given rise to considerable concern. The Texas Defender Service (2004) has documented numerous instances in which assessments of "future dangerousness" (a factor in the imposition of the death penalty) turned out to be woefully inaccurate. In a study of 155 prisoners on death row, those subsequently executed (67) spent an average of 12 years in prison before the punishment was carried out. Others had their sentences commuted to life or other lower penalties, and some had even been released; the latter group spent an average of 22 years in prison. Overall, only eight (5%) of those predicted to be dangerous committed a further serious assault, defined as behavior resulting in injury that requires more than the administration of first aid. In other words, risk assessments that determined whether someone would live or die were wrong 95% of the time. Echoing the comments of Pfohl just noted, these authors also remind us of the commonly observed tendency whereby "a person's worst act tells us everything about who he is" (Texas Defender Service, 2004, p. vi). The present author's experience is that many of the standard risk assessment tools (such as the PCL:R and HCR-20) are often used in a way such that all information about an individual is filtered through the details of his or her most serious offense when making broader judgments of the individual as a whole.

Such extreme situations aside, a more pervasive problem might be that as long as predictive accuracy remains below 100% (and it seems inconceivable that things will ever be otherwise), *ipso facto* some individuals will be wrongly classified (Litwack, 1993). As Mossman and Selke (2007, p. 561) have put it, "unless we are omniscient perfection is not an option." Thus risk assessment more or less inescapably leads to some people's rights being violated. Some may retort that the safety of the community takes precedence over individual rights; but this raises some challenging questions – given that the community is after all the assembly of its individual members.

There are also arguments against the probably widespread practice in which the same clinician who is working therapeutically with an individual may also be expected to prepare risk assessment reports concerning him or her. According to Grisso and Appelbaum (1992), these two roles are incompatible and from an ethical standpoint should be regarded as mutually exclusive. Assessing someone's risk level is likely to compromise and indeed may even be fatal to the "working alliance," the therapeutic relationship between a clinician and service user. Other authors have expressed the view that subject to certain safeguards regarding the clarity of these processes, dilemmas such as these can be resolved (McGuire, 1997).

As Pfohl (1979) found when studying the decision-making procedures in clinical teams, there is still a gap between what research shows to be important and what generally happens in practice. In a study of how information was used in risk assessments by mental health teams in four different settings, Elbogen, Mercado, Scalora, and Tomkins (2002) found that clinicians did accept that risk factors from various actuarial tools were relevant for the task of risk assessment. However, they perceived other indicators not derived from the research literature, such as violent fantasies, medication non-compliance, and impulsive behavior while in care, as being "significantly more relevant" (2002, p. 43). It may be that ethical questions are raised by this regarding whether it is acceptable to adhere to fixed but unfounded and potentially erroneous ideas when more systematic evidence tells us something different from what we think we know.

Taken in combination, these and other issues have been considered by some to be a cause of major worry over the risk assessment undertaking. According to Szmukler and Rose (2013), for example, it gives rise to a range of problems including possible conflicts in the roles of practitioners (perhaps more so in mental health than criminal justice). The "base rate problem," the fact that the kinds of serious events that risk assessment is intended to prevent have a relatively low rate of occurrence, means that the drawback of less than perfect accuracy is a very grave one. Even with a respectable AUC value of 0.75 there will be a high rate of wrong predictions and consequent risk of violating some individuals' rights.

A different kind of difficulty arises from the temptation to employ risk assessment instruments outside their designated areas of applicability. It is important to ensure prediction instruments have been validated on a similar population to the one with whom they are to be used (Otto, 2000). Thus assessment tools that had been developed for use in mental health settings and validated on clinically relevant samples are not suitable for use with other groups on whom no comparable data are available, such as persons convicted of terrorist offenses, for whom other types of assessments should be devised (Devernik, Beck, Grann, Hogue, & McGuire, 2009; Pressman & Flockton, 2012).

WIDER IMPLICATIONS

It is important to understand the broader context in which risk assessment has flourished. The study of risk has a paradox at its center. In the wealthier economies of the world, historical and sociological research indicates that by all conventional indicators of well-being, the present era is one in which the majority of the population are safer and healthier than at any time in their collective history (Fogel, 2004). The major killer diseases have been kept at bay for more than a generation; child mortality is a fraction of what it was a hundred years ago; average longevity has more than doubled. In most European countries, moreover, the rate of homicide has declined steadily from the thirteenth century to the present (Eisner, 2003). Iniquitously, grotesquely, commensurate improvements have not occurred in the poorer regions of the world, where in many places, over the same period, conditions have actually worsened. Yet despite large improvements in welfare in affluent, high-technology societies, many people remain intractably worried. This state of mind is very much at odds with what is known about the actual causes of mass human insecurity (Roberts, 2008). Yet in itself it is a source of extensive discomfort and distress (Gardner, 2009). There is an accompanying unease that concerted efforts to systematize and disseminate the process of risk assessment can be seen as one element in an insidious trend toward the "medicalized" control of society (Chriss, 2013) within which risk assessment constitutes a form of implicit political action.

ACKNOWLEDGMENTS

The author wishes to thank the following for permission to reproduce materials from their publications: the Risk Management Authority, Scotland and Professor David Farrington for Table 8.1; and the International Association for Correctional and Forensic Psychology and Sage, publishers of *Criminal Justice and Behavior*, for Figure 8.1.

REFERENCES

Ægisdóttir, S., White, M.J., Spengler, P.M., Maugherman, A.S., Anderson, L.A., ... & Rush, J.D. (2006). The meta-analysis of clinical judgment project: Fifty-six years of accumulated research on clinical versus statistical prediction. *Counseling Psychologist, 34*, 341–382.

American Psychiatric Association (2013). *Diagnostic and statistical manual of mental disorders* (5th ed.) (DSM-5). Washington, DC: American Psychiatric Association.

Andrade, J.T., O'Neill, K., & Diener, R.B. (2009). Violence risk assessment and risk management: A historical overview and clinical application. In J.T. Andrade (Ed.), *Handbook of violence risk assessment and treatment: New approaches for mental health professionals* (pp. 3–39). New York: Springer.

Andrews, D.A. (1989). Recidivism is predictable and can be influenced: Using risk assessments to reduce recidivism. *Forum on Corrections Research, 1*, 11–18.

Andrews, D.A., & Bonta, J. (2010a). Rehabilitating criminal justice policy and practice. *Psychology, Public Policy, and Law, 16*, 39–55.

Andrews, D.A., & Bonta, J. (2010b). *The psychology of criminal conduct* (5th ed.). Cincinnati, OH: LexisNexis/Anderson.

Andrews, D.A., Bonta, J., & Wormith, J.S. (2004). *Level of Service/Case Management Inventory*. North Tonawanda, NY: Multi-Health Systems.

Andrews, D.A., Bonta, J., & Wormith, J.S. (2006). The recent past and near future of risk and/or need assessment. *Crime & Delinquency, 52*, 7–27.

Andrews, D.A., & Dowden, C. (2006). Risk principle of case classification in correctional treatment: A meta-analytic investigation. *International Journal of Offender Therapy and Comparative Criminology, 50*, 88–100.

Angermeyer, M.C., & Matschinger, H. (1996). The effect of violent attacks by schizophrenic persons on the attitude of the public towards the mentally ill. *Social Science and Medicine, 43*, 1721–1728.

Appelbaum, P.S., Robbins, P.C., & Monahan, J. (2000). Violence and delusions: Data from the MacArthur Violence Risk Assessment study. *American Journal of Psychiatry, 157*, 566–572.

Appleby, L., Shaw, J., Kapur, N., Windfuhr, K., Ashton, A., Swinson, N., & White, D. (2006). *Avoidable deaths: Five year report of the National Confidential Inquiry into Suicide and Homicide by People with Mental Illness*. London: Department of Health.

Banks, S., Robbins, P.C., Silver, E., Vesselinov, R., Steadman, H.J., Monahan, J., Mulvey, E.P., Appelbaum, P.S., Grisso, T., & Roth, L.H. (2004). A multiple-models approach to violence risk assessment among people with mental disorder. *Criminal Justice and Behavior, 31*, 324–340.

Bjørkly, S., & Waage, L. (2005). Killing again: A review of research on recidivistic single-victim homicide. *International Journal of Forensic Mental Health, 4*, 99–106.

Blackburn, R. (2000). Risk assessment and prediction. In J. McGuire, T. Mason, & A. O'Kane (Eds.), *Behaviour, crime and legal processes: A guidebook for practitioners* (pp. 177–204). Chichester, UK: John Wiley & Sons, Ltd.

Blackburn, R. (2007). Personality disorder and antisocial deviance: Comments on the debate on the structure of the Psychopathy Checklist-Revised. *Journal of Personality Disorders, 21*, 142–159.

Bonta, J. (1996). Risk-needs assessment and treatment. In A.T. Harland (Ed.), *Choosing correctional options that work: Defining the demand and evaluating the supply* (pp. 18–32). Thousand Oaks, CA: Sage.

Bonta, J. (2002). Offender risk assessment: Guidelines for selection and use. *Criminal Justice and Behavior, 29*, 355–379.

Bonta, J., Law, M., & Hanson, K. (1998). The prediction of criminal and violent recidivism amongst mentally disordered offenders: A meta-analysis. *Psychological Bulletin, 123*, 123–142.

Bonta, J., & Wormith, S.J. (2008). Risk and need assessment. In G. McIvor & P. Raynor (Eds.), *Developments in social work with offenders* (pp. 131–152). London: Jessica Kingsley Publishers.

Buchanan, A. (1998). Criminal conviction after discharge from special (high security) hospital: Incidence in the first 10 years. *British Journal of Psychiatry, 172*, 472–476.

Campbell, M.A., French, S., & Gendreau, P. (2009). The prediction of violence in adult offenders: A meta-analytic comparison of instruments and methods of assessment. *Criminal Justice and Behavior, 36,* 567–590.

Chriss, J.J. (2013). *Social control: An introduction* (2nd ed.). Cambridge: Polity Press.

Clark, L.A., Watson, D., & Reynolds, S. (1995). Diagnosis and classification of psychopathology: Challenges to the current system and future directions. *Annual Review of Psychology, 46,* 121–153.

Coid, J., Hickey, N., Kahtan, N., Zhang, T., & Yang, M. (2007). Patients discharged from medium secure forensic psychiatry services: Reconvictions and risk factors. *British Journal of Psychiatry, 190,* 223–229.

Conroy, M.A., & Murrie, D.C. (2007). *Forensic assessment of violence risk: A guide for risk assessment and risk management.* Hoboken, NJ: John Wiley & Sons, Inc.

Cooke, D.J., Michie, C., Hart, S.D., & Clark, D. (2004). Reconstructing psychopathy: Clarifying the significance of antisocial and socially deviant behavior in the diagnosis of psychopathic personality disorder. *Journal of Personality Disorders, 18,* 337–357.

Copas, J., & Marshall, P. (1998). The offender group reconviction scale: A statistical reconviction score for use by probation officers. *Applied Statistics, 47,* 159–171.

Cunningham, M.D., Sorensen, J.R., & Reidy, T.J. (2009). Capital jury decision-making: The limitations of predictions of future violence. *Psychology, Public Policy, and Law, 15,* 223–256.

Davies, S., Clarke, M., Hollin, C., & Duggan, C. (2007). Long-term outcomes after discharge from medium-secure care: A cause for concern. *British Journal of Psychiatry, 191,* 70–74.

Devernik, M., Beck, A., Grann, M., Hogue, T., & McGuire, J. (2009). The use of psychiatric and psychological evidence in the assessment of terrorist offenders. *Journal of Forensic Psychiatry and Psychology, 20,* 508–515.

Douglas, K.S. (2014). Version 3 of the Historical-Clinical-Risk Management-20 (HCR-20^{V3}): Relevance to violence risk assessment and management in forensic conditional release. *Behavioral Sciences and the Law, 32,* 557–576.

Douglas, K.S., Guy, L.S., & Hart, S.D. (2009). Psychosis as a risk factor for violence to others: A meta-analysis. *Psychological Bulletin, 135,* 679–706.

Douglas, K.S., Hart, S.D., Webster, C.D., & Belfrage, H. (2013). *HCR-20 version 3 – Assessing Risk For Violence.* Ann Arbor, MI: Ann Arbor Publishers.

Eisner, M. (2003). Long-term historical trends in violent crime. *Crime and Justice, 30,* 83–142.

Elbogen, E.B., & Johnson, S.C. (2009). The intricate link between violence and mental disorder: Results from the National Epidemiologic Survey on alcohol and related conditions. *Archives of General Psychiatry, 66,* 152–161.

Elbogen, E.B., Mercado, C.C., Scalora, M.J., & Tomkins, A.J. (2002). Perceived relevance of factors for violence risk assessment: A survey of clinicians. *International Journal of Forensic Mental Health, 1,* 37–47.

Eronen, M., Hakola, P., & Tiihonen, J. (1996). Factors associated with homicide recidivism in a 13-year sample of homicide offenders in Finland. *Psychiatric Services, 47,* 403–406.

Farrington, D.P., Jolliffe, D., & Johnstone, L. (2008). *Assessing violence risk: A framework for practice*. Paisley, UK: Risk Management Authority.

Fazel, S., Gulati, G., Linsell, L., Geddes, J.R., & Grann, M. (2009). Schizophrenia and violence: Systematic review and meta-analysis. *PLoS Medicine, 6* (8), e100012. doi: 10.1371/journal.pmed.1000120

Fazel, S., Långström, N., Hjern, A., Grann M., & Lichtenstein, P. (2009). Schizophrenia, substance abuse, and violent crime. *Journal of the American Medical Association, 301*, 2016–2023.

Fazel, S., & Seewald, K. (2012). Severe mental illness in 33 588 prisoners worldwide: Systematic review and meta-regression analysis. *British Journal of Psychiatry, 200*, 364–373.

Fazel, S., Singh, J.P., Doll, H., & Grann. M. (2012). Use of risk assessment instruments to predict violence and antisocial behaviour in 73 samples involving 24 827 people: Systematic review and meta-analysis. *British Medical Journal, 345*, e4692. doi:10.1136/bmj.e4692

Fogel, M.H. (2009). Violence risk assessment evaluation: Practices and procedures. In J.C. Andrade (Ed.), *Handbook of violence risk assessment and treatment: New approaches for mental health professionals* (pp. 41–81). New York: Springer.

Fogel, R.W. (2004). *The escape from hunger and premature death 1700–2100: Europe, America and the Third World*. Cambridge: Cambridge University Press.

Gardner, D. (2009). *Risk: The science and politics of fear*. London: Virgin Publishing.

Gardner, D., Lidz, C.W., Mulvey, E.P., & Shaw, E.C. (1996). A comparison of actuarial methods for identifying repetitively violent patients with mental illnesses. *Law and Human Behaviour, 20*, 35–48.

Gendreau, P., & Cullen, F. (2008). Martinson redux. *Crime Scene: The Official Organ of Criminal Justice Psychology of the Canadian Psychological Association, 15*, 13–15.

Gendreau, P., Goggin, C., & Smith, P. (2002). Is the PCL-R really the "unparalleled" measure of offender risk? A lesson in knowledge cumulation. *Criminal Justice and Behavior, 29*, 397–426.

Gray, N.S., Snowden, R.J., MacCulloch, S., Phillips, H., Taylor, J., & MacCulloch, M.J. (2004). Relative efficacy of criminological, clinical and personality measures of future risk of offending in mentally disordered offenders: A comparative study of HCR-20, PCL:SV and OGRS. *Journal of Consulting and Clinical Psychology, 72*, 523–530.

Grisso, T., & Appelbaum, P.S. (1992). Is it unethical to offer predictions of future violence? *Law and Human Behavior, 16*, 621–633.

Grove, W.M., & Meehl, P.E. (1996). Comparative efficiency of informal (subjective, impressionistic) and formal (mechanical, algorithmic) prediction procedures. *Psychology, Public Policy and Law, 2*, 293–323.

Grove, W.M., Zald, D.H., Lebow, B.S., Snitz, B.E., & Nelson, C. (2000). Clinical versus mechanical prediction: A meta-analysis. *Psychological Assessment, 12*, 19–30.

Guy, L.S., Packer, I.K., & Warnken, W. (2012). Assessing risk of violence using structured professional judgment guidelines. *Journal of Forensic Psychology Practice, 12*, 270–283.

Hanson, R.K. (2009). The psychological assessment of risk for crime and violence. *Canadian Psychology, 50*, 172–182.

Hare, R.D. (1999). Psychopathy as a risk factor for violence. *Psychiatric Quarterly, 70*, 181–197.

Hare, R.D. (2003). *Hare Psychopathy Check List: Revised* (2nd ed.). North Tonawanda, NY: Multi-Health Systems.

Hare, R.D., & Neumann, C.S. (2008). Psychopathy as a clinical and empirical construct. *Annual Review of Clinical Psychology, 4*, 217–246.

Harris, G.T., Rice, M.E., & Cormier, C.A. (2002). Prospective replication of the Violence Risk Appraisal Guide in predicting violent recidivism among forensic patients. *Law and Human Behavior, 26*, 377–394.

Harris, G.T., Rice, M.E., & Quinsey, V.L. (2008). Shall evidence-based risk assessment be abandoned? *British Journal of Psychiatry, 192*, 154.

Hart, S.D., & Cooke, D.J. (2013). Another look at the (im-)precision of individual risk estimates made using actuarial risk assessment instruments. *Behavioral Sciences and the Law, 31*, 81–102.

Hart, S.D., Michie, C., & Cooke, D.J. (2007). Precision of actuarial risk assessment instruments: Evaluating the "margins of error" of group v. individual predictions of violence. *British Journal of Psychiatry, 190*, 60–65.

Heilbrun, K. (2003). Violence risk: From prediction to management. In D. Carson & R. Bull (Eds.), *Handbook of psychology in legal contexts* (2nd ed., pp. 127–142). Chichester, UK: John Wiley & Sons, Ltd.

Heilbrun, K., Douglas, K.S., & Yasuhara, K. (2009). Violence risk assessment: Core controversies. In J.L. Skeem, K.S. Douglas, & S.O. Lilienfeld (Eds.), *Psychological science in the courtroom: Consensus and controversy* (pp. 333–357). New York: Guilford Press.

Heilbrun, K., Dvoskin, J., Hart, S., & McNiel, D. (1999). Violence risk communication: Implications for research, policy and practice. *Health, Risk & Society, 1*, 91–105.

Heilbrun, K., O'Neill, M.L., Stevens, T.N., Strohman, L.K., Bowman, Q., & Lo, Y.-W. (2004). Assessing normative approaches to communicating violence risk: A national survey of psychologists. *Behavioral Sciences and the Law, 22*, 187–196.

Heilbrun, K., O'Neill, M.L., Strohman, L.K., Bowman, Q., & Philipson, J. (2000). Expert approaches to communicating violence risk. *Law and Human Behavior, 24*, 137–148.

Hill, A., Habermann, N., Klusmann, D., Berner, W., & Briken, P. (2008). Criminal recidivism in sexual homicide perpetrators. *International Journal of Offender Therapy and Comparative Criminology, 52*, 5–20.

Ho, H., Thomson, L., & Darjee, R. (2009). Violence risk assessment: The use of the PCL-SV, HCR-20 and VRAG to predict violence in mentally disordered offenders discharged from a medium secure unit in Scotland. *Journal of Forensic Psychiatry and Psychology, 20*, 523–541.

Hodgins, S. (2009). Violent behaviour among people with schizophrenia: A framework for investigations of causes, effective treatment, and prevention. In S. Hodgins, E. Viding, & A. Plodowski (Eds.), *The neurobiological basis of violence: Science and rehabilitation* (pp. 43–64). Oxford: Oxford University Press.

Hogan, N.R., & Olver, M.E. (2016). Assessing risk for aggression in forensic psychiatric inpatients: An examination of five measures. *Law and Human Behavior, 40*, 233–243.

Hollin, C.R. (2002). Risk-needs assessment and allocation to offender programmes. In J. McGuire (Ed.), *Offender rehabilitation and treatment: Effective programmes and policies to reduce re-offending* (pp. 309–332). Chichester, UK: John Wiley & Sons, Ltd.

Howard, P., Francis, B., Soothill, K., & Humphreys, I. (2009). *OGRS 3: The revised Offender Group Reconviction Scale*. London: Ministry of Justice. Available from: https://core. ac.uk/download/files/59/1556521.pdf (last retrieved July 16, 2016).

Jamieson, L., & Taylor, P.J. (2004). A reconviction study of special (high security) hospital patients. *British Journal of Criminology, 44*, 783–802.

Khiroya, R., Weaver, T., & Maden, T. (2009). Use and perceived utility of structured violence risk assessments in English medium secure forensic units. *Psychiatric Bulletin, 33*, 129–132.

Kröner, C., Stadtland, C., Eidt, M., & Nedopil, N. (2007). The validity of the Violence Risk Appraisal Guide (VRAG) in predicting criminal recidivism. *Criminal Behaviour and Mental Health, 17*, 89–100.

Kroner, D.G., Mills, J.F., & Reddon, J.R. (2005). A coffee can, factor analysis, and prediction of antisocial behavior: The structure of criminal risk. *International Journal of Law and Psychiatry, 28*, 360–374.

Large, M., Smith, G., & Nielssen, O. (2009). The relationship between the rate of homicide by those with schizophrenia and the overall crime rate: A systematic review and meta-analysis. *Schizophrenia Research, 112*, 123–129.

Large, M., Smith, G., Swinson, N., Shaw, J., & Nielssen, O. (2009). Homicide due to mental disorder in England and Wales over 50 years. *British Journal of Psychiatry, 193*, 130–133.

Leistico, A.R., Salekin, R.T., DeCoster, J., & Rogers, R. (2008). A large-scale meta-analysis relating the Hare measures of psychopathy to antisocial conduct. *Law and Human Behaviour, 32*, 28–45.

Link, B., Phelan, J.C., Bresnahan, M., Stueve, A., & Pescosolido, B.A. (1999). Public conceptions of mental illness: Labels, causes, dangerousness, and social distance. *American Journal of Public Health, 89*, 1328–1333.

Link, B., & Stueve, A. (1994). Psychotic symptoms and the violent/illegal behavior of mental patients compared to community controls. In J. Monahan & H.J. Steadman (Eds.), *Violence and mental disorder: Developments in risk assessment* (pp. 137–159). Chicago, IL: University of Chicago Press.

Litwack, T.R. (1993). On the ethics of dangerousness assessments. *Law and Human Behavior, 17*, 479–482.

Lowenkamp, C.T., Latessa, E.J., & Holsinger, A.M. (2006). The risk principle in action: What have we learned from 13,676 offenders and 97 correctional programs? *Crime & Delinquency, 52*, 77–93.

Loza, W. (2003). Predicting violent and nonviolent recidivism of incarcerated male offenders. *Aggression and Violent Behaviour, 8*, 175–203.

Maden, A. (2007). *Treating violence: A guide to risk management in mental health*. Oxford: Oxford University Press.

Maden, A., Scott, F., Burnett, R., Lewis, G.H., & Skapinakis, P. (2004). Offending in psychiatric patients after discharge from medium secure units: Prospective national cohort study. *British Medical Journal, 328*, 1534.

McGuire, J. (1997). Ethical dilemmas in forensic clinical psychology. *Legal and Criminological Psychology*, *2*, 177–192.

McGuire, J. (2004). Minimising harm in violence risk assessments: Practical solutions to ethical problems? *Health, Risk and Society*, *6*, 327–345.

McGuire, J. (2008). A review of effective interventions for reducing aggression and violence. *Philosophical Transactions of the Royal Society B*, *363*, 2577–2597.

McGuire, J. (2013). "What Works" to reduce reoffending: 18 years on. In L. Craig, J. Dixon, & T.A. Gannon (Eds.), *What Works in offender rehabilitation: An evidence based approach to assessment and treatment* (pp. 20–49). Oxford: Wiley-Blackwell.

McNiel, D.E. (1994). Hallucinations and violence. In J. Monahan & H.J. Steadman (Eds.), *Violence and mental disorder: Developments in risk assessment* (pp. 183–202). Chicago, IL: University of Chicago Press.

Medical News Today (2009). Rise in homicide by mentally ill in England and Wales. Available from: www.medicalnewstoday.com/articles/159123.php (last retrieved July 16, 2016).

Meehl, P.E. (1954). *Clinical and statistical prediction*. Minneapolis, MN: University of Minnesota Press.

Mehta, N., Kassam, A., Leese, M., Butler, G., & Thornicroft, G. (2009). Public attitudes towards people with mental illness in England and Scotland, 1994–2003. *British Journal of Psychiatry*, *194*, 278–284.

Melton, G.B., Petrila, J., Poythress, N.G., & Slobogin, C. (2007). *Psychological evaluations for the courts: A handbook for mental health professionals and lawyers* (3rd ed.). New York: Guilford Press.

Monahan, J. (1981). *The clinical prediction of violent behavior*. Washington, DC: Government Printing Office.

Monahan, J. (1984). The prediction of violent behaviour: Towards a second generation of theory and policy. *American Journal of Psychiatry*, *141*, 10–15.

Monahan, J., Steadman, H.J., Appelbaum, P.S., Grisso, T., Mulvey, E.P., Roth, L.H., … & Silver, E. (2006). The classification of violence risk. *Behavioral Sciences and the Law*, *24*, 721–730.

Monahan, J., Steadman, H.J., Robbins, P.C., Appelbaum, P.S., Banks, S., Grisso, T., … & Silver, E. (2005). An actuarial model of violence risk assessment for persons with mental disorders. *Psychiatric Services*, *56*, 810–815.

Monahan, J., Steadman, H.J., Silver, E., Appelbaum, P.S., Robbins, P.C., Mulvey, E.P., … & Banks, S. (2001). *Rethinking risk assessment: The MacArthur study of mental disorder and violence*. New York: Oxford University Press.

Mossman, D. (1994). Assessing predictions of violence: Being accurate about accuracy. *Journal of Consulting and Clinical Psychology*, *62*, 783–792.

Mossman, D. (2013). Evaluating risk assessments using receiver operating characteristics analysis: Rationale, advantages, insights, and limitations. *Behavioral Sciences and the Law*, *31*, 23–39.

Mossman, D., & Selke, T. (2007). Avoiding errors about "margins of error". *British Journal of Psychiatry*, *191*, 561.

National Confidential Inquiry into Suicide and Homicide by People with Mental Illness (2009). *Annual report: England and Wales*. London: Department of Health.

Nicholls, T.L., Pritchard, M.M., Reeves, K.A., & Hilterman, E. (2013). Risk assessment in intimate partner violence: A systematic review of contemporary approaches. *Partner Abuse*, *4*, 76–168.

Olweus, D. (1988). Environmental and biological factors in the development of aggressive behaviour. In W. Buikhuisen & S.A. Mednick (Eds.), *Explaining criminal behaviour* (pp. 90–120). Leiden: E.J. Brill.

Otto, R.K. (2000). Assessing and managing violence risk in outpatient settings. *Journal of Clinical Psychology*, *56*, 1239–1262.

Pfohl, S.J. (1979). From whom will we be protected? Comparative approaches to the assessment of dangerousness. *International Journal of Law and Psychiatry*, *2*, 55–78.

Phelan, J.C., Link, B.G., Stueve, A., & Pescosolido, B.A. (2000). Public conceptions of mental illness in 1950 and 1996: What is mental illness and is it to be feared? *Journal of Health and Social Behavior*, *41*, 188–207.

Phillips, H.K., Gray, N.S., MacCulloch, S.I., Taylor, J., Moore, S.C., Huckle, P., & MacCulloch, M.J. (2005). Risk assessment in offenders with mental disorders: Relative efficacy of personal demographic, criminal history, and clinical variables. *Journal of Interpersonal Violence*, *20*, 833–847.

Pressman, D.E., & Flockton, J. (2012). Calibrating risk for violent political extremists and terrorists: The VERA 2 structured assessment. *British Journal of Forensic Practice*, *14*, 237–251.

Prochaska, J., DiClemente, C., & Norcross, J. (1992). In search of how people change: Applications to addictive behaviors. *American Psychologist*, *47*, 1102–1114.

Quinsey, V.L., Harris, G.T., Rice, M.E., & Cormier, C.A. (2005). *Violent offenders: Appraising and managing risk* (2nd ed.), Washington, DC: American Psychological Association.

Roberts, A.R., Zgoba, K.M., & Shahidullah, S.M. (2007). Recidivism among four types of homicide offenders: An exploratory analysis of 336 homicide offenders in New Jersey. *Aggression and Violent Behavior*, *12*, 493–507.

Roberts, D. (2008). *Human insecurity: Global structures of violence*. London: Zed Books.

Rossegger, A., Gerth, J., Seewald, K., Urbaniok, F., Singh, J.P., & Endrass, J. (2013). Current obstacles in replicating risk assessment findings: A systematic review of commonly used actuarial instruments. *Behavioral Sciences and the Law*, *31*, 154–164.

Sartorius, N., & Schulze, H. (2005). *Reducing the stigma of mental illness: A report from a global association*. Cambridge: Cambridge University Press.

Sawyer, J. (1966). Measurement and prediction, clinical and statistical. *Psychological Bulletin*, *66*, 178–299.

Silver, E. (2006). Understanding the relationship between mental disorder and violence: The need for a criminological perspective. *Law and Human Behavior*, *30*, 685–706.

Silver, E., Mulvey, E.P., & Monahan, J. (1999). Assessing violence risk among discharged psychiatric patients. *Law and Human Behaviour*, *23*, 235–253.

Singh, J.P. (2013). Predictive validity performance indicators in violence risk assessment: A methodological primer. *Behavioral Sciences and the Law*, *31*, 8–22.

Singh, J.P., Desmarais, S.L., & Van Dorn, R.A. (2013). Measurement of predictive validity in violence risk assessment studies: A second-order systematic review. *Behavioral Sciences and the Law*, *31*, 55–73.

Singh, J.P., & Fazel, S. (2010). Forensic risk assessment. *Criminal Justice and Behavior*, *37*, 965–988.

Singh, J.P., Grann, M., & Fazel, S. (2011). A comparative study of violence risk assessment tools: A systematic review and meta-regression analysis of 68 studies involving 25,980 participants. *Clinical Psychology Review*, *31*, 499–513.

Sirdifield, C., Gojkovic, D., Brooker, C., & Ferriter, M. (2009). A systematic review of research on the epidemiology of mental health disorders in prison populations: A summary of findings. *Journal of Forensic Psychiatry and Psychology*, *20*, S78–S101.

Slovic, P., Monahan, J., & MacGregor, D.G. (2000). Violence risk assessment and risk communication: The effects of using actual cases, providing instruction, and employing probability versus frequency formats. *Law and Human Behavior*, *24*, 271–296.

Sorensen, J., Wrinkle, R., Brewer, V., & Marquart, J. (1999). Capital punishment and deterrence: Examining the effect of executions on rates of murder in Texas. *Crime and Delinquency*, *45*, 481–493.

Steadman, H.J., Mulvey, E.P., Monahan, J., Robbins, P.C., Appelbaum, P.S., Grisso, T., Roth, L.H., & Silver, E. (1998). Violence by people discharged from acute psychiatric inpatient facilities and by others in the same neighborhoods. *Archives of General Psychiatry*, *55*, 393–401.

Steadman, H.J., Osher, F.C., Robbins, P.C., Case, B., & Samuels, S. (2009). Prevalence of serious mental illness among jail inmates. *Psychiatric Services*, *60*, 761–765.

Szmukler, G., & Rose, N. (2013). Risk assessment in mental health care: Values and costs. *Behavioral Sciences and the Law*, *31*, 125–140.

Texas Defender Service (2004). *Deadly speculation: Misleading Texas capital juries with false predictions of future dangerousness*. Houston and Austin, TX: Texas Defender Service.

Tolman, A.O., & Rotzien, A.L. (2007). Conducting risk evaluations for future violence: Ethical practice is possible. *Professional Psychology: Research and Practice*, *38*, 71–79.

Tully, R.J., Chou, S., & Browne, K.D. (2013). A systematic review on the effectiveness of sex offender risk assessment tools in predicting sexual recidivism of adult male sex offenders. *Clinical Psychology Review*, *33*, 287–316.

Wallace, C., Mullen, P.E., & Burgess, P. (2004). Criminal offending in schizophrenia over a 25-year period marked by deinstitutionalization and increasing prevalence of comorbid substance use disorders. *American Journal of Psychiatry*, *161*, 716–727.

Webster, C.D., Douglas, K.S., Eaves, D., & Hart, S.D. (1997). *HCR-20: Assessing Risk for Violence, Version 2*. Burnaby, BC: Mental Health, Law and Policy Institute, Simon Fraser University.

Webster, C.D., & Hucker, S.J. (2007). *Violence risk: Assessment and management*. Chichester, UK: John Wiley & Sons, Ltd.

Whittington, R., Hockenhull, J.C., McGuire, J., Leitner, M., Barr, W., Cherry, M.G., ... & Dickson, R. (2013). A systematic review of risk assessment strategies for populations at high risk of engaging in violent behaviour: Update 2002-8. *Health Technology Assessment*, *17* (50), 1–128.

Wong, S.C.P., & Gordon, A. (2006). The validity and reliability of the Violence Risk Scale: A treatment-friendly violence risk assessment tool. *Psychology, Public Policy, and Law*, *12*, 279–309.

Wong, S.C.P., Gordon, A., & Gu, D. (2007). Assessment and treatment of violence-prone forensic clients: An integrated approach. *British Journal of Psychiatry*, *190*, S66–S74.

Wong, S.C.P., Olver, M.E., & Stockdale, K.C. (2009). The utility of dynamic and static factors in risk assessment, prediction, and treatment. In J.C. Andrade (Ed.), *Handbook of violence risk assessment and treatment: New approaches for mental health professionals* (pp. 83–118). New York: Springer.

World Health Organization (1992). *The international classification of mental and behavioural disorders* (10th ed.) (ICD-10). Geneva: World Health Organization.

World Health Organization (2001). *The World Health Report 2001. Mental health: New understanding, new hope*. Geneva: World Health Organization.

Yang, M., Wong, S.C.P., & Coid, J. (2010). The efficacy of violence prediction: A meta-analytic comparison of nine risk assessment tools. *Psychological Bulletin*, *136*, 740–767.

Zumkley, H. (1994). The stability of aggressive behavior: A meta-analysis. *German Journal of Psychology*, *18*, 273–281.

9

Assessing Mental Capacity and Fitness to Plead in Offenders with Intellectual Disabilities: Implications for Practice

LEAM A. CRAIG, IAN STRINGER AND ROGER B. HUTCHINSON

INTRODUCTION

This chapter considers the newly revised diagnostic criteria for intellectual developmental disorder (IDD) and the assessment process when determining whether a defendant with an IDD can demonstrate "capacity" to make decisions within the legal framework.

PREVALENCE OF OFFENDERS WITH INTELLECTUAL DISABILITIES

Before considering diagnostic criteria of intellectual disability, it is important to first consider the prevalence of individuals with intellectual disabilities within criminal justice settings. It is estimated that having a learning or intellectual disability is common, affecting 1% of the general population in the Western world (American Psychiatric Association: DSM-IV-TR, 2000; DSM-V, 2013). The presence of an intellectual disability usually leads to major functional impairment and lifelong

Assessments in Forensic Practice: A Handbook, First Edition. Edited by Kevin D. Browne,
Anthony R. Beech, Leam A. Craig, and Shihning Chou.
© 2017 John Wiley & Sons Ltd. Published 2017 by John Wiley & Sons Ltd.

need for support and interventions, not the least important of which are medical and health-care services (Gillberg & Soderstrom, 2003).

However, following the introduction of community care policies there has been a decrease in the provisions of custodial care for people with intellectual disabilities (Lindsay et al., 2002). There are more people with intellectual disabilities who have forensic problems living in the community and fewer individuals placed in large locked/secure institutions. Previously offenders with intellectual disabilities might have been diverted from criminal justice settings into mental health systems. However, it is apparent that more offenders with intellectual disabilities are being dealt with by the criminal justice system (Lindsay et al., 2002; Lindsay, Steptoe, Wallace, Haut, & Brewster, 2013). In his report, *The Incidence of Hidden Disabilities in the Prison Population*, Rack (2005) suggests that 20% of the prison population has some form of hidden disability. Murphy, Harnett, and Holland (1995) surveyed a sample of 157 men remanded in prison. Of those interviewed, 21% stated that they had an intellectual disability, reading problems, or had attended a special needs school. Similarly, Winter, Holland, and Collins (1997) surveyed people arrested who self-reported having difficulty reading or a history of attending special needs schools. Of the 212 offenders screened, 22% admitted having difficulty in reading.

Average estimates of prevalence of intellectual disability among offenders in the United Kingdom range from 1 to 10% (Loucks, 2007) with an estimated 25% falling within the borderline intellectual disabled range (IQ 70–79) (Mottram & Lancaster, 2006). On the other hand, Holland and Persson (2011) studied the prison population in Victoria, Australia and found a prevalence rate of around 1%, which is consistent with the prevalence of people with an intellectual disability in the general population. Holland and Persson compared a sample of 102 offenders with intellectual disabilities released from custody with 244 non-intellectually disabled prisoners released over the same period. They found that while prisoners with an intellectual disability are not over-represented among the Victorian prison population they do differ from non-intellectually disabled prisoners in a number of important ways. Prisoners with an intellectual disability were characterized by significant prior involvement with the criminal justice system, were at high risk of reoffending, and had difficulties moving to minimum security while in prison and in obtaining parole. These findings indicate that prisoners with an intellectual disability are a group with complex histories and needs, who present considerable challenges to the correctional system and the broader forensic disability and disability service systems in their management and rehabilitation.

Historically, the English legal system has recognized the relationship between intellectual status and criminal responsibility (Baroff, Gunn, & Hayes, 2004). In a study of defendants with intellectual disabilities, 90% of those with "mild retardation" (intellectual quotient – IQ scores between 55 and 69) were considered criminally responsible compared with two-thirds of defendants with "moderate retardation" (IQ score between 40 and 54) (Petrella, 1992).

Provisions within mental health laws are made regarding levels of responsibility for defendants with intellectual disabilities (for a review see Baroff, Gunn, & Hayes, 2004). While Acts such as the Police and Criminal Evidence (PACE) Act 1984 and the Criminal Procedure Act 1991 offer guidance when interviewing suspects with intellectual disabilities, the Mental Capacity Act (MCA) 2005 and the associated Codes of Practice make provisions for people who may lack capacity to make decisions about their welfare. The MCA offers guidance in circumstances where capacity can be enhanced, and, thus, individuals with intellectual disabilities who may previously been found unfit to plead may now be fit to stand trial.

Rather than discussing the various defenses relating to "diminished culpability" for defendants with intellectual disabilities, this review is more concerned with the assessment of mental capacity (decision-making) and fitness to plead and stand trial. In this chapter we summarize the diagnostic criteria when assessing offenders with intellectual disabilities and discuss the implications of fitness to plead and the application of the mental capacity legislation.

DIAGNOSTIC CRITERIA

A problem encountered in researching the topic of individuals with an intellectual disability is the range and interchange of terms used to describe individuals or groups of individuals with intellectual disabilities. Some authors use the term "learning disability," while others use "learning impairment," "learning disorders," "learning difficulties," "intellectual disabilities," and "developmentally delayed." This confuses and blurs the applicability of the research findings as sample sources vary, even though the aim is to encapsulate the same group.

Further, the diagnosis of an intellectual disability is not solely related to low intellect. It is a mistake to overemphasize the role of intelligence quotients (IQ)[1] as an indicator of appropriate treatment strategies, since IQ alone does not adequately describe a person's ability (Coleman & Haaven, 2001). Indeed, the British Psychological Society recommends that a classification of intellectual disability should only be made on the basis of assessed impairments of both intellectual functioning and adaptive/social functioning, which have been acquired before adulthood. Joyce et al. (2015) Guidance on the Assessment and Diagnosis of Intellectual Disabilities in Adulthood document outlines the features that make up the definition of "intellectual disability" and is consistent with that of the American Psychiatric Association (*Diagnostic and Statistical Manual of Mental Disorders: Text Revised;* DSM-IV-TR, 2000) and the Royal College of Psychiatrists (*Diagnostic Criteria for Psychiatric Disorders for Use with Adults with Intellectual Disabilities/Mental*

Retardation, DC-LD, 2001). They identify three core criteria for intellectual disability, all of which must be present for a person to be considered to have an intellectual disability:

1. Significant impairment of intellectual functioning (IQ <69).
2. Significant impairment of adaptive and social functioning (i.e., the person's effectiveness in meeting the standards expected of his/her age and cultural group in at least two of the following: communication, self-care, home living, social/ interpersonal skills, use of community resources, self-direction, functional academic skills, work, health and safety).
3. The onset before age 18 years.

Significant impairment of adaptive and social functioning is defined as "the individual requires significant assistance to provide for his/her own survival (eating and drinking needs, and to keep him/herself clean, warm and clothed), and/or with his/her social/ community adaptation (e.g. social problem solving and social reasoning)" (p. 6).

The Department of Health (2001) notes that this encompasses a large range of disabilities, with a basic categorization into four groups, based on IQ scores, which is the method most studies utilize: 50–70 – mild; 35–50 – moderate; 20–35 – severe; < 20 – profound. The DSM-IV-TR defines the degree of disability as "mild mental retardation" IQ range 50–55 – 70, "moderate retardation" IQ range 35–40 to 50–55, and "severe retardation" IQ range 20–25 to 35–40. The DC-LD defines the degree of disability as "mild intellectual disability" IQ range 50–69, mental age 9 to under 12 years; "moderate intellectual disability" IQ range 35–49, mental age 6 to under 9 years; "severe intellectual disability" IQ range 20–34, mental age 3 to under 6 years; and "profound intellectual disability" IQ range <20, mental age <3 years. Importantly, the IQ range "70–79" is often referred to as "borderline intellectual disability"; however, this term is not referred to in either the DSM-IV-TR or the DC-LD criteria.

The DC-LD criteria recommend that the diagnosis of a intellectual disability should be made in a hierarchical manner using the multiaxial system involving an assessment on several axes, each of which refers to a different domain of information that may help the clinician plan treatment and predict outcome. The following hierarchical system is suggested:

- Axis I – Refers to severity of intellectual disability.
- Axis II – Refers to the cause of intellectual disability.
- Axis III – Refers to psychiatric disorders.
- DC-LD Level A – Developmental disorders (includes autistic spectrum disorders, etc.).
- DC-LD Level B – Psychiatric illness (dementia – Alzheimer's and Huntington's disease, schizophrenia, delusional disorders, anxiety, and mood-related disorders, etc.).

- DC-LD Level C – Personality disorders.
- DC-LD Level D – Problem behaviors (aggressive behavior, self injury, sexually inappropriate behavior, etc.).
- DC-LD Level E – Other disorders (disorders related to drug/alcohol abuse, gender identity, and disorders of sexual preference such as paraphilias including fetishism, pedophilia, exhibitionism, sadomasochism behaviors, and psychosexual developmental disorders).

From the DC-LD criteria, developmental disorders have been listed as a separate level in view of the recognition that the developmental disorder may not be the underlying cause of a person's intellectual disabilities (Axis II). For example, pervasive developmental disorders may coexist with syndromes such as Fragile X syndrome and Down's syndrome, and are not invariably associated with intellectual disabilities (p. 13). The criterion distinguishes developmental disorders from psychiatric illness, although people with developmental disorders can develop co-morbid Axis II Levels B–D disorders. This can include brain damage, autism, intellectual disability, or all three. Therefore, if a person presents with a intellectual disability this is the primary Axis I disorder and any other disorders should be diagnosed taking account of both Axis I and Axis II disorders.

Unlike the DC-LD criteria, DSM-IV-TR (2000) "mental retardation" is coded as an Axis II disorder, whereas in United Kingdom it is considered an Axis I disorder. In the United Kingdom it is seen as the primary disorder and as such people with a severe intellectual disability who have in the past committed serious crimes have been contained within the health-care system. As previously highlighted, an individual with a severe intellectual disability in the United Kingdom could be diagnosed with a mild, moderate, or severe mental retardation in North America. In 1989 the US Supreme Court ruled that people with mental retardation could be executed as mental retardation could only be considered as one of a number of mitigating circumstances. In June 2002, the US Supreme Court decided that the execution of people with mental retardation was un-constitutional as execution was a "cruel and unusual punishment" and therefore was prohibited under the Eighth Amendment (Ellis, 2004). In the United States, individuals with severe mental retardation can still be considered to be criminally responsible and hence be prosecuted for criminal behavior. If found guilty of murder, they can no longer be executed, but can receive a sentence of life imprisonment.

With the introduction of DSM-V, the diagnosis of intellectual disability (intellectual developmental disorder: IDD) is revised from the DSM-IV diagnosis of mental retardation. As already mentioned, using DSM-IV, mental retardation was on Axis II to ensure that clinicians identified associated impairments alongside other mental disorders. However, under DSM-V, IDD is not a multiaxial classification as was DSM-IV-TR, and will no longer be on Axis II but instead listed along with other mental disorder diagnoses under Axis I. The change in terminology is designed to reflect deficits in cognitive capacity beginning in the developmental period. Together, these revisions bring DSM-V into alignment with terminology used by the World Health Organization's (WHO's) International Classification of Diseases (ICD-10, updated 2016, and ICD-11 scheduled for release in 2018). The diagnosis in DSM-V emphasizes both clinical judgment and standardized intelligence testing; however, with less emphasis on the IQ score (IQ below 70), but greater emphasis on the adaptive reasoning in academic, social, and practical settings. IQ testing is moved to the body of the text in DSM-V. However, DSM-V continues to specify that standardized psychological testing must be included in the assessment of affected persons but that psychological testing should accompany clinical assessment, emphasis being on adaptive behavior. The rationale for "de-emphasizing" IQ scores is that IQ test numbers have often been used inappropriately to define a person's overall ability in forensic cases without adequately considering adaptive functioning. DSM-V is consistent with the proposed ICD-11 criteria, which do not list IQ test score requirements in the formal diagnostic criteria and instead place testing requirements in the text.

In DSM-V, the clinical features remain largely unchanged, although greater emphasis is put on the assessment of impairments of general mental abilities that impact adaptive functioning. DSM-V does not list mild, moderate, severe, and profound subtypes, instead it lists mild, moderate, and severe severity levels. The severity levels are based on three domains: Conceptual (language, reading, writing, math, reasoning, knowledge, and memory, among others, used to solve problems); Social (awareness of others' experiences, empathy, interpersonal communication skills, friendship abilities, social judgment, and self-regulation, among others); and Practical (self-management across life settings, including personal care, job responsibilities, money management, recreation, managing one's behavior, and organizing school and work tasks, among others).

In the United Kingdom and Europe individuals are usually diagnosed as having either a mild (IQ 55 – 69) or severe intellectual disability (IQ 54 or less). In the United Kingdom it has usually been assumed that people with an IQ of 54 or less do not have the capacity to make decisions that will have a significant impact on their lives (to enter into a contract, have a sexual relationship, manage a bank account, etc.). In some circumstances the law is applied differently to people with an IQ of 54 or less compared with its application to people with an IQ of 55 or more.

FITNESS TO PLEAD AND STAND TRIAL

The Criminal Procedure Act, as Amended

When assessing offenders with intellectual disabilities it is important to consider their mental capacity and ability to plead. The guidelines for such cases where the accused might be deemed "unfit" are determined in accordance with tests laid down by Common Law. The procedure by which the court makes its decision is contained within the Criminal Procedure (Insanity) Act 1964 (section, 4, 4a (2), (3), and 5) amended by the Criminal Procedure (Insanity and Unfitness to Plead) Act 1991, which refers to a "disability such that it would constitute a bar to his being tried."

When a jury is impaneled for the purpose it must first hear appropriate medical evidence. If a jury determines that the defendant is not fit to plead, it must determine whether the defendant "did the act or made the omission charged against him as the offence" (section 4A(2), (3)). The jury acquits where it is not satisfied. Therefore, there is a so-called trial of the facts whereby the case against the defendant is tested, although this is not considered a trial. In cases where the defendant is found unfit to plead, the court may make one of the following orders:

1. an admission order to hospital;
2. a guardianship order under the Mental Health Act 1983, amended 2007;
3. a supervision and treatment order; or
4. an order for the defendant's absolute discharge.

Far from how the Criminal Procedure (Insanity) Act 1964 came about, today fitness to plead is primarily associated with mental illness or disability. However, there is a theoretical possibility that a person, who is otherwise mentally "normal," could be found unfit to plead. This was highlighted by the *R v. Pearson* case (cited by Emmins, 1986). *Pearson* was charged with burglary from a dwelling-house, and in the Crown Court the question was raised as of whether the accused was fit to plead. The jury found that *Pearson* was unfit to plead as he was deaf and of limited intellectual capacity, rendering him incapable of pleading guilty or not guilty. In consequence of the jury's finding, the Judge made an order that he was required to by section 5(1) of the 1964 Act, temporarily detaining him in prison and later admitting him to hospital, although it was doubtful that he was suffering from either mental illness or severe mental impairment as required by section 35(3) of the Mental Health Act 1983.

The case of trying a deaf-mute presented problems for the courts in terms of how to distinguish between the two and whether or not a deaf-mute was insane. *R v. Dyson* [1831]; a deaf-mute was indicted for the murder of her child. She was silent in court, and a jury, having heard the evidence that she has always been deaf and dumb, found her "mute by the visitation of God." Although a plea of *not guilty* was recorded, it was not possible to get *Dyson* to understand the complex process of challenging jurors. In directing the jury, Judge Parke J. told them:

> *If they were satisfied that the prisoner had not then, from the defects of her faculties,*
> *intelligence enough to understand the nature of the proceedings against her, they*
> *ought to find her not sane.*

The jury was satisfied and *Dyson* was declared insane and was detained under the Criminal Lunatics Act 1800. Two important points arose out of *Dyson*. First, it brought "idiocy" under the umbrella of insanity by establishing that those found unfit to plead were "not sane," and, second, it established intelligence as the foundation on which future decisions about fitness to plead were to be made. Such findings were to have great implications in the benchmark case of *R v. Prichard* [1836], who like *Dyson* was deaf and dumb. *Prichard* was indicted for bestiality, but did not plea to the indictment. A jury was impaneled and found *Prichard* mute by visitation of God. *Prichard* was able to read and write, and on reading the indictment he indicated by a sign that he was not guilty, from which the jury decided that he was able to plead. However, by referring to *Dyson*, Judge Alderson B. redirected the jury, asking them whether *Prichard* was sane or not (1836, pp. 304–305):

> *There are three points to be inquired into: – Firstly, whether the prisoner is mute of malice or not, secondly, whether he can plead to the indictment or not, thirdly, whether he is of sufficient intellect to comprehend the course of the proceedings on the trial, so as to make a proper defense – to know that he might challenge any jurors to whom he may object and to comprehend the details of the evidence… [I]f you think that there is no certain mode of communicating the details of the trial to the prisoner so that he can clearly understand them, and be able properly to make his defense to the charge, you ought to find that he is not of sane mind. It is not enough that he may have a general capacity of communicating in ordinary matters.*

As a result, *Prichard* was found unfit to plead, even though his disability also constitutes a classic example of muteness by visitation of God. In establishing whether or not the defendant was fit to plead, Judges Parke and Alderson primarily concerned themselves with each defendant's intelligence and his ability to communicate, neither referring to his ability to instruct his legal counsel.

In the case of *R v. Davies* [1853], *Davies* was an elderly man charged with murder who at first stood silent, and then answered in a confused manner. He was thought to be "mad", and the jury, when asked to consider his fitness to plead, was instructed to decide whether his madness was genuine. The question for the jury was not phrased in terms of cognitive ability or intelligence, instead the issue was whether the defendant was "incapable of properly instructing his counsel for his defense" (*R v. William J.* [1853]). The jury believed *Davies'* madness to be real, and he was found unfit to plead.

Such confusion in rulings was observed in the Appeal Court decision in *R v. Robertson* [1968], where the defendant, who suffered from a paranoid illness, was charged with a murder that he readily admitted. The Crown questioned *Robertson's* fitness to plead on the grounds that he could not properly defend himself. Although he was able to comprehend the court proceedings, he was found unfit to plead on the basis that his "delusional thinking might cause him to act unwisely than in his own best interests." On appeal, however, the finding of unfitness to plea was quashed, referring to *Prichard*, not *Davies*, that "the mere fact that the appellant was not capable of doing things which were in his own interest was insufficient ground for a jury to return a finding of disability."

Judge Alderson B.'s direction was upheld by the High Court in *Governor of Stafford Prison v. Ex Parte Emery* [1990] as a case of a deaf accused who could neither read or write nor communicate by sign language. On appeal, it was argued that *Ex Parte Emery* should have not been made the subject of an order under the Lunatics Act s.(2), because there was no evidence that he was insane as required by that section. The High Court held that in its context, "insane" merely meant under a disability, which prevented the accused from communicating with others or being communicated with them, therefore it was unnecessary to prove any mental illness. Although today it is unlikely that the issue of unfitness would be raised without the accused suffering from some degree of mental incapacity, Alderson B.'s direction in *Prichard* still remains the basis of the modern-day law:

   a. *An accused may be unfit to plead even though he is not sane within the meaning of the McNaghten Rules (Governor of Stafford Prison v Ex Parte Emery [1909] 2.K.B. 81) ... Similarly, it is submitted that the accused may be unfit even though he is not suffering from any of the forms of mental disorder defined in s.37 (1) of the Mental Health Act 1983, the existence of one of which is a precondition for making of a hospital order in the case of the convicted offender.*

   b. *The test of unfitness to plead is whether the accused will be able to comprehend the course of the proceedings as so to make a proper defense (Prichard [1836], 7 C&P. 303). Whether he can understand and reply rationally to the indictment is obviously a relevant factor, but the jury must also consider whether he would be able to exercise his right to challenge the jurors, understand details of evidence, instruct legal advisers and to give evidence himself.*

   c. *He will be fit to plead even though the jury take the view that he may act against his own best interests as a consequence of his mental condition (Robertson [1968] 3, All E.R 557). Similarly, a high degree of abnormality does not ipso facto render the accused unfit to plead.*

   d. *Loss of memory through hysterical amnesia does not amount to unfitness to plead if the accused is otherwise normal at the time of the trial (Podola [1960] 1. Q.B. 325). Such an accused will be able to comprehend the proceedings and communicate with his legal advisors.*

Returning to the problems raised by *Pearson's* case, it is now apparent why he had to be found unfit to plead. However, it was inappropriate to send him to a mental hospital by virtue of the order, s.5 (1) of the 1964 Act, as *Pearson* was mute by visitation, but not under disability. Consequently, an application was made to the Mental Health Review Tribunal discharging him three months later.

From *Prichard*, the inability to communicate is purely physical in origin (deaf-muteness) thus rendering the accused unfit to plead. In effect, *Pearson* was both at liberty and un-prosecutable.

The Law Commission undertook a consultation exercise (October, 2010) related to unfitness to plead in which unfitness to plead was considered in the broader context of the law relating to vulnerable defendants. The outcome of the consultation exercise (April, 2013) has resulted in draft legislation being produced (January, 2016) that considers the defendants capacity to effectively participate in a trial. In determining the question it is proposed that the court must take into account the assistance available to the defendant as regards the proceedings. The defendant's ability to understand the nature of the charge; ability to understand the evidence of the commission of the offense; ability to understand the trial process and consequences of being convicted; ability to give instructions to a legal representative; ability to make a decision about whether to plead guilty or not guilty; ability to make a decision about whether to give evidence; ability to make other decisions that might need to be made by the defendant in connection with the trial; ability to follow proceedings in court on the offense; ability to give evidence; and any other ability that appears to the court to be relevant in the particular case, must be considered. Ability to make a decision has four components that are described in the Mental Capacity Bill (2005). It is further proposed in this draft legislation that if the court determines that the defendant lacks capacity to participate effectively in the trial, the defendant may apply to the court for a determination that the defendant has the capacity to plead guilty, or that if the defendant has entered a plea of not guilty the defendant has the capacity to change the plea to guilty.

It is also proposed that the current approach to assessing unfitness to plead, which is reliant upon the opinion of two medical practitioners, changes to one in which the opinion of at least one medical practitioner and one other appropriately experienced practitioner is adopted. Within the draft legislation it is suggested that a registered psychologist can provide this second opinion. The Pritchard Criteria apply primarily to Crown Court proceedings. The draft legislation proposes that a defendant's capacity to participate effectively in a trial is extended to the magistrates' court.

IMPLICATIONS OF THE PRICHARD CRITERIA FOR PSYCHIATRIC AND PSYCHOLOGICAL ASSESSMENT

The Royal College of Psychiatrists' guidance to practitioners assessing "fitness to plead" includes an assessment of whether the individual concerned is able to follow the proceedings of the court. However, individuals' cognitive limitations may be such as to cause them to have great difficulty in following court proceedings and in particular remembering proceedings from one day to the next. Under these circumstances he is not fit to plead. It is not clear that he has the capacity to follow the details of the evidence and the proceedings of a trial so as to make a proper defense. Such individuals will have great difficulty comprehending and retaining information that arises during the trial, and without additional support, will be unable to weigh up information he has become aware of during the trial as part of the process of decision-making. This may adversely affect his ability to instruct Counsel.

In a review of the literature Petrella (1992) found that most defendants with intellectual disabilities were deemed competent to proceed to trial with only one-third deemed deficient in their understanding of the consequences of a conviction. When assessing competency to stand trial other studies have identified the difficulty to understand seven critical terms as important: guilty, testify, strategy, plead, prosecutor, jury, and trial (Smith, 1993; Smith & Hudson, 1995). In a study of 55 defendants with intellectual disabilities (mean IQ of 60.9), 96% and 92% have knowledge of "testify" and "plead" respectively and were judged as competent compared to 70% and 84% (of the same participants) who lacked knowledge of these terms and were judged as not competent (Smith & Hudson, 1995).

In a sample of 160 alleged offenders with intellectual disabilities, Smith and Broughton (1994) found that those with a mean IQ of 64.39 were considered competent to stand trial compared with those with a mean IQ of 58.02 who were not. Similar results were found with regard to the assessment of criminal responsibility. Related to the research on assessing competency to stand trial, Clare and Gudjonsson (1993) have also identified related problems of suggestibility in defendants with intellectual disabilities. The issue as to whether the standards for competency to plead and competency to stand trial are equivalent have been raised elsewhere (Baroff, Gunn, & Hayes, 2004).

In a prospective study of 479 referrals to a psychiatric service at a magistrates' court for assessment of fitness to plead, James et al. (2001) found that the two most important legal criteria in clinical decisions as to unfitness were whether the person could follow the proceedings of the trial or give adequate instructions to their solicitor. The legal criteria concerning trial were more predictive of unfitness than those concerning plea. Unfitness was significantly associated with the presence of positive psychotic symptomatology, in particular conceptual disorganization and delusional thinking, but not with symptoms of anxiety, depression, or withdrawal.

In England and Wales "fitness to plead" is judged by the court and is usually considered to be a function of five criteria (Murphy & Clare, 2003):

A. Ability to plead: *Does the defendant understand the charges against him/her and the differences between pleading guilty and not guilty and associated consequences.*
B. Ability to understand evidence: *Does the defendant understand the reason why s/he was arrested and charged. Although they may disagree with the reasons for being charged or the evidence against, the important issue is whether they understand the reason.*
C. Understanding of the court proceedings: *Is the defendant able to describe the relative positions of the Judge, defense, prosecution, and the role of witnesses?*

> *Does the defendant fully understand the role and selection of the jury. Does the defendant understand if s/he is found guilty s/he has the right to appeal? The defendant is not expected to demonstrate an understanding of the complexities of the law and its applications but rather to understand the court processes and proceedings.*
>
> D. Ability to instruct: *Does the defendant understand of his/her own solicitor's role. Is the defendant aware they can disagree with their solicitor, and if they wish, instruct a new solicitor? Is the defendant able to construct a legal strategy on their own or are they reliant upon others to do this for them?*
>
> E. Knowing that a juror can be challenged: *Does the defendant understand that the evidence will be heard by a jury and aware they (or their legal team) can challenge a juror. Does the defendant understand how a jury will reach a verdict?*

Some psychometric assessments may be of use when considering an individual's ability to plead. The Fitness Interview Test – Revised (FIT-R: Roesch, Zapf, & Eaves, 2006) is a structured interview for assessing a person's competence to stand trial. Originally designed for use in Canada, the revised version of the instrument is applicable for use in the United States, Canada, and the United Kingdom. The procedure involves a semi-structured interview, followed by the completion of a rating scale in which the evaluator assesses the degree of incapacity for each issue. All important aspects of competence to stand trial are assessed and the protocol allows uniformity of competency evaluation. The interrater reliability of items and sections on the FIT-R is good (Viljoen, Vincent, & Roesch, 2006). Using the FIT-R, Zapf and Roesch (1998) investigated the rate of (in)competence in individuals remanded to an inpatient setting for an assessment of fitness to stand trial in Canada. Their results indicate that only 11% of the remands were unfit to stand trial and, further, that with the use of a brief screening interview 82% of the remands could have been screened out at some earlier time as they were clearly fit to stand trial (Zapf & Roesch, 1997).

Consistent with the design of the FIT-R, confirmatory factor analysis supports a three-factor model, which includes understanding and reasoning about legal proceedings, appreciation of the charges and possible consequences of proceedings, and the ability to communicate with Counsel.

Case Example

An example of a criminal court assessment of an individual with intellectual disabilities is reported in Figure 9.1. Mr B suffers from an intellectual disability and demonstrates impairment of adaptive and social functioning. Psychometric results reveal that Mr B suffers deficits in memory processing skills and has limited cognitive ability and concentration skills. It would be expected that, under a period of lengthy questioning or court proceedings, he would be unable to assimilate newly acquired information with already existing information. Under these circumstances he may

Case Example: Mr B, 21 years of age.

Charge:	Mr B has been charged with Assault Occasioning Actual Bodily Harm and Wounding with Intent to Cause Harm. Mr B admits to be being present at the time of the offense but has pleaded not guilty.
WAIS–III:	Full Scale IQ = 59, Performance IQ = 59, Verbal IQ = 64. Verbal Comprehension Index score is 68 (range 64–75: 95% CI) Perceptual Organisation Index score is 60 (range 56–70; 95% CI) Working Memory Index score is 57 (range 53–66; 95% CI) Processing Speed Index score is 69 (range 64–82; 95% CI)
Developmental influences:	Mr B suffered a traumatic birth. He was born with the umbilical cord wrapped around his neck and there were signs of oxygen starvation (anoxia). He was incubated as a baby and was delayed in reaching his developmental milestones. He suffers from a speech impediment which impacts on his ability to form words.
Educational history:	Mr B was in trouble at school for difficult and demanding behavior. He struggled to read and write. He struggled to keep up with his peers academically and continued to misbehave. At about 12 years of age he attended a special school for children with intellectual disabilities and behavioral problems. He left school unable to read or write.
Social and adaptive functioning:	Members of his family confirm he is unable to wash or cook for himself. He has always lived with the support of his family. He often asks members of his family to buy items on his behalf feeling unable to communicate what he wants to shop assistants. He has never worked or operated a bank account and his finances are managed by members of his family.
Mental state examination:	He is easily distracted and his concentration is poor. His eye contact is fleeting and at times he is difficult to understand. Mr B has a marked stammer and has difficulty communicating. He was vague in recalling details of significant life events and his thoughts lacked focus.

Figure 9.1   Case example: Assessing mental capacity in Mr B.

well find it confusing and difficult to adequately follow the evidence and construct an argument in his defense. It would therefore be difficult to demonstrate that he has the capacity to follow the court process unaided. An assessment of his ability to attend to verbally presented information, to process information in memory, and then to formulate a response, is poor. Difficulties with working memory may make the processing of complex information more time consuming for him, will drain his mental energies more quickly, and will result in more frequent errors on a variety of intellectual tasks in comparison with other adults of his age. He will have great difficulty comprehending and retaining information that arises during the trial, and without additional support, will be unable to weigh up information he has become aware of during the trial as part of the process of decision-making. This may adversely affect his ability to instruct Counsel. The Royal College of Psychiatrists' guidance to practitioners assessing "fitness to plead" includes an assessment of whether the individual concerned is able to follow the proceedings of the court. Mr B's cognitive limitations will cause him to have a great deal of difficulty in following court proceedings and in particular remembering proceedings from one day to the next.

Under these circumstances he is not fit to plead. The Mental Capacity Act 2005 offers guidance on enhancing capacity in individuals in order for them to follow court processes. It is important to note that the fact the individual is competent at one juncture in the criminal proceedings does not mean that the individual necessarily is competent at all other stages of the proceedings, and an individual's ability to plead (i.e., understand proceedings and respond when required) may need to be tested at different stages of the court process (Whittemore, Ogloff, & Roesch, 1997). The assessment of mental capacity will be dealt with later in this chapter.

POLICE AND CRIMINAL EVIDENCE ACT (PACE) 1984

The Police and Criminal Evidence Act (PACE) 1984 and accompanying Codes of Practice are intended to provide assistance to the police when interviewing suspects and collating evidence. The Act came about following the inquiry into the convictions for Maxwell Confait's murder in 1972. Three "educationally sub-normal" boys (all under 18) were interviewed and two confessed to the murder after long periods of interrogation without having access to adult or legal guidance. Following the conviction further evidence revealed that one of the two boys had an incontrovertible alibi and could not have committed the murder. The subsequent Philips Inquiry led to the Police and Criminal Evidence Act 1984.

Of the Act, sections 76, 77, and 78 provide protection for vulnerable suspects or those with a mental disorder. Section 1(2) Mental Health Act 2007 amends section (2) Mental Health Act 1983 and provides a new definition of mental disorder as "any disorder or disability of the mind." The former categories of mental disorder (mental illness, mental impairment, severe mental impairment, and psychopathic disorder) have been abolished and the single definition applies throughout the Mental Health Act 1983 in England and Wales. Examples of clinically recognized mental disorders include personality disorders; eating disorders; autistic spectrum disorders; mental illnesses such as depression, bipolar disorder, and schizophrenia; and learning disabilities. Here, "learning disability" means "a state of arrested or incomplete development of the mind which includes significant impairment of intelligence and social functioning." Section 2(3) Mental Health Act 2007 inserts a new subsection 1(2A) into the Mental Health Act 1983.

Although people who are mentally disordered or otherwise mentally vulnerable are often capable of providing reliable evidence, they may, without knowing or wishing to do so, be particularly prone in certain circumstances to providing information that may be unreliable, misleading, or self incriminating. Care should always be taken when questioning such a person, and an "appropriate adult" should be involved if there is any doubt about a person's mental state or capacity (11C PACE Code C). The PACE revised Codes of Practice (July 2004) identify in cases where a person who is mentally disordered or mentally vulnerable an "appropriate adult" as (C1.7, b):

    i. *a relative, guardian, or other person responsible for their care or custody;*
    ii. *someone experienced in dealing with mentally disordered or mentally vulnerable people but who is not a police officer or employed by the police;*
    iii. *failing these, some other responsible adult aged 18 or over who is not a police officer or employed by the police.*

Under these criteria, having a solicitor present during the interview, and who does not have experience in working with people with mental health or intellectual disabilities, will not be considered as having an appropriate adult. A person who is mentally disordered or otherwise mentally vulnerable must not be interviewed regarding their involvement in a criminal offense or asked to provide or sign a written statement under caution or record of interview in the absence of an appropriate adult (Paragraph 11.15 PACE Code C). A confession by a mentally disordered offender may be excluded under section 76 or 78 PACE (Archbold 15–354 – 15–373). Where a confession is made by a "mentally handicapped" person and this is not excluded by the court, and the case depends wholly or substantially on that confession, the jury must be warned of the special need for caution before convicting in reliance on that confession (s77, PACE 1984).

There have been several cases where breaches of PACE or the Codes of Practice may result in evidence being excluded from the trial. For example, in the case of *R v. Moss* (Court of Appeal, March 1990). *Moss* was assessed as having a borderline intellectual disability (IQ-70-79). He confessed to committing indecent assault and, exclusively based on his confession, he was convicted and sentenced to five years' imprisonment. The Court of Appeal held that his confession should not have gone before the jury. His confession was elicited after he had been in custody for several days and was interviewed without a solicitor being present. His conviction was successfully appealed under sections 76 and 78.

The Youth Justice and Criminal Evidence Act 1999 created the provision for a range of Special Measures for cases involving vulnerable and intimidated witnesses to give their best evidence in court, one of which is the intermediary special measure. The Witness Intermediary Scheme (WIS) was set up by the Ministry of Justice (MoJ), and since 2008 there has been a national database of Registered Intermediaries selected, trained, and accredited by the MoJ. The Serious Organised Crime Agency now operates the WIS on behalf of the MoJ. Some vulnerable witnesses need assistance with communication and understanding to achieve best evidence during an investigation and at trial. Registered Intermediaries provide this assistance. The introduction of similar provisions for defendants has been gradual. Section 104 of the Coroners and Justice Act 2009 will allow for certain vulnerable accused to give oral evidence at trial with the assistance of a Registered Intermediary. This part of the Act has not yet been formally implemented but in the interim a practice has developed in the Crown Court in which judges, exercising their inherent jurisdiction to ensure that the accused has a fair trial, have granted applications by the defense to allow the defendant to be assisted by a Registered Intermediary during their evidence alone and, in many cases, throughout their trial (MoJ, 2015).

THE MENTAL CAPACITY ACT 2005

The legal position in relation to decision-making for adults who lack capacity is complex. The law has evolved over a long period of time and in a piecemeal fashion, resulting in different definitions and requirements in different legal domains, including, for example, capacity to consent to treatment, capacity to manage one's financial affairs, capacity to stand trial (fitness to plead), and capacity to consent to sexual relationships (Professional Practice Board and Social Care Institute for Excellence (2010)).

In England and Wales, there are some limited circumstances where if people do not have the capacity to make a decision, they can appoint (or have appointed for them) a proxy decision-maker, for example for financial matters. The Mental Capacity Act (MCA) 2005 offers provision for proxy decision-making for medical and other treatment, or for general health care, where people lack the capacity to make such decisions themselves. However, this does not extend to the ability to plead or stand trial.

In determining a person's ability to plead or stand trial, the MCA 2005, implemented in 2007, offers guidance on the assessment of capacity and the possibility of enhancing a person's capacity in order for them to make a decision or indeed to enter a plea. The MCA in England and Wales provides a framework to empower and protect people who may lack capacity to make some decisions for themselves. The MCA indicates that a person lacks capacity in relation to a matter if at the time he is unable to make a decision for himself in relation to the matter because of impairment or disturbance in the function of the mind or brain. The MCA sets out a number of principles:

1. A person must be assumed to have capacity unless it is established that he lacks capacity.
2. A person is not to be treated as unable to make a decision unless all practicable steps to help him to do so have been taken without success.

3. A person is not to be treated as unable to make a decision merely because he makes an unwise decision.
4. An act done, or decision made, under this Act for or on behalf of a person who lacks capacity must be done, or made, in his best interests.
5. Before the act is done, or the decision is made, regard must be had to whether the purpose for which it is needed can be as effectively achieved in a way that is less restrictive of the person's rights and freedom of action.

In a legal context mental capacity relates to a person's ability to do something including making a decision which may have legal consequences for the person or for someone else. It will be expected that those supporting people with an intellectual disability will maximize their decision-making capacity as a person will not be treated as unable to make a decision until all practicable steps to help him to do so have been taken without success. This may well result in individuals with an IQ below 55 being considered to be able to make decisions that in the past they were deemed to be unable to make. There are a number of "common law" tests of capacity in "case law." The new statutory definition of capacity may impinge on these "common law" tests, as judges consider the new statutory definition and use it to develop "common law" interpretations with respect to particular cases.

When making assessments of capacity, medical professions are concerned with diagnosis and prognosis whereas care professionals are concerned with the degree of independence, which involves consideration of levels of competence in performing skills such as eating, dressing, communication, and social skills. The Judicial Studies Board (JSB) suggests that a multidisciplinary approach is usually best in difficult or disputed cases and the assessment should not then be left entirely to the doctor. The legal profession is concerned with legal capacity, namely whether the individual is capable of making a reasoned and informed decision, and able to communicate that decision. The severity of the test and means of assessment may depend upon the nature and implications of the particular decision. The JSB note there is no universal test of mental capacity – the legal test to be applied relates to the decision made or not to be made. The JSB (2004) suggests three approaches to the question of mental capacity:

1. Outcome – determined by the content of a decision.
2. Status – judged according to the status of the individual such as age, a medical diagnosis, or place of residence.
3. Understanding – the ability of the individual to understand the nature and effect of a particular decision that is being assessed.

In considering these approaches the JSB suggest the "outcome" approach is flawed because we are entitled to be foolish (making decisions not in our best interests) and the "status" (or diagnostic) approach was abandoned some time ago.

This approach argues that a person is able or unable to make decisions, based on his or her membership of a specific group, characterized by such features as diagnosis, gender, or ethnic origin. Historically, this approach was widely used to limit the decision-making of men and women with intellectual disabilities and/or mental health needs, such that widespread injustices took place against these groups (see Grisso, 1986). The approach has not been upheld in recent case law, for example, in the case of *Re C* [1994], the man with schizophrenia who was deemed capable of making the decision to refuse amputation of his foot, nor does it form part of the MCA 2005. Moreover, research has suggested that it is not wise to judge people's capacity to make decisions on the basis of their clinical diagnosis, since diagnosis provides no direct information about the capacity of a specific individual to make decisions within a particular legal context (Grisso & Appelbaum, 1998; Wong et al., 2000). Therefore a test based on understanding is generally appropriate, although the outcome of decisions, or the individual's status, may result in capacity being questioned, and the appropriate test should then be applied. The British Psychological Society, Professional Practice Board Social Care Institute for Excellence (2010) offers guidance to practitioners on the assessment of capacity in adults.

It has been stated, in regard to medical treatment and issues relating to consent, that the individual must be (i) able to understand and retain information and (ii) weigh that information in the balance to arrive at a choice (*Re MB* 2 FCR 541; Butler-Sloss, 1997).

The JSB offers guidance where doubt is raised as to mental capacity. Specifically, the question to ask is not is he or she capable, or even is he or she incapable, but rather is he or she incapable of this particular act or decision. It is noted that capacity depends upon understanding rather than wisdom (i.e., outcome of a decision). For example, an individual may refuse life-saving medical treatment or intervention on the grounds of religious beliefs.

It is further suggested that in legal proceedings a judge should make the determination not as a medical expert, but as a lay person influenced by personal observation and on the basis of evidence not only from doctors, but also from others who know the individual. Medical evidence is admissible and usually important, but it must be considered whether the opinion of a medical witness as to capacity has been formed on sufficient grounds and on the basis of the correct legal test.

The MCA offers guidance on matters related to assessment of capacity. This guidance is based upon information made available previously from the Lord Chancellor's Department in the series of leaflets entitled "Making Decisions" published in 2002. In a practice note (Official Solicitor, 2004), it is stated that in the Official Solicitor's view the test of capacity to consent to or refuse treatment can be used for a wide range of decisions about capacity. Evidence from a psychiatrist or psychologist who has assessed the patient applying the *Re MB* test to a particular decision in question is generally required. It follows, from the terms of the *Re MB* test, that global psychometric test results are unlikely to be relevant. In the Official

Solicitor's experience, references to the outdated and discredited concept of mental age are of no assistance at all. In the case *Re MB*, to have capacity an individual must first comprehend and retain information, and second must be capable of weighing the information in the balance as part of a process of making a decision.

Capacity depends upon an individual's understanding rather than the status or outcome of any decisions made. Capacity is a question of fact to be determined by a court on all the available evidence of which the views of a doctor only comprise a part. The legal system relies on the assumption that people are capable of making, and thus responsible for, their own decisions and actions. The starting point for assessing someone's capacity to make a particular decision is always the assumption that the individual does have capacity. In legal proceedings, the burden of proof will fall on any person who asserts that capacity is lacking. A court must be satisfied that, on the balance of probabilities, capacity has been shown to be lacking.

The JSB note that there is no universal test of mental capacity but suggest a test based on understanding (the ability of the individual to understand the nature and effect of a particular decision that is being assessed) is generally appropriate, although the outcome of decisions, or the individual's status, may result in capacity being questioned, and the appropriate test should then be applied. The JSB (2004) suggest that a person is unable to make a decision for himself if he is unable:

A. *To understand the information relevant to the decision.*
B. *To retain that information.*
C. *To use or weigh that information as part of the process of making the decision.*
D. *To communicate his decision (whether by talking, using sign language, or any other means).*

The requirement to show that the inability to decide is caused by a form of mental disability sets a diagnostic threshold for a finding of incapacity. If there is no such impairment or disturbance, the individual cannot lack capacity within the meaning of the Act. The diagnostic threshold is intended to cover a wide range of situations. Examples include people who are affected by the symptoms of alcohol or drug misuse, delirium, or following head injury, as well as the more obvious categories of mental illness, intellectual disabilities, or the long-term effects of brain damage.

SUPPORTING DECISION-MAKING

There are some circumstances where, if people do not have the capacity to undertake a task, no one else can do it for them (e.g., voting, marrying, having sexual relationships, standing trial), and the government does not plan to provide proxy decision-making in these areas in the future.

However, the Guidance to the MCA notes that "a person is not to be treated as unable to make a decision unless all practicable steps to help him to do so have been taken without success (Sc.1/3)." There are a number of ways in which the case example of Mr B can be helped and supported to enable him to make his own decisions. These will vary depending on the decision to be made, the timescale for making the decision, and the individual circumstances of the person wishing to make it. Different methods may apply when seeking to give appropriate explanations, help, and support to a person with intellectual disabilities, for example, compared to those that will help to stimulate memory recall and recognition in a person with dementia.

In general terms, individuals who fall within the mild intellectual disability range (IQ<69) are likely to experience a range of important cognitive deficits. These may include reduced capacity for and reduced speed of processing information; difficulties learning new information; difficulties in solving problems; concrete thinking styles with difficulties in dealing with more abstract information; difficulties with language; and limited education-based knowledge and skills. These individuals often experience difficulties with time orientation, poor working memory, and limited effective short-term memory. These deficits can be subdivided into six main areas (Mackinnon, Bailey, & Pink, 2004):

1. Attention: *refers to the ability to tune in and concentrate and be able to recognize what is important. This is combated by providing a limited amount of information in order to reduce the number of distractions, looking at the person directly saying their name at the same time, providing practical examples (where possible) that are demonstrated and rehearsed with the use of pictures.*

2. Perception: *refers to the ability to make sense of and understand information. This is overcome using multiple sensory information (visual, auditory, and tactile), explaining clearly and simply the purpose of the exercise, with frequent opportunities to practice building familiarity and routine.*

3. Memory: *refers to the ability to acquire, hold and retrieve information from the short-term memory. Limiting the amount of information presented at any one time, using small chunks of information, visual prompts, gestures, and words to "jog" memory will assist in memory retention.*

4. Comprehension: *refers to the ability to understand what is being said. Here is it important to reduce the speed of what is being said, modifying the language being used, clarifying complex ideas and repeating and rephrasing key intellectual points increases the person's ability to understand the meaning.*

5. Expression: *refers to the ability to communicate messages to other people in a clear and concise way. The use of symbols, pictures and drawings can help explain complex concepts such as emotions and thoughts.*

6. Coping with change: *refers to the ability to be able to cope with changes in circumstances. In order to keep changes to a minimum and reduce anxiety, the room and layout are consistent across sessions. As far as possible the same persons attend increasing familiarity. Similarly, changes in circumstances need to be gradual and the client kept informed.*

The MCA suggests that an individual should not be deemed to have incapacity unless it can be demonstrated that all attempts have been made to enable the person to exercise capacity by enhancing their capacity. Various strategies are given in the Guidance that will enable an individual's capacity to be enhanced. If, following enhancement, the individual demonstrates that he is able to comprehend, retain, and weigh up information, this will demonstrate that he does have capacity with respect to the proceedings within which he currently finds himself. The Guidance makes the following suggestions:

1. *Relevant information:*
   - *Take time to explain anything thought to be relevant or that might help the person make the decision in question, trying not to burden the individual with more information than is required. This may be confusing.*
   - *Describe any foreseeable consequences of making the decision, or of not making any decision at all; what are the risks and benefits?*
   - *Explain the effects the decision might have on the person and on others, particularly those who have a close relationship with the person.*
   - *If there is a choice, give the same information in a balanced way on any alternative options.*
2. *Communication: General points to consider:*
   - *Consult family members, carers or whoever knows the person well on the best methods of communication (for example, using pictures or signing) with the person concerned, the best times to communicate and the best people to be involved in doing this.*
   - *Use simple language and, where appropriate, use pictures and objects rather than words.*
   - *Speak at the right volume and speed with appropriate vocabulary and sentence structure.*
   - *Awareness of any cultural or religious factors.*
   - *Consider the services of an independent advocate.*
3. *Communication: Aids for people with specific communication or cognitive problems:*
   - *Use any aids that might be helpful, such as pictures, photographs, pointing boards, or other signaling tools, symbols and objects, videos or tapes.*
4. *Choosing the best time and location:*
   - *Most people find it easier to make decisions if they are in an environment where they feel at ease or if the location is relevant to the decision in question. It is also important to recognize that some people are more alert or able to pay attention at different times of day. A judgment must be made as to which of the following pointers may be helpful and are possible and practicable in each situation:*
   Location
   - *Where possible, choose the best location where the person feels most at ease – for example a decision about consenting to treatment in hospital may be made easier by a visit to hospital to see what is involved.*

Timing
- *If possible, try to choose the best time of day when the person is most alert.*
- *Some medication could affect capacity. Consider delaying the decision until any negative effects of medication have subsided.*
- *Take one decision at a time – be careful to avoid tiring or confusing the person.*
- *Do not rush – allow time for reflection or clarification where appropriate.*

Enabling decision-making
- *The opportunity to talk things over with people they trust or who have been in a similar situation or faced similar dilemmas.*
- *Assistance from an advocate who is independent of the family or other agencies involved in the person's care.*

A distinction is made between instructed and non-instructed advocacy. An instructed advocate will help a person to put across their views and feelings when decisions are being made about the person's life. A non-instructed advocate will take affirmative action with or on behalf of the person who is unable to give clear indication of their views or wishes in a specific situation. The non-instructed advocate seeks to uphold the person's rights; ensures fair and equal treatment and access to services; and make certain that decisions are taken with due consideration for their unique preferences and perspectives. Independent Mental Capacity Advocate (IMCA) is a statutory advocate introduced by the MCA 2005 in England and Wales. Local authorities have commissioned IMCA services in England and Local Health Boards have commissioned them in Wales. IMCA services are provided by organizations that are independent from the NHS and local authorities. An IMCA service should be provided for any person aged 16 years or older who has no one able to support them, and who lacks capacity to make a decision about a long-term care move; serious medical treatment; adult protection procedures; or a care review (Office of the Public Guardian, 2007).

CONCLUSIONS

The aim of this chapter is to offer guidance to forensic practitioners on assessing mental capacity and fitness to plead in offenders with intellectual disabilities. The definitional difficulties associated with psychological capacities and processes are minimized with the MCA, which focuses on making provisions for people who lack the capacity to make various decisions about their welfare. For an individual to present with a mental impairment they must demonstrate a state of arrested or incomplete development of mind, not amounting to severe mental impairment, which includes significant impairment of intelligence and social functioning, and is associated with abnormally aggressive or seriously irresponsible conduct on the part of the person concerned (Mental Health Act 1983). When considering mental capacity, the JSB indicate that an adult who lacks mental capacity (in the legal sense) will not be able to make decisions that others would act upon, so may be unable to enter into contracts, administer their own affairs, or conduct litigation. The JSB suggest there is no universal test of mental capacity. The legal test to be applied relates to the decision made or not to be made. However, in some cases it may be possible to enhance a person's understanding of court processes and procedures and thus demonstrate capacity. However, with the introduction of the MCA it is probable that some individuals who would have been considered to lack the capacity to be prosecuted for criminal behavior under earlier legislation will in the future be considered to have this capacity, and hence may well be considered to be able to be held accountable for their criminal behavior. Behavior that was not labeled "criminal" or "prosecutable in the past" may well become "criminal" or "prosecutable" in the future.

NOTE

1 The principle method for determining levels of intellectual functioning is via use of psychometric assessment. The most commonly used assessment is the Wechsler Adult Intelligence Scale-Fourth version (WAIS-IV: Wechsler, 2008). The mean IQ score is 100 with a standard deviation of 15. A score of one standard deviation below the mean would correspond to an IQ of 85 or below, and two standard deviations below the mean would correspond to IQ of 70 or below. In addition to using the WAIS-IV assessment to determine IQ estimates, the ICD-10 and the British Psychological Society's Division of Clinical Psychology, Faculty for People with Intellectual Disabilities recommends the use of the Vineland Adaptive Behavior Scales (Sparrow, Balla, & Chichetti, 1984) as an assessment tool to measure impairment of adaptive/social functioning.

REFERENCES

American Psychiatric Association (2000). *Diagnostic and Statistical Manual of Mental Disorders – Text Revision (DSM-IV-TR)*. Washington, DC: American Psychiatric Association.

American Psychiatric Association (2013). *Diagnostic and Statistical Manual of Mental Disorders – V (DSM-V)*. Washington, DC: American Psychiatric Association.

Baroff, G.S., Gunn, M., & Hayes, S. (2004). Legal issues. In W.R. Lindsay, J.L. Taylor, & P. Sturmey (Eds.), *Offenders with developmental disabilities* (pp. 37–66). Chichester, UK: John Wiley & Sons, Ltd.

Butler-Sloss, L.J. (1997). *Assessment of capacity, Re MB* 2 FCR 541, Ca.

Clare, I., & Gudjonsson, G. (1993). Interrogative suggestibility, confabulation, and acquiescence in people with mild intellectual disabilities (mental handicap): Implications for reliability during police interrogations. *British Journal of Clinical Psychology, 32*, 295–301.

Coleman, E.M., & Haaven, J. (2001). Assessment and treatment of intellectual disabled sexual abusers. In M.S. Carich & S.E. Mussack (Eds.), *Handbook for sexual abuser assessment and treatment* (pp. 193–209). Brandon, VT: Safer Society Foundation, Inc.

Department of Health (2001). *Valuing people: A new strategy for learning disability for the 21st century*. London: The Stationery Office.

Ellis, J.W. (2004). Mental retardation and the death penalty: A guide to state legislature issues. Available from: www.deathpenaltyinfo.org/documents/MREllisLeg.pdf (last retrieved July 10, 2016).

Emmins, C. (1986). Unfitness to plead: Thoughts prompted by Glen Pearson's case. *Criminal Law Review* (Sept.), 604–618.

Gillberg, C., & Soderstrom, H. (2003). Learning disability. *The Lancet, 362* (9386), 811–821.

Governor of Stafford Prison v. Ex Parte Emery [1909] 2. K.B. 81.

Grisso, T. (1986). *Evaluating competencies: Forensic assessments and instruments*. New York: Plenum Press.

Grisso, T., & Appelbaum, P. (1998). *Assessing competence to consent to treatment: A guide for physicians and other health professionals*. New York: Oxford University Press.

Holland, S., & Persson, P. (2011). Intellectual disability in the Victorian prison system: Characteristics of prisoners with an intellectual disability released from prison in 2003–2006. *Psychology, Crime & Law, 17* (1), 25–41.

James, D.V., Duffield, G., Blizard, R., & Hamilton, L.W. (2001). Fitness to plead: A prospective study of the inter-relationships between expert opinion, legal criteria and specific symptomatology. *Psychological Medicine, 31*, 139–150.

Joyce, T., Bankhead, A. Davidson, T., King, S., Liddiard, H., & Willner, P. (2015). Guidance on the Assessment and Diagnosis of Intellectual Disabilities in Adulthood: Working Group of the British Psychological Society's Division of Clinical Psychology, Faculty for People with Intellectual Disabilities. Available from The British Psychological Society, St Andrews House, 48 Princess Road East, Leicester, LE1 7DR. Aviailable from http://www.bps.org.uk/system/files/Public%20files/DCP/guidance_on_the_assessment_and_diagnosis_of_intellectual_disabilities_in_adulthood.pdf.

Judicial Studies Board (2004). Section 5 Disability, Sub-section 5.4 Mental Incapacity. Available from: Judicial Office, 11th floor, Thomas More Building, Royal Courts of JusticeStrand, London WC2A 2LL.

Law Commission (October 2010). *Unfitness to plead. Consultation Paper Paper No. 197*. London: Law Commission. Available from: www.lawcom.gov.uk/wp-content/uploads/2015/06/cp197_Unfitness_to_Plead_web.pdf (last retrieved July 10, 2016).

Law Commission (April 2013). *Unfitness to plead: An analysis of responses*. London: Law Commission. Available from: www.lawcom.gov.uk/wp-content/uploads/2015/06/cp197_unfitness_to_plead_analysis-of-responses.pdf (last retrieved July 10, 2016).

Law Commission (January 2016). *Unfitness to plead. Volume 2: Draft legislation*. London: Law Commission. Available from: www.gov.uk/government/uploads/system/uploads/attachment_data/file/491959/53270_Law_Comm_HC_714_Vol-2_WEB.pdf.

Lindsay, W.R., Smith, A.H.W., Law, J., Quinn, L., Anderson, A., Smith, A., Overend, T., & Allan, R. (2002). A treatment service for sex offenders and abusers with intellectual disability: Characteristics of referral and evaluation. *Journal of Applied Research in Intellectual Disabilities, 15*, 166–174.

Lindsay, W.R., Steptoe, L., Wallace, L., Haut, F., & Brewster, E. (2013). An evaluation and 20-year follow-up of a community forensic intellectual disability service. *Criminal behaviour and mental health, 23* (2), 138–149.

Lord Chancellor's Department Consultation (2002). *Making decisions, Paper Leaflets 1–5.* London: LCD.

Loucks, N. (2007). *No one knows: Offenders with learning difficulties and learning disabilities – Review of prevalence and associated needs.* Prison Reform Trust. Available from: http://www.ohrn.nhs.uk/resource/policy/NoOneKnowPrevalence.pdf (last retrieved July 7, 2016).

Mackinnon, S., Bailey, B., & Pink, L. (2004). *Understanding intellectual disabilities: A video-based training resource for trainers and managers to use with staff.* Brighton, UK: Pavilion Publishing (Brighton) Ltd.

Ministry of Justice (2015). *Registered Intermediary Procedural Guidance Manual.* London: MoJ.

Mottram, P., & Lancaster, R. (2006). *HMPs Liverpool, Styal and Hindley YOI: Preliminary results.* Cumbria and Lancashire: NHS Specialised Services Commissioning Team.

Murphy, G.H., & Clare, I.C.H. (2003). Adults' capacity to make legal decisions. In D. Carson & Bull, R. (Eds.), *Handbook of psychology in legal contexts* (2nd ed., pp. 31–66). Chichester, UK: John Wiley & Sons, Ltd.

Murphy, G., Harnett, H., & Holland, A.J. (1995). A survey of intellectual disabilities among men on remand in prison. *Mental Handicap Research, 8,* 81–98.

Office of the Public Guardian (2007). *Making Decisions. OPG606. The Independent Mental Capacity Advocate (IMCA) service.*

Official Solicitor (2004). *Practice note: Declaratory proceedings: Medical and welfare decisions for adults who lack capacity).* Available from: www.offsol.demon.co.uk/adultdeclarations.htm.

Petrella, R.C. (1992). Defendants with mental retardation in the forensic services system. In R.W. Conley, R. Luckasson, & G.N. Bouthliet (Eds.), *The Criminal Justice System and mental retardation* (pp. 79–96). Baltimore, MD: Paul H. Brookes.

Professional Practice Board & Social Care Institute for Excellence (2010). Audit Tool for Mental Capacity Assessments. Available from The British Psychological Society, St Andrews House, 48 Princess Road East, Leicester, LE1 7DR. http://www.bps.org.uk/sites/default/files/documents/audit-tool-mental-capacity-assessments_0.pdf.

R v. Davies [1853] C.L.C. 326.

R v. Dyson [1831] 173 E.R. 303.

R v. Moss [1990] 91 Cr App R 371.

R v. Podola [1960] 1. Q.B. 325.

R v. Prichard [1836] 7 C&P. 303.

R v. Robertson [1968] 3, All E.R. 557.

R v. William J. [1853] C.L.C 326.

Rack, J. (2005). *The incidence of hidden disabilities in the prison population: Yorkshire and Humberside Research.* Available from The Dyslexia Institute, Park House, Wick Road, Egham, Surrey TW20 0HH. Also available electronically, www.alippe.eu/documents/HiddenDisabilities.pdf (last retrieved July 10, 2016).

Re C [1994] 1 All ER 819.

Re MB 2 FCR 541, Ca.

Roesch, R., Zapf, P., & Eaves, D. (2006). *Fitness Interview Test – Revised (FIT-R). A structured interview for assessing competency to stand trial.* Sarasota, FL: Professional Resource Press.

Royal College of Psychiatrists (2001). *Diagnostic criteria for psychiatric disorders for use with adults with intellectual disabilities/mental retardation (DC-LD)*. Occasional paper OP 48. London: Gaskell. Available from Gaskell, an imprint of the Royal College of Psychiatrists, 17 Belgrave Square, London, SW1X 8PG.

Smith, S.A. (1993). Confusing the terms "guilty!" and "not guilty": Implications for alleged offenders with mental retardation. *Psychological Reports, 73*, 675–678.

Smith, S.A., & Broughton, S.F. (1994). Competency to stand trial and criminal responsibility: An analysis in South Carolina. *Mental Retardation, 32*, 281–287.

Smith, S.A., & Hudson, R.L. (1995). A quick screening test for competency to stand trial for defendants with mental retardation. *Psychological Reports, 76*, 91–97.

Sparrow, S.S., Balla, D.A., & Chichetti, D.V. (1984). *Vineland adaptive behavior scales*. Circle Pines, MN: American Guidance Service.

Viljoen, J.L., Vincent, G.M., & Roesch, R. (2006). Assessing adolescent defendants' adjudicative competence interrater reliability and factor structure of the Fitness Interview Test–Revised. *Criminal Justice and Behavior, 33* (4), 467–487.

Wechsler, D. (2008). *Wechsler adult intelligence scale* (4th ed.). London: Psychological Corporation.

Whittemore, K.E., Ogloff, J.R., & Roesch, R. (1997). An investigation of competency to participate in legal proceedings in Canada. *Canadian Journal of Psychiatry, 42*, 869–875.

Winter, N., Holland, A.J., & Collins, S. (1997). Factors predisposing to suspected offending by adults with self-reported learning disabilities. *Psychological Medicine, 27* (3), 595–607.

Wong, J.G., Clare, I.C.H., Holland, A.J., Watson, P.C., & Gunn, M.J. (2000). The capacity of people with a "mental disability" to make a health care decision. *Psychological Medicine, 30*, 295–306.

World Health Organization (2016). *International statistical classification of diseases and related health problems 10th Revision (ICD-10)*. Available from: http://apps.who.int/classifications/icd10/browse/2016/en (last retrieved July 7, 2016).

Zapf, P.A., & Roesch, R. (1997). Assessing fitness to stand trial: A comparison of institution-based evaluations and a brief screening interview. *Canadian Journal of Community Mental Health, 16*, 53–66.

Zapf, P.A., & Roesch, R. (1998). Fitness to stand trial: Characteristics of remands since the 1992 Criminal Code amendments. *Canadian Journal of Psychiatry, 43*, 287–293.

10

Offenders with 'Personality Disorder' Diagnoses

LAWRENCE JONES AND PHIL WILLMOT

'Personality disorder' is very commonly diagnosed among offenders. Fazel and Danesh (2002), reviewing 62 surveys of mental disorder among prisoners from 12 countries, reported that 65% of male prisoners and 42% of female prisoners had a 'personality disorder.' The commonest diagnosis was antisocial 'personality disorder.' (47% of male prisoners and 21% of female prisoners). There is also evidence of a strong relationship between 'personality disorder,' particularly antisocial and borderline, and violent behavior (Egan, 2013; Jones 2011a; Fountoulakis, Leucht, & Kaprinis, 2008) though this link is by no means uncontested (Duggan & Howard 2009). Most people working with offenders will encounter significant levels of 'personality disorder' in their day-to-day work, most of which has not been formally diagnosed, much of which may be interpreted as offenders being "difficult," "antisocial," or "manipulative." Although 'personality disorder' is so common among offenders, specialist resources for offenders with 'personality disorder' are scarce in prison, the health sector, and the community.

Although both authors of this chapter work in specialist 'personality disorder' services, this chapter is aimed at the vast majority of practitioners working with offenders with 'personality disorder' who do not have access to specialist services. The chapter aims to provide an overview of issues involved in the assessment of offenders with 'personality disorders' and references for further reading. The emphasis will be on the central importance of case formulation (see Jones, 2010a;

Assessments in Forensic Practice: A Handbook, First Edition. Edited by Kevin D. Browne,
Anthony R. Beech, Leam A. Craig, and Shihning Chou.
© 2017 John Wiley & Sons Ltd. Published 2017 by John Wiley & Sons Ltd.

2011a) to the assessment of these individuals, rather than on simply administering a series of psychometric measures. Picking up on the observation by Westen, Gabbard, and Blagov (2006) that clinicians do not actually use either the categorical or the dimensional models of personality in their work (see also Jones, 2011a), it will highlight the importance of making personality theory relevant to the individual case.

THE ROLE OF CASE FORMULATION IN IDENTIFYING DOMAINS FOR ASSESSMENT

The construct of 'personality disorder' has been criticized on a number of grounds. As well as being an unhelpful and stigmatizing label for the individual who has offended, there is little evidence to support its use as a construct and it lacks conceptual coherence. Indeed, studies looking at validity and reliability have found them to be wanting (for a review see Livesley, 2001). As a consequence, diagnosis offers the clinician little by way of explanatory or causal models that can inform intervention to address the presenting problems brought by the client (e.g., Bentall, 2003). Knowing that an individual meets criteria for a particular 'personality disorder' does not help to identify the psychological mechanisms driving a particular problem. Consequently, knowing what to assess is dependent on having a formulation that attempts to explain why an individual is presenting in the way that they are (Jones, 2011a).

Applied psychologists typically argue that diagnostic frameworks do not assist practitioners because they often do not provide an explanatory framework that can be used to inform interventions. Current thinking is that, particularly for complex cases (Drake & Ward, 2003), individualized case formulation is the best approach to addressing the individual's needs (Jones, 2011a). This involves developing a causal model to account for why an individual presents in the way that they do, and then using this model to inform interventions and risk assessments. Once a model has been developed, it can be used to identify assessment strategies to explore the factors that have been identified in the model. Assessment then has one of the following roles: (i) exploratory work to explore how a particular factor is operating and to get more specific information about an individual; (ii) testing the veracity of the formulation based on predictions coming from the model; or (iii) testing whether a factor has changed using pre- and post-intervention assessments.

The alternative to using case formulation is to use a generic formulation from, for example, a treatment manual. This is usually a "one-size-fits-all" model that is then applied to every case. This strategy has the advantage of being simple. However, it runs the real risk of missing out on important treatment targets that could be critical in the individual case. Assessment in the absence of any case formulation, as well as being unethical, runs the risk of being directionless. In order to effectively bring about change it is important to identify what targets are going to be most effective in bringing about that change.

STANDARDIZED BATTERIES OF PSYCHOMETRICS

Prior to developing an initial case formulation, it can be useful to use psychometric measures to provide an overview of problems, needs, and symptoms which can later be addressed in the case formulation. Typically, standardized batteries for offenders with 'personality disorders' assess both features of 'personality disorder' and criminogenic factors. Offenders with 'personality disorder' are likely to have significant mental health and responsivity needs, in addition to their criminogenic needs, and the assessment and case formulation of these individuals should address all three areas of need. These three areas are not mutually exclusive and needs may fall into all three of these categories. For example, factors such as impulsivity or irritability could be a criminogenic need, a responsivity need, and mental health need for some offenders. Commonly used measures with this population are shown in Table 10.1.

There is a danger, however, when using batteries of assessments like this, that the clinician does not make use of the information in the case formulation. The information obtained can prove difficult to integrate in a manner that is meaningful and clinically useful.

Table 10.1 Widely used personality and criminogenic factor assessments.

Domain	Assessment instruments
Personality	International Personality Disorder Examination (IPDE; Loranger, 1999) NEO PI-R (Costa & McCrae, 1992) Personality Assessment Inventory (PAI; Morey, 1991) Comprehensive Assessment of Psychopathic Personality (CAPP; Cooke, Hart, Logan, & Kreis, 2009)
Mental disorder	Structured Clinical Interview for the DSM-IV (SCID; First, Spitzer, Gibbon, & Williams, 1994) PAI
Risk	HCR-20 (Webster, Douglas, Eaves, & Hart, 1997) Violence Risk Scale (VRS; Wong & Gordon, 2001) Violence Risk Scale: Sexual Offender Version (VRS-SO; Wong, Olver, Nicholaichuk, & Gordon, 2006)
Criminogenic need	Level of Service Inventory – Revised (LSI-R, Andrews & Bonta, 1995) Structured Assessment of Risk and Need (SARN; Thornton, 2002) VRS VRS-SO

ASSESSMENT METHODS

Triangulation

In order to improve the validity of an assessment it is useful to measure the construct in a number of different ways. This is particularly true in the forensic context where there are a number of factors that are likely to make it difficult for an individual to be open and honest in their responses to psychometric measures. It is always useful to contrast self-report with observational assessment. If there is congruence between different sources of information then they can be invested with a higher degree of confidence than if there are different outcomes from different modes of assessment. Much of the skill of forensic assessment is in the interpretation of different sources of information and the extent to which they support or contradict each other. This kind of interpretation can only be done with a good knowledge of the individual's current context and the various incentives to present in different ways at different stages of their treatment pathway.

Obtaining Norms

A critical problem for practitioners working with offenders with 'personality disorders' is the choice of norms to use when interpreting assessment results. The majority of assessment instruments have been developed on relatively non-disordered populations and, as such, the norms for these measures are difficult to use with offenders with 'personality disorders.' In addition, the complex combination of different problems encountered in this population makes norms very hard to use. The individual case generally does not match the profile of the normative data in several different and significant ways and consequently should only be used with great caution. For example, the chance of establishing or obtaining norms with individuals with paranoid, antisocial, and borderline 'personality disorder' diagnoses who have committed violent and sexual offenses and experience transient episodes of depression during which they self-harm is not high.

Supplementing the use of norms with single case designs where the individual's own scores are used as a baseline for later measures can be useful in some contexts. Idiographic assessment strategies come into their own with complex cases.

Assessing Personality Functioning

The personality assessments in Table 10.1 focus on assessing DSM-IV 'personality disorders' and are not as theory laden as measures such as the Millon Clinical Multiaxial Inventory (MCMI-III; Millon & Strack, 2007) which is based on Millon's theory of 'personality disorder.' Self-report measures of 'personality disorder' are notoriously prone to picking up a lot of state variance. The Personality Diagnostic Questionnaire (Hyler, 1994), for example, has been found to be "over diagnostic" of 'personality disorder' (Bagby & Farvolden, 2004) and this is thought to be because people answer the questionnaire based on their current functioning, rather than their functioning over a period of years, and so tend to overestimate their level of dysfunction. The IPDE and other structured interviews test whether a response is transient (due, for example, to an episode of mental illness, drug use stress, or similar state factor), in which case it is not rated as a feature of their personality.

Psychopathy Checklist – Revised (PCL-R)

This is the most discussed measure of personality in the forensic literature. It has gained in popularity because of its relatively strong predictive validity and because it was originally thought that people who were "psychopathic" were likely to get "worse" if they were put into treatment (based on Rice, Harris, & Cromier, 1992).

However, clinicians have increasingly criticized this finding (e.g., D'Silva, Duggan, & McCarthy, 2004), arguing that it has been given too much weight and that there are other studies that do not evidence adverse responses for "psychopaths." More recently, the instrument itself has been criticized on the grounds that (i) it is not clear what psychopathy is as different theorists conceptualize it in fundamentally different ways (see Blackburn, 2007 and Cooke, Michie, & Skeem, 2007 for discussion); and (ii) it has not been developed to be sensitive to change. It is problematic to have a measure that is looking at unchanging "personality" features but also can be used to measure change. In a clinical context, however, a measure of personality that can change is desirable. In recent years three such measures have been increasingly used in forensic settings:

Comprehensive Assessment of Psychopathic Personality (CAPP; Cooke et al., 2009)

This was developed as a measure of psychopathic personality traits that was sensitive to change, unlike the PCL-R. This measure assesses psychopathic personality in six domains: Attachment, Behavioral, Cognitive, Dominance, Emotional, and Self. This construct, developed though interviews with clinicians, has been redefined and in particular focuses more on personality descriptors and less on offending behavior.

Chart of Interpersonal Reactions in Closed Living Environments (CIRCLE; Blackburn & Renwick, 1996)

This was developed to assess the interpersonal presentations of people with 'personality disorder' in forensic settings. Blackburn's research has identified the two key personality dimensions of dominance–submission and friendliness–hostility as underpinning much of the interpersonal behavior of those with 'personality disorder' diagnoses. Jones (1997) proposed that this model was a clinically useful framework for conceptualizing the presentations of 'personality disordered' individuals. Jones (2009, 2010a) went on to propose that this model be used to conceptualize state repertoires linked with underlying traits following the work of evolutionary psychologists such as Gilbert (e.g., 2005). Assessment of this domain has been developed for forensic settings by Blackburn (e.g., Blackburn & Renwick, 1996). The CIRCLE has good test-retest reliability, has been trialed in secure settings, and offers norms that are usable with 'personality-disordered' populations.

Severity Indices of Personality Problems (SIPP: Andrea et al., 2007)

This is a self-report questionnaire aiming to measure the severity of the generic and changeable components of 'personality disorders' as identified by clinicians. Its authors claim that it aims to assess "core components of (mal)adaptive personality functioning that are regarded changeable by clinicians." Both a comprehensive diagnostic version (SIPP-118) and a short form (SIPP-SF) for research purposes are available. The scale has 16 facets (subscales) that have been found to have good psychometric properties, test-retest reliability, and which are "generic across various types of 'personality disorders,' and have good discriminative validity between various populations" (Andrea et al., 2007). The facets fit well into a common factor model with five higher-order domains; self-control, identity integration, responsibility, relational capacities, and social concordance. This instrument has been specifically tailored to measure the kinds of change targeted by psychotherapy with 'personality-disordered' individuals. Several facets of the scale, such as the measure of identity integration, are unique to the SIPP.

Other Assessment Areas

In addition to personality it is important to assess the other domains with this population, not least in order to avoid the mistake of seeing all of an individual's presentation as being due to their personality.

Readiness

A critical problem with people with 'personality disorder' diagnoses is their history of non-engagement and treatment drop out (McMurran, Huband, & Overton, 2010). The "multifactor offender readiness model" (MORM; Ward, Day, Howells, & Birgden, 2004) provides a framework for assessing a range of factors relevant to building a case formulation focusing on readiness (Jones, 2002). The aims of this assessment are to test and develop a readiness formulation that describes what kinds of input can result in treatment dropout or treatment engagement. Taking a motivational history (Jones, 2002), looking at episodes of engagement and/or drop out in the past, can be a useful supplementary approach providing critical qualitative information.

Assessing Neuropsychological Problems

A number of aspects of 'personality disorder' presentation can be underpinned by neuropsychological problems. Some of these are outlined below along with assessment strategies:

Impulsivity. There are a number of ways in which an individual can present in an impulsive way. They might, for example, have an attention deficit hyperactivity disorder (ADHD) and find it hard to stay attentive and focused in the context of goal-directed activity. There is evidence of high rates of adult ADHD among forensic populations (Young, 2007), and of a correlation between a diagnosis of ADHD during childhood and later diagnosis of borderline 'personality disorder' (Fossati, Novella, Donati, Donini, & Maffei, 2002). Assessment would look at measures of attention such as the Paced Auditory Serial-Addition Task (PASAT: Gronwall, 1977)

Alternatively an individual might have difficulty inhibiting a dominant response. This can be linked with frontal lobe deficits where an individual struggles to regulate behavior effectively or to change track when they are in the middle of a task. Frontal lobe assessments like the Hayling and Brixton test (Burgess & Shallice, 1997), Behavioral Assessment of the Dysexecutive Syndrome (BADS; Wilson, Alderman, Burgess, Emslie, & Evans, 1996), Wisconsin card sort (Berg, 1948), and trail making (Reitan, 1958) can help to identify if this is an issue.

Memory. It is not unusual for people with 'personality disorder' to have engaged in a range of activities that could expose them to the danger of head injury or the acquisition of neuropsychological deficits. Substance misuse, involvement with violence, and general risk-taking behavior can lead to this kind of problem. Memory problems can lead to difficulties learning and changing. This can then have a significant impact on relationships and other aspects of social functioning. Assessment of memory (e.g., The Adult Memory and Information Processing Battery, AMIPB: Coughlan & Hollows, 1985) can thus be useful in building an explanatory model to account for an individual's presentation.

Affective Recognition. Blair, Jones, Clark, and Smith (1995, 1997) have presented evidence suggesting that an individual's capacity to perceive distress in another's face is critical to their developing the capacity to inhibit violent behavior and has found that people who have been assessed as having high "psychopathy" as assessed by the PCL-R (Hare, 2003) perform relatively poorly on measures assessing perception of distressed emotion in pictures of faces (this may not be true for all individuals scoring on this instrument however). This can be assessed using Ekman and Friesen's (1976) Pictures of Facial Affect.

Theory of Mind. Another aspect of functioning that can be associated with offending behavior among people with 'personality disorder' is the individual's capacity to place themselves in others' shoes and think about others' minds. This can be assessed using a number of measures such as the Strange Story Test (Happé, 1994) or by self-report. If a deficit is identified it is important to conceptualize why the individual has the deficit: is it because they do not have the capacity for this kind of thinking, or is it a secondary consequence of another problem such as affective dysregulation or difficulty managing abstract concepts?

Social Cognition and Implicit Theories

Idiographic assessment using repertory grids (Fransella, Bell, & Bannister, 2004) is a useful approach for developing a detailed understanding of how an individual construes their personal and social world. Repertory grids can be useful in the context of both schema therapy and cognitive analytic therapy as a means of assessing an individual's core beliefs and the language they use to express these beliefs. The individual is asked to consider three "elements" (names of key aspects of the self, usually 12 or more are identified, or people in the individual's social world, e.g., "me now," "me when I was abused," and "the victim of my index offense") at a time and then asked how two of these are similar to each other and different from the third. The response to this categorization task is called a "construct"; in the example above this might be, for example, "me now" is different from "me when I was abused" and "the victim of my offense" in that I am "happy and safe now" whereas the other two are "terrified for their lives." This construct is then converted into a rating scale anchored at each end by the two contrasting poles of the construct: "happy and safe" might be rated as 0 and "terrified for their lives" 5 (on a 5-point scale). This procedure is called triadic elicitation and is continued until a number of constructs have been identified – either after a previously specified number of constructs have been identified or when the individual starts to repeat constructs that have previously been identified. Once a number of elements and a number of constructs have been identified, each of the elements is rated using each of the constructs, resulting in a matrix of ratings. This is then analyzed using a number of different statistical procedures used to identify underlying themes in the data (usually factor analysis or multidimensional scaling).

This process can also be used to analyze different stages of an offense (the elements) and the different states an individual was experiencing at the different stages of the offense (see Jones, 2004 for a worked example).

Narrative Assessment

Research into the links between offenders' narratives about themselves and desisting from offending (Maruna, 2001) suggests that how a person narrates their lives and thinks about their futures is linked with whether they go on to desist from offending. Assessment strategies for getting at this aspect of how an individual sees themselves needs to look for the extent to which the individual is using "condemnation narratives" – believing that you are fated to carry on offending and that you cannot redeem yourself; and "redemption narratives" – believing that you can stop offending and that it is possible to redeem yourself. This approach is critical also for

identifying the complex role of trauma and attachment turning-points in developing
the problems the individual needs to address. These can be seen when the individual
is asked to do a time line, a personal history that lists critical life events in a chrono-
logical fashion. Narratives can also provide useful information about the social context of patterns of schema and mode (or self-state) activation. Thematic analysis of
narrative material (Braun & Clarke, 2006) can be a useful strategy for identifying
significant ways of seeing the world and mechanisms for repetition of problematic
behavior in an individual's life.

Self-characterizations (Kelly, 1955) are another way of getting at an individual's
unique way of thinking about their lives by asking them to write a narrative account
of their life. The individual is asked to write an account of their lives from the perspective of a close friend or family member who both knows them and is willing to
give an honest account (see Fransella et al., 2004). This then can be used to explore
some of the ways the individual thinks about themselves and their offending behavior. The operation of core schemas and patterns of relating (reciprocal roles; Ryle &
Kerr, 2002) can also be identified in these narratives. Narratives can also be analyzed for coherence and fragmentation. Key "goods" and values can be identified
through thematic analysis of self-characterization work and these can then be used
in the context of therapy. Other forms of characterization can also be useful, for
example looking at the individual's account of "who I would like to be" or "who I
think I will become."

Criminogenic Needs

The NICE guidelines on antisocial 'personality disorder' (National Institute for
Health and Clinical Excellence, 2009) recommend that for individuals with
'personality disorder' the best form of intervention is to make use of the current
state of the art interventions for offending behavior (in adherence to the Risk-Needs-
Responsivity model by Andrews & Bonta, 2006). However, the literature on criminogenic needs should be applied with caution to offenders with 'personality
disorder' who are not necessarily typical of the offender populations on which many
of the meta-analytic and correlational studies of correctional research are based
(Willmot & Tetley, 2010). Assessments of criminogenic needs with this population
should be informed by the Risk-Needs-Responsivity literature but not constrained
by it. As Andrews (1995) has argued, "risk factors may be highly individualistic and
thus individualized reviews of high risk personal states, thought processes, thought
content, circumstances and situations are indicated" (p. 56).

States Associated with Traits

Westen et al. (2006) argue that neither personality assessments focusing on categorical
diagnoses nor those looking at personality dimensions are particularly useful for the
clinician trying to develop a formulation. For case formulation it is perhaps more
useful to have a model of states associated with traits and then some exploration of
how these states are linked with offending (Jones, 2011a) (see Table 10.2).

Table 10.2 Case formulation model: traits and links with offending (Jones, 2011a).

Enduring process	Related transient or state process
Trait including temperament	State including affect
Schema	Mode
Static risk	Dynamic risk
Attachment style	Specific attachment behaviors in reaction to attachment events (e.g., intimacy and loss)
Abuse history	Lived experience of abuse reminder in present
Offense history	Offense paralleling behavior

A number of therapeutic approaches to 'personality disorder' also highlight the general impact of frequent and rapid state shifting on the overall sense of self. States and state shifting are often linked with a range of traumatic/adverse experiences and associated experiences of dissociation. People who have 'personality disorder' diagnoses often have very fragmented self systems and experience themselves as being very different at different times and do not have access to an understanding of the range of self presentations they have when they are in a specific self state. Interventions such as Cognitive Analytic Therapy (e.g., Ryle, 1997a; Pollock, Stowell-Smith, & Gopfert, 2006) and mentalization-based interventions (e.g., Bateman & Fonagy, 2006) aim to build a more coherent sense of self through developing self and other monitoring skills which involve thinking about mental states and beliefs and how these impact on self and others. Assessment of the general integration of the experience and understanding of the self is generally a task for the clinician in interview using the therapeutic relationship as a tool that allows for the development of hypotheses about a specific individual's depth of insight. Some measures have been designed in order to assess this aspect of functioning (e.g., the Self Coherence subscale of the SIPP; Andrea et al., 2007).

VALIDITY AND RELIABILITY OF CASE FORMULATION

As an alternative to diagnosis, case formulation is not without its problems; Kuyken (2006) has highlighted issues around validity and reliability and questioned the assumption that formulation-based interventions have a greater impact than non-formulation-based interventions. Practitioners are now arguing that case formulation and causal modeling be seen as requiring the same kinds of evaluation as other psychological tools (Hart, Sturmey, Logan, & McMurran, 2011). Evaluation can take the form of interrater reliability or measures of adherence to an agreed format for doing case formulation. It can also be evaluated empirically on the basis of the predictions that can be made based on the formulation which can be tested using N=1 or single case methods.

Single Case Methodology and Behavioral Observation

Once a set of treatment targets has been identified using a case formulation it is important to assess the extent to which the target behavior is (i) present as predicted by the formulation and (ii) changing following intervention. The typical strategy for behavioral observation is to obtain a baseline set of measurements over a specified period of time and then monitor the same behavior, following the onset of an intervention. This design can be strengthened by then withdrawing the intervention and continuing to monitor behavior to see if the changes are sustained following the intervention (see Davies, Jones, & Howells 2010). It is generally unethical to deliberately engineer this kind of assessment strategy, but using natural contingencies such as a period on a waiting list prior to the onset of a group and breaks such as Christmas is acceptable. It is particularly important to ensure that the behaviors being monitored are clearly defined and are reasonable attempts to operationalize the underlying psychological construct. It sometimes makes sense not to monitor a specific behavior but, rather, to monitor an underlying psychological construct or behavioral function. For example, an individual may have a repertoire of different ways of dealing with trauma flashbacks such as self-harm, assaulting people, talking to staff, and listening to loud music. If the variable of interest is "flashbacks" then it would make sense to monitor all these indices of underlying psychological distress associated with trauma.

Offense Paralleling Behavior

A defining characteristic of 'personality disorder' is that individuals have a repertoire of dysfunctional behaviors which typically repeat themselves over time. There are a number of mechanisms that can drive this process of repetition and these same mechanisms can also be seen at play in the behavior of offenders who have repeatedly offended over time. The Offense Paralleling Behavior (OPB) approach (Jones, 2004) requires the clinician to identify ways in which these repeating patterns, and more specifically the psychological mechanisms that underlie them, are being evidenced in the current context. Within the OPB model, predictions are made, on the basis of the case formulation, about the kinds of behavior that would be expected if the individual was still engaging in the psychological processes that led to their offending. These behaviors can then be monitored to see if they are manifested.

Useful aspects of functioning to monitor with 'personality-disordered' offenders are schema mode/self-state switches, particularly in the context of crises. Examples of self-states or modes commonly encountered are "detached protector" or "zombie state," "enraged child," "critical/punishing parent," or "abuser rage" (Lobbestael, Arntz, & Sieswerda, 2005; Ryle, 1997a, 1997b). These patterns of state switching can be identified using thematic analysis and then monitored on the ward.

Strengths-Based Assessment

The potential for pathologizing is high for this population. However, it is useful to remember that dysfunctional and extreme behaviors were at some stage functional and had survival value for the individual. Moreover, current behaviors, though challenging or disruptive, will also meet the needs of the offender in some way. For example, Bowers (2003a) has pointed out that "manipulative" behavior in prisons or hospitals can be seen as a normal response to incarceration, protecting against institutionalization and generating status, respect, and self-esteem.

Unfortunately, assessment processes can often add to the sense of stigma for individuals. So much of the language used in the definitions of the symptoms of 'personality disorder' is pejorative and pathologizing. This highlights the need for strengths-based assessments and self-assessment. Strengths-based assessment focuses on working collaboratively with the offender to identify their capacities, competencies, and values. These are then seen as building blocks for development and validation. The Good Lives–Desistance model (e.g., Laws & Ward, 2011) aims to build a sense of agency with an individual engaging in a self-assessment process. Central to this model is the idea of "learning to apply intact skills in different contexts, or with some minor changes" (Laws & Ward, 2011, p. 235). Assessment involves careful questioning and a joint inquiry aimed at looking for exceptions and capacities in relation to managing offending. Solution-focused questioning (e.g., de Shazer, 1988; O'Connell, 1998), looking for a personalized conceptualization of problems, can offer a model for validating an individual's analytic skills as a strength – as opposed to offering them a "professional" analysis that implicitly undermines their own capacity to solve problems. Similarly "problem-free" conversations exploring times when offending was managed or not happening in order to identify an individualized "What Works" (Jones, 2010b) can be useful.

Assessment of Adjustment to Custody

There is a danger of seeing an individual's response to custody as evidence of their presenting with continued psychopathology. In order to avoid this and also in order to estimate what the impact of custody on risk is, it is important to have a basic natural history of emotional responses to custody (Jones, 2011b) that can then be worked with. Key areas suggested by Jones (2011b) to explore in interview are:

- Bereavement at the loss of freedom entailed by being in custody; for example, are they fighting "the system," surrendering to the "system"?
- Skills atrophy (see Benn, 2002). Assessment of the extent to which skills available when they entered custody are being allowed to atrophy through lack of use.
- Toxic reactions to custody, whereby the individual becomes more prone to offending in the custodial context due to an adverse reaction to the custodial experience.

There are few assessment instruments that allow the practitioner to assess this domain. The Custodial Adjustment Questionnaire (Thornton, 1987) can however be of some use. In interview it is useful to get a history of the individual's experience of and reactions to custody, looking in particular for toxic responses, such as reactance and hostile resistance to experiences of loss of agency; over-compliance and acceptance of custody as a long-term favored option; and panic reactions to the possibility of release or progression. The typology of institutional responses highlighted by Jones (1997) is also relevant.

THE ASSESSORS

The Assessor–Offender Relationship

Forensic psychological assessments can often be experienced by the offender as repetitive, aversive, and shaming experiences which largely focus on the most negative aspects of their lives such as their offending, substance misuse, failed relationships, and antisocial behavior and pay little attention to their positive achievements or to their experiences of victimization and trauma. Offenders who have been detained for a long time may well have faced very similar questions many times before. Repeating the same questions risks reinforcing the offender's negative beliefs about themselves as bad and defective, and about professionals as judgmental and rejecting. To begin a therapeutic relationship with an offender by focusing completely on their negative aspects can risk causing serious harm to the therapeutic relationship between psychologist and offender, not just for that psychologist but also for their successors.

Psychological assessment is always a two-way process and nowhere more so than with offenders with 'personality disorder.' As the clinician is assessing the offender, he or she is also being assessed. In any institution or service, the time spent in initial assessment will be the time when offenders form impressions and expectations about psychologists and other professionals, about relationships, about their environment, and about their own ability to engage in a process and to affect their own behavior. For offenders with 'personality disorder' in forensic settings, their prior experiences of institutions are often largely negative, so it is all the more important that their first impressions of staff and relationships in a new institution are positive.

Assessment and the Wider Team

Disagreement between professionals is likely when assessing offenders with 'personality disorder.' People with 'personality disorder' tend to behave in different and sometimes extreme ways with teams, particularly where different team members adopt different roles with the offender. Among people with 'personality disorder,' lifelong patterns of insecure attachment, abusive and transient relationships, and trauma are the norm (Paris & Zweig-Frank, 2001). It should be no surprise that this group should experience intense anxiety, discomfort, and negative transference reactions when faced with new relationships with people in authority, people who want to get close to them, health professionals, or other groups that may have previously been associated with trauma. Nor should it be a surprise that people who are perceived as caring, nurturing, or protecting should trigger equally intense positive transference reactions.

This tendency of people with 'personality disorder' to present very differently in different environments and with different people is often construed negatively by teams as the offender trying to deliberately "split the team." However, such behaviors can be seen as reflecting how the offender sees the world and key relationships. Also, as Bowers (2003b) has pointed out, most people are manipulative of others, but what distinguishes people with 'personality disorder' is their use of more coercive techniques and lack of concern for others. "Manipulative" behaviors can therefore provide an important source of assessment information both about the offender and their likely treatment needs.

Some of the more stigmatizing labels that are applied to offenders with 'personality disorders,' such as being "manipulative," "splitting teams," or "psychopathic," tend to locate the problem entirely in the offender. However, effective case formulation should involve a more systemic understanding of the problem behavior, which recognizes the role of the offender, other people, and the environment in triggering, maintaining, and managing the behavior.

Differences of opinion will inevitably occur within the team when faced with such different behaviors. Such disagreements should be seen as a natural manifestation of 'personality disorder' and healthy teams should be able to discuss such differences of opinion and synthesize them into a formulation that is shared by the whole team and the offender. The inevitability of such disagreements among teams working with offenders with 'personality disorders' highlights the need for regular and protected forums for team formulation and supervision.

As with any target of psychological therapy, a sound and thorough assessment is an essential foundation for subsequent treatment success. However, this is arguably even truer when assessing offenders with 'personality disorder' because the assessment not only provides important information to the clinical team but also should provide the offender with experiences of a safe, boundaried, and secure relationship, of being able to manage ruptures in that relationship, and of engaging collaboratively in a shared task. For some offenders these will be completely new experiences, but even when they are not, they will help to provide important disconfirming evidence of previously held beliefs about treatment and about people in authority, and a template for future therapeutic encounters. Assessment should therefore be seen not just as assessment, but as the first stage in the treatment process.

REFERENCES

Andrea, H., Verheul, R., Berghout, C.C., Dolan, C., van der Kroft, P.J.A., Bateman, A.W., Fonagy, P., & Busschbach, J.J. (2007). *Measuring the core components of maladaptive personality: Severity Indices of Personality Problems (SIPP-118). Report 005.* Viersprong Institute for Studies on Personality Disorders (VISPD) Medical Psychology and Psychotherapy. Available from: http://repub.eur.nl/res/pub/10066/ (last retrieved July 16, 2016).

Andrews, D.A. (1995). The psychology of criminal conduct and effective treatment. In J. McGuire (Ed.), *What Works: Reducing reoffending – Guidelines from research and practice* (pp. 35–62). Chichester, UK: John Wiley & Sons, Ltd.

Andrews, D., & Bonta, J. (1995). *The LSI–R: The Level of Service Inventory – Revised.* Toronto, ON: Multi-Health Systems.

Andrews, D.A., & Bonta, J. (2006). *The psychology of criminal conduct* (4th ed.). Cincinnati, OH: Anderson.

Bagby, R.M., & Farvolden, P. (2004). The Personality Diagnostic Questionnaire–4 (PDQ–4). In M.J. Hilsenroth & D.L. Segal (Eds.), *Comprehensive handbook of psychological assessment. Volume 2: Personality assessment* (pp. 122–133). Hoboken, NJ: John Wiley & Sons, Inc.

Bateman, A.W., & Fonagy, P. (2006). *Mentalization-based treatment for borderline personality disorder: A practical guide.* Oxford: Oxford University Press.

Benn, A. (2002). Cognitive Behaviour Therapy for psychosis in conditions of high security. In D.G. Kingdon & D. Turkington (Eds.), *The case study guide to Cognitive Behaviour Therapy of psychosis* (pp. 159–179). Chichester, UK: John Wiley & Sons, Ltd.

Bentall, R.P. (2003). *Madness explained: Psychosis and human nature.* London: Penguin Press.

Berg, E.A. (1948). A simple objective technique for measuring flexibility in thinking. *Journal of General Psychology, 39,* 15–22.

Blackburn, R. (2007). Personality disorder and antisocial deviance: Comments on the debate on the structure of the Psychopathy Checklist – Revised. *Journal of Personality Disorders, 21,* 142–159.

Blackburn, R., & Renwick, S.J. (1996). Rating scales for measuring the interpersonal circle in forensic psychiatric patients. *Psychological Assessment, 8,* 76–84.

Blair, R.J., Jones, L., Clark, F., & Smith, M. (1995). Is the psychopath "morally insane"? *Personality and Individual Differences, 19,* 741–752.

Blair, R.J., Jones, L., Clark, F., & Smith, M. (1997). The psychopathic individual: A lack of responsiveness to distress cues? *Psychophysiology, 34,* 192–198.

Bowers, L. (2003a). Manipulation: Searching for an understanding. *Journal of Psychiatric and Mental Health Nursing, 10,* 329–334.

Bowers, L. (2003b). Manipulation: Description, interpretation and ambiguity. *Journal of Psychiatric and Mental Health Nursing, 10,* 323–328.

Braun, V., & Clarke, V. (2006). Using thematic analysis in psychology. *Qualitative Research in Psychology, 3,* 77–101.

Burgess, P.W., & Shallice, T. (1997). *The Hayling and Brixton Tests.* Bury St Edmunds, UK: Thames Valley Test Company.

Cooke, D.J., Hart, S.D., Logan, C., & Kreis, M.K.F. (2009). *Recent developments in the use of the Comprehensive Assessment of Psychopathic Personality (CAPP)*. Symposium conducted at the Ninth International Association of Forensic Mental Health Services (IAFMHS) Annual Conference, Edinburgh, Scotland.

Cooke, D.J., Michie, C., & Skeem, J. (2007). Understanding the structure of the Psychopathy Checklist – Revised: An exploration of methodological confusion. *British Journal of Psychiatry*, *190* (Suppl. 49), s39–s50.

Costa, P.T., & McCrae, R.R. (1992). *The NEO PI-R professional manual*. Odessa, FL: Psychological Assessment Resources.

Coughlan, A.K., & Hollows, S.E. (1985). *The adult memory and information processing battery*. Leeds, UK. St James University Hospital.

Davies, J., Jones, L., & Howells, K. (2010). Evaluating individual change. In M. Daffern, L. Jones, & J. Shine (Eds.), *Offence Paralleling Behaviour: A case formulation approach to offender assessment and intervention* (pp. 287–302). Oxford: Wiley-Blackwell.

De Shazer, S. (1988). *Clues: Investigating solutions in brief therapy*. New York: W.W. Norton & Co.

Drake, C.R., & Ward, T. (2003). Treatment models for sex offenders: A move toward a formulation-based approach. In W. Ward, D.R. Laws, & S.M. Hudson (Eds.), *Sexual deviance: Issues and controversies* (pp. 226–243). Thousand Oaks, CA: Sage.

D'Silva, K., Duggan, C., & McCarthy, L. (2004). Does treatment really make psychopaths worse? A review of the evidence. *Journal of Personality Disorder*, *18*, 163–177.

Duggan, C., & Howard, R.C., (2009). The "functional link" between personality disorder and violence: A critical appraisal. In M. McMurran & R.C. Howard (Eds.), *Personality, personality disorder and violence* (pp. 19–37). Chichester, UK: John Wiley & Sons, Ltd.

Egan, V. (2013). What Works for personality-disordered offenders? In L.A. Craig, L. Dixon, & T. Gannon (Eds.), *What Works in offender rehabilitation: An evidence-based approach to assessment and treatment* (pp. 142–158). Chichester, UK: John Wiley & Sons, Ltd.

Ekman, P., & Friesen, W.V. (1976). Measuring facial movement. *Environmental Psychology and Nonverbal Behavior*, *1*, 56–75.

Fazel, S., & Danesh, J. (2002). Serious mental disorder in 23,000 prisoners: A systematic review of 62 surveys. *The Lancet*, *359*, 545–550.

First, M.B., Spitzer, R.L., Gibbon, M., & Williams, J.B.W. (1994). *Structured Clinical Interview for Axis I DSM–IV Disorders*. New York: Biometrics Research.

Fossati, A., Novella, L., Donati, D., Donini, M., & Maffei, C. (2002). History of childhood attention deficit/hyperactivity disorder symptoms and borderline personality disorder: A controlled study. *Comprehensive Psychiatry*, *43*, 369–377.

Fountoulakis, K., Leucht, S., & Kaprinis, G.S. (2008). Personality disorders and violence. *Current Opinion in Psychiatry*, *21*, 84–92.

Fransella, F., Bell, R., & Bannister, D. (2004). *A manual for Repertory Grid Technique* (2nd ed.). Chichester, UK: John Wiley & Sons, Ltd.

Gilbert, P. (2005). Compassion and cruelty: A bio-psychosocial approach. In P. Gilbert (Ed.), *Compassion: Conceptualisations, research and use in psychotherapy* (pp. 9–74). London: Routledge.

Gronwall, D.M. (1977). Paced auditory serial-addition task: A measure of recovery from concussion. *Perceptual Motor Skills*, *44* (2), 367–373.

Happé, F. (1994). An advanced test of theory of mind: Understanding of story characters' thoughts and feelings by able autistic, mentally handicapped, and normal children and adults. *Journal of Autism and Developmental Disorders*, *24*, 129–154.

Hare, R.D. (2003). *The Hare Psychopathy Checklist – Revised* (2nd ed.). Toronto: Multi-Health Systems.

Hart, S., Sturmey, P., Logan, C., & McMurran, M. (2011). Forensic case formulation. *International Journal of Forensic Mental Health*, *10*, 118–126.

Hyler, S.E. (1994). *Personality Diagnostic Questionnaire-4 (PDQ-4)*. New York: New York State Psychiatric Institute.

Jones, L. (1997). Developing models for managing treatment integrity and efficacy in a prison-based TC: The Max Glatt Centre. In E. Cullen, L. Jones, & R. Woodward (Eds.), *Therapeutic communities for offenders* (pp. 121–157). Chichester, UK: John Wiley & Sons, Ltd.

Jones, L. (2002). An individual case formulation approach to the assessment of motivation. In M. McMurran (Ed.), *Motivating offenders to change* (pp. 31–54). Chichester, UK: John Wiley & Sons, Ltd.

Jones, L. (2004). Offence Paralleling Behaviour (OPB) as a framework for assessment and interventions with offenders. In A. Needs & G. Towl (Eds.), *Applying psychology to forensic practice* (pp. 34–63). Oxford: Blackwell.

Jones, L. (2009). Working with sex offenders with personality disorder diagnoses. In A. Beech, L. Craig, & K. Browne (Eds.), *Assessment and treatment of sex offenders: A handbook* (pp. 217–235). Oxford: Wiley-Blackwell.

Jones, L. (2010a). Case formulation with personality disordered offenders. In A. Tennant and K. Howells (Eds.), *Using time, not doing time: Practitioner perspectives on personality disorder and risk* (pp. 45–62). Oxford: Wiley-Blackwell.

Jones, L. (2010b). Working with people who have committed sexual offences with personality disorder diagnoses. In A. Tennant & K. Howells (Eds.), *Using time, not doing time: Practitioner perspectives on personality disorder and risk* (pp. 125–140). Oxford: Wiley-Blackwell.

Jones, L. (2011a). Case formulation for Individuals with Personality Disorder. In P. Sturmey & M. McMurran (Eds.), *Forensic case formulation* (pp. 257–279). Oxford: Wiley-Blackwell.

Jones, L. (2011b). *Recovery in a high secure setting: The journey out of custody*. Paper presented at the British and Irish Group for the Study of Personality Disorder, Cambridge (March).

Kelly, G.A. (1955). *The psychology of personal constructs*. New York: W.W. Norton.

Kuyken, W. (2006). Evidence based case formulation: Is the emperor clothed? In N. Tarrier (Ed.), *Case formulation in Cognitive Behaviour Therapy: The treatment of challenging and complex cases* (pp. 12–35). London: Routledge.

Laws, D.R., & Ward, T. (2011). *Desistance from sexual offending: Alternatives to throwing away the keys*. New York: Guilford Press.

Livesley, J.W. (2001). *Handbook of personality disorders*. New York: Guilford Press.

Lobbestael, J., Arntz, A., & Sieswerda, S. (2005). Schema modes and childhood abuse in borderline and antisocial personality disorders. *Journal of Behavior Therapy and Experimental Psychiatry*, *36*, 240–253.

Loranger, A.W. (1999). *IPDE: International Personality Disorder Examination: DSM-IV and ICD-10 modules.* Washington, DC: American Psychiatric Press.

Maruna, S. (2001). *Making good: How ex-convicts reform and rebuild their lives.* Washington, DC: American Psychological Association.

McMurran, M., Huband, N., & Overton, E. (2010). Non-completion of personality disorder treatments: A systematic review of correlates, consequences, and interventions. *Clinical Psychology Review, 30,* 277–287.

Millon, T., & Strack, S. (2007). Contributions to the dimensional assessment of personality disorders using Millon's model and the Millon Clinical Multiaxial Inventory (MCMI-III). *Journal of Personality Assessment, 89,* 56–69.

Morey, L.C. (1991). *Personality Assessment Inventory.* Odessa, FL: Psychological Assessment Resources, Inc.

National Institute for Health and Clinical Excellence (2009). *Antisocial personality disorder: Treatment, management and prevention.* London: NICE.

O'Connell, B. (1998). *Solution focused therapy.* London: Sage.

Paris J., & Zweig-Frank, H. (2001). A 27-year follow-up of patients with borderline personality disorder. *Comprehensive Psychiatry, 42,* 482–487.

Pollock, P.H., Stowell-Smith, M., & Gopfert, M. (2006). *Cognitive Analytic Therapy for offenders: A new approach to forensic psychotherapy.* London: Taylor & Francis.

Reitan, R.M. (1958). Validity of the Trail Making test as an indicator of organic brain damage. *Perceptual Motor Skills, 8,* 271–276.

Rice, M., Harris, G., & Cormier, C. (1992). An evaluation of a maximum-security therapeutic community for psychopaths and other mentally disordered offenders. *Law and Human Behavior, 16,* 399–412.

Ryle, A. (1997a). The structure and development of borderline personality disorder: A proposed model. *British Journal of Psychiatry, 170,* 82– 87.

Ryle, A. (1997b). *Cognitive Analytic Therapy for Borderline Personality Disorder: The model and the method.* Chichester, UK: John Wiley & Sons, Ltd.

Ryle, A., & Kerr, I. (2002). *Introducing Cognitive Analytic Therapy: Principles and practice.* Chichester, UK: John Wiley & Sons, Ltd.

Thornton, D. (1987). Assessing custodial adjustment. In B.J. McGurk, D.M. Thornton, & M. Williams (Eds.), *Applying psychology to imprisonment* (pp. 445–462). London: HMSO.

Thornton, D. (2002). Constructing and testing a framework for dynamic risk assessment. *Sexual Abuse: A Journal of Research and Treatment, 14,* 139–153.

Ward, T., Day, A., Howells, K., & Birgden, A. (2004). The multifactor offender readiness model. *Aggression and Violent Behavior, 9,* 645–673.

Webster, C.D., Douglas, K.S., Eaves, D., & Hart, S.D. (1997). *HCR-20: Assessing risk for violence (Version 2).* Vancouver, BC: Simon Fraser University.

Westen, D., Gabbard, G., & Blagov, P. (2006). Back to the future: Personality structure as a context for psychopathology. In R.F. Krueger & J.L. Tackett (Eds.), *Personality and psychopathology: Building bridges* (pp. 335–384). New York: Guilford Press.

Willmot, P., & Tetley, A. (2010). What works with forensic patients with personality disorder? Integrating the literature on personality disorder, correctional programmes and psychopathy. In P. Willmot & N. Gordon (Eds.), *Working positively with personality disorder in secure settings* (pp. 35–48). Oxford: Wiley-Blackwell.

Wilson, B.A., Alderman, N., Burgess, P.W., Emslie, H., & Evans, J.J. (1996). *Behavioural assessment of the Dysexecutive Syndrome*. Bury St Edmunds, UK: Thames Valley Test Company.

Wong, S., & Gordon, A. (2001). *The Violence Risk Scale*. Saskatoon, SK: University of Saskatchewan.

Wong, S., Olver, M., Nicholaichuk, T., & Gordon, A. (2006). *Violence Risk Scale: Sexual Offender Version*. Saskatoon, SK: University of Saskatchewan.

Young, S. (2007). Forensic aspects of ADHD. In M. Fitzgerald, M. Bellgrove, & M. Gill (Eds.), *Handbook of Attention Deficit Hyperactivity Disorder* (pp. 91–108). Chichester, UK: John Wiley & Sons, Ltd.

11

Offenders and Substance Abuse

SIMON DUFF

The abuse of alcohol and drugs, separately and together, are recognized as issues for public and political scrutiny. For example, alcohol and aggression are seen as social problems across a variety of countries (Room & Rossow, 2001). Alcohol and drug use are also central to clinical scrutiny. When working with offenders and developing a formulation of their process of offending it is not uncommon to hear that at the time of the offense the individual had been drinking or had taken drugs. Prior to therapeutic intervention offenders frequently appear to perceive the effects of drugs (in this context we will also refer to alcohol as a drug/narcotic throughout) as diminishing their responsibility for the offending behavior, or believing that psychologists and others will accept that idea, which raises an interesting issue. One of the problems with considering the impact of narcotics on behavior is the extent to which they impact upon responsibility. Unless one is drugged then responsibility for taking the drug and the potential consequences of that decision could be assigned wholly to the individual. But if the drugs result in disinhibition does that also equate to a reduction in responsibility for the resultant offending behavior? For example, early research (e.g., Briddell et al., 1978) demonstrated that a participant's belief that he has consumed alcohol increases his arousal to stimuli of rape, indicating disinhibition concerning sexually inappropriate material. Is it reasonable to consider that the disinhibited person is less responsible if they then act under the influence of this disinhibition? A similar study compared the effects of alcohol on sexual arousal to rape in rapists and non-rapists (Wormith, Bradford, Pawlak, Borzecki, & Zohar, 1988). The control group comprising of six pedophiles, three exhibitionists,

Assessments in Forensic Practice: A Handbook, First Edition. Edited by Kevin D. Browne,
Anthony R. Beech, Leam A. Craig, and Shihning Chou.
© 2017 John Wiley & Sons Ltd. Published 2017 by John Wiley & Sons Ltd.

and one sexual sadist exhibited a decrease in erectile response to all stimuli after consuming enough alcohol to reach a .08 blood alcohol level (the level above which driving is illegal in the United Kingdom and all US states). The 13 rapists did not show a decrease in sexual response, following similar alcohol consumption, and appeared to show a slightly higher relative response to rape. In this case it does not appear that alcohol has a disinhibitory role for non-rapists, which might suggest that disinhibition only occurs in individuals who already have rape-potential beliefs, thoughts, or fantasies. Such findings provoke legal and philosophical debates that are central to forensic issues of investigation, conviction, disposal, and intervention and should be kept in mind while considering the material in this chapter, although they will not be directly addressed in this chapter. Of concern here is the issue of a potential relationship between the drugs that may be consumed by individuals and risk of offending and, possibly, the type of offending.

When considering the link between drugs and behavior we need to be aware that drug effects are not necessarily simple, that many drug users are exposed to a range of different drugs, and that current drug users may have complicated drug and pre-drug behavioral histories (e.g., developmental issues, mental health issues, experiences as victims, attachment issues) adding to the complexity of interpreting research findings with human participants, whether from the laboratory or the field. It is also possible that the factors that result in drug use will not be the same as those that maintain it, as, for example, whatever the trigger for drug use may be, if an individual develops a dependency for drug use that dependency may become the maintenance factor, regardless of the initiating trigger. As an example of the complex nature of drug interaction with human physiology, the psychostimulant methamphetamine can increase sexual arousal (e.g., Green & Halkitis, 2006) but is also linked to reduced sexual function in chronic users (e.g., Peugh & Belenko, 2001) and a similar pattern is found in opiate users (Peugh & Belenko, 2001). Studies have suggested that alcohol too can result in increased desire or impaired sexual function, raising another complicating factor; the effects of drugs may not be independent of an individual's expectation of the effect of the drug (as evidenced by the placebo effect, see Briddell et al., 1978) and recent studies suggest that with some drugs it is the personality of the drug taker that seems more important in determining the resultant effect of the drug than the known, population-based, pharmacological effects of the drug (Hoeken & Stewart, 2003). Despite these contradictory findings regarding the physiological effects of various drugs the majority appear to have the general effect of increasing what might be termed risky behaviors (e.g., inconsistent condom use, multiple partners, see Raj, Saitz, Cheng, Winter, & Samet, 2007; impaired decision-making in relation to gambling tasks, e.g., Bechara et al., 2001; George, Rogers, & Duka, 2005), though as yet the mechanism for this is unclear.

There are two key issues to consider with respect to offenders and substance abuse. The first is how substance abuse is related to offending behavior; the second, how the relationship between substance abuse and offending is understood by society. They are both important because they play a role in determining how society responds to offending behavior where substance abuse is involved.

SUBSTANCE ABUSE AND OFFENDING

In many nations there are specific offenses that name a substance as part of the offense, for example, offenses related to the possession and supply of drugs and the sale or supply of alcohol to children. In these cases it is simplistic to assume that the offenses "involve" alcohol rather than being directly related to other forms of specific offending (e.g., supplying alcohol to children as part of sexual grooming). Currently we are not aware of any research that has explored this potential link between what might be considered the index offense and an "intended" offense and this may be an important area to understand this potentially deeper relationship between alcohol and offending, but it is not clear how accurately it could be investigated. The concern of research and policy tends to center on the link between substance abuse, sexual crimes, and crimes of violence probably because they are seen as having the greatest impact on society from the position of cost (e.g., courts, imprisonment, and treatment) and victims. There are four ways in which the relationship between drug use and offending might be understood and each will be considered below. Clearly it is important to untangle these relationships to be able to develop efficient and effective interventions, whether these be aimed at individuals who offend or individuals who are using drugs, or more broadly take a societal approach by, for example, legalizing drug use or raising the cost of alcohol (see Chaloupka, Grossman, & Saffer, 2002). In each case we are ultimately attempting to appropriately assess the risk of offending and put into place systems to manage or reduce that risk.

In research concerned with real violence the relationship between drugs and offending is only correlational, thus studies indicating that, for example, alcohol use has been present in a range of offenses (e.g., sexual aggression, Testa, 2002; and child abuse, Widom & Hiller-Sturmhofel, 2001), may also be interpreted as the offending leading to alcohol consumption or that the two were coincidental rather than causal. This means that any of the studies reported below, to support one or other direction of causation, could be interpreted another way, so the approach here will be to represent the findings as the original researchers have suggested.

DRUG USE AS A TRIGGER FOR OFFENDING

Meta-analyses of laboratory studies, where the direction of causation can be determined, suggest that drugs increase behavior that could be offending if acted outside of the laboratory (e.g., Ito, Miller, & Pollock, 1996), supporting the view that drug use is a trigger for offending. A systematic review by Bennett, Holloway, and Farrington (2008) covering 30 studies showed that for drug users the odds of offending were on average three to four times higher (depending on the drug) than for non-drug users across a range of offense types. In a recent review of studies looking at the perinatal effects of cannabinoids, Sundram (2006) reports that impulsivity, inattention, and hyperactivity have all been identified as possible consequences of perinatal exposure. Babinski, Hartsough, and Lambert (1999) have shown that both impulsivity and hyperactivity in children are linked to higher involvement in offending in later life and, as such, if these are linked to perinatal exposure to alcohol, this suggests a direct link between alcohol exposure and offending behavior. Studies concerned with exposure to drugs during childhood have attempted to explain the psychological mechanism through which the potential influence of drugs on offending may occur. Hammersley, Marsland, and Reid (2003) report that a quarter of their sample of 269 young offenders indicated that they used drugs in order to have the courage to carry out their offenses, suggesting that in the absence of drugs the offenses would not have occurred despite the fact that the offenders had thought about or planned their behavior. However, Simpson's (2003) interviews suggest that while influenced by drugs, some offenders saw their behavior as "having a laugh" (p. 314), hinting at a different pathway for linking drugs and offending whereby there is no pre-drug intention to offend but rather offending is a side-effect of the narcotics. Other authors have identified similar mechanisms that may produce similar effects based on the idea that certain stimulants act to reduce anxiety that might normally be related to risky behaviors (such as aggression, see Felson & Staff, 2010). Increased sensation seeking may also be triggered by drugs that moderate the sensation of pain, either removing the negative aspect of pain thereby encouraging aggression, or increasing it, leading to defensive aggression (Durrant, 2011; Hoeken & Stewart, 2003). One factor identified as a moderator by Ito et al. (1996) is provocation, whereby the difference between drinking and sober participants on measures of aggression decreases as the intensity of the provocation increases, which may be an indicator that drugs increase sensitivity to provocation (known as alcohol myopia) or, as suggested above, reduce concerns regarding personal safety in responding to provocation.

A recent qualitative study concerned with sexual offenders and criminogenic need (Duff, 2010) found that only one participant from a total of 26 indicated that the use of alcohol and drugs was a contributory factor to his offending, writing in his victim apology letter, "I know that this may not be any comfort but I was under the influence of drugs and alcohol prior to the attack on you ... As I have said I had been drinking heavily and I am now aware that alcohol made me unaware of what I was doing and my personality altered when I was drinking ... I would take my actions to extremes" (p. 39). Interestingly the individual does not perceive his behavior as new but rather as routine behavior that became extreme. It is unclear if the extreme behavior referred to relates to acts (i.e., that without alcohol and drugs he would have still offended against a child, but not to the same degree) or to victim choice (i.e., the same behavior would have been enacted, but not on a child).

Earlier work has demonstrated the presence of alcohol in offenders. For example, Barbaree, Marshall, Yates, and Lightfoot (1983) report evidence suggesting that between 30% and 50% of rapists were intoxicated when they committed their offense and Grubin and Gunn (1990) have found that 58% of men convicted of rape in the United Kingdom report having been drinking prior to rape and 37% of these men were considered to be dependent on alcohol. More generally, Dunseith et al. (2004) report that elevated rates of substance abuse have been found among convicted sex offenders. Importantly though the research shows that a proportion of offenders are also users of drugs so drug use may be a part of offending behavior for some individuals rather than being a definitive risk factor for offending behavior. Some research suggests that once drugs have been factored out the link between mental disorder and sexual assaults disappears (e.g., Elbogen & Johnson, 2009). In a similar vein Shaw et al. (2006) have analyzed homicide data in England and Wales and conclude that drug use is a major contributor to homicide. It is important to note that these data were collected from reports written by and questionnaires to the mental health services rather than by the offenders and, as the authors acknowledge, this makes the findings dependent on the report writers' reliability in recording drug use. The British Crime Survey, based on victim reports of crime rather than on police data, reports over 2 million violent incidents in 2009/2010, of which 50% are estimated to have included the "involvement" of alcohol (Flatley, Kershaw, Smith, Chaplin, & Moon, 2010). These results are supported by the later work of Felson and Staff (2010) who investigated nearly 17,000 US inmates and determined that drunkenness is most strongly linked to homicide; they conclude that alcohol is particularly implicated in offenses linked to personal confrontation.

The availability of alcohol has been linked to non-lethal violence (e.g., robbery) by Nielsen and Martinez (2003) in Miami, as it has with other kinds of offending in Los Angeles (Scribner, MacKinnon, & Dwyer, 1995). Similarly, as Simpson (2003) suggests, for some offenders crime is the strategy that they use in order to support the purchase of drugs (i.e., to increase the likelihood of drugs being available, by having the finances to purchase them) and as such a need or desire for the drug may result in offending. This is supported by Rex (2002) who was concerned with how probationers desist from offending. One of the participants in her qualitative study remarked, "Sometimes, when [...] I've got nothing to do, I think of drugs or drink and then I think 'where am I going to get the money from?,' so I go and do it" (p. 371), where the "it" he refers to is offending. Based on these findings, and a wealth of other laboratory and field reports, there is support for the view that drugs can lead to offending behavior, whether planned or otherwise.

Of course we cannot assume that the role of alcohol is solely linked to the perpetrator of an offense, just as we cannot assume that the use of a weapon implies that it is the perpetrator who brings a weapon to offend (see Curtis, 1974). Brookman and Maguire (2002) report data indicating that in 52% of the cases of male-on-male homicide that they reviewed, alcohol had been consumed by either the victim or the perpetrator. In this case it is not clear if the victims are selected because their alcohol intake has made them more vulnerable or if their behavior while under the influence of alcohol may have provoked their murderer in some way (e.g., the victim, intoxicated, initiated a violent encounter), but in the former situation the alcohol-induced vulnerability may be understood as a trigger to offending. Indeed, in Felson and Staff's (2010) study approximately 39% of their violent offenders (N = 4,765) suggested that their victim was under the influence of drugs or alcohol although victims of violence are less likely to be intoxicated (Murdoch & Ross, 1990).

The above evidence supports the idea that drugs may be implicated in crime. However, as Giancola, Josephs, Dewall, and Gunn (2009) point out, this relationship is moderated by a range of other factors, explaining why, for example, alcohol does not increase aggression in all individuals. As Hammersley (2011) writes, "there can be a tendency to over-attribute the offending of known offenders to their substance use because, as offenders, they tautologously have 'problems' related to substance use" (p. 272).

OFFENDING AS A TRIGGER FOR DRUG USE

In direct contrast to the previous section, here we are concerned with the idea that offending behavior is the cause for drug abuse. One of the immediate problems with this approach is that it is not possible to carry out controlled, laboratory studies in order to investigate this relationship, unless we assume that virtual or artificial offending would be expected to produce the same effects as real offending and that participants would subsequently acknowledge a desire for narcotics. This does mean that any evidence in support of this position is more ecologically valid though more difficult to verify. For example, Hough (1996) has suggested that prostitution may lead to the use of drugs. Here the idea is that the drugs are used to make prostitution bearable, which is one of the relationships identified by Feucht (1993). However, it is also possible that the use of drugs leads to debt and that some women are forced into prostitution both to repay that debt and to have finances to continue drug use if they have developed a dependency on the drug. The difficulty here is the extent to which participants are willing and able to provide accurate information about the relationship between their behavior and their drug use, which may be further compromised in situations where one or other is considered demeaning or embarrassing. If we do accept the direction that drugs are a response to offending behavior, in this case to make it bearable (which may be either the behavior itself, any associated guilt, or the fear of being exposed to the associated risks), then presumably such an explanation might be plausible for any offense that an individual repeatedly engages in, such as mugging, burglary, or sexual offenses (e.g., against a child). Drug use could also be a response to trauma associated with having carried out a crime. A number of authors have suggested that trauma can be a reaction to having been the perpetrator of a crime (e.g., Byrne, 2003; Gray et al., 2003) and the use of drugs may be a coping mechanism, via self-medication, for some individuals.

Other explanations for this direction of the relationship include the idea that drugs may be used as part of the celebration of the successful commission of an offense (e.g., Goode, 1997; Menard, Mihalic, & Huizinga, 2001), just as alcohol may be used to celebrate the New Year, anniversaries, and so on. Menard et al. (2001) refer to this as chemical recreation. Through interviews with armed robbers who were still actively offending, Wright and Decker (1998) found that access to drugs was one of the ways in which the robbers used their money. This does not preclude the possibility that drugs were involved in the commission of the crimes (e.g., to increase confidence and courage) or that the robberies were necessary to fund pre-existing drug dependence. Research has demonstrated that the group process may be an important predictor for initial drug use (e.g., Freeland & Campbell, 1973), and one might suggest that in some circumstances, where a group of individuals are offending, this may lead to drug abuse, among other behaviors (e.g., gang-related activity).

OFFENDING AND DRUG USE ARE INDEPENDENT OF ONE ANOTHER (I.E., THERE IS NO RELATIONSHIP)

The fact that offending and drug use may co-occur does not imply causality. The difficulty with identifying if there is a link is that it often relies on self-report from offending populations. If offenders do suggest that there is a link we might have to be cautious in accepting this explanation as it may form a part of internal or external excuse making ("deviance disavowal," see McCaghy, 1968). Similar care is needed when a link is denied. Studies that have sought to explore this area have suggested that for a proportion of offenders, their view is that the two factors are not linked (e.g., see Liriano & Ramsey, 2003). Perhaps the most common explanation of there being no direct link between drug use and offending is the idea that using alcohol or drugs, to whatever extent, exposes an individual to more risk purely on the basis of the concomitant lifestyle choices (e.g., Felson & Staff, 2010).

In a review paper Braucht, Brakash, Follingstad, & Berry (1973) suggest that the use of narcotics co-occurs with poorer performance on a measure of social conformity. For some offenses low levels of social conformity may also be implicated, particularly those that are associated with antisocial characteristics (see Pihl & Peterson, 1992). Similarly Tarter, Kirisci, Feske, & Vanyukov (2007) have indicated that trait impulsivity seems to be linked to problematic drug use, and impulsivity also seems to be linked to offending such as violent crime (e.g., Krueger et al., 1994;

Caspi et al., 1997), thus the important factor for both offending and drug use is impulsivity. Linked to this, antisocial personality and psychopathy have been associated with sensation-seeking, which in turn has been associated with a greater likelihood of the initiation of drug use, particularly use of psychomotor stimulants (Pihl & Peterson, 1992). Recent research has demonstrated that cocaine-dependent individuals who are also identified as having antisocial personality disorder were more aggressive than controls and that cocaine-dependent individuals without antisocial personality disorder were not more aggressive than controls (Moeller et al., 2002), supporting the idea that offense-supporting behaviors and drug use are not directly connected.

Hammersley (2011) provides an interesting strand of evidence supporting the idea that drug abuse and crime are not necessarily linked, namely that the pattern of offending and drug use do not match one another. In teenagers the typical pattern is for drug use to gradually increase over the years and into a person's twenties; however, the typical pattern for crime is an increase in the teenage years and then decline. If the two were linked, either crime leading to drug use or drug use leading to crime, then the expectation would be that these two variables would mirror one another. What this pattern of data cannot answer is if initially there is a relationship, but then other factors uncouple drugs and offending. For example, more intense interpersonal relationships, employment, and families may be able to tolerate continued drug use more than they are able to tolerate continued criminal activity.

THE SUBSTANCE ABUSE/OFFENDING RELATIONSHIP IS MORE COMPLEX

As hinted at in the introduction, the relationship between drugs and offending may be complicated because of an individual's previous history, their use of drugs, the range of drugs they may have been exposed to, and the impact of other life events. Additionally it is possible that at times the relationship may be in one direction, at times in the other, and at times it may not exist for a given individual. This may be across the time course of an individual's relationship with drugs (as evidenced by the complex interaction between methamphetamine and sexual behavior, e.g., Green & Halkitis, 2006) or may be variable over a shorter time course linked to other factors such as the presence of other drug users or mood, and so on. A wealth of studies have identified factors that play a role in determining how alcohol interacts with behavior and some of these are state factors, some trait factors. For example, trait aggression, irritability, and anger have been identified as moderating factors (e.g., respectively, Smucker-Barnwell, Borders, & Earleywine, 2006; Giancola, 2002; Parrott & Zeichner, 2002). Similarly, cognitive function and marital conflict (e.g., respectively, Giancola, 2004; Quigley & Leonard, 1999) have been identified as trait factors. Regarding cognitive functioning, an interesting relationship between alcohol and sexual arousal has been identified when IQ is also considered. Using phallometric assessment Wilson, Lawson, and Abrams (1978) demonstrated that alcohol diminishes sexual arousal. However, Wormith et al. (1988) found that in individuals with lower IQ scores alcohol increases erectile response. This may be linked to different expectations, the possibility that lower IQ populations have reduced access to sex and so are less desensitized to it, or that the two studies are not entirely comparable. It does raise the question again as to what other factors may be involved in determining behavior under the influence of drugs as these contradictory results are not easily explained by an entirely psychopharmacological model of the relationship between alcohol and behavior.

This relationship is further complicated by, for example, social economic factors and issues regarding the type of drug used (e.g., Parker & Newcombe, 1987). For example, Eisner (2002) has interpreted a wealth of international data and concludes that whereas violence tends to occur in countries with high levels of inequality and low levels of affluence and social control, drug and alcohol abuse are more prevalent in countries with high gross domestic product per capita (considered an indicator of a nation's standard of living) and high urbanization. He did not attempt to draw a link between violence and drug use but the data do suggest that any such link will be complicated by social and economic forces too.

Issues such as irritability, anger, and marital conflict are found in both males and females and the expectation would be that they may similarly impact the two genders. However, gender research has suggested that there may be differences between males and females in their exposure to drugs and their effects. Sundram (2006) suggests that there may be effects of sex hormones as gender differences are routinely found; Bennett and Holloway (2010) report studies demonstrating that in the non-offending population more males than females have been exposed to drugs, but in the offending population the rates are about equal, although females may have been more likely to be taking drugs (based on drug testing at arrest). Adding to this gender complexity is research demonstrating that the effects of drugs may be, to some extent, dependent on the expectation one has regarding the use of a drug. For example, Bègue et al. (2009) have shown that expectancies significantly increase aggressive behavior, whereas the quantity of alcohol ingested was unrelated to aggression.

PUBLIC PERCEPTIONS

Although it is clearly important to understand the real relationship between drugs and offending in order to reduce offending and intervene with offenders, there is another practical issue to consider. From a wider perspective, behaviors that involve drugs will only be categorized as offenses and offenders under the influence of drugs will only be convicted if the general public and legal professionals understand that relationship. Although the great majority of the public have had the experience of the influence of drugs of some variety, even if only alcohol, on themselves and their friends and family, this understanding does not seem to be preserved when objectively considering offending. For example, Richardson and Campbell (1982) have demonstrated that rape victims are attributed more blame when they are raped and described as having been drinking, which may be based on the assumption that alcohol increases a woman's interest in sex (Abbey, Zawacki, Buck, Clinton, & McAuslan, 2004). Conversely, male rapists are attributed less blame for committing rape when they are depicted as drinking. To be entirely sure that this is an effect of the presence of alcohol, rather than a gender issue, the comparable study of male victims and female rapists would need to be done, but at first glance this at least suggests that the general public perceive the impact of alcohol in particular ways. Interestingly Schuller and Wall (1998) found that in mock jury studies a defendant was more likely to be found guilty of sexual assault if he had drunk alcohol rather than a soft drink, so there may be important differences between individual and group attributions of blame or the reduction in blame identified by Richardson and Campbell is not enough for an individual to be found not-guilty of an offense. Similarly, a victim described as having consumed alcohol is considered less credible and the defendant in their case is less likely to be found guilty (Schuller & Wall, 1998). This study is concerned with aspects of guilt and this may be the crucial difference between the Richardson and Campbell (1982) study and Schuller and Wall's mock jury study in that blame for an act and guilt for that act may not be construed as the same thing or that blame assumes some shared responsibility for an outcome whereas guilt precisely identifies the responsible party/parties. A later study explored the issue of causation. In a survey of 192 US citizens in Florida, Levenson, Brannon, Fortney, and Baker (2007) found that 65% answered "somewhat true" or "completely true" to the statement, "Alcohol and drugs play a moderate or major role in sex offending."

It is unlikely that the way that the public consider the relationship between drugs and behavior is limited to some kind of pharmacological understanding, or stereotyping, of the effects of drugs on, for example, planning, and decision-making. It is likely that there is a degree of categorization that takes place. This may be based on assumptions such as that people who use cocaine have a particular lifestyle linked to risk, that women who get drunk may be more promiscuous, and that smokers are less concerned with health. For example, Ross and Darke (1992) have demonstrated attitudes of distaste, personal avoidance, and assumptions of criminality with regard to intravenous drug users and Lyons and Willott (2008) have shown that drunk women are considered to be more deviant and less feminine than sober women. The fact that these biases may be a part of an individual's decision-making when determining the guilt or innocence of an alleged offender may influence how the courts and statistics come to respond to and understand (and thus determine) the relationship between drugs and offending.

CONCLUSIONS

In 2003 Hoeken and Stewart wrote, "The one thing that can be said unequivocally about the drug aggression relationship: We do not know enough about it" (p. 1547). The brief overview of literature in this chapter highlights this position. There is contrasting evidence speaking to each of the four potential relationships described above and each may suggest different social, legal, and psychological approaches to dealing with drug misuse and criminality. There does seem to be an assumption that by reducing substance abuse we will be reducing risk, but this argues for the position that drug abuse/use is a trigger for criminality. What if the abuse is self-medication, leading to a greater deterioration in various factors such as social functioning and problem solving, and so on? For example, McMurran (2011) suggests alcohol may be used as a coping strategy for the socially anxious. Would this possibly increase the likelihood of an individual offending? Reducing alcohol may increase sexual responsivity to inappropriate stimuli, leading to greater sexual fantasy and greater risk of sexual offending. It is possible an association between alcohol and aggression may actually be that there is an association between alcohol and men, and men and aggression (especially young men and aggression), rather than between aggression and alcohol. The view that alcohol is a disinhibitor and contributes to offending behavior, both with respect to the victim and the offender, may be a somewhat simplistic view, and although it may be useful from the perspective of aiding society to feel that the world is safe and predictable, from the perspective of assessing and working with offenders it is not necessarily helpful. This is because the relationship between alcohol and offending for a particular offender may be quite different, and in order to have the most accurate assessment, to lead to an accurate formulation for guiding intervention, this relationship must not be assumed, but explored.

REFERENCES

Abbey, A., Zawacki, T., Buck, P.O., Clinton, A.M., & McAuslan, P. (2004). Sexual assault and alcohol consumption: What do we know about their relationships and what types of research are still needed? *Aggression and Violent Behavior*, *9*, 271–303.

Babinski, L.M., Hartsough, C.S., & Lambert, N.M. (1999). Childhood conduct problems, hyperactivity-impulsivity, and inattention as predictors of adult criminal activity. *Journal of Child Psychology and Psychiatry*, *40*, 347–355.

Barbaree, H.E., Marshall, W.L., Yates, E. & Lightfoot, L.O. (1983). Alcohol intoxication and deviant sexual arousal in male social drinkers. *Behavioral Research and Therapy*, *21* (4), 365–373.

Bechara, A., Dolan, S., Denburg, N., Hindes, A., Anderson, S.W., & Nathan, P.E. (2001). Decision-making deficits, linked to a dysfunctional ventromedial prefrontal cortex, revealed in alcohol and stimulant abusers. *Neuropsychologia*, *39* (4), 376–389.

Bègue, L., Subra, B., Arvers, P., Muller, D., Bricout, V., & Zorman, M. (2009). A message in a bottle: Extrapharmacological effects of alcohol on aggression. *Journal of Experimental Social Psychology, 45,* 137–142.

Bennett, T., & Holloway, K. (2010). Understanding drugs, alcohol and crime. Maidenhead, UK: Open University Press.

Bennett, T., Holloway, K., & Farrington, D. (2008). The statistical association between drug misuse and crime: A meta-analysis. *Aggression and Violent Behavior, 13,* 107–118.

Braucht, G.N., Brakarsh, D., Follingstad, D., & Berry, K.L. (1973). Deviant drug use in adolescence: A review of psychosocial correlates. *Psychological Bulletin, 79,* 92–106.

Briddell, D.W., Rimm, D.C., Caddy, G.R., Krawitz, G., Sholis, D., & Wunderlin, R.J. (1978). Effects of alcohol and cognitive set on sexual arousal to deviant stimuli. *Journal of Abnormal Psychology, 87* (4), 418–430.

Brookman, F., & Maguire, M. (2002). Reducing homicide: A review of the possibilities. Home Office. Online report 01/03. Available from: http://webarchive.nationalarchives. gov.uk/20110218140618/rds.homeoffice.gov.uk/rds/pdfs2/rdsolr0103.pdf (last retrieved July 15, 2016).

Byrne, M.K. (2003). Trauma reactions in the offender. *International Journal of Forensic Psychology, 1* (1), 59–70.

Caspi, A., Begg, D., Dickson, N., Harrington, H., Langley, J., Moffitt, T.E., & Silva, P.A. (1997). Personality differences predict health-risk behaviors in young adulthood: Evidence from a longitudinal study. *Journal of Personality and Social Psychology, 73* (5), 1052–1063.

Chaloupka, F.J., Grossman, M., & Saffer, H. (2002). The effects of price on alcohol consumption and alcohol-related problems. *Alcohol Research & Health, 26* (1), 22–34.

Curtis, L.A. (1974). Victim precipitation and violent crime. *Social Problems, 21* (4), 594–605.

Duff, S.C. (2010). Exploring criminogenic need through victim apology letters: An Interpretative Phenomenological Analysis. *Journal of Aggression, Conflict and Peace Research, 2* (2), 33–43.

Dunseith, N.W., Nelson, E.B., Brusman-Lovins, L.A., Holcomb, J.L., Beckman, D., Weldge, J.A., … & McElroy, S.L. (2004). Psychiatric and legal features of 113 men convicted of sexual offenses. *Journal of Clinical Psychiatry, 65,* 293–300.

Durrant, R. (2011). Anxiety, alcohol use, and aggression: Untangling the causal pathways. *Legal and Criminal Psychology, 16,* 372–378.

Eisner, M. (2002). Crime, problem drinking, and drug use: Patterns of problem behaviour in cross-national perspective. *Annals of the American Academy of Political and Social Science, 508,* 201–225.

Elbogen, E.B., & Johnson, S.C. (2009). The intricate link between violence and mental disorder: Results from the National Epidemiologic Survey on alcohol and related conditions. *Archives of General Psychiatry, 66,* 152–161.

Felson, R.B., & Staff, J. (2010). The effects of alcohol intoxication on violent versus other offending. *Criminal Justice and Behavior, 37,* 1343–1360.

Feucht, T.E. (1993). Prostitutes on crack cocaine: Addiction, utility, and marketplace economies. *Deviant Behavior, 14,* 91–108.

Flatley, J., Kershaw, C., Smith, K., Chaplin, R., & Moon, D. (2010). Crime in England and Wales 2009/10. Home Office Statistical Bulletin 12/10. London: Home Office.

Freeland, J.B., & Campbell, R.S. (1973). The social context of first marijuana use. *International Journal of the Addictions, 8*, 317–324.

George, S., Rogers, R.D., & Duka, T. (2005). The acute effect of alcohol on decision making in social drinkers. *Psychopharmacology, 182*, 160–169.

Giancola, P.R. (2002). Irritability, acute alcohol consumption, and aggressive behavior in men and women. *Drug and Alcohol Dependence, 68*, 263–274.

Giancola, P.R. (2004). Executive functioning and alcohol-related aggression. *Journal of Abnormal Psychology, 113*, 541–555.

Giancola, P.R., Josephs, R.A., Dewall, C.N., & Gunn, R.L. (2009). Applying the attention-allocation model to the explanation of alcohol consumption-related aggression: Implications for prevention. *Substance Use & Misuse, 44*, 1263–1278.

Goode, E. (1997). Between politics and reason. New York: St. Martin's Press.

Gray, N.S., Carman, N.G., Rogers, P., MacCulloch, M.J., Hayward, P., & Snowden, R.J. (2003). Post-traumatic stress disorder caused in mentally disordered offenders by the committing of a serious violent or sexual offence. *Journal of Forensic Psychiatry & Psychology, 14* (1), 27–43.

Green, A.I., & Halkitis, P.N. (2006). Crystal methamphetamine and sexual sociality in an urban gay subculture: An elective affinity. *Culture, Health and Sex, 8*, 317–333.

Grubin, D., & Gunn, J. (1990). The imprisoned rapist and rape. London: Department of Forensic Psychiatry, Institute of Psychiatry.

Hammersley, R. (2011). Pathways through drugs and crime: Desistance, trauma and resilience. *Journal of Criminal Justice, 39*, 268–272.

Hammersley, R., Marsland, L., & Reid, M. (2003). Substance use by young offenders: The impact of the normalisation of drug use in the early years of the 21st century. Home Office Research Study #261. London: Home Office.

Hoeken, P.N.S., & Stewart, S.H. (2003). Drugs of abuse and the elicitation of human aggressive behaviour. *Addictive Behaviors, 28*, 1533–1554.

Hough, M. (1996). Drug misuse and the criminal justice system: A review of the literature. London: Home Office.

Ito, T.A., Miller, N., & Pollock, V.E. (1996). Alcohol and aggression: A meta-analysis on the moderating effects of inhibitory cues, triggering events, and self-focused attention. *Psychological Bulletin, 120*, 60–82.

Krueger, R.F., Schmutte, P.S., Caspi, A., Moffitt, T.E., Campbell, K., & Silva, P.A. (1994). Personality traits are linked to crime among men and women: Evidence from a birth cohort. *Journal of Abnormal Psychology, 103*, 328–338.

Levenson, J.S., Brannon, Y.N., Fortney, T., & Baker, J. (2007). Public perceptions about sex offenders and community protection policies. *Analysis of Social Issues and Public Policy, 7* (1), 137–161.

Liriano, S., & Ramsey, M. (2003). Prisoners' drug use before prison and the links with crime. In M. Ramsey (Ed.), Prisoners' drug use and treatment: Seven research studies. Home Office Research Study #267. London: Home Office.

Lyons, A.C., & Willott, S.A. (2008). Alcohol consumption, gender identities and women's changing social positions. *Sex Roles, 59*, 694–712.

McCaghy, C.H. (1968). Drinking and deviance disavowal: The case of child molesters. *Social Problems, 16* (1), 43–49.

McMurran, M. (2011). Anxiety, alcohol intoxication, and aggression. *Legal and Criminal Psychology, 16,* 357–371.

Menard, S., Mihalic, S., & Huizinga, D. (2001). Drugs and crime revisited. *Justice Quarterly, 18,* 269–299.

Moeller, F.G., Dougherty, D.M., Barratt, E.S., Oderinde, V., Mathias, C.W., Harper, R.A., & Swann, A.C. (2002). Increased impulsivity in cocaine dependent subjects independent of antisocial personality disorder and aggression. *Drug and Alcohol Dependence, 68,* 105–111.

Murdoch, D., & Ross, D. (1990). Alcohol and crimes of violence: Present issues. *Substance Use & Misuse, 25* (9), 1065–1081.

Nielsen, A.L., & Martinez, R. (2003). Reassessing the alcohol-violence linkage: Results from a multi-ethnic city. *Justice Quarterly, 20* (3), 445–469.

Parker, H., & Newcombe, R. (1987). Heroin use and acquisitive crime in an English community. *British Journal of Sociology, 38* (3), 331–350.

Parrott, D., & Zeichner, A. (2002). Effects of alcohol and trait anger on physical aggression. *Journal of Studies on Alcohol, 63,* 196–204.

Peugh, J., & Belenko, S. (2001). Alcohol, drugs and sexual function: A review. *Journal of Psychoactive Drugs, 33,* 223–232.

Pihl, R.O., & Peterson, J.B. (1992). Etiology. In P.E. Nathan, J.W. Langenbucher, B.S. McCrady, & W. Frankenstein (Eds.), *Annual review of addiction research and treatment* (pp. 153–175). Elmsford, NY: Pergamon Press.

Quigley, B.M., & Leonard, K.E. (1999). Husband alcohol expectancies, drinking, and marital-conflict styles as predictors of severe marital violence among newlywed couples. *Psychology of Addictive Behaviors, 13,* 49–59.

Raj, A., Saitz, R., Cheng, D.M., Winter, M., & Samet, J.H. (2007). Associations between alcohol, heroin, and cocaine use and high-risk sexual behaviors among detoxification patients. *American Journal of Drug and Alcohol Abuse, 33,* 169–178.

Rex, S. (2002). Desistance from offending: Experiences of probation. *Howard Journal, 38* (4), 366–383.

Richardson, D.R., & Campbell, J.L. (1982). Alcohol and rape: The effect of alcohol on attributions of blame for rape. *Personality and Social Psychology Bulletin, 8,* 468–476.

Room, R., & Rossow, I. (2001). The share of violence attributable to drinking. *Journal of Substance Abuse, 4,* 218–228.

Ross, M.W., & Darke, S. (1992). Mad, bad and dangerous to know: Dimensions and measurement of attitudes toward injecting drug users. *Drug and Alcohol Dependence, 30,* 71–74.

Schuller, R.A., & Wall, A. (1998). The effects of defendant and complainant intoxication on mock jurors judgements of sexual assault. *Psychology of Women Quarterly, 22* (4), 555–573.

Scribner, R.A., MacKinnon, D.P., & Dwyer, J.H. (1995). The risk of assaultive violence and alcohol availability in Los Angeles County. *American Journal of Public Health, 85,* 335–340.

Shaw, J., Hunt, I.M., Flynn, S., Amos, T., Meehan, J., Robinson, J., … & Appleby, L. (2006). The role of alcohol and drugs in homicides in England and Wales. *Addiction, 101* (8), 1117–1124.

Simpson, M. (2003). The relationship between drug use and crime: A puzzle inside an enigma. *International Journal of Drug Policy, 14*, 307–319.

Smucker-Barnwell, S., Borders, A., & Earleywine, M. (2006). Aggression expectancies and dispositional aggression moderate the relationship between alcohol consumption and alcohol related violence. *Aggressive Behavior, 32*, 517–525.

Sundram, S. (2006). Cannabis and neurodevelopment: Implications for psychiatric disorders. *Human Psychopharmacology, 21*, 245–254.

Tarter, R.E., Kirisci, L., Feske, U., & Vanyukov, M. (2007). Modeling the pathways linking childhood hyperactivity and substance use disorder in young adulthood. *Psychology of Addictive Behaviors, 21*, 266–271.

Testa, M. (2002). The impact of men's alcohol consumption on perpetration of sexual aggression. *Clinical Psychology Review, 22*, 1239–1263.

Widom, C.S., & Hiller-Sturmhofel, S. (2001). Alcohol abuse as a risk factor for and consequence of child abuse. *Alcohol Research and Health, 25*, 52–57.

Wislon, G.T., Lawson, D.M., & Abrams, D.B. (1978). Effects of alcohol on sexual arousal in male alcoholics. *Journal of Abnormal Psychology, 87* (6), 609–616.

Wormith, J.S., Bradford, J.M.W., Pawlak, A., Borzecki, M., & Zohar, A. (1988). The assessment of deviant sexual arousal as a function of intelligence, instructional set, and alcohol ingestion. *Canadian Journal of Psychiatry, 33*, 800–807.

Wright, R.T., & Decker, S.H. (1998). *Armed robbers in action: Stickups and street culture.* Boston, MA: Northeastern University Press.

PART THREE

Family Violence

12

Community Approaches to the Assessment and Prevention of Intimate Partner Violence and Child Maltreatment

KEVIN D. BROWNE, SHIHNING CHOU AND VICKI JACKSON-HOLLIS

INTRODUCTION

Family violence has been defined by the Council of Europe (1986) as:

> Any act or omission committed within the framework of the family by one of its members that undermines the life, the bodily or psychological integrity or the liberty of another member of the same family or that seriously harms the development of his or her personality. (Recommendation 85.4)

This definition incorporates all forms of violence involving physical, psychological, and/or sexual threats or use of aggression toward another, otherwise to treat or use persons or property in a way that causes injury and/or forcibly interferes with personal freedom. This may be of an emotional nature, for instance; verbal or non-verbal threats of violence, suicide, destroying pets, punching walls, throwing objects, locking a person in a room; and other aversive treatment, such as withholding money, food, and social interaction, or corrupting and exploiting the individual.

Therefore, family violence encompasses emotional, physical, and sexual acts by an adult or child that have the potential to harm other family members.

Assessments in Forensic Practice: A Handbook, First Edition. Edited by Kevin D. Browne,
Anthony R. Beech, Leam A. Craig, and Shihning Chou.
© 2017 John Wiley & Sons Ltd. Published 2017 by John Wiley & Sons Ltd.

Table 12.1 Two-way classification of family violence with example of major forms (from Browne & Herbert, 1997, p. 9).

	Physical violence	Psychological violence	Sexual violence
Active abuse	Non-accidental injury Forced coercion and restraint	Intimidation Emotional abuse Material abuse	Incest Assault and rape
Passive neglect	Poor health care Physical neglect	Lack of affection Emotional neglect Material neglect	Failure to protect Prostitution

They can be characterized in the same way and dichotomized into active (abuse) and passive (neglect) forms (see Table 12.1). Family violence is further classified into five types based on the victim: three types are perpetrated by adults in the family – child, spouse, or elder abuse and neglect; two types are perpetrated by children in the family – sibling and parent abuse (Browne & Herbert, 1997).

Research has established that different types of family violence often co-occur concurrently or across generations consecutively. This is especially the case for spousal abuse and child maltreatment. When more than one type of family violence co-occur then research has shown there is a greater likelihood of one or both types of maltreatment reoccurring both in terms of frequency and severity (see Table 12.2).

Edleson (1999a, b) estimated that between 30% and 60% of families had an overlap between child maltreatment and violence against the female partner in the family. In a recent survey of a nationally representative sample of 3,024 US adults (Klevens, Simon, & Chen, 2012), 27.5% of those who self-reported to have struck their partner also reported to have struck a child; 22.1% of those who admitted having struck a child also reported to have struck their partner. The experience of maltreatment in the family makes children more vulnerable to further abuse or exploitation inside and outside of the family. Indeed, Finkelhor, Ormrod, and Turner (2007) found that 22% of children experienced over four types of victimization within a 12-month period. Hamilton and Browne (1999) examined 400 referrals to police child protection units in England and found that 57% had suffered repeat victimization by the same perpetrator, 25% suffered re-victimization by a different perpetrator, and 18% suffered both.

Estimates of child maltreatment indicate that 22.6% of adults worldwide have suffered physical abuse in their childhood (Stoltenborgh, Bakermans-Kranenburg, van Ijzendoorn, & Alink, 2013), 36.3% experienced emotional abuse, and 16.3% experienced physical neglect, with no significant differences by sex (Stoltenborgh, Bakermans-Kranenburg, & van Ijzendoorn, 2013). However, the lifetime prevalence rates of child sexual abuse for boys and girls are 7.6% and 18% respectively (Stoltenborgh, van Ijzendoorn, Euser, & Bakermans-Kranenburg, 2011).

Victims of spousal abuse and child maltreatment are more likely to suffer from various types of physical or mental health problems, which incur significantly

Table 12.2 Severity of maltreatment (adapted from Browne & Herbert, 1997; Browne, 2002).

LESS SEVERE
Minor incidents of an occasional nature with little or no long-term damage – physical, sexual, or psychological.

Physical	e.g.	Injuries confined in area and limited to superficial tissues, including cases of light scratch marks, small slight bruising, minute burns, and small welts.
Sexual	e.g.	Inappropriate sexual touching, invitations and/or exhibitionism, sexualized behavior in the child.
Emotional	e.g.	Occasional verbal assaults, denigration, humiliation, scapegoating, confusing atmosphere.
Neglect	e.g.	Occasional withholding of love and affection, child weight paralleled to or slightly below third centile with no organic cause. Developmental delay. Unwashed skin and hair.

MODERATE SEVERE
More frequent incidents and/or of a more serious nature, but unlikely to be life-threatening or have such potentially long-term effects.

Physical	e.g.	Surface injuries of an extensive or more serious nature and small subcutaneous injuries, including cases of extensive bruising, large welts, lacerations, small hematomas and minor burns/scalds.
Sexual	e.g.	Non-penetrative sexual interaction of an indecent or inappropriate nature, such as fondling, masturbation, and digital penetration, sexualized behavior in the child.
Emotional	e.g.	Frequent verbal assaults, denigration and humiliation, occasional rejection. Child occasionally witnesses family violence and intoxicated parent(s).
Neglect	e.g.	Frequent withholding of love and affection, child non-organic failure to gain weight. Poor hygiene and cleanliness. Parent(s) occasionally depressed or mentally ill.

VERY SEVERE
Ongoing or very frequent maltreatment and/or less frequent incidents with potentially very severe physical or psychological harm. Delay in seeking help and/or incongruent story for injuries to child.

Physical	e.g.	All long and deep tissue injuries and broken bones including fractures, dislocations, subdural hematomas, serious burns, and damage to internal organs.
Sexual	e.g.	Sexual interaction involving attempted or actual oral and/or vaginal penetration. Symptoms include repeated urinary infections, vaginal discharge (STD), vaginal/anal bleeding and injury.

(*Continued*)

Table 12.2 (Continued)

VERY SEVERE

Ongoing or very frequent maltreatment and/or less frequent incidents with potentially very severe physical or psychological harm. Delay in seeking help and/or incongruent story for injuries to child.

Emotional   e.g.   Frequent rejection, occasional withholding of food and drink, enforced isolation and restriction of movement. Child frequently witnesses family violence and intoxicated parent(s).

Neglect   e.g.   Frequent unavailability of parent, guardian, or spouse, child sometimes left alone, non-organic failure to thrive, severe nappy rash with skin lesions. Parent(s) frequently depressed or mentally ill.

LIFE-THREATENING

Long-term or severe psychological and physical harm that results in life-threatening situations (including perpetrators failing to seek help for injuries to child, or victim harming self).

Physical   e.g.   Deliberate or persistent injuries which have the potential of victim death or near death (e.g., poisoning or choking the child).

Sexual   e.g.   Incest, coerced or forced penetration over a prolonged period. Underage pregnancy.

Emotional   e.g.   Persistent rejection, failure to nurture, frequent withholding of food and drink, enforced isolation and restriction of movement. Terrorizing and confining the child. Child witnesses psychotic episodes in parent(s).

Neglect   e.g.   Persistent unavailability of parent, guardian, or spouse, child often left alone, non-organic failure to maintain weight. Frequent illness and infection due to poor hygiene.

higher health care costs (Black & Frost, 2011; Krug, Mercy, Dahlberg, & Zwi, 2002). Children who grow up in environments without adequate care and nurturing relationships with a primary or other caregivers are more likely to have difficulty forming relationships with peers and developing empathy for others. Collectively, their impaired ability to work and fully contribute to the economy also results in loss of income for the society (World Health Organization, 2008).

INTIMATE PARTNER VIOLENCE

Since the World Health Assembly in 1996 adopted a resolution declaring violence a leading worldwide public health problem (WHA49.25), the World Health Organization (WHO) produced the first comprehensive global report on violence in 2002 (World Health Organization, 2002). It has devoted a considerable amount of resources to preventing violence against women and girls and intimate partner violence. The WHO published guidelines on preventing intimate partner and sexual violence against women in 2010 (World Health Organization, 2010). The first global and regional estimates of violence against women was published in 2013 and the WHO clinical and policy guidelines on responding to intimate partner violence (World Health Organization, Department of Reproductive Health and Research at London School of Hygiene and Tropical Medicine, & South African Medical Research Council, 2013) and sexual violence against women in the same year (World Health Organization, 2013).

The WHO adopts the term "intimate partner violence" (IPV), which describes any "behaviour within an intimate relationship that causes physical, sexual or psychological harm to those in the relationship, including acts of physical aggression, sexual coercion, psychological abuse and controlling behaviour" (World Health Organization, 2014, p. 82). Worldwide, approximately one in three women who have ever had a partner have experienced physical and/or sexual violence by a male intimate partner, and of those who have been physically or sexually abused by a partner, 42% have sustained injuries due to that violence (World Health Organization, 2013). It is worth noting that within intimate relationships, physical, sexual, and emotional violence also often co-occur. In the WHO multi-country study (World Health Organization, 2005a), it was estimated that between 23% and 56% of women who reported ever experiencing physical or sexual IPV had experienced both.

Risk Factors for Intimate Partner Violence

Women are more at risk from men who are generally violent or men with personality disorders than men who are only violent in the home. In incidents perpetrated by both generally violent men or men with personality disorders, the violence is more likely to be severe and even escalate to life-threatening violence and homicide (Aldridge & Browne, 2003; Holtzworth-Munroe & Stuart, 1994). In 81% of femicides, the woman had been physically abused by the perpetrator the year prior to the murder (Garcia, Soria, & Hurwitz, 2007). Women are nine times more likely to be killed by an intimate partner than by a stranger in the United States (Campbell et al., 2007). In England and Wales, 37% of all women killed were murdered by their current or former partner or lover (Aldridge & Browne, 2003). This is comparable to the most recent global estimates, which indicate that 38% of female homicides worldwide are committed by their male partners while the figure for male victims was 6% (Stockl et al., 2013; World Health Organization et al., 2013).

Risk factors associated with IPV can be associated with the victim and the perpetrator (Browne & Herbert, 1997). Victim characteristics that increase risk are those that increase the chances of the victim remaining in a violent relationship or returning to one, for example learned helplessness, negative self-concept, poor housing, unemployment and financial hardship, loneliness and dependence, victim of maltreatment as a child, and belief that partner will reform. Perpetrator characteristics that increase the risk of family violence are similar to those for all violent and antisocial offenders, for example history of violence, personality disorder, mental illness, substance misuse, social isolation, low self-esteem, poor impulse control and social skills, fear of abandonment and anxious emotional attachments, cognitive distortions, external locus of control and lack of empathy, poor housing, unemployment and financial hardship, life stress and redirected aggression, and exposure to violence as a child.

Mears (2003) states that alcohol, ethnicity, personality disorders, mental health problems, growing up in a violent home, patriarchal traditional views, unmarried marital status, poor education, poor income, and/or occupational disparity within the relationship are all consistently identified with increase risk of IPV. It is worth noting that women with a disability are at a higher risk of IPV due to their dependence on the abuser and the limited opportunities and resources they have to leave a violent partner. They also suffer from a higher rate of sexual assault by their abusers than non-disabled women and often report not being believed or not being taken seriously when speaking out about their abuse (Hague et al., 2008). The WHO (2002, 2006) adopts the ecological nested model to consider common risk factors for all forms of family violence. At the center are individual factors (child and parent), next relationship factors, followed by community/societal factors.

There is limited literature on risk factors associated with victimization in the romantic relationships of young women aged 12–24 years, although 31% of girls report being subjected to physical violence and 4% to sexual violence (Vezina & Hebert, 2007). The most recent review (Vezina & Hebert, 2007) identified 61 studies and found that there was inconsistent evidence that dating violence was associated with any ethnic minority group or socio-demographic background. However, family breakdown, depression, teenage pregnancy, dropping out of school, substance misuse, and conduct disorders were all associated with higher levels of dating violence. Not surprisingly, the same review found that prior victim experiences, lack of parental supervision, parental neglect, and delinquent behaviors were all associated with the young woman becoming a victim of dating violence. Early experiences of abuse and neglect in the victim's family of origin increase the risks of being a victim of physical and sexual violence at all ages (Browne & Herbert, 1997). The evidence to date indicates that risk factors for adolescents share many similarities to those described for adults (Lundgren & Amin, 2015).

Most recently, Jackson, Browne, and Joseph (2015) explored individual categories of victimization outside the family experienced by 730 English adolescents aged between 13 and 16 years over the lifetime: 1 in 4 experienced physical victimization, almost 1 in 2 experienced bullying, and 1 in 7 experienced sexual victimization. Even by the age of 16 years, 1 in 28 adolescents had experienced violence from a romantic partner during a date.

Assessment of Need in IPV (Screening for Targeted Prevention)

Targeted (i.e., secondary) prevention involves screening and targeting resources to individuals or families identified as being "in need" or "high priority" for additional services. This can be achieved by identifying known "risk" factors for intimate partner violence (please see the above section) and offering additional services before maltreatment occurs. Screening can be carried out either *universally* through community services available to all women/families or in a *targeted* manner, screening only at-risk groups who attend specialist services such as casualty emergency departments or mental health services.

Population-based surveys reveal that 20% to 60% of women have not disclosed the violence they suffer and fewer still have sought help from agencies, including health services. Of those who were injured due to violence, 48% reported needing health care but only 36% actually sought it. Therefore, it is important to implement measures that help enhance the level of disclosure by victims, such as asking questions about abusive experiences as part of a routine screening of those seeking medical advice and treatment (World Health Organization, 2005a).

In 30% of cases IPV starts in pregnancy (Lewis, 2007). It is also estimated that 4–8% of all pregnant women are victims of IPV, suggesting that this is an important topic for universal screening (Sharps, Laughon, & Giangrande, 2007). This can have a number of implications including maternal death during birth (Lewis, 2007). The onset of IPV during this period for many victims, and the serious implications it can have, highlights the importance of identifying IPV before pregnancy and recognizing and preventing violence during pregnancy. One way to do this would be through routine screening in health-care services, with a particular focus on services provided for pregnant and post-natal women (DeVoe & Kaufman Kantor, 2002; Dutton & Kropp, 2000). An inter-agency project in Leeds in the United Kingdom showed that 92% of women who were routinely questioned about IPV in maternity settings were in favor of this routine inquiry (Leeds Inter-Agency Project, 2005; Trotter et al., 2007).

Intimate partner violence was assessed in a large cohort study comprising a population of 14,252 families with newborn children in South East England (Browne, 1995; Browne & Herbert, 1997). Community nurse health visitors asked each mother "Is there a violent adult in the family?" as a part of a risk-factor screening tool to identify families at high risk for child maltreatment (Browne, Douglas, Hamilton-Giachritis, & Hegarty, 2006). It was found that 1.8% (n = 258) of mothers reported current, or a history of, IPV when asked this question. In the first five years of the child's life, 106 families from this population went on to maltreat their newborn with 30% of these reporting IPV, in comparison to 1.6% of the 14,146 non-maltreating parents (see Table 12.5). Therefore IPV was shown to increase the risk of child maltreatment by 23.4 times (risk ratio). This suggests that routine screening within maternity settings and home visits may be a way forward in identifying IPV. Indeed, research on screening by health staff has been found to be effective in some areas, with one study indicating that the majority of families who were brought to the attention of children's centers in England were done so mainly through their health staff (Pinney, Ball, & Niven, 2007).

Only a few good tools have been found for *targeted screening* in emergency departments, maternity services, and mental health care settings (Feder et al., 2009). Of these, a four-item tool used in the family practice setting which asks patients how many times had their partner Hurt, Insulted, Threatened with harm, and Screamed at them (HITS; Sherin, Sinacore, Li, Zitter, & Shakil, 1998) has been identified to be the best in terms of diagnostic accuracy, concurrent validity, and reliability compared to others (Feder et al., 2009). However, recent systematic reviews have concluded that the evidence is too limited to recommend a specific screening tool for healthcare settings (Macmillan et al., 2009; Rabin, Jennings, Campbell, & Bair-Merritt, 2009). Another systematic review suggested that poor performance of screening was related to a lack of staff training and inadequate knowledge among health professionals. There may also be a lack of acceptance as the identification of a victim increases the workload of already overstretched hospital and health services (Olive, 2007). In response to these assertions, the English Department of Health have issued professional guidelines to health visitors and school nurses of how to prevent, identify, and refer cases of domestic violence (Department of Health, 2013). The guidance emphasizes that routine screening needs to be combined with appropriate support and interventions, good multi-agency relationships, and referral services in order for it to be effective and for people to believe in its utility.

In terms of fatal assault, screening may be better applied to the identification of perpetrators and the Spousal Assault Risk Assessment (SARA; Kropp, Hart, Webster, & Eaves, 1999) containing 20 items relating to criminal history, psychosocial adjustment, spousal assault history, and current offense. Research by Kropp and Hart (2000) showed moderate levels of internal consistency and item homogeneity, high interrater reliability, and good convergent and discriminant validity with respect to other measures related to risk for general and violent criminality (see Chapter 14 by Louise Dixon in this volume).

HM Government (2016) state that health professionals can play an integral role in helping identify women who are suffering from IPV and helping them to leave their abuser, especially when the woman does not speak very good English, thus reducing the likelihood of them speaking out about their abuse. It may also be useful to place information regarding IPV and the help that is available in primary health care settings, in all languages relevant for that community, to increase the likelihood of women who have restricted freedom seeing them and being made aware of the services available (Izzidien, 2008).

Information Sharing and Multi-Agency Risk Assessment Conferences

In the United Kingdom, a multi-sector, interdisciplinary approach is seen as the most effective way of working together to provide protection to women and children in domestic settings (Home Office, 2005). In recent times there has been coordinated action against IPV with monthly meetings of multi-agency risk assessment conferences (MARACs) for IPV in most areas, as recommended by the Intimate Partner Violence, Crime and Victims Act 2004. The objective is to prevent spouse abuse by better sharing of information and risk assessment upon the identification of domestic abuse within a family and the provision of a multi-agency response to help protect women deemed as being at high risk (Douglas, Lilley, Kooper, & Diamond, 2004). The guidelines outline a structural framework and a pathway for information sharing between IPV and child protection agencies. Research so far suggests that the introduction of MARACs has been effective in reducing re-victimization and enhancing the safety of staff working with violent perpetrators, as well as information sharing (Robinson, 2006). Nevertheless, there are gaps in relation to sharing information to and from mental health care services. There is a need to improve the communication and sharing of information between health and social services and the law enforcement and criminal justice services in relation to violent perpetrators, for both MARACs and multi-agency public protection panels (MAPPAs). Furthermore, few black and ethnic minority services are involved in this information sharing and therefore the provision of support for women from ethnic minority backgrounds is restricted (Anitha, 2008, 2010; Izzidien, 2008).

CHILD MALTREATMENT

The WHO defines child maltreatment as "all forms of physical and/or emotional ill-treatment, sexual abuse, neglect or negligent treatment or commercial or other exploitation, resulting in actual or potential harm to the child's health, survival, development or dignity in the context of a relationship of responsibility, trust or power" (Browne, Hamilton-Giachritis, & Vettor, 2007a, b; Butchart, Harvey, Mian, & Furniss, 2006). Child maltreatment covers abuse and neglect of a child in physical, sexual, and emotional domains (see Table 12.1). Many children suffer more than one type of maltreatment at the same time and/or over a period of time, and in a minority of cases the child is victimized in a ritualistic and terrorizing way.

The perpetrators of child maltreatment are most often immediate family members (parents, stepparents, older siblings, and grandparents), although there is an equal probability of child maltreatment in foster families, adoptive families, and families with same-sex parents (Browne & Herbert, 1997). Extended family members (e.g., aunts, uncles, and cousins) may maltreat a child. Adults and older children who offend are also found outside the family in community and institutional settings: schools, sport centers, hospitals, children's homes, and residential and secure institutions. Men who sexually assault children often select these workplaces in order to be close to their intended victims (Elliott, Browne, & Kilcoyne, 1995). The more the victim knows and trusts the abuser, the more difficult it is for the child to disclose and share experiences.

Retrospective studies on the prevalence of child abuse and neglect among adolescents, teenagers, and adults, reporting these experiences earlier in their childhood, demonstrate that child maltreatment is a substantial burden on public health and social welfare. Every year, 4 to 16% of children are physically abused and 10% are neglected or psychologically abused. In addition between 5% and 10% of girls and up to 5% of boys are exposed to penetrative sexual abuse, and up to three times this number are exposed to any type of sexual abuse (Gilbert, Widom, et al., 2009).

By contrast, official government statistics (mainly from high-income countries) show that incidence rates for substantiated cases of child abuse and neglect, coming to the attention of the authorities, are less than 10% of the prevalence figures (Gilbert, Kemp, et al., 2009). Hence, child maltreatment significantly contributes to child mortality and morbidity, and it has been found that the consequences of passive neglect are at least as damaging in the long term as active physical or sexual abuse (Crittenden, 2002).

For many years, research has demonstrated the negative impact of abuse and neglect on children and adolescents and its long-term burden on physical and mental health and child development. The consequences of being a victim of abuse and/or neglect include death, physical and mental disabilities, stress and physical health problems, emotional and behavioral problems, low self-esteem and poor sense of self-worth, school absence and educational failure, sleep disorders, bed wetting and post-traumatic stress symptoms, mental health problems, eating disorders and self-injury, alcohol and drug abuse, risk of further victimization, antisocial behavior, delinquency and criminal acts, and victims becoming offenders (Browne et al., 2007a).

Risk Factors

Routine community clinic or home visit screening by health professionals for risk factors associated with child maltreatment and poor parenting is a means of ensuring that families with children who have additional needs are provided with additional services and support (Browne et al., 2006). Risk factors for child maltreatment are associated with the parent and/or the child and fall into four categories or levels: Individual, Relationship, Community, and Societal (see Table 12.3). Many of these risk factors are shared with increased risk of other forms of family violence (i.e., IPV, elder maltreatment, parent abuse, and sibling violence).

Child-Related Risk Factors (See Table 12.3)

Ethnicity: Although there is a limited amount of research regarding children from ethnic minority backgrounds, reports suggest that these children are at an increased risk of becoming the victims of child maltreatment. A recent systematic review looking at the maltreatment of children from ethnic minorities in the United States indicated that Asian American children suffer the highest rate of physical abuse compared to the national average and to other ethnic minority groups (Zhai & Gao, 2009). Asian American parents believe in parental authority and physical punishment, and also may have high expectations of their children. This may explain the increased rates of physical abuse in this group. Tzeng and Schwarzin (1990) report that children from "other" ethnic minorities, for example Oriental, Hispanic, and so on, are four times more likely to be sexually abused than white children, and three times more likely to be sexually abused than black children. By contrast to these US studies, a prospective cohort study on risk factors for child maltreatment in an English population (N=14,252) found little evidence for ethnicity being a risk factor for child maltreatment, as the number of cases from ethnic minorities were found to be representative of their (percent) proportion in the population in general (Browne & Herbert, 1997; Browne & Jackson, 2013).

Disability: An American record-linkage showed a cumulative prevalence of any child maltreatment in 31% of disabled children compared to 9% of non-disabled children. With regard to child physical abuse, Sullivan and Knutson (2000) found disabled children to be 3.8 times more likely to be physically abused than non-disabled children. However, the risk of physical abuse varies according to the type of disability, compared to children without a disability, as does other forms of child maltreatment (see Table 12.4). The English cohort study referred to above estimated the relative risk of child maltreatment to children with disabilities to be 2.6 times more than those without. Furthermore, prematurity or low birth rate increased the relative risk by 3.6 times and the child being separated for more than 24 hours post-delivery by 4.2 times (see Table 12.5).

Separated at birth: One suggested reason for a higher prevalence among children with low birth weight, prematurity, and disabilities is that these children may have been separated at birth for health needs, limiting the opportunity for the parent to bond and/or *not meeting the expectations of the parents* and relatives at birth. This in turn increases the risk of abandonment and rejection with higher levels of residential care for these children in comparison to non-disabled children (5.7% of the total population compared the 0.55% respectively)

Table 12.3 Global risk factors for child maltreatment. (Adapted from World Health Organization, 2006.)

Level	In parents/caregivers	In the child
Individual level	• Previous allegations of child abuse and neglect; • difficulty bonding with a newborn child; • does not show nurturing characteristics toward the child; • separation from child at birth; • history of own childhood maltreatment; • lack of awareness of child development or has unrealistic expectations; • inappropriate, excessive, or violent punishment or actions; • approval of/uses physical punishment or believes in its effectiveness; • physical or mental health problems or cognitive impairment; • impulsive and lack of self-control when upset or angry; • misuse of alcohol or drugs; • criminality activity; • social isolation; • depression, low self-esteem, or feeling of inadequacy; • poor parenting skills; • financial difficulties; • lack of engagement with health and social services.	• An unwanted baby or did not fulfill the parent's expectations or wishes; • separation from parent at birth; • physical or mental disability; • premature or low birth weight; • showing high needs; • symptoms of mental ill-health; • personality or temperament traits that are perceived by the parent as problematic; • multiple birth; • twins or siblings close in age; • exposed to dangerous behaviors (e.g., inter-parental violence or other types of adult violence in the home).
Relationship level	• Poor parent–child attachment and failure to bond; • physical, developmental, or mental health problems of a family member; • family breakdown; • violence in the family; • disrespectful gender roles and roles in intimate relationships; • isolated in the community or lack of a support network; • discrimination against the family; • involvement in criminal or violent activities in the community.	

Community level	• Tolerance of violence; • gender and social inequality; • lack of or inadequate housing; • lack of services to support families and institutions for specialized needs; • high levels of unemployment or poverty; • harmful levels of lead or other toxins in the environment; • transient neighborhood; • easy availability of alcohol; • a local drug trade.
Societal level	• Inadequate policies that lead to poor living standards, socioeconomic inequality, or instability; social and cultural norms that: • promote or glorify violence; • demand rigid gender roles for males and females; • diminish the status of the child in parent–child relationships; • existence of child pornography, child prostitution, and child labor.

Table 12.4 Relative risk of child maltreatment for children with disabilities compared to children without a disability (X 1). (Adapted from Kendall-Tackett, Lyon, Taliaferro, & Little, 2005, and based on data on 50,278 US children from Sullivan & Knutson, 2000.)

Children with	Neglect	Physical abuse	Sexual abuse	Psychological/ emotional abuse
Hearing difficulties	X 2	X 4	X 1	X 2
Speech/language difficulties	X 5	X 5	X 3	X 1
Developmental delays	X 4	X 4	X 4	X 4
Learning disabilities	X 2	X 2	X 2	X 2
Behavioral disorders	X 7	X 7	X 5.5	X 7
No disability	X 1	X 1	X 1	X 1

(Parker, Gordon, & Loughran, 2000). Consideration should therefore be given to the safeguarding of disabled children in general, and more specifically, for those children in residential settings in order to address the possible increased risk of abuse they may face there which is estimated to be two to three times more likely (Gilbert, Kemp, et al., 2009).

Although it has been recognized by the Department of Health (1999, 2013) that disabled children face an increased risk of abuse and maltreatment, a large proportion of local authorities fail to record details regarding disability when a child becomes involved in the child protection process. This is highlighted in a survey by Cooke in 2000 (cited in Cooke & Standen, 2002), in which only 51% of local authorities in England, Scotland, Wales, and Northern Ireland recorded whether the abused child suffered from any kind of disability. This lack of recording greatly affects the extent to which researchers can understand the relationship between disabilities and child maltreatment and therefore hinders the development of effective interventions.

Sibling abuse: In relation to sibling abuse, the availability of younger victims in the household and parents not providing adequate supervision are risk factors associated with inappropriate physical and/or sexual bullying from adolescents in the family (Browne & McManus, 2010). The presence of a child with special needs because of disability can increase the risk of sibling abuse in the family. The child with a disability may act as an offender when older than brothers or sisters or as a victim when younger than other siblings. Intervention with such families often involves adult members of the family being questioned on where the sexual and/or violent behaviors shown by their children were learned and how they developed to become abusive and problematic (e.g., exposed to inappropriate sexual behaviors such as observing parents' sexual intercourse, access to pornography, etc.) (Worling, 1995). Often there is a blurring of boundaries surrounding the identification of inappropriate sexual behavior, with it being referred to as exploratory; for example, the parents would say "boys will be boys." Likewise, the parents see it as mutually consenting sex play-acting "doctors and nurses" or "mothers and fathers." Consequently, the perpetrator is not held responsible for his/her actions and has a license to continue (O'Brien, 1991; Wiehe, 1997; Worling, 1995). This minimization and ignorance of wrongdoing is liable to have long-term consequences for the victim.

Parent-Related Factors (see Table 12.3)

Stepparent or cohabitee in the family: often considered to be a risk factor, although the relative risk (RR=5.5) would suggest stepparents are sometimes misrepresented for their relative contribution to child maltreatment in comparison to single or separated parents (RR=11.8). When the maternal caregiver is unavailable, disabled, or ill and/or where the child victim has a poor relationship with the mother, the situation may increase the possibility of sexual abuse to a child in all types of families (Browne, 1994; Browne 2009a, b). Usually children sexually abused within the family are victims of other forms of abuse such as physical and emotional abuse, either before or at the same time as being sexually abused (see Chapter 16).

Sex offenders outside the family sometimes target children living with a single parent. Indeed, children from separated/divorced families are vulnerable due to them experiencing *marital discord and divorce* (Mears, 2003). Children from broken families are more vulnerable than those from intact families because of their lack of confidence and low self-esteem. The children are unsure of themselves and as a consequence are more compliant to the approaches of a teenage or adult perpetrator, whether previously known or unknown (Browne, 1994; Elliott et al., 1995).

Intimate Partner Violence (IPV): This is highly associated with child physical and sexual abuse (RR=23.4), so that when the mother recognizes inappropriate parenting the perpetrator's response is usually violence toward her (Browne, 1993; Browne & Herbert, 1997). The importance of the links between intimate partner violence and child maltreatment has been recognized for family protection work for some time (Browne & Hamilton, 1999; Dietz & Craft, 1980; Jaffe, Wolfe, & Wilson, 1990). In the majority of cases this involves the father/stepfather seriously assaulting the mother as well as the children. An Australian study by Goddard and Hiller (1993) found that child sexual abuse (CSA) was evident in 40% of families with IPV. Truesdell, McNeil, and Deschner (1986) also claimed that IPV was more common than expected in North American incestuous families with nearly three-quarters (73%) of mothers from incestuous families experiencing at least one incident of intimate partner violence, a third of who were threatened or injured with a knife or a gun.

Where both spouse abuse and child maltreatment co-occur in the family, mental health problems and alcohol and drug dependency appear to be the most significant risk factors (RR=10.1) for violence (Browne & Hamilton, 1999). In the United States, surveys of battered women typically show that 60% of their partners have an alcohol problem and 20% have a drug problem (Kelley et al., 2009) and the majority of female victims suffer from mental health problems as a result. Some authors propose that these are the major causes of family violence (Pernanen, 1991).

Alcohol and drug dependency: relieves the man of the responsibility of his behavior and gives the wife justification for remaining in the relationship in the hope that he will control his addiction and end his aggression. It is true that alcohol and drugs appear to exacerbate pre-existing emotional problems, which increases the likelihood of violence. However, the majority of individuals who abuse drugs and alcohol admit they have been violent to their dependants while not under the influence of alcohol and drugs (Sonkin, Martin, & Walker, 1985). Indeed, mental health problems, and alcohol and drug dependency, are not the causes of family violence but rather conditions that coexist with it, along with many other factors. Nevertheless, they are often used as excuses for violent behavior – personally, socially, and legally. Interventions aimed at the protection of women and children must first address these associated factors as individuals addicted to alcohol and drugs or suffering from mental illness can rarely benefit from social services interventions. The interagency cooperation between health and social services is a necessary prerequisite in such cases (HM Government, 2015; Kelley et al., 2009). However, adult mental health services are considered by Reder and Duncan (2002) as the missing link in the child protection system since their mental health staff rarely contribute to the work of Local Authority Safeguarding Boards or to Case Conferences. This is despite the increasing evidence in the literature of a relationship between parental *mental health problems*, substance misuse, and violence toward women and children.

Assessment of Need in Families (Screening for Targeted Prevention)

The largest prospective cohort study on risk factors for child maltreatment in an English population of 14,252 families was carried out in Surrey (Browne & Herbert, 1997; Browne & Jackson, 2013). This study demonstrated that a family with IPV was 23 times more likely to abuse their child under five years of age compared to a family with a child under five without that characteristic (see Table 12.5). Parents with mental illness, alcohol abuse, or drug abuse were 10 times more likely to abuse and/or neglect their child. Likewise, an infant mentally or physically disabled was 2.6 times more likely to be abused under the age of five years compared to a child without a disability. Overall, health visitors using a 12-item checklist of risk factors (see Table 12.5) developed by Browne (1995) identified 7% of families in Surrey with a newborn child who showed a high number of predisposing factors (five or more) for child maltreatment. Of these high-risk families, 1 in 13 went on to abuse their children within the first five years of life in comparison to 1 in 400 low-risk families. Large effect sizes related to risk factors have also been reported in a meta-analytic review by Stith, Green, Smith, and Ward (2008).

In addition to risk factors, the quality of parenting (i.e., good enough parenting) is important to assess. Parents who were indifferent or intolerant toward their child were 13 times more likely to maltreat the child (see Table 12.5). Poor parenting can be identified by negative parental perceptions and uncaring attitudes toward the child together with insensitive and inconsistent caregiving. Indeed this has the potential to distinguish the true "hits" from the false alarms in health visitor screening and identify those parents most in need of positive parenting programs as a prevention strategy (Browne et al., 2006; Dixon, Browne, & Hamilton-Giachritsis, 2005; Dixon, Howie, & Starling, 2005).

Policymakers and practitioners who advocate positive parenting programs as a universal service directed at all new parents (e.g., Sanders & Cann, 2002) recognize the importance of caregiver–child interaction for the survival and healthy development of young children and the prevention of child abuse and neglect (World Health Organization, 2004, 2005b). Others (e.g., Olds, 2002) apply parenting programs to targeted populations that show risk factors associated with poor outcomes for children (i.e., mother under 21 at time of birth, and the presence of social isolation and/ or financial difficulties), as universally delivered programs are considered too costly. In the United Kingdom, targeting families who come into contact with health and social services is based on the "framework for assessment" (Department of Health, Department for Education and Employment, & Home Office, 2000) and their need is assessed by considering the following three areas (see Figure 12.1):

- Assessment of children's development needs in general.
- Assessment of the parent(s) capacity to respond appropriately to their child's needs.
- Assessment of the wider social and environmental factors that impact on the capacity to parent.

It has been suggested (Browne et al., 2006) that health visitors can play a significant role in the early assessment and identification of vulnerable women and children and ameliorate their potential for victimization. However this requires commitment and resources to maintain a universal home visitation program within the primary care setting, which is usually linked to services to children under five and a health needs assessment approach in public health practice (Thurtle, 2009). In addition, it requires an established referral network to services to provide preventative interventions (i.e., community psychiatric team, hospital services, social service departments, probation department, and housing department, as well as counseling and support services developed within the primary care trust). The provision and activities of "SureStart" children's centers are an essential component of working with vulnerable and disadvantaged families within the community (Department of Health & Department for Education and Skills, 2006).

Prevention of Child Maltreatment

To prevent violence to children and their separation from parents in difficulty, positive parenting programs can be offered to those families with a high number of risk factors that increase the likelihood of violence and neglect toward children (Sanders & Cann, 2002). These risk factors are associated with the child's immediate social environment of parents and family as well as the wider social environment of the community and society as a whole. The number and

Table 12.5 The number of families and the relative risk of child abuse and neglect associated with family characteristics screened at birth.*

Family characteristics at birth that are risk factors for child abuse and neglect	Relative risk for abuse and neglect RR	Abusing families (N=106) n	%	Non-abusing families (N=14,146) n	%	Total population (N=14,252) n	Families in total population with the characteristic (%)
1. History of spousal violence	23.4	32	30.2	226	1.6	258	1.81
2. Parent indifferent, intolerant, or over-anxious toward child	13.2	33	31.1	438	3.1	471	3.30
3. Single or separated parent	11.8	51	48.1	976	6.9	1027	7.21
4. Socioeconomic problems such as unemployment	15.7	75	70.8	1825	12.9	1900	13.33
5. History of mental illness, drug or alcohol addiction	10.1	37	34.9	679	4.8	716	5.02
6. Parent abused or neglected as a child	12.5	21	19.8	255	1.8	276	1.94
7. Infant premature, low birth rate	3.6	23	21.7	976	6.9	999	7.02
8. Infant separated from mother for more than 24 hours post-delivery	4.2	13	12.3	453	3.2	466	3.27
9. Mother less than 21 years old at time of birth	4.9	31	29.2	1089	7.7	1120	7.86
10. Stepparent or cohabitee present	5.5	29	27.4	877	6.2	906	6.36
11. Less than 18 months between birth of children	2.3	17	16.0	1061	7.5	1078	7.56
12. Infant mentally or physically handicapped	2.6	3	2.8	156	1.1	159	1.12

* As determined from a five-year prospective cohort study of 14,252 English families, from which 106 families were involved in child protection procedures by the time the child reached the age of five years. (Adapted from Browne & Herbert, 1997, p. 120.)

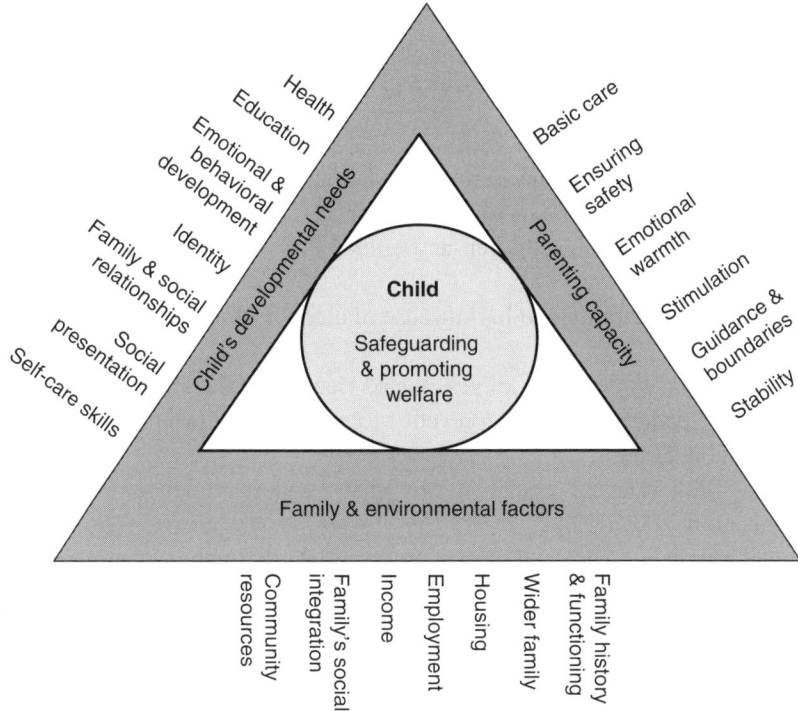

Figure 12.1 Framework for the assessment of children and families (Department of Health et al., 2000).

characteristics of risk factors present in the family will indicate the level of support required in the parenting training program.

A systematic review (Barlow, Simkiss, & Stewart-Brown, 2006) found insufficient evidence supporting the effectiveness of parenting programs to prevent child physical maltreatment but such programs may be effective in improving risk factors associated with physical maltreatment. For example, another systematic review found that parenting programs were effective in improving a number of aspects of parent–child interaction both in the short- and long-term, especially for teenage parents (Barlow, Jolley, & Hallam, 2011). While a direct impact of such programs on child maltreatment cannot be established, an early systematic review (Elkan et al., 2000) found parenting programs to be effective in improving the home environment and a recent systematic review found positive results for reducing unintentional injuries in childhood (Kendrick et al., 2013), some of which are associated with a lack of supervision and neglect.

There has been growing evidence demonstrating the effectiveness of prevention, more so for some strategies than others. However, most of the studies that generated the existing evidence were conducted in high-income countries and therefore the evidence may not be directly applicable to other societies (Gilbert, Widom, et al.,

2009; World Health Organization, 2006). Nevertheless, the WHO and its partners have recognized the overlaps of contributing factors for different types of violence and identified six prevention strategies and one response effort that tackle multiple forms of violence. These are:

- developing safe, stable, and nurturing relationships between children and their caregivers (World Health Organization, 2009 g);
- developing life skills in children and adolescents (World Health Organization, 2009c);
- reducing the availability and harmful use of alcohol (World Health Organization, 2009d);
- reducing access to guns and knives (World Health Organization, 2009b);
- promoting gender equality to prevent violence against women (World Health Organization, 2009e);
- changing cultural and social norms that support violence (World Health Organization, 2009a); and
- victim identification, care, and support programs (World Health Organization, 2009f).

The WHO (2014) conducted a survey to assess the extent to which the above seven prevention strategies have been implemented. Of the 113 participating countries, 49% had implemented programs that promote changes in social and cultural norms regarding IPV, 39% had implemented caregiver support programs, 38% had offered parenting education, 37% had implemented child sexual abuse prevention, 35% had offered home visiting, and 26% had launched professional awareness campaigns. It is worth noting that social and cultural norm changes and strategies still need to be evaluated more rigorously. Nevertheless, their implementation can be an important strategy to inform and create cultural shifts in the perception and acceptance of certain behaviors. However, it was also found that violence prevention activities are often addressed by multiple agencies without a lead agency for coordination. It is important to establish leadership in multidisciplinary prevention efforts.

Identification of Physical Abuse and Neglect (See Figure 12.2)

Children coming to the attention of health services through hospital/clinic visits offer the chance for health professionals to identify non-accidental injury, witting and unwitting neglect, and risks associated with child maltreatment. This is alongside standard procedures for dealing with developmental health checks, immunizations, and caring for physical injuries and illnesses. Good practice in hospitals and clinics involves routine screening and comprehensive history-taking by doctors and nurses. This should include components to promote the identification of child maltreatment:

- History of family circumstances (e.g., presence of isolation, violence, addiction, or mental illness).
- History of child's condition (e.g., story doesn't explain injury, delay in seeking help).

- Child's physical condition when undressed (e.g., presence of disability, lesions, previous injuries, or unusual marks).
- Child's physical care (e.g., cleanliness, teeth, hair, nails, hygiene).
- Child's behavior (e.g., frozen hyper-vigilance or aggressive hyperactivity).
- Parents/caretaker's behavior and demeanour (e.g., low self-esteem, depressed, over-anxious, insensitive, careless, punishing, defensive).

The integrated management of child health and illness by primary health care teams and community health professionals is aimed at the prevention of child disability, morbidity, and mortality, as well as at limiting the stress to parents in caring for a sick child (World Health Organization, 2005b). All children coming into contact with a health service, through home or clinic visits, can be observed and checked in the normal way for physical injuries and illnesses. During the consultation, the possibility of non-accidental injury and illnesses occurring because of abuse and/or neglect should be kept in mind. An algorithm developed for the WHO (Browne et al., 2007b) is currently being piloted and evaluated. This is presented in Figure 12.2 as an example of how child protection can be incorporated into health service provision for families and children.

Reactive surveillance and identification leads to intervention both to stop the current maltreatment and to prevent recurrent victimization. The poor cost effectiveness of this approach compared to primary and secondary prevention is highlighted by the fact that in England, at least a quarter of abused children are referred again to child protection professionals within two years (Hamilton & Browne, 1999).

However, a data paucity regarding the effectiveness of screening and identification has been recognized by Hall and Hall (2007) for the United Kingdom and Nygren et al. (2004) for the United States. It would often be necessary for health-care professionals to rely on statements given by the parent(s), who is/are most likely the perpetrator, or from observations reported by others. Hence, the detection and prevention of child abuse and neglect is said to be problematic (Gilbert, Widom et al., 2009). Therefore, the focus has tended to rest largely on ensuring health-care professionals and other service providers are educated in and vigilant to the signs of child abuse and neglect (World Health Organization, 2002).

Challenges for Risk Assessment and Prevention

In order to prevent family violence, it is important to target families with risk factors (prior to abuse) and place them in priority for health and social support services. The aim is to reduce the chances of spouse and child abuse by ameliorating the effects of adverse family characteristics that influence the personality and behavior of family members. Women and children from disruptive/violent homes may become socially withdrawn, shy, and unsure of themselves, with feelings of low self-esteem and a poor sense of self-worth. These women and children are especially vulnerable to the initial advances of a child sex offender inside or outside the family. Indeed, sex offenders report that these behavior components of a "submissive

Does the child have a condition associated with child abuse and neglect?

IF evidence of physical injury (especially head injury), OR growth failure, OR developmental delay and/or disability, OR delay in seeking health care, OR child discloses some form of maltreatment: THEN CHECK FOR SIGNS OF CHILD ABUSE AND NEGLECT (listen carefully to what the child says)

OBSERVE AND CHECK

- *Evidence of suspicious physical condition/injury*** (e.g., poisoning; facial bruises; multiple bruises in unusual sites; genital or anal injury; bite, belt or whip marks; contact burns or immersion scalds; and fractures in children less than one year).

- *Delay by parent/caregiver in seeking help for any injury with no valid reason.*

- *Lack of explanation or story inconsistent with injury or condition.*

- *Inadequate physical care of child:* growth failure; illness ignored; not-immunized; poor condition of skin, teeth, hair and nails; repeat attendances at clinic for child or sibling.

- *Abnormal child behavior:* indiscriminant affection, sexualized behavior, aggressive hyperactivity, frozen hyper-vigilance, self harm, avoids visual contact with caregiver.

- *Abnormal parent/caregiver behavior:* angry, defensive, punishing, threatening, insensitive, over-anxious, low self-esteem, depressed, negative attributions to child, poor supervision, rough handling.

- *Risky family circumstances:* history of violence, alcohol/drug misuse, mental illness, poor social support, child disability, child left alone, abandonment, denied access to child.

** (Note site pattern and color of all injuries)

Classify signs of child abuse

	CHILD ABUSE AND NEGLECT LIKELY	CHILD ABUSE AND NEGLECT POSSIBLE	CHILD ABUSE AND NEGLECT NOT LIKELY
• Evidence of suspicious physical condition/injury AND/OR • Delay in seeking help AND/OR • Lack of agreement between story and injury	➤URGENT referral to hospital specialist and services. ➤NOTIFY child protection team and/or social services in accordance with local protocols.		
• Inadequate physical care of child AND/OR • Abnormal child behavior AND/OR • Abnormal parent/caregiver behavior AND/OR • Risky family circumstances		• Schedule a follow-up clinic or home visit within 7 days. • Refer to community health and social services for family support and prevention work. • Counsel parents to reinforce positive parenting skills. • Inform parents about the developing child & appropriate routines and safety measures.	
• No signs consistent with the possibility of child abuse and neglect			• Counsel parents to reinforce positive parenting skills and sensitive interactions with child. • Inform parents about the developing child and appropriate routines and safety measures.

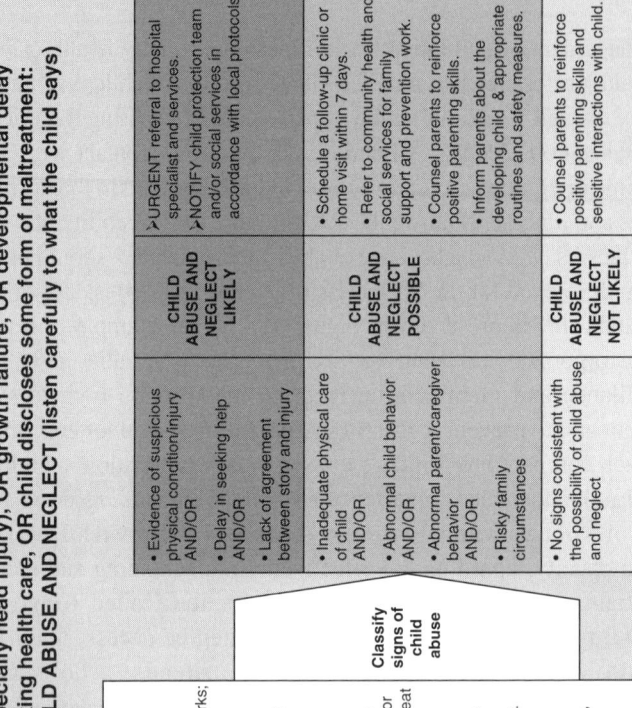

Figure 12.2 Integrated management of child abuse and neglect for children under five (Browne et al., 2007b).

personality" make women and children vulnerable and attractive to potential sex offenders and act as a signal for possible recruitment (Elliott et al., 1995). Hence certain family risk factors are the same for all forms of child and spouse abuse (see Table 12.3; Browne, 1993, 1994; Finkelhor, 1980; Finkelhor & Baron, 1986; Russell & Howell, 1983), such as:

- adult or child learning difficulties;
- adult or child physical health problems or disabilities;
- financial hardship and/or unemployment;
- poor relationships within family;
- marital conflict and/or family breakdown;
- single, separated, or divorced family;
- stepparent or cohabitee in family;
- family emotional and social isolation with social support deficits;
- adult or child victim of abuse and/or neglect in the past;
- adult or child alcohol and drug abuse;
- adult or child mental illness;
- adult antisocial behavior or child conduct disorder;
- adult or child criminal convictions; and
- adult or child with a history of violent or sexual offending.

The usual response to severe physical abuse or sexual abuse in the family and home environment is to take the children into public care and sometimes to offer shelter to the mother (the non-abusive carer in the vast majority of cases). This is to prevent "repeat victimization" by the same offender. Nevertheless, without victim support and therapeutic help for these women and children, the victims remain at a higher risk of "re-victimization" by a different offender (Coid et al., 2001; Hamilton & Browne, 1999). Indeed it has also been noted that despite professional intervention, many children remain vulnerable to further abuse (Jones & Ramchandani, 1999).

The conviction and imprisonment of the sexual or violent offender only occurs in a minority of cases (5 to 10%), when there is sufficient evidence to prove an antisocial crime "beyond all reasonable doubt" (Browne, 2009b). More often the alleged perpetrator of physical or sexual abuse is banned from contacting or approaching the victim by order of a family court (e.g., exclusion and/or occupation orders) working with the principle "on the balance of probability." The alleged offender may only then be convicted and imprisoned for breach of the order and contempt of court. However, he is at liberty to "befriend" other women and children and, hence, single parent families are at considerable risk (Browne & Herbert, 1997). Furthermore, the majority of convicted incest offenders attempt to return to their families. For example, Owen and Steele (1991) followed up 43 incest offenders a year after they had been released from a prison treatment program, and of those offenders who were married, 34% returned to live with their partners and 28% were living with partners and children.

CONCLUSION

A multi-sector, interdisciplinary approach is the most effective way of working together to promote children's rights to grow and develop in a safe family environment free from violence and provide care and protection to children. This requires interventions at all levels of the child's environment: the parents, the family, the community; and society in general. Hence, the public health approach has an ecological framework (Bronfenbrenner, 1979).

In order for children at risk of harm to be recognized and referred to appropriate services, appropriate reporting and referral systems need to be in place. The paucity of therapeutic services and poor referral networks (Allnock et al., 2009) have led to a concern as to whether "the process from recognition to reporting and subsequent interventions by child protection agencies improve lives of children overall." There is scarce evidence for effective interventions to prove that overall the harms of reporting are outweighed by the benefits of recognition in terms of care and protection (Gilbert, Kemp et al., 2009).

REFERENCES

Aldridge, M.L., & Browne, K.D. (2003). Perpetrators of spousal homicide: A review. *Trauma, Violence, & Abuse, 4* (3), 276.

Allnock, D., Bunting, L., Price, A., Morgan-Klein, N., Ellis, J., Radford, L., & Stafford, A. (2009). *Sexual abuse and therapeutic services for children and young people*. Retrieved from London: NSPCC.

Anitha, S. (2008). Neither safety nor justice: UK government response to domestic violence against immigrant women. *Journal of Social Welfare & Family Law, 30*, 189–202.

Anitha, S. (2010). No recourse, no support: State policy and practice towards South Asian women facing domestic violence in England. *British Journal of Social Work, 40*, 462–479.

Barlow, C.M., Jolley, R.P., & Hallam, J.L. (2011). Drawings as memory aids: Optimising the drawing method to facilitate young children's recall. *Applied Cognitive Psychology, 25* (3), 480–487. doi:10.1002/acp.1716

Barlow, J., Simkiss, D., & Stewart-Brown, S. (2006). Interventions to prevent or ameliorate child physical abuse and neglect: Findings from a systematic review of reviews. *Journal of Children's Services, 3*, 28.

Black, C. & Frost, D. (2011). Health at Work: An independent review of sickness absence (UK Parliamentary Report). London: HMSO. https://www.gov.uk/government/publications/review-of-the-sickness-absence-system-in-great-britain

Bronfenbrenner, U. (1979). *The ecology of human development*. Cambridge, MA: Harvard University Press.

Browne, K.D. (1993). Violence in the Family and its Links to Child Abuse. In C. Hobbs and J. Wynne (Eds.). *Child Abuse, Baillier's Clinical Paediatric Series, 1* (1): 149–164.

Browne, K.D. (1994). Child Sexual Abuse. In J. Archer (Ed.), *Male Violence*, Routledge: London, pp. 210–232.

Browne, K.D. (1995). Alleviating spouse relationship difficulties. *Counselling Psychology Quarterly, 8* (2), 109–122.

Browne, K.D. (2002). Child protection. In M. Rutter & E. Taylor (Eds.), *Child and adolescent psychiatry*. Oxford: Blackwell Science.

Browne, K.D. (2009a). Working to prevent sexual abuse in the family. In T. Beech, L. Craig, and K.D. Browne (Eds.) *Assessment and Treatment of Sexual Offenders: A Handbook*. Chichester: Wiley-Blackwell, pp. 491–514.

Browne, K.D. (2009b). Police work with sex offenders: Detection, Management and Treatment. In T. Beech, L. Craig, and K.D. Browne (Eds.) *Assessment and Treatment of Sexual Offenders: A Handbook*. Chichester: Wiley-Blackwell, pp. 515–534.

Browne, K.D., Douglas, J., Hamilton-Giachritis, C.E., & Hegarty, J. (2006). *A community health approach to the assessment of infants and their parents: The CARE Programme*. Chichester, UK: John Wiley & Sons, Ltd.

Browne, K.D., & Hamilton, C.E. (1999). Police recognition of the links between spouse abuse and child abuse. *Child Maltreatment, 4* (2), 136–147.

Browne, K.D., Hamilton-Giachritis, C.E., & Vettor, S. (2007a). The cycles of violence: The relationship between childhood maltreatment and the risk of later becoming a victim or perpetrator of violence. *World Health Organisation, regional office for Europe: Violence and Injury Prevention Programme*. Copenhagen & Rome.

Browne, K.D., Hamilton-Giachritis, C.E., & Vettor, S. (2007b). *Preventing Child Maltreatment in Europe: A Public Health Approach. Policy Briefing. World Health Organisation, regional office for Europe: Violence and Injury Prevention Programme*. Copenhagen & Rome.

Browne, K.D., & Herbert, M. (1997). *Preventing family violence*. Chichester, UK: John Wiley & Sons, Ltd.

Browne, K.D., & Jackson, V. (2013). Community intervention to prevent child maltreatment in England: Evaluating the contribution of the Family Nurse Partnership. *Journal of Public Health, 35* (3), 477–452.

Browne, K.D. & McManus, M. (2010). 'Adolescents with Intellectual Disability and Family Sexual Abuse' In L. Craig, W.R. Lindsay and K.D. Browne, (Eds.) *Assessment and Treatment of Sexual Offenders with Learning Disabilities*. Chichester: Wiley-Blackwell, pp. 47–69.

Butchart, A., Harvey, A.P., Mian, M., & Furniss, T. (2006). *Preventing child maltreatment: A guide to taking action and generating evidence*. Geneva: World Health Organization.

Campbell, J.C., Glass, N., Sharps, P.W., Laughon, K. B., & Bloom, T. (2007). Intimate partner homicide: Review and implications of research policy. *Trauma, Violence & Abuse, 8*(3), 246–269.

Coid, J., Petruckevitch, A., Feder, G., Chung, W., Richardson, J., & Moorey, S. (2001). Relation between childhood sexual and physical abuse and risk of revictimisation in women: A cross-sectional survey. *The Lancet, 358* (9280), 450–454.

Cooke, P., & Standen, P.J. (2002). Abuse and disabled children: Hidden needs? *Child Abuse Review, 11* (1), 1–18.

Council of Europe (1986). *Violence in the family*. Recommendation No. R(85)4. Strasbourg.

Crittenden, P. (2002). If I knew then what I know now: Integrity and fragmentation in the treatment of child abuse and neglect. In K.D. Browne, H. Hanks, P. Stratton, & C. Hamilton (Ed.), *Early prediction and prevention of child abuse: A handbook*. Chichester, UK: John Wiley & Sons, Ltd.

Department of Health (2013). Health Visiting and School Nursing Programmes: supporting implementation of the new service model No.5: Domestic Violence and Abuse – Professional

Guidance. London: Stationery Office. https://www.gov.uk/government/uploads/system/uploads/attachment_data/file/211018/9576-TSO-Health_Visiting_Domestic_Violence_A3_Posters_WEB.pdf

Department of Health, Home Office & Department for Education and Skills (1999) *Working Together to Safeguard Children: A Guide to Inter-Agency Working to Safeguard and Promote the Welfare of Children.* London: Stationery Office.

Department of Health, Department for Education and Employment, & Home Office (2000). *Framework for the assessment of children in need and their families.* London: The Stationery Office.

Department of Health, & Department for Education and Skills (2006). *SureStart children's centres: Practice guidance.* London.

DeVoe, E.R., & Kaufman Kantor, G. (2002). Measurement issues in child maltreatment and family violence prevention programs. *Trauma, Violence, & Abuse, 3* (1), 15–39.

Dietz, C.A., & Craft, J.L. (1980). Family dynamics of incest: A new perspective. *Social Case Work, 61,* 602–609.

Dixon, L., Browne, K., & Hamilton-Giachritsis, C. (2005). Risk factors of parents abused as children: A mediational analysis of the intergenerational continuity of child maltreatment (Part I). *Journal of Child Psychology and Psychiatry, 46* (1), 57.

Dixon, A., Howie, P., & Starling, J. (2005). Trauma exposure, post-traumatic stress, and psychiatric comorbidity in female juvenile offenders. *Journal of the American Academy of Child and Adolescent Psychiatry, 44* (8), 798–806.

Douglas, N., Lilley, S., Kooper, L., & Diamond, A. (2004). Safety and justice: Sharing personal information in the context of domestic violence – an overview. Retrieved from Social Care Online website: www.scie-socialcareonline.org.uk/safety-and-justice-sharing-personal-information-in-the-context-of-domestic-violence-an-overview/r/a11G00000017ssFIAQ.

Dutton, D.G., & Kropp, P.R. (2000). A review of domestic violence risk instruments. *Trauma, Violence, & Abuse, 1* (2), 171–181. doi:10.1177/1524838000001002004

Edleson, J.L. (1999a). Children's Witnessing of Adult Domestic Violence. *Journal of Interpersonal Violence, 14,* 839–870. doi: 10.1177/088626099014008004

Edleson, J.L. (1999b). The Overlap Between Child Maltreatment and Woman Battering. *Violence Against Women, 5,* 134–154. doi: 10.1177/107780129952003

Elkan, R., Kendrick, D., Hewitt, M., Robinson, J.J.A., Tolley, K., Blair, M.,… & Brummell, K. (2000). The effectiveness of domiciliary health visiting: A systematic review of international studies and a selective review of the British literature. *Health Technology Assessment, 4* (13), 1–338.

Elliott, M., Browne, K., & Kilcoyne, J. (1995). Child sexual abuse prevention: What offenders tell us. *Child Abuse & Neglect, 19* (5), 579–594.

Feder, G., Ramsay, J., Dunne, D., Rose, M., Arsene, C., Norman, R., … & Taket, A. (2009). How far does screening women for domestic (partner) violence in different health-care settings meet criteria for a screening programme? Systematic reviews of nine UK National Screening Committee criteria. *Health Technology Assessment, 13* (16), iii–iv, xi–xiii, 1–113, 137–347. doi:10.3310/hta13160

Finkelhor, D. (1980). Risk factors in the sexual victimization of children. *Child Abuse & Neglect, 4,* 265–273.

Finkelhor, D., & Baron, L. (1986). Risk factors for child sexual abuse. *Journal of Interpersonal Violence, 1* (1), 43–71.

Finkelhor, D., Ormrod, R.K., & Turner, H.A. (2007). Poly-victimization: A neglected component in child victimization. *Child Abuse & Neglect*, *31* (1), 7–26.

Garcia, L., Soria, C., & Hurwitz, E.L. (2007). Homicides and intimate partner violence: A literature review. *Trauma, Violence, & Abuse*, *8* (4), 370–383.

Gilbert, R., Kemp, A., Thoburn, J., Sidebotham, P., Radford, L., Glaser, D., & Macmillan, H.L. (2009). Recognising and responding to child maltreatment. *The Lancet*, *373* (9658), 167–180.

Gilbert, R., Widom, C.S., Browne, K., Fergusson, D., Webb, E., & Janson, S. (2009). Burden and consequences of child maltreatment in high-income countries. *The Lancet*, *373* (9657), 68–81. doi:10.1016/s0140-6736(08)61706-7

Goddard, C. & Hiller, P. (1993). Child sexual abuse: Assault in a violent context. *Australian Journal of Social Issues*, *28*, 20–33.

Hague, G., Thiara, R., Magowan, P. & Mullender, A. (2008). *Making the links Disabled women and domestic violence Final report*. London: Women's Aid Federation of England. https://1q7dqy2unor827bqjls0c4rn-wpengine.netdna-ssl.com/wp-content/uploads/2015/12/Disabled-women-Making_the_Links

Hall, D., & Hall, S. (2007). *The "family-nurse partnership": Developing an instrument for identification, assessment and recruitment of clients*. London: DCSF.

Hamilton, C.E., & Browne, K.D. (1999). Recurrent maltreatment during childhood: A survey of referrals to police child protection units in England. *Child Maltreatment*, *4* (4), 275–286.

HM Government (2015) Working together to safeguard children A guide to inter-agency working to safeguard and promote the welfare of children. London: Stationery Office. https://www.gov.uk/government/uploads/system/uploads/attachment_data/file/419595/Working_Together_to_Safeguard_Children.pdf

HM Government (2016). Ending violence to women and girls: Strategy 2016 to 2020. London: Stationery Office. https://www.gov.uk/government/uploads/system/uploads/attachment_data/file/522166/VAWG_Strategy_FINAL_PUBLICATION_MASTER_vRB.PDF

Holtzworth-Munroe, A., & Stuart, G.L. (1994). Typologies of male batterers: Three subtypes and the differences among them. *Psychological Bulletin*, *116*, 476–497.

Home Office (2005). *Domestic violence: A national report 2005*. London: Home Office.

Izzidien, S. (2008). Domestic abuse within South Asian communities: The specific needs of women, children and young people. Available from: www.nspcc.org.uk/services-and-resources/research-and-resources/ (last retrieved July 15, 2016).

Jackson, V., Browne, K.D., & Joseph, S. (2015). The prevalence of childhood victimization experienced outside of the family: Findings from an English prevalence study. *Child Abuse & Neglect, 51*, 343–357, doi:10.1016/j.chiabu.2015.08.006

Jaffe, P.G., Wolfe, D.A., & Wilson, S.K. (1990). *Children of battered women*. Thousand Oaks, CA: Sage.

Jones, D.P.H., & Ramchandani, P. (1999). *Child sexual abuse: Informing practice from research*. Abingdon, UK: Radcliffe.

Kelley, M.L., Klostermann, K., Doane, A.N., Mignone, T., Lam, W.K.K., LFals-Stewart, W., et al. (2009). The case for examining and treating the combined effects of parental drug use and interparental violence on children in their homes. *Aggression and violent behavior*, *15*, 76–82.

Kendall-Tackett, K.A., Lyon, T., Taliaferro, G., & Little, L. (2005). Why child maltreatment researchers should include children's disability status in their maltreatment studies. *Child Abuse and Neglect*, *29*, 147–151.

Kendrick, D., Mulvaney, C.A., Ye, L., Stevens, T., Mytton, J.A., & Stewart-Brown, S. (2013). Parenting interventions for the prevention of unintentional injuries in childhood. *Cochrane Database System Review*, *3*, Cd006020. doi:10.1002/14651858.CD006020.pub3

Klevens, J., Simon, T.R., & Chen, J. (2012). Are the perpetrators of violence one and the same? Exploring the co-occurrence of perpetration of physical aggression in the United States. *Journal of Interpersonal Violence*, *27* (10), 1987–2002. doi:10.1177/0886260511431441

Kropp, P.R., & Hart, S.D. (2000). The Spousal Assault Risk Assessment (SARA) Guide: Reliability and validity in adult male offenders. *Law and Human Behavior*, *24*, 101–118.

Kropp, P.R., Hart, S.D., Webster, C.D., & Eaves, D. (1999). *Spousal Assault Risk Assessment Guide (SARA)*. Toronto, ON: Multi-Health Systems.

Krug, E.G., Mercy, J.A., Dahlberg, L.L., & Zwi, A.B. (2002). The world report on violence and health. *The Lancet*, *360* (9339), 1083–1088.

Leeds Inter-Agency Project (2005). *Health and social care project report: Promoting good practice in health service responses to women and children experiencing domestic violence*. Retrieved from Leeds:

Lewis, G. (ed) (2007). *Saving Mothers' Lives*: reviewing maternal deaths to make motherhood safer. 2003-2005: Report on confidential enquiries into maternal deaths in the UK. London: CEMACH. http://www.publichealth.hscni.net/sites/default/files/Saving%20Mothers'%20Lives%202003-05%20.pdf

Lundgren, R., & Amin, A. (2015). Addressing intimate partner violence and sexual violence among adolescents: Emerging evidence of effectiveness. *Journal of Adolescent Health*, *56* (1 Suppl), S42–S50. doi:10.1016/j.jadohealth.2014.08.012

Macmillan, H.L., Wathen, C.N., Barlow, J., Fergusson, D.M., Leventhal, J., & Tousig, H.N. (2009). Interventions to prevent child maltreatment and associated impairment. *The Lancet*, *373* (9659), 250–266.

Mears, J. (2003). Survival is not enough: Violence against older women in Australia. *Violence Against Women*, *9*(12), 1478–1489. doi: 10.1177/1077801203259287

Nygren, P., Nelson, H.D. & Klein, J. (2004) Screening Children for Family Violence: A Review of the Evidence for the US Preventive Services Task Force. *Annauls of Family Medicine*, *2*, 161–169. doi: 10.1370/afm.113

O'Brien, M.J. (1991). Taking sibling incest seriously. In M. Parton (Ed.), *Family sexual abuse*. London: Sage.

Olds, D.L. (2002). Preventing child abuse and neglect with prenatal and infancy home visiting by nurses. In K.D. Browne, H. Hanks, P. Stratton, & C. Hamilton (Eds.), *Early prediction and prevention of child abuse: A handbook*. Chichester, UK: John Wiley & Sons, Ltd.

Olive, P. (2007). Care for Emergency Department Patients Who Have Experienced Domestic Violence: A Review of the Evidence Base. *Journal of Clinical Nursing*, *16*, 1736–1748. 10.1111/j.1365-2702.2007.01746.x

Owen, G., & Steele, N. (1991). Incest offenders after treatment. In M. Parton (Ed.), *Family sexual abuse* (pp. 178–198). London: Sage.

Parker, R., Gordon, D., & Loughran, F. (2000). *Disabled children in Britain: A re-analysis of the OPCS disability surveys*. London: HMSO.

Pernanen, K. (1991). *Alcohol in human violence*. London: Guilford Press.

Pinney, A., Ball, M., & Niven, L. (2007). *A better start: Children and families with special needs and disabilities in Sure Start local programmes*. London: DfES.

Rabin, R.F., Jennings, J.M., Campbell, J.C., & Bair-Merritt, M.H. (2009). Intimate Partner Violence Screening Tools. *American Journal of Preventive Medicine, 36* (5), 439–445. e434. doi:10.1016/j.amepre.2009.01.024

Reder, P., & Duncan, S. (2002). Predicting fatal child abuse and neglect. In K.D. Browne, H. Hanks, P. Stratton, & C. Hamilton (Eds.), *Early prediction and prevention of child abuse: A handbook (pp. 145–164).* Chichester, UK: John Wiley & Sons, Ltd.

Robinson, A.L. (2006). Reducing repeat victimization among high-risk victims of domestic violence: The benefits of a coordinated community response in Cardiff, Wales. *Violence Against Women, 12* (8), 761–788. doi:10.1177/1077801206291477

Russell, D.E., & Howell, N. (1983). The prevalence of rape in the United States revisited. *Signs, 8* (4), 688–695.

Sanders, M., & Cann, W. (2002). Promoting positive parenting as an abuse prevention strategy. In K.D. Browne, P. Stratton, H. Hanks, & C. Hamilton (Eds.), *Early prediction and prevention of child abuse: A handbook* (pp. 145–164). Chichester, UK: John Wiley & Sons, Ltd.

Sharps, P.W., Laughon, K., & Giangrande, S.K. (2007). Intimate Partner Violence and the childbearing year: Maternal and infant health consequences. *Trauma, Violence, & Abuse, 8* (2), 105–116. doi:10.1177/1524838007302594

Sherin, K.M., Sinacore, J.M., Li, X.Q., Zitter, R.E., & Shakil, A. (1998). HITS: a short domestic violence screening tool for use in a family practice setting. *Family Medicine, 30* (7), 508–512.

Sonkin, D., Martin, D., & Walker, L. (1985). *The male batterer: A treatment approach.* New York: Springer.

Stith, S.M., Green, N.M., Smith, D.B., & Ward, D.B. (2008). Marital satisfaction and marital discord as risk markers for intimate partner violence: A meta-analytic review. *Journal of Family Violence, 23* (3), 149–160.

Stockl, H., Devries, K., Rotstein, A., Abrahams, N., Campbell, J., Watts, C., & Moreno, C.G. (2013). The global prevalence of intimate partner homicide: A systematic review. *The Lancet, 382* (9895), 859–865. doi:10.1016/s0140-6736(13)61030-2

Stoltenborgh, M., Bakermans-Kranenburg, M.J., & van Ijzendoorn, M.H. (2013). The neglect of child neglect: A meta-analytic review of the prevalence of neglect. *Social Psychiatry and Psychiatric Epidemiology, 48* (3), 345–355. doi:10.1007/s00127-012-0549-y

Stoltenborgh, M., Bakermans-Kranenburg, M.J., van Ijzendoorn, M.H., & Alink, L.R. (2013). Cultural-geographical differences in the occurrence of child physical abuse? A meta-analysis of global prevalence. *International Journal of Psychology, 48* (2), 81–94. doi:10.1080/00207594.2012.697165

Stoltenborgh, M., van Ijzendoorn, M.H., Euser, E.M., & Bakermans-Kranenburg, M.J. (2011). A global perspective on child sexual abuse: Meta-analysis of prevalence around the world. *Child Maltreatment, 16* (2), 79–101.

Sullivan, P., & Knutson, J. (2000). Maltreatment and disabilities: A population based epidemiological study. *Child Abuse & Neglect, 24,* 1257–1274.

Thurtle, V. (2009). *Understanding the health of communities: Using a Health Needs Assessment Approach in public health practice.* London: CPCHVA and Unite the Union.

Trotter, J., Radford, J., & Harne, L. (2007). Changing relationships: services for disabled women experiencing domestic violence in the UK, *Research Policy and Planning, 25*(2/3), 155–166.

Truesdell, D., McNeil, J., & Deschner, J. (1986). Incidence of wife abuse in incestuous families. *Social Work, 31,* 38–40.

Tzeng, O.C.S., & Schwarzin, H.J. (1990). Gender and race differences in child sexual abuse correlates. *International Journal of Intercultural Relations, 14*, 135–161.

Vezina, J., & Hebert, M. (2007). Risk factors for victimization in romantic relationships of young women: A review of empirical studies and implications for prevention. *Trauma, Violence, & Abuse, 8* (1), 33–66.

Wiehe, V.R. (1997). *Sibling abuse: Hidden physical, emotional, and sexual trauma* (2nd ed.). Thousand Oaks, CA: Sage.

World Health Organization (2002). *The world report on violence and health.* Geneva: WHO.

World Health Organization (2004). *The importance of caregiver-child interactions for the survival and healthy development of young children: A review.* Geneva: WHO.

World Health Organization (2005a). *WHO multi-country study on women's health and domestic violence against women.* Geneva: WHO.

World Health Organization (2005b). *The World Health Report 2005: Making every mother and child count.* Geneva: WHO.

World Health Organization (2006). *Preventing child maltreatment: A guide to taking action and generating evidence.* Geneva: WHO.

World Health Organization (2008). *Manual for estimating the economic costs of injuries due to interpersonal and self-directed violence.* Geneva: WHO.

World Health Organization (2009a). *Violence prevention: The evidence.* Changing social and cultural norms that support violence. Geneva: WHO.

World Health Organization (2009b). *Violence prevention: The evidence. Guns, knives and pesticides: Reducing access to lethal means.* Geneva: WHO.

World Health Organization (2009c). *Violence prevention: The evidence. Preventing violence by developing life skills in children and adolescents.* Geneva: WHO.

World Health Organization (2009d). *Violence prevention: The evidence. Preventing violence by reducing the availability and harmful use of alcohol.* Geneva: WHO.

World Health Organization (2009e). *Violence prevention: The evidence. Promoting gender equality to prevent violence against women.* Geneva: WHO.

World Health Organization (2009f). *Violence prevention: The evidence. Reducing violence through victim identification, care and support programmes.* Geneva: WHO.

World Health Organization (2009g). *Violence prevention: The evidence. Preventing violence through the development of safe, stable and nurturing relationships between children and their parents or caregivers.* Geneva: WHO.

World Health Organization (2010). *Preventing intimate partner and sexual violence against women: Taking action and generating evidence.* Geneva: WHO.

World Health Organization (2013). *Responding to intimate partner violence and sexual violence against women: WHO clinical and policy guidelines.* Geneva: WHO.

World Health Organization (2014). *Global status report on violence prevention.* Geneva: WHO.

World Health Organization, Department of Reproductive Health and Research at London School of Hygiene and Tropical Medicine, & South African Medical Research Council. (2013). *Global and regional estimates of violence against women: Prevalence and health effects of intimate partner violence and non-partner sexual violence.* Geneva: WHO.

Worling, J.R. (1995). Adolescent sibling-incest offenders: Differences in family and individual functioning when compared to adolescent non-sibling sex offenders. *Child Abuse & Neglect, 19* (5), 633–643.

Zhai, F., & Gao, Q. (2009). Child maltreatment among Asian Americans: Characteristics and explanatory framework. *Child Maltreatment, 14* (2), 227–204.

13

Psychological Assessment of Parenting in Family Proceedings

KAREN BAILEY, EUGENE OSTAPIUK AND TALJINDER BASRA

INTRODUCTION

The Legislation

When parents fail to provide their children with a good enough and safe standard of care, or where there is evidence that a child has been subjected to physical, sexual, or emotional abuse, the state is obliged to intervene. The primary legislation affecting children in England and Wales is the Children Act 1989, amended 2004, for Northern Ireland, The Children (Northern Ireland) Order 1995, and for Scotland, The Children (Scotland) Act 1995. This legislation provides the legal framework that defines the responsibility of professionals, including psychologists, in respect of all matters relating to the welfare and development of the child. The term *family proceedings* is defined in section 8 of the Children Act 1989 and includes all public law (care, adoption, emergency protection, contact) and a large range of private law matters concerning divorce and separation, including those within applications under section 8 for contact, residence, specific issues, and prohibited steps. Professional practice in family proceedings reflects the core principles underpinning the 1989 Children Act, namely that the interests of the child are paramount; that delay in determining the questions concerning a child's upbringing is likely to prejudice the welfare of the child; and that non-intervention is preferred except in cases where it can be demonstrated that a court order would be better for a child than no order.

Assessments in Forensic Practice: A Handbook, First Edition. Edited by Kevin D. Browne, Anthony R. Beech, Leam A. Craig, and Shihning Chou.
© 2017 John Wiley & Sons Ltd. Published 2017 by John Wiley & Sons Ltd.

In 2000 the government published new guidelines for the assessment of children in need and their families (Department of Health, 2000). The *Framework for Assessment* specified that all professionals involved in *core assessments* (in-depth assessment that addresses the central or most important aspects of the child's needs) during family proceedings should have a thorough understanding of the developmental needs of children; the capacities of parents to respond appropriately to those needs; and the impact of wider family and environmental factors on parenting capacity and children. It was acknowledged that such assessments, though social work led, would invariably involve other agencies and independent professionals who would contribute specialist knowledge or advice or undertake specialist assessments. The *Framework* also acknowledged that psychologists were well placed to contribute to core assessments and to offer a range of services to support children and their families. In the year ending March 31, 2013, some 232,700 core assessments of children and their families were completed by local authorities in England (Department for Education, 2013) and 12,355 were completed in Wales (Welsh Assembly Government, 2013), representing an increase on previous years.

Over the years since the implementation of the Act, family proceedings had, for a variety of reasons, become subject to increasing delays. In an attempt to remedy this and promote best practice, the Department for Constitutional Affairs (2003) outlined the key stages in the management of care cases and set a guideline of 40 weeks for their completion, subsequently reduced to 25 weeks by the Public Law Outline (Ministry of Justice, 2010a), which offered a streamlined and simplified update of this protocol.

Use of Experts

Although it is not possible to give a definitive picture of the numbers and costs pertaining to use of experts in family proceedings because no central data are kept, Brophy (2006) provides the most authoritative and up-to-date review of the implementation of the Children Act 1989 and the use of expert evidence in family proceedings. Most cases involved in family proceedings contain multiple categories of child maltreatment, including physical, sexual, and emotional abuse and multiple allegations of failures of parenting. Between 80% and 90% of care order proceedings involve evidence from experts, and this figure appears to be relatively stable over the last decade. Local Authorities tend to engage most expert witnesses; the majority of the evidence from experts being commissioned during court proceedings. Children's guardians and, to a lesser degree, parents themselves are also responsible for requesting expert advice.

The clinical disciplines typically providing expert evidence include pediatrics, child and adolescent/family psychiatry, adult psychiatry, and psychology. Residential and non-residential *family center* assessments are also provided in a substantial proportion of childcare proceedings. Psychological reports may be based on an assessment of a child or an adult, or less frequently of both. Brophy, Wale, and Bates (1999) have shown that reports limited to an assessment of a parent were filed in up to 24% of cases; those based on an assessment of a child only were educational or clinical; educational psychological reports were filed in up to 13% of cases; and clinical reports were filed in up to 14% of cases.

Following a review of the quality and cost of expert witnesses, the government published a consultation paper, "The Use of Experts," concerning the quality, price, and procedures in publicly funded cases (Legal Services Commission, 2004). This proposed to raise the standard of services by encouraging the use of accredited experts; clear terms of instruction agreed in advance; with faster payment, simpler administration procedures, and greater control over the rising cost of experts' fees. The amount paid for experts' costs is not recorded separately by the Legal Services Commission, but is estimated to be around two-thirds of the total spent per year on disbursements in criminal, civil, and family cases. This total was £192m in 2007–2008, which increased to £205.4m in 2008–2009 and to £232.4m in 2009–2010. The most significant increase in disbursement spend was in public law family work, which increased by 46.6% between 2005–2006 and 2008–2009 (Ministry of Justice, 2010b). However, maximum rates for psychologists as expert witnesses were introduced in 2011 following on from the Ministry of Justice consultation "Proposals for the reform of Legal Aid in England and Wales." Further consultations were held in 2013 resulting in a reduction of these rates.

Psychologist as Expert

In the United Kingdom psychologists are increasingly offering their expertise to courts in family proceedings, although in other juridical systems, for example in the United States, they are considered the professionals of choice (Bow & Quinnell, 2002, 2004). There are no legal definitions for what is considered a competent psychological assessment, just as there are no legal definitions for who is qualified to perform a competent psychological assessment. The standards, procedures, and measures used are left to the professional bodies who promulgate guidance concerning best practice for psychologists acting as expert witnesses (American Psychological Association, 1998; British Psychological Society, 1998, 2004a, 2004b). These guidelines usually cover topics such as definition of an expert; criteria for competence required by the court; receiving and responding to instructions; confidentiality; conflict of interests; appearance at court; and practical and financial considerations. The British Psychological Society (2007) published a Child Protection Portfolio outlining a minimum standard of practice in relation to child protection.

There is a general expectation in family proceedings that the psychologist will act in the best interest of the child and that in so doing will rely on sound psychological knowledge, empirical data, and expert objective opinion to aid the court. The specific remit of any given assessment will depend upon the nature of the specific instructions issued to the psychologist acting as expert.

Instructing the Expert

In England and Wales, psychologists are instructed jointly by legal representatives of the parties involved in public law family proceedings (local authority, children's guardian, parents) to provide an assessment that addresses issues agreed by all parties. Less frequently, in private law proceedings the psychologist may be instructed at the request of one particular party, usually the parent(s). The scope of an assessment is determined by the nature of the opinion or recommendations requested of the psychologist. Referring parties or the court will ask specific questions to be answered by the assessment, normally following discussion with the psychologist.

A *letter of instruction* is sent to the psychologist expert by the lead solicitor acting on behalf of all the parties to proceedings. This is the person through whom all arrangements for the assessment are made and to whom the final report is sent. The letter follows a standard format: it lists the parties to the proceedings and their legal representatives; confirms the joint nature of the instructions; outlines the essential background details of the case; outlines the instructions to the expert; and presents specific questions to be answered by the assessment. The psychologist will typically be asked to address the impact of an individual's intellect, personality, experience of childhood abuse, chaotic lifestyle, substance abuse and dependency, criminal activity, and domestic violence on their capacity to provide safe parenting; nature of family dynamics; attachment between parent and child; support networks; therapeutic needs and timescale for completion of rehabilitation; capacity to change; and ability to work cooperatively with professionals.

The letter also gives guidance on how the psychologist should deal with any matters of fact before the court, that is, that unless specifically asked to do so, the psychologist should avoid expressing views about factual issues, which remain the preserve of the court, and where appropriate to express the expert's opinion in the context of a range of alternatives where these are available. Finally, the letter deals with issues of cost and timescale for completion of a report.

The Assessment Report

At the outset of the assessment, the psychologist must address issues of informed consent. This means not only obtaining consent from all adult participants, but, where appropriate, also informing the child subject to the assessment of the nature of their involvement with the psychologist. The psychologist must inform the parties how information obtained from them will be handled and disclosed and the limits of confidentiality by which the professional is bound. The psychologist is also obliged to remind all parties that his or her duty is to provide independent assistance to the court and that it overrides any obligation to anyone else.

Psychological assessments in family proceedings usually rely on multiple methods of data gathering, depending on the specific questions raised in instructions. Psychometric testing, clinical interviews, and review of relevant information from collateral sources such as social, health, education, and criminal justice agencies and the extended family system are important sources from which the psychologist derives a formulation of the significant factors in the case. Observation of parent–child interactions, especially in their home, is another important data source in evaluating parental capacity to care. Where this is not possible, for example in cases where the safety of the child is in jeopardy or parental contact with the child has been prohibited by the court, then observation of parent–child interactions may be undertaken in a family center or similar safe venue. For purposes of corroboration, balance, and context, the psychologist might also wish to interview extended family members and other individuals where appropriate (e.g., grandparents and teachers).

The psychologist must take care not to over-interpret nor inappropriately interpret assessment data from whatever source they are derived. The psychologist must be aware, in particular, that individuals involved in judicial proceedings are often defensive in their dealings with professionals and the circumstances of a compelled assessment may give rise to a biased presentation with potentially serious consequences of an adverse finding. Social desirability scales have been incorporated in many psychometric tests to detect this response tendency, which has long been known to confound psychological evaluations, particularly in legal proceedings where the stakes are high. The psychologist must be careful not to draw conclusions that are not adequately supported by the data; transparent about any limitations in methodology or data used; sensitive to the cultural context of the assessment; and present conclusions in a form that is understandable to all parties to the proceedings.

On completion of the psychological assessment, the psychologist may make recommendations regarding, but not limited to, psychological treatment for the parent(s) and/or child(ren), and may suggest other services or resources that would help parents to offer a good enough standard of care or create a safe environment for the child. Where recommendations are made, the primary focus must be the child's health and welfare, and the recommendations should be based on sound psychological data and interpretations based on generally accepted psychological theory and practice. There is no generally accepted view among psychologists as to whether it is appropriate to make recommendations to the court concerning disposal in family proceedings. However, where the psychologist is invited to do so in instructions, or if the psychologist chooses to make dispositional recommendations, these should be informed by evidence from best practice and reported outcomes, and should reflect the primacy of the child's interests and needs. Finally, the psychological report must be presented in an acceptable format and must contain appropriately worded sections regarding the expert's duty to the court and a statement of truth concerning the facts and opinions expressed in the report. Psychologists as experts are bound by the Family Procedure Rules 2012, Practice Direction 25B (The Duties of an Expert, the

Expert's Report, and Arrangements for an Expert to Attend Court), which came into force on January 31, 2013. Statements of Truth and Compliance must be stated at the end of each report in accordance with this Practice Direction.

REASONS FOR REFERRAL

Child Abuse

Child abuse, whether physical, sexual, or emotional, together with dysfunctional parenting skills are most likely to trigger the involvement of child welfare agencies, resulting in expert psychological advice being sought. The dynamics and factors associated with child abuse are complex issues because they differ markedly according to the victim's age, the setting in which the abuse occurs, and the relationship between victim and perpetrator (World Health Organization, 2006). It is this very complexity that prompts courts to seek psychological expertise in the assessment process.

In the United Kingdom, local authorities are obliged to enter the names of all children considered to be suffering from, or likely to suffer from, abuse or significant harm on the *Child Protection Register*. Data from these local child protection registers concerning the four key types of child maltreatment – physical, sexual, and emotional abuse and neglect – give some indication of the scale of the problem, though research indicates that abuse and neglect are both under-reported and under-registered. During the year 2013, 52,700 children became the subject of a Child Protection Plan in England with 43,100 remaining subject to the Plan at the end of the year; 41% of registrations related to children considered to be primarily at risk of neglect; emotional abuse accounted for 32% of registrations; physical abuse for 12%; sexual abuse 5%; and mixed categories made up the remaining 11% (Department for Education, 2013).

Child welfare services aim to prevent the occurrence of child abuse and neglect where children are at risk, and to prevent the recurrence of abuse or neglect where it has already occurred. In this context, psychological assessments of parenting in family proceedings often focus on identifying *risk factors* that increase and *protective factors* that decrease susceptibility to abuse and neglect. Although more research is required to fully understand the dynamics of these factors, there already exists a substantial body of knowledge about what can increase susceptibility to child abuse (see Table 13.1).

Parental Variables

Personal, financial, social, and environmental circumstances of parents as well as dysfunctional attitudes and behaviors may directly and significantly impair their ability to provide a good enough standard of care to a child. A number of significant factors have been identified in this respect and are discussed below.

Table 13.1 Risk factors associated with child abuse.

Type of factors	Research
Child factors	
Complications during birth/ separation from baby at birth	Browne & Herbert (1997); Browne, Hamilton, Heggarty, & Blissett (2000); Brown, Cohen, Johnson, & Salzinger (1998)
Twins, or less than 18 months between births of children	Browne & Herbert (1997); Browne et al. (2000)
Child has physical or mental disabilities	Browne & Herbert (1997); Browne et al. (2000)
The child was seriously ill, premature, or weighed under 2.5kg at birth	Wu et al. (2004); Browne & Herbert (1997); Browne et al. (2000); Brown et al. (1998)
Parental factors/individual factors	
Mother or partner under 21 years of age at birth of child	Browne & Herbert (1997); Browne et al. (2000); Dixon, Browne, & Hamilton-Giachritsis (2005); Egeland et al. (2002)
Either parent has been treated for mental illness or depression	Browne & Herbert (1997); Browne et al. (2000); Briere (1992); Berger (2005); Kotch, Browne, Dufort, & Winsor (1999)
Personality disorder	Famularo, Kinscherff, & Fenton (1992a); Dinwiddie & Bucholz (1993); Bools, Neale, & Meadow (1994); Stanley & Penhale (1999); Widiger & Trull (1994); Davison (2002)
Either parent has feelings of isolation	Browne & Herbert (1997); Browne et al. (2000); Crouch & Milner (2001); Egeland et al. (2002); Runtsz & Shallow (1997)
Mother or partner not biologically related to the child	Browne & Herbert (1997); Browne et al. (2000).
Living with stepparents	Finkelhor, Hotaling, Lewis, & Smith (1990); Brown et al. (1998)
Either parent has a dependency for drugs or alcohol	Browne & Herbert, (1997); Browne et al. (2000); Berger (2005); Walsh, MacMillan, & Jamieson (2003); Kotch et al. (1999); Reid, Macchetto, & Foster (1999); Wolfner & Gelles (1993); Chaffin et al. (1996); Jaudes, Ekwo, & Van Voohis (1995); Kelleher, Chaffin, Hooengerg, & Fischer (1994); Besinger, Garland, Litrownik, & Landsverk (1999); Famularo et al. (1992b); Murphy et al. (1991)
Either parent was physically or sexually abused as a child	Browne & Herbert (1997); Browne et al. (2000); Briere (1992); Dixon et al. (2005)
A single parent	Browne & Herbert (1997); Browne et al. (2000); Wu et al. (2004)

(Continued)

Table 13.1 (Continued)

Type of factors	Research
Either parent has indifferent feelings toward the child	Browne & Herbert (1997); Browne et al. (2000)
Mother smoking during pregnancy	Berger (2005); Wu et al. (2004)
Anxiety, poor self-esteem, and emotional problems	Briere (1992)
Parent had not completed secondary education	Kotch et al. (1999)
Poor interpersonal skills	Egeland et al. (2002)
Parents separated from their own mothers before the age of 14 years.	Kotch et al. (1999)
Relationship factors	
Adult in the household with violent tendencies	Browne & Herbert (1997); Browne et al. (2000); Dixon et al. (2005); Wu et al. (2004)
Societal factors	
Family has serious financial problems	Browne & Herbert (1997); Browne et al. (2000); Brown et al. (1998); Straus & Smith (1990); Berger (2005)
Low levels of social support.	Kotch et al. (1999)

Mental health: Child abuse by parents has been associated with a wide range of mental health problems ranging from depressive illness and personality disorders to severe psychiatric disorders including schizophrenia and related disorders (Masson, Oakley, & Pick, 2004). Falkov (1996) found that 30% of parents who killed their children were previously known to psychiatric services and 6% were diagnosed with a personality disorder. This is likely to be an underestimate, since co-morbidity of personality disorders with other psychiatric illnesses is the norm (Adshead, 2003) and prevalence of personality disorder in abusive mothers has been reported as being high as 70% in samples of mothers involved in childcare proceedings (Stanley & Penhale, 1999).

Learning disability: Parents with a learning disability are disproportionately represented in family proceedings and their children are more likely to be freed for adoption (Booth, Booth, & McConnell, 2005). Concerns generally relate to the child's developmental progress, issues of neglect, and parents' failure to protect, that is acts of omission rather than commission (James, 2004) resulting from their impaired cognitive, social, and adaptive functioning. Though a learning disability when considered in isolation should not preclude a parent's ability to provide a child with a good enough standard of care, it often impacts on their ability to identify and minimize potential risk factors as readily as parents who are not cognitively impaired.

Substance abuse: Misuse of and dependency on alcohol and illegal drugs also features among factors which impact significantly to impair parenting (National Research Council, 1993). Prevalence rates as high as 23% for drugs and 20% for alcohol abuse have been reported (Brophy, Jhutti-Johal, & Owen, 2003). Mothers who abuse substances during pregnancy may also place their children at risk of developmental problems by creating a chaotic and unsafe home environment. Though substance abuse alone is not directly predictive of child abuse, factors associated with it are also associated with child abuse risk (Hogan, Myers, & Elswick, 2006).

Domestic violence: Spousal or partner violence, whether partner on partner or reciprocal, is strongly represented in child protection cases in family proceedings. Children who witness or who are subjected to domestic violence face increased risks of exposure to traumatic events, neglect, and abuse that affect their well-being, safety, and emotional and psychological stability (Carlson, 2000; Edleson, 1999; Rossman, 2001). Reactions of distress; anger and/or aggression; as well as conduct disorder; social withdrawal and depression; school related problems; and deficits in cognitive and social problem solving, symptoms of Attention Deficit Hyperactivity Disorder, and poor self-esteem and health are some of the consequences for children following exposure to domestic violence (Herron & Holtzworth-Munroe, 2002; for a review, see Holt et al., 2008 and Carpenter & Stacks, 2009).

Chaotic lifestyle: A chaotic parental lifestyle, often associated with involvement in drugs, has been reported in over a third of the cases involved in family proceedings as a result of child abuse (Brophy et al., 2003). Factors associated with a chaotic lifestyle that impact adversely on an individuals ability to provide good enough parenting include multiple house moves and poor housing; multiple caregivers and unrelated/inexperienced caregivers; substance abuse; unemployment; and inconsistent and unpredictable childcare of infants and young children.

Crime: Although criminal activity has not been identified as a risk factor for child abuse per se (Saunders & Goddard, 1998), family criminality is a factor associated with referrals to child protection agencies for physical abuse, but not necessarily for sexual or emotional abuse or neglect (Hamilton & Browne, 1998). Parents who have committed *schedule one offenses* (sexual or violent offenses against a child under the age of 16 years, Children and Young Persons Act 1933) and are therefore considered a Person Posing a Risk to Children (PPRC) are of particular concern to child protection agencies.

Parenting knowledge: Abusive parents have higher and more unrealistic expectations of their children in terms of their abilities and also perceive their children to be more irritable and demanding, which influences their use of discipline and punishment (Browne & Saqi, 1987). Lack of knowledge may incline a parent to force their child to do something that may be beyond the child's developmental limitations. Neglectful parents show less empathy toward their children and have less caregiving skills, for example preparing food and keeping a clean home (Shahar, 2001); their management of stress is poor and they are less knowledgeable about child development (Burke, Chandy, Dannerbeck, & Watt, 1988). Abusing parents have irregular and lower-quality interactions with their children (Azar, 2002); respond inconsistently to their needs (Howe, Dooley, & Hinings, 2000); know less about child development and consequently expect more from their young infants and children. They attribute negative intent to their children's behavior (Dore & Lee, 1999), spank and punish more, and reason with them less (Koenig, Cicchetti, & Rogosch, 2000).

Personal, financial, social, and environmental circumstances: Parents subject to allegations of child abuse are likely to be poor; many live deprived and troubled lives in complex and dislocated social circumstances. A UK study by the NSPCC (2008) found that 65% of respondents who had experienced serious physical abuse or serious neglect and 71% who had experienced emotional maltreatment stated that they had experienced financial difficulties in their childhood. Gibbons, Conroy, & Bell (1995) found that approximately 54% of families involved in child protection were dependent on income support. Parents may often be known to social services because many of their children may already be on the child protection registers. Research suggests that about one-third of parents are likely to have been through care proceedings with a previous child (Hunt, MacLeod, & Thomas, 1999); and 73% of children were or had been on the child protection register (Brophy et al. 2003). Some parents may already have a child in care; and in other cases, children may already be living away from birth parents. Brophy et al. (2003) found that 50% of children subject to a care application were already living away from their birth parents at the point of application. The general consensus appears to be that parents with a history of childhood abuse are at increased risk of maltreating their own children (Egeland et al., 2002), resulting from the complex interaction between risk, protective, and mediating factors (Dixon et al., 2005). The prevalence of children with disabilities among maltreating families has been observed to be twice as high as in the general population (Goldson, 1998) with a significant proportion having a physical or learning disability (Hunt et al., 1999). A more detailed summary of risk factors reported in the literature is shown in Table 13.1.

THE FPP SURVEY

An Assessment Framework

Parents involved in childcare proceedings between 1998 and 2006 were referred for assessment to Forensic Psychology Practice Ltd (FPP), a private practice of clinical and forensic psychologists in Birmingham, UK. These assessments sought to identify the number and severity of risk factors associated with faulty parenting, and to determine how the risks could be dealt with. The purpose of the assessments was to direct courts to the best outcomes for the children, that is, should a child be permanently removed from its parents or should it be rehabilitated back to their care. The assessments involved psychometric testing; personal history and clinical interviews of the parent(s); review of information from other collateral sources; direct observation of contact between the parent(s) and their child; and interview and psychometric assessment of the child if deemed appropriate or if directed by the court. The data obtained from a retrospective survey of this cohort of parents are discussed below. Given that there are no set guidelines or frameworks to carry out such assessments, the data recorded varied from report to report, thus impacting on the sample sizes for different factors.

Biographical and Clinical Factors

During the personal history and clinical interviews, information was gathered on the parent's early development and childhood; family life; education and employment; relationships; adjustment problems (including criminal history, substance misuse, psychiatric history, traumatic events); parenting attitudes and behaviors; parents' insight into their difficulties and concerns of childcare professionals; and parents' empathy for their children, with a view to identifying potential risk factors. This information, in combination with the psychometric assessment, corroborating information, and direct observation of contact between the parent and child, was then used to formulate a psychological profile of the parent.

Table 13.2 shows the demographic factors of parents (N=293) involved in these assessments. In all, 41% had mental health problems (including depression, psychosis,

Table 13.2 Demographic factors and concerns of parents involved in childcare proceedings.

Factor	Previous research	FPP sample (N=293)
Mental health	43% (Brophy et al., 2003); 48% (Hunt et al., 1999)	41%
Drug abuse	23% (Brophy et al., 2003); 20% (Hunt et al., 1999)	20%
Alcohol abuse	20% (Brophy et al., 2003)	16%
Domestic violence	45% (Brophy et al., 2003); 51% (Hunt et al., 1999)	48%
Criminal activity	20% (Brophy et al., 2003); 61% (Hunt et al., 1999)	51%
Abused as a child	61% (Hunt et al., 1999)	53%
Learning disability	22% (Hunt et al., 1999)	19% (FSIQ<70)

self-harm/suicide); 20% had drug abuse problems; 16% had alcohol abuse problems; domestic violence was a concern in 48% of cases; 53% of parents had been abused as a child; and 19% were assessed as having a full scale IQ of less than 70.

A similar prevalence pattern has been reported by other researchers (Hunt et al., 1999; Brophy et al., 2003). A total of 51% of the sample had criminal convictions, though this may not have necessarily been of concern in terms of their parenting, for example if their conviction pre-dated the birth of their child and criminal activity had ceased.

Psychometric Measures

Psychometric measures of intelligence, personality style, emotional functioning, coping, substance abuse, and stress helped to build a psychological profile of the individual. In addition to assessing current levels of functioning, they can measure change over time; aid diagnosis; assess level of risk; inform intervention and treatment needs; support clinical judgment; explain past behavior; and predict future behavior. Decisions regarding which psychometric measures were administered were based upon the scope of the referral instructions, applicability to the case, and appropriateness of its use with the individual.

Intelligence: Standardized IQ tests, such as Wechsler Adult Intelligence Scale – 3rd
  edition (WAIS-III, Wechsler, 1997); Wechsler Abbreviated Scale of Intelligence
  (WASI, Wechsler, 1999); Raven's Progressive Matrices (Raven, Raven, & Court,
  1998); and the National Adult Reading Test (Nelson & Willison, 1982) provide a
  reliable indicator of cognitive ability. Though poor intellectual functioning alone
  does not preclude a person from offering a good enough standard of parenting, it
  can suggest best ways in which to approach intervention work with them. For
  example, someone who has deficits in verbal comprehension and reasoning may
  benefit from interventions using pictorial information and/or practical demon-
  strations and modeling. Measures of intelligence also inform decisions about the
  likely time course of rehabilitation.
    The average verbal IQ of parents (N=211) was 82 (low average range); rang-
  ing from 53 (extremely low) to 145 (very superior). The average performance IQ
  (N=212) was 93 (average range), ranging from 58 (extremely low) to 155 (very
  superior). The average full scale IQ (N=253) was 86 (low average), ranging from
  53 (extremely low) to 155 (very superior).
Personality: Personality is a complex set of characteristics specific to an individual
  whose assessment provides psychologists with an understanding of the clinical
  features that are idiosyncratic to the individual; it assists the formulation of presenting problems and identification of factors that may interfere with the outcome of intervention or likelihood of successful engagement. Understanding
  how these impact on parenting increases the individual's self-awareness and

determines the methodology of choice in any change-related work. Personality assessments most regularly used were the Millon Clinical Multiaxial Inventory (MCMI) – 3rd edition (Millon, 1994) and the Minnesota Multiphasic Personality Inventory (MMPI) – 2nd edition, (Butcher, Dahlstrom, Graham, Tellegen, & Kaemmer, 1989).

A total of 49% of parents (N=375) had significant scores on at least one clinical personality pattern, the largest groups being "depressive" (13.2%), "dependent" (11%), "self-defeating" (11%), and "paranoid" (10.8%) (see Table 13.3). In relation to clinical syndromes, 34% had significant scores on at least one clinical syndrome scale, 20.7% obtaining a significant score for "anxiety," 8.6% for "major depression," and 6.7 for "drug dependence."

Problem-solving style: Understanding how parents typically cope with problems or distressing life events and their typical behavioral, cognitive, and emotional responses in these situations are important to a parenting assessment. It is important to know, for example, whether someone approaches problems in a positive way or uses avoidance strategies as a means of coping. Assessment enables clinicians to identify the individual's strengths and weaknesses in stressful situations and suggest alternative coping strategies consistent with positive parenting. The Coping Response Inventory – CRI (Moos, 1993) or COPE (Carver, Scheier, & Weintraub, 1989) – were typically used in such assessments.

Table 13.4 shows that one-third (33.4%) of the parents assessed on the CRI (N=371) obtained the highest mean score for the coping strategy of "emotional discharge." This suggests that reducing tension by expressing strong emotions or getting angry was the most frequently used coping strategy. Unfortunately, individuals who consistently use emotional discharge are unlikely to resolve their problems and are at risk for distress; this type of coping is also related to depression, physical symptoms, and substance abuse. A total of 22% of parents also achieved elevated scores for "acceptance," indicating a tendency to accept their

Table 13.3 Percentage of parents (N=375) in childcare proceedings with significant personality characteristics and clinical syndromes.

Personality patterns	Percentage of parents with significant personality pattern
Avoidant	9.9
Depressive	13.2
Dependent	11.0
Self-defeating	11.0
Paranoid	10.8
Clinical Syndromes	
Anxiety	20.7
Drug dependence	6.7
Major depression	8.6

Table 13.4 Percentage of parents (N=371) involved in childcare proceedings achieving low or high scores for approach and avoidance coping strategies.

Coping strategy	Percentage of parents achieving low scores	Percentage of parents achieving high scores
Logical analysis	34.2	5.7
Positive reappraisal	20.5	7.3
Seeking support	15.4	21.6
Problem solving	12.1	15.6
Cognitive avoidance	14.6	17.8
Acceptance	8.1	22.4
Alternative rewards	21.3	16.2
Emotional discharge	6.5	33.4

problems as something they cannot change. Avoidance coping strategies were used more frequently than approach coping strategies, with over a third of parents (34%) achieving low scores for "logical analysis" (looking at a problem in a logical manner and breaking it down into smaller, more manageable parts), and a fifth (20.5%) achieving low scores for "positive reappraisal" (looking at the problem in a positive way).

Parenting stress: Being a parent can be extremely stressful. There are different sources of stress in parent–child relationships, which can point to relationships at risk for the development of dysfunctional parenting behavior or behavioral problems in the child. Psychometric measures of parenting stress included the Stress Index for Parents of Adolescents – SIPA (Sheras, Abidin, & Konold, 1998); Parenting Stress Index – PSI (Abidin, 1995); Parenting Alliance Measure – PAM (Abidin & Konold, 1999); and Child Abuse Potential Inventory – CAPI (Milner, 1986). Identifying difficult areas in their relationship with their child or in their role as a parent often constitutes a core component of a parenting rehabilitation plan.

Approximately one-fifth (21%) of all parents completing both the long form (N=223) and short form (N=202) versions of the PSI (see Tables 13.5 and 13.6) experienced a significant amount of stress in their role as a parent.

One in ten parents experienced significant levels of distress in their role as a parent; 28% of parents perceived significant difficulties in parent–child interactions, indicating either poor bonding between parent and child, or a perception that the child did not meet the parent's expectations and/or the interactions between them were not reinforcing to the parent. Furthermore, nearly one in five children were perceived to be difficult to manage. The results show that many parents perceive their problems to be attributable to the characteristics and behaviors of the child rather than their own shortcomings. Parents of nearly half the children (49.5%) reported significant levels of "life stress," that is, factors

Table 13.5 Percentage of parents achieving significant scores in relation to parenting stress of children (N=202), measured on a short form protocol.

Parenting stress factor	Percentage of parents achieving significant scores
Parental distress	10.4
Parent–child dysfunctional interaction	28.2
Difficult child	19.3
Total stress	21.8

Table 13.6 Percentage of parents achieving significant scores in relation to parenting stress of children (N=223), measured on a long form protocol.

Parenting stress factor	Percentage of parents achieving significant scores
Child domain	
Hyperactivity/distractibility	20.6
Adaptability	26.5
Reinforces parents	19.7
Demandingness	21.1
Mood	19.3
Acceptability	25.6
Child domain total stress	28.7
Parent domain	
Competence	14.3
Isolation	18.9
Attachment	10.8
Health	6.3
Role restriction	5.4
Depression	13.0
Spouse	21.5
Parent domain total stress	12.6
Total parenting stress	21.1
Life stress	49.5

outside of the parent–child system, which may further exacerbate the stress they experience in their role as a parent.

Anger: The stresses of parenting give rise to the experience and expression of strong emotions, especially anger, which impacts on the individual parent, the couple relationship, and the children. An understanding of how an individual experiences and expresses anger is, therefore, an important feature of a parenting assessment. Typical measures used included the State-Trait Anger Expression Inventory – STAXI-2 (Spielberger, 1999) and Novaco Anger Scale – NAS (Novaco, 1994). The STAXI measures an individual's disposition to perceive a wide range of situations as annoying or frustrating and the tendency to respond to such situations with the expression of anger toward other people or objects in the environment. Other measures include anger directed inward; the suppression of angry feelings; and the ability to monitor and prevent the outward expression of anger and calm down. Such assessments identify a parent's ability to control, maintain, and express their emotions in a manner that is not detrimental to the emotional or physical development of their child, and indicate where therapeutic intervention is needed.

Table 13.7 shows that 67.5% parents (N=362) obtained low scores for "angry reaction." This scale measures the individual's sensitivity to perceived criticism and negative evaluations by others under which circumstances intense feelings of anger are experienced. The results show that over two-thirds of parents (67%) did not readily react to such triggers, and nearly a quarter of parents (24%) achieved high scores for "anger expression-out," which measures an individual's tendency to express their anger in aggressive behavior directed toward other persons or objects in the environment. A similar number of parents (24%) attained a low score for "anger control-out," that is a person's propensity to expend energy in monitoring and preventing the outward experience and expression of anger. One-fifth of parents (19%) achieved low scores for "anger control-in," that is, a tendency to expend energy in calming down and reducing angry feelings as soon as possible.

Table 13.7 Percentage of parents (N=362) obtaining low (below 25th percentile) and high (above 75th percentile) scores in relation to the experience and expression of angry feelings.

Anger scale	Percentage of parents achieving low scores	Percentage of parents achieving high scores
State anger	0.5	6.9
State anger – feeling angry	0.5	10.5
Feel like expressing anger verbally	0	7.7
Feel like expressing anger physically	0	4.1
Trait anger	43.8	11.8
Trait – angry temperament	15.2	14.0
Trait – angry reaction	67.5	7.7
Anger expression-out	31.1	24.8
Anger expression-in	22.6	22.3
Anger control-out	24.8	30.9
Anger control-in	19.6	24.0
Anger expression-index	29.5	18.7

PARENTING INTERVENTIONS

It has long been recognized that acknowledging the initial problem and accepting the need to change are among the factors found to predict positive outcomes in parenting interventions (Littell & Girvin, 2005; Gelles, 2000). Furthermore, the multifactorial nature of poor parenting means that dysfunctional families require tailored intervention packages. A wide range of intervention measures are typically recommended by psychologists in family proceedings.

Parenting programs: Significant improvements in parenting with regard to child health care, home safety, and interactions between parent and child have been observed following parent training intervention programs (Berry, Charlson, & Dawson, 2003; Dore & Lee, 1999; Gershater-Molko, Lutzker, & Wesch, 2003; Timmer, Urquiza, Zebell, & McGrath, 2005; Calam, Sanders, Miller, Sadhnani, & Carmont, 2008), though efficacy of parent training appears to be lower in families with multiple problems (Brown & Dillenburger, 2004). Family-based interventions based on social learning principles have been shown to be beneficial in the treatment of child abuse (Sanders, Cann, & Markie-Dadds, 2003) and group-based parenting programs are effective in improving maternal psychosocial health, including depression, anxiety, self-esteem, and relationship with spouse/marital adjustment (Barlow, Coren, & Stewart-Brown, 2001; Dore & Lee, 1999). There is some research focused on the impact that Borderline Personality Disorder may have upon attachment and parenting (Crandell et al., 2003; Newman & Stevenson, 2005; Newman & Stevenson, 2008) and to a lesser extent, Narcissistic Personality Disorder (Brown, 2008). A systematic review of the literature pertaining to the link between personality disorder and parenting capacity largely supported the association between a diagnosis of personality disorder, poor parent–child interactions, and problematic parenting practices (Laulik, Chou, Browne, & Allam, 2013), although due to the number of confounding variables in the studies, causal inferences cannot be made. Adshead (2003) claims that the children of personality disordered parents may be placed at risk of physical and emotional harm as a consequence of the emotional difficulties, dysregulated affect, hostility, unusual cognitions, and preoccupation with the self that characterize aspects of personality disorder. The pervasive and enduring nature of personality suggests that any risks present are likely to remain long term, thus the question of what to do with parents with personality disorder is pressing.

Cognitive-behavioral interventions: Studies of cognitive-behavioral interventions in physical and emotional abuse and neglect (Dufour & Chamberland, 2004) report positive changes following intervention involving the modification of skills or parenting behaviors. These have shown that positive verbal responses and the reinforcement of desirable behaviors increased and aversive or coercive behaviors, aggressiveness, and physical punishment decreased following intervention. However, the longer-term effectiveness of cognitive-behavioral interventions may be impeded by inadequate personal resources and social isolation.

Support services: Interventions focusing on social support and integration include individual support where volunteers, relatives, or other informal or professional helpers provide different types of assistance to families in need (Dufour & Chamberland, 2004). Evaluation of antenatal parenting workshops; baby massage, dedicated crying, sleeping, and feeding clinics; and clinics to help parents manage toddler behavior showed approximately 75% of families at risk for child abuse having successful outcomes (Naughton & Heath, 2001). Furthermore, increasing informal support networks may reduce the amount of stressors and depression that parents experience and improve their positive parenting (Lyons, Henly, & Schuerman, 2005). Parental well-being and family functioning were found to improve with access to support services, though improvements were more profound among parenting couples and less so among families identified as having financial difficulties or problems with drug or alcohol abuse (Statham & Holtermann, 2004). In an evaluation of Family Preservation and Family Support programs, researchers found that programs designed to help families meet basic concrete needs and those using mentoring approaches were more effective than parenting and child-development-oriented programs (Chaffin, Bonner, & Hill, 2001). It has been suggested that parent training approaches using behavioral practice and modeling of parenting skills are more effective in changing abuse-related parenting behaviors and improving the parent–child relationships (Urquiza & McNeil, 1996). Furthermore, center-based services have been found to be more effective than home-based services, especially among higher risk parents (Chaffin et al., 2001), though other home-visiting program evaluations have suggested that early interventions with new parents reduce the incidence of child abuse and neglect (Olds et al., 1999), enhance parental efficacy and the use of non-violent discipline, and decrease stress and partner violence in the home (Duggan et al. 1999). Evaluation of individual programs, however, has its limitations because other known risk factors for child abuse and neglect, such as parental substance abuse, domestic violence, poverty, or depression may inhibit parenting behavior change (Chaffin et al., 1996). Mitigating these risk factors may be a more important treatment target than social support and increasing parenting knowledge, particularly in families at risk of child neglect (Chaffin et al., 2001).

Mental health, violence, and substance abuse: Problem-specific treatment programs have also been found to be effective with depression (McCabe, McGillivray, & Newton, 2006); domestic violence (Buttell & Mohr Carney, 2006); and substance abuse (Bottlender & Soyka, 2005; Holloway, Bennett & Farrington, 2005), though there were differences in treatment effectiveness between individuals based on gender, ethnic background, age, and type of drug abused. Furthermore, drug abusers involved in the legal system, and indeed parents in childcare proceedings, are more likely to complete treatment programs than those who are not (Choi & Ryan, 2006). The majority of outcome studies report that approximately two-thirds of men who complete domestic-violence-related treatment avoid re-assaulting their partners (Eisikovits & Edleson, 1989; Feder & Forde, 2000; Gondolf, 2002a; Rosenfeld, 1992; Tolman & Bennett, 1990), though the success rate for alcohol and drug addiction programs may be slightly lower (Gondolf, 2002b; Hubbard et al., 1989; Miller, Walters & Bennett, 2000). However, treatments for general mental health problems such as depression, anxiety, and marital distress appear to be more effective than those for domestic violence (Chambless & Gillis, 1993; Johnson, Hunsley, Greenberg, & Schindler, 1999; Lipsey & Wilson, 1993).

Sure Start: Programs that combine child-focused educational activities with explicit attention to parent–child interaction patterns and relationship building appear to have the greatest impacts, whereas services that are based on generic family support appear to be less effective (Shonkoff & Phillips, 2000). In the United Kingdom, Sure Start, a government initiative dating from 1999, aims to achieve better outcomes for children under the age of four years, parents, and communities by increasing the availability of childcare for all children; improving health and emotional development for young children; and supporting parents as parents and in their aspirations toward employment. Sure Start local programs have been shown to have beneficial effects, that is better parenting and better social functioning in children, with non-teenage mothers, but adverse effects, that is poorer social functioning, with children of teenage mothers and children of single parents or parents who were unemployed, and in the most disadvantaged families (Belsky et al., 2006; Rutter, 2006).

Family-based interventions: Abusive or neglectful parents who undertake a combination of individual, family, and/or group approaches based on a wide range of methods, such as individual psychological help, behavioral therapy, parent education, and family therapy show fewer inappropriate or neglectful behaviors, less psychological distress, and higher marital satisfaction (Dufour & Chamberland, 2004). The greatest benefit from family therapies is seen with neglectful families; families experiencing multiple forms of abuse or physical abuse are less likely to benefit from such interventions (Daro & McCurdy, 1994).

Compliance: Famularo, Kinscherff, Bunshaft, Spivak, & Fenton (1989) reviewed parental compliance with psychotherapeutic treatment orders made by courts in cases of child abuse. They found that 62% of parents were referred for alcohol or drug treatment, 60.9% for individual psychotherapy, and 29.4% for family treatment. Treatment compliance was significantly lowered in those parents presenting with substance abuse and those who sexually and/or physically abused their children in comparison to parents who neglected their children, but did not sexually or physically abuse them.

Treatment follow-up: There is little data available in the United Kingdom regarding the extent to which recommendations for treatment or rehabilitation made by psychologists are taken up by courts. However, the recently introduced guidance on case management (Ministry of Justice, 2010a) will ensure that in future all outcomes must be notified to experts who have been engaged by the court.

The FPP survey showed (see Table 13.8) that of parents (N=317) assessed during childcare proceedings, 49.2% were recommended to attend a parenting skills program; 41% needed to develop support networks; 31.2% were referred for anger management programs and 18.6% for assertiveness training; 30.6% needed help with coping skills; 31.5% required counseling for relationship difficulties and 22.4% for childhood abuse; and 14.2% were recommended for psycho-education and/or psychotherapeutic services to appreciate the impact of mental health problems on parenting. A similar number (12.6%) of parents were directed to address issues of domestic violence; 11.4% to undergo treatment for drug abuse and 8.8% for alcohol abuse. A smaller number (5.7%) were recommended for closer observation of their parenting skills in a residential assessment center; and 4.1% were considered in need of assistance with their living skills. However, a comparison of the figures for recognized need (i.e., Table 13.2) and recommended treatment (Table 13.8) reveals some inconsistencies. For example, while 53% of the sample had some history of childhood abuse, psychotherapy/counseling was only recommended in 22% of cases. Similarly, 41% had mental health problems, yet a recommendation for interventions to increase their understanding of mental health was made for only a third of this group; while a recommendation for intervention for domestic violence was made in only a quarter of

Table 13.8 Recommendations made for treatment/psychotherapeutic interventions following psychological assessment of parents in childcare proceedings (N=317).

Recommendations for treatment/intervention	Percentage of parents
Parenting skills – community based	49.2
Development of support networks	41.0
Relationship counseling	31.5
Anger management	31.2
Coping strategies/skills	30.6
Counseling for childhood abuse	22.4
Assertiveness training	18.6
Understanding mental health	14.2
Domestic violence counseling/program	12.6
Treatment for drugs	11.4
Treatment for alcohol	8.8
Parenting skills – residential family placement	5.7
Living skills	4.1

the number for whom domestic violence had been identified as an issue (12% compared to 48% respectively). With regard to drugs and alcohol, recommendations were made for related treatment in approximately half of the cases for whom these issues were identified (11% and 9% were recommended for treatment compared to a prevalence of 20% and 16% for drugs and alcohol respectively). Recommendations may not have been made in cases where the parent had already been referred to, begun engaging in, completed intervention work, or otherwise resolved historical issues; or in cases where the parent explicitly refused to engage in such work. The inconsistencies may also be accounted for by the range of recommendations made in relation to each type of presenting issue depending upon the individual needs of each parent. For example, in some cases, it may have been considered that the psychological sequelae of childhood abuse may be better addressed by interventions related to anger management, development of support networks, coping strategies, and/or parenting skills rather than individual psychotherapy/counseling if, for example, the parent was more motivated/had the capacity to engage in these more practical, skills-based interventions than they were to engage in in-depth, potentially traumatic and difficult psychotherapeutic work related to historical abuse.

A cohort of parents assessed during family proceedings were followed up after the final hearing (N=293) and provided outcome data on 110 children. Regarding the placement of the child, there was agreement in 65% of cases between psychologist recommendations and directions of the court at the final hearing. Table 13.9 shows that 82% of children were placed away from their biological family (33% were freed for adoption and 49% were placed with foster carers) and only 18% of children were returned to or remained with their biological family. These results are broadly in line with those of Brophy et al. (2003), who found that 72% of children in their study were permanently removed from their biological family and a further 13% were returned to a parent(s). However, Masson et al. (2004) in a survey of child protection disposals found that roughly half of the children (51%) were rehabilitated to family members; the other half (49%) were placed away from biological families in foster care, residential care, or were freed for adoption.

Table 13.9 Disposal of children (N=110) in family proceedings.

Disposal	FPP recommended (%)	Outcomes (%)		
		FPP	Brophy et al. (2003)	Masson et al. (2004)
Foster care (kinship or local authority)	58	49	72	13
Adoption	8	33		36
Remain/return to biological family	34	18	13	51

Such differences in outcomes may simply be due to methodological variations in data collection and analysis. However, they may reflect important differences in evaluation of risk factors between psychologists and other professionals involved in child protection and family proceedings. For example, FPP survey data show that courts were likely to heed psychological advice in more than three-quarters of cases (84%) where fostering away from biological parents was recommended, and in only half of cases (53%) where return to biological family was advocated. This may be because recommendations to return children to their family are often conditional on appropriate therapeutic help being offered to the parents by the local authority. In these cases lack of success may be due to lack of finances, resources, or services; or parental non-compliance with treatment or rehabilitation plans.

CONCLUSIONS

It is clear that dysfunctional parenting is a multifactorial phenomenon. A combination of physical and mental health problems and socioeconomic difficulties, coupled with personal vulnerability factors, are present in a large number of parents subject to statutory interventions resulting from abusive or neglectful parenting (Ammerman, 1990; McCoy & Keen, 2009). These risk factors may be located in the attitudes, behavior, or characteristics of parents; the children themselves; their immediate home and family environment; or the wider social and cultural context of the family. However, risk is dynamic and changeable across time and situation, and the presence of these risk factors can be mediated by protective factors, such as positive engagement with support networks; insight into the focal problem; and motivation to change. Although attempts to predict child abuse and poor parenting have, to date, met with only mixed success, the identification of risk and protective factors remains central to the psychological assessment of parenting and is an important reason why courts request psychological expertise (Hamilton & Browne, 2002).

As a result, the psychological assessment of parenting is inevitably going to be a complex and multifaceted process looking at the psychological, social, interpersonal, and environmental factors that combine to potentially impair or promote an individual's capacity to be a good parent. There is no formula to calculate the number or type of protective factors required to outweigh the presenting risk factors; and furthermore, given the complexity and uniqueness of parents involved in this type of assessment, there is no panacea. At its best, such an assessment can provide an informed, objective perspective that increases the fairness and accuracy of legal decisions; at its worst, it can contribute inaccurate, biased, or irrelevant information that violates a parent's rights and/or impairs the decision-making process (Budd, 2005). In order to ensure that such assessments have relevance to the legal decision-making in family proceedings they must be tailored to the referral questions; use a valid and reliable methodology; offer workable recommendations based on known outcomes; and suggest realistic timescales for rehabilitation where this is indicated.

Very little data are available in the United Kingdom on the quality, relevance, and impact of psychological assessment in family proceedings, though there is considerably more evidence from the United States, albeit in the context of child custody (Bow, 2006). What evidence there is suggests, among other things, a lack of standardized methodology, variable quality as perceived by commissioners, and a lack of communication between service users (i.e., courts and lawyers) and service providers (i.e., psychologists) (Saraw, 2008). However, current challenges facing practitioners not only relate to the legislation, the difficult nature of this client group, and lack of clear guidance and a framework as to how best to undertake assessments, but also to the need for enhanced professional training. The Mini Pupillage Scheme run by Warwickshire and Coventry Family Justice Council (2010) is a rare example of a free continuous professional development program for psychologists who wish to know more about court processes and observe live cross-examination of expert witnesses in real family cases. As psychologists become more involved in providing reports to court there is a growing need to ensure that guidance provided by professional bodies is matched by opportunities for hands-on experience during training.

REFERENCES

Abidin, R.R. (1995). *Parenting Stress Index: Manual*. Odessa, FL: Psychological Assessment Resources, Inc.

Abidin, R.R., & Konold, T.R. (1999). *Parenting Alliance Measure: Manual*. Odessa, FL: Psychological Assessment Resources, Inc.

Adshead, G. (2003). Dangerous and Severe Parenting Disorder? Personality disorder, parenting and new legal proposals. *Child Abuse Review*, *12*, 227–237.

American Psychological Association. Committee on Professional Practice and Standards (1998). *Guidelines for psychological evaluations in child protection matters*. Washington, DC: APA.

Ammerman, R.T. (1990). Predisposing child factors. In R.T. Ammerman & M. Hersen (Eds.), *Children at risk: An evaluation of factors contributing to child abuse and neglect*. New York: Plenum Press.

Azar, S. (2002). *Parenting and child maltreatment*. In M.H. Bornstein (Eds.), *Handbook of parenting. Volume 4: Social conditions and applied parenting* (2nd ed., pp. 361–388). Mahwah, NJ: Lawrence Erlbaum.

Barlow, J., Coren, E., & Stewart-Brown, S. (2001). *Systematic review of the effectiveness of parenting programmes in improving maternal psychosocial health*. Oxford: Health Services Research Unit, University of Oxford.

Belsky, J., Melhuish, E., Barnes, J., Leyland, A.H., Romaniuk, H., & National Evaluation of Sure Start Research Team (2006). Effects of Sure Start local programmes on children and families: Early findings from a quasi-experimental cross sectional study. *British Medical Journal*, *332*, 1476–1482.

Berger, L. (2005). Income, family characteristics and physical violence toward children. *Child Abuse & Neglect*, *29* (2), 107–133.

Berry, M., Charlson, R., & Dawson, K. (2003). Promising practices in understanding and treating child neglect. *Child & Family Social Work, 8* (1), 13–24.

Besinger, B.A., Garland, A.F., Litrownik, A.J., & Landsverk, J.A. (1999). Caregiver substance abuse among maltreated children placed in out-of-home care. *Child Welfare, 78,* 221–239.

Bools, C., Neale, B.A., & Meadow. R. (1994). Munchausen syndrome by proxy: A study of psychopathology. *Child Abuse & Neglect, 18,* 773–788.

Booth, T., Booth, W., & McConnell, D. (2005). The prevalence and outcomes of care proceedings involving parents with learning difficulties in the Family Courts, *Journal of Applied Research in Intellectual Disabilities, 18,* 7–17.

Bottlender, M., & Soyka, M. (2005). Outpatient alcoholism treatment: predictors of outcome after 3 years. *Drug and Alcohol Dependence, 80* (1): 83–89.

Bow, J.N. (2006). Review of empirical research on child custody practice. *Journal of Child Custody, 3* (1), 23–50.

Bow, J.N., & Quinnell, F.A. (2002). A critical review of child custody evaluation reports. *Family Court Review, 40* (2), 164–176.

Bow, J.N., & Quinnell, F.A. (2004). Critique of child custody evaluations by the legal profession. *Family Court Review, 42* (1), 115–127.

Briere, J. (1992). *Child abuse trauma: Theory and treatment of the fasting effects.* London: Sage.

British Psychological Society (1998). *Psychologists as expert witnesses.* Leicester: BPS.

British Psychological Society (2004a). *Safeguarding children and young people from abuse, harm and neglect: The responsibilities of chartered psychologists.* Leicester: BPS.

British Psychological Society (2004b). *Advice to members acting as an expert.* Leicester: BPS.

British Psychological Society (2007). *Child Protection Portfolio.* Leicester: Professional Affairs Board, BPS.

Brophy, J. (2006). *Research review: Child-care proceedings under the Children Act 1989.* Department for Constitutional Affairs, Research Series 5/06. London: DCA.

Brophy J., Jhutti-Johal, J., and Owen, C. (2003). *Significant harm in a multicultural setting.* Research Series 1/03, London: DCA.

Brophy, J., Wale, C., & Bates, P. (1999). *Myths and practices: A national survey of the use of experts in child-care proceedings.* London: BAAF.

Brown, N.W. (2008). *Children of the Self-Absorbed: A grown-up's guide to getting over narcissistic parents.* Second Edition. Oakland, CA: New Harbinger Publications, Inc.

Brown, E.A., & Dillenburger, K. (2004). An evaluation of the effectiveness of intervention in families with children with behavioural problems within the context of a Sure Start programme. *Child Care in Practice, 10* (1), 63–77.

Brown, J., Cohen, P., Johnson, J.G., & Salzinger, S. (1998). A longitudinal analysis of risk factors for child maltreatment: Findings of a 17-year prospective study of officially recorded and self-reported child abuse and neglect. *Child Abuse & Neglect, 22,* 1065–1078.

Browne, K.D., Hamilton, C.E., Heggarty, J., & Blissett, J. (2000). Identifying need and protecting children through community nursing home visits. *Representing Children, 13,* 111–123.

Browne, K.D., & Herbert, M. (1997). *Preventing family violence.* Chichester, UK: John Wiley & Sons, Ltd.

Browne, K.D., & Saqi, S. (1987). Parent–child interaction in abusing families: Possible causes and consequences. In P. Maher (Ed.), *Child abuse: An educational perspective* pp. 77–104. Oxford: Blackwell.

Budd, K.S. (2005). Assessing parenting capacity in a child welfare context. *Children and Youth Services Review, 27*, 429–444.

Burke, J., Chandy, J., Dannerbeck, A., & Watt, J. (1988). The parental environment cluster model of child neglect: An integrative conceptual model. *Journal of Child Welfare, 77* (4), 389–405.

Butcher, J.N., Dahlstrom, W.G., Graham, J.R., Tellegen, A., & Kaemmer, B. (1989). *Minnesota Multiphasic Personality Inventory (MMPI-2)*. Minneapolis, MN: University of Minnesota Press.

Buttell, F., & Mohr Carney, M. (2006). A large sample evaluation of a court-mandated batterer intervention program: Investigating differential program effect for African American and Caucasian men. *Research on Social Work Practice, 16* (2), 121–131.

Calam, R., Sanders, M.R., Miller, C., Sadhnani, V., & Carmont, S. (2008). Can technology and the media help to reduce dysfunctional parenting and increase engagement with preventative parenting interventions? *Child Maltreatment, 13*, 347–361.

Carlson, B.E. (2000). Children exposed to intimate partner violence: Research findings and implications for intervention. *Trauma, Violence, & Abuse, 1* (4), 321–340.

Carpenter, G.L., & Stacks, A.M. (2009). Developmental effects of exposure to intimate partner violence in early childhood: a review of the literature. *Children and Youth Services Review, 31*, 831–839

Carver, C.S., Scheier, M.F., & Weintraub, J.K. (1989). Assessing coping strategies: A theoretically based approach. *Journal of Personality and Social Psychology, 56*, 267–283.

Chaffin, M., Bonner, B.L., & Hill, R.F. (2001). Family preservation and family support programs: Child maltreatment outcomes across client risk levels and program types. *Child Abuse & Neglect, 25*, 1269–1289.

Chaffin, M., Kelleher, K., & Hollenbert, J. (1996). Onset of physical abuse and neglect: Psychiatric, substance abuse, and social risk factors from prospective community data. *Child Abuse & Neglect, 20*, 191–203.

Chambless, D.L., & Gillis, M.M. (1993). Cognitive therapy of anxiety disorders. *Journal of Consulting and Clinical Psychology, 61*, 248–260.

Choi, S., & Ryan, J. (2006). Completing substance abuse treatment in child welfare: The role of co-occurring problems and primary drug of choice. *Child Maltreatment, 11* (4), 313–325.

Crandell, L.E., Patrick, M.P.H., & Hobson, R.P. (2003). 'Still-face' interactions between mothers with borderline personality disorder and their 2-month-old infants. *British Journal of Psychiatry, 183*, 239–247.

Crouch, J.L., & Milner, J.S. (2001). Childhood physical abuse, early social support and risk for maltreatment: Current social support as a mediator of risk for child physical abuse. *Child Abuse and Neglect, 25*, 93–107.

Daro, D., & McCurdy, K. (1994). Preventing child abuse and neglect: Programmatic interventions. *Child Welfare, 73*, 405–422.

Davison, S. (2002). Principles of managing patients with personality disorder. *Advances in Psychiatric Treatment, 8*, 1–9.

Department for Constitutional Affairs (2003). *Protocol for judicial case management in public law Children Act cases*. London: Lord Chancellor's Department.

Department for Education (2013). Characteristics of children in need in England, 2012–13. London.

Department of Health (1988). *Protecting children: A guide for social workers undertaking a comprehensive assessment*. London: HMSO.

Department of Health (2000). *Framework for the assessment of children in need and their families*. London: The Stationery Office.

Dinwiddie, S., & Bucholz, K. (1993). Psychiatric diagnoses of self-reported child abusers. *Child Abuse & Neglect, 17*, 465–476.

Dixon, L., Browne, K.D., & Hamilton-Giachristis, C. (2005). Risk factors of parents abused as children: A mediational analysis of the intergenerational continuity of child maltreatment (Part 1). *Journal of Child Psychology and Psychiatry, 46*, 47–57.

Dixon, L., Hamilton-Giachritsis, C., & Browne, K.D. (2005). Attributions and behaviours of parents abused as children: A mediational analysis of the intergenerational continuity of child maltreatment (Part II). *Journal of Child Psychology and Psychiatry, 46*, 58–68.

Dore, M., & Lee, J. (1999). The role of parent training with abusive and neglectful parents. *Family Relations: Journal of Applied Family & Child Studies, 48* (3), 313–325.

Dufour, S., & Chamberland, C. (2004). The effectiveness of selected interventions for previous maltreatment: Enhancing the well-being of children who live at home. *Child & Family Social Work, 9*, 39–56.

Duggan, A.K., McFarlane, E.C., Windham, A.M., Rohde, C.A., Salvaker, D.S., Fuddy, L., … & Sia, C.C.J. (1999). Evaluation of Hawaii's healthy start program. *The Future of Children, 9* (1), 66–90.

Edleson, J.L. (1999). The overlap between child maltreatment and woman battering. *Violence Against Women, 5* (2), 134–154.

Egeland, B., Bosquet, M., & Chung, A.L. (2002). Continuities and discontinuities in the intergenerational transmission of child maltreatment: Implications for breaking the cycle of abuse. In K. Browne, H. Hanks, P. Stratton, & C. Hamilton (Eds.), *Early prediction and prevention of child abuse: A handbook* (pp. 217–232). Chichester, UK: John Wiley & Sons, Ltd.

Eisikovits, Z.C., & Edleson, J.L. (1989). Intervening with men who batter: A critical review of the literature. *Social Service Review, 63*, 384–413.

Falkov, A. (1996). Study of Working Together Part 8 reports. *Fatal Child Abuse and Parental Psychiatric Disorder: An analysis of 100 ACPC case reviews conducted under the terms of Part 8 of Working Together under the Children Act 1989*. London: Department of Health.

Famularo, R., Kinscerff, R., Bunshaft, D., Spivak, G., & Fenton, T. (1989). Parental compliance to court-ordered treatment interventions in cases of child maltreatment. *Child Abuse & Neglect, 13*, 507–514.

Famularo, R., Kinscherff, R., & Fenton, B. (1992a). Psychiatric diagnoses of abusive mothers: A preliminary report. *Journal of Nervous and Mental Disease, 180*, 658–661.

Famularo, R., Kinscherff, R., & Fenton, T. (1992b). Parental substance abuse and the nature of child maltreatment. *Child Abuse & Neglect, 16*, 475–483.

Feder, L., & Forde, D.R. (2000). *A test of the efficacy of court mandated counseling for domestic violence offenders: The Broward experiment (NIJ Publication No. 184752)*. Washington, DC.

Finkelhor, D., Hotaling, G., Lewis, I.A., & Smith, C. (1990). Sexual abuse in a national survey of adult men and women: Prevalence, characteristics, and risk factors. *Child Abuse and Neglect*, *14*, 19–28.

Gelles, R.J. (2000). Treatment-resistant families. In R.M. Reece (Ed.), *Treatment of child abuse: Common ground for mental health, medical, and legal practitioners*. Baltimore, MD: Johns Hopkins University Press.

Gershater-Molko, M., Lutzker, J.R., & Wesch, D. (2003). Project SafeCare: Improving health, safety and parenting skills in families reported for and at risk for child maltreatment. *Journal of Family Violence*, *18* (6): 377–386.

Gibbons, J., Conroy, S., & Bell, C. (1995). *Operating the Child Protection System*. London: HMSO.

Goldson, E. (1998). Children with disabilities and child maltreatment. *Child Abuse and Neglect*, *28*, 663–667.

Gondolf, E.W. (2002a). *Intensive outpatient treatment for alcohol and drug addiction: A three-year outcome study*. Pittsburgh, PA: Richard King Mellon Foundation.

Gondolf, E.W. (2002b). *Batterer treatment systems: Issues, outcomes, and recommendations*. Thousand Oaks, CA: Sage.

Hamilton, C.E., & Browne, K.D. (1998). The repeat victimisation of children: Should the concept be revised? *Aggression and Violent Behaviour*, *3* (1), 47–60.

Hamilton, C., & Browne, K. (2002). Predicting physical maltreatment. In K.D. Browne, H. Hanks, P. Stratton, & C. Hamilton (Eds.), *Early prediction and prevention of child abuse* pp. 41–56. Chichester, UK: John Wiley & Sons, Ltd.

Herron, K., & Holtzworth-Munroe, A. (2002). Child abuse potential: A comparison of subtypes of martially violent men and non-violent men. *Journal of Family Violence*, *17*, 1–21.

Hogan, T.M., Myers, B.J., & Elswick, R.K. (2006). Child abuse potential among mothers of substance-exposed and non-exposed infants and toddlers. *Child Abuse and Neglect*, *30*, 145–156.

Holloway, K., Bennett, T., & Farrington, D. (2005). *The effectiveness of Criminal Justice and Treatment programmes in reducing drug-related crime: A systematic review*. Home Office On-line Report 26/05. Available from: http://www.crim.cam.ac.uk/people/academic_research/david_farrington/olr2605.pdf.

Holt, S., Buckley, H., & Whelan, S. (2008). The impact of exposure to domestic violence on children and young people: A review of the literature. *Child Abuse & Neglect*, *32*, 797–810.

Howe, D., Dooley, T., & Hinings, D. (2000). Assessment and decision-making in a case of child neglect and abuse using an attachment perspective. *Child & Family Social Work*, *5*, 143–155.

Hubbard, R., Marsden, M.E., Rachal, J.V., Harwood, H., Cavenaugh, E., & Ginzburg, H. (1989). *Drug abuse treatment: A national survey of effectiveness*. Chapel Hill, NC: University of North Carolina Press.

Hunt, J., Macleod, A., & Thomas, C. (1999). *The last resort: Child protection, the courts and the 1989 Children Act*. London: The Stationery Office.

James, H. (2004). Promoting effective working with parents with learning disabilities. *Child Abuse Review*, *13*, 31–41.

Jaudes, P.K., Ekwo, E., & Van Voorhis, J. (1995). Association of drug abuse and child abuse. *Child Abuse & Neglect*, *19*, 1065–1075.

Johnson, S.M., Hunsley, J., Greenberg, L., & Schindler, D. (1999). Emotionally focused couples therapy: Status and challenges. *Clinical Psychology: Science and Practice*, 6, 67–79.

Kellehcr, K., Chaffin, M., Hooengerg, J., & Fischer, E. (1994). Alcohol and drug disorders among physically abusive and neglectful parents in a community-based sample. *American Journal of Public Health*, 84, 1586–1590.

Koenig, A., Cicchetti, D., & Rogosch, F. (2000). Child compliance/noncompliance and maternal contributors to internalization in maltreating and non-maltreating dyads. *Child Development*, 71, 1018–1032.

Kotch, J., Browne, D., Dufort, V., & Winsor, J. (1999). Predicting child maltreatment in the first 4 years of life from characteristics assessed in the neonatal period. *Child Abuse & Neglect*, 23 (4), 305–319.

Laulik, S., Chou, S., Browne, K.D., & Allam, J. (2013). The link between personality disorder and parenting behaviours: A systematic review. *Aggression and Violent Behaviour*, 18, 644–655.

Legal Services Commission (2004). The use of experts: Consultation paper. *Quality, price, and procedures in publicly funded cases*. London: LSC.

Lipsey, M., & Wilson, D. (1993). The efficacy of psychological, educational, and behavioral treatment: Confirmation from meta-analysis. *American Psychologist*, 48, 1181–1209.

Littell, J.H., & Girvin, H. (2005). Caregivers readiness for change: Predictive validity in a child welfare sample. *Child Abuse and Neglect*, 2, 59–80.

Lyons, S.J., Henly, J.R., & Schuerman, J.R. (2005). Informal support in maltreating families: Its effect on parenting practices. *Children and Youth Services Review*, 27 (1), 21–38.

Masson, J., Oakley, W.M., & Pick, K. (2004). Emergency protection orders: Court orders for child protection cases. Warwick University. In J. Brophy, *Child Care Proceedings under the Children Act 1989*. Research Series 5/06. London: DCA.

McCabe, M.P., McGillivray, J.A., & Newton, D.C. (2006). Effectiveness of treatment programmes for depression among adults with mild/moderate intellectual disability. *Journal of Intellectual Disability Research*, 50 (4), 239–247.

McCoy, M.L., and Keen, S.M. (2009). *Child abuse and neglect*. New York: Psychology Press.

Miller, W.R., Walters, S.T., & Bennett, M.E. (2000). How effective is alcoholism treatment in the United States? *Journal of Studies on Alcohol*, 62, 211–220.

Millon, T (1994). *Millon Clinical Multiaxial Inventory–III: Manual*. Minneapolis, MN: National Computer Systems, Inc.

Milner, J.S. (1986). *The Child Abuse Potential Inventory Manual* (2nd ed.). Webster, NC: Psytec.

Ministry of Justice (2010a). *The Public Law Outline: Guide to case management in public law proceedings*. London: Lord Chancellor's Department.

Ministry of Justice (2010b). *Proposals for the reform of legal aid in England and Wales*. London: The Stationery Office.

Moos, R.H. (1993). *Coping Response Inventory-Adult Form: Professional Manual*. Odessa, FL: PAR, Inc.

Murphy, J.M., Jellinek, M., Quinn, D., Smith, G., Poitrast, F., & Goshko, M. (1991). Substance abuse and serious child maltreatment: Prevalence, risk, and outcome in a court sample. *Child Abuse & Neglect*, 15, 197–211.

National Research Council (1993). *Understanding child abuse and neglect.* Washington, DC: National Academy Press.

Naughton, A., & Heath, A. (2001). Developing an early intervention programme to prevent child maltreatment. *Child Abuse Review, 10*, 85–96.

Nelson, H.E., & Willison, J. (1982). *The National Adult Reading Test* (2nd ed.). London: NFER-NELSON,

Newman, L., & Stevenson, C. (2005). Parenting and borderline personality disorder: ghosts in the nursery. *Clinical Child Psychology and Psychiatry, 10*, 385–394.

Newman, L., & Stevenson, C. (2008). Issues in infant-parent psychotherapy for mothers with borderline personality disorder. *Clinical Child Psychology and Psychiatry 13* (4): 505–514.

Novaco, R.W. (1994). Anger as a risk factor for violence among the mentally disordered. In J. Monahan & H.J. Steadman (Eds.), *Violence and mental disorder: Developments in risk assessment* pp. 21–60. Chicago, IL: University of Chicago Press.

NSPCC (2008). *Child protection research briefing: Poverty and child maltreatment.* London: NSPCC.

Olds, D.L., Henderson, C.R., Kitzman, H.J., Eckenrode, J.J., Cole, R.E., & Tatelbaum, R.C. (1999). Prenatal and infancy home visitation by nurses: Recent findings. *The Future of Children, 9* (1), 44–65.

Raven, J., Raven, J.C., & Court, J.H. (1998). *Raven's Progressive Matrices and Vocabulary Scales.* Oxford: Psychologists Press Ltd.

Reid, J., Macchetto, P., & Foster, S. (1999). *No safe haven: Children of substance-abusing parents.* New York: National Center on Addiction and Substance Abuse at Columbia University.

Rosenfeld, B.D. (1992). Court-ordered treatment of spouse abuse. *Clinical Psychology Review, 12*, 205–226.

Rossman, B.B. (2001). Longer term effects of children's exposure to domestic violence. In S.A. Graham-Bermann & J.L. Edleson (Eds.), *Domestic violence in the lives of children: The future of research, intervention, and social policy* (pp. 35–66). Washington, DC: American Psychological Association.

Runtz, M.G., & Shallow, J.R (1997). Social support and coping strategies as mediators of adult adjustment following childhood maltreatment. *Child Abuse and Neglect, 21*, 211–266.

Rutter, M. (2006). Is Sure Start and effective preventive intervention? *Child and Adolescent Mental Health, 11* (3), 135–141.

Sanders, M., Cann, W., & Markie-Dadds, C. (2003). Why a universal population-level approach to the prevention of child abuse is essential. *Child Abuse Review, 12*, 145–154.

Saraw, S. (2008). *An investigation into psychologist parental assessment processes in child protection cases.* Unpublished master's research project. University of Birmingham, Centre for Forensic and Family Psychology.

Saunders, B., & Goddard, C. (1998). *A critique of structured risk assessment procedures. Instruments of abuse?* Child Abuse and Family Violence Research Unit, Malaysia: Monash University.

Shahar, G. (2001). Maternal personality and distress as predictors of child neglect. *Journal of Research in Personality, 35*, 537–545.

Sheras, P., Abidin, R., & Konold, T. (1998). *Stress Index for Parents of Adolescents: Professional Manual.* Florida: PAR, Inc.

Shonkoff, J., & Phillips, D. (Eds.) (2000). *From neurons to neighbourhoods: The science of early childhood development*. Washington, DC: National Academy Press.

Spielberger, C.D. (1999). *State-Trait Anger Expression Inventory: Second edition (STAXI-2)*. Florida: PAR, Inc.

Stanley, N., & Penhale, B. (1999). The mental health problems of mothers experiencing the child protection system: Identifying needs and appropriate responses. *Child Abuse Review*, *8* (1), 34–45.

Statham, J., & Holtermann, S. (2004). Families on the brink: The effectiveness of family support services. *Child & Family Social Work*, *9* (2), 153–166.

Straus, M.A., & Smith, C. (1990). Violence in Hispanic families in the United States: Incidence rates and structural interpretations. In M.A. Straus & R.J. Gelles (Eds.), *Physical violence in American families: Risk factors and adaptations in violence in families* (pp. 341–363). New Brunswick, NJ: Transactions Publishers.

Timmer, S.G., Urquiza, A.J., Zebell, N.M. & McGrath, J.M. (2005). Parent-child interaction therapy: Application to maltreating parent-child dyads. *Child Abuse and Neglect*, *2* (7), 825–842.

Tolman, R.M., & Bennett, L.W. (1990). A review of quantitative research on men who batter. *Journal of Interpersonal Violence*, *5*, 87–118.

Urquiza, A.J., & McNeil, C.B. (1996). Parent-child interaction therapy: An intensive dyadic intervention for physically abusive families. *Child Maltreatment*, *1*, 134–144.

Walsh, C., MacMillan, H., & Jamieson, E. (2003). The relationship between parental substance abuse and child maltreatment: Findings from the Ontario Health Supplement. *Child Abuse & Neglect*, *27*, 1409–1425.

Warwickshire and Coventry Family Justice Council (2010). *Mini Pupillage Scheme: Free Family Court CPD opportunities for psychologists*. Available from: www.wcfjc.org.uk/mini-pupillage-scheme-3 (last retrieved July 15, 2016).

Wechsler, D. (1997). *Wechsler Adult Intelligence Scale – 3rd UK Edition (WAISR-IIIUK)*. San Antonio, TX: The Psychological Corporation.

Wechsler, D. (1999). *Wechsler Abbreviated Scale of Intelligence (WASI)*. San Antonio, TX: The Psychological Corporation.

Welsh Assembly Government (2013). Referrals, Assessments and Social Services for Children, 2012–13.

Widiger, T.A., & Trull, T.J. (1994). Personality disorders and violence. In J. Monahan & H.J. Steadman (Eds.), *Violence and mental disorder: Developments in risk assessment* pp. 203–279. Chicago, IL: University of Chicago Press.

Wolfner, G.D., & Gelles, R.J. (1993). A profile of violence toward children: A national study. *Child Abuse & Neglect*, *17*, 197–212.

World Health Organization (2006). *Preventing child maltreatment: A guide to taking action and generating evidence*. Geneva: WHO.

Wu, S.S., Ma, C.X., Carter, R.L., Ariet, M., Feaver, E., Resnick, M., & Roth, J. (2004). Risk factors for infant maltreatment: A population-based study. *Child Abuse & Neglect*, *28*, 1253–1264.

14

Perpetrators of Intimate Partner Violence

LOUISE DIXON

INTRODUCTION

Intimate partner violence (IPV) has been recognized and increasingly acknowledged as a public issue since the 1970s. Documented as a common event internationally (e.g., Esquivel Santovena & Dixon, 2012), research has shown IPV can occur between two people (more than two in polygamous relationships) in a current or past relationship from various social backgrounds, nationalities, ethnicities, and educational levels (Dixon & Graham-Kevan, 2010; Esquivel Santovena & Dixon, 2012). Recognition of the magnitude of this public health issue has resulted in many societal efforts to prevent and reduce it including the development of laws, policies, specific services, and assessment and intervention strategies with both victims and perpetrators.

Research has highlighted the need to adopt a theory-driven, evidence-based approach to the reduction of interpersonal violence (e.g., Andrews & Bonta, 1998). A non-biased scientific approach to understanding the problem provides valid and reliable outcomes that professionals can use to guide practice with victims and perpetrators. Arguably, despite this recognition, the value of such work has not been accepted in the domain of IPV (Dixon & Graham-Kevan, 2011; Dixon, Archer, & Graham-Kevan, 2012). This chapter provides the reader with a critical overview of the IPV literature that highlights discrepancies in theoretical explanations of IPV and empirical research methodology and findings derived from these theories. It considers the merits of responding to this societal problem from a psychological

Assessments in Forensic Practice: A Handbook, First Edition. Edited by Kevin D. Browne, Anthony R. Beech, Leam A. Craig, and Shihning Chou.
© 2017 John Wiley & Sons Ltd. Published 2017 by John Wiley & Sons Ltd.

perspective, and understanding the role of individual factors in its etiology. The implications of this knowledge for risk assessment of IPV are considered throughout.

DEFINITIONS OF IPV

If professionals are to adopt a valid and reliable approach to the assessment of IPV, consensus must be reached as to what constitutes this type of interpersonal violence. However, this is not an easy task as many definitions have been developed from different theoretical perspectives for various settings (e.g., legal, medical, welfare, educational). Many terms and adjectives are used to describe violence and aggression that take place between intimate partners. However, professionals should consider these terms and their meaning carefully. For instance, "domestic violence" is the most widely used term to describe violence between intimate partners and has been frequently used to coin male assault of female partners in the academic literature (Dixon & Graham-Kevan, 2010). However, this term is ambiguous as there are five forms of violence that can take place within a family unit (sibling, parent, child, elder, partner maltreatment) (Browne & Herbert, 1997) and therefore "domestic violence" is also legitimately used to refer to any one of these forms. Definitions should also consider whether partner violence occurring outside of marital and cohabiting relationships and in same sex relationships is encompassed in the terminology used. Furthermore, as will be revealed in the ensuing discussion, terms that refer to unidirectional abuse of a woman only (such as "wife assault") are limited, as the possibility of male victimization and mutual (or reciprocal) aggression or violence also need to be captured by a definition (Dixon & Browne, 2003).

In addition to the above, professionals must consider the adjective used to describe the violence that takes place (Dixon & Graham-Kevan, 2010). For example, words that depict severe and chronic violence (such as battering) exclude acts of a less severe and frequent nature, which should arguably be included in any definition. Some researchers have distinguished between terms of physical violence and physical aggression, reserving "aggression" to refer to acts which are unlikely to result in injury to the victim and "violence" for acts that are likely to result in injury (Archer, 2000). In a similar vein, other researchers noted the importance of this distinction several years earlier. Straus, Gelles, & Steinmetz (1980) distinguished between "normal violence" and "abusive violence" in their first comprehensive national study of violence in the American family. They coined the term "normal violence" to describe acts that were not traditionally perceived as violent in order to draw attention to these acts occurring in families. "Abusive violence" was defined as "an act which has the high potential for injuring the person being hit" (p. 22). Injuries resulting from both forms of violence were considered separately.

To adhere to the above considerations, the academic literature mostly uses the term "partner violence." This is in contrast to the clinical literature, which continues to use the term domestic violence; therefore consensus is currently lacking (Dixon & Graham-Kevan, 2010). However, most definitions provide reference to the myriad of behaviors that IPV may encompass, commonly citing physical, psychological, and sexual violence and emphasizing that it can take more than one form. Furthermore, many definitions also include reference to more subtle "controlling behaviors" such as sulking, withholding affection, jealous and possessive behaviors, and financial control. Indeed, the Home Office definition of domestic violence has been revised to reflect this concept (Home Office, 2013). This term is preferable in describing such behaviors in comparison to "psychological violence or abuse" as it places emphasis on the perpetrator's motivation rather than the impact of these behaviors on the victim and can be used to describe behaviors in non-clinical samples (Graham-Kevan, 2007). Indeed, research has demonstrated the importance of incorporating such behaviors into research definitions. For instance, unlike physical aggression, controlling behaviors do not diminish over time and longitudinal research shows they may be a precursor to physical aggression (Graham-Kevan, 2007). Certainly empirical research shows controlling behaviors and physical aggression co-occur and women have reported controlling behaviors to be more damaging than physical aggression (Graham-Kevan, 2007).

PREVALENCE OF IPV

Variations in definitions of IPV have often stemmed from discrepancies in the theoretical approach used to understand it. Such inconsistencies have notoriously resulted in different methodological approaches to research in this area. As a result it is very difficult to compare prevalence and incidence rates across surveys and time, which is problematic because it is important to establish the base rates of IPV experienced by men and women to inform service provision and guide assessment (Dixon & Graham-Kevan, 2011).

Surveys which tap into representative community samples and ask about victimization and perpetration in the context of conflict in relationships (such as the 1975 and 1985 National Family Violence Surveys) (Straus, 1990; Straus & Gelles, 1985; Straus et al., 1980) reveal high prevalence and incidence rates carried out at approximately equal rates by both sexes. Reciprocal violence was found to be the most common form accounting for approximately 50% of reported cases. Recent research has further highlighted the necessity to measure the reciprocal nature of violence within relationships, showing it results in high levels of injury (e.g., LaRoche 2008; Whitaker, Haileyesus, Swahn, & Saltzman, 2007) and increases risk of physical harm to children present in the household (Slep & O'Leary, 2005).

These aforementioned findings are not replicated in surveys which only ask about victimization, such as the National Violence Against Women Survey (Tjaden & Thoennes, 1998), or crime surveys which assume respondents will perceive acts of aggression from an intimate partner as criminal. Such surveys typically find high rates of female victimization and male perpetration. However, if surveys fail to ask questions about perpetration (and perpetration by both members of the couple), or frame the context of violence as criminal rather than behaviors which take place within conflict in a relationship, underreporting is likely to be common, particularly in respect to female perpetration and male victimization (Straus, 1999).

Therefore, the accuracy of surveys that do not adopt a neutral context to assess the rate of male and female perpetration and victimization in couples, in national representative community samples, can be questioned (Dixon et al., 2012; Dixon & Graham-Kevan, 2011; Esquivel Santovena & Dixon, 2012). It is important to give careful consideration to the methodology used in studies before citing their figures as representing the true nature and prevalence of IPV experienced by all members of the general population. As Bachman (2000) asserts: "Until agreed-on conceptual and operational definitions are used in research, the question of 'how many' may continue to dominate in this field of study" (p. 886). However, he continues to highlight that even conservative estimates demonstrate the seriousness of IPV for society. Indeed, various large-scale self-report community studies would suggest that an estimate between 20% and 30% for the lifetime incidence of physical IPV victimization in Western countries is a sensible approximation (Dixon & Graham-Kevan, 2010).

The discrepancies in definitions and rates of IPV described above have stemmed from years of controversy over the best theoretical stance and resultant methodological procedures to explain why this social problem occurs. It is therefore necessary to describe the main theoretical camps that have led to these distinctions.

THEORETICAL DEBATE

Theoretical frameworks allow professionals to understand the nature of a problem which implicitly suggests the course of action that should be taken to eliminate it (Loseke, Gelles, & Cavanaugh, 2005). Therefore, the theoretical stance taken is an important issue as it impacts greatly on how the problem is perceived and responded to by professionals and society as a whole. Two main theoretical perspectives dominate the IPV literature to date.

The gendered perspective, often termed Feminist or Radical Feminist theory, grew out of the women's movement in the 1970s and highlighted violence against women as an important social problem. This stance views IPV as an event that is commonly acted out by men toward their female partner and one that is caused by societal rules which support male dominance and female subordination. Yllö (2005) reflects this in her assertion:

> *violence grows out of inequality within marriage (and other intimate relations that are modelled on marriage) and reinforces male dominance and female subordination*

within the home and outside it. In other words violence against women ... is a part of male control ... It is not gender neutral any more than the economic division of labor or the institution of marriage is gender neutral. (p. 22)

From this perspective it is understood that patriarchy is a direct cause of men's violence toward their female partner. Therefore, in order to address this problem it is conceded that societies' and individual perpetrators' belief structures needs to change. Perpetrator intervention programs designed from this perspective do not address individual factors, such as psychological issues, which, from the gendered perspective, can be seen to potentially exonerate a man of his actions (Dutton, 2006).

The gendered perspective has historically been very influential in understanding the causes of men's violence against their female partner and highlighting violence against women as an important political issue in Western societies to date. Indeed, it has been instrumental in building shelters for women and children, developing charities, changing laws and policies, and, importantly, in changing societies' acceptance of violence against women through educational campaigns and legal reforms (e.g., Dutton, 2006). However, it has been criticized as an ideologically driven perspective that has not been developed from sound empirical evidence (Dutton, 2006). Dutton states that gendered theory has led to several bedrock beliefs about IPV such as:

Domestic violence is used by men against women and men are violent whenever they can get away with it ... Women are never violent except in self-defence ... Males choose to be violent and have a gender based need for power ... When a man is injured by a woman she is acting in self-defence ... (p. 98)

He further goes onto discuss that while these beliefs have led to laws about the type of intervention a man must receive in several US states, they have not been supported by research adopting a gender inclusive approach (i.e., research that starts with no assumptions about gender – see below). Indeed, little support for the relationship between patriarchy and IPV exists (e.g., Sugarman & Frankel, 1996). Therefore, if such "bed rock" beliefs are not an accurate representation of the true nature of the problem they may prove detrimental to the successful reduction and prevention of IPV (Dixon & Graham-Kevan; 2011; Dixon et al. 2012).

A "gender inclusive" perspective offers an alternative view. This considers the possibility that both sexes can be perpetrators and/or victims of IPV, stemming from research with representative community samples showing men and women engage in violent acts at approximately the same rates (e.g., National Family Violence surveys; see Straus, 1990). This perspective seeks to understand why individuals or couples engage in IPV. Therefore, the emphasis is on understanding individual differences rather than the wider effects of society on men's behavior. This perspective would deem the use of psychological input in the design of assessment and intervention programs appropriate. From this stance psychological assessment and therapy aimed at the individual or couple (if appropriate) is warranted.

Research from this perspective typically adopts a systematic approach to the study of IPV. Rates and severity of aggression are commonly measured using the Conflict Tactics Scale (CTS), a self-report tool initially developed in the late 1970s and now revised to form a second version (CTS2; Straus, Hamby, Boney-McCoy, & Sugarman, 1996). The CTS scales ask respondents to report on a range of predetermined behavioral acts that both they and their partner have engaged in during times of conflict with each other. The CTS2 contains five subscales that distinguish negotiation tactics, physical assault, psychological aggression, sexual coercion, and injury. Furthermore, minor acts of physical and psychological aggression, sexual coercion, and injury are differentiated from more severe forms of these acts. This is particularly useful as the less severe acts of physical assault that might not otherwise be considered as constituting partner violence (slapping, pushing, grabbing) are also measured. The behavioral acts listed form clearly defined behavioral categories. Therefore, results can be systematically compared within and across samples. Indeed, this tool allowed the systematic collection of large data sets from which international prevalence and incidence rates have been calculated (e.g., National Family Violence Surveys; see Straus, 1990).

The National Family Violence Surveys (Straus, 1990; Straus & Gelles, 1985; Straus et al., 1980) conducted with representative US community samples found conflict rates of approximately 12% of men and women experiencing IPV within a 12-month period (Straus, 1999). In addition, the research demonstrated the reciprocal nature of much IPV, a finding that proved to be a contentious point for researchers and activists adopting a gendered approach. To date many studies and meta-analytic reviews have supported this finding, which refutes many of the beliefs held by the gendered perspective (Dutton, 2006).

Archer (2000) provided the most comprehensive study on gender differences in heterosexual intimate partner violence to date. He included 82 independent studies from which data were available for comparing rates of abuse perpetration by men and women. In total a combined data set of 64,487 people was analyzed. Results showed that women were slightly more likely than men to use physical aggression against a partner (d = −.05), but that overall women were slightly more likely to be injured (d = +0.15) and require medical treatment for their injuries than men (d = +0.08). He also reported that the sample studied was an important moderator of effect size. For example, studies using shelter samples produced very high effect sizes in the male direction; community and student samples were slightly more likely to be in the female direction.

Archer (2002) conducted a subsequent meta-analysis in response to claims that he only found gender symmetry because his research did not take into account the seriousness of acts carried out by men and women. He went onto analyze the frequency and severity of each gender's aggressive acts. Results showed that women used more minor acts of physical aggression unlikely to result in physical harm in comparison to men ("throw something at" and "slap"). However, both were just as likely to use severe acts, although the nature of these severe acts differed. Women were more likely to use severe acts of "throw something at" and "slap" or "kick, bite, punch and hit with an object" than men. The severe acts of "beat up" and "choke or strangle" were in the male direction. Finally, the severe acts of "threatening with a knife or gun" and "using a knife or gun" showed effect sizes close to zero, with men and women equally likely to adopt this strategy as each other. These findings remained consistent whether reports were derived from self, partner, or a composite of both, and using any one of four different measurement techniques. Therefore, while qualitative differences did exist between some of the acts that men and women perpetrated, both sexes were just as likely to enact severe physical aggression as each other.

In sum, gender-inclusive research asks the same questions of both male and female respondents and highlights that a proportion of men *and* women can be both aggressors and victims within their intimate relationships. This runs counter to the common assertion that female aggression in relationships is uncommon. It is clear that the theoretical perspective and methodology used to investigate IPV can effect how the problem is understood and therefore which sex is resultantly more likely to be seen as the aggressor in couples. It is concluded that the methodology used in research studies should be critically evaluated before reaching conclusions about the implications it holds for furthering understanding about the nature of IPV. Furthermore, professionals should understand the potential for both sexes to aggress so that unbiased and open-minded assessments can take place (Dixon & Graham-Kevan, 2011).

UNDERSTANDING IPV USING A NESTED ECOLOGICAL MODEL

Perpetrators of IPV are not a homogenous group. Bearing this in mind, and also the disagreement between the theories proposed to explain the etiology of IPV, Dutton (2006) proposed a "Nested Ecological Model" of IPV. This social psychological perspective seeks to explain how the interplay between an individual's internal events and wider society can shape their development and behavior. It can be used to understand which risk factors increase the likelihood of an individual aggressing against their intimate partner at different social levels.

The Nested Ecological Model details four levels of analysis which each describe individual or social factors that may contribute to the risk of IPV occurring. It provides a comprehensive guide about the potential causes of IPV and individual's behavioral patterns from which theories can be proposed and tested. The reader is referred to Dutton's (2006) text for a detailed review of this model. Briefly, the four levels consist of the Macrosystem Level (broad cultural values and beliefs such as women's political and socioeconomic power); the Exosystem Level (subculture factors such as peer group influence, work-related stress); the Microsystem Level (immediate context in which violence occurs such as couple or family interaction pattern); and the Ontogenic Level (individual factors such as personality, cognitions, and emotions). Potential risk factors of IPV are described at each level. This explanation accounts for the fact that people who exist in similar social circumstances do not all aggress against their partner; individual differences are important moderators or mediators in a complex web of interacting factors. From this perspective there is room for psychological assessment and intervention. Importantly, it highlights the necessity of considering the interaction of factors at all social levels. Most research to date has examined the influence of risk factors at one level only.

One study that has considered the utility of this model in identifying risk factors for IPV is that by Stith et al. (2004). Stith and her colleagues provided an empirical test of the Nested Ecological Model by conducting a meta-analysis of 85 studies that investigated risk factors associated with physical violence in heterosexual, married, or cohabiting partners. The levels of analysis in the Nested Ecological Model were used to identify and organize risk factors for perpetration and victimization of IPV. Only studies that matched their systemic criteria for inclusion were examined. Furthermore, only information on multiple risk factors related to physical male aggression and female physical victimization were gathered, as there was a lack of evidence available regarding factors related to male victimization. The relationship of one factor (marital satisfaction) could be explored with female physical perpetration.

For male physical perpetration large effect sizes were found for emotional verbal abuse, forced sex, marital satisfaction, illicit drug use, and attitudes condoning marital violence. Moderate effect sizes were found for several other factors, including traditional sex role ideology; however, Dutton (2006) does question the quality of some research included in the meta-analysis to test the contribution of this particular risk factor. For female physical perpetration, marital satisfaction was found to have a moderate effect size. For female physical victimization, large effect sizes were found for the woman using violence toward her male partner and moderate effect sizes for depression and fear of future abuse. The authors go onto to stress the importance of understanding female perpetration as a large risk factor for her victimization in practice settings:

> *Clinical services to victims of abuse, whether male or female, have focused on empowering the victim but have not addressed methods for helping the victim to manage their own anger. Results from this meta-analysis highlight the need for clinicians to address this issue with victims. (p. 92)*

Adopting a different approach to this area of study, O'Leary, Smith Slep, and O'Leary (2007) used Structural Equation Modeling to investigate the direct and indirect relationships that various risk factors identified by different theoretical perspectives (feminist, psychopathological, and dyadic) had with relationship aggression. Aggression was defined as physical and psychological aggression measured by the CTS2 (Straus et al., 1996). From tests with 453 representatively sampled US couples they proposed multivariate models of men's and women's partner aggression. Both male and female models display a complicated path of direct and indirect predictors of aggression, which account for 47% and 50% of the variance respectively. The three strongest direct predictors of partner aggression for men and women were dominance/jealousy; marital adjustment; and partner responsibility attributions. In addition, for men three direct paths were identified: exposure to family-of-origin aggression; anger expression; and perceived social support. For women, one additional direct path was found, namely a history of their own aggression as a child or teenager.

Taken together the results of these empirical studies highlight the complicated nature of IPV and the importance of examining this phenomenon from a multifactorial perspective. This has important implications for which factors professionals should aim to investigate during risk assessment. It is clear that a narrow focus will inevitably miss the complexities that can help professionals begin to understand an offender's violent behavior.

CHARACTERISTICS OF PERPETRATORS

Risk assessment requires the professional to determine factors that are present in the individual that may increase their risk of offending and/or reoffending against their intimate partner. Thus, it is important for professionals to be aware of what the evidence base tells us about individual characteristics associated with IPV so that assessments can be carried out comprehensively and with an open mind, aiding the professional to determine all the facts without bias. A considerable amount of research has investigated the role of individual differences to date, often with a focus on exploring typologies of men who offend against their female intimate partner. However, some work into typologies of couples has been carried out. Such typologies of perpetrators and couples are useful to help professionals synthesize the wide array of information available in the literature and to organize and interpret the meaning of data gathered during assessment.

While little knowledge has been gathered about the characteristics of female perpetrators to date, research has consistently demonstrated across time that men who are violent to their female partner are a heterogeneous group (e.g., Faulk, 1974; Gondolf, 1988; Holtzworth-Munroe & Meehan, 2004; Saunders, 1992). However, considering gender inclusive research findings it is not unrealistic to assume similar risk profiles for both sexes; indeed researchers have begun to find evidence of this similarity (e.g., Babcock, Miller, & Siard, 2003). Classification systems of men who have been violent to their female partner have been successfully developed and tested. For example, Holtzworth-Munroe and Stuart (1994) constructed a hypothetical typology from a review of the literature. They identified three types of perpetrator using three descriptive dimensions of severity and generality of violence and psychopathology/personality disorder of the perpetrator. Each type is labeled by a title that reflects the nature of their violence: Family Only (FO), Generally Violent/Antisocial (GVA), and Dysphoric/Borderline (DB). A summary describing each type's suggested characteristics can be found in Table 14.1. They are proposed to account for 50%, 25%, and 25% of abusive men residing in the community respectively.

Considering the described characteristics of each subtype it is possible to suggest reasons for why violence may be enacted, specific to each type. For the FO perpetrator

Table 14.1 Summary of IPV perpetrator subtype characteristics proposed by Holtworth-Munroe and Stuart (1994).

Family Only (FO)	Generally Violent/ Antisocial (GVA)	Dysphoric/Borderline (DB)
• Violent acts are of low severity and frequency • These perpetrators most closely resemble non-violent men, but some differences exist • They are more likely to have the following risk factors compared to non-violent men: Distal Risk Factors: exposure to violence in their family of origin Proximal Risk Factors: insecure attachment patterns, mild marital social skill problems, low levels of impulsivity	• Violent acts are of moderate to severe severity both within and outside the family • These perpetrators are likely to have: Distal Risk Factors: the highest genetic predisposition for aggressive and impulsive behavior and experience of severe violence in their childhood of origin Proximal Risk Factors: involvement with delinquent and deviant peers, antisocial behavior and criminality, dismissive attachment style, rigid conservative attitudes about women, attitudes supportive of violence, lack of conflict resolution skills, narcissistic traits, moderate anger, and low empathy	• Violent acts are of moderate to high severity, mainly limited to family members • These perpetrators are likely to have: Distal Risk Factors: some genetic predisposition for psychopathology, impulsivity and aggression and some experience of family of origin violence Proximal Risk Factors: some involvement with deviant peer groups, preoccupied or fearful attachment, high dependency on and preoccupation with partner, hostile attitudes to women, moderate attitudes supportive of violence, characteristics of borderline personality, the highest levels of depression and anger, moderate impulsivity, low to moderate empathy levels, low to moderate levels of criminality and substance abuse, and low marital communication skills

violence may result from a combination of poor communication skills with their partner, mild impulsivity, and preoccupation or dependency on their partner, and on occasion physical aggression is introduced during conflict. However protective factors such as remorse, low levels of psychopathology, negative attitudes about violence, and positive attitudes to women limit the frequency of violence. The GVA offenders view violence as an appropriate script to respond with in many situations, such as those where they feel anger or the need to exert control, resulting in them being a high risk for marital and general violence. For the DB offender, when they perceive they have been slighted, rejected, or abandoned (such as during times of marital conflict) they may react impulsively with high levels of distress and anger.

Empirical support for the typology has been successfully gathered across many studies over the years (Chase, O'Leary, & Heyman, 2001; Dixon & Browne, 2003; Gottman et al., 1995; Hamberger, Lohr, Bonge, & Tolin, 1996; Tweed & Dutton, 1998; Waltz, Babcock, Jacobson, & Gottman, 2000; White & Gondolf, 2000). Of particular interest, Holtzworth-Munroe et al. (2000) found support using a community sample of 102 men who had been violent toward their intimate partner during the previous 12 months. However, cluster analysis revealed four types of men, rather than the three types initially predicted. The three hypothesized subtypes were found (FO, N=37; DB, N=15; GVA, N=16) and differed as stated on distal and proximal risk and behavioral variables. In addition, a low-level antisocial type (LLA, N=34) was found, who fell in between the GVA and FO subtypes on several variables.

The heterogeneity of perpetrators committing the most severe form of IPV – femicide – has received less attention than non-lethal violence occurring in the community. Research investigating the two phenomena has reliably found differences between lethal and non-lethal partner assault (Aldridge & Browne, 2003; Campbell et al., 2003b; Dutton & Kerry, 1999), which has played an important role in the development of risk assessment tools (e.g., Campbell, 1986). This has led some researchers to conclude that they are distinct entities that should not be viewed along a continuum of severity. However, while this may be true for some cases, a large proportion of lethal cases do occur in the context of previous IPV, with studies reporting victims in 65–85% of cases being abused by the same perpetrator prior to their death (Campbell et al., 2003b; Campbell, 2004; Moracco, Runyan, & Butts, 1998). Therefore, it is plausible that the main characteristics thought to define types of partner violent men in the community are representative of those men committing lethal intimate partner violence. Dixon, Hamilton-Giachritsis, and Browne (2008) used a multidimensional approach to empirically construct a classification system of 90 men convicted and incarcerated for the murder of their female partner in the United Kingdom, based on the Holtzworth-Munroe and Stuart (1994) typology. The resultant framework classified 80% (N=72) of the sample into three subgroups of men characterized by Low Criminality/Low Psychopathology (15%); Moderate–High Criminality/High Psychopathology (36%); and High Criminality/ Low–Moderate Psychopathology (49%). The last two groups were thought to be akin to Holtzworth-Munroe and Stuart's (1994) GVA and DB offender respectively and thus suggests that men characteristic of these offenders will be most likely to commit femicide. The high frequency of men classified by the High Criminality/ Low–Moderate Psychopathology region is contrary to work by Saunders and Browne (2000) who propose that men resembling the DB category will be most at risk of murdering their partner. However, it must be noted that as a high percentage of men resembling the DB profile are likely to commit femicide (Dutton & Kerry, 1999) they may be underrepresented in a prison sample.

In summary, the above information provides an empirical guide as to which individual factors may be useful to examine during the assessment of perpetrators and the possible functions of such behaviors for different types of offenders.

CHARACTERISTICS OF COUPLES

While typologies of violent men provide useful information for professionals working with male perpetrators, researchers have suggested that such typologies provide a narrow focus as they do not consider other important factors that may contribute to the cause and maintenance of IPV, such as the family context and the role that both partners play in the intimate relationship (e.g., Dixon & Browne, 2003). Indeed, it has been stipulated that aggression in the family is a product of the person environment interaction (Frude, 1991) and therefore a dyadic approach to understanding IPV seems useful.

Researchers have focused on classifying the couple involved in the violent relationship. Johnson (1995, 1999) classified people in couples on the basis of their own and their partner's use of controlling behaviors and aggression. Couples were labeled as participating in "Common Couple Violence" (later renamed "Situational Couple Violence") when one or both members used non-controlling physical aggression toward the other, borne out of conflict in particular situations that occasionally result in aggression rather than the need for power and control. Perpetrators involved in the more traditionally understood dominating relationship were labeled "Intimate Terrorists" as they used controlling aggression toward their partner who uses either no aggression or non-controlling aggression and were referred to as "Violent Resistant" partners. Couples were labeled "Mutual Violence Control" when essentially two intimate terrorists were aggressing against one another in a bid for control. While Johnson (1999) stipulated the majority of Intimate Terrorists were male and Violent Resistants female, more recent research using a very large representative Canadian sample by Laroche (2008) demonstrates that both men and women can be classified into these categories at approximately equal rates.

In addition to Johnson's work, Bartholomew, Henderson, and Dutton (2001) report different patterns of aggression between couples as a result of the interacting attachment styles, further emphasizing the importance of considering both members of the couple. Such research highlights the difficulty in identifying one person as "the victim" and the other as "the perpetrator"; couples do not always present with such a clear-cut dichotomy. This highlights the need for professionals to consider the role that both partners play in the violent interaction. Indeed, Hamel (2005) recommends that professionals should aim to interview both members of the couple where possible (separately, at least at first) in order to glean information from both and to avoid making predetermined judgments about the type of relationship, and who is the victim and who is the perpetrator.

RISK ASSESSMENT TOOLS

Risk assessments are useful in a number of important domains such as sentence planning, safety planning for victims or other family members, developing a treatment plan, and evaluating post-treatment risk. As such it is imperative that professionals can determine risk of harm in an accurate and reliable manner; therefore tried and tested methods of violence risk assessment are essential in this area.

Approaches to violence risk assessment can be divided into categories of clinical, actuarial, and structured professional judgment (SPJ). For a more detailed commentary on each of these the reader is guided to Nicholls, Desmarais, Douglas, and Kropp (2007). Briefly, an unaided clinical approach to risk assessment is subjective and has been found to be open to many biases. On the contrary the actuarial approach derives risk factors through empirical methods. However, while deemed more robust than the less formal unaided clinical judgment, problems have been noted with this approach. For example, they mainly focus on static risk factors and often fail to account for protective factors. SJP combines these approaches to provide a structure for professionals to systematically follow. This structure is developed from the empirical literature and ensures salient information is included in any assessment. However, unlike other actuarial tools they do not provide the practitioner with specific cut-off scores, which has been both commended because of its flexibility and criticized because of the subjectivity this also affords.

Several tools currently exist which are designed to assess the risk of IPV, such as the Danger Assessment (Campbell, 1986; Campbell, Webster, & Glass, 2009); Spousal Assault Risk Assessment (Kropp, Hart, Webster, and Eaves, 1999); Brief Spousal Assault Form for the Evaluation of Risk (Kropp, Hart, & Belfrage, 2004); Ontario Domestic Assault Risk Assessment (Hilton et al., 2004); Domestic Violence Screening Inventory (Williams & Houghton, 2004), and the Partner Abuse Scale (Dutton, Landolt, Starzomski, & Bodnarchuk, 2001). Several police forces in the United Kingdom now implement the Domestic Abuse, Stalking, and Honor Based Violence (DASH; Richards, 2009) risk identification checklist to aid professionals identify early risk for victims of domestic abuse and their children, stalking and harassment, and honor-based violence. This model is different to other IPV tools listed in that it provides a focus on three related domestic violence events. It is important to understand the specific purpose of each tool before its use, as the focus can shift from risk of assault, to recidivism, or homicide. Furthermore, to date tools have been developed with male perpetrators and their relevance to female perpetrators is not known. An introduction to two of these tools that have received substantial attention due to published validity data is provided below.

Spousal Assault Risk Assessment (SARA; Kropp et al., 1999)

The SARA is a structured professional tool that is used to assess the risk for repeated spousal violence. It is the most widely used SPJ tool for risk assessments of IPV risk. As with any tool of this nature, the quality of the professional judgment is dependent on the skills and training of the assessor and the quality of available information. Therefore, it is stipulated that users should have expertise in individual assessment and in the area of IPV.

The SARA was developed from a review of the clinical and empirical literature on wife assault (Cooper, 1993) and is therefore applicable to the assessment of male violence against women. It consists of 20 items that are grouped into five content areas of Criminal history; Psychosocial adjustment; Spousal assault history; Current offense; and Other considerations.

The recommended assessment procedure emphasizes that the user should access multiple sources of information and methods of data collection to ensure a more accurate reflection of the offender and his circumstances is collated. The assessment should consist of structured or semi-structured interviews with the accused and victim(s); standardized measures of physical and emotional abuse; standardized measures of drug and alcohol abuse; review of collateral records (police reports, criminal records, victim impact statements): and other assessment procedures where applicable (such as personality inventories, IQ testing, interview with probation officers/relatives/children). Users are advised to track down any missing information and avoid completing the assessment if information is incomplete. If this is unavoidable it is recommended that the completeness of the information on which the SARA is based is discussed in the final report and conclusions limited accordingly (Kropp, 2008).

As the SARA was not designed to provide a predictive scale of risk, absolute cut-off scores are not produced. Rather, the user is asked to make three coding judgments on a summary form, using detailed criteria that map onto a three-point scale. The presence of each individual item is coded as absent (0); subthreshold (1); or present (2). In general, risk is expected to increase with the more items coded as present. However, in addition to consideration of the number of items present, the SARA allows for subjective clinical interpretation. The user can mark the presence of "critical items," which may be deemed sufficient on their own to conclude an imminent risk of harm. Critical items are scored on a two-point scale of absent (0) or present (1). Finally, the users overall professional opinion of overall perceived risk in two domains ("risk of imminent harm to spouse" and "risk of harm to some other identifiable person") is also summarized using a three-point scale of low (1), moderate (2), and high (3).

The SARA's reliability and validity has been determined. Kropp and Hart (2000) analyzed SARA ratings in six samples of adult male offenders (N=2,681) and concluded that interrater reliability for individual items and overall risk was high. Ratings also showed good convergent and discriminant validity in relation to measures of risk for general and violent criminality. Furthermore, Williams and Houghton (2004) reported findings from a study with 434 male perpetrators who were assessed with the SARA on release into the community and their reoffense rates examined 18 months later. Receiver Operator Curves (ROC) were computed to estimate predictive accuracy of the total score, producing an area under the curve (AUC) of .70 (where 0.5 indicates chance and 1 perfect prediction). However, while predictive validity for the SARA has been found in some studies, it should be remembered that the SARA was not designed as a predictive tool; it provides a guide and not a replacement for clinical judgment.

Danger Assessment (DA: Campbell, 1986; Campbell et al., 2009)

Murder of an intimate partner has been shown to have distinct risk factors in comparison to assault; hence specific tools have been developed using retrospective studies of femicide and serious injury to predict lethal violence. The DA (Campbell, 1986) and its revised version (Campbell et al., 2009) assesses the risk of male severe and lethal violence toward female intimate partners and has been used in a variety of multidisciplinary settings.

It was originally designed to help women assess their risk of being murdered or seriously injured by their intimate or ex-intimate partner. Thus, it was developed as an informal risk factor tool to guide clinical decision-making, rather than as a predictive instrument per se. Until recently, published information only existed on its construct validity, not predictive validity. However, Campbell et al. (2003a, 2003b) carried out an 11-city case-control study to identify risk factors for intimate partner femicide in abusive relationships and to inform the potential revision of the DA. Campbell et al. (2009) used the information from this study to revise the DA. In this article they describe the development, psychometric validation, and suggestions for its use.

The DA and its recently revised version are structurally the same and consist of two parts. The woman can complete it by herself or with the professional. The first part assesses the severity and frequency of violence the woman has experienced. The professional presents her with a calendar of the past year and asks her to approximate days on which she experienced physically abusive incidents and the severity of these incidents using a scale of 1 (slap, pushing, no injuries, and/or lasting pain) to 5 (use of weapon, wounds from weapon). In its original development, use of the calendar proved to increase recall and reduce denial and minimization of the abuse (Campbell, 1986). The second part lists risk factors associated with partner femicide, which requires the respondent to answer in a yes/no format. The DA contains 15 items and the revised version 20 items, as four additional items have been added and one original item has been split into two. In total the instrument takes approximately 20 minutes to complete.

In the revised version of the DA, Campbell et al. (2009) developed a scoring algorithm to identify four levels of danger: variable danger (score of 0–7); increased danger (score of 9–13); severe danger (score of 14–17); and extreme danger (18 and above). The authors go onto determine the predictive validity of the revised DA and the weighted scores using ROC curves. An independent sample of 194 attempted femicide cases included .90 of the cases in the area under the ROC curve. The authors conclude:

> *The revised 20-item DA can accurately identify the vast majority of abused women who are at increased risk of femicide or attempted femicide as well as distinguish most of the IPV cases that are at lowest risk of femicide or attempted femicide, at least in this urban sample of women. However, further development and testing of the DA is needed, as with all of the IPV risk assessment strategies. (p. 669)*

The predictive accuracy of the DA has also been tested in female same-sex populations who experience severe and lethal assault from an intimate partner (Glass et al., 2008). In this publication appropriate amendments are made to the DA to increase predictive validity within this population.

Utility of General Violence Risk Assessment Tools

It is apparent that considerable overlap exists between risk factors used by tools that specifically assess risk of IPV and tools that assess risk of interpersonal violence in general. A recent meta-analysis by Hanson, Helmus, and Bourgon (2007) demonstrated similar predictive accuracy of both types of tools in assessing risk of recidivism of male IPV offenders. Hanson et al. (2007) suggest further research is needed to determine the utility of specific risk tools for IPV above and beyond the valid and reliable risk tools designed to assess general and violence recidivism.

In conclusion, there is not enough evidence to suggest a gold standard instrument for assessment of IPV to date. However, it is suffice to say that development of such tools should be based on the empirical literature and that any assessment should be guided by the knowledge discussed in this chapter.

CONCLUSION

This chapter intended to provide an overview of the IPV literature in order to convey the importance of adopting a non-biased, evidence-based understanding and to highlight that this knowledge should be reflected in assessments with perpetrators, victims, or couples (where applicable). The need to focus on the role of individual factors within the context of other social levels is clearly highlighted. Indeed, other areas of general violence risk assessment have demonstrated the importance of using empirical methods in determining risk factors and IPV should be no exception to this rule.

Empirical research has highlighted key risk factors and multifactorial models to guide professionals in their assessment of IPV and useful tools have been developed to guide best practice assessments. While precise risk assessment of IPV is far from accomplished we have come a long way from understanding the cause of partner violence as patriarchy resulting from a male-dominated society. Adopting a psychological perspective allows the development of individual risk assessment and functional analysis, evidence-based risk assessment tools, and psychologically guided intervention programs, and provides hope for the future of rehabilitation and prevention in this domain. Collectively the empirical research demonstrates the complex nature of IPV and the need to recognize the benefits of understanding this phenomenon from a multifactorial perspective.

REFERENCES

Aldridge, M., & Browne, K.D. (2003). Spousal homicide: A review. *Trauma, Violence and Abuse*, *4*, 265–276.

Andrews, D.A., & Bonta, J. (1998). *The psychology of criminal conduct* (2nd ed.). Cincinnati, OH: Anderson.

Archer, J. (2000). Sex differences in aggression between heterosexual partners: A meta-analytic review. *Psychological Bulletin*, *126*, 651–680.

Archer, J. (2002). Sex differences in physically aggressive acts between heterosexual partners: A meta-analytic review. *Aggression and Violent Behavior*, *7*, 313–351.

Babcock, J.C., Miller, S.A., & Siard, C. (2003). Toward a typology of abusive women: Differences between partner-only and generally violent women in the use of violence. *Psychology of Women Quarterly*, *27*, 153–161.

Bachman, R. (2000). A comparison of annual incidence rates and contextual characteristics of intimate partner violence against women from the National Crime Victimization Survey (NCVS) and the National Violence Against Women Survey (NVAWS). *Violence Against Women*, *6*, 839–867.

Bartholomew, K., Henderson, A.J.Z., & Dutton, D.G. (2001). Insecure attachment and partner abuse. In C.C. Clulow (Ed.). *Attachment and couple work: Applying the secure base concept in research and practice*. London: Routledge.

Browne, K.D., & Herbert, M. (1997). *Preventing family violence*. Chichester, UK: John Wiley & Sons, Ltd.

Campbell, J.C. (1986). Nursing assessment of risk of homicide for battered women. *Advances in Nursing Science*, *8*, 36–51.

Campbell, J.C. (2004). Helping women understand their risk in situations of intimate partner violence. *Journal of Interpersonal Violence*, *19*, 1464–1477.

Campbell, J.C., Webster, D.W., & Glass, N. (2009). The Danger Assessment: Validation of a Lethality Risk Assessment Instrument for Intimate Partner Femicide. *Journal of Interpersonal Violence*, *24*, 653–674.

Campbell, J.C., Webster, D., Koziol-McLain, J., Block, C.R., Campbell, D.W., Curry, M.A., …, & Wilt, S.A. (2003a). Assessing risk factors for intimate partner homicide. *National Institute of Justice Journal*, *250*, 14–19.

Campbell, J.C., Webster, D., Koziol-McLain, J., Block, C.R., Campbell, D.W., Curry, M.A., …, & Laughon, K. (2003b). Risk factors for femicide in abusive relationships: Results from a multisite case control study. *American Journal of Public Health*, *93*, 1089–1097.

Chase, K.A., O'Leary, K.D., & Heyman, R.E. (2001). Categorizing partner-violent men within the reactive-proactive typology model. *Journal of Consulting and Clinical Psychology*, *69*, 567–572.

Cooper, M. (1993). *Assessing the risk of repeated violence among men arrested for wife assault: A review of the literature*. Vancouver, BC: British Columbia Institute on Family Violence.

Dixon, L., Archer, J.A., & Graham-Kevan, N. (2012). Perpetrator programmes for partner violence: Are they based on ideology or evidence? *Legal and Criminological Psychology*, *17*, 196–215.

Dixon, L., & Browne, K.D. (2003). The heterogeneity of spouse abuse: A review. *Aggression and Violent Behavior*, *268*, 1–24.

Dixon, L., & Graham-Kevan, N. (2010). Spouse abuse. In B.S. Fisher and S.P. Lab (Eds.), *Encyclopedia of victimology and crime prevention* (pp. 6–10). Thousand Oaks, CA: Sage.

Dixon, L., & Graham-Kevan, N. (2011). Understanding the nature and aetiology of intimate partner violence and implications for practice: A review of the evidence base. *Clinical Psychology Review*, *31*, 1145–1155.

Dixon, L., Hamilton-Giachritsis, C., & Browne, K.D. (2008). Classifying partner femicide. *Journal of Interpersonal Violence*, *23*, 74–93.

Dutton, D.G. (2006). *Rethinking domestic violence*. Vancouver, BC: UCB Press.

Dutton, D.G., & Kerry, G. (1999). Modus operandi and personality disorder in incarcerated spousal killers. *International Journal of Law and Psychiatry*, *22*, 287–299.

Dutton, D.G., Landolt, M.A., Starzomski, A., & Bodnarchuk, M. (2001). Validation of the propensity for abusiveness scale in diverse male populations. *Journal of Family Violence*, *16*, 59–73.

Esquivel Santovena, E., & Dixon, L. (2012). Investigating the true rate of physical intimate partner violence: A review of nationally representative surveys. *Aggression and Violent Behavior*, *17*, 208–219.

Faulk, M. (1974). Men who assault their wives. *Medicine, Science and the Law*, July, 180–183.

Frude, N. (1991). *Understanding family problems: A psychological approach.* Chichester, UK: John Wiley & Sons, Ltd.

Glass, N., Perrin, N., Hanson, G., Bloom, T., Gardner, E., & Campbell, J.C. (2008). Risk for re-assault in abusive female same-sex relationships. *American Journal of Public Health, 98,* 1021–1027.

Gondolf, E.W. (1988). Who are these guys? Toward a behavioural typology of batterers. *Violence and Victims, 3,* 187–203.

Gottman, J.M., Jacobson, N.S., Rushe, R.H., Shortt, J.W., Babcock, J., La Taillade, J.J., & Waltz, J. (1995). The relationship between heart rate reactivity, emotionally aggressive behaviour and general violence in batterers. *Journal of Family Psychology, 9,* 227–248.

Graham-Kevan, N. (2007). Power and control in relationship aggression. In J. Hamel & T.L. Nicholls (Eds.), *Family interventions in domestic violence: A handbook of gender-inclusive theory and treatment* (pp. 87–108). New York: Springer.

Hamberger, L.K., Lohr, J.M., Bonge, D., & Tolin, D.F. (1996). A large sample empirical typology of male spouse abusers and its relationship to dimensions of abuse. *Violence and Victims, 11,* 277–292.

Hamel, J. (2005). *Gender inclusive treatment of intimate partner abuse: A comprehensive approach.* New York: Springer.

Hanson, R.K., Helmus, L., & Bourgon, G. (2007). The validity of risk assessments for intimate partner violence: A meta-analysis. *Public Safety Canada,* 2007–07.

Hilton, N.Z., Harris, G.T., Rice, M.E., Lang, C., Cormier, C.A., & Lines, K.J. (2004). A brief actuarial assessment for the prediction of wife assault recidivism: The Ontario Domestic Assault Risk Assessment. *Psychological Assessment, 16,* 267–275.

Holtzworth-Munroe, A., & Meehan, J.C. (2004). Typologies of men who are martially violent: Scientific and clinical implications. *Journal of Interpersonal Violence, 19,* 1369–1389.

Holtzworth-Munroe, A., Meehan, C., Herron, K., Rehman, U., & Stuart, G.L. (2000). Testing the Holtzworth-Munroe and Stuart (1994) Batterer Typology. *Journal of Consulting and Clinical Psychology, 68,* 1000–1019.

Holtzworth-Munroe, A., & Stuart, G.L. (1994). Typologies of male batterers: Three subtypes and the differences among them. *Psychological Bulletin, 116,* 476–497.

Home Office (2013). Domestic violence and abuse. Available from: www.gov.uk/domestic-violence-and-abuse (last retrieved July 16, 2016).

Johnson, M.P. (1995). Patriarchal terrorism and common couple violence: Two forms of violence against women. *Journal of Marriage and the Family, 57,* 283–294.

Johnson, M.P. (1999). *Two types of violence against women in the American family: Identifying intimate terrorism and common couple violence.* Paper presented at the annual meetings of the National Council on Family Relations, Irvine, California.

Kropp, P.R. (2008). Development of the Spousal Assault Risk Assessment Guide (SARA) and the Brief Spousal Assault Form (B-SAFER). In A.C. Baldry & F.W. Winkel (Eds.), *Intimate partner violence prevention and intervention: The risk assessment and management approach* (pp. 19–31) New York: Nova Science Publishers.

Kropp, P.R., & Hart, S.D. (2000). The Spousal Assault Risk Assessment (SARA) Guide: Reliability and validity in adult male offenders. *Law and Human Behavior, 24* (1), 101–118.

Kropp, P.R., Hart, S.D., & Belfrage, H. (2004). *Brief Spousal Assault Form for the Evaluation of Risk (B-SAFER): User manual.* Vancouver, BC: British Columbia Institute on Family Violence.

Kropp, P.R., Hart, S.D., Webster, C.D., & Eaves, D. (1999). *Manual for the spousal assault risk assessment guide* (3rd ed.). Toronto, ON: Multi-Health Systems.

Laroche, D. (2008). *Context and consequences of domestic violence against men and women in Canada 2004: Living conditions, April.* Québec: Institut de la Statistique du Québec.

Loseke, D.R., Gelles, R.J., & Cavanaugh, M.M. (2005). Section I: Controversies in conceptualisation. In D.R. Loseke., R.J. Gelles, & M.M. Cavanaugh (Eds.), *Current controversies on family violence* (pp. 1–4). Thousand Oaks, CA: Sage.

Moracco, K.E., Runyan, C.W., & Butts, J.D. (1998). Femicide in north Carolina, 1991–1993: A statewide study of patterns and precursors. *Homicide Studies, 2,* 422–446.

Nicholls, T.N., Desmarais, S.L., Douglas, K.S., & Kropp, P.R. (2007). Violence risk assessments with perpetrators of intimate partner abuse. In J. Hamel & T.L. Nicholls (Eds.), *Family interventions in domestic violence: A handbook of gender-inclusive theory and treatment* (pp. 275–301). New York: Springer.

O'Leary, K.D., Smith Slep, A.M., & O'Leary, S.G. (2007). Multivariate models of men's and women's partner aggression. *Journal of Consulting and Clinical Psychology, 75,* 752–764.

Richards, L. (2009). Domestic Abuse, Stalking and Harassment and Honour Based Violence (DASH, 2009) Risk Identification and Assessment and Management Model. Available from: www.dashriskchecklist.co.uk/index.php?page=dash-2009-model-for-practitioners (last retrieved July 16, 2016).

Saunders, D.G. (1992). A typology of men who batter women: Three types derived from cluster analysis. *American Orthopsychiatry, 62,* 264–275.

Saunders, D.G., & Browne, A. (2000). Intimate partner homicide. In R.T. Ammerman & M. Hersen (Eds.), *Case studies in family violence* (2nd ed., pp. 415–449). New York: Kluwer Academic/Plenum Publishers.

Slep, A.M.S., & O'Leary, S.G. (2005). Parent and partner violence in families with young children: Rates, patterns and connections. *Journal of Consulting and Clinical Psychology, 73,* 435–444.

Stith, S.M., Smith, D.B., Penn, C.E., Ward, D.B., & Tritt, D. (2004). Intimate partner physical abuse perpetration and victimization risk factors: A meta-analytic review. *Aggression and Violent Behavior, 10,* 65–98.

Straus, M.A. (1990). The National Family Violence Surveys. In M.A. Straus & R.J. Gelles (Eds.), *Physical violence in American families: Risk factors and adaptations to violence in 8145 families* (pp. 3–15). New Brunswick, NJ: Transaction Publishers.

Straus, M.A. (1999). The controversy over domestic violence by women: A methodological, theoretical and sociology of science analysis. In X. Arriaga & S. Oskamp (Eds.), *Violence in intimate relationships* (pp. 17–44). Thousand Oaks, CA: Sage.

Straus, M.A., & Gelles, R.J. (1985). *Is family violence increasing? A comparison of 1975 and 1985 national survey rates.* Paper presented at the American Society of Criminology, San Diego, California.

Straus, M.A., Gelles, R.J., & Steinmetz, S.K. (1980). *Behind closed doors: Violence in the American family.* New York: Anchor Books.

Straus, M.A., Hamby, S.L., Boney-McCoy, S., & Sugarman, D. (1996). The revised Conflict Tactic Scales (CTS2): Development and preliminary psychometric data. *Journal of Family Issues, 17*, 283–316.

Sugarman, D.B., & Frankel, S.L. (1996). Patriarchal ideology and wife-assault: A meta-analytic review. *Journal of Family Violence, 11*, 13–40.

Tjaden, P., & Thoennes, N. (1998). *Prevalence, incidence, and consequence of violence against women: Findings from the National Violence Against Women Survey. Research in Brief*, November. National Institute of Justice Centers for Disease Control and Prevention, USA.

Tweed, R.G., & Dutton, D.G. (1998). A comparison of impulsive and instrumental subgroups of batterers. *Violence and Victims, 13*, 217–230.

Waltz, J., Babcock, J.C., Jacobson, N.S., & Gottman, J. (2000). Testing a typology of batterers. *Journal of Consulting and Clinical Psychology, 68*, 658–669.

Whitaker, D.J., Haileyesus, T., Swahn, M., & Saltzman, L.S. (2007). Differences in frequency of violence and reported injury between relationships with reciprocal and non-reciprocal intimate partner violence. *American Journal of Public Health, 97*, 941–947.

White, R.J., & Gondolf, E.W. (2000). Implications of personality profiles for batterer treatment. *Journal of Interpersonal Violence, 15*, 467–488.

Williams, K.R., & Houghton, A.B. (2004). Assessing the risk of domestic violence re-offending: A validation study. *Law and Human Behavior, 28* (4), 437–455.

Yllö, K.A. (2005). Through a feminist lens: Gender, diversity, and violence: Extending the feminist framework. In D.R. Loseke., R.J. Gelles, & M.M. Cavanaugh (Eds.), *Current controversies on family violence* (pp. 19–34). Thousand Oaks, CA: Sage.

PART FOUR

Policy and Practice

15

Assessment of Hostage Situations and Their Perpetrators: In the Context of Domestic Violence

CAROL A. IRELAND

The assessment and consequent management of a hostage situation can be varied in response to the motivation and presenting traits of the hostage-taker. While a model of crisis negotiation can be utilized, it nonetheless requires modification in the context of the presenting situation. Models of crisis negotiation present with a structure to manage a chaotic situation, with the appreciation of the need to modify any approach dependent upon the presenting crisis. This chapter will present a crisis model that has been regularly utilized through a variety of hostage situations. The chapter will also propose modifications in response to the presenting situation in regard to the perpetrators motivations, traits, and characteristics, which are important considerations as part of the negotiation process. Crisis incidents focusing on domestic violence will be a main consideration. Before describing the crisis model and adaptions to it, it is important to clarify what is meant by "hostage" situations.

Hostage-taking would be considered as the "holding of one or more persons against their will with the actual or implied use of force" (Lanceley, 1999). McMains and Mullins (2001) further report a hostage situation is any incident in which people are being held by another person or persons against their will, usually by force or coercion, and demands are being made by the hostage-taker. It can be regarded as a crisis incident where the perpetrator's ability to manage the presenting problem has diminished. Crisis situations, such as hostage-taking, have been regarded as "a

Assessments in Forensic Practice: A Handbook, First Edition. Edited by Kevin D. Browne, Anthony R. Beech, Leam A. Craig, and Shihning Chou.
© 2017 John Wiley & Sons Ltd. Published 2017 by John Wiley & Sons Ltd.

temporary state of upset and disorganization, characterized chiefly by an individual's inability to cope with a particular situation using customary methods of problem solving" (Slaikeu, 1990). Hostage-taking is certainly not a new concept. The term "hostage" comes from the Latin *hospes* meaning "hospitality." Clearly this definition is no longer an accurate representation of the term. Faure (2004) argues that, historically, the practice of hostage-taking dates back many centuries to ancient Egypt, Persia, the Middle East, Greece, and the Roman Empire. In some circumstances it was to even be found as a clause in political contracts, such as treaties. The first "hostages" were more often individuals regarded as prominent, even members of royalty, and who were given to adversaries in order to guarantee the fulfillment of commitments. Commitments may be varied, but included exchanging prisoners or leaving land and territory (Faure, 2004). Indeed, the practice of hostage-taking did not become illegal until the eighteenth century. In today's society, hostage-taking can include a variety of situations, such as skyjacking, barricade with a hostage (such as in a domestic dispute), attacks on public buildings, such as embassies, and kidnapping (Hayes, 2002). Further, and as argued by Faure (2004), according to the definition adopted by the European Union in 2001, hostage-taking falls into the category of terrorist offenses and includes activities such as extortion, seizure of aircraft, kidnapping for the purpose of seriously intimidating a population, and any efforts to alter or destroy the political, economic, or social structure of a country.

MODEL OF CRISIS NEGOTIATION

The management of a hostage situation is through the use of crisis negotiation. This is an approach first introduced in the 1970s by the New York Police Department following substantial crisis incidents which ended in tragedy, such as the Munich Olympics where a number of Israeli athletes were taken hostage and later killed, as well as the Attica prison riots where a number of prisoners and hostages were killed by the authorities (Vecchi, Van Hasselt, & Romano, 2005). Crisis negotiation is considered to be an approach that focuses on the safe release of the hostages, the non-violent arrest of the perpetrator, and where efforts are made to calm a situation and to increase rational thought.

Crisis negotiation focuses on establishing communication with the perpetrator, buying time in order to defuse emotions and enable planning. Such planning can involve the gathering of intelligence to determine the best negotiation or intervention strategies and/or tactics (Lanceley, 1999; Romano & McCann, 1997). The playing for time can allow the perpetrator time to consider their actions more rationally, as opposed to simply responding impulsively and more reactively to the presenting situation (Whyte, 2005). Ultimately the aim of crisis negotiation is to demonstrate that the method chosen by the perpetrator, namely the taking of a hostage, is not an effective strategy for dealing with their problem. Hatcher, Mohandie, Turner, and Gelles

(1998) argue that "the goal or mission of crisis/hostage negotiation is to utilize verbal strategies to buy time and intervene so that the emotions of the perpetrator can decrease and rationality can increase" (p. 455).

The use of crisis negotiation strategies is not restricted to a hostage situation. A hostage situation can be considered to have parallels with a variety of other crisis situations, such as roof top protests and barricades, and where the use of the crisis negotiation model can enhance the management of the situation. The model has been used in a variety of crisis situations and has been reported to have between an 80 and 95% success rate (McMains & Mullins, 2001), in contrast to a high rate of injuries when a more forceful approach is utilized. Taking by force is not to be preferred over negotiation, with armed assaults resulting in a 78% injury or death rate (Dolnik, 2004). A total of 75% of all casualties in a hostage incident arise from the rescue attempt (Poland & McCrystle, 1999).

One of the most utilized models of crisis negotiation is arguably the Behavioral Influence Stairway Model (BISM) developed by the FBI (Vecchi et al., 2005, revised Van Hasselt, Romano, & Vecchi, 2008). This model is presented in Figure 15.1.

This model focuses on developing an effective relationship between the person in crisis and the negotiator, leading to behavioral change in the person in crisis, leading to a peaceful resolution (Dalfonzo, 2002). This approach has been consistently effective in the resolution of a wide range of volatile crisis situations (Flood, 2003), including community crisis situations such as domestic violence. This model is a development from earlier approaches, which focused on a more problem-solving aim to the crisis situation, and identifying motivations, looking to separate the individual from the problem, focusing on their interests as opposed to their positions, generating options, with a view to creating behavioral change (Fisher, Ury, & Patton, 1991).

The substantial emphasis on the relationship-building process of crisis negotiation highlights the importance of having a supportive and trusting relationship between the perpetrator and negotiator in order to maximize the chances of a peaceful resolution.

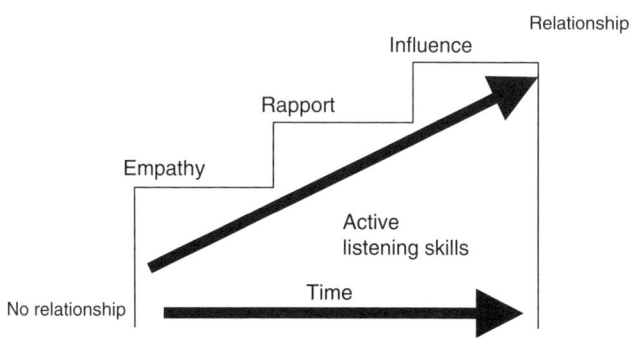

Figure 15.1 Behavioral Influence Stairway Model (Van Hasselt et al., 2008). Reproduced with permission of Sage Publications.

While the motivation of the perpetrator is undoubtedly important, the model empha-sizes the need to develop an appropriate relationship as a key factor in managing the situation, and not with an over-focus on the perpetrators motivations alone. This further demonstrates a clear shift in the literature with regard to key factors in peaceful resolutions. Arguably, an over-focus on problem solving can potentially lead a negotiator to focus too heavily on seeking the motivation behind the crisis, which may potentially lead to a tendency to rush the perpetrator to a resolution.

The BISM (Van Hasselt et al., 2008) focuses on four key elements that are considered important in the developing of an effective relationship between the negotiator and perpetrator: active listening, empathy, rapport, and influence. While presented as steps, an effective consideration of this approach is to view each of the four key elements as building on one another. For example, once active listening is felt to have been achieved, the next step would be empathy. Yet, this would not mean that active listening is no longer incorporated, but rather, it is continually built upon by the negotiator. This model is designed to be flexible and dynamic, where an individual may quickly move up the steps, or even skip some steps altogether. It is regarded as very much a starting point in the negotiation process, and is used in order to provide a structure to a usually chaotic situation.

Active listening is considered the crucial first step in this model, with the view that little can be achieved without this as a fundamental basis. Vecchi et al. (2005) argue that active listening is an attempt to lower the perpetrator's emotions, and to return them to more rational thinking. Empathy follows as an appreciation of the situation and the person's circumstances as part of this. Rapport is then developed, where trust between the negotiator and perpetrator enhances as a result of such understanding and demonstration of empathy. Finally, influence occurs as the perpetrator is persuaded to change their behavior from the maladaptive to the more adaptive (Van Hasselt et al., 2008).

PERPETRATOR MOTIVATIONS

The motivations and interests of a perpetrator can be varied (Dolnik, 2004) and are of key consideration when a crisis negotiator attempts to develop a relationship with the person in crisis. Dolnik (2004) argues that a perpetrator may try to provoke a confrontation as part of the crisis situation, and in order to give permission to commit suicide, financial gain, or even avoid a prison term. There may be political, religious, or financial motivations. The perpetrator may be responding to propa-ganda or a feeling of a need to seek revenge. Importantly, the perpetrators interests may not be that obvious, and may be more hidden, such as a desire to be admired by others, to fulfill another need, or to demonstrate their commitment to a particular cause (Dolnik, 2004). Whyte (2005) argues that such differing motivations can include prisoners taking staff hostage in order to bargain for better living conditions or terrorists viewing hostage-taking as a means by which they can gain international media attention for a political motivation.

Whyte (2005) further argues that motivations may again be different for an estranged husband barricaded in a house with his estranged partner, and who may be less clear as to his demands in the "heat of the moment." For example, a perpetrator may inform the authorities that they have taken their child hostage as their estranged partner who cares for their child will not allow them enough access to the child and they wish for more contact. Arranging for more contact may actually exacerbate the situation as this may not be the true reason for the perpetrators distress. Indeed, the lack of contact with the child may actually relate to a feeling that the perpetrator has little control over their life, often feeling that decisions are made without collaboration and discussion. They may feel that the limited contact with their child is a further example of their estranged partner making decisions to suit their own needs without consideration of the other. To not explore this in detail, and to indeed focus on increasing contact, may potentially lead the perpetrator to further feel that they are not being listened too, and the presenting issue is considered only at a superficial level, therefore prolonging the prospect of a resolution.

Similarly, a perpetrator who has taken their child hostage following the breakdown of their relationship with their partner, may make a number of demands, such as wishing to see their partner, or desiring to see their doctor. It is important to consider that these demands may not actually be the true motive and the situation may be more about an expression of their distress or even a need to seek revenge on their partner in the hope that the crisis situation will evoke the same level of distress they felt when their relationship with their partner came to an end. As such, to consider meeting such requested demands might potentially lead a perpetrator to feel that their true needs, such as an opportunity to express their distress or seek revenge, are not considered by the authorities, which may exacerbate the situation further.

Noesner and Webster (1997), expanding on the earlier work of Miron and Goldstein (1979), have categorized such demands and consequent motivations of hostage-taking, into two types of behavior: instrumental behavior and expressive behavior. Instrumental behavior consists of demands and objectives that focus on meeting the goals of the hostage-taker, that are rational and focused on achieving an aim, or changing some aspect of society. Some terrorist hostage-taking fits the more instrumental behavior, or an offender who decides to take hostages as part of leverage during a robbery. Expressive behavior refers more to the hostage-taker expressing their internal emotions and impulses in the given situation, and which are often personal to the hostage-taker. Here the focus appears less rational and is directed more toward an expression of emotion than an attempt to seek specific demands. Indeed, the demands may not be the point. It has further been argued that the instrumental and expressive behavior should be regarded more as along a continuum, as opposed to an individual clearly fitting in to either at any one time. Hostage-takers may have a mixture of both instrumental and expressive motivations. For example, an individual who makes the decision to take their ex-partner hostage may have planned the event some time in advance, with a clear focus and goal of distressing the ex-partner. Yet, this may further be a result of the emotional distress they feel following the relationship breakdown, and a lack of rational thinking. As such, and while appearing to have clear goals and planning, the actual focus of the crisis itself may be more toward the perpetrator demonstrating to the ex-partner their distress at the relationship deteriorating, and their uncertainty as to how they can continue their day-to-day life without their partner. As such, this would present with both instrumental and expressive behaviors, and is something that crisis negotiators need to be mindful of.

ADDITIONAL CONSIDERATIONS IN RESPONSE TO DOMESTIC VIOLENCE

Domestic violence can be defined as:

> *Any incident of threatening behaviour, violence or abuse (psychological, physical, sexual, financial or emotional) between adults, aged 18 or over, who are or have been intimate partners or family members, regardless of gender and sexuality. Family members are defined as mother, father, son, daughter, brother, sister and grandparents, whether directly or indirectly related, in-laws or step-family. (ACPO, 2008, p. 7)*

Reports indicate that, in the United Kingdom, domestic violence can account for around 15% of all violent crime, involving one in four women and one in six men at some point in their lives. A total of 35% of all murders are driven by domestic violence. It is documented that domestic violence has the highest rate of repeat victimization (Home Office, 2006). Domestic violence does not focus on any particular culture or gender, with it occurring across society, regardless of age, gender, ethnicity, sexuality, wealth, and geography (Home Office, 2006).

Previous research in the United States has indicated that almost 80% of all hostage situations are relationship driven, such as perceived relationship difficulties and resentments, including abandonment and rejection (Flood, 2003). Domestic violence has reportedly been identified as presenting with a range of risks. In the United States, and when looking at rates of domestic violence toward women, it is noted that a woman is more likely to be assaulted, injured, raped, or killed by a male partner than by any other types of assailant (National Coalition Against Domestic Violence, 1995). Van Hasselt et al. (2005) argue that the crisis incident involving domestic violence presents with a range of complex and varied issues, much in the same way as any crisis incident. Van Hasselt et al. (2005) further argue that a range of risk factors can be present, such as substance abuse, possession of a weapon, prior history of domestic violence, threats or actual separation or divorce, and other criminal activity, much as would be related to general risk factors in violent domestic incidents. Van Hasselt et al. (2005) argue that there was a proportion of crisis incidents where the hostage-taker was under the influence of substances. In their study, they present five cases of hostage-taking as part of domestic violence, arguing that in three out of the five cases presented, substance use was a factor, with the use of a deadly weapon being a further factor in all five cases, leading to the death of the victim (hostage) in two out of the five cases, and before the police and negotiators had arrived at the scene. Yet, such presentations are not unique to crisis incidents driven by domestic violence, with Michaud, St-Yves, and Guay (2008) reporting that substance misuse is found in two-thirds of perpetrators in crisis incidents, which exacerbates the impaired judgment, irritability, and increased risk of violence (Parker & Auerhahn, 1998).

CONSIDERATIONS IN RESPONSE TO PERPETRATORS' BEHAVIOR, CHARACTERISTICS, AND TRAITS

As presented earlier, the behavior change stairway model of crisis negotiation is an important consideration to the management of a crisis situation, offering structure to a highly stressful and potentially chaotic situation. Yet, the model on its own offers only guidance on management, and there needs to be further consideration and modification in response to the presenting traits, behaviors, and characteristics of a perpetrator, and which may interfere with the relationship-building aim of the model. Exploration of all possible behaviors, characteristics, and traits would not be achievable within the context of this chapter, yet examples of perpetrator's behavior, characteristics, and traits are presented and discussed below. It is further of note that perpetrators may potentially fall into more than one of the presented categories, or demonstrate elements from a combination of categories. The categories here are presented for ease of presentation.

Hostile and Aggressive Perpetrator

This individual may be described as potentially deceitful and persistently lying. They may be unclear with the negotiator regarding information around the crisis or other issues, or, alternatively, their reasons behind certain decisions may change without a clear reason or understanding. They may present as impulsive and irritable, making quick decisions regarding how to manage the crisis and expressing frustration when the situation appears not to be moving in their chosen direction. For example, if the perpetrator has taken their ex-partner hostage and is demanding to see their child, they may become extremely agitated and irritable if this demand is not met. They may further present as aggressive, with a reckless disregard for themselves and others, caring little for the distress caused to the hostage and their families. As such, they may further find it difficult to consider the negative aspects of the crisis situation, demonstrating little remorse for their actions.

The negotiator would have to consider some crucial issues with such an individual and as part of the crisis situation. It would be helpful for the negotiator to ensure that the attention is kept on the perpetrator as a way of managing any impulsivity. This further ensures that the perpetrator is kept occupied, reducing the potential for them to over-focus on the hostage(s). Over-focusing on any hostages by the negotiator would be unhelpful here, especially as the perpetrator can present with a high level of aggression and a lack of remorse, which may heighten any risk of harming the hostage. Such individuals may find it challenging to engage successfully with negotiators perceived to be in an authoritarian role, and indeed might find it difficult to relate and work with such individuals. This is an important consideration for the negotiating team, and any individuals who are felt to present with a perceived level of authority to the perpetrator are best not to become directly involved in the negotiations. Further, discussions around what is morally right and wrong may not be the most effective here as they may present with little respect for this. For example, when considering the perpetrator who presents in this way and who has held their ex-partner hostage, any discussions around such a decision being ineffective or unhelpful is likely to be disregarded. Negotiators would need to consider the varying levels of irritability and aggression carefully, particularly when any demands are not met, such as the perpetrator asking to see his child and this not taking place. As such, any decision to discuss demands need to take place carefully and with due consideration as to the potential consequences.

Importantly the negotiator needs to be mindful that they may not be able to trust the information provided by the perpetrator. This may be considered accurate in any crisis situation but particularly so with the perpetrator who presents with these traits. Also, a consideration in crisis situations that involve a hostage is the effort to develop a positive relationship between the hostage and the perpetrator, and where the perpetrator is less likely to harm the hostage. Traditionally this has been referred to as the Stockholm Syndrome, where the hostage begins to relate positively to the perpetrator, developing negative feelings toward the authorities, which are further reciprocated by the perpetrator (Fuselier, 1988). Although this syndrome is very rare, it is even less likely with the hostile and aggressive perpetrator as described here. As such, discussions with the perpetrator on the benefits to them for ending the situation, namely "what's in it for me?" may be the most helpful. Similarly they may show little regard for the safety of the hostages, leading to the negotiator to attempt full focus on themselves as part of the crisis resolution.

Part of the crisis negotiations, and as presented earlier in this chapter, is the development of a positive relationship between the perpetrator and crisis negotiator, and as part of the BISM (Van Hasselt et al., 2008). As such, appropriate personal disclosures can be a crucial factor in developing this relationship. Yet, careful consideration with this perpetrator needs to take place, where personal information that is sensitive should be avoided. It would be true to state that personal information that is sensitive to the negotiator is generally best avoided as part of the negotiation process, but this is particularly important here. For example, the perpetrator may use such information to attempt to distress or to blame the negotiator in some way. An example may be a negotiator, as part of developing the relationship, disclosing to the perpetrator that they have in the past become angry when dealing with a stressful situation. The perpetrator, later in the negotiations, and in an effort to control the situation and to disregard the negotiator, may use such information to comment to the negotiator that the current situation is stressful and it appears to them that the negotiator is actually becoming angry and finding it difficult to cope. Of additional consideration when the negotiator attempts to develop an effective relationship is that the perpetrator may simply give the impression that a relationship is developing, when this may indeed not be the case. As part of the perpetrator's presentation, the development of rapport, a key aspect in relationship development, may not be a viable option.

Paranoid Perpetrator

This individual can present with a range of anxieties, such as feeling that others are exploiting or deceiving them. For example, they may have taken their partner hostage as they feel they have been unfaithful to them, exploiting them in front of their friends, taking advantage of them in a variety of ways, which has no basis of truth. They may struggle to trust others, which may be particularly challenging as part of the crisis situation. For example, they may feel that their ex-partner has continually lied to them without true basis. They may fear that information may be used against them such as to "trick" them into agreeing something that they do not wish for. They may read threats into messages or situations, where most would not. For example, his partner may have, prior to the crisis incident, had a friend visit the home. Without due cause, the perpetrator may regard this visit as one where his partner and their friend were discussing him in negative terms, interpreting this simply due to the friend looking at him when he entered the room. In particular, this individual may present as bearing substantial grudges toward others for a long duration, of at least 12 months or more. Such grudges may be unfounded but present with a high level of emotion nonetheless. For example, the perpetrator may report to have not spoken to his partner's mother for over 12 months as a result of a perceived slight against him. He may report that the mother chose not to say her farewells to him when leaving a family party and where he interpreted this as a threat toward him. As a result, he may develop strong feelings of dislike toward the mother, which have continued and been persistent. As such, this individual may perceive attacks to his character or reputation, without founding, with a further level of heightened suspicion.

Following such a presentation the negotiator needs to consider a variety of issues. In particular, they may regard the negotiator with suspicion. As such, sincerity and active listening are important considerations. A key aspect of crisis negotiation, and indeed of developing the relationship, is for the negotiator to present with honesty. As such, and particularly relevant for this individual, it is very important not to lie. There is a substantial risk that the negotiator may be "caught out," which will seriously compromise their relationship with the perpetrator. In some instances this may even lead to a decision to change negotiators. Honesty is important here and is something that the perpetrator may look for to a substantial degree. More senior authorities managing the crisis situation can assist here by ensuring the negotiator is made aware only of critical information that is needed as part of the negotiations and not that which may potentially compromise the situation. For example, the authorities may choose not to inform the negotiator that a tactical assault is being planned, so as not to place them in a difficult position with the perpetrator, and where they are being asked to lie. Further, and a key strategy in negotiation, is the playing of time in order to increase rational thinking and maximize the chance of a peaceful resolution. As part of this the negotiator is not in a position to make executive decisions, such as whether the perpetrator can have some food or not. The negotiator is asked to pass these requests on. Yet, for a perpetrator who is paranoid it is useful to consider how to respond to their queries as to who the information is being passed on to. A solution for the negotiator is simply to say "I suspect it is probably my boss, but I'm not sure as I'm here talking to you, so I can only guess…"

As the negotiator attempts to gather information about the presenting situation the perpetrator may be suspicious as to why the negotiator appears interested in seeking information about them. For example, the negotiator may be attempting to gather information about how they respond when they feel angry and, indeed, what kind of issues raise their emotions in this way. The perpetrator who is paranoid may respond with suspicion and be fearful of confiding in the negotiator, demanding why the negotiator is seeking such information, and alleging to the negotiator that they only wish to seek such information so that others may know what makes them angry and who may then make efforts to anger them as a result. As such, gaining trust and consequent rapport in the model may present with a number of challenges.

It is important for the negotiator to remain calm in the situation. For example, the perpetrator with paranoid behaviors and characteristics may react angrily toward the negotiator if they feel they are getting too close to them. For example, the perpetrator may have started to discuss issues with the negotiator and it appears that indeed some form of a relationship is beginning to develop. Yet, the perpetrator may then recognize this, become suspicious of the negotiators motives, and look to remove this developing relationship using anger as a perceived method of ending this relationship quickly. As such, it is important for the negotiator to persevere, to remain calm, and to continue to present honestly to the perpetrator. Alternatively, the perpetrator may consider hidden meaning in the negotiator's discussions that may make little sense to those around them. For example, the perpetrator may report that when the negotiator turns to look at the floor when talking to them this is indeed a message to them that the negotiator does not value them and might simply be trying to "con" them in some way. While invariably this cannot be avoided altogether, all discussions and non-verbal interactions need to be considered carefully. For example, it is useful for the negotiator to ensure that they are clear in their discussions with no ambiguity. As there can be a risk that the perpetrator may well perceive attacks on their character in some way, such as them feeling they are managing the crisis situation ineffectively, and which is simply further evidence of their inadequacies, then the "saving of face" could be an important consideration. Here the negotiator will aim to highlight the positive characteristics of the individual, and attempt to place a "positive spin" on the situation, without suggesting the decision to take an individual hostage was an effective strategy. For example, the negotiator may indicate that "you strike me as the kind of person that likes to do the right thing, and I think you are showing that now by taking the time to talk to me, and I thank you for that."

Depressed Perpetrator

This individual can present with a range of behaviors and characteristics that require considerations as part of a crisis situation. Clearly, they may present as low in mood. They may have little interest in what is going on around them other than the immediate situation itself. Yet, and as part of the low mood, there may be a number of challenges when attempting to engage the individual in conversation. They may present with little motivation to continue a conversation with others and appear tired and fatigued. As such, they may find it difficult to concentrate on aspects of the crisis situation, presenting with a high level of distractibility. They may present with feelings of worthlessness, even displaying feelings of guilt. For example, during a crisis situation where an individual takes their partner hostage as part of an altercation, as time progresses, they may feel that they are not dealing with the situation well, and may feel a level of guilt for distressing loved ones, leading to an exacerbation of low self-worth. This may further exacerbate any thoughts of self-harm or suicide, and may be potential serious considerations in the depressed perpetrator. They may further present with a number of challenges when decisions are required, such as struggling to make any specific choices about their presenting options.

As such, the negotiator must consider a variety of presenting issues with such an individual. For example, any decision to perhaps withhold food and water from the individual, and in an effort to perhaps increase a basic need for food and increase the chances of them ending the crisis situation, may have less of an impact on such individuals. Indeed, they may present with little interest in food and water as a result of such low mood. In particular, it may be challenging to engage the individual in conversation, and they may further present as relatively "flat" in their emotions. The depressed perpetrator may feel they do not have the motivation or energy to maintain such discussions. This clearly presents with challenges for the negotiator as conversation can be an important aspect of developing a relationship with the individual, and as part of the behavioral influence stairway. If the negotiator is able to initiate a level of conversation, then the topic must be considered carefully, such as one that will not exacerbate feelings of worthlessness and guilt. If such worthlessness and guilt were enhanced, then so may the potential for negative feelings on behalf of the perpetrator. The use of active listening and empathy would be important here, with the negotiator making efforts to appreciate the presenting distress of the perpetrator.

A useful approach for the negotiator may be to focus on previous occasions where the perpetrator has felt in a similar way, but where the situation got better. For example, it may be discussed that part of the crisis situation is around the perpetrators feelings that they are worthless and can offer nothing positive to those around them. The negotiator may then focus on previous situations where they have felt the same but where their emotions improved, and even what improved such emotions. This is with a view of emphasizing to the perpetrator that negative emotions do not always remain and can improve. In addition, focusing on successful events in their lives may further promote a more positive mindset for the individual in crisis.

When the negotiator is conversing with the depressed perpetrator it may be important to consider that, due to a lower motivation, lessening in their concentration, and fatigue, they may benefit from further time to consider any questions posed. As such, the negotiator not rushing the perpetrator to a response may be helpful here, as well as expecting that the individual may on occasions "drift" away from the conversation. If the perpetrator does discuss issues around suicide and/or self-harm, it is important for this not to be ignored. The nature of such discussions should be considered carefully including:

- How long have they thought like this?
- Is any proposed plan they make a well considered plan?
- Have they attempted this in the past, and if so, what happened?
- Have they thought of this in the past, but changed their mind? If so, what caused them to change their mind?
- Have they the means of carrying out their plans?

It is crucial that the negotiator is wary of any sudden improvements in the perpetrator which appear unrelated to the negotiations. For example, does the perpetrator suddenly appear more elated and positive in their thinking which is not felt to be a result of the negotiation process? This may indeed reflect a decision in the individual to seriously self-harm or even commit suicide. Importantly the negotiators role here is not to provide therapy to the individual around the function of their self-harm or attempted suicides but rather to postpone suicidal action as opposed to changing the individual's mood. For example, the negotiator may discuss that the perpetrator delays any decision to self-harm as opposed to persuading them not to do this and engaging in therapy with them. It is important that the perpetrator feels that, even if they choose to end the crisis situation, they still have choices, as opposed to an "all or nothing debate," and where the authorities can do little to manage the outcome. The view would be that, once outside of the crisis situation, their risk of self-harm and suicide could be more carefully managed.

CONCLUSIONS

It is hoped this chapter has highlighted that crisis negotiation is a complex and varied area. The behavioral influence stairway is an effective model by which to begin the negotiation process and to consider the development of clear approaches and tactics that are relevant for the presenting situation. The management of a crisis situation that is related to a domestic incident would not be unique to any other crisis situation; the same model would be applied, with appropriate modifications. Exploration of the presenting traits, characteristics, and behavior of the perpetrator is an important focus which requires careful consideration and thought on behalf of the crisis negotiator. While the motivation of a perpetrator is an important consideration in a crisis situation, this should not be to the exclusion of developing an effective relationship between the negotiator and perpetrator, and should refrain from an overemphasis on attempting to solve the presenting or perceived problem.

REFERENCES

ACPO (2008). *Guidance on investigating domestic violence*. Wybaston, UK: Association of Chief of Police Officers/National Police Improvement Agency.

Dalfonzo, V. (2002). *National crisis negotiation course*. Quantico, VA: FBI Academy.

Dolnik, A. (2004). Contrasting dynamics of crisis negotiations: Barricade versus kidnapping incidents. *International Negotiation, 8*, 495–526.

Faure, G.O. (2004). Negotiating with terrorists: The hostage case. *International Negotiation, 8*, 469–494.

Fisher, R., Ury, W., & Patton, B. (1991). Getting to yes: Negotiating agreement without giving in (2nd ed.). New York: Penguin.

Flood, J.J. (2003). *A report of findings from the Hostage Barricade Database System (HOBAS)*. Quantico, VA: Crisis Negotiation Unit, Critical Incident Response Group, FBI Academy.

Fuselier, G.D. (1988). Hostage negotiation consultant: Emerging role for the clinical psychologist. *Professional Psychology: Research and Practice, 19* (2), 175–179.

Hatcher, C., Mohandie, K., Turner, J., & Gelles, M.G. (1998). The role of the psychologist in crisis/hostage negotiations. *Behavioural Sciences and the Law, 16*, 455–472.

Hayes, R.E. (2002). *Negotiations with terrorists*. In V. Kremenyuk (Ed.), *International negotiation* (pp. 416–430). San Francisco, CA: Jossey-Bass.

Home Office (2006). *Lessons learned from the domestic violence enforcement campaigns 2006*. Police and Crime Standards Directorate. London: Home Office.

Lanceley, F.J. (1999). *On-scene guide for crisis negotiators*. New York: CRS Press, Inc.

McMains, M.J., & Mullins, W.C. (2001). *Crisis negotiations: Managing critical incidents and hostage situations in law enforcement and corrections* (2nd ed.). Cincinnati, OH: Anderson.

Michaud, P., St-Yves, M., & Guay, J. (2008). Predictive modeling in hostage and barricade incidents. *Criminal Justice and Behavior, 35* (9), 1136–1155.

Miron, M.S., & Goldstein, A.P. (1979). *Hostage*. Elmsford, NY: Pergamon Press.

National Coalition Against Domestic Violence (1995). PO Box 18749, Denver, CO 80218–0749.

Noesner, G.W., & Webster, M. (1997). Crisis intervention. *FBI Law Enforcement Bulletin, 66*, 13.

Parker, R.N., & Auerhahn, K. (1998). Alcohol, drugs, and violence. In J. Hagan & K.S. Cook (Eds.), *Annual Review of Sociology, 24*. Palo Alto, CA: Annual Reviews.

Poland, J.M., & McCrystle, M.J. (1999). *Practical, tactical, and legal perspectives of terrorism and hostage-taking*. Lewiston, NY: E. Mellon Press.

Romano, S.J., & McCann, M.F. (Eds.) (1997). *Crisis negotiation: A compendium*. Quantico, VA: Crisis Negotiation Unit, Critical Incident Response Group, FBI Academy.

Slaikeu, K.S. (1990). *Crisis intervention: A handbook for practice and research*. Boston, MA: Allyn and Bacon.

Van Hasselt, V.B., Flood, J.J., Romano, S.J., Vecchi, G.M., de Fabrique, N., & Dalfonzo, V.A. (2005). Hostage-taking in the context of domestic violence: Some case examples. *Journal of Family Violence, 20* (1), 21–27.

Van Hasselt, V.B., Romano, S.J., & Vecchi, G.M. (2008). Role playing: Applications in hostage and crisis negotiation skills training. *Behaviour Modification, 32* (2), 248–263.

Vecchi, G.M., Van Hasselt, V.B., & Romano, S.S. (2005). Crisis (hostage) negotiation: Current strategies and issues in high-risk conflict resolution. *Aggression and Violent Behaviour, 10*, 533–551.

Whyte, P. (2005). Negotiation and hostage-taking: The 1996 Japanese experience in Lima, Peru. Unpublished paper. Faculty of Law, University of British Columbia.

16

Assessing the Sexually Abused Child as a Witness

KEVIN D. BROWNE

INTRODUCTION

The debate on child witnesses has centered on the credibility of children and guidance on the optimum conditions for interviewing children to obtain valid and reliable reports of sexual and violent assaults and incidences of child maltreatment (Bottoms & Goodman, 1996; Faller, 2007; Ney, 2013; Selkin, 1991). In the United Kingdom, the *Memorandum of good practice on video recorded interviews with child witnesses for criminal proceedings* (Home Office, 1992) introduced into courts screens and video links for children to give evidence without coming into direct contact with the alleged offender (Westcott & Jones, 1997). This initiative was partly driven by the need to protect the child in the courtroom and partly because the credibility of the child witness had been undermined by cross-examination, with children being upset and wrongly deemed unreliable witnesses (Davies & Drinkwater, 1988). A number of publications, some aimed at children, are now available to prepare families for the courtroom (e.g., Copen, 2000; Copen, Martin, & Pucci, 2000; Harvey & Watson-Russell, 1991; Plotnikoff & Woolfson, 1998). The aim is to alleviate the child's anxiety and improve their testimony. Additionally, the *Speaking up for justice* report (Home Office, 1998) influenced the implementation of other special measures to help protect and support child witnesses, including therapy provision where identified as appropriate for the child (Smallbone, Marshall, & Wortley, 2008). Guidelines followed (Crown Prosecution Service,

Assessments in Forensic Practice: A Handbook, First Edition. Edited by Kevin D. Browne, Anthony R. Beech, Leam A. Craig, and Shihning Chou.
© 2017 John Wiley & Sons Ltd. Published 2017 by John Wiley & Sons Ltd.

Home Office, & Department of Health, 2001; Home Office, 2002) to help balance the need to ensure the child is prepared and informed about the investigative interview and potential legal proceedings and at the same time not to corrupt or influence the child's evidence.

Since these developments more than a decade ago, measures to protect child victims and children as witnesses in investigative interviews, legal proceedings, and the courtroom have been implemented worldwide (Crawford & Bull, 2006; McWilliams et al. 2014; Teoh & Lamb, 2010). Guidelines for safeguarding children as victims and witnesses was produced in the United Kingdom by the Crown Prosecution Service (CPS) in 2009 (http://www.cps.gov.uk/legal/vtoz/safeguarding_children_ as_victims_and_witnesses), based on policies on prosecuting criminal cases involving children and young people as victims and witnesses published in 2006 (https:// www.cps.gov.uk/victims_witnesses/children_policy.pdf). The purpose of this chapter is to assess the psychological factors within the individual that influence the validity and reliability of the child victim of sexual abuse as a witness. One criteria applied in these cases has been the boundary between fact and "fantasy" sometimes referred to as "false (traumatic) memory syndrome" (Donovan, 1997).

There seems to be a number of myths that surround the layman's view of child sexual abuse that permeates legal professionals and processes. First, that there has been a recent increase in the problem; second, that the phenomenon is rare; third, that such offenses are committed by adult male strangers to the child; and fourth, that the child will fully recover from the adverse sexual experience in time. Research evidence contests all these common beliefs.

The increase in the number of reported cases of sexual abuse over the last three decades reflects a greater recognition of the problem (Gilbert et al., 2009; Kempe, 1980; Search, 1988). Child sexual abuse has always been present in society; evidence suggests it was common in Victorian times in the United Kingdom and classical writings indicate its presence in Greek and Roman cultures. The age when child sexual abuse occurs is different to that of physical abuse and neglect. The majority of sexual abuse cases occur to children aged five upwards. This is not to say that children under five aren't sexually abused but it is less common (Hobbs & Wynne, 2002). A meta-analysis of eight victim surveys found that on average 2.5% of female victims and 21.3% of male victims report that they were abused by female perpetrators (Fergusson & Mullen, 1999). Hence, the vast majority of victims are sexually assaulted by male perpetrators. In the United Kingdom, teenage male perpetrators aged 20 and younger account for about one-third of all allegations of sexual abuse (Glasgow, Horne, Calam, & Cox, 1994; Watkins & Bentovim, 1992) and 20% of those convicted of a sexual offense are aged under 18 (Home Office, 2003). Vizard, Hickley, French, and McCrory (2007) reported that across several studies, 30% to 50% of sexual abuse is perpetrated by adolescents, with the majority of these being male.

EXTENT OF CHILD SEXUAL ABUSE

An early study of the *prevalence* of child sexual abuse in the United Kingdom (Baker & Duncan, 1985) found that 12% of women and 8% of men recall sexually abusive experiences in their childhood. The prevalence of child sexual abuse has been also assessed through a "victim survey" in the United States by David Finkelhor and his colleagues (1990). They interviewed 1,145 men and 1,481 women in the United States and found that 9.5% of men said that they had been involved in unwanted sexual intercourse during childhood, whereas 15% of women were found to have been victims of sexual intercourse during childhood. In addition, 5% of men and 20% of women admitted to being touched, grabbed, or kissed as a child. There were much smaller figures for non-contact abuse (e.g., exhibitionism). Therefore, it was claimed that at least 1 in 10 males and 1 in 5 females in the United States have been sexually abused during childhood. A similar study of English young adults (18–24 years) who gave retrospective self-reports for their childhood (Cawson, Wattam, Brooker, & Kelly, 2000; May-Chahal & Cawson, 2005) showed that 16% had reported sexual abuse (11% contact sexual abuse). Young women reported more sexual and emotional abuse than young men. When young teenagers (aged 13 to 14 years) were surveyed in Romania about maltreatment in the family home (Browne, 2002), 9% claimed to have been sexually abused.

An international overview of child sexual abuse (Finkelhor, 1994) exemplifies the variation for prevalence rates in the European countries that have conducted surveys (Austria, Belgium, Denmark, Finland, France, Germany, Greece, Great Britain, Ireland, the Netherlands, Norway, Spain, Sweden, and Switzerland). In these countries, the prevalence rates for sexual abuse of female children ranged from 7% to 36% and for male children ranged from 3% to 29% (Finkelhor, 1994). The differences in prevalence rates can partly be explained by the variations in methods, samples used, and response rates experienced by the different surveys undertaken to obtain this information across Europe and other countries. It should be noted that there is no reliable evidence to suggest that some ethnic groups are more likely to maltreat their children than others, although children from ethnic minorities may be over-represented in residential care due to poverty and social neglect.

More recently, the prevalence of all forms of maltreatment to children was estimated for high-income countries (Gilbert et al., 2009). It was found that 16% of children are physically abused, 10% are neglected, and 10% are psychologically abused. With regard to sexual abuse before the age of 18 years, 10% of girls and up to 5% of boys are exposed to penetrative sexual abuse, and up to three times this number are exposed to any type of sexual abuse.

The *incidence* of cases that come to the attention of the police and social services may seem a high number (see Table 16.1), but in reality it is a small proportion of the overall *prevalence* of child sexual abuse cases in society, as indicated by the above

Table 16.1 Rate of children on child protection plans or registers, per 10,000 children aged 0–17, at March 31, 2014 (July 31 for Scotland). (From Bywaters et al., 2016.)

	Number	Rate per 10,000 children	Increase since 2009
England	48,300	42.1	+41.6
Wales	3,135	49.5	+24.9
Scotland	1,406	27.8	+7.5
Northern Ireland	1,914	44.3	−19.5

Table 16.2 Percentage of children in England, Northern Ireland, and Wales on child protection plans or registers in year to March 31, 2014, by form of maltreatment. (Adapted from Bywaters et al., 2016.)

	Physical abuse	Neglect	Emotional abuse	Sexual abuse	Multiple
England	10	41	35	5	9
Wales	11	39	38	5	6
Northern Ireland	33	27	12	5	23

studies. Evidence from victim surveys and prevalence studies consistently indicates that the number of people reporting abuse in childhood is approximately 10 times that reported to the authorities, referred to as the "incidence rate" (Creighton, 2002; Gilbert et al., 2009). For example, in England on March 31, 2014, there were 42 children per 10,000 (aged 0–17 years) on child protection plans or registers, following reports of actual or highly suspected abuse and/or neglect. Of the 48,300 children that were the subject of a child protection plan register only 2,000 were registered for sexual abuse, which represents only 5% of cases (see Table 16.2). At March 31, 2015, 49,700 children in England were subject of a child protection plan; this represents half of all "children in need" (Department for Education, 2016), and domestic violence between parents was found associated with 1 in 2 cases (see Chapter 12). However, sexually abused children were only 5% of cases with child protection plans (see Table 16.2), which means that the vast majority of sexually abused children do *not* come to the attention of the police and social services suggesting that false denials are more common than false allegations (Browne, 1991a). This is a very important fact for social service, law enforcement, and legal professionals to grasp.

RELATIONSHIP WITH PERPETRATOR

According to the American Humane Association (McDonald & Associates, Inc., 2005), cases of child sexual abuse represented 7% of all child maltreatment referrals. In terms of adult sex offenders, biological parents were alleged perpetrators in only 3% of these cases. The parents' male partners were thought to be responsible for 11% of cases, other relatives 30%, child caregivers in institutional and day care settings 23%, teachers 11%, and foster carers 6%. In the other 16% of cases, the perpetrators were unknown to the victim and involved a sex offender who was a stranger to the child.

However, in a UK survey of convicted sex offenders by Elliott, Browne, and Kilcoyne (1995) it was found that approximately one-third of convicted sex offenders against children were intra-familial, one-third were extra-familial acquaintances and known to the child, and one-third were strangers. One in three offenders who were in a parental/caregiver role sexually abused both their own and other children. This suggests that at least one-third of "incest" perpetrators could be regarded as "true" pedophiles with a primary "fixated" sexual interest in children and not merely "situational" sex offenders as suggested by Howells (1981).

A United Nation's review of research on violence against children in the community, the *Secretary General's study on violence against children*, estimates that between 21% and 34% of sexual assaults on children are committed by strangers (Pinheiro, 2006). The review confirms previous findings that the majority of child sexual abuse is perpetrated by someone in a position of trust in or outside the family. For example, a recent report (John Jay College of Criminal Justice, 2004) claimed that approximately 4% of US Catholic priests had been accused of abusing 10,700 children.

More recently, Jackson, Browne, and Joseph (2016) explored the victim experiences of young people within the school and community environments (extra-familial victimization) in the English Midlands. This study examined the prevalence of 24 different types of extra-familial victimization experienced by a sample of 730 young people, aged 13 to 16 years (mean 13.8 years). The findings showed that 1 in 4 suffered physical victimization and 1 in 7 experienced sexual victimization, the majority of which was perpetrated by their peers. The findings suggest that violent peer victimization is not an isolated event.

Child sex offenders outside the family target single parent families and families where there is marital discord. They regard children from these families to be more vulnerable than those from intact families and easier to bully. This is because such children lack confidence and have low self-esteem as a result of their experiences in a separated or disrupted family. The children are unsure of themselves and as a consequence are more compliant to the approaches of teenage or adult perpetrators, whether previously known or unknown (Browne, 1994, 2009a, 2009b).

The relationship between perpetrator and victim will affect the frequency and duration of the abuse and strategies used to engage the victim in the abuse (Faller, 1990). For example, those that are family or acquainted with the victim are more likely to employ psychological strategies such as coercion and bribery, whereas strangers are more likely to rely on physical force and surprise as a means of overcoming their victims. Partly for this reason, family members, friends, and acquaintances have fewer reported victims than strangers to the victim. Hence, proximity in the relationship context will also influence disclosure of abuse. Close relationships are less likely to be disclosed than those that are more distant or involving a stranger (Browne, 2009a, 2009b).

A stepparent or cohabitee in the family is often considered to be a risk factor for sexual abuse, although the early figure for stepfathers in the United Kingdom representing 12% of cases (Mrazek, Lynch, and Bentovim, 1981) would suggest stepparents are somewhat maligned considering their relative contribution to child sexual abuse. When the maternal caregiver is unavailable, disabled, or ill and where the child victim has a poor relationship with the maternal caregiver, these conditions may enhance the possibility of child sexual abuse (Browne, 1994, 2009a, 2009b). Usually children sexually abused within the family are victims of other forms of abuse such as physical and emotional abuse. These forms coexist with child sexual abuse or have a previous history. Research shows that one-third of all sexually abused children have been previously physically abused or neglected under age five (Finkelhor & Baron, 1986).

Other types of family violence such as wife abuse are also highly associated with child physical and sexual abuse in the family, so that where the mother is present in the home and recognizes there is a problem, the perpetrator's response is usually violence (Browne, 1993, 2009a, 2009b; Browne & McManus, 2010).

LONG-TERM EFFECTS OF SEXUAL ABUSE

A review by Ruth Gilbert et al. (2009) concluded that child maltreatment had long-term effects on mental health, drug and alcohol misuse, risky sexual behavior, obesity, delinquency, and criminal behavior for both boys and girls. It was stated that these effects were long-lasting and continued as an adult, but this has been known for some time.

There is now no doubt that child maltreatment has long-lasting effects on the behavior and mental processes of the victim (Peters, 1988). The impact of child sexual abuse for the victim leads to an overwhelming sense of anxiety that can negatively interfere with the development of self-esteem and self-perception (Kilgore, 1988). These effects can lead to feelings of depression, low self-esteem, powerlessness, loss of control, and lack of trust in others (Jehu, 1988; Peters, 1988; Watkins & Bentovim, 1992). Thus the victim has difficulties in managing emotions and feelings in relation to others and shows poor social skills and may express her distress through the abuse of drugs and alcohol (Watkins & Bentovim, 1992).

Previous research and clinical evidence has demonstrated that fear, anxiety, depression, lack of self-confidence, guilt, and shame are emotional disturbances commonly associated with victims of physical and sexual child abuse and that these feelings often compromise and inhibit the development and enjoyment of intimate relationships in later years (Browne & Finkelhor, 1986; McCann, Sakheim, & Abrahamson, 1988).

Long-term trauma is especially associated with the victim's feelings of stigmatization and self-blame (Finkelhor, 1984, 1986). Indeed, Wyatt and Mickey (1987) have found that psychological disturbance was higher for women who blamed themselves for the abuse, and that self-attribution of blame was more common in women who had not disclosed their own experiences of child sexual abuse due to fear of not being believed.

Non-disclosure, leading to long-term trauma, is more likely in cases of intrafamilial sexual abuse, coerced by family members, as these experiences are very traumatic for the child due to the abuse of trust and unquestioning power inherent in family relationships. Nevertheless, the presence of force during sexual abuse by friends and acquaintances also has been found to have a strong influence on long-term trauma (Finkelhor, 1979; Russell, 1986).

Summitt (1983) claims that female victims, unlike male victims, tend to internalize their inner rage and hostility as a result of their abuse, hence they are more likely to harm themselves than to harm others as a consequence of their own victimization. However, research has shown that the phenomenon is not so clear-cut and a significant minority of girls become violent and antisocial to others and a significant number of boys harm themselves directly and through risk-taking behaviors (Falshaw & Browne, 1997; Falshaw, Browne, & Hollin, 1996; Hamilton, Falshaw, & Browne, 2002).

VALIDITY OF THE CHILD'S DISCLOSURE

False Allegations

Mandatory reporting laws in the United States and other countries demand that all those who have professional contact with children must report any suspicions of abuse or neglect to the relevant authorities. Understandably, professionals err on the side of caution and a number of unsubstantiated allegations emerge. Previously, as much as 65% of child abuse and neglect allegations in the United States have been claimed to be unfounded (Besharov, 1985). This figure represents child abuse allegations *in general* and does not distinguish between allegations arising from children and those arising from adults. By contrast clinical research about false allegations arising from children quotes figures of between 1% and 6%. For example, Peters (1988) reported only four false accusations from a total of 64 children brought to a hospital emergency room for suspected sexual abuse. Goodwin, Sahd, and Rada (1978) also discovered that only 3 of 46 sexual abuse cases reported to a child abuse agency were based upon false allegations. Thus, in both studies, only 6% of reported cases of child sexual abuse could not be substantiated.

Another keynote publication was the research paper by Jones and McGraw (1987) who reviewed 576 reports of child sexual abuse made to the Denver

Department of Social Services during 1983. They found that 49% of reports were reliable accounts of child sexual abuse and action by social services and the police followed. In 24% of reports, there was insufficient information to continue with any health, social, or legal intervention. For 17% of the reports there was not enough evidence but unsubstantiated suspicions remained, while 4% of the time the children recanted their allegation and nothing could be done. Only 5% of reports from adults proved to be fictitious and only 1% of the time were reports by children proven to be fictitious. Altogether, the fictitious reports were again found to be 6% of cases. The 1% of children initiating false allegations demonstrated little or no accompanying emotion while describing their victimization. Their descriptions frequently lack detail and threats from the offender were absent from their accounts. Most of the mothers who made false allegations were involved in custody/visitation disputes. Larger-scale studies (Everson & Boat, 1989) have confirmed these figures as representative.

There is little doubt that unfounded allegations for child abuse and neglect occur when parents are involved in custody and/or visitation disputes over a child (Ney, 2013). A National Canadian study of 7,672 child maltreatment cases (Trocme & Bala, 2005) estimated that a third of cases were unsubstantiated and 4% involved intentional false allegations. Where the parents were separated the number of intentional false allegations increased to 12% of these cases. Another North American study of 257 sexual abuse allegations from a child (Malloy, Lyon, & Quas, 2007) found that 46.3% of parents found it difficult to believe and consequently 23.1% of children recanted (denied the abuse post-disclosure) and withdrew the allegation. This was more likely for younger children: those abused by a parent and those who received a lack of support from the non-abusive parent, friends, and family. Hence, the two important questions of an investigation into alleged sexual abuse of a child are (i) Where did the allegation originate from (adult or child)? and (ii) Are the parents separated?

It is evident that a false denial from a child is six times more likely that a false allegation and that if the allegation originates from the child then 99 times out of 100, the child is telling the truth.

Reliability of the Child Witness

The credibility of the child witness in court has been questioned by lawyers in four main ways in relation to children being considered unreliable witnesses:

1. inconsistent statement details of the abuse allegation;
2. inconsequent past behavior of the victim in relation to alleged abuser;
3. unreasonable delay in disclosing abuse; *or*
4. no disclosure at all.

Inconsistent Statement Details

It is common for people with a history of abuse and neglect as a child to give inconsistent details of their maltreatment (Smith & Tilney, 2007). In both law enforcement and legal work, the assumption is that a memory for a particular event would be clear, accurate, and authentic, as might be expected when providing supporting evidence in court for an accusation of theft against an alleged offender (Wattam, 1991). This assumption is incorrect in a number of ways:

• Abuse is not an event but a process of many events occurring over a certain duration of time (Faller, 2007).
• An individual subjected to one type of abuse is often subjected to another (Gilbert et al., 2009).
• Memories for any one abusive incident would be influenced by other abusive incidents, such that details of any one event would become confused with other events (Browne & Hamilton, 1997).

Ironically, an exact same account with an absence of inconsistency may indicate the possibility of a false allegation (Green & Schetkey, 1988; see Table 16.3). The inconsistencies shown in the details of statements made by individuals with a history of abuse are associated with the person attempting to accommodate their experiences and cope with the unhappy and painful memories. Therefore, on one occasion their subconscious may allow them to reveal their inner feelings that relate to their maltreatment and on other occasions their psychological defense mechanisms will

Table 16.3 Characteristics of true and unsubstantiated cases of child sexual abuse in the family. (Adapted from Green & Schetky, 1988.)

True cases	Unsubstantiated cases
Child initially reticent to discuss abuse with mother or others	Child discusses the abuse when prompted by mother. Child checks with mother
Child rarely will confront father with the allegation, even with mother present	Child will often confront father with allegation in mother's presence, while seeking mother's approval
Child usually fearful in father's presence, congruent with affect and ideation unless molestation was gentle and non-threatening	Discrepancy between the child's angry accusations and the apparent comfort in father's presence
Mothers often depressed; no other specific psychopathology	Prominent paranoid and hysterical psychopathology in mothers
Child usually demonstrates signs and symptoms of child sexual abuse	Child might be sexually preoccupied, but does not exhibit signs and symptoms of child sexual abuse

help them to minimize or even deny the memories that were previously recalled (Aldridge & Wood, 1998). This occurs with all forms of child maltreatments and especially in cases of sexual abuse (Summitt, 1983).

Inconsequent Past Behavior

Those who have worked with victims of child maltreatment sometimes observe (what would appear to others to be) conflicting actions. For example, making allegations of child maltreatment and having a history of sending "Father's Day" cards and letters to the alleged abuser. Indeed, these inconsistencies in behavior are often used in cross-examination. There is little recognition that the "splitting" of the abuser into the bad parent/carer (i.e., the part of the abusive parent/carer that maltreats the child at night) and the good parent/carer (i.e., the part of the abusive parent/carer that eats meals with them, cuddles them to watch TV, takes them on outings, and provides a home for them) is a defense mechanism that helps the victim tolerate their torture without mental breakdown. The way such victims can cope with their conflicting experiences is to on occasions address the good parts of the parent and send letters and cards to that part. This helps them to suppress the bad feelings and experiences they might remember. However, when directly interviewed about their abuse experiences it is difficult for them to recall those good parts and they may even deny that they existed or that they could have even sent cards and letters.

In addition to the notion of splitting described above, there is of course the concept of compliance. In respect of letters and photographs indicating non-abusive experiences the abused children learn to comply with their parents' wishes to avoid punishment inside the home. This compliance may extend to letters, diaries, and cards that the sexually abusive parent might read. Therefore, a more simple explanation is that the victim fears the abuser and wishes to appease them (Browne, 1994). It is well established in research on parenting that parental abuse and/or neglect is more likely to result in the child having an insecure attachment to their caregiver (Morton & Browne, 1998). Such insecure attachments in early childhood lead to mistrust and fear of strange adults and as such an abused child illogically clings to their abusive parent. Perhaps the phrase "better the devil you know rather than the devil you don't know" ironically applies to this situation.

It is well established that victims of abuse just want the abuse to stop rather than being removed from the home or totally rejected by the parent. Crittenden (2002) indicates that rejection and neglect is more difficult for the child to cope with than physical violence. Generally these two aspects of maltreatment go hand in hand. It might be hypothesized that, for some victims of incest, sending a Father's Day card to an abusive father may be a better way of coping than not having a father at all. Hence, the relevance of such evidence in a case involving child maltreatment is questionable if not irrelevant.

Delayed Memory for Childhood Abuse

The child's testimony is usually acceptable to the court if he or she is old enough to verbalize, knows what the truth is, and can distinguish right from wrong. The child's verbalizations during cross-examination or during an investigation cannot always be accepted at face value, because they are subjected to powerful distorting influences from within such as fear, shame, and guilt and externally by the power of suggestion and wanting to please the interviewer (Doris, 1993; Eisen, Quas, & Goodman, 2002; Faller, 2007; Myers, 2005; Westcott, Davies, & Bull, 2002). In addition, external threats of retaliation and punishment for betraying the perpetrator might engender fear and anxiety, such that the victim experiences sexual abuse for months or years before disclosing the maltreatment suffered (Ney, 2013).

Many factors may influence childhood memory: developmental sophistication of the child, the events and details to be remembered, the child's ability to use memory, and the stress associated with the initial event (Finkelhor, 1995). Therefore, forgetting may be caused by a variety of problems: failure to perceive an event, difficulties in coding or storing material, or problems in recalling the event. In addition, how the child is interviewed is likely to have a profound effect on the child's ability to recall and report information from memory (Aldridge & Wood, 1998; Poole & Lamb, 1998; Pipe, Lamb, Orbach, & Cederborg, 2007). Nevertheless, once an event is stored a child's memory is likely to be as enduring as an adult's (Bull, 2001; Dent & Flin, 1992; Faller, 2007). However, children and adults with an intellectual disability show poorer memory and greater suggestibility (Gudjonsson & Henry, 2003). The problem of suggestibility during investigative interviews involving eyewitness memory in young children has recently been reviewed (Goodman & Melinder, 2007) with the conclusion that courts and legal professionals should not be negative about this matter, neither should they be overly optimistic about the abilities of young children.

In relation to an adult client who reports recollections of child sexual abuse often many years or even decades after the abuse has taken place, there are two possibilities to consider:

1. That there is a relatively common phenomenon called amnesia in which childhood traumas are forgotten until somehow restimulated at a later point in time, or
2. Some clients lie about or are deluded into believing childhood abuse has occurred in their past, as a result of a False Memory Syndrome (Freyd, 1992).

There are at least two models to explain why someone who is abused as a child might forget such an event. The classic notion of repression as presented by Freud in 1966, suggests that child abuse memories may be blocked from conscious awareness by virtue of their potential to produce extreme psychological conflict. For example, a victim who receives bribes or special privileges for not disclosing abuse might actively repress her abuse memories, in the interests of avoiding feelings of guilt or shame.

A second explanation is the concept of amnesia, when describing absent abuse memories. This suggests a dissociative defense against re-experiencing the anxiety and distress associated with the recall of traumatic abuse. From this perspective, dissociation is adaptive: "It allows relatively normal functioning for the duration of the traumatic event and leaves a large part of the personality unaffected by the trauma" (Van der Kolk & Kadiash, 1987, pp. 195–196).

Indeed, there is much evidence from clinical samples that many women sexually abused as children experience periods when they cannot remember the abuse. Briere and Conte (1993) found that 59% of 450 women in treatment had at some time forgotten the sexual abuse they suffered during childhood. Likewise, Herman and Schatzow (1987) report 64% of women had incomplete memories for their sexual abuse and 28% of this clinical sample had total amnesia about the event.

A follow-up study of a community sample by Meyer Williams (1992) showed that 38% of women who were reported as being sexually abused in childhood failed to disclose they were victims of sexual abuse when asked about it years later. At the time of the adult interviews the women's age was between 18 and 31 years old. Qualitative analysis of the sensitive questions used in the interview showed that the vast majority of the 38% of women actually did not remember the abuse and a minority chose not to report their sexual victimization to the interviewers. The results of interviews with these women help determine how widespread non-disclosures are in retrospective reports and highlight the association between amnesia for the abuse and social and psychological difficulties.

In all the studies outlined there was a significant relationship between being physically injured during the abuse and amnesia. The threat of violence or where the victim feared that they would die, if they ever reported the abuse, also contributed to amnesia. The large percentage of subjects reporting some level of amnesia in each study appears to suggest that abuse-related amnesia is a common and real phenomenon and that abuse-specific amnesia may be associated more with violence than with internal conflict. This suggests that amnesia may be associated with dissociative avoidance of the distress suffered from recalling the abuse. Therefore, evidence for lying or the concept of the False Memory Syndrome is very limited.

NON-DISCLOSURE OF SEXUAL ABUSE AS A CHILD

Where the experiences of abuse are constantly remembered by the victim, other factors inhibit the child from disclosing facts about their situation. For example, Hershkowitz, Lores, and Lamb (2007) explored disclosure of sexual abuse with alleged child victims and their parents, where the alleged perpetrator was not in the child's family. They found that 53% of the victims took between one week and two years to disclose and 40% did not disclose until prompted to do so. Only half the children disclosed to their parents, the other half reported to be too ashamed and afraid of their parent's response. Hence, two of the most important factors for non-disclosure is the fear of what might happen and the learned helplessness that follows as a consequence of this fear.

Fear

The most obvious source of fear is the offender's violence or threat of violence to the victim on disclosure. In addition, the offender will often claim that bad things will happen to the victim, and/or the people and things the victim cares about, as a consequence of their disclosure (Browne, 1994; Elliott et al., 1995). The victim fear response may stay with them for many years after the abuse has stopped. As a consequence of physical and sexual maltreatment, the child victim fears and mistrusts all adults. The child associates the offender's maltreatment with adult behavior in general and, thus, may consider other adults as having the potential for physical and sexual abuse. A second source of fear is associated with the personal consequences of disclosure such as not being believed, being blamed for the sexual activity, being labeled as promiscuous, and being sent away from their family.

Learned Helplessness

Children taken into care often show signs of low self-esteem and lack self-confidence. They feel stigmatized, bewildered, abandoned, and stressed by the change of environment, family, and friends (Roberts, 1993; Rowe, Cain, Hindleby, & Keone, 1984). This makes them particularly vulnerable to further abuse and victimization (Browne, 1991b; Hamilton & Browne, 1998). Children from disrupted families internalize their feelings of being unloved and blame themselves as not worthy of love and affection (Browne, 1993, 1994). For example, the case of Anna, an eight-year-old girl who was sexually abused by one of the male care staff while living in a children's home:

Anna's case

It was impossible for Anna to challenge the views of her social worker and that of other staff who worked in the children's home, as they all regarded Mr Charming as a "model care worker" with ten years' experience of working in residential care. The victim was left with the feeling that in some way the sexual abuse was her own fault. Hence, the victim thinks that she will be blamed for the sexual abuse if she is believed at all. She also feared his violent reprisal as he

> claimed he would smother her with a pillow in the night if she told anyone. Anna passively cried out for help many times, through bed-wetting, cutting her arms, and running away, for which she was punished by her care worker and ignored by her social worker. With such negative rejections to Anna's help-seeking behavior, she developed feelings of learned helplessness (that nothing will or could be done) and this became an integral part of her personality to remain with her into adulthood. Even now she is unsure of the consequences of her disclosure as an adult and whether anything will be done to punish her offender.

The risk for the victim on disclosure is whether or not they will be believed. This can result in more long-term adverse consequences for the victim, as secondary trauma, sometimes worse than the abuse itself (Davenport, Browne, & Palmer, 1994). This secondary trauma often occurs in the courtroom (Butler-Smith, 1987; Quas et al., 2005).

A British study on the experiences of disclosure by Waller and Ruddock (1993) indicated that of the 45 adult women in their clinical care who reported that they had been sexually abused as a child, only 27 had attempted some form of disclosure during their childhood. Reasons for not telling anyone seem to center on fear of blame and fear of not being believed. Furthermore, only half of those women who had disclosed in their childhood did so in an active way, half being passive respondents to investigations (Waller & Ruddock, 1993).

An Australian study of adults (Waldby, 1985) endorses this finding and gives a breakdown of reasons for not reporting:

- 25.1% were prevented from talking about the abuse because of fear of disbelief or punishment;
- 20.8% gave shame, guilt, or social stigma as their reason;
- 10.2% referred to intimidation or threats from the abuser;
- 9.6% did not know who to tell;
- 9.2% feared family breakdown,;
- 7.5% denied or wanted to forget the experience; and
- 4.5% felt powerless and didn't think anyone would believe them.

Thus, the majority did not disclose because of considerations related to the response of others, of which fear of disbelief was a feature in up to 30% of cases.

Overall, there are significant pressures that tend to inhibit disclosure of sexual abuse, causing victims to deny any knowledge of the molestation. Hence, denial of sexual abuse allegations by the child has limited validity. On the other hand, if the child is able to describe the sexual abuse, one must give this credence. Therefore "False denials are common but false disclosures are rare" (Browne, 1991a).

CONCLUSIONS

Sexual abuse toward a child must be considered within context, as a process not an event. In addition, for many children, victimization occurs on more than one occasion, with the same perpetrator or different perpetrators. It is generally considered that repeat or re-victimization will lead to more severe trauma and a greater potential for antisocial behavior toward others (Browne & Hamilton, 1997; Hamilton et al., 2002). Some memory for victimizing events may be lost from conscious memory, while those children who experience a single event may be less traumatized and details of the incident will be remembered and better supported (Terr, 1991; Whitfield, 1995). This may be because memories from different abusive incidents become confused, particularly when the same perpetrator is involved and the incidents occur frequently. Furthermore, denial, repression, and disassociation may be more often associated with repeated victimization and re-victimization, whereas single incidents are more likely to be recollected and talked about freely, particularly if the victim experiences a supportive and understanding environment (Whitfield, 1995). These facts need to be taken into account when interviewing a child about the sexual abuse that they may have suffered. It is good practice to allow the child's disclosure and their narrative account to be expressed at the child's pace and in their preferred modality (verbally, written statement, or through drawings and/or play). During an interview, only limited indirect questions should be asked and direct prompts and questions such as "were you sexually abused by him?" should never be asked. Observations of appropriate interviews, following guidelines on good practice, have found little evidence for "false memory syndrome" in relation to the sexual abuse of children.

Research evidence has indicated that the sexual abuse of children has a long history and is a common experience affecting at least 1 in 5 children. Most sex offenders (95%) are male and a third commit sex offenses as an adolescent and/or teenager on younger peers. For the victim there are long-lasting effects on physical and mental health that can reduce the quality of life in adulthood and place the victim at risk of further victimization. These vulnerabilities influence the credibility of children's and adult's evidence to the police and to the courts, which is often associated with a fear of potential consequences. For the majority of victims the costs of disclosure outweigh the benefits and it is estimated that only 1 in 10 child victims disclose their sexually abusive experiences to police and/or health and social service professionals (Gilbert et al., 2009).

Research studies have shown that family and professional responses to a child's disclosure can strongly influence the content and details of the disclosure (Faller, 2007; Ney, 2013). One in four children recants the disclosure and withdraws their allegations, many as a consequence of the reaction of family and professionals to the disclosure and inappropriate interview procedures. Other children minimize the seriousness and limit the detailed descriptions of the sexual assaults they have experienced to protect their family. Hence, it is poor practice to interview a child victim in the presence of the non-abusing mother or close relative, and the presence of a professional "appropriate adult" would be a better option during investigative interviews (Hooper & Browne, 2016). Evidence of false allegations is limited to 1% of children and up to 6% overall, although it is acknowledged that these rates double where parents are separated (Trocme & Bala, 2005). Therefore false denials are common but false disclosures are rare.

REFERENCES

Aldridge, M., & Wood, J. (1998). *Interviewing children: A guide for childcare and forensic practitioners*. Chichester, UK: John Wiley & Sons, Ltd.

Baker, A.W., & Duncan, S.P. (1985). Child sexual abuse: A study of prevalence in Britain. *Child Abuse & Neglect, 8* (4), 457–467.

Besharov, E. (1985). "Doing something" about child abuse: The need to narrow the grounds for state intervention. *Harvard Journal of Law and Public Policy, 8,* 539–589.

Bottoms, B.L., & Goodman, G.S. (1996). *International perspectives on child abuse and children's testimony: Psychological research and law*. Thousand Oaks, CA: Sage.

Briere, J., & Conte, J. (1993). Self-reported amnesia for abuse in adults molested as children. *Journal of Traumatic Stress, 6,* 21–31.

Browne, A., & Finkelhor, D. (1986). Impact of child sexual abuse: A review of the research. *Psychological Bulletin, 99,* 66–77.

Browne, K.D. (1991a). Can children be relied upon to tell the truth and how reliable is the child witness? In M.S. Kasim (Ed.), *Child abuse and the law* (pp. 50–54). Kuala Lumpur: Malaysian Council for Child Welfare.

Browne, K.D. (1991b). When is it safe for the abused child to return home? In M.S. Kasim (Ed.), *Child abuse and the law* (pp. 23–24). Kuala Lumpur: Malaysian Council for Child Welfare.

Browne, K.D. (1993). Violence in the family and its links to child abuse. In C. Hobbs & J. Wynne (Eds.), *Child abuse: Baillier's Clinical Paediatric Series, 1* (1), 149–164.

Browne, K.D. (1994). Child sexual abuse. In J. Archer (Ed.), *Male violence* (pp. 210–232). Routledge: London.

Browne, K.D. (2002). *National prevalence study of child abuse and neglect in Romanian Families*. Copenhagen: WHO Regional Office for Europe.

Browne, K.D. (2009a). Working to prevent sexual abuse in the family. In T. Beech, L. Craig, & K.D. Browne (Eds.), *Assessment and treatment of sexual offenders: A handbook* (pp. 491–514). Oxford: Wiley-Blackwell.

Browne, K.D. (2009b). Police work with sex offenders: Detection, management and treatment. In T. Beech, L. Craig, & K.D. Browne (Eds.), *Assessment and treatment of sexual offenders: A handbook* (pp. 515–534). Oxford: Wiley-Blackwell.

Browne, K.D., & Hamilton, C. (1997). The repeat and revictimisation of children: Possible influences on recollections for trauma. In D. Read & S. Lindsay (Eds.), *Recollections of Trauma* (pp. 425–433). New York: Plenum Press.

Browne, K.D., & McManus, M. (2010). Adolescents with intellectual disability and family sexual abuse. In L. Craig, W.R. Lindsay, & K.D. Browne (Eds.), *Assessment and treatment of sexual offenders with learning disabilities* (pp. 47–69). Oxford: Wiley-Blackwell.

Bull, R. (2001). *Children and the law* (Essential Readings in Developmental Psychology). Oxford: Blackwell.

Butler-Smith, S. (1987). *Children's story: Sexually molested children in criminal court.* London: HMSO.

Bywaters, P., Bunting, L., Davidson, G., Hanratty, J., Mason, W., Mc Cartan, C., & Steils, N. (2016). *The relationship between poverty, child abuse and neglect: A rapid evidence review*. York, UK: Joseph Rowntree Foundation. Available from: www.jrf.org.uk/file/48920/download?token=P (last retrieved July 15, 2016).

Cawson, P., Wattam, C., Brooker, S., & Kelly, G. (2000). *Child maltreatment in the United Kingdom: A study of prevalence of child abuse and neglect.* London: NSPCC.

Copen, L.M. (2000). *Preparing children for court: A practitioner's guide* (Interpersonal Violence: The Practice Series). Beverly Hills, CA: Sage.

Copen, L.M., Martin, S., & Pucci, L.M. (2000). *Getting ready for court: Civil court edition: A book for children* (Interpersonal Violence: The Practice Series). Beverly Hills, CA: Sage.

Crawford, E., & Bull, R. (2006). Child witness support and preparation: Are parents and caregivers ignored? *Child Abuse Review, 15* (4), 243–256.

Creighton, S.J. (2002). Recognising changes in incidence and prevalence. In K.D. Browne, H. Hanks, P. Stratton, & C.E. Hamilton (Eds.), *Early prediction and prevention of child abuse: A handbook* (pp. 5–22). Chichester, UK: John Wiley & Sons, Ltd.

Crittenden, P. (2002). If I knew then what I know now: Integrity and fragmentation in the treatment of child abuse and neglect. In K.D. Browne, H. Hanks, P. Stratton, & C.E. Hamilton (Eds.), *Early prediction and prevention of child abuse: A handbook* (pp. 111–126). Chichester, UK: John Wiley & Sons, Ltd.

Crown Prosecution Service, Home Office, & Department of Health (2001). *Provision of therapy for child witnesses prior to a criminal trail.* London: CPS, Home Office.

Davenport, C., Browne, K.D., & Palmer, R. (1994). Opinions on the traumatising effects of child sexual abuse: Evidence for consensus. *Child Abuse & Neglect, 18* (9), 725–738.

Davies, G., & Drinkwater J. (1998). *Child witness: Do the courts abuse children?* (Issues in Criminological and Legal Psychology). Leicester, UK: British Psychological Society.

Dent, H.R., & Flin, R. (1992). *Children as witnesses.* Chichester, UK: John Wiley & Sons, Ltd.

Department for Education (2016). Referrals, assessments and children who were the subject of a child protection plan year ending 31 March 2015. London: National Statistics Service.

Donovan, D.M. (1997). Why memory is a red herring in the recovered (traumatic) memory debate. In D. Read & S. Lindsay (Eds.), *Recollections of trauma* (pp. 403–415). New York: Plenum Press.

Doris, J. (1993). *The suggestibility of children's recollections: Implications for eyewitness testimony*. Washington, DC: American Psychological Association.

Eisen, M., Quas, J.A., & Goodman, G.S. (2002). *Memory and suggestibility in the forensic interview*. New Jersey: LEA.

Elliott, M., Browne, K.D., & Kilcoyne, J. (1995). Child sexual abuse prevention: What offenders tell us. *Child Abuse & Neglect, 19*, 579–594.

Everson, M.D., & Boat, B.W. (1989). False allegations of sexual abuse by children and adolescents. *Journal of the American Academy of Child and Adolescent Psychiatry*, *28*, 230–235.

Faller, K.C. (1990). *Understanding child sexual maltreatment*. Beverley Hills, CA: Sage.

Faller, K.C. (2007). *Interviewing children about sexual abuse: Controversies and best practice*. New York: Oxford University Press.

Falshaw, L., & Browne, K.D. (1997). Adverse childhood experiences and violent acts of young people in secure accommodation. *Journal of Mental Health*, *6* (5), 443–456.

Falshaw, L., Browne, K.D., & Hollin, C.R. (1996). Victim to offender: A review. *Aggression and Violent Behavior*, *1* (4), 389–404.

Fergusson, D.M., & Mullen, P.E. (1999). *Childhood sexual abuse: An evidence based perspective* (Developmental Clinical Psychology and Psychiatry, Volume 40). London: Sage.

Finkelhor, D. (1979). *Sexually victimized children*. New York: Free Press.

Finkelhor, D. (1984). *Child sexual abuse: New theory and research*. New York: Free Press.

Finkelhor, D. (1986). *A sourcebook on child sexual abuse*. Beverly Hills, CA: Sage.

Finkelhor, D. (1994). The international epidemiology of child sexual abuse. *Child Abuse & Neglect*, *18* (5), 409–418.

Finkelhor, D. (1995). The victimisation of children: A developmental perspective. *American Journal of Orthopsychiatry*, *65* (2), 177–193.

Finkelhor, D., & Baron, L. (1986). Risk factors for child sexual abuse. *Journal of Interpersonal Violence*, *1*, 43–71.

Finkelhor, D., Hotaling, G., Lewis, I.A., & Smith, C. (1990). Sexual abuse in a national survey of adult men and women: Prevalence, characteristics and risk factors. *Child Abuse & Neglect*, *14*, 19–28.

Freud, S. (1966). In J. Strachey (Ed. and Trans.), *The standard edition of the complete psychological works of Sigmund Freud*. London: Hogarth Press.

Freyd, P. (1992). *FMS Foundation Newsletter*. Philadelphia: FMS Foundation, May 1.

Gilbert, R., Spatz-Widom, C., Browne, K., Fergusson, D., Webb, E., & Janson, S. (2009). Child maltreatment: Burden and consequences in high-income countries (Lancet Series on Child Maltreatment, 1). *The Lancet*, *373* (9657), 68–81.

Glasgow, D., Horne, L., Calam, R., & Cox. A. (1994). Evidence, incidence, gender and age in sexual abuse of children perpetrated by children: Towards a developmental analysis of child sexual abuse. *Child Abuse Review*, *3*, 196–210.

Goodman, G.S., & Melinder, A. (2007). Child witness research and forensic interviews: A review. *Legal and Criminological Psychology*, *12* (1), 1–19.

Goodwin, J., Sahd, D., & Rada, R. (1978). Incest hoax: False accusations, false denials. *Bulletin of the American Academy of Psychiatry and the Law*, *6*, 269–276.

Green, A.H., & Schetky, D.H. (1988). True and false allegations of child sexual abuse. In D.H. Schetky & A.H. Green (Eds.), *Child sexual abuse: A handbook for health care and legal professionals* (pp. 104–124). New York: Brunner/Mazel.

Gudjonsson, G.H., & Henry, L. (2003). Child and adult witnesses with intellectual disability: The importance of suggestibility. *Legal and Criminological Psychology*, *8* (2), 241–252.

Hamilton, C., & Browne, K.D. (1998). The repeat victimisation of children: Should the concept be revised? *Aggression and Violent Behavior*, *3* (1), 47–60.

Hamilton, C.E., Falshaw, L., & Browne, K.D. (2002). The link between recurrent maltreatment and offending behaviour. *International Journal of Offender Therapy and Comparative Criminology, 46* (1), 75–94.

Harvey, W., & Watson-Russell, A. (1991). *So you have to go to court!: Child's guide to testifying as a witness in child abuse cases.* Toronto, ON: Butterworths.

Herman, J.L., & Schatzow, E. (1987). Recovery and verification of memories of childhood sexual trauma. *Psychoanalytic Psychology, 4,* 1–14.

Hershkowitz, I., Lores, O., & Lamb, M.E. (2007). Exploring disclosure of child sexual abuse with alleged victims and their parents. *Child Abuse and Neglect, 31* (2), 11–123.

Hobbs, C., & Wynne, J. (2002). Predicting child sexual abuse and neglect. In K.D. Browne, H. Hanks, P. Stratton, & C.E. Hamilton (Eds.), *Early prediction and prevention of child abuse: A handbook* (pp. 71–91). Chichester, UK: John Wiley & Sons, Ltd.

Home Office (1992). *Memorandum of good practice on video recorded interviews with child witnesses for criminal proceedings.* London: The Stationary Office.

Home Office (1998). *Speaking up for justice: Report of the interdepartmental working group on the treatment of vulnerable or intimidated witnesses in the criminal justice system.* London: Home Office.

Home Office (2002). *Achieving best evidence in criminal proceedings: Guidance on interviewing victims and witnesses, and using special measures.* London: Home Office.

Home Office (2003). *Criminal statistics: England and Wales 2002. Statistics relating to criminal proceedings for the year 2002.* London: The Stationary Office.

Hooper, R., & Browne, K.D. (2016). Use of appropriate adults during investigative interviews with vulnerable people. *International Journal of Offender Therapy and Comparative Criminology.* (In Submission).

Howells, K. (1981). Adult sexual interest in children: Considerations relevant to theories of etiology. In M. Cook & K. Howells (Eds.), *Adult sexual interest in children* (pp. 55–94). London: Academic Press.

Jackson, V., Browne, K.D., & Joseph, S. (2016). The prevalence of childhood victimization experienced outside of the family: Findings from an English prevalence study. *Child Abuse & Neglect, 51,* 343–357.

Jehu, D. (1988). *Beyond sexual abuse: Therapy with women who were childhood victims.* Chichester, UK: John Wiley & Sons, Ltd.

John Jay College of Criminal Justice (2004). *The nature and scope of the problem of sexual abuse of minors by catholic priests and deacons in the United States.* Report to the United States Conference of Catholic Bishops. New York: John Jay College of Criminal Justice.

Jones, D.P.H., & McGraw, J.M. (1987). Reliable and fictitious accounts of sexual abuse in children. *Journal of Interpersonal Violence, 2,* 27–45.

Kempe, C.H. (1980). Incest and other forms of sexual abuse. In C.H. Kempe & R.E. Helfer (Eds.), *The battered child* (3rd ed., pp. 198–214). Chicago, IL: Chicago University Press.

Kilgore, L.C. (1988). Effects of early childhood sexual abuse on self and ego development. *Social Casework: The Journal of Contemporary Social Work, 9,* 224–225.

Malloy, L.C., Lyon, T.D., & Quas, J.A. (2007). Filial dependency and recantation of child sexual abuse allegations. *Journal of the American Academy of Child and Adolescent Psychiatry, 46* (2), 162–170.

May-Chahal, C., & Cawson, P. (2005). Measuring child maltreatment in the United Kingdom: A study of the prevalence of child abuse and neglect. *Child Abuse & Neglect*, *29* (9), 969–984.

McCann, I.L., Sakheim, D.K., & Abrahamson, D.J. (1988). Trauma and victimisation: A model of psychological adaptation. *Counselling Psychologist*, *16* (4), 531–594.

McDonald, W.R., & Associates (2005). *Child maltreatment 2003: Reports from the States to the National Child Abuse and Neglect Data System*. Washington, DC: US Department of Health and Human Services, Children's Bureau.

McWilliams, K., Augusti, E.M., Dion, J., Block, S.D., Melinder, A., Cashmore, J., & Goodman, G.S. (2014). Children as witnesses (Chapter 16). In G.B. Melton, A. Ben-Arieh, J. Cashmore, G.S. Goodman, & N.K. Worley (Eds.), *The Sage handbook of child research* (pp. 285–299). Beverley Hills, CA: Sage.

Meyer Williams, L. (1992). Adult memories of childhood abuse: Preliminary findings from a longitudinal study. *The Advisor*, *5* (3), 19–21. (American Professional Society on the Abuse of Children, Summer 1992.)

Morton, N.J., & Browne, K.D. (1998). Theory and observation of attachment and its relation to child maltreatment. *Child Abuse & Neglect*, *22* (11), 1093–1104.

Mrazek, P., Lynch, M., & Bentovim, A. (1981). Sexual abuse of children in the United Kingdom. *Child Abuse & Neglect*, *7*, 147–153.

Myers, J.E.B. (2005). *Myers on evidence in child, domestic and elder abuse cases, Volume 2*. New York: Aspen.

Ney, T. (Ed.) (2013). *True or false allegations of child sexual abuse: Assessment and case management*. New York: Brunner/Mazel.

Peters, S.D. (1988). Child sexual abuse and later psychological problems. In G. Wyatt & G. Powell (Eds.), *Lasting effects of child sexual abuse* (pp. 101–118). Berverly Hills, CA: Sage.

Pinheiro P.S. (Ed.) (2006). *World report on violence against children: Secretary General's study on violence against children*. New York: United Nations.

Pipe, M.E., Lamb, M.E., Orbach, Y., & Cederborg, A. (Eds.) (2007). *Child sexual abuse: Disclosure, delay and denial*. Oxford: Routledge/Taylor Francis.

Plotnikoff, J., & Woolfson, R. (1998). Preparing young witnesses for court: A handbook for child witness supporters. London: NSPCC.

Poole, D.A., & Lamb, M.E. (1998). *Investigative interviews of children: A guide for helping professionals*. Washington, DC: American Psychological Association.

Quas, J., Goodman, G., Ghetti, S., Alexander, K., Edelstein, R., Redich, A.D., Corden, I.M., & Jones, D.P.H. (2005). *Childhood sexual assault victims: Long-term outcome after testifying in court* (Monographs of the Society for Research in Child Development).

Roberts, J. (1993). Abused children and foster care: The need for specialist resources. *Child Abuse Review*, *2* (1), 3–14.

Rowe, J., Cain, H., Hindleby, M., & Keone, A. (1984). *Long-term foster care*. Batsford, London.

Russell, D.E. (1986). *The secret trauma: Incest in the lives of girls and women*. New York: Basic Books.

Search, G. (1988). *The last taboo: Sexual abuse of children*. London: Penguin Books.

Selkin, J. (1991). *The child sexual abuse case in the courtroom*. Denver, CO: J. Selkin.

Smallbone, S., Marshall, W.L., & Wortley, R. (2008). *Preventing child sexual abuse: Evidence, policy and practice*. Cullompton, UK: Willan Publishing.

Smith, K., & Tilney, S. (2007). *Vulnerable adult and child witnesses*. London: Blackstones.

Summitt, R.C. (1983). The child sexual accommodation syndrome. *Child Abuse & Neglect*, 7, 177–193.

Teoh, Y.S., & Lamb, M.E. (2010). Preparing children for investigative interviews: Rapport building, instruction and evaluation. *Applied Developmental Science*, 14 (3), 154–163.

Terr, L.C. (1991). Childhood traumas: An outline and overview. *American Journal of Psychiatry*, 148, 10–20.

Trocme, N., & Bala, N. (2005). False allegations of abuse and neglect when parents separate. *Child Abuse & Neglect*, 29 (12), 1333–1345.

Van der Kolk, B.A., & Kadish, W. (1987). Amnesia, dissociation and the return of the repressed. In B.A. van der Kolk, *Psychological trauma* (pp. 190–215). Washington, DC: American Psychiatric Press.

Vizard, E., Hickely, N., French, L., & McCrory, E. (2007). Children and adolescents who present with sexually abusive behaviour: A UK descriptive study. *Journal of Forensic Psychiatry and Psychology*, 18 (1), 59–73.

Waldby, C. (1985). *Breaking the silence*. Sydney: Honeysett.

Waller, G., & Ruddock, A. (1993). Experiences of disclosure of child sexual abuse and psychopathology. *Child Abuse Review*, 2 (3), 71–81.

Watkins, B., & Bentovim, A. (1992). The sexual abuse of male children and adolescents: A review of current research. *Journal of Child Psychology and Psychiatry*, 33 (1), 197–248.

Wattam, C. (1991). *Truth and belief in the "disclosure" process*. London: NSPCC.

Westcott, H.L., & Jones, J. (1997). *Perspectives on the memorandum*. London: NSPCC.

Westcott, H.L., Davies, G., & Bull, R. (2002). *Children's testimony: A handbook of psychological research and forensic practice* (Wiley Series in Psychology of Crime, Policing and Law). Chichester, UK: John Wiley & Sons, Ltd.

Whitfield, C.L. (1995). *Memory and abuse: Remembering and healing the effects of trauma*. Florida: Health Communications, Inc.

Wyatt, G.E., & Mickey, M.R. (1987). Ameliorating the effects of child sexual abuse an exploratory study of support by parents and others. *Journal of Interpersonal Violence*, 2 (4), 403–414.

17

Working with Young Offenders

CLIVE R. HOLLIN AND RUTH M. HATCHER

INTRODUCTION

Which young people are most at risk of entering a life of crime? What are the individual factors that increase the risk that a particular child or adolescent will become involved in crime? What are the circumstances that increase the likelihood that a young offender will grow up to become an adult offender?

There are several methodologies that researchers can use to try to answer these questions. However, prospective longitudinal surveys are taken to be the methodology of choice. The basis of a prospective longitudinal study is that a cohort, generally of several hundred people, is followed over a long period of time. Information is periodically gathered on the cohort's characteristics, including their personal details and social circumstances, through repeated interviews and record checks. In this way, longitudinal studies can show relationships between individual development and life events over the lifespan that are associated with an increase or decrease in offending. However, the multitude of variables in longitudinal research together with their complex interrelationships poses difficulties in making firm statements about causality.

The *Cambridge Study in Delinquent Development* is an excellent example of a prospective longitudinal study. The Cambridge study started in 1961 with a cohort of 411 males aged 8–9 years and to date there have been nine follow-up interviews providing a wealth of information on the lives of those involved (Farrington, 2003; Farrington et al., 2006). There have been a substantial number of prospective

Assessments in Forensic Practice: A Handbook, First Edition. Edited by Kevin D. Browne, Anthony R. Beech, Leam A. Craig, and Shihning Chou.

longitudinal surveys with a focus on offending: Farrington and Welsh (2007) provide details of 32 major longitudinal surveys, mainly carried out with males in Western industrialized countries.

WHO BECOMES DELINQUENT?

The longitudinal studies provide information that help to identify the individual, familial, and social factors linked with offending. In the main, this research is concerned with the more serious types of offenses such as theft, car crime, burglary, and violence, and less so with minor offenses and status offenses such as truancy.

The Cambridge study found that when the cohort was aged 8–10 years there were a range of factors that distinguished the later delinquents from the non-delinquents. These factors fell into six categories: (i) the child's disruptive behavior; (ii) the child's low intelligence or low school attainment; (iii) the child's impulsiveness, risk taking, and poor concentration; (iv) a family member, parent or sibling, involved in criminal activity; (v) poor parenting as seen with a lack of discipline and supervision, or the child's separation from his parents; (vi) the family's poor economic standing as seen by low income and poor housing, compounded by a large family size. These six categories could independently predict delinquency after the age 8–10 years. Further, there is a cumulative effect so that the more categories that are prevalent for an individual, the greater the likelihood of later offending.

Individual Factors

Any child's behavior will be a product of their individual capability, itself perhaps with a heritable component, in interaction with their physical and social environment. *Intelligence* is one individual factor for which there is a weight of evidence associating low intelligence, particularly regarding the ability to comprehend abstract concepts, with conduct disorder. In turn, conduct disorder in childhood is linked with offending in adolescence (Lahey et al., 1995). This does not mean that young offenders have abnormally low IQs; rather that their IQs are consistently lower than those of their non-delinquent peers. If intelligence and delinquency are related then it is not unexpected that delinquency is also closely associated with poor school attainment.

It is the case that delinquents are more likely than their non-offending peers to truant from school, to be seen as difficult by teachers, and to fail academically. In terms of causality, it is possible that lower intelligence precipitates conduct problems, school failure, and concomitant psychological and social functioning. Alternatively, there could be a third factor, such as temperament, which plays a mediating role across the other factors.

The concept of *temperament* has proved to have an enduring popularity (Thomas, Chess, & Birch, 1968), and the type of temperament most associated with delinquent behavior is one in which the child is uninhibited with frequent displays of impulsive and aggressive behavior. The notion of temperament is close to personality and it is not difficult to see an overlap with the high extraversion and high neuroticism in Eysenck's (1977) theory of antisocial behavior.

The trait of *impulsiveness* is one that figures in accounts of offending from both temperament and personality. The term "impulsive" is generally used in the context of moving rapidly from perception of the situation to taking action without thinking of the potential consequences. Impulsivity is strongly associated with delinquency, particularly violent acts against other people (Jolliffe & Farrington, 2009). The emotion of *anger* is closely associated with impulsivity and with delinquency, typically acts involving violence toward people or property (Swaffer & Hollin, 2000). In addition, chronic anger may have a deleterious effect upon the young person's health (Swaffer & Hollin, 2001).

The term *social cognitive skills* refers to a range of psychological abilities such as empathy, social perspective taking, and social problem solving, and there is a relationship between cognitive skills and delinquency (McMurran & McGuire, 2005; Ross & Fabiano, 1985). Socially competent behavior relies on accurate perception of the other person's intentions and emotions. Aggressive children may have difficulties in the selection and interpretation of appropriate social cues (Akhtar & Bradley, 1991; Marsh & Blair, 2008). The misperception of social cues can, in turn, lead to misattribution of intent so that the other person's actions are mistakenly seen as hostile or threatening (Crick & Dodge, 1996). The next step is, of course, that the young person acts in line with their (mis)perceptions, either by withdrawing from the situation or responding to the perceived aggression with aggressive behavior. Empathy is another aspect of cognition often associated with antisocial behavior, particularly acts of violence. Jolliffe and Farrington (2007) found that, for any type of offense, male but not female offenders had lower empathy than non-offenders. However, for acts of violence, both male and female offenders had lower empathy than their non-offending counterparts.

Family Factors

A large family size, with five or more siblings, is a reliable predictor of delinquency. It is possible that family size stretches the family's resources, limiting parental attention and supervision, reducing physical space and privacy, and causing financial difficulties. A shortage of physical and psychological resources can have adverse effects on family functioning. As parents struggle so their supervision and monitoring of their children's behavior may be affected, sometimes to the point of emotional neglect and physical abuse (Iwaniec, 2006; Stith et al., 2009). The parental child-rearing patterns may be characterized by low levels of involvement in the child's everyday life and by the use of harsh and inconsistent physical chastisement (Widom & White, 1997). In addition, a delinquent sibling may be a potent model to be followed by his or her brothers and sisters.

It is possible that the family will be disrupted by parental conflict so that the children observe arguments and even physical violence. Such conflict can affect a parent's mental health, typically associated with episodes of depression and substance use, and may cause the breakup of their relationship. The family backgrounds of many delinquents are characterized by broken homes in which one parent, generally the father, leaves the family, sometimes to be replaced by a sequence of short-term partners, at other times leaving one parent to cope with looking after the family. A broken home is not in itself criminogenic: Wells and Rankin (1991) found that it was the cause of the breakdown that was important, with parental separation having a greater association with delinquency than parental death.

When the individual and familial risk factors are present there is a heightened probability that a young person will become entangled in the criminal justice system. However, Moffitt (1993) makes the observation that:

When official rates of crime are plotted against age, the rates for both prevalence and incidence of offending appear highest during adolescence; they peak sharply at about age 17 and drop precipitously in young adulthood. The majority of criminal offenders are teenagers; by the early 20s, the number of active offenders decreases by over 50%, and by age 28, almost 85% of former delinquents desist from offending ... With slight variations, this general relationship between age and crime obtains among males and females, for most types of crimes, during recent historical periods and in numerous Western nations. (p. 675)

Thus, some young people commit offenses during adolescence but the number peaks at around age 17 years and declines thereafter. However, some adolescent offenders continue their life trajectory ensconced in a life of crime. A Home Office report (Roe & Ashe, 2008), which details the main findings of a survey of crime among 4,554 young people aged between 10 and 25 years, gives details that complement the longitudinal research.

The survey asked the young people about 20 offenses that they may have committed in the past 12 months; these offenses fell into three clusters: (i) property-related offenses, including burglary, vehicle-related thefts, and thefts from work, school, shops, and other people, and criminal damage to property; (ii) violent offenses including robbery and assault; and (iii) selling drugs. The first point to make is that the majority of young people were not offenders: over three-quarters of the sample had not committed any of the 20 offenses, and for those who had the pattern was one of committing infrequent trivial offenses. In all, only 6% of the sample had committed an offense six or more times in the past 12 months; while 10% said they had committed at least one of the serious offenses. The most common offenses were assault, reported by 12% of the sample, followed by thefts (10%), criminal damage (4%), selling drugs (3%), and vehicle-related thefts (2%). Only a very small number of young people, around 1% or less, had committed burglary or robbery, and a few young people (3%) said they had carried a knife. As in the wider literature (e.g., Moffitt, 1993), the survey found that the peak age for offending was 14 to 17 years.

The survey also shows how blurred the distinction can become between offender and victim: the young people who had committed offenses were also more likely to be victims. In all, one-half of the young people who had committed an offense had also been victims of a personal crime compared to about one-fifth of the non-offenders. In total, just over one-quarter of the whole sample had been a victim of either personal theft or of assault in the last 12 months. The experience of victimization was more frequent among the 10 to 15 year olds, with the majority of incidents taking place at school. It is unlikely that many of these incidents would have been brought to the attention of the police. In the older, 16 to 25 year age group, the incidents that resulted in the young person becoming the victim of a crime were most likely to occur in a public house, nightclub, or in the street.

LIFE-COURSE PERSISTENT OFFENDERS

It is a stable finding in the research literature that offending peaks during the period of adolescence and most young people grow out of crime. However, some adolescents, mainly males, mature to an adult life in which antisocial behavior and crime is a part of their everyday existence. Moffitt (1993) suggested that in fact there are two distinct groups of adolescents: first, there are young people for who offending is *adolescent limited*; second, there are others for whom antisocial behavior and crime are *life-course persistent*. Moffitt argues that these two groups, adolescent limited and life-course persistent, are qualitatively distinct and require different theoretical explanations. Moffitt's theory generated a great deal of research concerning the two categories, their specific etiology, and their applicability to males and females (Moffitt, 2003; Moffitt, Caspi, Rutter, & Silva, 2001). Smith (2007) provides an excellent overview of the issues involved.

As theory progresses so too does practice: if we can identify the risk factors associated with juvenile crime with some confidence then how can this knowledge be used to inform efforts to prevent crime? There are two ways in which research informs practice: first, the assessment of young people involved in delinquency; second, the design of programs to work with young people to reduce the likelihood that they will enter a life of crime.

RESEARCH INTO PRACTICE

If practice is to be evidence based then, given the plethora of risk factors for young people's involvement in crime, there is potentially a great deal of ground to cover. Thus, efforts to prevent juvenile crime could be directed at societal factors, such as school and peer group; or at the family circumstances and functioning; or at the individual young person.

Indeed, each of these areas – broad social factors, the family, and the individual – have generated substantial literatures (Farrington & Welsh, 2007; LeMarquand & Tremblay, 2004; Piquero, Farrington, Welsh, Tremblay, & Jennings, 2009; Swenson, Henggeler, & Schoenwald, 2004). The focus here, however, is on what works with the individual young person.

What Works?

In the field of offender treatment there have been a number of meta-analytic studies (Andrews et al., 1990; Garrett, 1985; Lipsey, 1992), with several syntheses also available (Hollin, 1993, 1994; Lipsey, 1995; Lösel, 1995), of the effectiveness of interventions designed to reduce offending. The meta-analyses showed that, given substantial variability, treatment produces an overall positive net gain when compared to no treatment of about a 10% reduction in offending (Lipsey, 1992; Lösel, 1995). However, not all interventions have the same effect: Lipsey (1992) suggests that "high effect" interventions are associated with a fall in rates of reoffending in the order of 20% when set against baseline levels from mainstream criminal sanctioning. The characteristics of successful treatments are described in Figure 17.1.

To guide practice, Andrews and Bonta (1994) formulated the *risk principle* which suggests that for maximum effect intensive treatment should be directed at offenders assessed as medium to high risk of reoffending. There is evidence to show that when the risk principle is not adhered to the effect of treatment is diminished, with expensive resources directed unnecessarily at low risk offenders (Palmer, McGuire, Hatcher, Hounsome, Bilby, & Hollin, 2008). Andrews and Bonta (1994) also formulated the *need principle*, drawing the distinction between *criminogenic* and *non-criminogenic* needs. Criminogenic needs are the dynamic subset of the

---

1 Indiscriminate targeting of treatment programs is counterproductive in reducing recidivism: medium- to high-risk offenders should be selected and programs should focus on criminogenic targets.

2 The type of treatment program is important with stronger evidence for structured behavioral and multimodal approaches than for less focused approaches.

3 The most successful studies, while behavioral in nature, include a cognitive component to focus on the offender's attitudes and beliefs.

4 Treatment programs should be designed to engage high levels of offender responsivity.

5 Treatment programs conducted in the community have a stronger effect than residential programs. While residential programs can be effective, they should be linked structurally with community-based interventions.

6 The most effective programs have high treatment integrity in that they are closely monitored for compliance with the treatment model, and they are conducted by trained staff.

Figure 17.1 Characteristics of effective treatments.

offender's overall risk level: they are dynamic factors because they can change and any such changes impact on the likelihood of further offending. Non-criminogenic needs, such as self-image or headaches, are also dynamic and changeable but any changes are not associated with the reduced reoffending (which does not mean that they should be dismissed as unimportant). Static factors, such as criminal history and family background, are also related to the probability of further offending but, unlike dynamic factors, cannot be changed.

Thus, assessment for treatment intended to reduce offending must be concerned with dynamic needs and be able to discriminate between criminogenic and non-criminogenic needs. Further, if the assessment is directed toward a particular program, then the assessment may be able both to screen for suitability for treatment and, if sensitive to change, inform program evaluation.

The practice that has grown around the evidence from the meta-analyses has become known as "What Works" (McGuire, 1995, 2002). The increasing sophistication of this research is reflected in the growth in knowledge about what works for specific types of offending, such as reducing acts of aggression and violence (McGuire, 2008) and sexual offenses (Lösel & Schmucker, 2005). These findings can inform the design of interventions for use with offenders that may have significantly greater than chance impact on rates of offending. The "What Works" approach should not stand in isolation from other initiatives. There are advantages to nesting work with individual offenders within, say, school-based programs or family interventions. However, to return to individually focused treatment to reduce offending, there are three areas to consider; these three are *assessment*, *treatment design*, and *treatment management*.

ASSESSMENT

The risk principle – that the intensity of intervention should be varied according to the risk level of the young offender – gives rise to the need to accurately assess the likelihood that a young offender will commit further offenses. Likewise, the need principle – that interventions should focus on dynamic criminogenic needs – requires the reliable identification of the criminogenic areas of an individual's life. Over recent years, there has been a growing sophistication in the assessment of risk and need. Indeed, the offender assessment field has witnessed a shift away from the use of clinical assessment, whereby professionals draw on their training and experience to derive a risk assessment, to the development of evidence-based, actuarial, structured approaches to measuring risk and need.

Within adult services risk/need assessment tools such as the Level of Service Inventory – Revised (LSI-R; Andrews & Bonta, 1995) and the Offender Assessment System (OASys; Home Office, 1999; Howard, 2006) have changed the way that custodial and community services establish an offender's risk and criminogenic needs. As measurement becomes more refined so criminal justice agencies are able to plan interventions and offender management with greater precision. Similar developments in assessment have taken place within youth offending services. For example, the adult LSI-R has been adapted for use with 12 to 17 year olds: the Youth Level of Service/Case Management Inventory (YLS/CMI; Hoge & Andrews, 2002) is a 42-item assessment completed by the practitioner on the basis of offender interviews, file material, and other available assessments. The YLS/CMI gives an overall risk/need score and an associated risk banding, low, medium, high, very high, which indicates the likelihood of future reconviction. Eight category scores are also produced – prior and current offenses/dispositions, family circumstances/ parenting, education/employment, peer relations, substance abuse, leisure/recreation, personality/behavior, and attitudes/orientation – which provide a more detailed assessment of the young person's criminogenic needs. The outputs of the YLS/CMI can be used to guide the courts in their sentencing and to inform practitioners with regard to the management of the young offender through their custodial or community sentence.

Within the United Kingdom, the Youth Justice Board for England and Wales (YJB) have adapted their own assessment tool, *Asset*, to guide the assessment of individual, lifestyle, familial, and community factors. The main section of Asset, like the YLS/CMI, is completed by the practitioner, but there is also a self-assessment section for the young offenders to complete, along with an assessment of risk of harm in those instances where there are indicators that serious harm may be an issue. A complementary referral and assessment framework, *Onset*, has also been developed by the YJB for use with young people at risk of antisocial or delinquent behavior (as opposed to those who are already on the offending pathway).

Tools such as the YLS/CMI and Asset have been developed through close examination of research literature exploring risk factors for offending, as discussed above, plus any factors that may have a protective effect. Once identified, the risk factors are studied in a large cohort of offenders over a period of time (usually 2 years) to determine how much each factor contributes to offending behavior. On the basis of this research evidence weightings are then given to the various factors: the factors that contribute more to the likelihood of future offending receive a greater weighting than those that contribute less. A risk score for an individual is determined by summing the weighted risk factor scores and then making a subsequent adjustment if any protective factors are present.

The YLS/CMI and *Asset* have both been evaluated to confirm their predictive utility among the general young offender population. *Asset* has been found to predict reconviction with up to 70% accuracy (Baker, Jones, Roberts, & Merrington, 2003; Baker, Jones, Merrington, & Roberts, 2005). This level of accuracy, the authors argue, is similar to the predictive accuracies found with evaluations of adult risk assessment tools. The YLS/CMI has been found to have predictive efficacy in relation to general, violent, and non-violent recidivism (Olver, Stockdale, & Wormith, 2009).

Evidence-based, structured risk, and need assessments for young offenders can be used to inform service delivery: for example, young offenders can be allocated to specific interventions, say for alcohol use or anger management, on the basis of their assessed criminogenic need. In addition, assessment of dynamic risk factors that are changeable over time can be repeated to assess for change across time to evaluate the impact of the intervention at both an individual and cohort level. The outcomes from such evaluations are important in refining the development and delivery of interventions for young offenders.

TREATMENT DESIGN

The "What Works?" research gave rise to the articulation of several principles for effective practice: (i) focus on criminogenic need to reduce risk of reoffending; (ii) use a structured approach; (iii) aim to change both cognition and behavior. These principles are further informed by two other findings from the meta-analyses. The first finding concerns the theoretical orientation of successful treatment programs: Lipsey (1992) comments that "More structured and focused treatments (e.g. behavioral, skill-orientated) and multimodal treatments seem to be more effective than the less structured and focused approaches (e.g. counseling)" (p. 123). Andrews et al. (1990) take this finding a step further in proposing that some therapeutic approaches are ill-advised for general use with offenders. They suggest that "Traditional psychodynamic and nondirective client-centred therapies are to be avoided within general samples of offenders" (p. 376).

The high-effect interventions are behavioral in orientation and they include a cognitive component to address the "Attitudes, values, and beliefs that support anti-social behavior" (Gendreau & Andrews, 1990, p. 182). Thus, alongside the skills the young person may need to develop in order to avoid crime and engage in pro-social activities, interventions should aim to address offenders' antisocial thinking. For example, offenders may not consider the effects of their actions on others, including those who directly suffer as a result of the crime as well as their family, dependents, and so on. It follows that working to help offenders mature in moral responsibility and empathy toward others may be a step toward reducing offending. Roberts and Camasso (1991) also stress the importance of working with the families of young offenders – a point reinforced by the findings of Piquero et al. (2009).

The second finding relates to the style of delivery of an intervention. Andrews and Bonta (1994) refer to the *responsivity principle* in describing the advantages of delivering interventions in a manner that is appropriate to the capabilities of the offender. As well as individual differences in intelligence, verbal ability, and so on, young offenders will not all come from the same social and cultural backgrounds. It cannot therefore be assumed that all young offenders have a high degree of verbal ability, or high levels of personal insight, or an aptitude to benefit from in-depth group discussion.

Thus, in order to design interventions to which young offenders will be responsive, these issues should be addressed by engaging offenders in a way that is commensurate with their individual ability and learning style. In practice, this indicates an active style of interaction, using role-play and dynamic exercises, rather than lots of talking. The design and delivery of the intervention should be sensitive to the offenders' gender and culture in order to be engaging and to be seen to be relevant. As shown by Blanchette and Brown (2006), it is unwise to assume that risk, needs, and responsivity are the same for women as for men. When responsivity is increased this maximizes the likelihood of the success of the intervention.

Offending Behavior Programs

As the "What Works?" findings grew in influence the method that emerged of delivering interventions that were structured, focused on criminogenic needs, and could be delivered with consistency drew on the mainstream clinical psychology literature regarding manualized treatment programs (Wilson, 1996). The first manualized offending behavior program to be adopted for widespread use was Reasoning and Rehabilitation (R&R; Ross, Fabiano, & Ewles, 1988). R&R is a cognitive-behavioral program aimed at reducing offending, drawing on research showing associations between cognition and offending (Ross & Fabiano, 1985). R&R applies methods such as modeling and role-play to encourage offenders to think constructively and in ways that are likely to promote social behavior. The outcome evidence suggests that R&R is successful in reducing rates of offending (Tong & Farrington, 2006).

As the use of offending behavior programs increased so they became more widely used with a range of offenders (Hollin & Palmer, 2006), including violent offenders (Polaschek, 2006). With particular regard to aggressive young offenders, *Aggression Replacement Training* provides an excellent example of a program-based intervention.

Aggression Replacement Training (ART)

ART was developed during the 1980s (Goldstein & Glick, 1987), later substantially revised (Goldstein, Glick, & Gibbs, 1998), and further refined in light of the increasing practice and evidence base (Goldstein, Nensén, Daleflod, & Kalt, 2004). ART consists of the three components of *Skillstreaming*, *Anger Control Training*, and *Moral Reasoning Training*, all drawn from cognitive-behavioral theory and practice (Hollin, 2004).

Skillstreaming develops the interpersonal skills that will allow the young person to use socially acceptable behaviors rather than destructive, violent behavior. Anger Control Training assists the young person to identify the triggers for their anger, to gain awareness of their own angry thoughts and reactions, and to develop effective coping and social problem solving strategies to control their anger. Moral Reasoning Training is concerned with the values the young person places on their own behavior and that of other people. This phase of ART uses established methods of cognitive and behavioral change to develop the young person's moral reasoning skills and to broaden their social perspective taking. Overall, the outcome evidence suggests that ART is an effective method by which to reduce aggressive behavior (Goldstein, 2004).

TREATMENT MANAGEMENT

The meta-analyses strongly indicate that *treatment integrity* is a feature of effective programs. The notion of treatment integrity includes the professional and organization structures and practices that are necessary to ensure that treatment is designed and delivered to the highest possible standard (Hollin, 1995). In the case of established treatment programs, such as ART or R&R, high levels of treatment integrity are achieved when the intervention is delivered in a way that is consistent with the intentions of the program developers. When treatment integrity is taken seriously it cuts across many aspects of the organizational functioning of the treatment service, including management of standards of staff training and supervision, quality assurance procedures, and a flow of management information to allow continued improvement of services and to detect failings in delivery (Hollin, Epps, & Kendrick, 1995; Serin & Preston, 2001).

When an established intervention is implemented within an organization there are various barriers to its continued use in the way it was intended to be applied (Perepletchikova, Hilt, Chereji, & Kazdin, 2009). The net effect of low integrity, typically, is *treatment drift*, where the focus of the intervention gradually shifts over time, or *treatment non-compliance*, in which there are misallocations to the program or it is changed in an ad hoc manner by individual practitioners. If organizational efforts to ensure high levels of treatment integrity are made in the spirit of consultation rather than scrutiny then there may be benefits in terms of staff retention (Aarons, Sommerfeld, Hecht, Silovsky, & Chaffin, 2009).

CONCLUSION

The impact of research, particularly the longitudinal and the "What Works?" studies, have given rise to a wave of optimism in services for young people at risk of slipping into a life of crime. There is much that remains to be learned: for example, a greater understanding of gender differences is a priority for research (Kjelsberg & Friestad, 2009). Nonetheless, a renewed confidence in our ability to design effective strategies to reduce juvenile crime is manifest at several levels: (i) at the level of primary prevention enough is known so that it is not unreasonable to think in terms of a national prevention strategy to divert children from a life of crime (Farrington & Coid, 2003; Farrington & Welsh, 2007); (ii) at secondary prevention, the research has helped define the risk factors predictive of crime so that, given accurate assessment, services can be directed to at-risk young people; (iii) at tertiary prevention, the delivery of effective services such as offending behavior programs to offenders is achieving notable successes (Hollin & Palmer, 2009), although more work specifically with young offenders would be welcome.

The gains to be made from effective prevention strategies, at all three levels, are significant. A reduction in crime not only spares victims the personal effects of crime, there are also significant economic benefits associated with effective crime reduction. A crime prevented results in a reduction on criminal justice costs as well as a reduction in costs to health and social service budgets (Cohen, 2005). In addition, for the young person themselves a life outside the criminal justice system may be significantly happier then one locked within it.

REFERENCES

Aarons, G.A., Sommerfeld, D.H., Hecht, D.B., Silovsky, J.F., & Chaffin, M.J. (2009). The impact of evidence-based practice implementation and fidelity monitoring on staff turnover: Evidence for a protective effect. *Journal of Consulting and Clinical Psychology*, *77*, 270–280.

Akhtar, N., & Bradley, E.J. (1991). Social information processing deficits of aggressive children: Present findings and implications for social skills training. *Clinical Psychology Review*, *11*, 621–644.

Andrews, D.A., & Bonta, J.L. (1994). *The psychology of criminal conduct*. Cincinnati, OH: Anderson.

Andrews, D.A., & Bonta, J.L. (1995). *Level of Service Inventory-Revised Manual*. North Tonawanda, NY: Multi-Heath Systems.

Andrews, D.A., Zinger, I., Hoge, R.D., Bonta, J., Gendreau, P., & Cullen, F.T. (1990). Does correctional treatment work? A clinically relevant and informed meta-analysis. *Criminology*, *28*, 369–404.

Baker, K., Jones, S., Merrington, S., & Roberts, C. (2005). *Further development of Asset*. London: Youth Justice Board for England and Wales.

Baker, K., Jones, S., Roberts, C., & Merrington, S. (2003). *The evaluation of the validity and reliability of the Youth Justice Board's Assessment for Young Offenders: Findings from the first two years of ASSET*. London: Youth Justice Board for England and Wales.

Blanchette, K., & Brown, S.L. (2006). *The assessment and treatment of women offenders: An integrative approach*. Chichester, UK: John Wiley & Sons, Ltd.

Cohen, M.A. (2005). *The costs of crime and justice*. London: Routledge.

Crick, N.R., & Dodge, K.A. (1996). Social information – processing mechanisms in reactive and proactive aggression. *Child Development*, *67*, 993–1002.

Eysenck, H.J. (1977). *Crime and personality* (3rd ed.). London: Routledge & Kegan Paul.

Farrington, D.P. (2003). Key results from the first 40 years of the Cambridge Study in Delinquent Development. In T.P. Thornberry & M.D. Krohn (Eds.), *Taking stock of delinquency: An overview of findings from contemporary longitudinal studies* (pp. 137–183). New York: Kluwer/Plenum.

Farrington, D.P., & Coid, J.W. (Eds.) (2003). *Early prevention of adult antisocial behaviour*. Cambridge: Cambridge University Press.

Farrington, D.P., Coid, J.W., Harnett, L.M., Jolliffe, D., Soteriou, N., Turner, R.E., & West, D.J. (2006). *Criminal careers up to age 50 and life success up to age 48: New findings from the Cambridge Study in Delinquent Development* (2nd ed.). Home Office Research Study 299. London: Home Office Research, Development, and Statistics Directorate.

Farrington, D.P., & Welsh, B.C. (2007). *Saving children from a life of crime: Early risk factors and effective interventions*. Oxford: Oxford University Press.

Garrett, C.G. (1985). Effects of residential treatment on adjudicated delinquents: A meta-analysis. *Journal of Research in Crime and Delinquency, 22*, 287–308.

Gendreau, P., & Andrews, D.A. (1990). Tertiary prevention: What the meta-analyses of the offender treatment literature tell us about "What Works". *Canadian Journal of Criminology, 32*, 173–184.

Goldstein, A.P. (2004). Evaluations of effectiveness. In A.P. Goldstein, R. Nensén, B. Daleflod, & M. Kalt (Eds.), *New perspectives on Aggression Replacement Training* (pp. 231–244). Chichester, UK: John Wiley & Sons, Ltd.

Goldstein, A.P., & Glick, B. (1987). *Aggression Replacement Training: A comprehensive intervention for adolescent youth*. Champaign, IL: Research Press.

Goldstein, A.P., Glick, B., & Gibbs, J.C. (1998). *Aggression Replacement Training* (rev. ed.). Champaign, IL: Research Press.

Goldstein, A.P., Nensén, R., Daleflod, B., & Kalt, M. (Eds.) (2004). *New perspectives on Aggression Replacement Training*. Chichester, UK: John Wiley & Sons, Ltd.

Hoge, R.D., & Andrews, D.A. (2002). *Youth Level of Service/Case Management Inventory (YLS/CMI: User's manual)*. North Tonawanda, NY: Multi-Health Systems.

Hollin, C.R. (1993). Advances in the psychological treatment of delinquent behaviour. *Criminal Behaviour and Mental Health, 3*, 142–157.

Hollin, C.R. (1994). Designing effective rehabilitation programmes for young offenders. *Psychology, Crime and Law, 1*, 193–199.

Hollin, C.R. (1995). The meaning and implications of "programme integrity." In J. McGuire (Ed.), *What Works: Reducing reoffending* (pp. 195–208). Chichester, UK: John Wiley & Sons, Ltd.

Hollin, C.R. (2004). Aggression Replacement Training: The cognitive-behavioral context. In A.P. Goldstein, R. Nensén, B. Daleflod, & M. Kalt (Eds.), *New perspectives on Aggression Replacement Training* (pp. 3–19). Chichester, UK: John Wiley & Sons, Ltd.

Hollin, C.R., Epps, K., & Kendrick, D. (1995). *Managing behavioural treatment: Policy and practice with delinquent adolescents*. London: Routledge.

Hollin, C.R., & Palmer, E.J. (Eds.) (2006). *Offending behaviour programmes: Development, application, and controversies*. Chichester, UK: John Wiley & Sons, Ltd.

Hollin, C.R., & Palmer, E.J. (2009). Cognitive skills programmes for offenders. *Psychology, Crime & Law, 15*, 147–164.

Home Office (1999). *Effective Practice Initiative: A Joint Risk/Needs Assessment System for the Prison and Probation Services*. Probation Circular PC16/1999. London: Home Office.

Howard, P. (2006). *The Offender Assessment System: An evaluation of the second pilot*. Home Office Findings 278. London: Home Office.

Iwaniec, D. (2006). *The emotionally abused and neglected child*. Chichester, UK: John Wiley & Sons, Ltd.

Jolliffe, D., & Farrington, D.P. (2007). The relationship between low empathy and self-reported offending. *Legal and Criminological Psychology*, *12*, 265–286.

Jolliffe, D., & Farrington, D.P. (2009). A systematic review of the relationship between childhood impulsiveness and later violence. In M. McMurran & R. Howard (Eds.), *Personality, personality disorder and violence* (pp. 41–61). Chichester, UK: John Wiley & Sons, Ltd.

Kjelsberg, E., & Friestad, C. (2009). Exploring gender issues in the development of conduct disorder in adolescence to criminal behaviour in adulthood. *International Journal of Law and Psychiatry*, *32*, 18–22.

Lahey, B.B., Loeber, R., Frick, P.J., Hart, E.L., Applegate, B., Zhang, Q., Green, S.M., & Russoet, M.F. (1995). Four-year longitudinal study of conduct disorder in boys: Patterns and predictors of persistence. *Journal of Abnormal Psychology*, *104*, 83–93.

LeMarquand, D., & Tremblay, R.E. (2004). Delinquency prevention in schools. In C.R. Hollin (Ed.), *The essential handbook of offender assessment and treatment* (pp. 237–258). Chichester, UK: John Wiley & Sons, Ltd.

Lipsey, M.W. (1992). Juvenile delinquency treatment: A meta-analytic inquiry into the variability of effects. In T.D. Cook, H. Cooper, D.S. Cordray, H. Hartmann, L.V. Hedges, R.J. Light, T.A. Louis, & F. Mosteller (Eds.), *Meta-analysis for explanation: A casebook* (pp. 83–127). New York: Russell Sage Foundation.

Lipsey, M.W. (1995). What do we learn from 400 studies on the effectiveness of treatment with juvenile delinquents? In J. McGuire (Ed.), *What Works: Reducing reoffending* (pp. 63–111). Chichester, UK: John Wiley & Sons, Ltd.

Lösel, F. (1995). Increasing consensus in the evaluation of offender rehabilitation: Lessons from recent research syntheses. *Psychology, Crime & Law*, *2*, 19–39.

Lösel, F., & Schmucker, M. (2005). The effectiveness of treatment for sexual offenders: A comprehensive meta-analysis. *Journal of Experimental Criminology*, *1*, 117–146.

Marsh, A.A., & Blair R.J.R. (2008). Deficits in facial affect recognition among antisocial populations: A meta-analysis. *Neuroscience & Biobehavioral Reviews*, *32*, 454–465.

McGuire, J. (Ed.) (1995). *What Works: Reducing reoffending*. Chichester, UK: John Wiley & Sons, Ltd.

McGuire, J. (Ed.) (2002). *Offender rehabilitation and treatment: Effective programmes and policies to reduce reoffending*. Chichester, UK: John Wiley & Sons, Ltd.

McGuire, J. (2008). A review of effective interventions for reducing aggression and violence. *Philosophical Transactions of the Royal Society B*, *363*, 2577–2597.

McMurran, M., & McGuire, J. (Eds.) (2005). *Social problem solving and offending: Evidence, evaluation and evolution*. Chichester, UK: John Wiley & Sons, Ltd.

Moffitt, T.E. (1993). Adolescence-limited and life-course-persistent antisocial behavior: A developmental taxonomy. *Psychological Review*, *100*, 674–701.

Moffitt, T.E. (2003). Life-course persistent and adolescent-limited antisocial behavior: A 10-year research review and a research agenda. In B.B. Lahey, T.E. Moffitt, & A. Caspi (Eds.), *Causes of conduct disorder and juvenile delinquency* (pp. 49–75). New York: Guilford Press.

Moffitt, T.E., Caspi, C., Rutter, M., & Silva, P.A. (2001). *Sex differences in antisocial behaviour: Conduct disorder, delinquency, and violence in the Dunedin Longitudinal Study.* Cambridge: Cambridge University Press.

Olver, M.E., Stockdale, K.C., & Wormith, J.S. (2009). Risk assessment with young offenders: A meta-analysis of three assessment measures. *Criminal Justice and Behavior, 36,* 329–353.

Palmer, E.J., McGuire, J., Hatcher, R.M., Hounsome, J.C., Bilby, C.A.L., & Hollin, C.R. (2008). The importance of appropriate allocation to offending behavior programs. *International Journal of Offender Therapy and Comparative Criminology, 52,* 206–221.

Perepletchikova, F., Hilt, L.M., Chereji, E., & Kazdin, A.E. (2009). Barriers to implementing treatment integrity procedures: Survey of treatment outcome researchers. *Journal of Consulting and Clinical Psychology, 77,* 212–218.

Piquero, A.R., Farrington, D.P., Welsh, B.C., Tremblay, R., & Jennings, W.G. (2009). Effects of early family/parent training programs on antisocial behavior and delinquency. *Journal of Experimental Criminology, 5,* 83–120.

Polaschek, D.L.L. (2006). Violent offender programmes: Concept, theory, and practice. In C.R. Hollin & E.J. Palmer (Eds.), *Offending behaviour programmes: Development, application, and controversies* (pp. 113–154). Chichester, UK: John Wiley & Sons, Ltd.

Roberts, A.R., & Camasso, M.J. (1991). The effect of juvenile offender treatment programs on recidivism: A meta-analysis of 46 studies. *Notre Dame Journal of Law, Ethics, and Public Policy, 5,* 421–441.

Roe, S., & Ashe, J. (2008). *Young people and crime: Findings from the 2006 Offending, Crime and Justice Survey.* Home Office Statistical Bulletin, 09/08. London: Home Office.

Ross, R.R., & Fabiano, E.A. (1985). *Time to think: A cognitive model of delinquency prevention and offender rehabilitation.* Johnson City, TN: Institute of Social Sciences and Arts.

Ross, R.R., Fabiano, E.A., & Ewles, C.D. (1988). Reasoning and rehabilitation. *International Journal of Offender Therapy and Comparative Criminology, 32,* 29–35.

Serin, R.C., & Preston, D.L. (2001). Designing, implementing and managing treatment programs for violent offenders. In G.A. Bernfeld, D.P. Farrington, & A.W. Leschied (Eds.), *Offender rehabilitation in practice: Implementing and evaluating effective programs* (pp. 205–221). Chichester, UK: John Wiley & Sons, Ltd.

Smith, D.J. (2007). Crime and the life course. In M. Maguire, R. Morgan, & R. Reiner (Eds.), *The Oxford handbook of criminology* (4th ed., pp. 641–681). Oxford: Oxford University Press.

Stith, S.M., Liu, T., Davies, C., Boykin, E.L., Alder, M.C., Harris, J.M., Som, A., McPherson, M., & Dees, J.E.M.E.G. (2009). Risk factors in child maltreatment: A meta-analytic review of the literature. *Aggression and Violent Behavior, 14,* 13–29.

Swaffer, T., & Hollin, C. (2000). Anger and impulse control. In R. Newell & K. Gournay (Eds.), *Mental health nursing: An evidence-based approach* (pp. 265–289). Edinburgh: Churchill Livingstone.

Swaffer, T., & Hollin, C.R. (2001). Anger and general health in young offenders. *Journal of Forensic Psychiatry*, *12*, 90–103.

Swenson, C.C., Henggeler, S.W., & Schoenwald, S.K. (2004). Family based treatments. In C.R. Hollin (Ed.), *The essential handbook of offender assessment and treatment* (pp. 79–94). Chichester, UK: John Wiley & Sons, Ltd.

Thomas, A., Chess, S., & Birch, H.G. (1968). *Temperament and behavior disorders in children*. New York: New York University Press.

Tong, L.S.J., & Farrington, D.P. (2006). How effective is the "Reasoning and Rehabilitation" programme in reducing re-offending? A meta-analysis of evaluations in four countries. *Psychology, Crime & Law*, *12*, 3–24.

Wells, L.E., & Rankin, J.H. (1991). Families and delinquency: A meta-analysis of the impact of broken homes. *Social Problems*, *38*, 71–93.

Widom, C.S., & White, H.R. (1997). Problem behaviours in abused and neglected children grown up: Prevalence and co-occurrence of substance use, crime, and violence. *Criminal Behaviour and Mental Health*, *7*, 287–310.

Wilson, G.T. (1996). Manual-based treatments: The clinical application of research findings. *Behaviour Research and Therapy*, *34*, 294–314.

18

The Ethics of Risk Assessment

JAMES VESS, TONY WARD AND PAMELA M. YATES

INTRODUCTION

Ethical and knowledge-related values are embedded in the practice arena and inform both assessment and treatment decision-making (Day & Ward, 2010). Failure to take into account the ethical principles that underpin such decisions can occur because of lack of knowledge of the core ethical values they express. For example, standards advocating respect for offenders' confidentiality and consent matter because they underpin their autonomy and basic well-being, fundamental aspects of human agency. When a clinician fails to adequately inform a sex offender of his treatment options or of the reasons for undergoing assessment, crucial information required to make an informed decision will be missing. In a nutshell, ethical concepts such as human rights and the values they protect are important because they ensure offenders are accorded the respect due to them as fellow members of the human race. Respect they should not forfeit, although in forensic contexts their potential for harm needs to be carefully balanced with concern for their own interests and wants (Vess, 2009; Ward & Birgden, 2007).

Forensic risk assessments take place in a variety of cases and legal contexts, including sentencing and release decisions by courts and parole boards, security ratings and treatment access in correctional settings, and recommendations to judicial decision-makers in situations ranging from civil commitment to child custody conditions. The primary focus of this chapter is ethical considerations in current risk assessment practices with violent and sexual offenders, although many of the issues

Assessments in Forensic Practice: A Handbook, First Edition. Edited by Kevin D. Browne, Anthony R. Beech, Leam A. Craig, and Shihning Chou.
© 2017 John Wiley & Sons Ltd. Published 2017 by John Wiley & Sons Ltd.

will have broader application in forensic risk assessment. This focus results in part from the most recent generation of legislative initiatives to protect the public from the perceived threat posed by violent and especially sex offenders, which has been accompanied by a burgeoning empirical research literature as well as a vigorous professional debate over issues of the legality and ethics of risk assessments that can weigh heavily in decisions that must balance public safety and individual human rights. The perspective taken in this chapter is shaped by a review of the current professional literature and from the professional experiences of the authors in forensic risk assessment practice. We concentrate our comments on the ethical implications of risk assessment practices, particularly those relevant for human rights, in the context of a description of risk assessment. For a broader treatment of ethical issues related to sex offenders, the articles by Vess (2008), Day and Ward (2010), Ward and Salmon (2009), and Ward and Birgden (2007) should be consulted.

ETHICS AND HUMAN RIGHTS

To understand the ethical issues posed by recent legislation, it is necessary to have a clearly articulated framework for understanding human rights. Ward and colleagues have discussed human rights in correctional clinical practice, and have specifically applied their model to the treatment of sex offenders (Ward & Birgden, 2007; Ward, Gannon, & Birgden, 2007). Drawing from the work of Freeden (1991), these authors develop a conceptual model in which human rights serve a protective function, so that individuals can pursue their own intentions in creating meaningful lives. Human rights thereby create a space within which individuals can lead lives that maintain a basic sense of human dignity.

In the model presented by Ward, Gannon, and Vess (2009), human rights reflect the core values of freedom and well-being, based on Gewirth's (1998) assertion that these conditions are necessary for the attainment of the individual's personal goals. Freedom involves the ability to act on the basis of one's particular intentions, and well-being involves conditions that support basic levels of physical and mental functioning, as well as access to necessary social, material, and psychological resources. The structure of human rights begins with these broad, intangible core values and moves toward more specific human rights objects, as formulated by Orend (2002), including personal security, personal freedom, material subsistence, elemental equality, and social recognition. It is in support of these human rights objects that the more tangible rights delineated by current human rights policies are defined, such as freedom from discrimination, the right to a fair trial, and due process of law (Ward & Birgden, 2007). The utility of this model for forensic clinical practice is that all professional ethics can be seen as serving to protect underlying human rights, and all human rights can be seen as stemming from the core values of freedom and well-being (Ward et al., 2009). Human rights confer both entitlements and obligations on individuals and therefore create pressure on the community as a whole to ensure that each person is not subject to unreasonable restrictions on his or her actions. Furthermore, while practitioners are obligated to take the welfare of the community into account when working with sex offenders, they also have a responsibility to act in ways that protect the core interests of the offenders themselves.

RISK ASSESSMENT MEASURES

An important, and in our view often under-appreciated, ethical issue, concerns the duty of practitioners to ensure that the measures they use meet the highest scientific standards possible. Furthermore, interpretations of data collected by assessment measures should be made with their limitations clearly in mind, and such deficits explicitly communicated to the relevant forensic actors. In this respect the science of risk assessment ought to be conducted within a justifiable and comprehensive ethical framework.

Applying the above human rights foundation of professional ethics to the area of forensic risk assessment, the key issue is the potential threat to the freedom and well-being of both the individual being assessed and those whom he or she may harm as a result of the findings of the assessment. The underlying concern here is the limited level of predictive accuracy of current methods for assessing risk. There are several aspects to this concern. One is the distinction between the reliability and the predictive validity or accuracy of risk assessment measures. Reliability is a statistical term used to refer to the consistency of results obtained from a measure. There are a variety of ways in which reliability is evaluated or characterized, including internal consistency (Do the items of the instrument correlate with each other and the total score?), test-retest (Are the results consistent from one point in time to another?), and interrater reliability (Do two different assessors obtain similar results on the measure?).

For the purposes of applied risk assessment with offenders, the most immediate concern regarding reliability is interrater reliability. The key issue here is whether different assessment experts arrive at similar findings regarding risk, using standardized assessment measures. Actuarial measures such as the STATIC-99 (Hanson & Thornton, 2000) have demonstrated consistently high levels of interrater reliability, largely because of the highly specific scoring criteria involved in this form of standardized assessment measure. Doren (2004) states:

> *A major reason these instruments have made it to the head of their class is the degree and findings of research to date concerning their accuracy. For instance, the interrater reliability for the RRASOR has been studied on at least seven occasions with each study showing very supportive results (Barbaree, Setto, Lanton, & Peacock, 2001; Bartosh, Garby, Lewis, & Gray, 2003; de Vogel, de Ruiter, van Beek, & Mead, 2004;*

Harris et al., 2003; Langton, 2003; Sjostedt, & Langstrom, 2001, 2002). The Static-99 has demonstrated even more frequently supportive results (Barbaree et al. 2001; Bartosch et al. 2003; de Vogel et al., 2004; Hanson, 2001; Harris et al., 2003; Langton, 2003; Sjostedt & Langstrom, 2001; Wong et al., 2000). Neither instrument has ever to date failed to show a high degree of interrater reliability when empirically studied. (p. 26)

Standardized measures of dynamic risk factors such as the STABLE-2000 and STABLE-2007 have also demonstrated adequate interrater reliability when administered by trained assessors according to specified scoring criteria (Hanson & Harris, 2000, 2001).

Predictive Accuracy

Examples of measures with research evidence of predictive validity include the Violence Risk Appraisal Guide (VRAG) (Harris, Rice, & Quinsey, 1993), the Sex Offender Risk Appraisal Guide (SORAG) (Quinsey, Harris, Rice, & Cormier, 1998), the Rapid Risk Assessment of Sexual Offense Recidivism (RRASOR) (Hanson, 1997), and the STATIC-99 (Hanson & Thornton, 2000). Actuarial measures such as these form the foundation of the best-validated risk assessment procedures currently available. Professionals practicing in the role of risk assessment expert must know, and be able to convey to the judicial decision-maker, the accuracy of the measures they use to assess risk. But how accurate are the currently available measures, and under what circumstances are they accurate? It is important to recognize that none of the statistical indices yet developed can completely answer the question of how accurate a risk assessment measure is (Gottfredson & Moriarty, 2006). Some researchers (e.g., Quinsey, Harris, Rice, & Cormier, 2006) argue that Relative Operating Characteristic (ROC) analysis offers the best index of statistical accuracy because it is independent of the base-rate variations in different samples of offenders.

ROC analysis is widely used in medical and scientific research to assess the performance of a diagnostic test. ROC analysis produces a curve that is a graphic illustration of the test's performance to establish the best cut-off point for making a diagnosis or prediction. This procedure was developed in the early days of radar and sonar detection used in the Second World War, from which the name is derived, and later applied to other fields. The ROC curve is produced by plotting the false positive rate and the true positive rate associated with each score of a test (such as the Static-99). The area under this curve (AUC) then provides a value that reflects the predictive accuracy of the test. A test with no predictive accuracy (no greater than chance) results in a diagonal line across the graph and an AUC value of .50, while a perfectly accurate test produces an AUC value of 1.0. Typical levels of predictive accuracy observed for measures of sexual recidivism range from around .60 to above .70, and are considered to provide moderate levels of accuracy.

Harris and Rice (2003) state:

> *The best available statistic to express the true accuracy of a test comes for the Relative Operating Characteristic or ROC, which is a plot of the hit rate (or sensitivity) as a function of the test's false alarm rate (1–specificity). ROCs illustrate a test universal – there is always a trade-off between sensitivity and specificity. Unless the test is modified to increase its accuracy, sensitivity cannot be improved without worsening specificity (and vice versa). The area subtended by the ROC is a good overall index of the test's accuracy; several studies have shown that this area statistic is independent of the base rate and serves as a good way to summarize and compare predictive accuracies. (p. 200)*

Yet others argue convincingly that the base rate of sexual recidivism cannot be ignored in considering the accuracy of a given measure in a particular application. The base rate is the frequency with which an event occurs within a given sample or population. In the current context, it refers to the frequency with which violent or sexual offenders reoffend. Knowing the relevant base rate, and its impact on the accuracy of risk predictions based on various measures as discussed below, is important for making sense of the various statements made about the risk measures used in a particular case.

What is clear is that indices that are sensitive to base rates and those that are not can lead to dramatically different conclusions concerning the value of risk assessment measures (Gottfredson & Moriarty, 2006). Campbell (2003) addresses this issue directly in the context of actuarial risk assessment of sex offenders for legal proceedings. He questions:

> *If informed that a probability that the score of a randomly selected recidivist exceeds the score of a randomly selected non-recidivist, on a given actuarial instrument, can this information assist the trier of fact? Does identifying the ROC values of the Static-99 and RRASOR as 0.71 and 0.68 respectively (Hanson & Thornton, 2000) aid decision-making in commitment proceedings? Possibly, then, reporting raw scores and corresponding recidivism rates, ROC values, regression analyzes, and correlational data misleads a trier of fact. (p. 270)*

Different samples of sexual offenders reoffend at substantially different rates, and this rate will affect the accuracy of an actuarial measure when used with different groups of offenders. Using the optimal cut-off score for distinguishing sexual recidivists from non-recidivists reported by Sjöstedt and Langström (2001), Campbell (2003) reports that 51% of the sexual recidivists would be missed (i.e., the false negative rate), and 31% of those predicted to be recidivists would not reoffend (i.e., the false positive rate). What is crucial to note in this situation is that as the base rate changes, the rates of false positives and false negatives for a given score on the prediction measure will also change. This is why it is incomplete, and potentially misleading, to report indices like ROC values with the implication that they provide sufficient accuracy information without reference to the base rate. While these figures are associated with a significant improvement over predictions made without using empirically derived actuarial risk measures, they specify the degree of uncertainty still inherent in this approach.

Experience in court and parole board hearings in cases of sexual and violent offenders suggests that critical information about the limitations of accuracy with current risk assessment measures is often not made clear by those reporting the risk. This violates both scientific and ethical norms related to autonomy. A number of different statistical properties have been used to convey information about accuracy, including sensitivity, specificity, correlation, effect size, and ROC analysis. Without sufficient clarification of the relative accuracy of available risk measures, offenders face the risk of "trial by mathematics" (Tribe, 1971, as cited by Janus & Prentky, 2003, p. 18). Assuming that the meaning of a particular statistic is explained to the court, it remains uncertain as to whether this information actually advances the court's understanding of a measure's accuracy or a risk factor's importance in any meaningful way.

In light of the margin for error inherent in current actuarial measures, more individualized risk assessments are desirable from both scientific and ethical perspectives, preferably those that take into account dynamic and etiological factors. However, adjusted actuarial assessments (i.e., actuarial assessments adjusted by considering dynamic factors and other clinical information) may represent unstandardized procedures that can be conducted in an inconsistent, ad hoc way. This criticism may be minimized by considering only factors clearly associated with increased rates of sexual recidivism in the empirical research literature in the formulation of risk in an individual case. It is noted, however, that "Without a well defined decision-making procedure for adjusted actuarial assessment, these improvised judgements can also be expected to vary inconsistently from one case to another" (Campbell, 2003, p. 275).

There is still a lack of peer-reviewed research identifying the accuracy levels of adjusted actuarial assessment. While some like Quinsey et al. (2006) maintain that adjusting purely actuarial risk predictions can only diminish their accuracy, most experts in the field are advocating a more thorough understanding of individual cases through the consideration of dynamic risk factors. The point here is that there is no clear method for adjusting actuarial results, and limited empirical data to provide estimates of accuracy with adjusted risk assessments. As John La Fond has stated, "Actuarial instruments reduce much of the variability in predictions that can generate very different results when individual clinicians bring their different training, experience, and normative preferences to the task of assessing sex offenders for risk." La Fond goes on to note, "No serious dispute exists about the fact that these instruments only allow experts to conclude that a particular individual belongs to a group with certain risk factors. However, they cannot be used to state authoritatively that an individual has a certain probability of reoffending." He then adds, "Even if experts can identify a range of risk for a group, they do not know where within that range each individual with those characteristics falls. To mathematically compile the range of risk for the group, we need to aggregate individuals into a group calculation. This necessarily distorts any judgment about individual risk" (2005, p. 53).

An empirically informed approach using standardized measures to categorize offenders represents a significant advance in our approach to risk assessment, and now forms the foundation for current best practice standards in the field. Yet this leaves the issue of needing to make release decisions in the face of largely unchanging actuarial assessments of risk based on static factors. As pointed out by Hart (2001), risk is inherently contextual. The violence risk posed by offenders will depend on where they will reside, what their employment is, what kinds of clinical and supervision services they will have, their involvement with antisocial associates, their motivation and ability to establish a prosocial adjustment, their responses to adverse life events, and so on. Hart has suggested that the task of the mental health professional is to understand how and why a person has chosen to act violently in the past and to determine whether the factors involved in those decisions, such as perceptual distortions, antisocial attitudes, irrational beliefs, labile affect, or interpersonal stressors, might lead the person to make similar choices in the future. Besides being reliable and accurate, risk assessments need to be prescriptive; they should identify the treatment and supervision interventions that can be used to manage the individual's risk. Adherence to these requirements will increase the chances of making a risk prediction that is scientifically justifiable and ethically acceptable – from the perspectives of both the offender and the community.

Other factors that are especially important to assess properly in the context of violent and sexual offenders are psychopathy and deviant arousal, as these factors, particularly in combination, have been associated with some of the highest observed rates of sexual reoffending. For example, Hildebrand, de Ruiter, and de Vodel (2004) examined the sexual recidivism rates among a sample of treated rapists. They reported a sexual reconviction rate of 82% over an average follow-up of 11.8 years for offenders who were both psychopathic and sexually deviant, compared to 18% for offenders who were both non-psychopathic and non-deviant. Similar outcomes have been observed with other samples including child molesters (Rice & Harris, 1997).

The assessment of these two factors in relation to judicial decision-making with sex offenders therefore warrants specific consideration. Psychopathy is a severe form of personality disorder with distinctive emotional, interpersonal, and antisocial features. Highly psychopathic offenders are characterized by emotional deficits such as a lack of empathy or remorse, a manipulative and exploitative interpersonal style, and a blatant disregard for the rights of others. Research has consistently found psychopathy to have a strong relationship to a variety of negative criminal justice outcomes. These include poor response to available treatment interventions, increased involvement in institutional misconduct while incarcerated, and higher levels of violent and sexual reoffending as compared to less psychopathic offenders.

There is wide agreement that the best standardized measure for assessing psychopathy is the Revised Psychopathy Checklist (PCL-R) developed by Robert Hare. It assesses 20 emotional and behavioral features that define psychopathy, based on a thorough review of file and interview information. There is also a 12 item screening version (the PCL:SV). When conducted by adequately trained individuals, both the PCL-R and PCL:SV produce highly reliable scores. Hare (2003) has reviewed a variety of studies that demonstrate a predictive relationship between psychopathy and sexual reoffending. Although the studies reviewed used different cut-off scores on the PCL-R and often mixed rapists and child molesters in their samples, higher levels of psychopathy were found to be associated with higher rates of sexual reoffending.

There is a concern, however, that although the PCL instruments have shown consistently high interrater reliability in the context of research studies, evidence for consistency in scoring across different professionals in adversarial legal proceedings is not as well established. These concerns reflect concerns about the reliability and validity of the measure, and also raise ethical worries about decisions based on its clinical application. A study by Murrie, Boccaccini, Johnson, and Janke (2008) found that scoring discrepancies for the PCL-R in Sexually Violent Predator (SVP) hearings were both significantly larger than expected in light of the established Standard Error of Measure, and consistently in the direction favoring the legal side who retained each expert (i.e., the departmental expert, representing the "prosecution" side of the state in pursuing an SVP commitment, was consistently higher in PCL-R scoring than the expert retained by the respondent, considered the "defendant" seeking to avoid commitment). It appears that the clinicians in this study were all qualified and experienced risk assessors. This finding, albeit based on a relatively small sample of cases, raises concerns about the applied reliability of an important measure such as the PCL-R in actual legal procedures where issues of personal freedom and public safety are at stake.

Because of its potential importance as a risk factor, the assessment of sexual deviance also requires careful consideration. It appears that risk assessment experts sometimes conclude that deviant sexual arousal must be present based on the presence of convictions for sexual offenses. Yet sexual offending alone is not sufficient evidence for the presence of sexual deviance. Stephen Hart and Randall Kropp (2008) have stated:

Mental health professionals should attempt a direct and comprehensive evaluation of sexual deviance, gathering information about normal and abnormal sexual thoughts, urges, images, fantasies, behavior, and physiological arousal. An important corollary of this standard is that assessments of sexual deviance should avoid over-focusing on convictions for sexual offenses. Sexual offenses are neither necessary nor sufficient for a diagnosis of sexual deviance. Many people with sexual deviance never act on their thoughts, images, urges, or fantasies; and many of those who act in a manner consistent with their sexual deviance do so in a way that may be perfectly legal (e.g., see Marshall, 2006). Also, many – perhaps the majority – of people who commit sexual offenses do not suffer from sexual deviance. Sexual offenses may be the result of many other causal factors, including such things as anger, generalized negative attitudes toward women, poor impulse control, poor heterosexual skills, and inappropriate sexualization of nonsexual needs. Assuming that all sexual offenders have sexual deviance is as illogical as assuming that all thieves have kleptomania or that all arsonists have pyromania. (p. 560)

Assessing Individuals Outside the Actuarial Framework

As alluded to earlier, there is a now a broad consensus that empirically validated actuarial risk measures form the foundation of the most accurate risk assessment methods currently available, and therefore provide the most ethical basis for risk assessment in forensic applications. Actuarial measures function by placing an individual into a clearly defined group of individuals with similar levels of specified risk factors, for whom the group rates of an outcome such as violent or sexual offending are known. A critical caveat to this approach, however, is the degree to which a given individual may fundamentally differ from the reference group with whom the measure has been developed and validated.

One example of this issue is the risk assessment of female sex offenders. International experts in the area of risk assessment with sex offenders have been clear and consistent in their position regarding the use of static actuarial measures with female sex offenders. In the revised coding rules for the STATIC-99 (Harris, Phenix, Hanson, & Thornton, 2003), the authors state, "The STATIC-99 is an actuarial risk prediction instrument designed to estimate the probability of sexual and violent reconviction for adult males who have already been charged with or convicted of at least one sexual offense against a child or a non-consenting adult" and "This instrument is not recommended for females, young offenders (those having an age of less than 18 years at time of release), or offenders who have only been convicted of prostitution related offenses … or possession of pornography/indecent materials" (p. 5). In their review of sexual recidivism in females, Cortoni & Hanson (2005) conclude:

The results of this review have implications for those professionals working with female sexual offenders. First, it appears that evaluators should be more concerned about the risk of non-sexual recidivism than sexual recidivism in female sexual offenders. Second, the substantial difference in recidivism rates suggests that risk tools developed on male sexual offenders are unlikely to apply to females. Simply extrapolating from the male sexual offender literature to assess risk in female offenders is likely to lead to invalid risk appraisal and unintended consequences. (pp. 12–13)

As for measures of dynamic risk factors, the most recent revision of the commonly used STABLE and ACUTE instruments is presented by Hanson, Harris, Scott, and Helmus (2007). Their report of the ongoing study and validation of these instruments at that time relied upon risk assessment and reoffending data for 997 sexual offenders across 16 jurisdictions. The authors state, "There were six women in the sample; one of them reoffended with a non-sexual violent crime. Given that the recidivism rates of the female sexual offenders would be expected to differ from the rates for males (Cortoni & Hanson, 2005), the female offenders were not considered further" (p. 3).

The issue of cases "beyond the actuarial scheme" is also addressed by Doren (2002). Although Doren does not specifically address risk assessment with female sex offenders, he notes that there are two features that are critical to consider in determining whether a risk assessment measure should be used with a particular individual. One is whether the individual possesses some characteristic that has a known or essentially obvious relationship with recidivism potential, and the other is the degree to which the person is thereby different from the general distribution of this feature in the instrument's researched samples. In the case of female offenders, both these considerations quite obviously apply. Therefore, Doren suggests, there is reason to believe that the recidivism base rates underlying the instrument may not be representative of the sex offender being evaluated. The same concerns may apply to other subgroups of offenders who have not been adequately represented in the normative groups for whom risk measures have been validated. This may include ethnic minorities, those with intellectual deficits or psychiatric conditions, or those who fall outside the age range of the validation samples. Conducting risk assessments with individuals such as these presents significant ethical concerns regarding the use of current actuarial risk measures.

THE RISK ASSESSMENT PROCESS

The preceding portion of the chapter has focused on the properties of current risk measures and the implications for ethical forensic risk assessment. There are also a variety of issues associated with the risk assessment process itself that have implications for ethical practice.

Professional Roles

The process of assessing and reporting risk to judicial decision-makers highlights the issue of the various roles that mental health professionals may play, and the potentially problematic boundaries of these roles. One issue in this area is being clear about who the client is. In most cases in these proceedings, the client is the court or other judicial decision-making body. The role of the risk assessor is to provide the most accurate and objective evidence regarding risk relevant to the matters to be decided by the court. This role should be non-partisan, regardless of which side has retained the expertise of the assessor. This neutral position may be difficult to maintain, however, in the face of expectations by the prosecution or defense to assist in obtaining the desired judicial outcome.

There is also the potential for role conflict when the expert explicitly occupies dual roles, resulting in potential conflicts of interest. This most directly occurs in instances in which a psychologist is in both a treatment role and a court assessment role, but it also applies when the psychologist engages in advocacy in the role of trial consultant. As a trial consultant the psychologist essentially joins the retaining attorney's team "to bring psychological expertise to the partisan adversarial process. Impartiality is not required of the trial consultant, but the psychologist trial consultant who holds a place on the 'trial team' is cautioned against agreeing to transition into or concurrently participate in the case as an examining or testifying expert" (Bush, Connell, & Denney, 2006, p. 40).

The clarity of these role boundaries may be difficult to maintain. As Bush et al. (2006) go on to say:

> *Although there is no clear line distinguishing the appropriate contribution of a testifying expert from that of a non-testifying, consulting expert, practitioners may help clarify the appropriate course of action by examining their motivations. Being motivated to clarify genuine professional disagreement and its genesis, to assist an attorney in making appropriate use of one's opinion, the testifying expert is on solid ground. When the motivation is to contribute as a member of the trial team, sharing its goal to win the case, the psychologist has become an advocate whose opinions should not be offered as objective expertise. (p. 40)*

This concern is amplified when there is a lack of risk assessment expertise available to offenders that is independent of a government department seeking a judicial decision against them. When such expertise is not available it may be difficult for offenders to present a competent challenge to the findings and recommendations of the state. This raises human rights issues related to equal protection under the law, and the underlying principles of freedom and well-being.

Consent

Obtaining informed consent in the context of forensic risk assessment requires careful consideration of several issues addressed in this chapter. It is crucial that the individual to be assessed understands clearly the role to be played by the assessor, who the client is (typically the judicial decision-maker, not the individual being assessed), the nature of the information to be obtained, how it will be used, and who will have access to it both during the current proceedings and in the future.

This information must be presented explicitly and in a form that the individual can comprehend. Only when this is understood can the individual give *informed* consent.

Another concern is raised by cases in which the offender refuses to participate in the assessment process. The question has been debated as to whether it is ethical to produce an assessment report in the absence of an interview with the individual whose risk is being assessed. One concern is whether a report of sufficient accuracy and relevance can be written without a direct interaction with the offender. Actuarial risk assessment measures depend primarily upon static, historical factors that are obtained from the official record, and do not therefore require an interview. Factors such as psychopathy, an important consideration in formulating risk for reoffending, can reliably be assessed based on a thorough review of adequate file documentation, although the optimal assessment process for the revised Psychopathy Checklist (PCL-R) includes interview data (Hare, 2003).

The primary limitation to the potential accuracy of assessments conducted without interviewing the individual is that current cognitive, affective, and behavioral factors that might influence the formulation of risk cannot be assessed. Whether this is considered an important limitation depends in part on the position the forensic clinician takes regarding the relative accuracy of clinically adjusted actuarial assessments. Although empirical evidence for improved accuracy of risk assessments that include current dynamic risk factors is only beginning to emerge, many risk assessment experts believe that to be optimally useful in risk management, risk assessments should include an individualized case formulation that cannot be derived from the static factors covered by actuarial instruments. Current dynamic risk factors are important not only for understanding the individual's particular pathway to offending, but also for developing effective approaches to risk management. Unless this information is available in file documentation (and has been adequately assessed in previous reports), it will be difficult to obtain this information in the absence of a clinical interview.

Confidentiality

Related to informed consent is the issue of confidentiality. It has been established that in cases of assessing risk for civil commitment or extended supervision proceedings, the offender cannot maintain confidentiality of information contained in official records associated with his offending. But the parameters of what information may remain confidential is less clear. In New Zealand, for example, the law allows for the protection of information disclosed by the offender in the context of treatment activities. It requires specific consent from the offender in order to access and include this information in any reports, including risk assessment reports to the court. The importance of this protection emphasizes a critical aspect of the treatment process: the individual undertaking treatment must be able to disclose information without fear of recrimination, punishment, or other adverse outcomes, or the entire therapeutic process is compromised. Future curtailment of liberty resulting in part from disclosures made in the typically confidential therapeutic context becomes possible unless clear boundaries are maintained between information revealed in the treatment context and information used in forensic risk assessments. This raises profound and far-reaching ethical issues in the interface between correctional or forensic treatment and subsequent risk assessments, which are beyond the scope of this chapter to address.

This issue of confidentiality also requires special consideration in the risk assessment process. It must be made clear to the offender that the evaluator is acting as an agent of the state, so that information disclosed in the risk assessment process will not be held as confidential, and will be reported to the court as part of the formulation of risk. This sets up a potential conflict that distinguishes forensic assessments in this context from most other clinical activities. On the one hand, the evaluator is encouraging the offender to open up about the factors related to his offending and potential for reoffending, and on the other this information may result in a finding of higher risk that will provide the basis for the court to substantially curtail the offender's liberty.

Confidentiality is therefore one of the fundamental differences of the role of the forensic risk assessor as compared to other clinical roles. In order to most effectively assess an individual, including a sex offender, a certain amount of rapport is necessary, and rapport involves an element of trust. The clinician is encouraging the individual to reveal personal information that can be helpful in understanding the risk for reoffending, and therefore perhaps helpful in preventing future offending. And yet this may not be best for the offender's interests, especially in light of the limited accuracy of current risk assessment methods, and the opportunity for the offender to be among the false positives whose freedom will be diminished on the mistaken determination that they will reoffend.

CONCLUSIONS

Offenders retain their fundamental human rights, even when the state imposes limitations on the exercising of these rights (Schopp, 2003; Ward & Birgden, 2007; Ward et al., 2009). Risk assessment experts must be properly trained and sufficiently skilled in the use of empirically validated measures and procedures. The role of the expert in such cases must always remain clear: the client is the judicial decision-maker, and the expert's responsibility is to provide the best available risk assessment evidence in a way that does not imply or directly overstate the predictive accuracy of the findings. It is an ethical responsibility to make clear the limitations in our current knowledge and error rates in our current procedures in our risk assessment reports.

The clarity of role boundaries presents another set of ethical considerations in forensic risk assessment. The primary client is seldom the offender, yet we are inviting an individual to engage in a process of self-revelation that will have a direct effect on decisions made about his or her liberty. There is an inherent ethical tension between the trust and rapport that is essential to an optimal assessment process and the utilization of information in reports to the courts or other state agencies that have the power to determine the offender's freedom. The role of the assessor and the boundaries involved in the assessment process must be made explicitly clear to the offender, even when this may result in more limited disclosure in the assessment process. It is the offender's right to make an informed decision about what he or she discloses, in full awareness of the likely consequences resulting from the use of this information in a risk assessment report.

Unless hired as an expert consultant to the legal team rather than the assessor of risk, the role of the risk assessor is to be a source of unbiased clinical and scientific information to the judicial decision-maker, rather than as an advisor to legal counsel whose role it is to obtain a ruling favorable to their side in the matter before the court. This may be difficult for experts retained by either the prosecution or the defense. Even if attorneys accept the need for an objective and unbiased assessment of risk, both sides may expect the active advice and guidance of the expert they are working with to best present their case, attack the evidence of the opposing side, and obtain their desired judicial outcome. The degree to which the assessor engages in this role of advisor or strategist in the hearing process potentially increases the risk of becoming a partisan participant rather than an objective expert.

Forensic risk assessment requires substantial expertise in current risk measures, a thorough familiarity with the constantly evolving research literature, and a clear understanding of the unique role boundaries in this specialized area of professional practice. Informed consent, confidentiality, and the usual clinical approach to client relationships, therapeutic alliance, and trust, all involve unique considerations in this context. In our view, practitioners require a strong grounding in relevant ethical concepts and theory if they are to avoid ethical blindness and subsequent clinical actions that violate the fundamental rights of offenders. It is only through ongoing professional development and constant attention to these issues that practitioners can proceed ethically to protect the human rights of those they assess.

REFERENCES

Barbaree, H.E., Seto, M.C., Langton, C.M., & Peacock, E.J. (2001). Evaluating the predictive accuracy of six risk assessment instruments for adult sex offenders. *Criminal Justice and Behavior*, *28*, 490–521.

Bartosh, D.L., Garby, T., Lewis, D., & Gray, S. (2003). Differences in the predictive validity of actuarial risk assessments in relation to sex offender type. *International Journal of Offender Therapy and Comparative Criminology*, *47*, 422–438.

Bush, S.S., Connell, M.A., & Denney, R.L. (2006). *Ethical practice in forensic psychology: A systematic model for decision-making*. Washington, DC: American Psychological Association.

Campbell, T.W. (2003). Sex offenders and actuarial risk assessments: Ethical considerations. *Behavioral Sciences and the Law*, *21*, 269–279.

Cortoni, F., & Hanson, R.K. (2005). *A review of the recidivism rates of adult female sexual offenders*. Correctional Service of Canada, Research Report R-169. Available from: www.csc-scc.gc.ca/research/092/r169_e.pdf (last retrieved July 16, 2016).

Day, A., & Ward, T. (2010). Offender rehabilitation as a value laden process. *International Journal of Offender Therapy and Comparative Criminology*, *54*, 289–306.

De Vogel, V., de Ruiter, C., van Beek, D., & Mead, G. (2004). Predictive validity of the SVR-20 and Static-99 in a Dutch sample of treated sex offenders. *Law and Human Behavior*, *28* (3), 235–251.

Doren, D. (2002). *Evaluating sex offenders: A manual for civil commitments and beyond*. London: Sage.

Doren, D.M. (2004). Stability of the interpretative risk percentages for the RRASOR and Static-99. *Sexual Abuse: A Journal of Research and Treatment*, *16*, 25–36.

Freeden, M. (1991). *Rights*. Minneapolis, MN: University of Minnesota Press.

Gewirth, A. (1998). *Self-fulfillment*. Princeton, NJ: Princeton University Press.

Gottfredson, S.D., & Moriarty, L.J. (2006). Statistical risk assessment: Old problems and new applications. *Crime & Delinquency*, *52*, 178–200.

Hanson, R.K. (1997). *The development of a brief actuarial risk scale for sexual offense recidivism* (User report 1997-04). Ottawa: Department of the Solicitor General of Canada.

Hanson, R.K. (2001). Note on the reliability of STATIC-99 as used by the California Department of Mental Health evaluators (unpublished report). Sacramento, CA: California Department of Mental Health.

Hanson, R.K., & Harris, A.J.R. (2000). Where should we intervene? Dynamic predictors of sex offense recidivism. *Criminal Justice and Behavior*, *27*, 6–35.

Hanson, R.K., & Harris, A.J.R. (2001). A structured approach to evaluating change among sexual offenders. *Sexual Abuse: A Journal of Research and Treatment*, *13*, 105–122.

Hanson, R.K., Harris, A.J.R., Scott, T.L., & Helmus, L. (2007). *Assessing the risk of sexual offenders on community supervision: The Dynamic Supervision Project*. Available from: www.static99.org/pdfdocs/hansonharrisscottandhelmus2007.pdf (last retrieved July 16, 2016).

Hanson, R.K., & Thornton, D. (2000). Improving risk assessment for sex offenders: A comparison of three actuarial scales. *Law and Human Behaviour*, *24*, 119–136.

Hare, R.D. (2003). *Hare Psychopathy Checklist – Revised (PCL-R)* (2nd ed.). Toronto, ON: Multi-Health Systems.

Harris, A.J.R., Phenix, A., Hanson, R.K., & Thornton, D. (2003). *Static-99 Coding Rules: Revised – 2003*. Available from: www.static99.org/pdfdocs/static-99-coding-rules_e.pdf (last retrieved July 15, 2016).

Harris, G.T., & Rice, M.E. (2003). Actuarial assessment of risk among sex offenders. *Annuls of the New York Academy of Science*, *989*, 198–210.

Harris, G.T., Rice, M.E., & Quinsey, V.L. (1993). Violent recidivism of mentally disordered offenders: The development of a statistical prediction instrument. *Criminal Justice and Behavior*, *20*, 315–335.

Harris, G.T., Rice, M.E., Quinsey, V.L., Lalumiere, M.L., Boer, D., & Lang, C. (2003). A multisite comparison of actuarial risk instruments for sex offenders. *Psychological Assessment*, *15*, 413–425.

Hart, S.D. (2001). Assessing and managing violence risk. In K.S. Douglas, C.D. Webster, S.D. Hart, D. Eaves, & J.R.P. Ogloff (Eds.), *HCR-20 violence risk management guide* (pp. 27–40). Burnaby, BC: Simon Fraser University.

Hart, S.D., & Kropp, P.R. (2008). Sexual deviance and the law. In D.R. Laws & W.T. O'Donohue (Eds.), *Sexual deviance: Theory, assessment, and treatment* (pp. 557–570). New York: Guilford Press.

Hildebrand, M., de Ruiter, C., & de Vogel, V. (2004). Psychopathy and sexual deviance in treated rapists: Association with sexual and nonsexual recidivism. *Sexual Abuse: A Journal of Research and Treatment, 16*, 1–24.

Janus, E.S., & Prentky, R.A. (2003). Forensic use actuarial risk assessment with sex offenders: Accuracy, admissibility and accountability. *American Criminal Law Review, v40*. Available from: http://www.antoniocasella.eu/nume/Janus_2003.pdf (last retrieved July 16, 2016).

La Fond, J.Q. (2005). *Preventing sexual violence: How society should cope with sex offenders.* Washington, DC: American Psychological Association.

Langton, C.M. (2003). Contrasting approaches to risk assessment with adult male sexual offenders: An evaluation of recidivism prediction schemes and the utility of supplementary clinical information for enhancing predictive accuracy. Dissertation. Institute of Medical Science, University of Toronto, Canada.

Marshall, W.L. (2006). Diagnostic problems with sexual offenders. In W.L. Marshall, Y.M. Fernandez, L.E. Marshall, & G.A. Serran (Eds.), *Sexual offender treatment: Controversial issues* (pp. 33–44). Chichester, UK: John Wiley & Sons, Ltd.

Murrie, D.C., Boccaccini, M.T., Johnson, J.T., & Janke, C. (2008). Does interrater (dis) agreement on Psychopathy Checklist scores in Sexually Violent Predator trials suggest partisan allegiance in forensic evaluations? *Law and Human Behaviour, 32*, 352–362.

Orend, B. (2002). *Human rights: Concept and context.* Ontario, Canada: Broadview Press.

Quinsey, V.L., Harris, G.T., Rice, M.E., & Cormier, C.A. (1998). *Violent offenders: Appraising and managing risk.* Washington, DC: American Psychological Association.

Quinsey, V.L., Harris, G.T., Rice, M.E., & Cormier, C.A. (2006). *Violent offenders: Appraising and managing risk* (2nd ed.). Washington, DC: American Psychological Association.

Rice, M.E., & Harris, G.T. (1997). Cross validation and extension of the Violence Risk Appraisal Guide for child molesters and rapists. *Law and Human Behavior, 21*, 231–241.

Schopp, R.F. (2003). Sexual aggression: Mad, bad, and mad. *Annals of the New York Academy of Science, 989*, 324–336.

Sjöstedt, G., & Langstrom, N. (2001). Actuarial assessment of sex offender recidivism risk: A cross-validation of the RRASOR and Static-99 in Sweden. *Law and Human Behavior, 25* (6), 629–645.

Sjöstedt, G., & Langstrom, N. (2002). Assessment of risk for criminal recidivism among rapists in Sweden: A comparison of different procedures. *Psychology, Crime & Law, 8*, 25–40.

Tribe, L.H. (1971). Trial by mathematics: Precision and ritual in the legal process. *Harvard Law Review, 84*, 1329–1355.

Vess, J. (2008). Sex offender risk assessment: Consideration of human rights in Community Protection Legislation. *Legal and Criminological Psychology, 13*, 245–256.

Vess, J. (2009). Fear and loathing in public policy: Ethical issues in laws for sex offenders. *Aggression and Violent Behavior, 14*, 264–272.

Ward, T., & Birgden, A. (2007). Human rights and correctional clinical practice. *Aggression and Violent Behavior, 12*, 628–643.

Ward, T., Gannon, T.A., & Birgden, A. (2007). Human rights and the treatment of sex offenders. *Sexual Abuse: A Journal of Research and Treatment, 19*, 195–216.

Ward, T., Gannon, T.A., & Vess, J. (2009). Human rights, ethical principles, and standards in forensic practice. *International Journal of Offender Therapy and Comparative Criminology, 53* (2), 126–144.

Ward, T., & Salmon, K. (2009). The ethics of punishment: Correctional practice implications. *Aggression and Violent Behavior, 14*, 239–247.

Wong, K., Flahr, L., Maire, B., Wilde, S., Gu, D., & Wong, S. (2000, June). *Inter-rater reliability of the violence risk scale and the violence risk scale: Sex offender version.* Poster presented at the Annual Conference of the Canadian Psychological Association, Ottawa, Ontario.

Index

Page numbers in **bold** indicate figures/tables.

Assessments in Forensic Practice: A Handbook, First Edition. Edited by Kevin D. Browne, Anthony R. Beech, Leam A. Craig, and Shihning Chou.
© 2017 John Wiley & Sons Ltd. Published 2017 by John Wiley & Sons Ltd.